Information and Divergence Measures

Information and Divergence Measures

Editors

Alex Karagrigoriou
Andreas Makrides

MDPI • Basel • Beijing • Wuhan • Barcelona • Belgrade • Manchester • Tokyo • Cluj • Tianjin

Editors
Alex Karagrigoriou
Lab of Stat and Data Analysis,
University of the Aegean,
Karlovasi, Greece

Andreas Makrides
Lab of Stat and Data Analysis,
University of the Aegean,
Karlovasi, Greece

Editorial Office
MDPI
St. Alban-Anlage 66
4052 Basel, Switzerland

This is a reprint of articles from the Special Issue published online in the open access journal *Entropy* (ISSN 1099-4300) (available at: https://www.mdpi.com/journal/entropy/special_issues/diverg_measure).

For citation purposes, cite each article independently as indicated on the article page online and as indicated below:

LastName, A.A.; LastName, B.B.; LastName, C.C. Article Title. *Journal Name* **Year**, *Volume Number*, Page Range.

ISBN 978-3-0365-8386-0 (Hbk)
ISBN 978-3-0365-8387-7 (PDF)

© 2023 by the authors. Articles in this book are Open Access and distributed under the Creative Commons Attribution (CC BY) license, which allows users to download, copy and build upon published articles, as long as the author and publisher are properly credited, which ensures maximum dissemination and a wider impact of our publications.

The book as a whole is distributed by MDPI under the terms and conditions of the Creative Commons license CC BY-NC-ND.

Contents

About the Editors vii

Alex Karagrigoriou and Andreas Makrides
Information and Divergence Measures
Reprinted from: *Entropy* **2023**, 25, 683, doi:10.3390/e25040683 1

Frank Nielsen
Statistical Divergences between Densities of Truncated Exponential Families with Nested Supports: Duo Bregman and Duo Jensen Divergences
Reprinted from: *Entropy* **2022**, 24, 421, doi:10.3390/e24030421 5

Christos Meselidis and Alex Karagrigoriou
Contingency Table Analysis and Inference via Double Index Measures
Reprinted from: *Entropy* **2022**, 24, 477, doi:10.3390/e24040477 27

Igal Sason
Information Inequalities via Submodularity and a Problem in Extremal Graph Theory
Reprinted from: *Entropy* **2022**, 24, 597, doi:10.3390/e24050597 45

Mark Levene
A Skew Logistic Distribution for Modelling COVID-19 Waves and Its Evaluation Using the Empirical Survival Jensen–Shannon Divergence
Reprinted from: *Entropy* **2022**, 24, 600, doi:10.3390/e24050600 77

María Jaenada, Pedro Miranda and Leandro Pardo
Robust Test Statistics Based on Restricted Minimum Rényi's PseudodistanceEstimators
Reprinted from: *Entropy* **2022**, 24, 616, doi:10.3390/e24050616 91

Nizar Bouhlel and David Rousseau
A Generic Formula and Some Special Cases for the Kullback–Leibler Divergence between Central Multivariate Cauchy Distributions
Reprinted from: *Entropy* **2022**, 24, 838, doi:10.3390/e24060838 119

Daohua Yu, Xin Zhou, Yu Pan, Zhendong Niu and Huafei Sun
Application of Statistical K-Means Algorithm for University Academic Evaluation
Reprinted from: *Entropy* **2022**, 24, 1004, doi:10.3390/e24071004 145

Florentina Suter, Ioana Cernat and Mihai Drăgan
Some Information Measures Properties of the GOS-Concomitants from the FGM Family
Reprinted from: *Entropy* **2022**, 24, 1361, doi:10.3390/e24101361 169

Andres Dajles and Joseph Cavanaugh
Probabilistic Pairwise Model Comparisons Based on Bootstrap Estimators of the Kullback–Leibler Discrepancy
Reprinted from: *Entropy* **2022**, 24, 1483, doi:10.3390/e24101483 189

Jun Chen, Jie Wang, Yidong Zhang, Fei Wang and Jianjiang Zhou
Spatial Information-Theoretic Optimal LPI Radar Waveform Design
Reprinted from: *Entropy* **2022**, 24, 1515, doi:10.3390/e24111515 207

Răzvan-Cornel Sfetcu, Sorina-Cezarina Sfetcu and Vasile Preda
Some Properties of Weighted Tsallis and Kaniadakis Divergences
Reprinted from: *Entropy* **2022**, 24, 1616, doi:10.3390/e24111616 221

Trevor Herntier and Adrian M. Peter
Transversality Conditions for Geodesics on the Statistical Manifold of Multivariate Gaussian Distributions
Reprinted from: *Entropy* **2022**, *24*, 1698, doi:10.3390/e24111698 . . . . **233**

Aida Toma
Robust Z-Estimators for Semiparametric Moment Condition Models
Reprinted from: *Entropy* **2023**, *25*, 1013, doi:10.3390/e25071013 . . . . **255**

About the Editors

Alex Karagrigoriou

He studied at the University of Patras, Greece, and the University of Maryland, USA. He has worked at the University of Maryland, the United States Department of Agriculture (USDA) and the Institute of Statistical Sciences, Taiwan, and taught at the Universities of Maryland, Athens, the Aegean, and Cyprus. He is currently Professor of Probability and Statistics and Director of the Laboratory of Statistics and Data Analysis at the University of the Aegean, Greece. ir mechanisms of action (pore-forming activity, safety of antibiotics to human and animal cells).

His research activities cover various areas of statistics, such as applied probability, probability theory, mathematical statistics, applied and computational statistics, statistical and stochastic modeling, model selection criteria, biostatistics, information theory and divergence measures, time series analysis, goodness of fit tests, economic demography, actuarial mathematics, risk theory, Markov and semi-Markov processes, statistical quality control, big data analytics, multivariate analysis, and reliability theory. He has published more than 100 articles (journals and collective volumes) and has given more than 80 invited presentations at international conferences, symposia, and universities all over the world. He has supervised 3 postdoc, 6 PhD and 50 master's theses, published 2 textbooks in Greek, and edited 9 collective volumes (Wiley, ISAST, Springer, iSTE Wiley).

He has extensive experience as a Principal Scientific and Financial Investigator in the design and execution of research projects which involve the statistical analysis of medical, biomedical, socioeconomic, and economic data and has been involved in a number of research programs with external funding over the last 20 years, as well as the organization of conferences, seminars, workshops, and summer schools.

Andreas Makrides

He received his PhD in Statistics (2016) from the Department of Mathematics and Statistics, University of Cyprus, his M.Sc. in Statistics and Modeling (with excellence, 2010) from the Department of Mathematics of the Aristotle University of Thessaloniki, Greece, and his B.Sc. (Hons, with excellence, 2008) from the Department of Mathematics of the Aristotle University of Thessaloniki, Greece.

He has worked as a postdoctoral researcher (2018–2019) at the Laboratoire de Mathématiques Raphaël Salem, University of Rouen, France, and (2020–2022) at the Department of Statistics and Actuarial–Financial Mathematics, University of the Aegean, Greece. His research interests lie in fields including stochastic modeling, stochastic processes, applied probability, mathematical statistics, semi-Markov processes, reliability theory, multi-state systems, entropy and divergence, goodness of fit tests, and control charts—statistical quality control. He has co-supervised one master's thesis, edited two volumes on data analysis models and methods (2022, iSTE Wiley), been involved in the organization of conferences and workshops, and served as a guest editor for a special issue of the journal Entropy.

He was a representative of both Cyprus and France at the 21st EYSM in Belgrade, Serbia (selected by the Regional Committee of the Bernoulli Society). He was the recipient of two excellence awards from the State Scholarships Foundations of Greece and Cyprus (2005–2008).

He also has teaching experience, having started working in 2017 as an Associate Lecturer at the University of Cyprus, the Cyprus University of Technology, and the Uclan University, Cyprus, on various undergraduate and postgraduate courses.

Editorial

Information and Divergence Measures

Alex Karagrigoriou [1,*] and Andreas Makrides [1,2]

1. Laboratory of Statistics and Data Analysis, Department of Statistics and Actuarial-Financial Mathematics, University of the Aegean, GR-83200 Karlovasi, Greece; makrides.an@unic.ac.cy
2. Department of Computer Science, University of Nicosia, CY-1700 Nicosia, Cyprus
* Correspondence: alex.karagrigoriou@aegean.gr

Citation: Karagrigoriou, A.; Makrides, A. Information and Divergence Measures. *Entropy* **2023**, *25*, 683. https://doi.org/10.3390/e25040683

Received: 31 March 2023
Accepted: 13 April 2023
Published: 19 April 2023

Copyright: © 2023 by the authors. Licensee MDPI, Basel, Switzerland. This article is an open access article distributed under the terms and conditions of the Creative Commons Attribution (CC BY) license (https://creativecommons.org/licenses/by/4.0/).

The present Special Issue of *Entropy*, entitled Information and Divergence Measures, covers various aspects and applications in the general area of Information and Divergence Measures.

Measures of information appear everywhere in probability and statistics. They play a fundamental role in communication theory. They have a long history dating back to the papers of Fisher, Shannon, and Kullback. There are many measures each claiming to capture the concept of information or simply being measures of divergence or distance between two probability distributions. Numerous generalizations of such measures also exist.

The concept of distance is important in establishing the degree of similarity and/or closeness between functions, populations, and distributions. The intense engagement of many authors with entropy and divergence measures demonstrates the significant role they are playing in the sciences. Indeed, distances and entropies are related to inferential statistics, including both estimation and hypothesis testing problems [1–6], model selection criteria [7–9] and probabilistic and statistical modelling with applications in multivariate analysis, actuarial science, portfolio optimization, survival analysis, reliability theory, change-point problems, etc. [10–15]. Thus, the significance of entropy and divergence measures that emerges in these and many more scientific fields is a topic of great interest to scientists, researchers, medical experts, engineers, industrial managers, computer experts, data analysts, etc.

All the articles included in this Special Issue were reviewed and accepted for publication because they have been found to contribute research works of the highest quality and at the same time, they highlight the diversity of the topics in this scientific area. The issue presents twelve original contributions that span a wide range of topics. In [16], the authors demonstrate how to employ the techniques of the calculus of variations with a variable endpoint to search for the closest distribution from a family of distributions generated via a constraint set on the parameter manifold. In [17], the authors consider weighted Tsallis and Kaniadakis divergences and establish inequalities between these measures and Tsallis and Kaniadakis logarithms. In [18], LPI waveforms are designed within the constraints of the detection performance metrics of radar and PISs, both of which are measured by the Kullback–Leibler divergence, and the resolution performance metric, measured by joint entropy with the solution based on the sequential quadratic programming method. In [19], a bootstrap approximation of the Kullback–Leibler discrepancy is utilized to estimate the probability that the fitted null model is closer to the underlying generating model than the fitted alternative model. The authors also propose a bias correction either by adding a bootstrap-based correction or by adding the number of parameters in the candidate model. In [20], the authors extend, and compute information measures related to Shannon and Tsallis entropies, for the concomitants of the generalized order statistics from the Farlie–Gumbel–Morgenstern family. In [21], the evaluation of academic performance by using the statistical K-means (SKM) algorithm to produce clusters is investigated. A simulation experiment on the top 20 universities in China shows the advantages of the SKM algorithm over traditional methods. In [22], the authors introduce a closed-form expression for the Kullback–Leibler divergence between two central multivariate Cauchy distributions used in different signal and image processing applications where non-Gaussian models are needed. In [23], restricted minimum Rényi's pseudodistance estimators are defined, and their asymptotic distribution and influence function are derived. Further, robust Rao-type and divergence-type tests based on minimum Rényi's pseudodistance and restricted minimum Rényi's pseudodistance estimators are considered, and their asymptotic properties are obtained. In [24], a skew logistic distribution is proposed and extended to the skew bi-logistic distribution to allow the modelling of multiple waves in epidemic time series data. The proposed distribution is validated by COVID-19 data from the UK and is evaluated for goodness-of-fit using the empirical survival Jensen–Shannon divergence and the Kolmogorov–Smirnov two-sample test statistic. In [25], an approach for the derivation of families of inequalities for set functions is suggested and applied to obtain information inequalities with Shannon information measures that satisfy sub/supermodularity and monotonicity properties. The author also applies the generalized Han's inequality to analyse a problem in extremal graph theory, with an information–theoretic proof and interpretation. In [26], the authors focus on a general family of measures of divergence and purpose a restricted minimum divergence estimator under constraints and a new double-index (dual) divergence test statistic which is thoroughly examined. Finally, in [27], by calculating the Kullback–Leibler divergence between two probability measures belonging to different exponential families dominated by the same measure, the authors obtain a formula that generalizes the ordinary Fenchel–Young divergence and define the duo Fenchel–Young divergence which is equivalent to a duo Bregman divergence. The author also proves that the skewed Bhattacharyya distances between truncated exponential families amount to equivalent skewed duo Jensen divergences.

Acknowledgments: We wish to thank the authors for their contributions and their willingness to share innovative ideas and techniques to furnish this issue. In addition, we would like to thank and express our appreciation to the reviewers since they spent a considerable amount of time providing accurate and fair manuscript evaluations. Finally, we would like to express our pleasure for working with staff of the Editorial Office of Entropy for the fruitful and excellent cooperation.

Conflicts of Interest: The authors declare no conflict of interest.

References

1. Alin, A.; Kurt, S. Ordinary and penalized minimum power-divergence estimators in two-way contingency tables. *Comput. Stat.* **2008**, *23*, 455–468. [CrossRef]
2. Basu, A.; Harris, I.R.; Hjort, N.L. Robust and efficient estimation by minimising a density power divergence. *Biometrika* **1998**, *85*, 549–559. [CrossRef]
3. Jiménez-Gamero, M.D.; Batsidis, A. Minimum distance estimators for count data based on the probability generating function with applications. *Metrika* **2017**, *80*, 503–545. [CrossRef]
4. Patra, S.; Maji, A.; Basu, A.; Pardo, L. The Power Divergence and the Density Power Divergence Families: The Mathematical Connection. *Sankhya B* **2013**, *75*, 16–28. [CrossRef]
5. Toma, A.; Broniatowski, M. Dual divergence estimators and tests: Robustness results. *J. Multivar. Anal.* **2011**, *102*, 20–36. [CrossRef]
6. Vonta, F.; Mattheou, K.; Karagrigoriou, A. On properties of the (φ,α)-power divergence family with applications to goodness of fit tests. *Methodol. Comput. Appl. Probab.* **2012**, *14*, 335–356. [CrossRef]
7. Shang, J.; Cavanaugh, J.E. Bootstrap variants of the Akaike information criterion for mixed model selection. *Comput. Stat. Data Anal.* **2008**, *52*, 2004–2021. [CrossRef]
8. Neath, A.A.; Cavanaugh, J.E.; Weyhaupt, A.G. Model evaluation, discrepancy function estimation, and social choice theory. *Comput. Stat.* **2015**, *30*, 231–249. [CrossRef]
9. Mattheou, K.; Lee, S.; Karagrigoriou, A. A model selection criterion based on the BHHJ measure of divergence. *J. Stat. Plan. Inference* **2009**, *139*, 228–235. [CrossRef]
10. Barbu, V.S.; D'Amico, G.; Makrides, A. A continuous-time semi-Markov system governed by stepwise transitions. *Mathematics* **2022**, *10*, 2745. [CrossRef]
11. Batsidis, A.; Martin, N.; Pardo Llorente, L.; Zografos, K. φ-Divergence Based Procedure for Parametric Change-Point Problems. *Methodol. Comput. Appl. Probab.* **2016**, *18*, 21–35. [CrossRef]

12. Nielsen, F. Revisiting Chernoff Information with Likelihood Ratio Exponential Families. *Entropy* **2022**, *24*, 1400. [CrossRef]
13. Sachlas, A.; Papaioannou, T. Residual and past entropy in actuarial science and survival models. *Methodol. Comput. Appl. Probab.* **2014**, *16*, 79–99. [CrossRef]
14. Preda, V.; Dedu, S.; Iatan, I.; Cernat, I.D.; Sheraz, M. Tsallis Entropy for Loss Models and Survival Models Involving Truncated and Censored Random Variables. *Entropy* **2022**, *24*, 1654. [CrossRef] [PubMed]
15. Zografos, K.; Nadarajah, S. Survival exponential entropies. *IEEE Trans. Inf. Theory* **2005**, *51*, 1239–1246. [CrossRef]
16. Herntier, T.; Peter, A.M. Transversality Conditions for Geodesics on the Statistical Manifold of Multivariate Gaussian Distributions. *Entropy* **2022**, *24*, 1698. [CrossRef]
17. Sfetcu, R.-C.; Sfetcu, S.-C.; Preda, V. Some Properties of Weighted Tsallis and Kaniadakis Divergences. *Entropy* **2022**, *24*, 1616. [CrossRef]
18. Chen, J.; Wang, J.; Zhang, Y.; Wang, F.; Zhou, J. Spatial Information-Theoretic Optimal LPI Radar Waveform Design. *Entropy* **2022**, *24*, 1515. [CrossRef]
19. Dajles, A.; Cavanaugh, J. Probabilistic Pairwise Model Comparisons Based on Bootstrap Estimators of the Kullback–Leibler Discrepancy. *Entropy* **2022**, *24*, 1483. [CrossRef]
20. Suter, F.; Cernat, I.; Drăgan, M. Some Information Measures Properties of the GOS-Concomitants from the FGM Family. *Entropy* **2022**, *24*, 1361. [CrossRef]
21. Yu, D.; Zhou, X.; Pan, Y.; Niu, Z.; Sun, H. Application of Statistical K-Means Algorithm for University Academic Evaluation. *Entropy* **2022**, *24*, 1004. [CrossRef] [PubMed]
22. Bouhlel, N.; Rousseau, D. A Generic Formula and Some Special Cases for the Kullback–Leibler Divergence between Central Multivariate Cauchy Distributions. *Entropy* **2022**, *24*, 838. [CrossRef] [PubMed]
23. Jaenada, M.; Miranda, P.; Pardo, L. Robust Test Statistics Based on Restricted Minimum Rényi's Pseudodistance Estimators. *Entropy* **2022**, *24*, 616. [CrossRef] [PubMed]
24. Levene, M. A Skew Logistic Distribution for Modelling COVID-19 Waves and Its Evaluation Using the Empirical Survival Jensen–Shannon Divergence. *Entropy* **2022**, *24*, 600. [CrossRef]
25. Sason, I. Information Inequalities via Submodularity and a Problem in Extremal Graph Theory. *Entropy* **2022**, *24*, 597. [CrossRef]
26. Meselidis, C.; Karagrigoriou, A. Contingency Table Analysis and Inference via Double Index Measures. *Entropy* **2022**, *24*, 477. [CrossRef]
27. Nielsen, F. Statistical Divergences between Densities of Truncated Exponential Families with Nested Supports: Duo Bregman and Duo Jensen Divergences. *Entropy* **2022**, *24*, 421. [CrossRef]

Disclaimer/Publisher's Note: The statements, opinions and data contained in all publications are solely those of the individual author(s) and contributor(s) and not of MDPI and/or the editor(s). MDPI and/or the editor(s) disclaim responsibility for any injury to people or property resulting from any ideas, methods, instructions or products referred to in the content.

Article

Statistical Divergences between Densities of Truncated Exponential Families with Nested Supports: Duo Bregman and Duo Jensen Divergences

Frank Nielsen

Sony Computer Science Laboratories, Tokyo 141-0022, Japan; frank.nielsen.x@gmail.com

Abstract: By calculating the Kullback–Leibler divergence between two probability measures belonging to different exponential families dominated by the same measure, we obtain a formula that generalizes the ordinary Fenchel–Young divergence. Inspired by this formula, we define the duo Fenchel–Young divergence and report a majorization condition on its pair of strictly convex generators, which guarantees that this divergence is always non-negative. The duo Fenchel–Young divergence is also equivalent to a duo Bregman divergence. We show how to use these duo divergences by calculating the Kullback–Leibler divergence between densities of truncated exponential families with nested supports, and report a formula for the Kullback–Leibler divergence between truncated normal distributions. Finally, we prove that the skewed Bhattacharyya distances between truncated exponential families amount to equivalent skewed duo Jensen divergences.

Keywords: exponential family; statistical divergence; truncated exponential family; truncated normal distributions

1. Introduction

1.1. Exponential Families

Let $(\mathcal{X}, \Sigma)$ be a measurable space, and consider a regular minimal exponential family [1] $\mathcal{E}$ of probability measures P_θ all dominated by a base measure μ ($P_\theta \ll \mu$):

$$\mathcal{E} = \{P_\theta \ :\ \theta \in \Theta\}. \tag{1}$$

The Radon–Nikodym derivatives or densities of the probability measures P_θ with respect to μ can be written canonically as

$$p_\theta(x) = \frac{dP_\theta}{d\mu}(x) = \exp\left(\theta^\top t(x) - F(\theta) + k(x)\right), \tag{2}$$

where θ denotes the natural parameter, $t(x)$ the sufficient statistic [1–4], and $F(\theta)$ the log-normalizer [1] (or cumulant function). The optional auxiliary term $k(x)$ allows us to change the base measure μ into the measure ν such that $\frac{d\nu}{d\mu}(x) = e^{k(x)}$. The order D of the family is the dimension of the natural parameter space Θ:

$$\Theta = \left\{\theta \in \mathbb{R}^D\ :\ \int_\mathcal{X} \exp\left(\theta^\top t(x) + k(x)\right) d\mu(x) < \infty\right\}, \tag{3}$$

where $\mathbb{R}$ denotes the set of reals. The sufficient statistic $t(x) = (t_1(x), \ldots, t_D(x))$ is a vector of D functions. The sufficient statistic $t(x)$ is said to be minimal when the $D+1$ functions $1, t_1(x), \ldots, t_D(x)$ are linearly independent [1]. The sufficient statistics $t(x)$ are such that the probability $\Pr[X|\theta] = \Pr[X|t(X)]$. That is, all information necessary for the statistical inference of parameter θ is contained in $t(X)$. Exponential families are characterized as

families of parametric distributions with finite-dimensional sufficient statistics [1]. Exponential families $\{p_\lambda\}$ include among others the exponential, normal, gamma/beta, inverse gamma, inverse Gaussian, and Wishart distributions once a reparameterization $\theta = \theta(\lambda)$ of the parametric distributions $\{p_\lambda\}$ is performed to reveal their natural parameters [1].

When the sufficient statistic $t(x)$ is x, these exponential families [1] are called natural exponential families or tilted exponential families [5] in the literature. Indeed, the distributions P_θ of the exponential family $\mathcal{E}$ can be interpreted as distributions obtained by tilting the base measure μ [6]. In this paper, we consider either discrete exponential families like the family of Poisson distributions (univariate distributions of order $D = 1$ with respect to the counting measure) or continuous exponential families like the family of normal distributions (univariate distributions of order $D = 2$ with respect to the Lebesgue measure). The Radon–Nikodym derivative of a discrete exponential family is a probability mass function (pmf), and the Radon–Nikodym derivative of a continuous exponential family is a probability density function (pdf). The support of a pmf $p(x)$ is $\mathrm{supp}(p) = \{x \in \mathbb{Z} : p(x) > 0\}$ (where $\mathbb{Z}$ denotes the set of integers) and the support of a d-variate pdf $p(x)$ is $\mathrm{supp}(p) = \{x \in \mathbb{R}^d : p(x) > 0\}$. The Poisson distributions have support $\mathbb{N} \cup \{0\}$ where $\mathbb{N}$ denotes the set of natural numbers $\{1, 2, \ldots, \}$. Densities of an exponential family all have coinciding support [1].

1.2. Truncated Exponential Families with Nested Supports

In this paper, we shall consider truncated exponential families [7] with nested supports. A truncated exponential family is a set of parametric probability distributions obtained by truncation of the support of an exponential family. Truncated exponential families are exponential families but their statistical inference is more subtle [8,9]. Let $\mathcal{E}_{\mathrm{Trunc}} = \{q_\theta\}$ be a truncated exponential family of $\mathcal{E} = \{p_\theta\}$ with nested supports $\mathrm{supp}(q_\theta) \subset \mathrm{supp}(p_\theta)$. The canonical decompositions of densities p_θ and q_θ have the following expressions:

$$p_\theta(x) = \exp\left(\theta^\top t(x) + k(x) - F(\theta)\right), \tag{4}$$

$$q_\theta(x) = \frac{p_\theta(x)}{Z^{\mathcal{X}_{\mathrm{Trunc}}}(\theta)} = \exp\left(\theta^\top t(x) + k(x) - F_{\mathrm{Trunc}}(\theta)\right), \tag{5}$$

where the log-normalizer of the truncated exponential family is:

$$F_{\mathrm{Trunc}}(\theta) = F(\theta) + \log Z^{\mathcal{X}_{\mathrm{Trunc}}}(\theta), \tag{6}$$

where $Z^{\mathcal{X}_{\mathrm{Trunc}}}(\theta)$ is a normalizing term that takes into account the truncated support $\mathcal{X}_{\mathrm{Trunc}}$. These equations show that densities of truncated exponential families only differ by their log-normalizer functions. Let $\mathcal{X}_{\mathrm{Trunc}}$ denote the support of the distributions of $\mathcal{E}_{\mathrm{Trunc}} = \mathrm{supp}(q_\theta)$ and $\mathcal{X} = \mathrm{supp}(p_\theta)$ the support of $\mathcal{E}$. Family $\mathcal{E}_{\mathrm{Trunc}}$ is a truncated exponential family of $\mathcal{E}$ that can be notationally written as $\mathcal{E}_{\mathcal{X}_{\mathrm{Trunc}}}$. Family $\mathcal{E}$ can also be interpreted as the (un)truncated exponential family $\mathcal{E}_\mathcal{X}$ with densities $p_\theta^\mathcal{X} = p_\theta$. A truncated exponential family $\mathcal{E}_{\mathcal{X}_{\mathrm{Trunc}}}$ of $\mathcal{E}$ is said to have nested support when $\mathcal{X}_{\mathrm{Trunc}} \subset \mathcal{X}$. For example, the family of half-normal distributions defined on the support $\mathcal{X}_{\mathrm{Trunc}} = [0, \infty)$ is a nested truncated exponential family of the family of normal distributions defined on the support $\mathcal{X} = (-\infty, \infty)$.

1.3. Kullback–Leibler Divergence Between Exponential Family Distributions

For two σ-finite probability measures P and Q on $(\mathcal{X}, \Sigma)$ such that P is dominated by Q ($P \ll Q$), the Kullback–Leibler divergence between P and Q is defined by

$$D_{\mathrm{KL}}[P : Q] = \int_\mathcal{X} \log \frac{dP}{dQ} dP = E_P\left[\log \frac{dP}{dQ}\right], \tag{7}$$

where $E_P[X]$ denotes the expectation of a random variable $X \sim P$ [10]. When $P \not\ll Q$, we set $D_{\mathrm{KL}}[P : Q] = +\infty$. Gibbs' inequality [11] $D_{\mathrm{KL}}[P : Q] \geq 0$ shows that the Kullback–Leibler divergence (KLD for short) is always non-negative. The proof of Gibbs' inequality relies on Jensen's inequality and holds for the wide class of f-divergences [12] induced by convex generators $f(u)$:

$$I_f[P:Q] = \int_\mathcal{X} f\left(\frac{dQ}{dP}\right) dP \geq f\left(\int_\mathcal{X} \frac{dQ}{dP} dP\right) \geq f(1). \tag{8}$$

The KLD is an f-divergence obtained for the convex generator $f(u) = -\log u$.

1.4. Kullback–Leibler Divergence Between Exponential Family Densities

It is well-known that the KLD between two distributions P_{θ_1} and P_{θ_2} of $\mathcal{E}$ amounts to computing an equivalent Fenchel–Young divergence [13]:

$$D_{KL}[P_{\theta_1}:P_{\theta_2}] = \int_\mathcal{X} p_{\theta_1}(x) \log \frac{p_{\theta_1}(x)}{p_{\theta_2}(x)} d\mu(x) = Y_{F,F^*}(\theta_2, \eta_1), \tag{9}$$

where $\eta = \nabla F(\theta) = E_{P_\theta}[t(x)]$ is the moment parameter [1] and

$$\nabla F(\theta) = \left[\frac{\partial}{\partial \theta_1} F(\theta), \ldots, \frac{\partial}{\partial \theta_D} F(\theta)\right]^\top, \tag{10}$$

is the gradient of F with respect to $\theta = [\theta_1, \ldots, \theta_D]^\top$. The Fenchel–Young divergence is defined for a pair of strictly convex conjugate functions [14] $F(\theta)$ and $F^*(\eta)$ related by the Legendre–Fenchel transform by

$$Y_{F,F^*}(\theta_1, \eta_2) := F(\theta_1) + F^*(\eta_2) - \theta_1^\top \eta_2. \tag{11}$$

Amari (1985) first introduced this formula as the canonical divergence of dually flat spaces in information geometry [15] (Equation 3.21), and proved that the Fenchel–Young divergence is obtained as the KLD between densities belonging to the same exponential family [15] (Theorem 3.7). Azoury and Warmuth expressed the KLD $D_{KL}[P_{\theta_1}:P_{\theta_2}]$ using dual Bregman divergences in [13] (2001):

$$D_{KL}[P_{\theta_1}:P_{\theta_2}] = B_F(\theta_2:\theta_1) = B_{F^*}(\eta_1:\eta_2), \tag{12}$$

where a Bregman divergence [16] $B_F(\theta_1:\theta_2)$ is defined for a strictly convex and differentiable generator $F(\theta)$ by:

$$B_F(\theta_1:\theta_2) := F(\theta_1) - F(\theta_2) - (\theta_1 - \theta_2)^\top \nabla F(\theta_2). \tag{13}$$

Acharyya termed the divergence Y_{F,F^*} the Fenchel–Young divergence in his PhD thesis [17] (2013), and Blondel et al. called such divergences Fenchel–Young losses (2020) in the context of machine learning [18] (Equation (9) in Definition 2). This term was also used by the author the Legendre–Fenchel divergence in [19]. The Fenchel–Young divergence stems from the Fenchel–Young inequality [14,20]:

$$F(\theta_1) + F^*(\eta_2) \geq \theta_1^\top \eta_2, \tag{14}$$

with equality if and only if $\eta_2 = \nabla F(\theta_1)$.

Figure 1 visualizes the 1D Fenchel–Young divergence and gives a geometric proof that $Y_{F,F^*}(\theta_1, \eta_2) \geq 0$ with equality if and only if $\eta_2 = F'(\theta_1)$. Indeed, by considering the behavior of the Legendre–Fenchel transformation under translations:

- if $F_t(\theta) = F(\theta + t)$ then $F_t^*(\eta) = F^*(\eta) - \eta^\top t$ for all $t \in \mathbb{R}$, and
- if $F_\lambda(\theta) = F(\theta) + \lambda$ then $F_\lambda^*(\eta) = F^*(\eta) - \lambda$ for all $\lambda \in \mathbb{R}$,

we may assume without loss of generality that $F(0) = 0$. The function $F'(\theta)$ is strictly increasing and continuous since $F(\theta)$ is a strictly convex and differentiable convex function. Thus we have $F(\theta) = \int_0^\theta F'(\theta) \, d\theta$ and $F^*(\eta) = \int_0^\eta F^{*\prime}(\eta) \, d\eta = \int_0^\eta F'^{-1}(\eta) \, d\eta$.

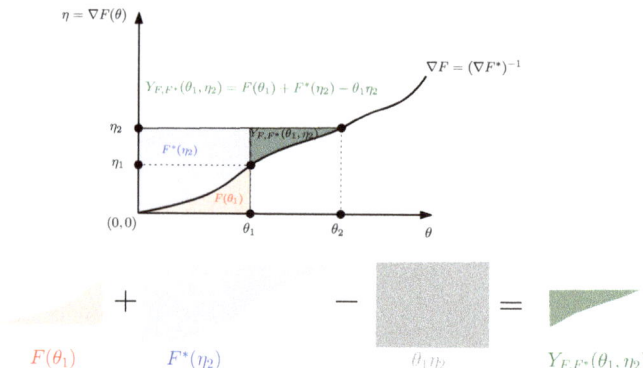

Figure 1. Visualizing the Fenchel–Young divergence.

The Bregman divergence $B_F(\theta_1 : \theta_2)$ amounts to a dual Bregman divergence [13] between the dual parameters with swapped order: $B_F(\theta_1 : \theta_2) = B_{F^*}(\eta_2 : \eta_1)$ where $\eta_i = \nabla F(\theta_i)$ for $i \in \{1,2\}$. Thus the KLD between two distributions P_{θ_1} and P_{θ_2} of $\mathcal{E}$ can be expressed equivalently as follows:

$$D_{\mathrm{KL}}[P_{\theta_1} : P_{\theta_2}] = Y_{F,F^*}(\theta_2 : \eta_1) = B_F(\theta_2 : \theta_1) = B_{F^*}(\eta_1 : \eta_2) = Y_{F^*,F}(\eta_1 : \eta_2). \tag{15}$$

The symmetrized Kullback–Leibler divergence $D_J[P_{\theta_1} : P_{\theta_2}]$ between two distributions P_{θ_1} and P_{θ_2} of $\mathcal{E}$ is called Jeffreys' divergence [21] and amounts to a symmetrized Bregman divergence [22]:

$$\begin{aligned} D_J[P_{\theta_1} : P_{\theta_2}] &= D_{\mathrm{KL}}[P_{\theta_1} : P_{\theta_2}] + D_{\mathrm{KL}}[P_{\theta_2} : P_{\theta_1}], & (16)\\ &= B_F(\theta_2 : \theta_1) + B_F(\theta_1 : \theta_2), & (17)\\ &= (\theta_2 - \theta_1)^\top (\eta_2 - \eta_1) := S_F(\theta_1, \theta_2). & (18) \end{aligned}$$

Note that the Bregman divergence $B_F(\theta_1 : \theta_2)$ can also be interpreted as a surface area:

$$B_F(\theta_1 : \theta_2) = \int_{\theta_2}^{\theta_1} (F'(\theta) - F'(\theta_2)) \, d\theta. \tag{19}$$

Figure 2 illustrates the sided and symmetrized Bregman divergences.

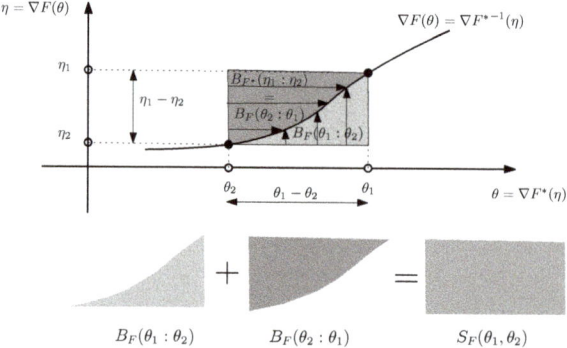

Figure 2. Visualizing the sided and symmetrized Bregman divergences.

1.5. Contributions and Paper Outline

We recall in Section 2 the formula obtained for the Kullback–Leibler divergence between two exponential family densities equivalent to each other [23] (Equation (29)). Inspired by this formula, we give a definition of the duo Fenchel–Young divergence induced by a pair of strictly convex functions F_1 and F_2 (Definition 1) in Section 3, and prove that the divergence is always non-negative provided that F_1 upper bounds F_2. We then define the duo Bregman divergence (Definition 2) corresponding to the duo Fenchel–Young divergence. In Section 4, we show that the Kullback–Leibler divergence between a truncated density and a density of a same parametric exponential family amounts to a duo Fenchel–Young divergence or equivalently to a duo Bregman divergence on swapped parameters (Theorem 1). That is, we consider a truncated exponential family [7] $\mathcal{E}_1$ of an exponential family $\mathcal{E}_1$ such that the common support of the distributions of $\mathcal{E}_1$ is contained in the common support of the distributions of $\mathcal{E}_2$ and both canonical decompositions of the families coincide (see Equation (2)). In particular, when $\mathcal{E}_2$ is also a truncated exponential family of $\mathcal{E}$, then we express the KLD between two truncated distributions as a duo Bregman divergence. As examples, we report the formula for the Kullback–Leibler divergence between two densities of truncated exponential families (Corollary 1), and illustrate the formula for the Kullback–Leibler divergence between truncated exponential distributions (Example 6) and for the Kullback–Leibler divergence between truncated normal distributions (Example 7).

In Section 5, we further consider the skewed Bhattacharyya distance between densities of truncated exponential families and prove that it amounts to a duo Jensen divergence (Theorem 2). Finally, we conclude in Section 6.

2. Kullback–Leibler Divergence Between Different Exponential Families

Consider now two exponential families [1] $\mathcal{P}$ and $\mathcal{Q}$ defined by their Radon–Nikodym derivatives with respect to two positive measures $\mu_\mathcal{P}$ and $\mu_\mathcal{Q}$ on $(\mathcal{X}, \Sigma)$:

$$\mathcal{P} = \{P_\theta : \theta \in \Theta\}, \tag{20}$$
$$\mathcal{Q} = \{Q_{\theta'} : \theta' \in \Theta'\}. \tag{21}$$

The corresponding natural parameter spaces are

$$\Theta = \left\{\theta \in \mathbb{R}^D : \int_\mathcal{X} \exp(\theta^\top t_\mathcal{P}(x) + k_\mathcal{P}(x)) \, d\mu_\mathcal{P}(x) < \infty\right\}, \tag{22}$$

$$\Theta' = \left\{\theta' \in \mathbb{R}^{D'} : \int_\mathcal{X} \exp(\theta'^\top t_\mathcal{Q}(x) + k_\mathcal{Q}(x)) \, d\mu_\mathcal{Q}(x) < \infty\right\}, \tag{23}$$

The order of $\mathcal{P}$ is D, $t_\mathcal{P}(x)$ denotes the sufficient statistics of P_θ, and $k_\mathcal{P}(x)$ is a term to adjust/tilt the base measure $\mu_\mathcal{P}$. Similarly, the order of $\mathcal{Q}$ is D', $t_\mathcal{Q}(x)$ denotes the sufficient statistics of $Q_{\theta'}$, and $k_\mathcal{Q}(x)$ is an optional term to adjust the base measure $\mu_\mathcal{Q}$. Let p_θ and $q_{\theta'}$ denote the Radon–Nikodym derivatives with respect to the measures $\mu_\mathcal{P}$ and $\mu_\mathcal{Q}$, respectively:

$$p_\theta = \frac{dP_\theta}{d\mu_\mathcal{P}} = \exp(\theta^\top t_\mathcal{P}(x) - F_\mathcal{P}(\theta) + k_\mathcal{P}(x)), \tag{24}$$

$$q_{\theta'} = \frac{dQ_{\theta'}}{d\mu_\mathcal{Q}} = \exp(\theta'^\top t_\mathcal{Q}(x) - F_\mathcal{Q}(\theta') + k_\mathcal{Q}(x)), \tag{25}$$

where $F_\mathcal{P}(\theta)$ and $F_\mathcal{Q}(\theta')$ denote the corresponding log-normalizers of $\mathcal{P}$ and $\mathcal{Q}$, respectively.

$$F_\mathcal{P}(\theta) = \log\left(\int \exp(\theta^\top t_\mathcal{P}(x) + k_\mathcal{P}(x)) \, d\mu_\mathcal{P}(x)\right), \tag{26}$$

$$F_\mathcal{Q}(\theta) = \log\left(\int \exp(\theta^\top t_\mathcal{Q}(x) + k_\mathcal{Q}(x)) \, d\mu_\mathcal{Q}(x)\right). \tag{27}$$

The functions $F_\mathcal{P}$ and $F_\mathcal{Q}$ are strictly convex and real analytic [1]. Hence, those functions are infinitely many times differentiable on their open natural parameter spaces.

Consider the KLD between $P_\theta \in \mathcal{P}$ and $Q_{\theta'} \in \mathcal{Q}$ such that $\mu_\mathcal{P} = \mu_\mathcal{Q}$ (and hence $P_\theta \ll Q_{\theta'}$). Then the KLD between P_θ and $Q_{\theta'}$ was first considered in [23]:

$$D_{\mathrm{KL}}[P_\theta : Q_{\theta'}] = E_P\left[\log\left(\frac{\mathrm{d}P_\theta}{\mathrm{d}Q_{\theta'}}\right)\right], \tag{28}$$

$$= E_{P_\theta}\left[\left(\theta^\top t_\mathcal{P}(x) - {\theta'}^\top t_\mathcal{Q}(x) - F_\mathcal{P}(\theta) + F_\mathcal{Q}(\theta') + k_\mathcal{P}(x) - k_\mathcal{Q}(x)\right)\underbrace{\frac{\mathrm{d}\mu_\mathcal{P}}{\mathrm{d}\mu_\mathcal{Q}}}_{=1}\right],$$

$$= F_\mathcal{Q}(\theta') - F_\mathcal{P}(\theta) + \theta^\top E_{P_\theta}[t_\mathcal{P}(x)] - {\theta'}^\top E_{P_\theta}[t_\mathcal{Q}(x)] + E_{P_\theta}[k_\mathcal{P}(x) - k_\mathcal{Q}(x)].$$

Recall that the dual parameterization of an exponential family density P_θ is P^η with $\eta = E_{P_\theta}[t_\mathcal{P}(x)] = \nabla F_\mathcal{P}(\theta)$ [1], and that the Fenchel–Young equality is $F(\theta) + F^*(\eta) = \theta^\top \eta$ for $\eta = \nabla F(\theta)$. Thus the KLD between P_θ and $Q_{\theta'}$ can be rewritten as

$$D_{\mathrm{KL}}[P_\theta : Q_{\theta'}] = F_\mathcal{Q}(\theta') + F^*_\mathcal{P}(\eta) - {\theta'}^\top E_{P_\theta}[t_\mathcal{Q}(x)] + E_{P_\theta}[k_\mathcal{P}(x) - k_\mathcal{Q}(x)]. \tag{29}$$

This formula was reported in [23] and generalizes the Fenchel–Young divergence [17] obtained when $\mathcal{P} = \mathcal{Q}$ (with $t_\mathcal{P}(x) = t_\mathcal{Q}(x)$, $k_\mathcal{P}(x) = k_\mathcal{Q}(x)$, and $F(\theta) = F_\mathcal{P}(\theta) = F_\mathcal{Q}(\theta)$ and $F^*(\eta) = F^*_\mathcal{P}(\eta) = F^*_\mathcal{Q}(\eta)$).

The formula of Equation (29) was illustrated in [23] with two examples: the KLD between Laplacian distributions and zero-centered Gaussian distributions, and the KLD between two Weibull distributions. Both these examples use the Lebesgue base measure for $\mu_\mathcal{P}$ and $\mu_\mathcal{Q}$.

Let us report another example that uses the counting measure as the base measure for $\mu_\mathcal{P}$ and $\mu_\mathcal{Q}$.

Example 1. *Consider the KLD between a Poisson probability mass function (pmf) and a geometric pmf. The canonical decompositions of the Poisson and geometric pmfs are summarized in Table 1. The KLD between a Poisson pmf p_λ and a geometric pmf q_p is equal to*

$$D_{\mathrm{KL}}[P_\lambda : Q_p] = F_\mathcal{Q}(\theta') + F^*_\mathcal{P}(\eta) - E_{P_\theta}[t_\mathcal{Q}(x)] \cdot \theta' + E_{P_\theta}[k_\mathcal{P}(x) - k_\mathcal{Q}(x)], \tag{30}$$
$$= -\log p + \lambda \log \lambda - \lambda - \lambda \log(1-p) - E_{P_\lambda}[\log x!] \tag{31}$$

Since $E_{P_\lambda}[-\log x!] = -\sum_{k=0}^\infty e^{-\lambda} \frac{\lambda^k \log(k!)}{k!}$, we have

$$D_{\mathrm{KL}}[P_\lambda : Q_p] = -\log p + \lambda \log \frac{\lambda}{1-p} - \lambda - \sum_{k=0}^\infty e^{-\lambda} \frac{\lambda^k \log(k!)}{k!}. \tag{32}$$

Note that we can calculate the KLD between two geometric distributions Q_{p_1} and Q_{p_2} as

$$D_{\mathrm{KL}}[Q_{p_1} : Q_{p_2}] = B_{F_\mathcal{Q}}(\theta(p_2) : \theta(p_1)), \tag{33}$$
$$= F_\mathcal{Q}(\theta(p_2)) - F_\mathcal{Q}(\theta(p_1)) - (\theta(p_2) - \theta(p_1))\eta(p_1), \tag{34}$$

We obtain:

$$D_{\mathrm{KL}}[Q_{p_1} : Q_{p_2}] = \log\left(\frac{p_1}{p_2}\right) - \left(1 - \frac{1}{p_1}\right)\log\frac{1-p_1}{1-p_2}.$$

Table 1. Canonical decomposition of the Poisson and the geometric discrete exponential families.

Quantity	Poisson Family $\mathcal{P}$	Geometric Family $\mathcal{Q}$
support	$\mathbb{N} \cup \{0\}$	$\mathbb{N} \cup \{0\}$
base measure	counting measure	counting measure
ordinary parameter	rate $\lambda > 0$	success probability $p \in (0,1)$
pmf	$\frac{\lambda^x}{x!} \exp(-\lambda)$	$(1-p)^x p$
sufficient statistic	$t_\mathcal{P}(x) = x$	$t_\mathcal{Q}(x) = x$
natural parameter	$\theta(\lambda) = \log \lambda$	$\theta(p) = \log(1-p)$
cumulant function	$F_\mathcal{P}(\theta) = \exp(\theta)$	$F_\mathcal{Q}(\theta) = -\log(1 - \exp(\theta))$
	$F_\mathcal{P}(\lambda) = \lambda$	$F_\mathcal{Q}(p) = -\log(p)$
auxiliary term	$k_\mathcal{P}(x) = -\log x!$	$k_\mathcal{Q}(x) = 0$
moment $\eta = E[t(x)]$	$\eta = \lambda$	$\eta = \frac{e^\theta}{1-e^\theta} = \frac{1}{p} - 1$
negentropy	$F^*_\mathcal{P}(\eta(\lambda)) = \lambda \log \lambda - \lambda$	$F^*_\mathcal{Q}(\eta(p)) = \left(1 - \frac{1}{p}\right) \log(1-p) + \log p$
$(F^*(\eta) = \theta \cdot \eta - F(\theta))$		

3. The Duo Fenchel–Young Divergence and Its Corresponding Duo Bregman Divergence

Inspired by formula of Equation (29), we shall define the *duo Fenchel–Young divergence* using a *dominance condition* on a pair $(F_1(\theta), F_2(\theta))$ of strictly convex generators.

Definition 1 (duo Fenchel–Young divergence). *Let $F_1(\theta)$ and $F_2(\theta)$ be two strictly convex functions such that $F_1(\theta) \geq F_2(\theta)$ for any $\theta \in \Theta_{12} = \mathrm{dom}(F_1) \cap \mathrm{dom}(F_2)$. Then the duo Fenchel–Young divergence $Y_{F_1,F_2^*}(\theta, \eta')$ is defined by*

$$Y_{F_1,F_2^*}(\theta, \eta') := F_1(\theta) + F_2^*(\eta') - \theta^\top \eta'. \tag{35}$$

When $F_1(\theta) = F_2(\theta) =: F(\theta)$, we have $F_1^*(\eta) = F_2^*(\eta) =: F^*(\eta)$, and we retrieve the ordinary Fenchel–Young divergence [17]:

$$Y_{F,F^*}(\theta, \eta') := F(\theta) + F^*(\eta') - \theta^\top \eta' \geq 0. \tag{36}$$

Note that in Equation (35), we have $\eta' = \nabla F_2(\theta')$.

Property 1 (Non-negative duo Fenchel–Young divergence). *The duo Fenchel–Young divergence is always non-negative.*

Proof. The proof relies on the reverse dominance property of strictly convex and differentiable conjugate functions:

Lemma 1 (Reverse majorization order of functions by the Legendre–Fenchel transform). *Let $F_1(\theta)$ and $F_2(\theta)$ be two Legendre-type convex functions [14]. Then if $F_1(\theta) \geq F_2(\theta)$ then we have $F_2^*(\eta) \geq F_1^*(\eta)$.*

Proof. This property is graphically illustrated in Figure 3. The reverse dominance property of the Legendre–Fenchel transformation can be checked algebraically as follows:

$$\begin{align}
F_1^*(\eta) &= \sup_{\theta \in \Theta} \{\eta^\top \theta - F_1(\theta)\}, \tag{37}\\
&= \eta^\top \theta_1 - F_1(\theta_1) \quad (\text{with } \eta = \nabla F_1(\theta_1)), \tag{38}\\
&\leq \eta^\top \theta_1 - F_2(\theta_1), \tag{39}\\
&\leq \sup_{\theta \in \Theta} \{\eta^\top \theta - F_2(\theta)\} = F_2^*(\eta). \tag{40}
\end{align}$$

□

Thus we have $F_1^*(\eta) \leq F_2^*(\eta)$ when $F_1(\theta) \geq F_2(\theta)$. Therefore it follows that $Y_{F_1, F_2^*}(\theta, \eta') \geq 0$ since we have

$$Y_{F_1, F_2^*}(\theta, \eta') := F_1(\theta) + F_2^*(\eta') - \theta^\top \eta', \tag{41}$$
$$\geq F_1(\theta) + F_1^*(\eta') - \theta^\top \eta' = Y_{F_1, F_1^*}(\theta, \eta') \geq 0, \tag{42}$$

where Y_{F_1, F_1^*} is the ordinary Fenchel–Young divergence, which is guaranteed to be non-negative from the Fenchel–Young inequality. □

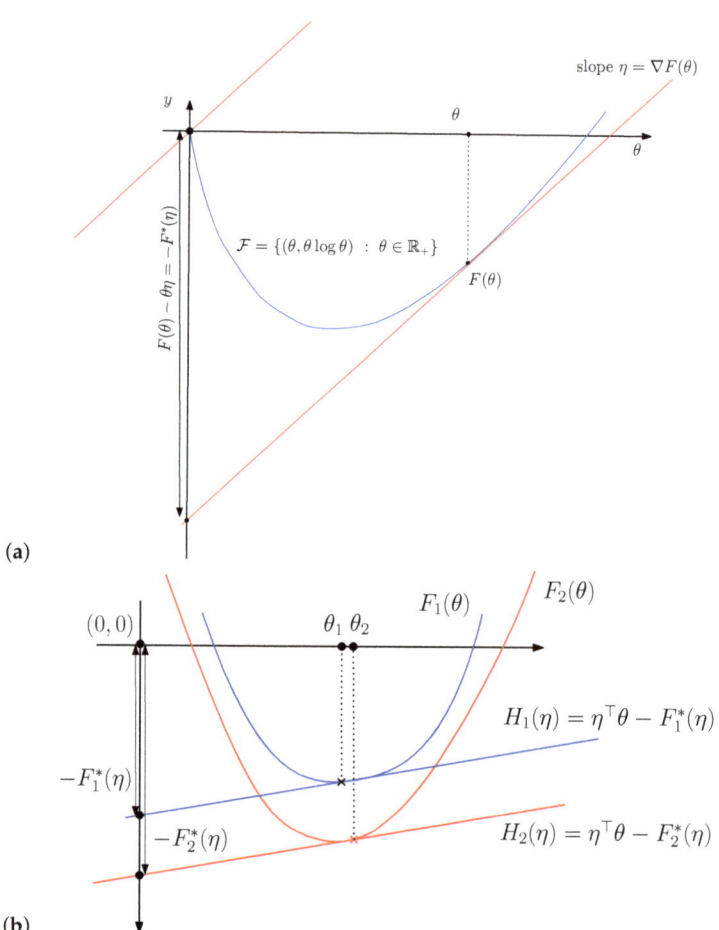

Figure 3. (**a**) Visual illustration of the Legendre–Fenchel transformation: $F^*(\eta)$ is measured as the vertical gap (left long black line with both arrows) between the origin and the hyperplane of the "slope" η tangent at $F(\theta)$ evaluated at $\theta = 0$. (**b**) The Legendre transforms $F_1^*(\eta)$ and $F_1^*(\eta)$ of two functions $F_1(\theta)$ and $F_2(\theta)$ such that $F_1(\theta) \geq F_2(\theta)$ reverse the dominance order: $F_2^*(\eta) \geq F_1^*(\eta)$.

We can express the duo Fenchel–Young divergence using the primal coordinate systems as a generalization of the Bregman divergence to two generators that we term the duo Bregman divergence (see Figure 4):

$$B_{F_1, F_2}(\theta : \theta') := Y_{F_1, F_2^*}(\theta, \eta') = F_1(\theta) - F_2(\theta') - (\theta - \theta')^\top \nabla F_2(\theta'), \tag{43}$$

with $\eta' = \nabla F_2(\theta')$.

This generalized Bregman divergence is non-negative when $F_1(\theta) \geq F_2(\theta)$. Indeed, we check that

$$B_{F_1,F_2}(\theta:\theta') = F_1(\theta) - F_2(\theta') - (\theta - \theta')^\top \nabla F_2(\theta'), \quad (44)$$

$$\geq F_2(\theta) - F_2(\theta') - (\theta - \theta')^\top \nabla F_2(\theta') = B_{F_2}(\theta:\theta') \geq 0. \quad (45)$$

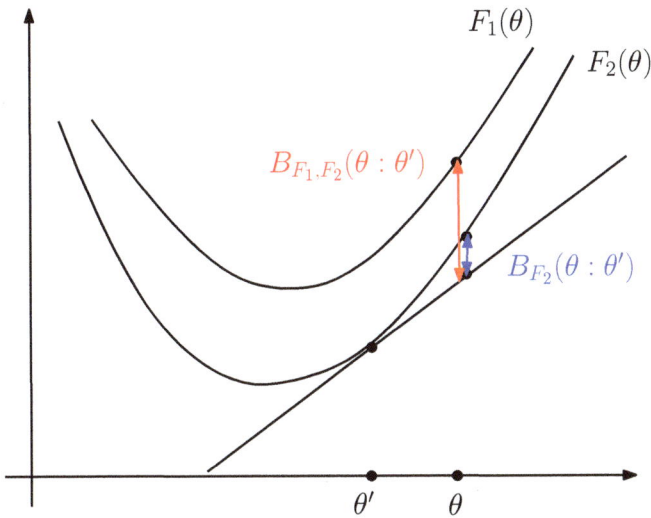

Figure 4. The duo Bregman divergence induced by two strictly convex and differentiable functions F_1 and F_2 such that $F_1(\theta) \geq F_2(\theta)$. We check graphically that $B_{F_1,F_2}(\theta:\theta') \geq B_{F_2}(\theta:\theta')$ (vertical gaps).

Definition 2 (duo Bregman divergence). *Let $F_1(\theta)$ and $F_2(\theta)$ be two strictly convex functions such that $F_1(\theta) \geq F_2(\theta)$ for any $\theta \in \Theta_{12} = \mathrm{dom}(F_1) \cap \mathrm{dom}(F_2)$. Then the generalized Bregman divergence is defined by*

$$B_{F_1,F_2}(\theta:\theta') = F_1(\theta) - F_2(\theta') - (\theta - \theta')^\top \nabla F_2(\theta') \geq 0. \quad (46)$$

Example 2. Consider $F_1(\theta) = \frac{a}{2}\theta^2$ for $a > 0$. We have $\eta = a\theta$, $\theta = \frac{\eta}{a}$, and

$$F_1^*(\eta) = \frac{\eta^2}{a} - \frac{a}{2}\frac{\eta^2}{a^2} = \frac{\eta^2}{2a}. \quad (47)$$

Let $F_2(\theta) = \frac{1}{2}\theta^2$ so that $F_1(\theta) \geq F_2(\theta)$ for $a \geq 1$. We check that $F_1^*(\eta) = \frac{\eta^2}{2a} \leq F_2^*(\eta)$ when $a \geq 1$. The duo Fenchel–Young divergence is

$$Y_{F_1,F_2^*}(\theta,\eta') = \frac{a}{2}\theta^2 + \frac{1}{2}\eta'^2 - \theta\eta' \geq 0, \quad (48)$$

when $a \geq 1$. We can express the duo Fenchel–Young divergence in the primal coordinate systems as

$$B_{F_1,F_2}(\theta,\theta') = \frac{a}{2}\theta^2 + \frac{1}{2}\theta'^2 - \theta\theta'. \quad (49)$$

When $a = 1$, $F_1(\theta) = F_2(\theta) = \frac{1}{2}\theta^2 := F(\theta)$, and we obtain $B_F(\theta,\theta') = \frac{1}{2}\|\theta - \theta'\|_2^2$, half the squared Euclidean distance as expected. Figure 5 displays the graph plot of the duo Bregman divergence for several values of a.

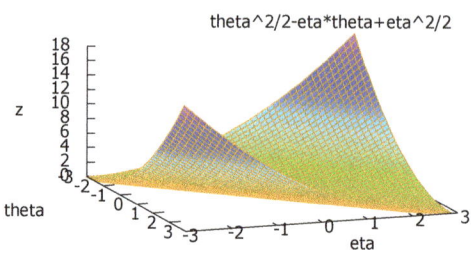

(a)

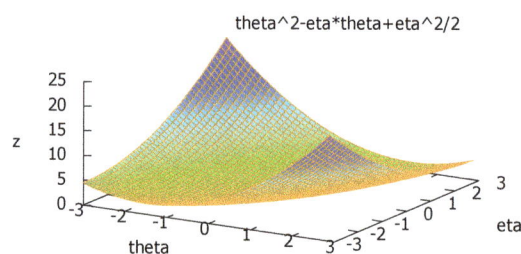

(b)

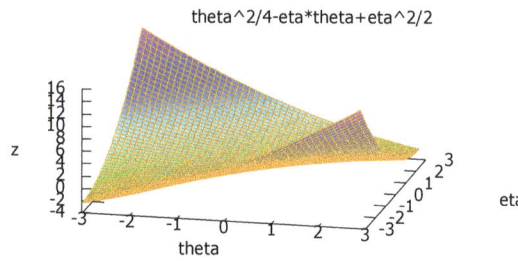

(c)

Figure 5. The duo half squared Euclidean distance $D_a^2(\theta:\theta') := \frac{a}{2}\theta^2 + \frac{1}{2}\theta'^2 - \theta\theta'$ is non-negative when $a \geq 1$: (**a**) half squared Euclidean distance ($a = 1$), (**b**) $a = 2$, (**c**) $a = \frac{1}{2}$, which shows that the divergence can be negative then since $a < 1$.

Example 3. *Consider $F_1(\theta) = \theta^2$ and $F_2(\theta) = \theta^4$ on the domain $\Theta = [0,1]$. We have $F_1(\theta) \geq F_2(\theta)$ for $\theta \in \Theta$. The convex conjugate of $F_1(\eta)$ is $F_1^*(\eta) = \frac{1}{4}\eta^2$. We have*

$$F_2^*(\eta) = \eta^{\frac{4}{3}}\left(\left(\frac{1}{4}\right)^{\frac{1}{3}} - \left(\frac{1}{4}\right)^{\frac{4}{3}}\right) = \frac{3}{4^{\frac{4}{3}}}\eta^{\frac{4}{3}} \tag{50}$$

with $\eta_2(\theta) = 4\theta^3$. Figure 6 plots the convex functions $F_1(\theta)$ and $F_2(\theta)$, and their convex conjugates $F_1^*(\eta)$ and $F_2^*(\eta)$. We observe that $F_1(\theta) \geq F_2(\theta)$ on $\theta \in [0,1]$ and that $F_1^*(\eta) \leq F_2^*(\eta)$ on $H = [0,2]$.

We now state a property between dual duo Bregman divergences:

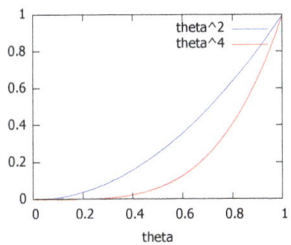
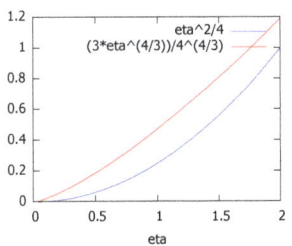

Convex functions $F_1(\theta) \geq F_2(\theta)$ Conjugate functions $F_1^*(\eta) \leq F_2^*(\eta)$

Figure 6. The Legendre transform reverses the dominance ordering: $F_1(\theta) = \theta^2 \geq F_2(\theta) = \theta^4 \Leftrightarrow F_1^*(\eta) \leq F_2^*(\eta)$ for $\theta \in [0,1]$.

Property 2 (Dual duo Fenchel–Young and Bregman divergences). *We have*

$$Y_{F_1,F_2^*}(\theta:\eta') = B_{F_1,F_2}(\theta:\theta') = B_{F_2^*,F_1^*}(\eta':\eta) = Y_{F_2^*,F_1}(\eta':\theta) \tag{51}$$

Proof. From the Fenchel–Young equalities of the inequalities, we have $F_1(\theta) = \theta^\top \eta - F_1^*(\eta)$ for $\eta = \nabla F_1(\theta)$ and $F_2(\theta') = \theta'^\top \eta' - F_2^*(\eta')$ with $\eta' = \nabla F_2(\theta')$. Thus we have

$$\begin{aligned}
B_{F_1,F_2}(\theta:\theta') &= F_1(\theta) - F_2(\theta') - (\theta - \theta')^\top \nabla F_2(\theta'), \tag{52}\\
&= \theta^\top \eta - F_1^*(\eta) - \theta'^\top \eta' + F_2^*(\eta') - (\theta - \theta')^\top \eta', \tag{53}\\
&= F_2^*(\eta') - F_1^*(\eta) - (\eta' - \eta)^\top \theta, \tag{54}\\
&= B_{F_2^*,F_1^*}(\eta':\eta). \tag{55}
\end{aligned}$$

Recall that $F_1(\theta) \geq F_2(\theta)$ implies that $F_1^*(\eta) \leq F_2^*(\eta)$ (Lemma 1), $\theta = \nabla F_1^*(\eta)$, and therefore the dual duo Bregman divergence is non-negative:

$$\begin{aligned}
B_{F_2^*,F_1^*}(\eta':\eta) &= F_2^*(\eta') - F_1^*(\eta) - (\eta' - \eta)^\top \theta,\\
&\geq \underbrace{F_1^*(\eta') - F_1^*(\eta) - (\eta' - \eta)^\top \nabla F_1^*(\eta)}_{B_{F_1^*}(\eta':\eta) \geq 0}.
\end{aligned}$$

□

4. Kullback–Leibler Divergence between Distributions of Truncated Exponential Families

Let $\mathcal{E}_1 = \{P_\theta : \theta \in \Theta_1\}$ be an exponential family of distributions all dominated by μ with Radon–Nikodym density $p_\theta(x) = \exp(\theta^\top t(x) - F_1(\theta) + k(x)) \, d\mu(x)$ defined on the support $\mathcal{X}_1$. Let $\mathcal{E}_2 = \{Q_\theta : \theta \in \Theta_2\}$ be another exponential family of distributions all dominated by μ with Radon–Nikodym density $q_\theta(x) = \exp(\theta^\top t(x) - F_2(\theta) + k(x)) \, d\mu(x)$ defined on the support $\mathcal{X}_2$ such that $\mathcal{X}_1 \subseteq \mathcal{X}_2$. Let $\tilde{p}_\theta(x) = \exp(\theta^\top t(x) + k(x)) \, d\mu(x)$ be the common unnormalized density so that

$$p_\theta(x) = \frac{\tilde{p}_\theta(x)}{Z_1(\theta)} \tag{56}$$

and

$$q_\theta(x) = \frac{\tilde{p}_\theta(x)}{Z_2(\theta)} = \frac{Z_1(\theta)}{Z_2(\theta)} p_\theta(x), \tag{57}$$

with $Z_1(\theta) = \exp(F_1(\theta))$ and $Z_2(\theta) = \exp(F_2(\theta))$ being the log-normalizer functions of $\mathcal{E}_1$ and $\mathcal{E}_2$, respectively.

We have

$$D_{KL}[p_{\theta_1} : q_{\theta_2}] = \int_{\mathcal{X}_1} p_{\theta_1}(x) \log \frac{p_{\theta_1}(x)}{q_{\theta_2}(x)} d\mu(x), \tag{58}$$

$$= \int_{\mathcal{X}_1} p_{\theta_1}(x) \log \frac{p_{\theta_1}(x)}{p_{\theta_2}(x)} d\mu(x) + \int_{\mathcal{X}_1} p_{\theta_1}(x) \log\left(\frac{Z_2(\theta_2)}{Z_1(\theta_2)}\right) d\mu(x), \tag{59}$$

$$= D_{KL}[p_{\theta_1} : p_{\theta_2}] + \log Z_2(\theta_2) - \log Z_1(\theta_2). \tag{60}$$

Since $D_{KL}[p_{\theta_1} : p_{\theta_2}] = B_{F_1}(\theta_2 : \theta_1)$ and $\log Z_i(\theta) = F_i(\theta)$, we obtain

$$D_{KL}[p_{\theta_1} : q_{\theta_2}] = B_{F_1}(\theta_2 : \theta_1) + F_2(\theta_2) - F_1(\theta_2), \tag{61}$$

$$= F_1(\theta_2) - F_1(\theta_1) - (\theta_2 - \theta_1)^\top \nabla F_1(\theta_1) + F_2(\theta_2) - F_1(\theta_2), \tag{62}$$

$$= F_2(\theta_2) - F_1(\theta_1) - (\theta_2 - \theta_1)^\top \nabla F_1(\theta_1) =: B_{F_2,F_1}(\theta_2 : \theta_1). \tag{63}$$

Observe that since $\mathcal{X}_1 \subseteq \mathcal{X}_2$, we have:

$$F_2(\theta) = \log \int_{\mathcal{X}_2} \tilde{p}_\theta(x) \, d\mu(x) \geq \log \int_{\mathcal{X}_1} \tilde{p}_\theta(x) \, d\mu(x) := F_1(\theta). \tag{64}$$

Therefore $\Theta_2 \subseteq \Theta_1$, and the common natural parameter space is $\Theta_{12} = \Theta_1 \cap \Theta_2 = \Theta_2$.

Notice that the reverse Kullback–Leibler divergence $D^*_{KL}[p_{\theta_1} : q_{\theta_2}] = D_{KL}[q_{\theta_2} : p_{\theta_1}] = +\infty$ since $Q_{\theta_2} \not\ll P_{\theta_1}$.

Theorem 1 (Kullback–Leibler divergence between truncated exponential family densities). *Let $\mathcal{E}_2 = \{q_{\theta_2}\}$ be an exponential family with support $\mathcal{X}_2$, and $\mathcal{E}_1 = \{p_{\theta_1}\}$ a truncated exponential family of $\mathcal{E}_2$ with support $\mathcal{X}_1 \subset \mathcal{X}_2$. Let F_1 and F_2 denote the log-normalizers of $\mathcal{E}_1$ and $\mathcal{E}_2$ and η_1 and η_2 the moment parameters corresponding to the natural parameters θ_1 and θ_2. Then the Kullback–Leibler divergence between a truncated density of $\mathcal{E}_1$ and a density of $\mathcal{E}_2$ is*

$$D_{KL}[p_{\theta_1} : q_{\theta_2}] = Y_{F_2,F_1^*}(\theta_2 : \eta_1) = B_{F_2,F_1}(\theta_2 : \theta_1) = B_{F_1^*,F_2^*}(\eta_1 : \eta_2) = Y_{F_1^*,F_2}(\eta_1 : \theta_2). \tag{65}$$

For example, consider the calculation of the KLD between an exponential distribution (view as half a Laplacian distribution, i.e., a truncated Laplacian distribution on the positive real support) and a Laplacian distribution defined on the real line support.

Example 4. *Let $\mathbb{R}_{++} = \{x \in \mathbb{R} : x > 0\}$ denote the set of positive reals. Let $\mathcal{E}_1 = \{p_\lambda(x) = \lambda \exp(-\lambda x), \lambda \in \mathbb{R}_{++}, x > 0\}$ and $\mathcal{E}_2 = \{q_\lambda(x) = \lambda \exp(-\lambda|x|), \lambda \in \mathbb{R}_{++}, x \in \mathbb{R}\}$ denote the exponential families of exponential distributions and Laplacian distributions, respectively. We have the sufficient statistic $t(x) = -|x|$ and natural parameter $\theta = \lambda$ so that $\tilde{p}_\theta(x) = \exp(-|x|\theta)$. The log-normalizers are $F_1(\theta) = -\log \theta$ and $F_2(\theta) = -\log \theta + \log 2$ (hence $F_2(\theta) \geq F_1(\theta)$). The moment parameter $\eta = \nabla F_1(\theta) = \nabla F_2(\theta) = -\frac{1}{\theta} = -\frac{1}{\lambda}$. Thus using the duo Bregman divergence, we have:*

$$D_{KL}[p_{\theta_1} : q_{\theta_2}] = B_{F_2,F_1}(\theta_2 : \theta_1), \tag{66}$$

$$= F_2(\theta_2) - F_1(\theta_1) - (\theta_2 - \theta_1)^\top \nabla F_1(\theta_1), \tag{67}$$

$$= \log 2 + \log \frac{\lambda_1}{\lambda_2} + \frac{\lambda_2}{\lambda_1} - 1. \tag{68}$$

Moreover, we can interpret that divergence using the Itakura–Saito divergence [24]:

$$D_{IS}[\lambda_1 : \lambda_2] := \frac{\lambda_1}{\lambda_2} - \log \frac{\lambda_1}{\lambda_2} - 1 \geq 0. \tag{69}$$

we have

$$D_{KL}[p_{\theta_1} : q_{\theta_2}] = D_{IS}[\lambda_2 : \lambda_1] + \log 2 \geq 0. \tag{70}$$

We check the result using the duo Fenchel–Young divergence:

$$D_{\mathrm{KL}}[p_{\theta_1}:q_{\theta_2}] = Y_{F_2,F_1^*}(\theta_2:\eta_1), \tag{71}$$

with $F_1^*(\eta) = -1 + \log\left(-\frac{1}{\eta}\right)$:

$$\begin{aligned}
D_{\mathrm{KL}}[p_{\theta_1}:q_{\theta_2}] &= Y_{F_2,F_1^*}(\theta_2:\eta_1), & (72)\\
&= -\log\lambda_2 + \log 2 - 1 + \log\lambda_1 + \frac{\lambda_2}{\lambda_1}, & (73)\\
&= \log\frac{\lambda_1}{\lambda_2} + \frac{\lambda_2}{\lambda_1} + \log 2 - 1. & (74)
\end{aligned}$$

Next, consider the calculation of the KLD between a half-normal distribution and a (full) normal distribution:

Example 5. *Consider $\mathcal{E}_1$ and $\mathcal{E}_2$ to be the scale family of the half standard normal distributions and the scale family of the standard normal distribution, respectively. We have $\tilde{p}_\theta(x) = \exp\left(-\frac{x^2}{2\sigma^2}\right)$ with $Z_1(\theta) = \sigma\sqrt{\frac{\pi}{2}}$ and $Z_2(\theta) = \sigma\sqrt{2\pi}$. Let the sufficient statistic be $t(x) = -\frac{x^2}{2}$ so that the natural parameter is $\theta = \frac{1}{\sigma^2} \in \mathbb{R}_{++}$. Here, we have both $\Theta_1 = \Theta_2 = \mathbb{R}_{++}$. For this example, we check that $Z_1(\theta) = \frac{1}{2}Z_2(\theta)$. We have $F_1(\theta) = -\frac{1}{2}\log\theta + \frac{1}{2}\log\frac{\pi}{2}$ and $F_2(\theta) = -\frac{1}{2}\log\theta + \frac{1}{2}\log(2\pi)$ (with $F_2(\theta) \geq F_1(\theta)$). We have $\eta = -\frac{1}{2\theta} = -\frac{1}{2}\sigma^2$. The KLD between two half scale normal distributions is*

$$\begin{aligned}
D_{\mathrm{KL}}[p_{\theta_1}:p_{\theta_2}] &= B_{F_1}(\theta_2:\theta_1), & (75)\\
&= \frac{1}{2}\left(\log\frac{\sigma_2^2}{\sigma_1^2} + \frac{\sigma_1^2}{\sigma_2^2} - 1\right). & (76)
\end{aligned}$$

Since $F_1(\theta)$ and $F_2(\theta)$ differ only by a constant and the Bregman divergence is invariant under an affine term of its generator, we have

$$\begin{aligned}
D_{\mathrm{KL}}[q_{\theta_1}:q_{\theta_2}] &= B_{F_2}(\theta_2:\theta_1), & (77)\\
&= B_{F_1}(\theta_2:\theta_1) = \frac{1}{2}\left(\log\frac{\sigma_2^2}{\sigma_1^2} + \frac{\sigma_1^2}{\sigma_2^2} - 1\right). & (78)
\end{aligned}$$

Moreover, we can interpret those Bregman divergences as half of the Itakura–Saito divergence:

$$D_{\mathrm{KL}}[p_{\theta_1}:p_{\theta_2}] = D_{\mathrm{KL}}[q_{\theta_1}:q_{\theta_2}] = B_{F_2}(\theta_2:\theta_1) = \frac{1}{2}D_{\mathrm{IS}}[\sigma_1^2:\sigma_2^2]. \tag{79}$$

It follows that

$$\begin{aligned}
D_{\mathrm{KL}}[p_{\theta_1}:q_{\theta_2}] &= B_{F_2,F_1}(\theta_2:\theta_1) = F_2(\theta_2) - F_1(\theta_1) - (\theta_2 - \theta_1)^\top \nabla F_1(\theta_1), & (80)\\
&= \frac{1}{2}\left(\log\frac{\sigma_2^2}{\sigma_1^2} + \frac{\sigma_1^2}{\sigma_2^2} + \log 4 - 1\right), & (81)\\
&= D_{\mathrm{KL}}[q_{\theta_1}:q_{\theta_2}] + \log 2. & (82)
\end{aligned}$$

Since $\log 2 > 0$, we have $D_{\mathrm{KL}}[p_{\theta_1}:q_{\theta_2}] \geq D_{\mathrm{KL}}[q_{\theta_1}:q_{\theta_2}]$.

Thus the Kullback–Leibler divergence between a truncated density and another density of the same exponential family amounts to calculate a duo Bregman divergence on the reverse parameter order: $D_{\mathrm{KL}}[p_{\theta_1}:q_{\theta_2}] = B_{F_2,F_1}(\theta_2:\theta_1)$. Let $D_{\mathrm{KL}}^*[p:q] := D_{\mathrm{KL}}[q:p]$ be the reverse Kullback–Leibler divergence. Then $D_{\mathrm{KL}}^*[q_{\theta_2}:p_{\theta_1}] = B_{F_2,F_1}(\theta_2:\theta_1)$.

Notice that truncated exponential families are also exponential families but those exponential families may be non-steep [25].

Let $\mathcal{E}_1 = \{p_\theta^{a_1,b_1}\}$ and $\mathcal{E}_2 = \{p_\theta^{a_2,b_2}\}$ be two truncated exponential families of the exponential family $\mathcal{E} = \{p_\theta = \frac{dP_\theta}{d\mu}\}$ with log-normalizer $F(\theta)$ such that

$$p_\theta^{a_i,b_i}(x) = \frac{p_\theta(x)}{Z_{a_i,b_i}(\theta)}, \tag{83}$$

with $Z_{a_i,b_i}(\theta) = \Phi_\theta(b_i) - \Phi_\theta(a_i)$, where $\Phi_\theta(x)$ denotes the CDF of $p_\theta(x)$. Then the log-normalizer of $\mathcal{E}_i$ is $F_i(\theta) = F(\theta) + \log(\Phi_\theta(b_i) - \Phi_\theta(a_i))$ for $i \in \{1,2\}$.

Corollary 1 (Kullback–Leibler divergence between densities of truncated exponential families). *Let $\mathcal{E}_i = \{p_\theta^{a_i,b_i}\}$ be truncated exponential families of the exponential family $\mathcal{E} = \{p_\theta\}$ with support $\mathcal{X}_i = [a_i, b_i] \subset \mathcal{X}$ (where $\mathcal{X}$ denotes the support of $\mathcal{E}$) for $i \in \{1,2\}$. Then the Kullback–Leibler divergence between $p_{\theta_1}^{a_1,b_1}$ and $p_{\theta_2}^{a_2,b_2}$ is infinite if $[a_1, b_1] \not\subset [a_2, b_2]$ and has the following formula when $[a_1, b_1] \subset [a_2, b_2]$:*

$$D_{\mathrm{KL}}[p_{\theta_1}^{a_1,b_1} : p_{\theta_2}^{a_2,b_2}] = D_{\mathrm{KL}}[p_{\theta_1}^{a_1,b_1} : p_{\theta_2}^{a_1,b_1}] + \log \frac{Z_{a_2,b_2}(\theta_2)}{Z_{a_1,b_1}(\theta_2)}. \tag{84}$$

Proof. We have $p_\theta^{a_1,b_1} = \frac{p_\theta}{Z_{a_1,b_1}(\theta)}$ and $p_\theta^{a_2,b_2} = \frac{p_\theta}{Z_{a_2,b_2}(\theta)}$. Therefore $p_\theta^{a_2,b_2} = p_\theta^{a_1,b_1} \frac{Z_{a_1,b_1}(\theta)}{Z_{a_2,b_2}(\theta)}$. Thus we have

$$D_{\mathrm{KL}}[p_{\theta_1}^{a_1,b_1} : p_{\theta_2}^{a_2,b_2}] = \int_{\mathcal{X}_1} p_{\theta_1}^{a_1,b_1}(x) \log \frac{p_{\theta_1}^{a_1,b_1}(x)}{p_{\theta_2}^{a_2,b_2}} d\mu(x), \tag{85}$$

$$= \int_{\mathcal{X}_1} p_{\theta_1}^{a_1,b_1}(x) \log \frac{p_{\theta_1}^{a_1,b_1}(x)}{p_{\theta_2}^{a_1,b_1}} d\mu(x) + \log \frac{Z_{a_2,b_2}(\theta_2)}{Z_{a_1,b_1}(\theta_2)}, \tag{86}$$

$$= D_{\mathrm{KL}}[p_{\theta_1}^{a_1,b_1} : p_{\theta_2}^{a_1,b_1}] + \log \frac{Z_{a_2,b_2}(\theta_2)}{Z_{a_1,b_1}(\theta_2)}. \tag{87}$$

□

Thus the KLD between truncated exponential family densities $p_{\theta_1}^{a_1,b_1}$ and $p_{\theta_2}^{a_2,b_2}$ amounts to the KLD between the densities with the same truncation parameter with an additive term depending on the log ratio of the mass with respect to the truncated supports evaluated at θ_2. We shall illustrate with two examples the calculation of the KLD between truncated exponential families.

Example 6. Consider the calculation of the KLD between a truncated exponential distribution $p_{\lambda_1}^{a_1,b_1}$ with support $\mathcal{X}_1 = [a_1, b_1]$ ($b_1 > a_1 \geq 0$) and another truncated exponential distribution $p_{\lambda_2}^{a_2,b_2}$ with support $\mathcal{X}_2 = [a_2, b_2]$ ($b_2 > a_2 \geq 0$). We have $p_\lambda(x) = \lambda \exp(-\lambda x)$ (density of the untruncated exponential family with natural parameter $\theta = \lambda$, sufficient statistic $t(x) = -x$ and log-normalizer $F(\theta) = -\log \theta$), $p_{\lambda_1}^{a_1,b_1} = \frac{1}{Z_{a_1,b_1}(\lambda)} p_{\lambda_1}(x)$, and $p_{\lambda_2}^{a_2,b_2} = \frac{1}{Z_{a_2,b_2}(\lambda)} p_{\lambda_2}(x)$. Let $\Phi_\lambda(x) = 1 - \exp(-\lambda x)$ denote the cumulative distribution function of the exponential distribution. We have $Z_{a,b}(\lambda) = \Phi_b(\lambda) - \Phi_a(\lambda)$ and

$$F_{a,b}(\lambda) = F(\lambda) + \log(\Phi_b(\lambda) - \Phi_a(\lambda)) = -\log \lambda + \log(e^{-\lambda a} - e^{-\lambda b}). \tag{88}$$

If $[a_1, b_1] \not\subseteq [a_2, b_2]$ then $D_{\text{KL}}[p_{\lambda_1} : q_{\lambda_2}] = +\infty$. Otherwise, $[a_1, b_1] \in [a_2, b_2]$, and the exponential family $\{p_\lambda\}$ is the truncated exponential family $\{q_\lambda\}$. Using the computer algebra system Maxima (https://maxima.sourceforge.io/ accessed on 15 March 2022), we find that

$$- E_{p_\lambda}[x] = \frac{(1 + \lambda b)e^{\lambda a} - (1 + \lambda a)e^{\lambda b}}{\lambda(e^{\lambda b} - e^{\lambda a})} = F'_{a,b}(\lambda). \tag{89}$$

Thus we have:

$$\begin{aligned}
D_{\text{KL}}[p_{\lambda_1}^{a_1,b_1} : q_{\lambda_2}^{a_2,b_2}] &= B_{F_2,F_1}(\theta_2 : \theta_1), &(90)\\
&= F_{a_2,b_2}(\lambda_2) - F_{a_1,b_1}(\lambda_1) - (\lambda_2 - \lambda_1)F'_{a_1,b_1}(\lambda_1),\\
&= \log\frac{\lambda_1}{\lambda_2} + (\lambda_2 - \lambda_1)E_{p_{\lambda_1}}[x] + \log\frac{e^{-\lambda_2 a_2} - e^{-\lambda_2 b_2}}{e^{-\lambda_1 a_1} - e^{-\lambda_1 b_1}}. &(91)
\end{aligned}$$

When $a_1 = a_2 = 0$ and $b_1 = b_2 = +\infty$, we recover the KLD between two exponential distributions p_{λ_1} and p_{λ_2}:

$$\begin{aligned}
D_{\text{KL}}[p_{\lambda_1} : p_{\lambda_2}] &= B_F(\lambda_2 : \lambda_1), &(92)\\
&= F(\theta_2) - F(\theta_1) - (\theta_2 - \theta_1)F'(\theta_1), &(93)\\
&= \frac{\lambda_2}{\lambda_1} - \log\frac{\lambda_2}{\lambda_1} - 1 = D_{\text{IS}}[\lambda_2 : \lambda_1]. &(94)
\end{aligned}$$

Note that the KLD between two truncated exponential distributions with the same truncation support $\mathcal{X} = [a, b]$ is

$$D_{\text{KL}}[p_{\lambda_1}^{a,b} : p_{\lambda_2}^{a,b}] = \log\frac{\lambda_2}{\lambda_1} + \log\frac{\Phi_{\lambda_2}(b) - \Phi_{\lambda_2}(a)}{\Phi_{\lambda_1}(b) - \Phi_{\lambda_1}(a)} + (\lambda_2 - \lambda_1)E_{p_1^{a,b}}[x]. \tag{95}$$

We also check Corollary 1:

$$D_{\text{KL}}[p_{\lambda_1}^{a_1,b_1} : p_{\lambda_2}^{a_2,b_2}] = D_{\text{KL}}[p_{\lambda_1}^{a_1,b_1} : p_{\lambda_2}^{a_1,b_1}] + \log\frac{Z_{a_2,b_2}(\lambda_2)}{Z_{a_1,b_1}(\lambda_2)}, \tag{96}$$

The next example shows how to compute the Kullback–Leibler divergence between two truncated normal distributions:

Example 7. Let $N_{a,b}(m, s)$ denote a truncated normal distribution with support the open interval (a, b) ($a < b$) and probability density function defined by:

$$p_{m,s}^{a,b}(x) = \frac{1}{Z_{a,b}(m, s)}\exp\left(-\frac{(x - m)^2}{2s^2}\right), \tag{97}$$

where $Z_{a,b}(m, s)$ is related to the partition function [26] expressed using the cumulative distribution function (CDF) $\Phi_{m,s}(x)$:

$$Z_{a,b}(m, s) = \sqrt{2\pi}s\left(\Phi_{m,s}(b) - \Phi_{m,s}(a)\right), \tag{98}$$

with

$$\Phi_{m,s}(x) = \frac{1}{2}\left(1 + \text{erf}\left(\frac{x - m}{\sqrt{2}s}\right)\right), \tag{99}$$

where $\text{erf}(x)$ is the error function:

$$\text{erf}(x) := \frac{2}{\sqrt{\pi}}\int_0^x e^{-t^2}dt. \tag{100}$$

Thus we have $\mathrm{erf}(x) = 2\,\Phi(\sqrt{2}x) - 1$ where $\Phi(x) = \Phi_{0,1}(x)$.

The pdf can also be written as

$$p_{m,s}^{a,b}(x) = \frac{1}{s}\frac{\phi(\frac{x-m}{s})}{\Phi(\frac{b-m}{s}) - \Phi(\frac{a-m}{s})}, \qquad (101)$$

where $\phi(x)$ denotes the standard normal pdf ($\phi(x) = p_{0,1}^{-\infty,+\infty}(x)$):

$$\phi(x) := \frac{1}{\sqrt{2\pi}} \exp\left(-\frac{x^2}{2}\right), \qquad (102)$$

and $\Phi(x) = \Phi_{0,1}(x) = \int_{-\infty}^{x} \phi(t)\,dt$ is the standard normal CDF. When $a = -\infty$ and $b = +\infty$, we have $Z_{-\infty,\infty}(m,s) = \sqrt{2\pi}\,s$ since $\Phi(-\infty) = 0$ and $\Phi(+\infty) = 1$.

The density $p_{m,s}^{a,b}(x)$ belongs to an exponential family $\mathcal{E}_{a,b}$ with natural parameter $\theta = \left(\frac{m}{s^2}, -\frac{1}{2s^2}\right)$, sufficient statistics $t(x) = (x, x^2)$, and log-normalizer:

$$F_{a,b}(\theta) = -\frac{\theta_1^2}{4\theta_2} + \log Z_{a,b}(\theta) \qquad (103)$$

The natural parameter space is $\Theta = \mathbb{R} \times \mathbb{R}_{--}$ where $\mathbb{R}_{--} = \{x \in \mathbb{R} : x < 0\}$ denotes the set of negative real numbers.

The log-normalizer can be expressed using the source parameters (m,s) (which are not the mean and standard deviation when the support is truncated, hence the notation m and s):

$$\begin{aligned}
F_{a,b}(m,s) &= \frac{m^2}{2s^2} + \log Z_{a,b}(m,s), & (104) \\
&= \frac{m^2}{2s^2} + \frac{1}{2}\log 2\pi s^2 + \log(\Phi_{m,s}(b) - \Phi_{m,s}(a)). & (105)
\end{aligned}$$

We shall use the fact that the gradient of the log-normalizer of any exponential family distribution amounts to the expectation of the sufficient statistics [1]:

$$\nabla F_{a,b}(\theta) = E_{p_{m,s}^{a,b}}[t(x)] = \eta. \qquad (106)$$

Parameter η is called the moment or expectation parameter [1].

The mean $\mu(m,s;a,b) = E_{p_{m,s}^{a,b}}[x] = \frac{\partial}{\partial \theta_1} F_{a,b}(\theta)$ and the variance $\sigma^2(m,s;a,b) = E_{p_{m,s}^{a,b}}[x^2] - \mu^2$ (with $E_{p_{m,s}^{a,b}}[x^2] = \frac{\partial}{\partial \theta_2} F_{a,b}(\theta)$) of the truncated normal $p_{m,s}^{a,b}$ can be expressed using the following formula [26,27] (page 25):

$$\begin{aligned}
\mu(m,s;a,b) &= m - s\,\frac{\phi(\beta) - \phi(\alpha)}{\Phi(\beta) - \Phi(\alpha)}, & (107) \\
\sigma^2(m,s;a,b) &= s^2\left(1 - \frac{\beta\phi(\beta) - \alpha\phi(\alpha)}{\Phi(\beta) - \Phi(\alpha)} - \left(\frac{\phi(\beta) - \phi(\alpha)}{\Phi(\beta) - \Phi(\alpha)}\right)^2\right), & (108)
\end{aligned}$$

where $\alpha := \frac{a-m}{s}$ and $\beta := \frac{b-m}{s}$. Thus we have the following moment parameter $\eta = (\eta_1, \eta_2)$ with

$$\begin{aligned}
\eta_1(m,s;a,b) &= E_{p_{m,s}^{a,b}}[x] = \mu(m,s;a,b), & (109) \\
\eta_2(m,s;a,b) &= E_{p_{m,s}^{a,b}}[x^2] = \sigma^2(m,s;a,b) + \mu^2(m,s;a,b). & (110)
\end{aligned}$$

Now consider two truncated normal distributions $p_{m_1,s_1}^{a_1,b_1}$ and $p_{m_2,s_2}^{a_2,b_2}$ with $[a_1,b_1] \subseteq [a_2,b_2]$ (otherwise, we have $D_{\mathrm{KL}}[p_{m_1,s_1}^{a_1,b_1} : p_{m_2,s_2}^{a_2,b_2}] = +\infty$). Then the KLD between $p_{m_1,s_1}^{a_1,b_1}$ and $p_{m_2,s_2}^{a_2,b_2}$ is equivalent to a duo Bregman divergence:

$$D_{\mathrm{KL}}[p_{m_1,s_1}^{a_1,b_1} : p_{m_2,s_2}^{a_2,b_2}] = F_{m_2,s_2}(\theta_2) - F_{m_1,s_1}(\theta_1) - (\theta_2 - \theta_1)^\top \nabla F_{m_1,s_1}(\theta_1),$$
$$= \frac{m_2}{2s_2^2} - \frac{m_1}{2s_1^2} + \log \frac{Z_{a_2,b_2}(m_2,s_2)}{Z_{a_1,b_1}(m_1,s_1)} - \left(\frac{m_2}{s_2^2} - \frac{m_1}{s_1^2}\right)\eta_1(m_1,s_1;a_1,b_1)$$
$$- \left(\frac{1}{2s_1^2} - \frac{1}{2s_2^2}\right)\eta_2(m_1,s_1;a_1,b_1). \tag{111}$$

Note that $F_{m_2,s_2}(\theta) \geq F_{m_1,s_1}(\theta)$.

This formula is valid for (1) the KLD between two truncated normal distributions, or for (2) the KLD between a truncated normal distribution and a (full support) normal distribution. Note that the formula depends on the erf function used in function Φ. Furthermore, when $a_1 = a_2 = -\infty$ and $b_1 = b_2 = +\infty$, we recover (3) the KLD between two univariate normal distributions, since $\log \frac{Z_{a_2,b_2}(m_2,s_2)}{Z_{a_1,b_1}(m_1,s_1)} = \log \frac{\sigma_2}{\sigma_1} = \frac{1}{2}\log\frac{\sigma_2^2}{\sigma_1^2}$:

$$D_{\mathrm{KL}}[p_{m_1,s_1} : p_{m_2,s_2}] = \frac{1}{2}\left(\log \frac{s_2^2}{s_1^2} + \frac{\sigma_1^2}{\sigma_2^2} + \frac{(m_2-m_1)^2}{s_2^2} - 1.\right). \tag{112}$$

Note that for full support normal distributions, we have $\mu(m,s;-\infty;+\infty) = m$ and $\sigma^2(m,s;-\infty;+\infty) = s^2$.

The entropy of a truncated normal distribution (an exponential family [28]) is $h[p_{m,s}^{a,b}] = -\int_a^b p_{m,s}^{a,b}(x)\log p_{m,s}^{a,b}(x)dx = -F^*(\eta) = F(\theta) - \theta^\top \eta$. We find that

$$h[p_{m,s}^{a,b}] = \log\left(\sqrt{2\pi e}s\left(\Phi(\beta) - \Phi(\alpha)\right)\right) + \frac{\alpha\phi(\alpha) - \beta\phi(\beta)}{2(\Phi(\beta) - \Phi(\alpha))}. \tag{113}$$

When $(a,b) = (-\infty, \infty)$, we have $\Phi(\beta) - \Phi(\alpha) = 1$ and $\alpha\phi(\alpha) - \beta\phi(\beta) = 0$ since $\beta = -\alpha$, $\phi(-x) = \phi(x)$ (an even function), and $\lim_{\beta \to +\infty} \beta\phi(\beta) = 0$. Thus we recover the differential entropy of a normal distribution: $h[p_{\mu,\sigma}] = \log\left(\sqrt{2\pi e}\sigma\right)$.

5. Bhattacharyya Skewed Divergence Between Truncated Densities of an Exponential Family

The Bhattacharyya α-skewed divergence [29,30] between two densities $p(x)$ and $q(x)$ with respect to μ is defined for a skewing scalar parameter $\alpha \in (0,1)$ as:

$$D_{\mathrm{Bhat},\alpha}[p:q] := -\log \int_{\mathcal{X}} p(x)^\alpha q(x)^{1-\alpha} d\mu(x), \tag{114}$$

where $\mathcal{X}$ denotes the support of the distributions. The Bhattacharyya distance is

$$D_{\mathrm{Bhat}}[p,q] = D_{\mathrm{Bhat},\frac{1}{2}}[p:q] = -\log \int_{\mathcal{X}} \sqrt{p(x)q(x)} d\mu(x). \tag{115}$$

The Bhattacharyya distance is not a metric distance since it does not satisfy the triangle inequality. The Bhattacharyya distance is related to the Hellinger distance [31] as follows:

$$D_H[p,q] = \sqrt{\frac{1}{2}\int_{\mathcal{X}} \left(\sqrt{p(x)} - \sqrt{q(x)}\right)^2 d\mu(x)} = \sqrt{1 - \exp(-D_{\mathrm{Bhat}}[p,q])}. \tag{116}$$

The Hellinger distance is a metric distance.

Let $I_\alpha[p:q] := \int_{\mathcal{X}} p(x)^\alpha q(x)^{1-\alpha} d\mu(x)$ denote the skewed affinity coefficient so that $D_{\mathrm{Bhat},\alpha}[p:q] = -\log I_\alpha[p:q]$. Since $I_\alpha[p:q] = I_{1-\alpha}[q:p]$, we have $D_{\mathrm{Bhat},\alpha}[p:q] = D_{\mathrm{Bhat},1-\alpha}[q:p]$.

Consider an exponential family $\mathcal{E} = \{p_\theta\}$ with log-normalizer $F(\theta)$. Then it is well-known that the α-skewed Bhattacharyya divergence between two densities of an exponential family amounts to a skewed Jensen divergence [30] (originally called Jensen difference in [32]):

$$D_{\text{Bhat},\alpha}[p_{\theta_1} : p_{\theta_2}] = J_{F,\alpha}(\theta_1 : \theta_2), \tag{117}$$

where the skewed Jensen divergence is defined by

$$J_{F,\alpha}(\theta_1 : \theta_2) = \alpha F(\theta_1) + (1-\alpha) F(\theta_2) - F(\alpha \theta_1 + (1-\alpha)\theta_2). \tag{118}$$

The convexity of the log-normalizer $F(\theta)$ ensures that $J_{F,\alpha}(\theta_1 : \theta_2) \geq 0$. The Jensen divergence can be extended to full real α by rescaling it by $\frac{1}{\alpha(1-\alpha)}$, see [33].

Remark 1. *The Bhattacharyya skewed divergence $D_{\text{Bhat},\alpha}[p : q]$ appears naturally as the negative of the log-normalizer of the exponential family induced by the exponential arc $\{r_\alpha(x) \, \alpha \in (0,1)\}$ linking two densities p and q with $r_\alpha(x) \propto p(x)^\alpha q(x)^{1-\alpha}$. This arc is an exponential family of order 1:*

$$r_\alpha(x) = \exp(\alpha \log p(x) + (1-\alpha) \log q(x) - \log Z_\alpha(p : q)), \tag{119}$$

$$= \exp\left(\alpha \log \frac{p(x)}{q(x)} - F_{pq}(\alpha)\right) q(x). \tag{120}$$

The sufficient statistic is $t(x) = \frac{p(x)}{q(x)}$, the natural parameter $\alpha \in (0,1)$, and the log-normalizer $F_{pq}(\alpha) = \log Z_\alpha(p : q) = \log \int p(x)^\alpha q(x)^{1-\alpha} d\mu(x) = -D_{\text{Bhat},\alpha}[p : q]$. This shows that $D_{\text{Bhat},\alpha}[p : q]$ is concave with respect to α since log-normalizers $F_{pq}(\alpha)$ are always convex. Grünwald called those exponential families the likelihood ratio exponential families [34].

Now, consider calculating $D_{\text{Bhat},\alpha}[p_{\theta_1} : q_{\theta_2}]$ where $p_{\theta_1} \in \mathcal{E}_1$ with $\mathcal{E}_1$ a truncated exponential family of $\mathcal{E}_2$ and $q_{\theta_2} \in \mathcal{E}_2 = \{q_\theta\}$. We have $q_\theta(x) = \frac{Z_1(\theta)}{Z_2(\theta)} p_\theta(x)$, where $Z_1(\theta)$ and $Z_2(\theta)$ are the partition functions of $\mathcal{E}_1$ and $\mathcal{E}_2$, respectively. Thus we have

$$I_\alpha[p_{\theta_1} : q_{\theta_2}] = \left(\frac{Z_1(\theta_2)}{Z_2(\theta_2)}\right)^{1-\alpha} I_\alpha[p_{\theta_1} : p_{\theta_2}], \tag{121}$$

and the α-skewed Bhattacharyya divergence is

$$D_{\text{Bhat},\alpha}[p_{\theta_1} : q_{\theta_2}] = D_{\text{Bhat},\alpha}[p_{\theta_1} : p_{\theta_2}] - (1-\alpha)(F_1(\theta_2) - F_2(\theta_2)). \tag{122}$$

Therefore we obtain

$$D_{\text{Bhat},\alpha}[p_{\theta_1} : q_{\theta_2}] = J_{F_1,\alpha}(\theta_1 : \theta_2) - (1-\alpha)(F_1(\theta_2) - F_2(\theta_2)), \tag{123}$$
$$= \alpha F_1(\theta_1) + (1-\alpha) F_2(\theta_2) - F_1(\alpha \theta_1 + (1-\alpha)\theta_2), \tag{124}$$
$$=: J_{F_1,F_2,\alpha}(\theta_1 : \theta_2). \tag{125}$$

We call $J_{F_1,F_2,\alpha}(\theta_1 : \theta_2)$ the duo Jensen divergence. Since $F_2(\theta) \geq F_1(\theta)$, we check that

$$J_{F_1,F_2,\alpha}(\theta_1 : \theta_2) \geq J_{F_1,\alpha}(\theta_1 : \theta_2) \geq 0. \tag{126}$$

Figure 7 illustrates graphically the duo Jensen divergence $J_{F_1,F_2,\alpha}(\theta_1 : \theta_2)$.

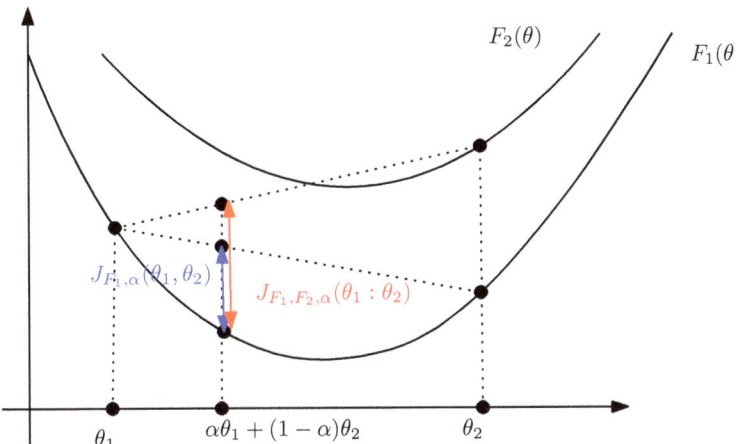

Figure 7. The duo Jensen divergence $J_{F_1,F_2,\alpha}(\theta_1:\theta_2)$ is greater than the Jensen divergence $J_{F_1,\alpha}(\theta_1:\theta_2)$ for $F_2(\theta) \geq F_1(\theta)$.

Theorem 2. *The α-skewed Bhattacharyya divergence for $\alpha \in (0,1)$ between a truncated density of $\mathcal{E}_1$ with log-normalizer $F_1(\theta)$ and another density of an exponential family $\mathcal{E}_2$ with log-normalizer $F_2(\theta)$ amounts to a duo Jensen divergence:*

$$D_{\mathrm{Bhat},\alpha}[p_{\theta_1}:q_{\theta_2}] = J_{F_1,F_2,\alpha}(\theta_1:\theta_2), \qquad (127)$$

where $J_{F_1,F_2,\alpha}(\theta_1:\theta_2)$ is the duo skewed Jensen divergence induced by two strictly convex functions $F_1(\theta)$ and $F_2(\theta)$ such that $F_2(\theta) \geq F_1(\theta)$:

$$J_{F_1,F_2,\alpha}(\theta_1:\theta_2) = \alpha F_1(\theta_1) + (1-\alpha)F_2(\theta_2) - F_1(\alpha\theta_1 + (1-\alpha)\theta_2). \qquad (128)$$

In [30], it is reported that

$$\begin{aligned}
D_{\mathrm{KL}}[p_{\theta_1}:p_{\theta_2}] &= B_F(\theta_2:\theta_1), &(129)\\
&= \lim_{\alpha\to 0}\frac{1}{\alpha}J_{F,\alpha}(\theta_2:\theta_1) = \lim_{\alpha\to 0}\frac{1}{\alpha}J_{F,1-\alpha}(\theta_1:\theta_2), &(130)\\
&= \lim_{\alpha\to 0}\frac{1}{\alpha}D_{\mathrm{Bhat},\alpha}[p_{\theta_2}:p_{\theta_1}] = \lim_{\alpha\to 0}\frac{1}{\alpha}D_{\mathrm{Bhat},1-\alpha}[p_{\theta_1}:p_{\theta_2}]. &(131)
\end{aligned}$$

Indeed, using the first-order Taylor expansion of

$$F(\theta_1 + \alpha(\theta_2 - \theta_1)) \underset{\alpha\to 0}{\approx} F(\theta_1) + \alpha(\theta_2 - \theta_1)^\top \nabla F(\theta_1) \qquad (132)$$

when $\alpha \to 0$, we check that we have

$$\begin{aligned}
\frac{1}{\alpha}J_{F,\alpha}(\theta_2:\theta_1) &:= \frac{F(\theta_1) + \alpha(F(\theta_2) - F(\theta_1)) - F(\theta_1 + \alpha(\theta_2 - \theta_1))}{\alpha}, &(133)\\
&\underset{\alpha\to 0}{\overset{\text{Equation }(132)}{\approx}} \frac{\cancel{F(\theta_1)} + \alpha(F(\theta_2) - F(\theta_1)) - \cancel{F(\theta_1)} - \alpha(\theta_2 - \theta_1)^\top\nabla F(\theta_1)}{\alpha}, &(134)\\
&= F(\theta_2) - F(\theta_1) - (\theta_2 - \theta_1)^\top \nabla F(\theta_1), &(135)\\
&=: B_F(\theta_2:\theta_1). &(136)
\end{aligned}$$

Thus we have $\lim_{\alpha\to 0}\frac{1}{\alpha}J_{F,\alpha}(\theta_2:\theta_1) = B_F(\theta_2:\theta_1)$.

Moreover, we have

$$\lim_{\alpha\to 0}\frac{1}{\alpha}D_{\mathrm{Bhat},1-\alpha}[p:q] = D_{\mathrm{KL}}[p:q]. \qquad (137)$$

Similarly, we can prove that

$$\lim_{\alpha \to 1} \frac{1}{1-\alpha} J_{F_1,F_2,\alpha}(\theta_1 : \theta_2) = B_{F_2,F_1}(\theta_2 : \theta_1), \tag{138}$$

which can be reinterpreted as

$$\lim_{\alpha \to 1} \frac{1}{1-\alpha} D_{\text{Bhat},\alpha}[p_{\theta_1} : q_{\theta_2}] = D_{\text{KL}}[p_{\theta_1} : q_{\theta_2}]. \tag{139}$$

6. Concluding Remarks

We considered the Kullback–Leibler divergence between two parametric densities $p_\theta \in \mathcal{E}_1$ and $q_{\theta'} \in \mathcal{E}_2$ belonging to truncated exponential families [7] $\mathcal{E}_1$ and $\mathcal{E}_2$, and we showed that their KLD is equivalent to a duo Bregman divergence on swapped parameter order (Theorem 1). This result generalizes the study of Azoury and Warmuth [13]. The duo Bregman divergence can be rewritten as a duo Fenchel–Young divergence using mixed natural/moment parameterizations of the exponential family densities (Definition 1). This second result generalizes the approach taken in information geometry [15,35]. We showed how to calculate the Kullback–Leibler divergence between two truncated normal distributions as a duo Bregman divergence. More generally, we proved that the skewed Bhattacharyya distance between two parametric densities of truncated exponential families amounts to a duo Jensen divergence (Theorem 2). We showed asymptotically that scaled duo Jensen divergences tend to duo Bregman divergences generalizing a result of [30,33]. This study of duo divergences induced by pair of generators was motivated by the formula obtained for the Kullback–Leibler divergence between two densities of two different exponential families originally reported in [23] (Equation (29)).

It is interesting to find applications of the duo Fenchel–Young, Bregman, and Jensen divergences beyond the scope of calculating statistical distances between truncated exponential family densities. Note that in [36], the authors exhibit a relationship between densities with nested supports and quasi-convex Bregman divergences. However, those considered parametric densities are not exponential families since their supports depend on the parameter. Recently, Khan and Swaroop [37] used this duo Fenchel–Young divergence in machine learning for knowledge-adaptation priors in the so-called change regularizer task.

Funding: This research received no external funding.

Institutional Review Board Statement: Not applicable

Informed Consent Statement: Not applicable.

Data Availability Statement: Not applicable.

Acknowledgments: The author would like to thank the three reviewers for their helpful comments, which led to this improved paper.

Conflicts of Interest: The author declares no conflicts of interest.

References

1. Sundberg, R. *Statistical Modelling by Exponential Families*; Cambridge University Press: Cambridge, UK, 2019; Volume 12.
2. Pitman, E.J.G. *Sufficient Statistics and Intrinsic Accuracy*; Mathematical Proceedings of the cambridge Philosophical Society; Cambridge University Press: Cambridge, UK, 1936; Volume 32, pp. 567–579.
3. Darmois, G. Sur les lois de probabilitéa estimation exhaustive. *CR Acad. Sci. Paris* **1935**, *260*, 85.
4. Koopman, B.O. On distributions admitting a sufficient statistic. *Trans. Am. Math. Soc.* **1936**, *39*, 399–409. [CrossRef]
5. Hiejima, Y. Interpretation of the quasi-likelihood via the tilted exponential family. *J. Jpn. Stat. Soc.* **1997**, *27*, 157–164. [CrossRef]
6. Efron, B.; Hastie, T. *Computer Age Statistical Inference: Algorithms, Evidence, and Data Science*; Cambridge University Press: Cambridge, UK, 2021; Volume 6.
7. Akahira, M. *Statistical Estimation for Truncated Exponential Families*; Springer: Berlin/Heidelberg, Germany, 2017.

8. Bar-Lev, S.K. Large sample properties of the MLE and MCLE for the natural parameter of a truncated exponential family. *Ann. Inst. Stat. Math.* **1984**, *36*, 217–222. [CrossRef]
9. Shah, A.; Shah, D.; Wornell, G. A Computationally Efficient Method for Learning Exponential Family Distributions. *Adv. Neural Inf. Process. Syst.* **2021**, *34*. Available online: https://proceedings.neurips.cc/paper/2021/hash/84f7e69969dea92a925508f7c1f9579a-Abstract.html (accessed on 15 March 2022).
10. Keener, R.W. *Theoretical Statistics: Topics for a Core Course*; Springer: Berlin/Heidelberg, Germany, 2010.
11. Cover, T.M. *Elements of Information Theory*; John Wiley & Sons: Hoboken, NJ, USA, 1999.
12. Csiszár, I. Eine informationstheoretische Ungleichung und ihre Anwendung auf Beweis der Ergodizitaet von Markoffschen Ketten. *Magyer Tud. Akad. Mat. Kutato Int. Koezl.* **1964**, *8*, 85–108.
13. Azoury, K.S.; Warmuth, M.K. Relative loss bounds for on-line density estimation with the exponential family of distributions. *Mach. Learn.* **2001**, *43*, 211–246. [CrossRef]
14. Rockafellar, R.T. *Convex Analysis*; Princeton University Press: Princeton, NJ, USA, 2015.
15. Amari, S.I. Differential-geometrical methods in statistics. *Lect. Notes Stat.* **1985**, *28*, 1.
16. Bregman, L.M. The relaxation method of finding the common point of convex sets and its application to the solution of problems in convex programming. *Ussr Comput. Math. Math. Phys.* **1967**, *7*, 200–217. [CrossRef]
17. Acharyya, S. Learning to Rank in Supervised and Unsupervised Settings Using Convexity and Monotonicity. Ph.D. Thesis, The University of Texas at Austin, Austin, TX, USA, 2013.
18. Blondel, M.; Martins, A.F.; Niculae, V. Learning with Fenchel-Young losses. *J. Mach. Learn. Res.* **2020**, *21*, 1–69.
19. Nielsen, F. An elementary introduction to information geometry. *Entropy* **2020**, *22*, 1100. [CrossRef] [PubMed]
20. Mitroi, F.C.; Niculescu, C.P. *An Extension of Young's Inequality*; Abstract and Applied Analysis; Hindawi: London, UK, 2011; Volume 2011.
21. Jeffreys, H. *The Theory of Probability*; OUP Oxford: Oxford, UK, 1998.
22. Nielsen, F.; Nock, R. Sided and symmetrized Bregman centroids. *IEEE Trans. Inf. Theory* **2009**, *55*, 2882–2904. [CrossRef]
23. Nielsen, F. On a variational definition for the Jensen-Shannon symmetrization of distances based on the information radius. *Entropy* **2021**, *23*, 464. [CrossRef]
24. Itakura, F.; Saito, S. Analysis synthesis telephony based on the maximum likelihood method. In Proceedings of the 6th International Congress on Acoustics, Tokyo, Japan, 21–28 August 1968; pp. 280–292.
25. Del Castillo, J. The singly truncated normal distribution: A non-steep exponential family. *Ann. Inst. Stat. Math.* **1994**, *46*, 57–66. [CrossRef]
26. Burkardt, J. *The Truncated Normal Distribution*; Technical Report; Department of Scientific Computing Website, Florida State University: Tallahassee, FL, USA, 2014.
27. Kotz, J.; Balakrishan. *Continuous Univariate Distributions, Volumes I and II*; John Wiley and Sons: Hoboken, NJ, USA, 1994.
28. Nielsen, F.; Nock, R. Entropies and cross-entropies of exponential families. In Proceedings of the 2010 IEEE International Conference on Image Processing, Hong Kong, China, 26–29 September 2010; pp. 3621–3624.
29. Bhattacharyya, A. On a measure of divergence between two statistical populations defined by their probability distributions. *Bull. Calcutta Math. Soc.* **1943**, *35*, 99–109.
30. Nielsen, F.; Boltz, S. The Burbea-Rao and Bhattacharyya centroids. *IEEE Trans. Inf. Theory* **2011**, *57*, 5455–5466. [CrossRef]
31. Hellinger, E. Neue Begründung der Theorie Quadratischer Formen von unendlichvielen Veränderlichen. *J. Reine Angew. Math.* **1909**, *1909*, 210–271. [CrossRef]
32. Rao, C.R. Diversity and dissimilarity coefficients: A unified approach. *Theor. Popul. Biol.* **1982**, *21*, 24–43. [CrossRef]
33. Zhang, J. Divergence function, duality, and convex analysis. *Neural Comput.* **2004**, *16*, 159–195. [CrossRef] [PubMed]
34. Grünwald, P.D. *The Minimum Description Length Principle*; MIT Press: Cambridge, MA, USA, 2007.
35. Nielsen, F. The Many Faces of Information Geometry. *Not. Am. Math. Soc.* **2022**, *69*. [CrossRef]
36. Nielsen, F.; Hadjeres, G. *Quasiconvex Jensen Divergences and Quasiconvex Bregman Divergences*; Workshop on Joint Structures and Common Foundations of Statistical Physics, Information Geometry and Inference for Learning; Springer: Berlin/Heidelberg, Germany, 2020; pp. 196–218.
37. Emtiyaz Khan, M.; Swaroop, S. Knowledge-Adaptation Priors. *arXiv* **2021**, arXiv:2106.08769.

Article

Contingency Table Analysis and Inference via Double Index Measures

Christos Meselidis * and Alex Karagrigoriou

Laboratory of Statistics and Data Analysis, Department of Statistics and Actuarial-Financial Mathematics, University of the Aegean, Karlovasi, GR-83200 Samos, Greece; alex.karagrigoriou@aegean.gr
* Correspondence: meselidis@aegean.gr

Abstract: In this work, we focus on a general family of measures of divergence for estimation and testing with emphasis on conditional independence in cross tabulations. For this purpose, a restricted minimum divergence estimator is used for the estimation of parameters under constraints and a new double index (dual) divergence test statistic is introduced and thoroughly examined. The associated asymptotic theory is provided and the advantages and practical implications are explored via simulation studies.

Keywords: double index divergence test statistic; multivariate data analysis; conditional independence; cross tabulations

1. Introduction

The concept of distance or divergence is known since at least the time of Pearson, who, in 1900, considered the classical goodness-of-fit (gof) problem by considering the distance between observed and expected frequencies. The problem for both discrete and discretized continuous distributions have been in the center of attention for the last 100+ years. The classical set-up is the one considered by Pearson where a hypothesized m-dimensional multinomial distribution, say $Multi(N, p_1, \ldots, p_m)$ is examined as being the underlying distributional mechanism for producing a given sample of size N. The problem can be extended to examine the homogeneity (in terms of the distributional mechanisms) among two independent samples or the independence among two population characteristics. In all such problems we are dealing with cross tabulations or crosstabs (or contingency tables). Problems of such nature appear frequently in a great variety of fields including biosciences, socio-economic and political sciences, actuarial science, finance, business, accounting, and marketing. The need to establish for instance, whether the mechanisms producing two phenomena are the same or not is vital for altering economic policies, preventing socio-economic crises or enforcing the same economic or financial decisions to groups with similar underlying mechanisms (e.g., retaining the insurance premium in case of similarity or having different premiums in case of diversity). It is important to note that divergence measures play a pivotal role also in statistical inference in continuous settings. Indeed, for example, in [1] the authors investigate the multivariate normal case while in a recent work [2], the modified skew-normal-Cauchy (MSNC) distribution is considered, against normality.

Let us consider the general case of two m-dimensional multinomial distributions for which each probability depends on an s-dimensional unknown parameter, say $\boldsymbol{\theta} = (\theta_1, \ldots, \theta_s)^\top$. A general family of measures introduced by [3] is the d_Φ^α family defined by

$$d_\Phi^\alpha(\mathbf{p}(\boldsymbol{\theta}), \mathbf{q}(\boldsymbol{\theta})) = \sum_{i=1}^m q_i(\boldsymbol{\theta})^{1+\alpha} \Phi\left(\frac{p_i(\boldsymbol{\theta})}{q_i(\boldsymbol{\theta})}\right); \ \alpha > 0, \ \Phi \in F^* \tag{1}$$

where α is a positive indicator (index) value, $\mathbf{p}(\boldsymbol{\theta}) = (p_1(\boldsymbol{\theta}), \ldots, p_m(\boldsymbol{\theta}))^\top$ and $\mathbf{q}(\boldsymbol{\theta}) = (q_1(\boldsymbol{\theta}), \ldots, q_m(\boldsymbol{\theta}))^\top$, F^* is a class of functions s.t. $F^* = \{\Phi(\cdot) : \Phi(x) \text{ strictly convex}, x \in \mathbb{R}^+, \Phi(1) = \Phi'(1) = 0, \Phi''(1) \neq 0 \text{ and by convention, } \Phi(0/0) = 0 \text{ and } 0\Phi(p/0) = \lim_{x \to \infty}[\Phi(x)/x]\}$.

Note that the well known Csiszar family of measures [4] is obtained for the special case where the indicator is taken to be equal to 0 while the classical Kullback–Leibler (KL) distance [5] is obtained if the indicator α is equal to 0 and at the same time the function $\Phi(\cdot)$ is taken to be $\Phi(x) \equiv \Phi_{KL}(x) = x \log(x)$ or $x \log(x) - x + 1$.

The function
$$\Phi_\lambda(x) = \frac{1}{\lambda(\lambda+1)}\left[x(x^\lambda - 1) - \lambda(x-1)\right] \in F^*, \lambda \neq 0, -1$$

is associated with the Freeman–Tukey test when $\lambda = -1/2$, with the recommended Cressie and Read (CR) power divergence [6] when $\lambda = 2/3$, with the Pearson's chi-squared divergence [7] when $\lambda = 1$ and with the classical KL distance when $\lambda \to 0$.

Finally, the function
$$\Phi_\alpha(x) \equiv (\lambda+1)\Phi_\lambda(x)|_{\lambda=\alpha} = \frac{1}{\alpha}[x(x^\alpha - 1) - \alpha(x-1)], \alpha \neq 0$$

produces the BHHJ or Φ_α-power divergence [8] given by

$$d^\alpha_{\Phi_\alpha}(\mathbf{p}(\boldsymbol{\theta}), \mathbf{q}(\boldsymbol{\theta})) = \sum_{i=1}^m q_i^\alpha(\boldsymbol{\theta})\{q_i(\boldsymbol{\theta}) - p_i(\boldsymbol{\theta})\} + \frac{1}{\alpha}\sum_{i=1}^m p_i(\boldsymbol{\theta})\{p_i^\alpha(\boldsymbol{\theta}) - q_i^\alpha(\boldsymbol{\theta})\}.$$

Assume that the underlying true distribution of an m-dimensional multinomial random variable with N experiments, is

$$\mathbf{X} = (X_1, \ldots, X_m)^\top \sim Multi(N, \mathbf{p} = (p_1, \ldots, p_m)^\top)$$

where $\mathbf{p}$ is, in general, unknown, belonging to the parametric family

$$\mathcal{P} = \left\{\mathbf{p}(\boldsymbol{\theta}) = (p_1(\boldsymbol{\theta}), \ldots, p_m(\boldsymbol{\theta}))^\top : \boldsymbol{\theta} = (\theta_1, \ldots, \theta_s)^\top \in \Theta \subset \mathbb{R}^s\right\}. \quad (2)$$

The sample estimate $\hat{\mathbf{p}} = (\hat{p}_1, \ldots, \hat{p}_m)^\top$ of $\mathbf{p}$ is easily obtained by $\hat{p}_i = x_i/N$ where x_i is the observed frequency for the i-th category (or class).

Divergence measures can be used for estimating purposes by minimizing the associated measure. The classical estimating technique is the one where (1) we take $\alpha = 0$ and $\Phi(x) = \Phi_{KL}(x)$. Then, the resulting KL minimization is equivalent to the classical maximization of the likelihood producing the well-known Maximum Likelihood Estimator (MLE, see ([9], Section 5.2)). In general, the minimization with respect to the parameter of interest of the divergence measure, gives rise to the corresponding minimum divergence estimator (see, e.g., [6,10,11]). For the case where constraints are involved the case associated with Csiszar's family of measures was recently investigated [12]. For further references, please refer to [13–21].

Consider the hypothesis

$$H_0: \mathbf{p} = \mathbf{p}(\boldsymbol{\theta}_0) \text{ vs. } H_1: \mathbf{p} \neq \mathbf{p}(\boldsymbol{\theta}_0), \boldsymbol{\theta}_0 = (\theta_{01}, \ldots, \theta_{0s})^\top \in \Theta \subset \mathbb{R}^s \quad (3)$$

where $\mathbf{p}$ is the vector of the true but unknown probabilities of the underlying distribution and $\mathbf{p}(\boldsymbol{\theta}_0)$ the vector of the corresponding probabilities of the hypothesized distribution which is unknown and falls within the family of $\mathcal{P}$ with the unknown parameters satisfying in general, certain constraints, e.g., of the form $c(\boldsymbol{\theta}) = 0$, under which the estimation of the parameter will be performed. The purpose of this work is twofold: having as a reference the divergence measure given in (1), we will first propose a general double index divergence class of measures and make inference regarding the parameter estimators involved. Then, we proceed with the hypothesis problem with the emphasis given to the concept of conditional independence. The innovative idea proposed in this work is the duality in choosing among the members of the general class of divergences, one for estimating and one for testing purposes which may not be necessarily, the same. In that sense, we propose a double index divergence test statistic offering the greatest possible range of options, both for the strictly convex function Φ and the indicator value $\alpha > 0$.

Thus, the estimation problem can be examined considering expression (1) using a function $\Phi_2 \in F^*$ and an indicator $\alpha_2 > 0$:

$$d^{\alpha_2}_{\Phi_2}(\mathbf{p}, \mathbf{p}(\boldsymbol{\theta})) = \sum_{i=1}^{m} p_i^{1+\alpha_2}(\boldsymbol{\theta}) \Phi_2\left(\frac{p_i}{p_i(\boldsymbol{\theta})}\right) \qquad (4)$$

the minimization of which with respect to the unknown parameter, will produce the restricted minimum (Φ_2, α_2) divergence (rMD) estimator

$$\hat{\boldsymbol{\theta}}^r_{(\Phi_2, \alpha_2)} = \arg\inf_{\boldsymbol{\theta} \in \Theta : c(\boldsymbol{\theta}) = 0} d^{\alpha_2}_{\Phi_2}(\hat{\mathbf{p}}, \mathbf{p}(\boldsymbol{\theta})) \qquad (5)$$

for some constraints $c(\boldsymbol{\theta}) = 0$. Observe that the unknown vector of underlying probabilities has been replaced by the vector of the corresponding sample frequencies $\hat{\mathbf{p}}$. Then, the testing problem will be based on

$$d^{\alpha_1}_{\Phi_1}\left(\hat{\mathbf{p}}, \mathbf{p}(\hat{\boldsymbol{\theta}}^r_{(\Phi_2, \alpha_2)})\right) = \sum_{i=1}^{m} p_i^{1+\alpha_1}(\hat{\boldsymbol{\theta}}^r_{(\Phi_2, \alpha_2)}) \Phi_1\left(\frac{\hat{p}_i}{p_i(\hat{\boldsymbol{\theta}}^r_{(\Phi_2, \alpha_2)})}\right) \qquad (6)$$

where $\Phi_1(\cdot)$ and α_1 may be different from the corresponding quantities used for the estimation problem in (4). Finally, the duality of the proposed methodology surfaces when the testing problem is explored via the dual divergence test statistic formulated on the basis of the double-α-double-Φ divergence given by

$$d^{\alpha_1}_{\Phi_1}\left(\hat{\mathbf{p}}, \mathbf{p}(\hat{\boldsymbol{\theta}}^r_{(\Phi_2, \alpha_2)})\right) \qquad (7)$$

where $\Phi_1, \Phi_2 \in F^*$ and $\alpha_1, \alpha_2 > 0$.

The remaining parts of this work are: Section 2 presents the formal definition and the asymptotic properties of the rMD estimator (rMDE). Section 3 deals with the general testing problem with the use of rMDE. The associated set up for the case of three-way contingency tables is developed in Section 4 with a simulation section emphasizing on the conditional independence of three random variables. We close this work with some conclusions.

2. Restricted Minimum (Φ, α)-Power Divergence Estimator

In what follows, we will provide the formal definition and the expansion of the rMD estimator and prove its asymptotic normality. The assumptions required for establishing the results of this section for the rMD estimator under constraints, are provided below:

Assumption 1.

(A_0) $f_1(\boldsymbol{\theta}), \ldots, f_\nu(\boldsymbol{\theta})$ are the constrained functions on the s-dimensional parameter $\boldsymbol{\theta}$, $f_k(\boldsymbol{\theta}) = 0$, $k = 1, \ldots, \nu$ and $\nu < s < m - 1$;

(A_1) There exists a value $\boldsymbol{\theta}_0 \in \Theta$, such that $\mathbf{X} = (X_1, \ldots, X_m)^\top \sim \text{Multi}(N, \mathbf{p}(\boldsymbol{\theta}_0))$;

(A_2) Each constraint function $f_k(\boldsymbol{\theta})$ has continuous second partial derivatives;

(A_3) The $\nu \times s$ and $m \times s$ matrices

$$Q(\boldsymbol{\theta}_0) = \left(\frac{\partial f_k(\boldsymbol{\theta}_0)}{\partial \theta_j}\right)_{\substack{k=1,\ldots,\nu \\ j=1,\ldots,s}} \quad \text{and} \quad J(\boldsymbol{\theta}_0) = \left(\frac{\partial p_i(\boldsymbol{\theta}_0)}{\partial \theta_j}\right)_{\substack{i=1,\ldots,m \\ j=1,\ldots,s}}$$

are of full rank;

(A_4) $p(\theta)$ has continuous second partial derivatives in a neighbourhood of θ_0;

(A_5) θ_0 satisfies the Birch regularity conditions (see Appendix A and [22]).

Definition 1. *Under assumptions* (A_0)–(A_3) *the rMD estimator of* θ_0 *is any vector in* Θ, *such that*

$$\hat{\theta}^r_{(\Phi,\alpha)} = \arg\inf_{\{\theta \in \Theta \subset \mathbb{R}^s:\, f_k(\theta)=0, k=1,\ldots,v\}} d^\alpha_\Phi(\hat{p}, p(\theta)). \tag{8}$$

In order to derive the decomposition of $\hat{\theta}^r_{(\Phi,\alpha)}$ the Implicit Function Theorem (IFT) is exploited according to which if a function has an invertible derivative at a point then itself is invertible in a neighbourhood of this point but it cannot be expressed in closed form [23].

Theorem 1. *Under Assumptions* (A_0)–(A_5), *the rMD estimator of* θ_0 *is such that*

$$\hat{\theta}^r_{(\Phi,\alpha)} = \theta_0 + H(\theta_0)\left(B(\theta_0)^\top B(\theta_0)\right)^{-1} B(\theta_0)^\top diag(p(\theta_0)^{\alpha/2}) \times$$
$$\times diag(p(\theta_0)^{-1/2})(\hat{p} - p(\theta_0)) + o(\|\hat{p} - p(\theta_0)\|) \tag{9}$$

where $\hat{\theta}^r_{(\Phi,\alpha)}$ *is unique in a neighbourhood of* θ_0 *and*

$$H(\theta_0) = I - \left(B(\theta_0)^\top B(\theta_0)\right)^{-1} Q(\theta_0)^\top \times$$
$$\times \left(Q(\theta_0)\left(B(\theta_0)^\top B(\theta_0)\right)^{-1} Q(\theta_0)^\top\right)^{-1} Q(\theta_0),$$

$$B(\theta_0) = diag(p(\theta_0)^{\alpha/2}) A(\theta_0), \text{ while } A(\theta_0) = diag(p(\theta_0)^{-1/2}) J(\theta_0).$$

Proof. Let V be a neighbourhood of θ_0 on which $p(\cdot): \Theta \to \mathcal{P} \subset I^m$ has continuous second partial derivatives where I^m is the interior of the unit cube of dimension m. Let

$$F = (F_1, \ldots, F_{v+s}): I^m \times \mathbb{R}^{v+s} \to \mathbb{R}^{v+s}$$

with

$$F_j(\mathbf{p}, \lambda, \theta) = \begin{cases} f_j(\theta), & j = 1, \ldots, v \\ \dfrac{\partial d^\alpha_\Phi(\mathbf{p}, p(\theta))}{\partial \theta_{j-v}} + \sum_{k=1}^{v} \lambda_k \dfrac{\partial f_k(\theta)}{\partial \theta_{j-v}}, & j = v+1, \ldots, v+s. \end{cases}$$

where $(\mathbf{p}, \lambda, \theta) = (p_1, \ldots, p_m, \lambda_1, \ldots, \lambda_v, \theta_1, \ldots, \theta_s)$ and $\lambda_k, k = 1, \ldots, v$ are the coefficients of the constraints.

It holds that

$$F_j(p_1(\theta_0), \ldots, p_m(\theta_0), 0, \ldots, 0, \theta_{01}, \ldots, \theta_{0s}) = 0,\ j = 1, \ldots, v+s$$

and by denoting $\gamma = (\gamma_1, \ldots, \gamma_{v+s}) = (\lambda_1, \ldots, \lambda_v, \theta_1, \ldots, \theta_s)$, the matrix

$$\frac{\partial F}{\partial \gamma} = \left(\frac{\partial F_j}{\partial \gamma_k}\right)_{\substack{j=1,\ldots,v+s \\ k=1,\ldots,v+s}} = \begin{pmatrix} 0_{v \times v} & Q(\theta_0) \\ Q(\theta_0)^\top & \Phi''(1) B(\theta)^\top B(\theta) \end{pmatrix}$$

is nonsingular at $(\mathbf{p}, \lambda, \theta) = (p(\theta_0), \gamma_0) = (p_1(\theta_0), \ldots, p_m(\theta_0), 0, \ldots, 0, \theta_{01}, \ldots, \theta_{0s})$ with $\gamma_0 = (0_v, \theta_0)$.

Using the IFT a neighbourhood U of $(\mathbf{p}(\theta_0), \gamma_0)$ exists, such that $\partial F/\partial \gamma$ is nonsingular and a unique differentiable function $\gamma^* = (\lambda^*, \theta^*): A \subset I^m \to \mathbb{R}^{v+s}$, such that

$p(\theta_0) \in A$ and $\{(p, \gamma) \in U \colon F(p, \gamma) = 0\} = \{(p, \gamma^*(p)) \colon p \in A\}$ and $\gamma^*(p(\theta_0)) = (\lambda^*(p(\theta_0)), \theta^*(p(\theta_0))) = \gamma_0$. By the chain rule and for $p = p(\theta_0)$ we obtain

$$\frac{\partial F}{\partial p(\theta_0)} + \frac{\partial F}{\partial \gamma_0} \frac{\partial \gamma_0}{\partial p(\theta_0)} = 0.$$

Then

$$\frac{\partial \theta_0}{\partial p(\theta_0)} = \begin{pmatrix} E(\theta_0) \\ W(\theta_0) \end{pmatrix}$$

where

$$E(\theta_0) = \Phi''(1) \left(Q(\theta_0) \left(B(\theta_0)^\top B(\theta_0) \right)^{-1} Q(\theta_0)^\top \right)^{-1} \times$$

$$\times Q(\theta_0) \left(B(\theta_0)^\top B(\theta_0) \right)^{-1} B(\theta_0)^\top diag(p(\theta_0)^{\alpha/2}) diag(p(\theta_0)^{-1/2})$$

and

$$W(\theta_0) = H(\theta_0) \left(B(\theta_0)^\top B(\theta_0) \right)^{-1} B(\theta_0)^\top diag(p(\theta_0)^{\alpha/2}) diag(p(\theta_0)^{-1/2}) \quad (10)$$

since

$$\frac{\partial F}{\partial p(\theta_0)} = \begin{pmatrix} 0_{\nu \times m} \\ -\Phi''(1) B(\theta_0)^\top diag(p(\theta_0)^{\alpha/2}) diag(p(\theta_0)^{-1/2}) \end{pmatrix}.$$

Expanding $\theta^*(p)$ around $p(\theta_0)$ and using (10) gives, for $\theta^*(p(\theta_0)) = \theta_0$,

$$\theta^*(p) = \theta_0 + H(\theta_0) \left(B(\theta_0)^\top B(\theta_0) \right)^{-1} B(\theta_0)^\top diag(p(\theta_0)^{\alpha/2}) \times$$

$$\times diag(p(\theta_0)^{-1/2}) (\hat{p} - p(\theta_0)) + o(\|\hat{p} - p(\theta_0)\|).$$

Since $\hat{p} \xrightarrow{p} p(\theta_0)$ eventually $\hat{p} \in A$ and then $\gamma^*(\hat{p}) = (\lambda^*(\hat{p}), \theta^*(\hat{p}))$ is the unique solution of the system

$$f_k(\theta) = 0, \qquad k = 1, \ldots, \nu$$

$$\frac{\partial d_\Phi^\alpha(p, p(\theta))}{\partial \theta_j} + \sum_{k=1}^\nu \lambda_k \frac{\partial f_k(\theta)}{\partial \theta_j} = 0, \quad j = 1, \ldots, s$$

and $(\hat{p}, \gamma^*(\hat{p})) \in U$. Hence, $\theta^*(\hat{p})$ coincides with rMDE $\hat{\theta}^r_{(\Phi, \alpha)}$ given in (9). □

The theorem below establishes the asymptotic normality of rMDE which is a straightforward extension of Theorem 2.4 [11] since by the Central Limit Theorem we know that

$$\sqrt{N}(\hat{p} - p(\theta_0)) \xrightarrow[N \to \infty]{L} N(0, \Sigma_{p(\theta_0)}) \quad (11)$$

with the asymptotic variance-covariance matrix $\Sigma_{p(\theta_0)}$ given by $diag(p(\theta_0)) - p(\theta_0) p(\theta_0)^\top$.

Theorem 2. *Under Assumptions (A_0)–(A_5), by (11) and for $W(\theta_0)$ given in (10), the asymptotic distribution of rMDE is the s-dimensional Normal distribution given by*

$$\sqrt{N}(\hat{\theta}^r_{(\Phi, \alpha)} - \theta_0) \xrightarrow[N \to \infty]{L} N_s(0, W(\theta_0) \Sigma_{p(\theta_0)} W(\theta_0)^\top).$$

Remark 1. *The proposed class of estimators forms a family of estimators that goes beyond the indicator α since it is easy to see that estimators obtained for the Csiszar's φ family are given for $\alpha = 0$ in (1) and also the standard equiprobable model.*

3. Statistical Inference

In this section, we introduce the double index divergence test statistic

$$T^{\alpha_1}_{\Phi_1}\left(\hat{\theta}^r_{(\Phi_2,\alpha_2)}\right) = \frac{2N}{\Phi''_1(1)} d^{\alpha_1}_{\Phi_1}\left(\hat{p}, \mathbf{p}(\hat{\theta}^r_{(\Phi_2,\alpha_2)})\right) \quad (12)$$

with $\Phi_1, \Phi_2 \in F^*$ and $\alpha_1, \alpha_2 > 0$ and make the additional assumptions by which we focus on the Csiszar's family of measures for testing purposes (the notation φ is used for clarity) and the equiprobable model:

Assumption 2.
(A_6) $p_i = 1/m, \forall i$
(A_7) $\Phi_1 = \varphi, \alpha_1 = 0$.

The Theorem below provides the asymptotic distribution of (12) under Assumptions (A_0)–(A_7). Assumption (A_7) will be later relaxed and a general asymptotic result will be presented in the next subsection. A discussion about Assumption A_6 will also be made in the sequel.

Theorem 3. *Under Assumptions (A_0)–(A_7) and for the hypothesis in (3) we have*

$$T^0_\varphi\left(\hat{\theta}^r_{(\Phi_2,\alpha_2)}\right) = \frac{2N}{\varphi''(1)} d_\varphi\left(\hat{p}, \mathbf{p}(\hat{\theta}^r_{(\Phi_2,\alpha_2)})\right) \xrightarrow[N \to \infty]{L} \chi^2_{m-1-s-v}$$

with $\hat{\theta}^r_{(\Phi_2,\alpha_2)}$ given in (9).

Proof. It is straightforward that

$$\mathbf{p}(\hat{\theta}^r_{(\Phi_2,\alpha_2)}) = \mathbf{p}(\theta_0) + \mathbf{J}(\theta_0)(\hat{\theta}^r_{(\Phi_2,\alpha_2)} - \theta_0) + o(\|\hat{\theta}^r_{(\Phi_2,\alpha_2)} - \theta_0\|)$$

which by Theorem 2, expression (11), and for $\mathbf{M}(\theta_0) = \mathbf{J}(\theta_0)\mathbf{W}(\theta_0)$ reduces to

$$\mathbf{p}(\hat{\theta}^r_{(\Phi_2,\alpha_2)}) - \mathbf{p}(\theta_0) = \mathbf{M}(\theta_0)(\hat{p} - \mathbf{p}(\theta_0)) + o_p(N^{-1/2})$$

which implies that

$$\sqrt{N}(\mathbf{p}(\hat{\theta}^r_{(\Phi_2,\alpha_2)}) - \mathbf{p}(\theta_0)) \xrightarrow[N \to \infty]{L} N(0, \mathbf{M}(\theta_0)\Sigma_{\mathbf{p}(\theta_0)}\mathbf{M}(\theta_0)^\top). \quad (13)$$

Combining the above we obtain

$$\sqrt{N}\begin{pmatrix} \hat{p} - \mathbf{p}(\theta_0) \\ \mathbf{p}(\hat{\theta}^r_{(\Phi_2,\alpha_2)}) - \mathbf{p}(\theta_0) \end{pmatrix} \xrightarrow[N \to \infty]{L} N\left(0, \begin{pmatrix} I \\ \mathbf{M}(\theta_0) \end{pmatrix} \Sigma_{\mathbf{p}(\theta_0)}(I, \mathbf{M}(\theta_0)^\top)\right)$$

and

$$\sqrt{N}(\hat{p} - \mathbf{p}(\hat{\theta}^r_{(\Phi_2,\alpha_2)})) \xrightarrow[N \to \infty]{L} N(0, \mathbf{L}(\theta_0))$$

where

$$\mathbf{L}(\theta_0) = \Sigma_{\mathbf{p}(\theta_0)} - \mathbf{M}(\theta_0)\Sigma_{\mathbf{p}(\theta_0)} - \Sigma_{\mathbf{p}(\theta_0)}\mathbf{M}(\theta_0)^\top + \mathbf{M}(\theta_0)\Sigma_{\mathbf{p}(\theta_0)}\mathbf{M}(\theta_0)^\top. \quad (14)$$

The expansion of $d_\varphi(\mathbf{p}, \mathbf{q})$ around $(\mathbf{p}(\theta_0), \mathbf{p}(\theta_0))$ yields

$$T^0_\varphi\left(\hat{\theta}^r_{(\Phi_2,\alpha_2)}\right) = \sum_{i=1}^m \frac{N}{p_i(\theta_0)}\left(\hat{p}_i - p_i(\hat{\theta}^r_{(\Phi_2,\alpha_2)})\right)^2 + o_p(1) = \mathbf{X}^\top \mathbf{X} + o_p(1)$$

where

$$\mathbf{X} = \sqrt{N} diag(\mathbf{p}(\boldsymbol{\theta}_0)^{-1/2})(\hat{\mathbf{p}} - \mathbf{p}(\hat{\boldsymbol{\theta}}^r_{(\Phi_2,\alpha_2)})) \xrightarrow[N\to\infty]{L} N(\mathbf{0}, \mathbf{T}(\boldsymbol{\theta}_0)).$$

Then, under A_7, $\mathbf{T}(\boldsymbol{\theta}_0)$ (see (14)) is a projection matrix of rank $m - 1 - s + \nu$ since the trace of the matrices $\mathbf{A}(\boldsymbol{\theta}_0)(\mathbf{A}(\boldsymbol{\theta}_0)^\top \mathbf{A}(\boldsymbol{\theta}_0))^{-1}\mathbf{A}(\boldsymbol{\theta}_0)^\top$ and $\mathbf{A}(\boldsymbol{\theta}_0)(\mathbf{A}(\boldsymbol{\theta}_0)^\top \mathbf{A}(\boldsymbol{\theta}_0))^{-1}\mathbf{Q}(\boldsymbol{\theta}_0)^\top$ $(\mathbf{Q}(\boldsymbol{\theta}_0)(\mathbf{A}(\boldsymbol{\theta}_0)^\top \mathbf{A}(\boldsymbol{\theta}_0))^{-1}\mathbf{Q}(\boldsymbol{\theta}_0)^\top)^{-1}\mathbf{Q}(\boldsymbol{\theta}_0)(\mathbf{A}(\boldsymbol{\theta}_0)^\top\mathbf{A}(\boldsymbol{\theta}_0))^{-1}\mathbf{A}(\boldsymbol{\theta}_0)^\top$ is equal to s and ν, respectively.

Then, the result follows from the fact (see ([24], p. 57)) that $\mathbf{X}^\top \mathbf{X}$ has a chi-squared distribution with degrees of freedom equal to the rank of the variance-covariance matrix of the random vector $\mathbf{X}$ as long as it is a projection matrix. □

Remark 2. *Relaxation of Assumption (A_6): Arguing as in [11], when the true model is not the equiprobable the result of Theorem 3 holds true as long as $\alpha_2 = 0$ and approximately true when $\alpha_2 \to 0$.*

Asymptotic Theory of the Dual Divergence Test Statistic

Having established the two main results of the work, namely the decomposition of the proposed restricted estimator (Theorem 1) together with its asymptotic properties (Theorem 2), as well as the asymptotic distribution of the associated test statistic under the class of Csiszar φ-functions (Theorem 3) we continue below extended in a natural way the results of [11] for the dual divergence test statistic. The extensions presented in this section are considered vital due to their practical impication on cross tabulations discussed in Section 4. The proofs will be omitted since both results (Theorems 4 and 5) follow along the lines of previous results (see Theorems 3.4 and 3.9 of [11]). In what follows we adopt the following notation:

$$b = m^{-\alpha_1},\ p^{\alpha_1}_{(1)} = \min_{i\in\{1,\ldots,m\}} p_i(\boldsymbol{\theta}_0)^{\alpha_1},\ p^{\alpha_1}_{(m)} = \max_{i\in\{1,\ldots,m\}} p_i(\boldsymbol{\theta}_0)^{\alpha_1},\ k = m - 1 - s + \nu.$$

Theorem 4. *Under Assumptions (A_0)–(A_7) we have*

$$T^{\alpha_1}_{\Phi_1}(\hat{\boldsymbol{\theta}}^r_{(\Phi_2,\alpha_2)}) \xrightarrow[N\to\infty]{L} b\chi^2_k.$$

Remark 3. *Consider the case where Assumption (A_6) is relaxed. Then, the asymptotic distribution of the test statistic $T^{\alpha_1}_{\Phi_1}(\hat{\boldsymbol{\theta}}^r_{(\Phi_2,\alpha_2)})$ is estimated to be approximately $b\chi^2_k$ where*

$$b = \frac{p^{\alpha_1}_{(1)} + p^{\alpha_1}_{(m)}}{2} \tag{15}$$

as long as $\alpha_2 = 0$ or $\alpha_2 \to 0$. For further elaboration of this remark we refer to [11].

Remark 4. *Observe that if $\alpha_1 \to 0$ then $b \to 1$ and the asymptotic distribution becomes χ^2_k, while for α_1 away from 0 the distribution is proportional to χ^2_k with proportionality index $b \neq 1$. However, for not equiprobable models these statements hold true as long as α_2 is close to zero.*

Consider now the hypothesis with contiguous alternatives [25,26]

$$H_0 : \mathbf{p} = \mathbf{p}(\boldsymbol{\theta}_0)\ vs.\ H_{1,N} : \mathbf{p} = \mathbf{p}(\boldsymbol{\theta}_0) + \frac{\mathbf{d}}{\sqrt{N}} \tag{16}$$

where $\mathbf{d}$ is an m-dimensional vector of known real values with components d_i satisfying the assumption $\sum_{i=1}^{m} d_i = 0$.

Observe that as N tends to infinity, the local contiguous alternative converges to the null hypothesis at the rate $O(N^{1/2})$. Alternatives, such as those in (16), are known as *Pitman transition alternatives* or *Pitman (local) alternatives* or *local contiguous alternatives* to the null hypothesis H_0 [25].

Theorem 5. *Under Assumptions (A_0)–(A_7) and for the hypothesis (16) we have*

$$T_{\Phi_1}^{\alpha_1}(\hat{\boldsymbol{\theta}}_{(\Phi_2,\alpha_2)}^r) \xrightarrow[N\to\infty]{L} b\chi_k^2(\boldsymbol{\xi}^\top \boldsymbol{\xi})$$

which represents a non-central chi-squared distribution with k degrees of freedom and non-centrality parameter $\boldsymbol{\xi}^\top \boldsymbol{\xi}$ for which $\boldsymbol{\xi} = diag(\boldsymbol{p}(\boldsymbol{\theta}_0)^{-1/2})(I - J(\boldsymbol{\theta}_0)W(\boldsymbol{\theta}_0))\boldsymbol{d}$.

Remark 5. Observe that under Assumption (A_6) $(p_i = 1/m)$ the asymptotic distribution is independent of Φ, α_1 and α_2. As a result the associated power of the test is $\Pr(\chi_k^2(\boldsymbol{\xi}^\top \boldsymbol{\xi}) \geq \chi_{k,a}^2)$ where a the $100(1-a)\%$ percentile of the distribution. If assumption A_6 is relaxed then the distribution is approximately non-central chi-squared with proportionality index $b = \frac{p_{(1)}^{\alpha_1} + p_{(m)}^{\alpha_1}}{2}$.

4. Cross Tabulations and Dual Divergence Test Statistic

In this section, we try to take advantage of the methodology proposed earlier for the analysis of cross tabulations. In particular we focus on the case of three categorical variables, say X, Y, and Z with corresponding, I, J, and K. Then, assume that the probability mass of a realization of a randomly selected subject is denoted by $p_{ijk}(\boldsymbol{\theta}) = Pr(X = i, Y = j, Z = k) > 0$, where here and in what follows $i = 1, \ldots, I, j = 1, \ldots, J, k = 1, \ldots, K$ unless otherwise stated. The associated probability vector is given as $\mathbf{p}(\boldsymbol{\theta}) = \{p_{ijk}(\boldsymbol{\theta})\}$ where

$$p_{ijk}(\boldsymbol{\theta}) = \begin{cases} \theta_{ijk}, & (i,j,k) \neq (I,J,K) \\ 1 - \sum_{\substack{i=1 \\ (i,j,k)\neq(I,J,K)}}^{I}\sum_{j=1}^{J}\sum_{k=1}^{K} \theta_{ijk}, & (i,j,k) = (I,J,K) \end{cases}$$

and the parameter space as $\Theta = \{\theta_{ijk}, (i,j,k) \neq (I,J,K)\}$. The sample estimator of $p_{ijk}(\boldsymbol{\theta})$ is $\hat{p}_{ijk} = n_{ijk}/N$, where n_{ijk} is the frequency of the corresponding (i,j,k) cell.

In this set up the dual divergence test statistics is given as

$$T_{\Phi_1}^{\alpha_1}\left(\hat{\boldsymbol{\theta}}_{(\Phi_2,\alpha_2)}^r\right) = \frac{2N}{\Phi_1''(1)}\sum_{i=1}^{I}\sum_{j=1}^{J}\sum_{k=1}^{K} p_{ijk}(\hat{\boldsymbol{\theta}}_{(\Phi_2,\alpha_2)}^r)^{1+\alpha}\Phi_1\left(\frac{\hat{p}_{ijk}}{p_{ijk}(\hat{\boldsymbol{\theta}}_{(\Phi_2,\alpha_2)}^r)}\right) \quad (17)$$

where $\hat{p}_{ijk}$ as above and the rMD estimator as

$$\hat{\boldsymbol{\theta}}_{(\Phi_2,\alpha_2)}^r = \arg\inf_{\{\boldsymbol{\theta}\in\Theta\subset\mathbb{R}^s: f_k(\boldsymbol{\theta})=0, k=1,\ldots,\nu\}}\sum_{i=1}^{I}\sum_{j=1}^{J}\sum_{k=1}^{K} p_{ijk}(\boldsymbol{\theta})^{1+\alpha_2}\Phi_2\left(\frac{\hat{p}_{ijk}}{p_{ijk}(\boldsymbol{\theta})}\right). \quad (18)$$

For $\alpha_1, \alpha_2 = 0$ and special cases of the functions Φ_1 and Φ_2, classical restricted minimum divergence estimators and associated test statistics can be derived from (18) and (17), respectively. For example, for $\alpha_1, \alpha_2 = 0$, and $\Phi_1, \Phi_2 = \Phi_{KL}$ the likelihood ratio test statistic with the restricted maximum likelihood estimator $(G^2(\hat{\boldsymbol{\theta}}^r))$ can be derived, while for $\Phi_1, \Phi_2 = \Phi_\lambda$ and $\lambda = 1$ we obtain the chi-squared test statistic with the restricted minimum chi-squared estimator $(X^2(\hat{\boldsymbol{\theta}}_{X^2}^r))$. For $\Phi_1, \Phi_2 = \Phi_\lambda$ and $\lambda = 2/3$ the dual divergence test statistic reduces to the power divergence test statistic with the restricted minimum power divergence estimator $(CR(\hat{\boldsymbol{\theta}}_{CR}^r))$ whereas for $\lambda = -1/2$ reduces to the Freeman–Tukey test statistic with the restricted minimum Freeman–Tukey estimator $(FT(\hat{\boldsymbol{\theta}}_{FT}^r))$.

The hypothesis of conditional independence between X, Y, and Z is given for any triplet i, j, k by

$$H_0 : p_{ijk}(\theta_0) = \frac{p_{i*k}(\theta_0) p_{*jk}(\theta_0)}{p_{**k}(\theta_0)}, \; \theta_0 \in \Theta \text{ unknown}$$

where

$$p_{i*k}(\theta_0) = \sum_{j=1}^{J} p_{ijk}(\theta_0), \; p_{*jk}(\theta_0) = \sum_{i=1}^{I} p_{ijk}(\theta_0) \text{ and } p_{**k}(\theta_0) = \sum_{i=1}^{I}\sum_{j=1}^{J} p_{ijk}(\theta_0).$$

Under the $(I-1)(J-1)K$ constrained functions

$$f_{ijk}(\theta) = p_{11k}(\theta) p_{ijk}(\theta) - p_{1jk}(\theta) p_{i1k}(\theta) = 0$$

$i = 2, \ldots, I$, $j = 2, \ldots, J$, $k = 1, \ldots, K$ the above H_0 hypothesis with θ_0 unknown, becomes

$$H_0 : \mathbf{p} = \mathbf{p}(\theta_0), \text{ for } \theta_0 \in \Theta_0,$$

where $\Theta_0 = \{\theta \in \Theta : f_{ijk}(\theta) = 0, \; i = 2, \ldots, I, \; j = 2, \ldots, J, \; k = 1, \ldots, K\}$.

Remark 6. *For practical purposes, the choice of the values of the indices is motivated by the work of [8] where, in an attempt to achieve a compromise between robustness and efficiency of estimators, they recommended the use of small values in the $(0, 1)$ region. In the following subsection, our analysis will reconfirm their findings since as it will be seen, values of both indices close to (0) (than to one (1)) will be found to be associated with a good performance not only in terms of estimation but also in terms of goodness of fit as it will be reflected in the size and the power of the test.*

Simulation Study

In this simulation study, we use the rMD estimator and the associated dual divergence test statistic for the analysis of cross tabulations. Specifically, we are going to compare in terms of size and power classical tests with those that can be derived through the proposed methodology, for the problem of conditional independence of three random variables in contingency tables. We test the hypothesis of conditional independence for a $2 \times 2 \times 2$ contingency table, thus in this case we have $m = 8$ probabilities of the multinomial model, $s = 7$ unknown parameters to estimate and two constraint functions ($\nu = 2$) which are given by

$$f_{221}(\theta) = \theta_{111}\theta_{221} - \theta_{121}\theta_{211} \text{ and } f_{222}(\theta) = \theta_{112}\left(1 - \sum_{\substack{i=1 \\ (i,j,k) \neq (2,2,2)}}^{2}\sum_{j=1}^{2}\sum_{k=1}^{2} \theta_{ijk}\right) - \theta_{122}\theta_{212}.$$

For a better understanding of the behaviour of the dual divergence test statistic given in (17) we compare it with the four classical tests-of-fit mentioned earlier in Section 4, namely with the $G^2(\hat{\theta}^r)$, $X^2(\hat{\theta}^r_{X^2})$, $CR(\hat{\theta}^r_{CR})$ and $FT(\hat{\theta}^r_{FT})$. The proposed test $T^{\alpha_1}_{\Phi_1}\left(\hat{\theta}^r_{(\Phi_2,\alpha_2)}\right)$ is applied for $\Phi_1 = \Phi_{\alpha_1}$, $\Phi_2 = \Phi_{\alpha_2}$ and six different values of α_1 and α_2, $\alpha_1, \alpha_2 = 10^{-7}, 0.01, 0.05, 0.10, 0.50,$ and 1.50. Note that, the critical values used in this simulation study, are the asymptotic critical values based on the asymptotic distribution $b\chi^2_2$ with b as in (15) for the double index family of test statistics, and the χ^2_2 for the classical test statistics. For the analysis we used 100,000 simulations and sample sizes equal to $n = 20, 25$ (small sample sizes) and $n = 40, 45$ (moderate sample sizes).

In this study, we have used the model previously considered by [27] given by

$$p_{111} = \pi_{111} - \pi_{111}w \qquad p_{211} = \pi_{211} + \pi_{222}w - \pi_{111}w$$
$$p_{112} = \pi_{112} + \pi_{111}w - \pi_{222}w \qquad p_{212} = \pi_{212} + \pi_{111}w - \pi_{222}w$$
$$p_{121} = \pi_{121} + \pi_{222}w \qquad p_{221} = \pi_{221} + \pi_{222}w - \pi_{111}w$$
$$p_{122} = \pi_{122} + \pi_{111}w \qquad p_{222} = \pi_{222} - \pi_{222}w$$

where $0 \leq w < 1$ and $\pi_{ijk} = p_{i**} \times p_{*j*} \times p_{**k}$ $i, j, k = 1, 2$ with

$$\pi_{111} = 0.036254 \qquad \pi_{112} = 0.164994 \qquad \pi_{121} = 0.092809 \qquad \pi_{122} = 0.133645$$
$$\pi_{211} = 0.092809 \qquad \pi_{212} = 0.133645 \qquad \pi_{221} = 0.237591 \qquad \pi_{222} = 0.108253.$$

For $w = 0$ we take the model under the null hypothesis of conditional independence while for values $w \neq 0$ we take the models under the alternative hypotheses. We considered the following values of $w = 0.00, 0.30, 0.60,$ and 0.90. Note that the larger the value of w the more we deviate from the null model. For the simulation study, we used the R software [28], while for the constrained optimization the **auglag** function from the **nloptr** package [29].

From Table 1, we can observe that in terms of size the performance of the $T_{\Phi_1}^{\alpha_1}(\hat{\theta}^r_{(\Phi_2,\alpha_2)})$ is adequate for values of $\alpha_1, \alpha_2 \leq 0.5$ both for small and moderate sample sizes. In addition, we can see that for $\alpha_1 \leq 0.10$, $T_{\Phi_1}^{\alpha_1}(\hat{\theta}^r_{(\Phi_2,\alpha_2)})$ appears to be liberal while for $\alpha_1 \geq 0.5$ appears to be conservative. We also note that the size becomes smaller as α_1 and α_2 increase with $\alpha_1 \geq \alpha_2$. Table 2 provides the size of the classical tests-of-fit from where we can observe that $CR(\hat{\theta}^r_{CR})$ has the best performance among all competing tests for every sample size. In contrast, $FT(\hat{\theta}^r_{FT})$ has the worst performance among all competing tests and appears to be very liberal. Furthermore, $X^2(\hat{\theta}^r_{X^2})$ appears to be conservative while $G^2(\hat{\theta}^r)$ appears to be liberal. Note that for $\alpha_1 \in [0.01, 0.5]$ and $\alpha_2 \leq 0.10$, $T_{\Phi_1}^{\alpha_1}(\hat{\theta}^r_{(\Phi_2,\alpha_2)})$ behaves better than the $G^2(\hat{\theta}^r)$ test statistic and its performance is quite close to the performance of the $X^2(\hat{\theta}^r_{X^2})$.

Table 1. Size ($w = 0.00$) calculations (%) of the $T_{\Phi_1}^{\alpha_1}(\hat{\theta}^r_{(\Phi_2,\alpha_2)})$ test statistic for sample sizes $n = 20, 25, 40, 45$. Sizes that satisfy Dale's criterion are presented in bold.

α_1	α_2										
	10^{-7}	0.01	0.05	0.10	0.50	1.50	10^{-7}	0.01	0.05	0.10	0.50	1.50
	$n = 20$						$n = 25$					
10^{-7}	8.256	8.257	8.260	8.263	9.216	13.856	7.863	7.865	7.878	7.920	8.927	13.192
0.01	8.207	8.206	8.209	8.224	9.224	13.623	7.753	7.754	7.763	7.817	8.797	12.930
0.05	7.896	7.849	7.879	7.886	8.719	12.916	7.340	7.334	7.327	7.350	8.313	12.277
0.10	7.403	7.404	7.378	7.356	8.046	11.994	6.965	6.959	6.940	6.934	7.675	11.364
0.50	3.873	3.850	3.769	3.612	3.023	4.050	3.857	3.819	3.722	3.604	3.191	4.304
1.50	0.920	0.893	0.807	0.758	0.509	0.202	1.046	1.019	0.948	0.885	0.602	0.203
	$n = 40$						$n = 45$					
10^{-7}	7.016	7.016	7.027	7.055	7.887	11.362	6.858	6.858	6.870	6.908	7.732	11.099
0.01	6.933	6.933	6.940	6.957	7.778	11.183	6.760	6.760	6.770	6.805	7.601	10.941
0.05	6.590	6.589	6.580	6.593	7.342	10.505	6.427	6.422	6.415	6.426	7.153	10.340
0.10	6.246	6.239	6.228	6.222	6.794	9.758	6.082	6.070	6.053	6.043	6.612	9.586
0.50	3.854	3.832	3.762	3.661	3.367	4.362	3.813	3.789	3.716	3.635	3.331	4.269
1.50	1.172	1.160	1.115	1.066	0.760	0.383	1.183	1.170	1.119	1.068	0.773	0.437

In order to examine the closeness of the estimated (true) size to the nominal size $\alpha = 0.05$ we consider the criterion given by Dale [30]. The criterion involves the following inequality

$$|\text{logit}(1 - \hat{\alpha}_n) - \text{logit}(1 - \alpha)| \leq d \qquad (19)$$

where logit$(p) = \log(p/(1-p))$ and $\hat{\alpha}_n$ is the estimated (true) size. The estimated (true) size is considered to be close to the nominal size if (19) is satisfied with $d = 0.35$. Note that in this situation the estimated (true) size is close to the nominal one if $\hat{\alpha}_n \in [0.0357, 0.0695]$ and is presented in Tables 1 and 2 in bold. This criterion has been used previously among others by [27,31].

Regarding the proposed test we can see that for small sample sizes the estimated (true) size is close to the nominal for $\alpha_1 \in [0.10, 0.50]$ and $\alpha_2 \leq 0.10$ while for moderate sample sizes for $\alpha_1 \in [10^{-7}, 0.50]$ and $\alpha_2 \leq 0.10$. With reference to the classical tests-of-fit we can observe that the size of the $CR(\hat{\theta}^r_{CR})$ is close to the nominal for every sample size whereas the size of $G^2(\hat{\theta}^r)$ and $X^2(\hat{\theta}^r_{X^2})$ is close only for moderate sample sizes. Finally, we note that the estimated (true) size of $FT(\hat{\theta}^r_{FT})$ fails to be close to the nominal both for small and moderate sample sizes.

In Tables 3–5, we provide the results regarding the power of the proposed family of test statistics for the three alternatives and sample sizes $n = 20, 25, 40, 45$, while Table 2 provides the results regarding the power of the classical tests-of-fit. The performance tends to be better as we deviate from the null model and as the sample size increases both for the classical and the proposed tests.

Table 2. Size ($w = 0.00$) and power ($w = 0.30, 0.60, 0.90$) calculations (%) for the classical tests-of-fit. Sizes that satisfy Dale's criterion are presented in bold.

Sample size	FT	G^2	CR	X^2	FT	G^2	CR	X^2
		$w = 0.00$				$w = 0.30$		
$n = 20$	14.715	8.261	**4.219**	3.140	18.366	9.072	4.200	2.966
$n = 25$	13.664	7.865	**4.333**	3.477	19.674	9.846	4.783	3.646
$n = 40$	11.154	7.016	**4.722**	4.059	21.920	12.192	6.935	5.548
$n = 45$	10.787	**6.858**	**4.703**	4.082	22.467	12.992	7.471	6.081
		$w = 0.40$				$w = 0.45$		
$n = 20$	29.707	14.936	7.096	4.910	47.859	26.721	13.789	9.704
$n = 25$	35.768	18.966	9.469	7.118	62.810	38.023	20.147	15.296
$n = 40$	48.366	31.513	18.780	15.030	85.773	69.599	47.644	39.481
$n = 45$	50.821	35.381	22.367	18.217	89.108	76.685	57.000	48.451

Table 3. Power ($w = 0.30$) calculations (%) of the $T^{\alpha_1}_{\Phi_1}(\hat{\theta}^r_{(\Phi_2,\alpha_2)})$ test statistic for sample sizes $n = 20, 25, 40, 45$.

						α_2					
α_1	10^{-7}	0.01	0.05	0.10	0.50	1.50	10^{-7}	0.01	0.05	0.10	0.50	1.50
			$n = 20$						$n = 25$			
10^{-7}	9.073	9.072	9.071	9.076	9.993	15.062	9.846	9.846	9.868	9.895	10.924	15.729
0.01	8.990	8.989	8.988	9.006	9.948	14.724	9.630	9.630	9.651	9.727	10.712	15.343
0.05	8.350	8.278	8.340	8.357	9.231	13.819	9.033	9.008	8.990	9.022	9.876	14.332
0.10	7.694	7.696	7.626	7.616	8.273	12.656	8.225	8.216	8.194	8.188	8.890	13.111
0.50	3.751	3.717	3.607	3.418	2.889	4.199	3.797	3.761	3.656	3.581	3.252	4.620
1.50	0.793	0.764	0.676	0.630	0.415	0.163	0.820	0.810	0.756	0.718	0.479	0.158
			$n = 40$						$n = 45$			
10^{-7}	12.192	12.193	12.207	12.231	13.142	17.775	12.992	12.992	13.003	13.052	14.014	18.490
0.01	11.935	11.934	11.942	11.979	12.853	17.387	12.724	12.724	12.730	12.764	13.721	18.148
0.05	11.075	11.075	11.069	11.074	11.844	16.046	11.799	11.786	11.760	11.768	12.628	16.815
0.10	10.072	10.060	10.039	10.022	10.565	14.549	10.747	10.729	10.688	10.669	11.218	15.183
0.50	4.863	4.842	4.743	4.648	4.342	5.815	5.214	5.179	5.078	4.977	4.648	6.116
1.50	0.979	0.970	0.928	0.890	0.662	0.379	1.032	1.019	0.978	0.928	0.693	0.412

Table 4. Power ($w = 0.60$) calculations (%) of the $T_{\Phi_1}^{\alpha_1}(\hat{\theta}^r_{(\Phi_2,\alpha_2)})$ test statistic for sample sizes $n = 20, 25, 40, 45$.

α_1	α_2										
	10^{-7}	0.01	0.05	0.10	0.50	1.50	10^{-7}	0.01	0.05	0.10	0.50	1.50
	$n = 20$						$n = 25$					
10^{-7}	14.928	14.937	14.932	14.944	16.186	22.900	18.965	18.964	19.004	19.042	20.607	27.684
0.01	14.807	14.813	14.808	14.833	16.117	22.486	18.565	18.564	18.598	18.702	20.235	27.069
0.05	13.711	13.583	13.726	13.735	14.939	21.143	17.436	17.383	17.360	17.422	18.733	25.365
0.10	12.612	12.619	12.529	12.525	13.217	19.545	15.794	15.767	15.743	15.726	16.869	23.368
0.50	6.088	5.994	5.811	5.416	4.553	6.403	6.879	6.821	6.656	6.473	5.912	8.458
1.50	1.118	1.077	0.944	0.889	0.553	0.215	1.275	1.240	1.152	1.081	0.729	0.260
	$n = 40$						$n = 45$					
10^{-7}	31.513	31.518	31.533	31.608	33.469	40.799	35.381	35.381	35.404	35.465	37.411	44.556
0.01	30.904	30.903	30.925	30.999	32.868	40.221	34.848	34.845	34.863	34.941	36.744	43.942
0.05	28.949	28.946	28.938	28.956	30.509	37.756	32.727	32.716	32.697	32.715	34.310	41.510
0.10	26.504	26.485	26.434	26.398	27.631	34.747	30.146	30.110	30.051	30.014	31.289	38.456
0.50	11.949	11.867	11.598	11.409	10.830	14.703	14.052	13.966	13.632	13.321	12.731	16.901
1.50	1.797	1.761	1.692	1.578	1.142	0.716	1.973	1.945	1.870	1.776	1.295	0.838

Table 5. Power ($w = 0.90$) calculations (%) of the $T_{\Phi_1}^{\alpha_1}(\hat{\theta}^r_{(\Phi_2,\alpha_2)})$ test statistic for sample sizes $n = 20, 25, 40, 45$.

α_1	α_2										
	10^{-7}	0.01	0.05	0.10	0.50	1.50	10^{-7}	0.01	0.05	0.10	0.50	1.50
	$n = 20$						$n = 25$					
10^{-7}	26.712	26.710	26.707	26.711	28.495	37.924	38.017	38.016	38.132	38.191	40.982	50.954
0.01	26.589	26.586	26.585	26.613	28.718	37.421	37.365	37.364	37.456	37.645	40.482	50.206
0.05	25.437	25.267	25.531	25.502	27.170	35.979	35.674	35.559	35.526	35.643	38.260	48.187
0.10	24.287	24.284	24.232	24.172	24.868	33.946	33.014	32.939	32.867	32.854	35.184	45.569
0.50	12.003	11.780	11.424	10.772	8.807	11.665	14.353	14.226	13.870	13.560	12.312	16.886
1.50	1.731	1.662	1.489	1.422	0.904	0.298	2.268	2.226	2.026	1.916	1.387	0.506
	$n = 40$						$n = 45$					
10^{-7}	69.599	69.605	69.637	69.755	72.196	79.363	76.685	76.685	76.731	76.805	78.802	84.683
0.01	68.923	68.923	68.954	69.049	71.518	79.003	76.177	76.173	76.192	76.264	78.143	84.344
0.05	66.310	66.309	66.306	66.365	68.576	77.069	73.760	73.745	73.732	73.766	75.748	82.751
0.10	62.500	62.455	62.372	62.343	64.660	74.161	70.295	70.264	70.144	70.131	72.172	80.319
0.50	30.094	29.904	29.349	28.848	27.895	36.902	36.612	36.465	35.792	35.073	34.056	43.732
1.50	3.748	3.678	3.472	3.210	2.269	1.562	4.349	4.274	4.017	3.747	2.665	1.927

As general comments regarding the behaviour of the proposed and the classical tests-of-fit in terms of power we state that the best results for the $T_{\Phi_1}^{\alpha_1}(\hat{\theta}^r_{(\Phi_2,\alpha_2)})$ are obtained for small values of α_1 in the range $(0, 0.1]$ and large values of α_2 with $\alpha_1 \leq \alpha_2$. Note that although in terms of power results become better as α_2 increases in terms of size these are adequate only for $\alpha_2 \leq 0.5$. In addition, we can observe that the performance of $T_{\Phi_1}^{\alpha_1}(\hat{\theta}^r_{(\Phi_2,\alpha_2)})$ is better than the $CR(\hat{\theta}^r_{CR})$ and $X^2(\hat{\theta}^r_{X^2})$ for every alternative and every sample size for $\alpha_1 \leq 0.1$ and $\alpha_2 \leq 0.5$ and slightly better than $G^2(\hat{\theta}^r)$ for small values of α_1 and large values of α_2, for example for $\alpha_1 = 0.01$ and $\alpha_2 = 0.50$. Furthermore, we can observe that for $\alpha_1 = 0.1$ and $\alpha_2 \leq 0.1$ the size of the test is better than the size of the $G^2(\hat{\theta}^r)$ and slightly worst form the size of the $CR(\hat{\theta}^r_{CR})$ and $X^2(\hat{\theta}^r_{X^2})$ test statistics while its power is quite better than the power of the $CR(\hat{\theta}^r_{CR})$ and $X^2(\hat{\theta}^r_{X^2})$ and slightly worst than the $G^2(\hat{\theta}^r)$. Additionally, we can see that as α_1 and α_2 tend to 0 the behaviour of the $T_{\Phi_1}^{\alpha_1}(\hat{\theta}^r_{(\Phi_2,\alpha_2)})$ test statistic coincides with the $G^2(\hat{\theta}^r)$ test both in terms of size and power as it was expected.

In order to attain a better insight about the behaviour of the test statistics, we apply Dale's criterion, not only for the nominal size $\alpha = 0.05$, but also for a range of nominal sizes that are of interest. Based on the previous analysis, beside the classical tests, we will focus our interest on the $T_{\Phi_1}^{0.05}(\hat{\theta}_{(\Phi_2,0.05)}^r)$, $T_{\Phi_1}^{0.10}(\hat{\theta}_{(\Phi_2,0.10)}^r)$, and $T_{\Phi_1}^{0.20}(\hat{\theta}_{(\Phi_2,0.20)}^r)$. The following simplified notation is used in every Figure, FT $\equiv FT(\hat{\theta}_{FT}^r)$, ML $\equiv G^2(\hat{\theta}^r)$, CR $\equiv CR(\hat{\theta}_{CR}^r)$, Pe $\equiv X^2(\hat{\theta}_{X^2}^r)$, T1 $\equiv T_{\Phi_1}^{0.05}(\hat{\theta}_{(\Phi_2,0.05)}^r)$, T2 $\equiv T_{\Phi_1}^{0.10}(\hat{\theta}_{(\Phi_2,0.10)}^r)$, and T3 $\equiv T_{\Phi_1}^{0.20}(\hat{\theta}_{(\Phi_2,0.20)}^r)$. From Figure 1a, we can see that for small sample sizes ($n = 25$) $T_{\Phi_1}^{0.20}(\hat{\theta}_{(\Phi_2,0.20)}^r)$ and $CR(\hat{\theta}_{CR}^r)$ satisfy Dale's criterion for every nominal size while $T_{\Phi_1}^{0.10}(\hat{\theta}_{(\Phi_2,0.10)}^r)$ and $X^2(\hat{\theta}_{X^2}^r)$ for nominal sizes greater than 0.03 and 0.06, respectively. Note that the dashed line in Figure 1 denotes the situation in which the estimated (true) size equals to the nominal size and thus lines that lie above this reference line refer to liberal tests while those that lie below to conservative ones. On the other hand, for moderate sample sizes ($n = 45$) all chosen test statistics satisfy Dale's criterion except $FT(\hat{\theta}_{FT}^r)$.

Taking into account the fact that the actual size of each test differs from the targeted nominal size, we have to make an adjustment in order to proceed further with the comparison of the tests in terms of power. We focus our interest in those tests that satisfy Dale's criterion and follow the method proposed in [32] which involves the so-called receiver operating characteristic (ROC) curves. In particular, let $G(t) = Pr(T \geq t)$ be the survivor function of a general test statistic T, and $c = \inf\{t : G(t) \leq \alpha\}$ be the critical value, then ROC curves can be formulated by plotting the power $G_1(c)$ against the size $G_0(c)$ for various values of the critical value c. Note that with $G_0(t)$ we denote the distribution of the test statistic under the null hypothesis and with $G_1(t)$ under the alternative.

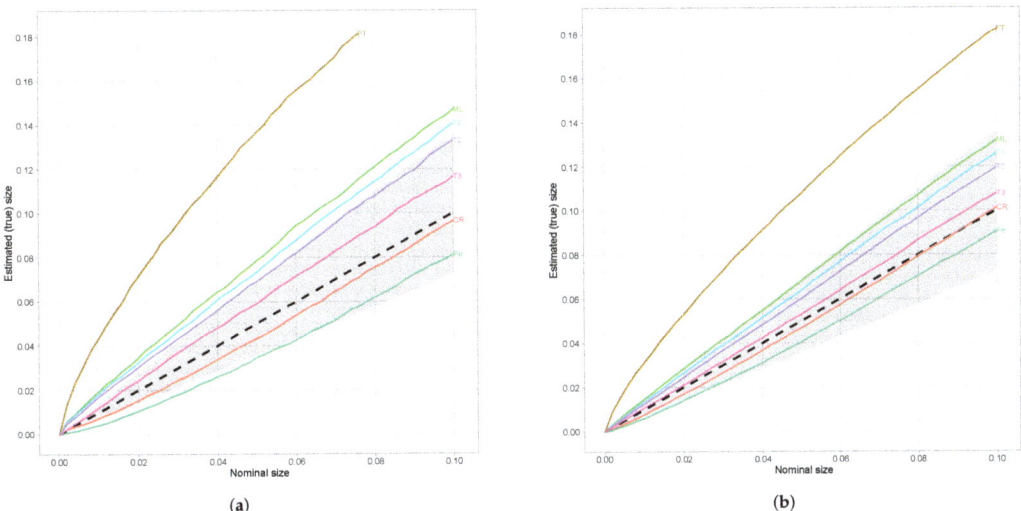

Figure 1. Estimated (true) sizes against nominal sizes. The shaded area refers to Dale's criterion. (**a**) $n = 25$. (**b**) $n = 45$.

Since results are similar for every alternative we restrict ourselves to $w = 0.60$ which refers to an alternative that is neither too close nor too far from the null. For small sample sizes ($n = 25$) results are presented in Figure 2, where we can see that the proposed test is superior from the classical tests-of-fit in terms of power. However, for moderate sample sizes ($n = 45$) we can observe in Figure 3 that $G^2(\hat{\theta}^r)$ has the best performance among all competing tests followed by the proposed test-of-fit.

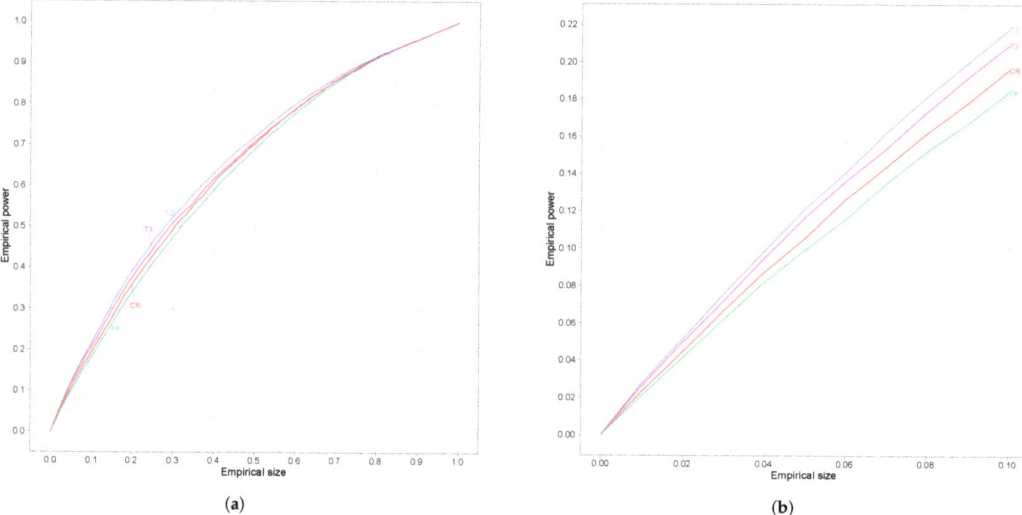

Figure 2. (**a**) Empirical ROC curves for $n = 25$. (**b**) The same curves magnified over a relevant range of empirical sizes.

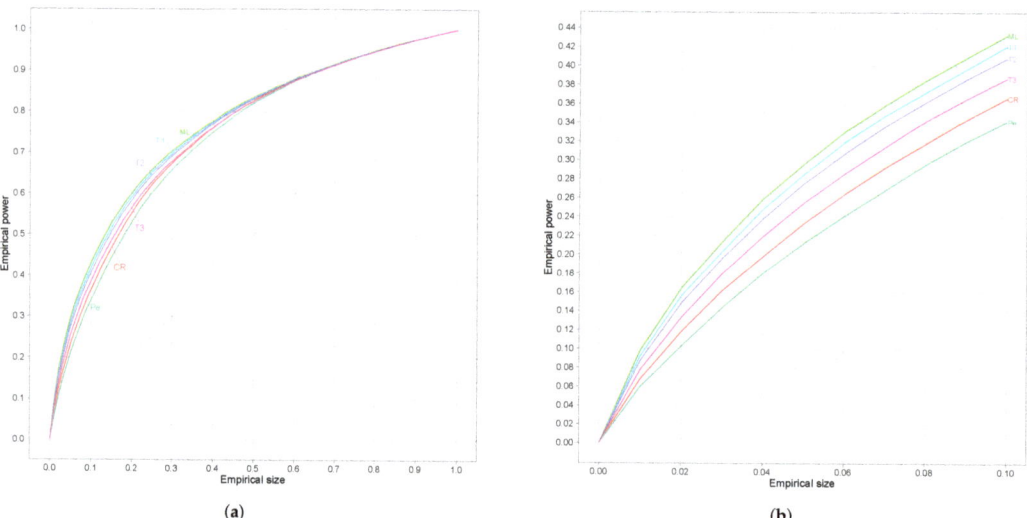

Figure 3. (**a**) Empirical ROC curves for $n = 45$. (**b**) The same curves magnified over a relevant range of empirical sizes.

From the conducted analysis we conclude that regarding the proposed test there is a trade off between size and power for different choices of the indices α_1 and α_2. In particular, we can see that as α_1 increases the size becomes smaller in the expense of smaller power, while as α_2 increases the power becomes better and the tests more liberal. In conclusion, we could state that for values of α_1 and α_2 in the range $(0.05, 0.25)$ the resulting test statistic provides a fair balance between size and power which makes it an attractive alternative to the classical tests-of-fit where for small sample sizes larger values of the indices are preferable whereas for moderate sample sizes, smaller ones are recommended.

5. Conclusions

In this work, a general divergence family of test statistics is presented for hypothesis testing problems as in (3), under constraints. For estimating purposes, we introduce, discuss and use the rMD (restricted minimum divergence) estimator presented in (8). The proposed double index (dual) divergence test statistic involves two pairs of elements, namely (Φ_2, α_2) to be used for the estimation problem and (Φ_1, α_1) to be used for the testing problem. The duality refers to the fact that the two pairs may or may not be the same providing the researcher with the greatest possible flexibility.

The asymptotic distribution of the dual divergence test statistic is found to be proportional to the chi-squared distribution irrespectively of the nature of the multinomial model, as long as the values of the two indicators involved are relative close to zero (less than 0.5). Such values are known to provide a satisfactory balance between efficiency and robustness (see, for instance, [8] or [3]).

The methodology developed in this work can be used in the analysis of contingency tables which is applicable in various scientific fields: biosciences, such as genetics [33] and epidemiology [34]; finance, such as the evaluation of investment effectiveness or business performance [35]; insurance science [36]; or socioeconomics [37]. This work concludes with a comparative simulation study between classical test statistics and members of the proposed family, where the focus is placed on the conditional independence of three random variables. Results indicate that, by selecting wisely the values of the α_1 and α_2 indices, we can derive a test statistic that can be thought of as a powerful and reliable alternative to the classical tests-of-fit especially for small sample sizes.

Author Contributions: Conceptualization, A.K. and C.M.; data curation, C.M.; methodology, A.K. and C.M; software, C.M.; formal analysis, A.K. and C.M.; writing—original draft preparation, C.M.; writing—review and editing, A.K. and C.M.; supervision, A.K. All authors have read and agreed to the published version of the manuscript.

Funding: The research received no external funding.

Institutional Review Board Statement: Not applicable.

Informed Consent Statement: Not applicable.

Data Availability Statement: Not applicable.

Acknowledgments: The authors wish to express their appreciation to the anonymous referees and the Associated Editor for their valuable comments and suggestions. The authors wish also to express their appreciation to the professor A. Batsidis of the University of Ioannina for bringing to their attention citation [31] which helped greatly the comparative analysis performed in this work. This work was completed as part of the first author PhD thesis and falls within the research activities of the Laboratory of Statistics and Data Analysis of the University of the Aegean.

Conflicts of Interest: The authors declare no conflict of interest.

Appendix A

The Birch regularity conditions mentioned in Assumption (A5) of Section 2 are stated below (for details see [22])

1. The point θ_0 is an interior point of Θ;
2. $p_i = p_i(\theta_0) > 0$ for $i = 1, \ldots, m$;
3. The mapping $\mathbf{p}(\theta) \colon \Theta \to \mathcal{P}$ is totally differentiable at θ_0 so that the partial derivatives of $p_i(\theta_0)$ with respect to each θ_j exist at θ_0 and $\mathbf{p}(\theta)$ has a linear approximation at θ_0 given by

$$p_i(\theta) = p_i(\theta_0) + \sum_{j=1}^{s}(\theta_j - \theta_{0j})\frac{\partial p_i(\theta_0)}{\partial \theta_j} + o(\|\theta - \theta_0\|), \ i = 1, \ldots, m$$

as $\theta \to \theta_0$.

4. The Jacobian matrix

$$\mathbf{J}(\boldsymbol{\theta}_0) = \left(\frac{\partial \mathbf{p}(\boldsymbol{\theta})}{\partial \boldsymbol{\theta}}\right)_{\boldsymbol{\theta}=\boldsymbol{\theta}_0} = \left(\frac{\partial p_i(\boldsymbol{\theta}_0)}{\partial \theta_j}\right)_{\substack{i=1,\ldots,m \\ j=1,\ldots,s}}$$

is of full rank;
5. The mapping inverse to $\boldsymbol{\theta} \to \mathbf{p}(\boldsymbol{\theta})$ exists and is continuous at $\boldsymbol{\theta}_0$;
6. The mapping $\mathbf{p}: \Theta \to \mathcal{P}$ is continuous at every point $\boldsymbol{\theta} \in \Theta$.

References

1. Salicru, M.; Morales, D.; Menendez, M.; Pardo, L. On the Applications of Divergence Type Measures in Testing Statistical Hypotheses. *J. Multivar. Anal.* **1994**, *51*, 372–391. [CrossRef]
2. Contreras-Reyes, J.E.; Kahrari, F.; Cortés, D.D. On the modified skew-normal-Cauchy distribution: Properties, inference and applications. *Commun. Stat. Theory Methods* **2021**, *50*, 3615–3631. [CrossRef]
3. Mattheou, K.; Karagrigoriou, A. A New Family of Divergence Measures for Tests of Fit. *Aust. N. Z. J. Stat.* **2010**, *52*, 187–200. [CrossRef]
4. Csiszár, I. Eine Informationstheoretische Ungleichung und Ihre Anwendung auf Beweis der Ergodizitaet von Markoffschen Ketten. *Magyer Tud. Akad. Mat. Kut. Int. Koezl.* **1963**, *8*, 85–108.
5. Kullback, S.; Leibler, R.A. On Information and Sufficiency. *Ann. Math. Stat.* **1951**, *22*, 79–86. [CrossRef]
6. Cressie, N.; Read, T.R.C. Multinomial Goodness-of-Fit Tests. *J. R. Stat. Soc. Ser. B Methodol.* **1984**, *46*, 440–464. [CrossRef]
7. Pearson, K. On the criterion that a given system of deviations from the probable in the case of a correlated system of variables is such that it can be reasonably supposed to have arisen from random sampling. *Lond. Edinb. Dublin Philos. Mag. J. Sci.* **1900**, *50*, 157–175. [CrossRef]
8. Basu, A.; Harris, I.R.; Hjort, N.L.; Jones, M.C. Robust and Efficient Estimation by Minimising a Density Power Divergence. *Biometrika* **1998**, *85*, 549–559. [CrossRef]
9. Pardo, L. *Statistical Inference Based on Divergence Measures*; Chapman and Hall/CRC: New York, NY, USA, 2006.
10. Morales, D.; Pardo, L.; Vajda, I. Asymptotic Divergence of Estimates of Discrete Distributions. *J. Stat. Plan. Inference* **1995**, *48*, 347–369. [CrossRef]
11. Meselidis, C.; Karagrigoriou, A. Statistical Inference for Multinomial Populations Based on a Double Index Family of Test Statistics. *J. Stat. Comput. Simul.* **2020**, *90*, 1773–1792. [CrossRef]
12. Pardo, J.; Pardo, L.; Zografos, K. Minimum φ-divergence Estimators with Constraints in Multinomial Populations. *J. Stat. Plan. Inference* **2002**, *104*, 221–237. [CrossRef]
13. Read, T.R.; Cressie, N.A. *Goodness-of-Fit Statistics for Discrete Multivariate Data*; Springer: New York, NY, USA, 1988.
14. Alin, A.; Kurt, S. Ordinary and Penalized Minimum Power-divergence Estimators in Two-way Contingency Tables. *Comput. Stat.* **2008**, *23*, 455–468. [CrossRef]
15. Toma, A. Optimal Robust M-estimators Using Divergences. *Stat. Probab. Lett.* **2009**, *79*, 1–5. [CrossRef]
16. Jiménez-Gamero, M.; Pino-Mejías, R.; Alba-Fernández, V.; Moreno-Rebollo, J. Minimum ϕ-divergence Estimation in Misspecified Multinomial Models. *Comput. Stat. Data Anal.* **2011**, *55*, 3365 – 3378. [CrossRef]
17. Kim, B.; Lee, S. Minimum density power divergence estimator for covariance matrix based on skew t distribution. *Stat. Methods Appl.* **2014**, *23*, 565–575. [CrossRef]
18. Neath, A.A.; Cavanaugh, J.E.; Weyhaupt, A.G. Model Evaluation, Discrepancy Function Estimation, and Social Choice Theory. *Comput. Stat.* **2015**, *30*, 231–249. [CrossRef]
19. Ghosh, A. Divergence based robust estimation of the tail index through an exponential regression model. *Stat. Methods Appl.* **2016**, *26*, 181–213. [CrossRef]
20. Jiménez-Gamero, M.D.; Batsidis, A. Minimum Distance Estimators for Count Data Based on the Probability Generating Function with Applications. *Metrika* **2017**, *80*, 503–545. [CrossRef]
21. Basu, A.; Ghosh, A.; Mandal, A.; Martin, N.; Pardo, L. Robust Wald-type tests in GLM with random design based on minimum density power divergence estimators. *Stat. Methods Appl.* **2021**, *30*, 973–1005. [CrossRef]
22. Birch, M.W. A New Proof of the Pearson-Fisher Theorem. *Ann. Math. Stat.* **1964**, *35*, 817–824. [CrossRef]
23. Krantz, S.G.; Parks, H.R. *The Implicit Function Theorem: History, Theory, and Applications*; Birkhäuser: Basel, Swiztherland, 2013.
24. Ferguson, T.S. *A Course in Large Sample Theory*; Chapman and Hall: Boca Raton, FL, USA, 1996.
25. McManus, D.A. Who Invented Local Power Analysis? *Econom. Theory* **1991**, *7*, 265–268. [CrossRef]
26. Neyman, J. "Smooth" Test for Goodness of Fit. *Scand. Actuar. J.* **1937**, *1937*, 149–199. [CrossRef]
27. Pardo, J.A. An approach to multiway contingency tables based on φ-divergence test statistics. *J. Multivar. Anal.* **2010**, *101*, 2305–2319. [CrossRef]
28. R Core Team. *R: A Language and Environment for Statistical Computing*; R Foundation for Statistical Computing: Vienna, Austria, 2016.

29. Johnson, S.G. The NLopt Nonlinear-Optimization Package. 2014. Available online: http://ab-initio.mit.edu/nlopt (accessed on 27 March 2022).
30. Dale, J.R. Asymptotic Normality of Goodness-of-Fit Statistics for Sparse Product Multinomials. *J. R. Stat. Soc. Ser. B Methodol.* **1986**, *48*, 48–59. [CrossRef]
31. Batsidis, A.; Martin, N.; Pardo Llorente, L.; Zografos, K. φ-Divergence Based Procedure for Parametric Change-Point Problems. *Methodol. Comput. Appl. Probab.* **2016**, *18*, 21–35. [CrossRef]
32. Lloyd, C.J. Estimating test power adjusted for size. *J. Stat. Comput. Simul.* **2005**, *75*, 921–933. [CrossRef]
33. Dubrova, Y.E.; Grant, G.; Chumak, A.A.; Stezhka, V.A.; Karakasian, A.N. Elevated Minisatellite Mutation Rate in the Post-Chernobyl Families from Ukraine. *Am. J. Hum. Genet.* **2002**, *71*, 801–809. [CrossRef]
34. Znaor, A.; Brennan, P.; Gajalakshmi, V.; Mathew, A.; Shanta, V.; Varghese, C.; Boffetta, P. Independent and combined effects of tobacco smoking, chewing and alcohol drinking on the risk of oral, pharyngeal and esophageal cancers in Indian men. *Int. J. Cancer* **2003**, *105*, 681–686. [CrossRef]
35. Merková, M. Use of Investment Controlling and its Impact into Business Performance. *Procedia Econ. Financ.* **2015**, *34*, 608–614. [CrossRef]
36. Geenens, G.; Simar, L. Nonparametric tests for conditional independence in two-way contingency tables. *J. Multivar. Anal.* **2010**, *101*, 765–788. [CrossRef]
37. Bartolucci, F.; Scaccia, L. Testing for positive association in contingency tables with fixed margins. *Comput. Stat. Data Anal.* **2004**, *47*, 195–210. [CrossRef]

Article

Information Inequalities via Submodularity and a Problem in Extremal Graph Theory

Igal Sason [1,2]

[1] Andrew & Erna Viterbi Faculty of Electrical and Computer Engineering, Technion-Israel Institute of Technology, Haifa 3200003, Israel; eeigal@technion.ac.il; Tel.: +972-4-8294699
[2] Faculty of Mathematics, Technion-Israel Institute of Technology, Haifa 3200003, Israel

Abstract: The present paper offers, in its first part, a unified approach for the derivation of families of inequalities for set functions which satisfy sub/supermodularity properties. It applies this approach for the derivation of information inequalities with Shannon information measures. Connections of the considered approach to a generalized version of Shearer's lemma, and other related results in the literature are considered. Some of the derived information inequalities are new, and also known results (such as a generalized version of Han's inequality) are reproduced in a simple and unified way. In its second part, this paper applies the generalized Han's inequality to analyze a problem in extremal graph theory. This problem is motivated and analyzed from the perspective of information theory, and the analysis leads to generalized and refined bounds. The two parts of this paper are meant to be independently accessible to the reader.

Keywords: extremal combinatorics; graphs; Han's inequality; information inequalities; polymatroid; rank function; set function; Shearer's lemma; submodularity

1. Introduction

Information measures and information inequalities are of fundamental importance and wide applicability in the study of feasibility and infeasibility results in information theory, while also offering very useful tools which serve to deal with interesting problems in various fields of mathematics [1,2]. The characterization of information inequalities has been of interest for decades (see, e.g., [3,4] and references therein), mainly triggered by their indispensable role in proving direct and converse results for channel coding and data compression for single and multi-user information systems. Information inequalities, which apply to classical and generalized information measures, have also demonstrated far-reaching consequences beyond the study of the coding theorems and fundamental limits of communication systems. One such remarkable example (among many) is the usefulness of information measures and information inequalities in providing information–theoretic proofs in the field of combinatorics and graph theory (see, e.g., [5–22]).

A basic property that is commonly used for the characterization of information inequalities relies on the nonnegativity of the (conditional and unconditional) Shannon entropy of discrete random variables, the nonnegativity of the (conditional and unconditional) relative entropy and the Shannon mutual information of general random variables, and the chain rules which hold for these classical information measures. A byproduct of these properties is the sub/supermodularity of some classical information measures, which also prove to be useful by taking advantage of the vast literature on sub/supermodular functions and polymatroids [22–31]. Another instrumental information inequality is the entropy power inequality, which dates back to Shannon [32]. It has been extensively generalized for different types of random variables and generalized entropies, studied in regard to its geometrical relations [33], and it has been also ubiquitously used for the analysis of various information–theoretic problems.

Among the most useful information inequalities are Han's inequality [34], its generalized versions (e.g., [15,25,30,31]), and Shearer's lemma [7] with its generalizations and refinements (e.g., [15,31,35]). In spite of their simplicity, these inequalities prove to be useful in information theory, and other diverse fields of mathematics and engineering (see, e.g., [6,35]). More specifically in regard to these inequalities, in Proposition 1 of [22], Madiman and Tetali introduced an information inequality which can be specialized to Han's inequality, and which also refines Shearer's lemma while also providing a counterpart result. In [30], Tian generalized Han's inequality by relying on the sub/supermodularity of the unconditional/conditional Shannon entropy. Likewise, the work in [31] by Kishi et al., relies on the sub/supermodularity properties of Shannon information measures, and it provides refinements of Shearer's lemma and Han's inequality. Apart of the refinements of these classical and widely-used inequalities in [31], the suggested approach in the present work can be viewed in a sense as a (nontrivial) generalization and extension of a result in [31] (to be explained in Section 3.2).

This work is focused on the derivation of information inequalities via submodularity and nonnegativity properties, and on a problem in extremal graph theory whose analysis relies on an information inequality. The field of extremal graph theory, which is a subfield of extremal combinatorics, was among the early and fast developing branches of graph theory during the 20th century. Extremal graph theory explores the relations between properties of graphs such as its order, size, chromatic number or maximal and minimal degrees, under some constraints on the graph (by, e.g., considering graphs of a fixed order, and by also imposing a type of a forbidden subgraph). The interested reader is referred to the comprehensive textbooks [10,36] on the vast field of extremal combinatorics and extremal graph theory.

This paper suggests an approach for the derivation of families of inequalities for set functions, and it applies it to obtain information inequalities with Shannon information measures that satisfy sub/supermodularity and monotonicity properties. Some of the derived information inequalities are new, while some known results (such as the generalized version of Han's inequality [25]) are reproduced as corollaries in a simple and unified way. This paper also applies the generalized Han's inequality to analyze a problem in extremal graph theory, with an information–theoretic proof and interpretation. The analysis leads to some generalized and refined bounds in comparison to the insightful results in Theorems 4.2 and 4.3 of [6]. For the purpose of the suggested problem and analysis, the presentation here is self-contained.

The paper is structured as follows: Section 2 provides essential notation and preliminary material for this paper. Section 3 presents a new methodology for the derivation of families of inequalities for set functions which satisfy sub/supermodularity properties (Theorem 1). The suggested methodology is then applied in Section 3 for the derivation of information inequalities by relying on sub/supermodularity properties of Shannon information measures. Section 3 also considers connections of the suggested approach to a generalized version of Shearer's lemma, and to other results in the literature. Most of the results in Section 3 are proved in Section 4. Section 5 applies the generalized Han's inequality to a problem in extremal graph theory (Theorem 2). A byproduct of Theorem 2, which is of interest in its own right, is also analyzed in Section 5 (Theorem 3). The presentation and analysis in Section 5 is accessible to the reader, independently of the earlier material on information inequalities in Sections 3 and 4. Some additional proofs, mostly for making the paper self-contained or for suggesting an alternative proof, are relegated to the appendices (Appendices A and B).

2. Preliminaries and Notation

The present section provides essential notation and preliminary material for this paper.
- $\mathbb{N} \triangleq \{1, 2, \ldots\}$ denotes the set of natural numbers.
- $\mathbb{R}$ denotes the set of real numbers, and $\mathbb{R}_+$ denotes the set of nonnegative real numbers.
- $\varnothing$ denotes the empty set.

- $2^\Omega \triangleq \{\mathcal{A} : \mathcal{A} \subseteq \Omega\}$ denotes the power set of a set Ω (i.e., the set of all subsets of Ω).
- $\mathcal{T}^c \triangleq \Omega \setminus \mathcal{T}$ denotes the complement of a subset $\mathcal{T}$ in Ω.
- $\mathbb{1}\{E\}$ is an indicator of E; it is 1 if event E is satisfied, and zero otherwise.
- $[n] \triangleq \{1, \ldots, n\}$ for every $n \in \mathbb{N}$;
- $X^n \triangleq (X_1, \ldots, X_n)$ denotes an n-dimensional random vector;
- $X_\mathcal{S} \triangleq (X_i)_{i \in \mathcal{S}}$ is a random vector for a nonempty subset $\mathcal{S} \subseteq [n]$; if $\mathcal{S} = \emptyset$, then $X_\mathcal{S}$ is an empty set, and conditioning on $X_\mathcal{S}$ is void.
- Let X be a discrete random variable that takes its values on a set $\mathcal{X}$, and let P_X be the probability mass function (PMF) of X. The *Shannon entropy* of X is given by

$$\mathsf{H}(X) \triangleq - \sum_{x \in \mathcal{X}} \mathsf{P}_X(x) \log \mathsf{P}_X(x), \tag{1}$$

where throughout this paper, we take all logarithms to base 2.
- The *binary entropy function* $\mathsf{H}_{\mathsf{b}} : [0,1] \to [0, \log 2]$ is given by

$$\mathsf{H}_{\mathsf{b}}(p) \triangleq -p \log p - (1-p) \log(1-p), \quad p \in [0,1], \tag{2}$$

where, by continuous extension, the convention $0 \log 0 = 0$ is used.
- Let X and Y be discrete random variables with a joint PMF P_{XY}, and a conditional PMF of X given Y denoted by $\mathsf{P}_{X|Y}$. The *conditional entropy* of X given Y is defined as

$$\mathsf{H}(X|Y) \triangleq - \sum_{(x,y) \in \mathcal{X} \times \mathcal{Y}} \mathsf{P}_{XY}(x,y) \log \mathsf{P}_{X|Y}(x|y) \tag{3a}$$

$$= \sum_{y \in \mathcal{Y}} \mathsf{P}_Y(y) \, \mathsf{H}(X|Y=y), \tag{3b}$$

and

$$\mathsf{H}(X|Y) = \mathsf{H}(X,Y) - \mathsf{H}(Y). \tag{4}$$

- The *mutual information* between X and Y is symmetric in X and Y, and it is given by

$$\mathsf{I}(X;Y) = \mathsf{H}(X) + \mathsf{H}(Y) - \mathsf{H}(X,Y) \tag{5a}$$
$$= \mathsf{H}(X) - \mathsf{H}(X|Y) \tag{5b}$$
$$= \mathsf{H}(Y) - \mathsf{H}(Y|X). \tag{5c}$$

- The *conditional mutual information* between two random variables X and Y, given a third random variable Z, is symmetric in X and Y and it is given by

$$\mathsf{I}(X;Y|Z) = \mathsf{H}(X|Z) - \mathsf{H}(X|Y,Z) \tag{6a}$$
$$= \mathsf{H}(X,Z) + \mathsf{H}(Y,Z) - \mathsf{H}(Z) - \mathsf{H}(X,Y,Z). \tag{6b}$$

- For continuous random variables, the sums in (1) and (3) are replaced with integrals, and the PMFs are replaced with probability densities. The entropy of a continuous random variable is named *differential entropy*.
- For an n-dimensional random vector X^n, the *entropy power* of X^n is given by

$$\mathsf{N}(X^n) \triangleq \exp\left(\tfrac{2}{n} \, \mathsf{H}(X^n)\right), \tag{7}$$

where the base of the exponent is identical to the base of the logarithm in (1).

We rely on the following basic properties of the Shannon information measures:

- Conditioning cannot increase the entropy, i.e.,

$$H(X|Y) \leq H(X), \qquad (8)$$

with equality in (8) if and only if X and Y are independent.
- Generalizing (4) to n-dimensional random vectors gives the chain rule

$$H(X^n) = \sum_{i=1}^{n} H(X_i|X^{i-1}). \qquad (9)$$

- The *subadditivity property of the entropy* is implied by (8) and (9):

$$H(X^n) \leq \sum_{i=1}^{n} H(X_i), \qquad (10)$$

with equality in (10) if and only if $X_1, \ldots, X_n$ are independent random variables.
- *Nonnegativity of the (conditional) mutual information*: In light of (5) and (8), $I(X;Y) \geq 0$ with equality if and only if X and Y are independent. More generally, $I(X;Y|Z) \geq 0$ with equality if and only if X and Y are conditionally independent given Z.

Let Ω be a finite and non-empty set, and let $f\colon 2^{\Omega} \to \mathbb{R}$ be a real-valued set function (i.e., f is defined for all subsets of Ω). The following definitions are used.

Definition 1 (Sub/Supermodular function). *The set function $f\colon 2^{\Omega} \to \mathbb{R}$ is submodular if*

$$f(\mathcal{T}) + f(\mathcal{S}) \geq f(\mathcal{T} \cup \mathcal{S}) + f(\mathcal{T} \cap \mathcal{S}), \qquad \forall\, \mathcal{S}, \mathcal{T} \subseteq \Omega \qquad (11)$$

Likewise, f is supermodular if $-f$ is submodular.

An identical characterization of submodularity is the diminishing return property (see, e.g., Proposition 2.2 in [23]), where a set function $f\colon 2^{\Omega} \to \mathbb{R}$ is submodular if and only if

$$\mathcal{S} \subset \mathcal{T} \subset \Omega,\ \omega \in \mathcal{T}^c \implies f(\mathcal{S} \cup \{\omega\}) - f(\mathcal{S}) \geq f(\mathcal{T} \cup \{\omega\}) - f(\mathcal{T}). \qquad (12)$$

This means that the larger is the set, the smaller is the increase in f when a new element is added.

Definition 2 (Monotonic function). *The set function $f\colon 2^{\Omega} \to \mathbb{R}$ is monotonically increasing if*

$$\mathcal{S} \subseteq \mathcal{T} \subseteq \Omega \implies f(\mathcal{S}) \leq f(\mathcal{T}). \qquad (13)$$

Likewise, f is monotonically decreasing if $-f$ is monotonically increasing.

Definition 3 (Polymatroid, ground set and rank function). *Let $f\colon 2^{\Omega} \to \mathbb{R}$ be submodular and monotonically increasing set function with $f(\emptyset) = 0$. The pair (Ω, f) is called a polymatroid, Ω is called a ground set, and f is called a rank function.*

Definition 4 (Subadditive function). *The set function $f\colon 2^{\Omega} \to \mathbb{R}$ is subadditive if, for all $\mathcal{S}, \mathcal{T} \subseteq \Omega$,*

$$f(\mathcal{S} \cup \mathcal{T}) \leq f(\mathcal{S}) + f(\mathcal{T}). \qquad (14)$$

A nonnegative and submodular set function is subadditive (this readily follows from (11) and (14)). The next proposition introduces results from [25,28,37]. For the sake of completeness, we provide a proof in Appendix A.

Proposition 1. Let Ω be a finite and non-empty set, and let $\{X_\omega\}_{\omega \in \Omega}$ be a collection of discrete random variables. Then, the following holds:

(a) The set function $f\colon 2^\Omega \to \mathbb{R}$, given by

$$f(\mathcal{T}) \triangleq \mathrm{H}(X_\mathcal{T}), \quad \mathcal{T} \subseteq \Omega, \tag{15}$$

is a rank function.

(b) The set function $f\colon 2^\Omega \to \mathbb{R}$, given by

$$f(\mathcal{T}) \triangleq \mathrm{H}(X_\mathcal{T} | X_{\mathcal{T}^c}), \quad \mathcal{T} \subseteq \Omega, \tag{16}$$

is supermodular, monotonically increasing, and $f(\varnothing) = 0$.

(c) The set function $f\colon 2^\Omega \to \mathbb{R}$, given by

$$f(\mathcal{T}) \triangleq \mathrm{I}(X_\mathcal{T}; X_{\mathcal{T}^c}), \quad \mathcal{T} \subseteq \Omega, \tag{17}$$

is submodular, $f(\varnothing) = 0$, but f is not a rank function. The latter holds since the equality $f(\mathcal{T}) = f(\mathcal{T}^c)$, for all $\mathcal{T} \subseteq \Omega$, implies that f is not a monotonic function.

(d) Let $\mathcal{U}, \mathcal{V} \subseteq \Omega$ be disjoint subsets, and let the entries of the random vector $X_\mathcal{V}$ be conditionally independent given $X_\mathcal{U}$. Then, the set function $f\colon 2^\mathcal{V} \to \mathbb{R}$ given by

$$f(\mathcal{T}) \triangleq \mathrm{I}(X_\mathcal{U}; X_\mathcal{T}), \quad \mathcal{T} \subseteq \mathcal{V}, \tag{18}$$

is a rank function.

(e) Let $X_\Omega = \{X_\omega\}_{\omega \in \Omega}$ be independent random variables, and let $f\colon 2^\Omega \to \mathbb{R}$ be given by

$$f(\mathcal{T}) \triangleq \mathrm{H}\!\left(\sum_{\omega \in \mathcal{T}} X_\omega\right), \quad \mathcal{T} \subseteq \Omega. \tag{19}$$

Then, f is a rank function.

The following proposition addresses the setting of general alphabets.

Proposition 2. For general alphabets, the set functions f in (15) and (17)–(19) are submodular, and the set function f in (16) is supermodular with $f(\varnothing) \triangleq 0$. Moreover, the function in (18) stays to be a rank function, and the function in (19) stays to be monotonically increasing.

Proof. The sub/supermodularity properties in Proposition 1 are preserved due to the nonnegativity of the (conditional) mutual information. The monotonicity property of the functions in (18) and (19) is preserved also in the general alphabet setting due to (A10) and (A14c), and the mutual information in (18) is nonnegative. □

Remark 1. In contrast to the entropy of discrete random variables, the differential entropy of continuous random variables is not functionally submodular in the sense of Lemma A.2 in [38]. This refers to a different form of submodularity, which was needed by Tao [38] to prove sumset inequalities for the entropy of discrete random variables. A follow-up study in [39] by Kontoyiannis and Madiman required substantially new proof strategies for the derivation of sumset inequalities with the differential entropy of continuous random variables. The basic property which replaces the discrete functional submodularity is the data-processing property of mutual information [39]. In the context of the present work, where the commonly used definition of submodularity is used (see Definition 1), the Shannon entropy of discrete random variables and the differential entropy of continuous random variables are both submodular set functions.

We rely, in this paper, on the following standard terminology for graphs. An undirected graph G is an ordered pair $G = (V, E)$ where $V = V(G)$ is a set of elements, and $E = E(G)$

is a set of 2-element subsets (pairs) of V. The elements of V are called the vertices of G, and the elements of E are called the edges of G. We use the notation $V = V(G)$ and $E = E(G)$ for the sets of vertices and edges, respectively, in the graph G. The number of vertices in a finite graph G is called the order of G, and the number of edges is called the size of G. Throughout this paper, we assume that the graph G is undirected and finite; it is also assumed to be a simple graph, i.e., it has no loops (no edge connects a vertex in G to itself) and there are no multiple edges which connect a pair of vertices in G. If $e = \{u,v\} \in E(G)$, then the vertices u and v are the two ends of the edge e. The elements u and v are adjacent vertices (neighbors) if they are connected by an edge in G, i.e., if $e = \{u,v\} \in E(G)$.

3. Inequalities via Submodularity

3.1. A New Methodology

The present subsection presents a new methodology for the derivation of families of inequalities for set functions, and in particular inequalities with information measures. The suggested methodology relies, to large extent, on the notion of submodularity of set functions, and it is presented in the next theorem.

Theorem 1. *Let Ω be a finite set with $|\Omega| = n$. Let $f \colon 2^\Omega \to \mathbb{R}$ with $f(\varnothing) = 0$, and $g \colon \mathbb{R} \to \mathbb{R}$. Let the sequence $\{t_k^{(n)}\}_{k=1}^n$ be given by*

$$t_k^{(n)} \triangleq \frac{1}{\binom{n}{k}} \sum_{\mathcal{T} \subseteq \Omega \colon |\mathcal{T}|=k} g\!\left(\frac{f(\mathcal{T})}{k}\right), \qquad k \in [n]. \tag{20}$$

(a) *If f is submodular, and g is monotonically increasing and convex, then the sequence $\{t_k^{(n)}\}_{k=1}^n$ is monotonically decreasing, i.e.,*

$$t_1^{(n)} \geq t_2^{(n)} \geq \cdots \geq t_n^{(n)} = g\!\left(\frac{f(\Omega)}{n}\right). \tag{21}$$

In particular,

$$\sum_{\mathcal{T} \subseteq \Omega \colon |\mathcal{T}|=k} g\!\left(\frac{f(\mathcal{T})}{k}\right) \geq \binom{n}{k} g\!\left(\frac{f(\Omega)}{n}\right), \qquad k \in [n]. \tag{22}$$

(b) *If f is submodular, and g is monotonically decreasing and concave, then the sequence $\{t_k^{(n)}\}_{k=1}^n$ is monotonically increasing.*

(c) *If f is supermodular, and g is monotonically increasing and concave, then the sequence $\{t_k^{(n)}\}_{k=1}^n$ is monotonically increasing.*

(d) *If f is supermodular, and g is monotonically decreasing and convex, then the sequence $\{t_k^{(n)}\}_{k=1}^n$ is monotonically decreasing.*

Proof. See Section 4.1. □

Corollary 1. *Let Ω be a finite set with $|\Omega| = n$, $f \colon 2^\Omega \to \mathbb{R}$, and $g \colon \mathbb{R} \to \mathbb{R}$ be convex and monotonically increasing. If*

- *f is a rank function,*
- *$g(0) > 0$ or there is $\ell \in \mathbb{N}$ such that $g(0) = \ldots = g^{(\ell-1)}(0) = 0$ with $g^{(\ell)}(0) > 0$,*
- *$\{k_n\}_{n=1}^\infty$ is a sequence such that $k_n \in [n]$ for all $n \in \mathbb{N}$ with $k_n \xrightarrow[n \to \infty]{} \infty$,*

then

$$\lim_{n\to\infty}\left\{\frac{1}{n}\log\left(\sum_{\mathcal{T}\subseteq\Omega:|\mathcal{T}|=k_n}g\left(\frac{f(\mathcal{T})}{k_n}\right)\right)-\mathsf{H}_\mathsf{b}\left(\frac{k_n}{n}\right)\right\}=0, \quad (23)$$

and if $\lim_{n\to\infty}\frac{k_n}{n}=\beta\in[0,1]$, then

$$\lim_{n\to\infty}\frac{1}{n}\log\left(\sum_{\mathcal{T}\subseteq\Omega:|\mathcal{T}|=k_n}g\left(\frac{f(\mathcal{T})}{k_n}\right)\right)=\mathsf{H}_\mathsf{b}(\beta). \quad (24)$$

Proof. See Section 4.2. □

Corollary 2. *Let Ω be a finite set with $|\Omega|=n$, and $f\colon 2^\Omega\to\mathbb{R}$ be submodular and nonnegative with $f(\varnothing)=0$. Then,*
(a) *For $\alpha\geq 1$ and $k\in[n-1]$*

$$\sum_{\mathcal{T}\subseteq\Omega:|\mathcal{T}|=k}\left(f^\alpha(\Omega)-f^\alpha(\mathcal{T})\right)\leq c_\alpha(n,k)\,f^\alpha(\Omega), \quad (25)$$

with

$$c_\alpha(n,k)\triangleq\left(1-\frac{k^\alpha}{n^\alpha}\right)\binom{n}{k}. \quad (26)$$

For $\alpha=1$, (25) holds with $c_1(n,k)=\binom{n-1}{k}$ regardless of the nonnegativity of f.
(b) *If f is also monotonically increasing (i.e., f is a rank function), then for $\alpha\geq 1$*

$$\left(\frac{k}{n}\right)^{\alpha-1}\binom{n-1}{k-1}f^\alpha(\Omega)\leq\sum_{\mathcal{T}\subseteq\Omega:|\mathcal{T}|=k}f^\alpha(\mathcal{T})\leq\binom{n}{k}f^\alpha(\Omega),\quad k\in[n]. \quad (27)$$

Proof. See Section 4.3. □

Corollary 2 is next specialized to reproduce Han's inequality [34], and a generalized version of Han's inequality (Section 4 of [25]).

Let $X^n=(X_1,\ldots,X_n)$ be a random vector with finite entropies $\mathsf{H}(X_i)$ for all $i\in[n]$. The set function $f\colon 2^{[n]}\to[0,\infty)$, given by $f(\mathcal{T})=\mathsf{H}(X_\mathcal{T})$ for all $\mathcal{T}\subseteq[n]$, is submodular [25] (see Proposition 1a and Proposition 2). From (25), the following holds:
(a) Setting $\alpha=1$ in (25) implies that, for all $k\in[n-1]$,

$$\sum_{1\leq i_1<\ldots<i_k\leq n}(\mathsf{H}(X^n)-\mathsf{H}(X_{i_1},\ldots,X_{i_k}))\leq\left(1-\frac{k}{n}\right)\binom{n}{k}\mathsf{H}(X^n) \quad (28a)$$

$$=\binom{n-1}{k}\mathsf{H}(X^n), \quad (28b)$$

(b) Consequently, setting $k=n-1$ in (28) gives

$$\sum_{i=1}^n(\mathsf{H}(X^n)-\mathsf{H}(X_1,\ldots,X_{i-1},X_{i+1},\ldots,X_n))\leq\mathsf{H}(X^n), \quad (29)$$

which gives Han's inequality.

Further applications of Theorem 1 lead to the next corollary, which partially introduces some known results that have been proved on a case-by-case basis in Theorems 17.6.1–17.6.3 of [1] and Section 2 of [2]. In particular, the monotonicity properties of the sequences in (30) and (32)–(34) were proved in Theorems 1 and 2, and Corollaries 1 and 2 of [2]. Both known and new results are readily obtained here, in a unified way, from Theorem 1. The utility of one of these inequalities in extremal combinatorics is discussed in the continuation to this subsection (see Proposition 3), providing a natural generalization of a beautiful combinatorial result in Section 3.2 of [19].

Corollary 3. Let $\{X_i\}_{i=1}^n$ be random variables with finite entropies. Then, the following holds:
(a) The sequences

$$h_k^{(n)} \triangleq \frac{1}{\binom{n}{k}} \sum_{\mathcal{T} \subseteq [n]: |\mathcal{T}|=k} \frac{H(X_\mathcal{T})}{k}, \quad k \in [n], \tag{30}$$

$$\ell_k^{(n)} \triangleq \frac{1}{\binom{n}{k}} \sum_{\mathcal{T} \subseteq [n]: |\mathcal{T}|=k} \frac{I(X_\mathcal{T}; X_{\mathcal{T}^c})}{k}, \quad k \in [n] \tag{31}$$

are monotonically decreasing in k. If $\{X_i\}_{i=1}^n$ are independent, then also the sequence

$$m_k^{(n)} \triangleq \frac{1}{\binom{n-1}{k-1}} \sum_{\mathcal{T} \subseteq [n]: |\mathcal{T}|=k} H\left(\sum_{\omega \in \mathcal{T}} X_\omega\right), \quad k \in [n] \tag{32}$$

is monotonically decreasing in k.
(b) The sequence

$$r_k^{(n)} \triangleq \frac{1}{\binom{n}{k}} \sum_{\mathcal{T} \subseteq [n]: |\mathcal{T}|=k} \frac{H(X_\mathcal{T} | X_{\mathcal{T}^c})}{k}, \quad k \in [n] \tag{33}$$

is monotonically increasing in k.
(c) For every $r > 0$, the sequences

$$s_k^{(n)}(r) \triangleq \frac{1}{\binom{n}{k}} \sum_{\mathcal{T} \subseteq [n]: |\mathcal{T}|=k} N^r(X_\mathcal{T}), \quad k \in [n], \tag{34}$$

$$u_k^{(n)}(r) \triangleq \frac{1}{\binom{n}{k}} \sum_{\mathcal{T} \subseteq [n]: |\mathcal{T}|=k} \exp\left(-\frac{r\, H(X_\mathcal{T} | X_{\mathcal{T}^c})}{k}\right), \quad k \in [n], \tag{35}$$

$$v_k^{(n)}(r) \triangleq \frac{1}{\binom{n}{k}} \sum_{\mathcal{T} \subseteq [n]: |\mathcal{T}|=k} \exp\left(\frac{r\, I(X_\mathcal{T}; X_{\mathcal{T}^c})}{k}\right), \quad k \in [n] \tag{36}$$

are monotonically decreasing in k. If $\{X_i\}_{i=1}^n$ are independent, then also the sequence

$$w_k^{(n)}(r) \triangleq \frac{1}{\binom{n}{k}} \sum_{\mathcal{T} \subseteq [n]: |\mathcal{T}|=k} N^r\left(\sum_{\omega \in \mathcal{T}} X_\omega\right), \quad k \in [n] \tag{37}$$

is monotonically decreasing in k.

Proof. The finite entropies of $\{X_i\}_{i=1}^n$ assure that the entropies involved in the sequences (30)–(37) are finite. Item (a) follows from Theorem 1a, where the submodular set functions f which correspond to (30)–(32) are given in (15), (17) and (19), respectively, and g is the identity function on the real line. The identity $k\binom{n}{k} = n\binom{n-1}{k-1}$ is used for (32). Item (b) follows from Theorem 1c, where f is the supermodular function in (16) and g is the identity function on the real line. We next prove Item (c). The sequence (34) is monotonically decreasing by Theorem 1a, where f is the submodular function in (15), and $g \colon \mathbb{R} \to \mathbb{R}$ is the monotonically increasing and convex function defined as $g(x) = \exp(2rx)$ for $x \in \mathbb{R}$ (with $r > 0$). The sequence (35) is monotonically decreasing by Theorem 1d, where f is the supermodular function in (16), and $g \colon \mathbb{R} \to \mathbb{R}$ is the monotonically decreasing and convex function defined as $g(x) = \exp(-rx)$ for $x \in \mathbb{R}$. The sequence (36) is monotonically decreasing by Theorem 1a, where f is the submodular function in (17) and g is the monotonically increasing and convex function defined as $g(x) = \exp(rx)$ for $x \in \mathbb{R}$. Finally, the sequence (37) is monotonically decreasing by Theorem 1a, where f is the submodular function in (19) and g is the monotonically increasing and convex function defined as $g(x) = \exp(2rx)$ for $x \in \mathbb{R}$. □

Remark 2. *From Proposition 2, since the proof of Corollary 3 only relies on the sub/supermodularity property of f, the random variables $\{X_i\}_{i=1}^n$ do not need to be discrete in Corollary 3. In the reproduction of Han's inequality as an application of Corollary 2, the random variables $\{X_i\}_{i=1}^n$ do not need to be discrete as well since f is not required to be nonnegative if $\alpha = 1$ (only the submodularity of f in (15) is required, which holds due to Proposition 2).*

The following result exemplifies the utility of the monotonicity result of the sequence (30) in extremal combinatorics. It also generalizes the result in Section 3.2 of [19] for an achievable upper bound on the cardinality of a finite set in the three-dimensional Euclidean space, expressed as a function of its number of projections on each of the planes XY, XZ and YZ. The next result provides an achievable upper bound on the cardinality of a finite set of points in an n-dimensional Euclidean space, expressed as a function of its number of projections on each of the k-dimensional Euclidean subspaces with an arbitrary $k < n$.

Proposition 3. *Let $\mathcal{P} \subseteq \mathbb{R}^n$ be a finite set of points in the n-dimensional Euclidean space with $|\mathcal{P}| \triangleq M$. Let $k \in [n-1]$, and $\ell \triangleq \binom{n}{k}$. Let $\mathcal{R}_1, \ldots, \mathcal{R}_\ell$ be the projections of $\mathcal{P}$ on each of the k-dimensional subspaces of $\mathbb{R}^n$, and let $|\mathcal{R}_j| = M_j$ for all $j \in [\ell]$. Then,*

$$|\mathcal{P}| \leq \left(\prod_{j=1}^{\binom{n}{k}} M_j \right)^{\frac{1}{\binom{n-1}{k-1}}}. \tag{38}$$

Let $R \triangleq \frac{\log M}{n}$, and $R_j \triangleq \frac{\log M_j}{k}$ for all $j \in [\ell]$. An equivalent form of (38) is given by the inequality

$$R \leq \frac{1}{\ell} \sum_{j=1}^{\ell} R_j. \tag{39}$$

Moreover, if $M_1 = \ldots = M_\ell$ and $\sqrt[k]{M_1} \in \mathbb{N}$, then (38) and (39) are satisfied with equality if $\mathcal{P}$ is a grid of points in $\mathbb{R}^n$ with $\sqrt[k]{M_1}$ points on each dimension (so, $M = M_1^{\frac{n}{k}}$).

Proof. Pick uniformly at random a point $X^n = (X_1, \ldots, X_n) \in \mathcal{P}$. Then,

$$H(X^n) = \log |\mathcal{P}|. \tag{40}$$

The sequence in (30) is monotonically decreasing, so $h_k^{(n)} \geq h_n^{(n)}$, which is equivalent to

$$\binom{n-1}{k-1} H(X^n) \leq \sum_{\mathcal{T} \subseteq [n]: |\mathcal{T}|=k} H(X_\mathcal{T}). \tag{41}$$

Let $\mathcal{S}_1, \ldots, \mathcal{S}_\ell$ be the k-subsets of the set $[n]$, ordered in a way such that M_j is the cardinality of the projection of the set $\mathcal{P}$ on the k-dimensional subspace whose coordinates are the elements of the subset $\mathcal{S}_j$. Then, (41) can be expressed in the form

$$\binom{n-1}{k-1} H(X^n) \leq \sum_{j=1}^{\ell} H(X_{\mathcal{S}_j}), \tag{42}$$

and also
$$H(X_{\mathcal{S}_j}) \leq \log M_j, \quad j \in [\ell], \tag{43}$$

since the entropy of a random variable is upper bounded by the logarithm of the number of its possible values. Combining (40), (42) and (43) gives

$$\binom{n-1}{k-1} \log |\mathcal{P}| \leq \sum_{j=1}^{\ell} \log M_j. \tag{44}$$

Exponentiating both sides of (44) gives (38). In addition, using the identity $\binom{n}{k} = \frac{n}{k}\binom{n-1}{k-1}$ gives (39) from (44). Finally, the sufficiency condition for equalities in (38) or (39) can be easily verified, which is obtained if $\mathcal{P}$ is a grid of points in $\mathbb{R}^n$ with the same finite number of projections on each dimension. □

3.2. Connections to a Generalized Version of Shearer's Lemma and Other Results in the Literature

The next proposition is a known generalized version of Shearer's Lemma.

Proposition 4. *Let Ω be a finite set, let $\{\mathcal{S}_j\}_{j=1}^M$ be a finite collection of subsets of Ω (with $M \in \mathbb{N}$), and let $f: 2^\Omega \to \mathbb{R}$ be a set function.*

(a) *If f is non-negative and submodular, and every element in Ω is included in at least $d \geq 1$ of the subsets $\{\mathcal{S}_j\}_{j=1}^M$, then*

$$\sum_{j=1}^M f(\mathcal{S}_j) \geq d\, f(\Omega). \tag{45}$$

(b) *If f is a rank function, $\mathcal{A} \subset \Omega$, and every element in $\mathcal{A}$ is included in at least $d \geq 1$ of the subsets $\{\mathcal{S}_j\}_{j=1}^M$, then*

$$\sum_{j=1}^M f(\mathcal{S}_j) \geq d\, f(\mathcal{A}). \tag{46}$$

The first part of Proposition 4 was pointed out in Section 1.5 of [35], and the second part of Proposition 4 is a generalization of Remark 1 and inequality (47) in [20]. We provide a (somewhat different) proof of Proposition 4a, as well as a self-contained proof of Proposition 4b in Appendix B.

Let $\{X_i\}_{i=1}^n$ be discrete random variables, and consider the set function $f: 2^{[n]} \to \mathbb{R}_+$ which is defined as $f(\mathcal{A}) = H(X_\mathcal{A})$ for all $\mathcal{A} \subseteq [n]$. Since f is a rank function [25], Proposition 4 then specializes to Shearer's Lemma [7] and a modified version of this lemma (see Remark 1 of [20]).

In light of Proposition 1e and Proposition 4b, Corollaries 4 and 5 are obtained as follows.

Corollary 4. *Let $\{X_i\}_{i=1}^n$ be independent discrete random variables, $\{\mathcal{S}_j\}_{j=1}^M$ be subsets of $[n]$, and $\mathcal{A} \subseteq [n]$. If each element in $\mathcal{A}$ belongs to at least $d \geq 1$ of the sets $\{\mathcal{S}_j\}_{j=1}^M$, then*

$$d\, H\left(\sum_{i \in \mathcal{A}} X_i\right) \leq \sum_{j=1}^M H\left(\sum_{i \in \mathcal{S}_j} X_i\right). \tag{47}$$

In particular, if every $i \in [n]$ is included in at least $d \geq 1$ of the subsets $\{\mathcal{S}_j\}_{j=1}^M$, then

$$d \, \mathrm{H}\left(\sum_{i=1}^n X_i\right) \leq \sum_{j=1}^M \mathrm{H}\left(\sum_{i \in \mathcal{S}_j} X_i\right). \tag{48}$$

Remark 3. *Inequality* (48) *is also a special case of* [37] *(Theorem 2), and they coincide if every element* $i \in [n]$ *is included in a fixed number* (d) *of the subsets* $\{\mathcal{S}_j\}_{j=1}^M$.

A specialization of Corollary 4 gives the next result.

Corollary 5. *Let* $\{X_i\}_{i=1}^n$ *be independent and discrete random variables with finite variances. Then, the following holds:*

(a) *For every* $k \in [n-1]$,

$$\mathrm{H}\left(\sum_{i=1}^n X_i\right) \leq \frac{1}{\binom{n-1}{k-1}} \sum_{\mathcal{T} \subseteq [n]:\, |\mathcal{T}|=k} \mathrm{H}\left(\sum_{\omega \in \mathcal{T}} X_\omega\right), \tag{49}$$

and equivalently,

$$\mathrm{N}\left(\sum_{i=1}^n X_i\right) \leq \left\{\prod_{\mathcal{T} \subseteq [n]:\, |\mathcal{T}|=k} \mathrm{N}\left(\sum_{\omega \in \mathcal{T}} X_\omega\right)\right\}^{\frac{1}{\binom{n-1}{k-1}}}. \tag{50}$$

(b) *For every* $k \in [n-1]$,

$$\mathrm{N}\left(\sum_{i=1}^n X_i\right) \leq \frac{1}{\binom{n}{k}} \sum_{\mathcal{T} \subseteq [n]:\, |\mathcal{T}|=k} \mathrm{N}^{\frac{k}{k}}\left(\sum_{\omega \in \mathcal{T}} X_\omega\right), \tag{51}$$

where (51) *is in general looser than* (50), *with equivalence if* $\{X_i\}_{i=1}^n$ *are i.i.d.; in particular,*

$$\mathrm{N}\left(\sum_{i=1}^n X_i\right) \leq \left\{\prod_{j=1}^n \mathrm{N}\left(\sum_{i \neq j} X_i\right)\right\}^{\frac{1}{n-1}} \tag{52a}$$

$$\leq \frac{1}{n} \sum_{j=1}^n \left\{\mathrm{N}\left(\sum_{i \neq j} X_i\right)\right\}^{\frac{n}{n-1}}. \tag{52b}$$

Proof. Let $\{\mathcal{S}_j\}_{j=1}^M$ be all the k-element subsets of $\Omega = [n]$ (with $M = \binom{n}{k}$). Then, every element $i \in [n]$ belongs to $d = \frac{kM}{n} = \binom{n-1}{k-1}$ such subsets, which then gives (49) as a special case of (48). Alternatively, (49) follows from Corollary 3b, which yields $m_k^{(n)} \geq m_n^{(n)}$ for all $k \in [n-1]$. Exponentiating both sides of (49) gives (50). Inequality (51) is a loosened version of (50), which follows by invoking the AM-GM inequality (i.e., the geometric mean of nonnegative real numbers is less than or equal to their arithmetic mean, with equality between these two means if and only if these numbers are all equal), in conjunction with the identity $\frac{k}{n}\binom{n}{k} = \binom{n-1}{k-1}$. Inequalities (50) and (51) are consequently equivalent if $\{X_i\}_{i=1}^n$ are i.i.d. random variables, and (52) is a specialized version of (50) and the loosened inequality (51) by setting $k = n-1$. □

The next remarks consider information inequalities in Corollaries 3–5, in light of Theorem 1 here, and some known results in the literature.

Remark 4. *Inequality* (49) *was derived by Madiman as a special case of Theorem 2 in* [37]. *The proof of Corollary 5a shows that* (49) *can be also derived in two different ways as special cases of both Theorem 1a and Proposition 4a.*

Remark 5. Inequality (51) can be also derived as a special case of Theorem 1a, where f is the rank function in (19), and $g \colon \mathbb{R} \to \mathbb{R}$ is given by $g(x) \triangleq \exp(2nx)$ for all $x \in \mathbb{R}$. It also follows from the monotonicity property in Corollary 3c, which yields $w_k^{(n)}(n) \geq w_n^{(n)}(n)$ for all $k \in [n-1]$.

Remark 6. The result in Theorem 8 of [31] is a special case of Theorem 1a here, which follows by taking the function g in Theorem 1a to be the identity function. The flexibility in selecting the function g in Theorem 1 enables to obtain a larger collection of information inequalities. This is in part reflected from a comparison of Corollary 3 here with Corollary 9 of [31]. More specifically, the findings about the monotonicity properties in (30), (31) and (33) were obtained in Corollary 9 of [31], while relying on Theorem 8 of [31] and the sub/supermodularity properties of the considered Shannon information measures. It is noted, however, that the monotonicity results of the sequences (34)–(37) (Corollary 3c) are not implied by Theorem 8 of [31].

Remark 7. Inequality (52) forms a counterpart of an entropy power inequality by Artstein et al., (Theorem 3 of [40]), where for independent random variables $\{X_i\}_{i=1}^n$ with finite variances:

$$\mathrm{N}\left(\sum_{i=1}^n X_i\right) \geq \frac{1}{n-1} \sum_{j=1}^n \mathrm{N}\left(\sum_{i \neq j} X_i\right). \tag{53}$$

Inequality (50), and also its looser version in (51), form counterparts of the generalized inequality by Madiman and Barron, which reads (see inequality (4) in [41]):

$$\mathrm{N}\left(\sum_{i=1}^n X_i\right) \geq \frac{1}{\binom{n-1}{k-1}} \sum_{\mathcal{T} \subseteq [n] : |\mathcal{T}|=k} \mathrm{N}\left(\sum_{\omega \in \mathcal{T}} X_\omega\right), \quad k \in [n-1]. \tag{54}$$

4. Proofs

The present section provides proofs of (most of the) results in Section 3.

4.1. Proof of Theorem 1

We prove Item (a), and then readily prove Items (b)–(d). Define the auxiliary sequence

$$f_k^{(n)} \triangleq \frac{1}{\binom{n}{k}} \sum_{\mathcal{T} \subseteq \Omega : |\mathcal{T}|=k} f(\mathcal{T}), \quad k \in [0:n], \tag{55}$$

averaging f over all k-element subsets of the n-element set $\Omega \triangleq \{\omega_1, \ldots, \omega_n\}$. Let the permutation $\pi \colon [n] \to [n]$ be arbitrary. For $k \in [n-1]$, let

$$\mathcal{S}_1 \triangleq \{\omega_{\pi(1)}, \ldots, \omega_{\pi(k-1)}, \omega_{\pi(k)}\}, \tag{56a}$$

$$\mathcal{S}_2 \triangleq \{\omega_{\pi(1)}, \ldots, \omega_{\pi(k-1)}, \omega_{\pi(k+1)}\}, \tag{56b}$$

which are k-element subsets of Ω with $k-1$ elements in common. Then,

$$f(\mathcal{S}_1) + f(\mathcal{S}_2) \geq f(\mathcal{S}_1 \cup \mathcal{S}_2) + f(\mathcal{S}_1 \cap \mathcal{S}_2), \tag{57}$$

which holds by the submodularity of f (by assumption), i.e.,

$$f(\{\omega_{\pi(1)}, \ldots, \omega_{\pi(k)}\}) + f(\{\omega_{\pi(1)}, \ldots, \omega_{\pi(k-1)}, \omega_{\pi(k+1)}\})$$
$$\geq f(\{\omega_{\pi(1)}, \ldots, \omega_{\pi(k+1)}\}) + f(\{\omega_{\pi(1)}, \ldots, \omega_{\pi(k-1)}\}). \tag{58}$$

Averaging the terms on both sides of (58) over all the $n!$ permutations π of $[n]$ gives

$$\frac{1}{n!} \sum_\pi f(\{\omega_{\pi(1)}, \ldots, \omega_{\pi(k)}\}) = \frac{k! \, (n-k)!}{n!} \sum_{\mathcal{T} \subseteq \Omega : |\mathcal{T}|=k} f(\mathcal{T}) \tag{59a}$$

$$= \frac{1}{\binom{n}{k}} \sum_{\mathcal{T} \subseteq \Omega: |\mathcal{T}|=k} f(\mathcal{T}) \tag{59b}$$

$$= f_k^{(n)}, \tag{59c}$$

and similarly

$$\frac{1}{n!} \sum_{\pi} f(\{\omega_{\pi(1)}, \ldots, \omega_{\pi(k-1)}, \omega_{\pi(k+1)}\}) = f_k^{(n)}, \tag{60a}$$

$$\frac{1}{n!} \sum_{\pi} f(\{\omega_{\pi(1)}, \ldots, \omega_{\pi(k+1)}\}) = f_{k+1}^{(n)}, \tag{60b}$$

$$\frac{1}{n!} \sum_{\pi} f(\{\omega_{\pi(1)}, \ldots, \omega_{\pi(k-1)}\}) = f_{k-1}^{(n)}, \tag{60c}$$

with $f_0^{(n)} = 0$ since by assumption $f(\varnothing) = 0$. Combining (58)–(60) gives

$$2 f_k^{(n)} \geq f_{k+1}^{(n)} + f_{k-1}^{(n)}, \quad k \in [n-1], \tag{61}$$

which is rewritten as

$$f_k^{(n)} - f_{k-1}^{(n)} \geq f_{k+1}^{(n)} - f_k^{(n)}, \quad k \in [n-1]. \tag{62}$$

Consequently, it follows that

$$\frac{f_k^{(n)}}{k} - \frac{f_{k+1}^{(n)}}{k+1} = \frac{1}{k} \sum_{j=1}^{k} \left(f_j^{(n)} - f_{j-1}^{(n)} \right) - \frac{1}{k+1} \sum_{j=1}^{k+1} \left(f_j^{(n)} - f_{j-1}^{(n)} \right) \tag{63a}$$

$$= \left(\frac{1}{k} - \frac{1}{k+1} \right) \sum_{j=1}^{k} \left(f_j^{(n)} - f_{j-1}^{(n)} \right) - \frac{1}{k+1} \left(f_{k+1}^{(n)} - f_k^{(n)} \right) \tag{63b}$$

$$= \frac{1}{k(k+1)} \sum_{j=1}^{k} \left\{ \left(f_j^{(n)} - f_{j-1}^{(n)} \right) - \left(f_{k+1}^{(n)} - f_k^{(n)} \right) \right\} \tag{63c}$$

$$\geq 0, \tag{63d}$$

where equality (63a) holds since $f_0^{(n)} = 0$, and inequality (63d) holds by (62). The sequence $\left\{ \frac{f_k^{(n)}}{k} \right\}_{k=1}^{n}$ is therefore monotonically decreasing, and in particular

$$f_k^{(n)} \geq \frac{k f_n^{(n)}}{n} = \frac{k}{n}. \tag{64}$$

We next prove (25) when $\alpha = 1$, and then proceed to prove Theorem 1. By (64)

$$\frac{f_n^{(n)}}{n} \leq \frac{f_{n-1}^{(n)}}{n-1}, \tag{65}$$

where, by (55),

$$f_n^{(n)} = f(\Omega), \quad f_{n-1}^{(n)} = \frac{1}{n} \sum_{\mathcal{T} \subseteq \Omega: |\mathcal{T}|=n-1} f(\mathcal{T}). \tag{66}$$

Combining (65) and (66) gives

$$(n-1) f(\Omega) \leq \sum_{\mathcal{T} \subseteq \Omega: |\mathcal{T}|=n-1} f(\mathcal{T}). \tag{67}$$

Since there are n subsets $\mathcal{T} \subseteq \Omega$ with $|\mathcal{T}| = n - 1$, rearranging terms in (67) gives (25) for $\alpha = 1$; it is should be noted that, for $\alpha = 1$, the set function f does not need to be nonnegative for the satisfiability of (25) (however, this will be required for $\alpha > 1$).

We next prove Item (a). By (20), for $k \in [n]$,

$$t_k^{(n)} = \frac{1}{\binom{n}{k}} \sum_{\mathcal{T} \subseteq \Omega: |\mathcal{T}|=k} g\left(\frac{f(\mathcal{T})}{k}\right) \tag{68a}$$

$$= \frac{1}{\binom{n}{k}} \sum_{\mathcal{T}=\{t_1,\ldots,t_k\} \subseteq \Omega} g\left(\frac{f(\{t_1,\ldots,t_k\})}{k}\right). \tag{68b}$$

Fix $\Omega_k \triangleq \{t_1, \ldots, t_k\} \subseteq \Omega$, and let $\tilde{f} \colon 2^{\Omega_k} \to \mathbb{R}$ be the restriction of the function f to the subsets of Ω_k. Then, $\tilde{f}$ is a submodular set function with $\tilde{f}(\varnothing) = 0$; similarly to (55), (65) and (66) with f replaced by $\tilde{f}$, and n replaced by k, the sequence $\left\{\frac{\tilde{f}_j^{(k)}}{j}\right\}_{j=1}^k$ is monotonically decreasing. Hence, for $k \in [2:n]$,

$$\frac{\tilde{f}_k^{(k)}}{k} \leq \frac{\tilde{f}_{k-1}^{(k)}}{k-1}, \tag{69}$$

where

$$\tilde{f}_k^{(k)} = \tilde{f}(\Omega_k) = f(\{t_1, \ldots, t_k\}), \tag{70a}$$

$$\tilde{f}_{k-1}^{(k)} = \frac{1}{k} \sum_{\mathcal{T} \subseteq \Omega_k: |\mathcal{T}|=k-1} \tilde{f}(\mathcal{T}) \tag{70b}$$

$$= \frac{1}{k} \sum_{\mathcal{T} \subseteq \Omega_k: |\mathcal{T}|=k-1} f(\mathcal{T}) \tag{70c}$$

$$= \frac{1}{k} \sum_{i=1}^{k} f(\{t_1, \ldots, t_{i-1}, t_{i+1}, \ldots, t_k\}). \tag{70d}$$

Combining (69) and (70) gives

$$f(\{t_1, \ldots, t_k\}) \leq \frac{1}{k-1} \sum_{i=1}^{k} f(\{t_1, \ldots, t_{i-1}, t_{i+1}, \ldots, t_k\}), \tag{71}$$

and, since by assumption g is monotonically increasing,

$$g\left(\frac{f(\{t_1, \ldots, t_k\})}{k}\right) \leq g\left(\frac{1}{k} \sum_{i=1}^{k} \frac{f(\{t_1, \ldots, t_{i-1}, t_{i+1}, \ldots, t_k\})}{k-1}\right). \tag{72}$$

From (68) and (72), for all $k \in [2:n]$,

$$t_k^{(n)} \leq \frac{1}{\binom{n}{k}} \sum_{\mathcal{T}=\{t_1,\ldots,t_k\} \subseteq \Omega} g\left(\frac{1}{k} \sum_{i=1}^{k} \frac{f(\{t_1, \ldots, t_{i-1}, t_{i+1}, \ldots, t_k\})}{k-1}\right), \tag{73}$$

and

$$t_k^{(n)} \leq \frac{1}{k\binom{n}{k}} \sum_{i=1}^{k} \sum_{\mathcal{T}=\{t_1,\ldots,t_k\} \subseteq \Omega} g\left(\frac{f(\{t_1, \ldots, t_{i-1}, t_{i+1}, \ldots, t_k\})}{k-1}\right) \tag{74a}$$

$$= \frac{n-k+1}{k\binom{n}{k}} \sum_{i=1}^{k} \left\{ \sum_{\{t_1,\ldots,t_{i-1},t_{i+1},\ldots,t_k\} \subseteq \Omega} g\left(\frac{f(\{t_1, \ldots, t_{i-1}, t_{i+1}, \ldots, t_k\})}{k-1}\right) \right\} \tag{74b}$$

$$= \frac{k!\,(n-k)!\,(n-k+1)}{n!\,k} \sum_{\mathcal{S} \subseteq \Omega: |\mathcal{S}|=k-1} g\left(\frac{f(\mathcal{S})}{k-1}\right) \tag{74c}$$

$$= \frac{(k-1)!\,(n-k+1)!}{n!} \sum_{\mathcal{S} \subseteq \Omega: |\mathcal{S}|=k-1} g\left(\frac{f(\mathcal{S})}{k-1}\right) \tag{74d}$$

$$= \frac{1}{\binom{n}{k-1}} \sum_{\mathcal{S} \subseteq \Omega: |\mathcal{S}|=k-1} g\left(\frac{f(\mathcal{S})}{k-1}\right) \tag{74e}$$

$$= t_{k-1}^{(n)}, \tag{74f}$$

where (74a) holds by invoking Jensen's inequality to the convex function g; (74b) holds since the term of the inner summation in the right-hand side of (74a) does not depend on t_i, so for every $(k-1)$-element subset $\mathcal{S} = \{t_1, \ldots, t_{i-1}, t_{i+1}, \ldots, t_k\} \subseteq \Omega$, there are $n-k+1$ possibilities to extend it by a single element (t_i) into a k-element subset $\mathcal{T} = \{t_1, \ldots, t_k\} \subseteq \Omega$; (74e) is straightforward, and (74f) holds by the definition in (20). This proves Item (a).

Item (b) follows from Item (a), and similarly Item (d) follows from Item (c), by replacing g with $-g$. Item (c) is next verified. If f is a supermodular set function with $f(\emptyset) = 0$, then (57) and (58), and (61)–(63) hold with flipped inequality signs. Hence, if g is monotonically decreasing, then inequalities (72) and (73) are reversed; finally, if g is also concave, then (by Jensen's inequality) (74) holds with a flipped inequality sign, which proves Item (c).

4.2. Proof of Corollary 1

By assumption $f \colon 2^{\Omega} \to \mathbb{R}$ is a rank function, which implies that $0 \leq f(\mathcal{T}) \leq f(\Omega)$ for every $\mathcal{T} \subseteq \Omega$. Since (by definition) f is submodular with $f(\emptyset) = 0$, and (by assumption) the function g is convex and monotonically increasing, then (from (22), while replacing k with k_n)

$$\binom{n}{k_n} g\left(\frac{f(\Omega)}{n}\right) \leq \sum_{\mathcal{T} \subseteq \Omega: |\mathcal{T}|=k_n} g\left(\frac{f(\mathcal{T})}{k_n}\right) \leq \binom{n}{k_n} g\left(\frac{f(\Omega)}{k_n}\right), \quad n \in \mathbb{N}. \tag{75}$$

By the second assumption in Corollary 1, for positive values of x that are sufficiently close to zero, we have

- $g(x) \approx g(0) > 0$ if $g(0) > 0$;
- $g(x)$ scales like $\frac{1}{\ell!} g^{(\ell)}(0) x^{\ell}$ if $g(0) = \ldots = g^{(\ell-1)}(0) = 0$ with $g^{(\ell)}(0) > 0$ for some $\ell \in \mathbb{N}$.

In both cases, it follows that

$$\lim_{x \to 0^+} x \log g(x) = 0. \tag{76}$$

In light of (75) and (76), and since (by assumption) $k_n \xrightarrow[n \to \infty]{} \infty$, it follows that

$$\lim_{n \to \infty} \frac{1}{n} \left[\log\left(\sum_{\mathcal{T} \subseteq \Omega: |\mathcal{T}|=k_n} g\left(\frac{f(\mathcal{T})}{k_n}\right) \right) - \log \binom{n}{k_n} \right] = 0. \tag{77}$$

By the following upper and lower bounds on the binomial coefficient:

$$\frac{1}{n+1} \exp\left(n\, \mathsf{H_b}\!\left(\frac{k_n}{n}\right) \right) \leq \binom{n}{k_n} \leq \exp\left(n\, \mathsf{H_b}\!\left(\frac{k_n}{n}\right) \right), \tag{78}$$

the combination of equalities (77) and (78) gives equality (23). Equality (24) holds as a special case of (23), under the assumption that $\lim_{n \to \infty} \frac{k_n}{n} = \beta \in [0, 1]$.

4.3. Proof of Corollary 2

For $\alpha = 1$, Corollary 2 is proved in (67). Fix $\alpha > 1$, and let $g \colon \mathbb{R} \to \mathbb{R}$ be

$$g(x) \triangleq \begin{cases} x^\alpha, & x \geq 0, \\ 0, & x < 0, \end{cases} \tag{79}$$

which is monotonically increasing and convex on the real line. By Theorem 1a,

$$t_k^{(n)} \geq t_n^{(n)}, \quad k \in [n]. \tag{80}$$

Since by assumption f is nonnegative, it follows from (20) and (79) that

$$t_k^{(n)} = \frac{1}{\binom{n}{k}} \sum_{\mathcal{T} \subseteq \Omega \colon |\mathcal{T}|=k} g\left(\frac{f(\mathcal{T})}{k}\right) \tag{81a}$$

$$= \frac{1}{k^\alpha \binom{n}{k}} \sum_{\mathcal{T} \subseteq \Omega \colon |\mathcal{T}|=k} f^\alpha(\mathcal{T}). \tag{81b}$$

Combining (80)–(81) and rearranging terms gives, for all $\alpha > 1$,

$$\sum_{\mathcal{T} \subseteq \Omega \colon |\mathcal{T}|=k} f^\alpha(\mathcal{T}) \geq \left(\frac{k}{n}\right)^\alpha \binom{n}{k} f^\alpha(\Omega) \tag{82a}$$

$$= \left(\frac{k}{n}\right)^{\alpha-1} \binom{n-1}{k-1} f^\alpha(\Omega), \tag{82b}$$

where equality (82b) holds by the identity $\frac{k}{n} \binom{n}{k} = \binom{n-1}{k-1}$. This further gives

$$\sum_{\mathcal{T} \subseteq \Omega \colon |\mathcal{T}|=k} \bigl(f^\alpha(\Omega) - f^\alpha(\mathcal{T}) \bigr) = \binom{n}{k} f^\alpha(\Omega) - \sum_{\mathcal{T} \subseteq \Omega \colon |\mathcal{T}|=k} f^\alpha(\mathcal{T}) \tag{83a}$$

$$\leq \left(1 - \frac{k^\alpha}{n^\alpha}\right) \binom{n}{k} f^\alpha(\Omega) \tag{83b}$$

$$= c_\alpha(n,k) f^\alpha(\Omega), \tag{83c}$$

where equality (83c) holds by the definition in (26). This proves (25) for $\alpha > 1$.

We next prove Item (b). The function f is (by assumption) a rank function, which yields its nonnegativity. Hence, the leftmost inequality in (27) holds by (82). The rightmost inequality in (27) also holds since $f \colon 2^\Omega \to \mathbb{R}$ is monotonically increasing, which yields $f(\mathcal{T}) \leq f(\Omega)$ for all $\mathcal{T} \subseteq \Omega$. For $k \in [n]$ and $\alpha \geq 0$ (in particular, for $\alpha \geq 1$),

$$\sum_{\mathcal{T} \subseteq \Omega \colon |\mathcal{T}|=k} f^\alpha(\mathcal{T}) \leq \binom{n}{k} f^\alpha(\Omega), \tag{84}$$

where (84) holds since there are $\binom{n}{k}$ k-element subsets $\mathcal{T}$ of the n-element set Ω, and every summand $f^\alpha(\mathcal{T})$ (with $\mathcal{T} \subseteq \Omega$) is upper bounded by $f^\alpha(\Omega)$.

5. A Problem in Extremal Graph Theory

This section applies the generalization of Han's inequality in (28) to the following problem.

5.1. Problem Formulation

Let $\mathcal{A} \subseteq \{-1,1\}^n$, with $n \in \mathbb{N}$, and let $\tau \in [n]$. Let $G = G_{\mathcal{A},\tau}$ be an un-directed simple graph with vertex set $V(G) = \mathcal{A}$, and pairs of vertices in G are adjacent (i.e., connected by an edge) if and only if they are represented by vectors in $\mathcal{A}$ whose Hamming distance is less than or equal to τ:

$$\{x^n, y^n\} \in \mathsf{E}(G) \Leftrightarrow (x^n, y^n \in \mathcal{A}, \ x^n \neq y^n, \ \mathsf{d_H}(x^n, y^n) \leq \tau). \tag{85}$$

The question is how large can the size of G be (i.e., how many edges it may have) as a function of the cardinality of the set $\mathcal{A}$, and possibly based also on some basic properties of the set $\mathcal{A}$?

This problem and its related analysis generalize and refine, in a nontrivial way, the bound in Theorem 4.2 of [6] which applies to the special case where $\tau = 1$. The motivation for this extension is next considered.

5.2. Problem Motivation

Constraint coding is common in many data recording systems and data communication systems, where some sequences are more prone to error than others, and a constraint on the sequences that are allowed to be recorded or transmitted is imposed in order to reduce the likelihood of error. Given such a constraint, it is then necessary to encode arbitrary user sequences into sequences that obey the constraint.

From an information–theoretic perspective, this problem can be interpreted as follows. Consider a communication channel $\mathsf{W} \colon \mathcal{X} \to \mathcal{Y}$ with input alphabet $\mathcal{X}$ and output alphabet $\mathcal{Y}$, and suppose that a constraint is imposed on the sequences that are allowed to be transmitted over the channel. As a result of such a constraint, the information sequences are first encoded into codewords by an error-correction encoder, followed by a constrained encoder that maps these codewords into constrained sequences. Let them be binary n-length sequences from the set $\mathcal{A} \subseteq \{-1, 1\}^n$. A channel modulator then modulates these sequences into symbols from $\mathcal{X}$, and the received sequences at the channel output, with alphabet $\mathcal{Y}$, are first demodulated, and then decoded (in a reverse order of the encoding process) by the constrained decoder and error-correction decoder.

Consider a channel model where pairs of binary n-length sequences from the set $\mathcal{A}$ whose Hamming distance is less than or equal to a fixed number τ share a common output sequence with positive probability, whereas this halts to be the case if the Hamming distance is larger than τ. In other words, we assume that by design, pairs of sequences in $\mathcal{A}$ whose Hamming distance is larger than τ cannot be confused in the sense that there does not exist a common output sequence which may be possibly received (with positive probability) at the channel output.

The confusion graph G that is associated with this setup is an undirected simple graph whose vertices represent the n-length binary sequences in $\mathcal{A}$, and pairs of vertices are adjacent if and only if the Hamming distance between the sequences that they represent is not larger than τ. The size of G (i.e., its number of edges) is equal to the number of pairs of sequences in $\mathcal{A}$ which may not be distinguishable by the decoder.

Further motivation for studying this problem is considered in the continuation (see Section 5.5).

5.3. Analysis

We next derive an upper bound on the size of the graph G. Let $X^n = (X_1, \ldots, X_n)$ be chosen uniformly at random from the set $\mathcal{A} \subseteq \{-1, 1\}^n$, and let P_{X^n} be the PMF of X^n. Then,

$$\mathsf{P}_{X^n}(x^n) = \begin{cases} \dfrac{1}{|\mathcal{A}|}, & \text{if } x^n \in \mathcal{A}, \\ 0, & \text{if } x^n \notin \mathcal{A}, \end{cases} \tag{86}$$

which implies that

$$\mathsf{H}(X^n) = \log |\mathcal{A}|. \tag{87}$$

The graph G is an un-directed and simple graph with a vertex set $\mathsf{V}(G) = \mathcal{A}$ (i.e., the vertices of G are in one-to-one correspondence with the binary vectors in the set $\mathcal{A}$). Its set of edges $\mathsf{E}(G)$ are the edges which connect all pairs of vertices in G whose Hamming distance is less than or equal to τ. For $d \in [\tau]$, let $\mathsf{E}_d(G)$ be the set of edges in G which connect all pairs of vertices in G whose Hamming distance is equal to d, so

$$|\mathsf{E}(G)| = \sum_{d=1}^{\tau} |\mathsf{E}_d(G)|. \qquad (88)$$

For $x^n \in \{-1,1\}^n$, $d \in [n]$, and integers $k_1, \ldots, k_d$ such that $1 \leq k_1 < \ldots < k_d \leq n$, let

$$\widetilde{x}^{(k_1,\ldots,k_d)} \triangleq (x_1, \ldots, x_{k_1-1}, x_{k_1+1}, \ldots, x_{k_d-1}, x_{k_d+1}, \ldots, x_n) \qquad (89)$$

be a subvector of x^n of length $n - d$, obtained by dropping the bits of x^n in positions $k_1, \ldots, k_d$; if $d = n$, then $(k_1, \ldots, k_n) = (1, \ldots, n)$, and $\widetilde{x}^{(k_1,\ldots,k_d)}$ is an empty vector. By the chain rule for the Shannon entropy,

$$\mathsf{H}(X^n) - \mathsf{H}\big(\widetilde{X}^{(k_1,\ldots,k_d)}\big)$$

$$= \mathsf{H}\big(X_{k_1}, \ldots, X_{k_d} \mid \widetilde{X}^{(k_1,\ldots,k_d)}\big) \qquad (90\mathrm{a})$$

$$= -\sum_{x^n \in \{-1,1\}^n} \mathsf{P}_{X^n}(x^n) \log\!\Big(\mathsf{P}_{X_{k_1},\ldots,X_{k_d} \mid \widetilde{X}^{(k_1,\ldots,k_d)}}\big(x_{k_1}, \ldots, x_{k_d} \mid \widetilde{x}^{(k_1,\ldots,k_d)}\big)\Big) \qquad (90\mathrm{b})$$

$$= -\frac{1}{|\mathcal{A}|} \sum_{x^n \in \mathcal{A}} \log\!\Big(\mathsf{P}_{X_{k_1},\ldots,X_{k_d} \mid \widetilde{X}^{(k_1,\ldots,k_d)}}\big(x_{k_1}, \ldots, x_{k_d} \mid \widetilde{x}^{(k_1,\ldots,k_d)}\big)\Big), \qquad (90\mathrm{c})$$

where equality (90c) holds by (86).

For $x^n \in \{-1,1\}^n$, $d \in [n]$, and integers $k_1, \ldots, k_d$ such that $1 \leq k_1 < \ldots < k_d \leq n$, let

$$\overline{x}^{(k_1,\ldots,k_d)} \triangleq (x_1, \ldots, x_{k_1-1}, -x_{k_1}, x_{k_1+1}, \ldots, x_{k_d-1}, -x_{k_d}, x_{k_d+1}, \ldots, x_n), \qquad (91)$$

where the bits of x^n in position $k_1, \ldots, k_d$ are flipped (in contrast to $\widetilde{x}^{(k_1,\ldots,k_d)}$ where the bits of x^n in these positions are dropped), so $\overline{x}^{(k_1,\ldots,k_d)} \in \{-1,1\}^n$ and $\mathsf{d}_\mathsf{H}\big(x^n, \overline{x}^{(k_1,\ldots,k_d)}\big) = d$. Likewise, if $x^n, y^n \in \{-1,1\}^n$ satisfy $\mathsf{d}_\mathsf{H}(x^n, y^n) = d$, then there exist integers $k_1, \ldots, k_d$ such that $1 \leq k_1 < \ldots < k_d \leq n$ where $y^n = \overline{x}^{(k_1,\ldots,k_d)}$ (i.e., the integers $k_1, \ldots, k_d$ are the positions (in increasing order) where the vectors x^n and y^n differ).

Let us characterize the set $\mathcal{A}$ by its cardinality, and the following two natural numbers:

(a) If $x^n \in \mathcal{A}$ and $\overline{x}^{(k_1,\ldots,k_d)} \in \mathcal{A}$ for any $(k_1, \ldots, k_d)$ such that $1 \leq k_1 < \ldots < k_d \leq n$, then there are at least $m_d \triangleq m_d(\mathcal{A})$ vectors $y^n \in \mathcal{A}$ whose subvectors $\widetilde{y}^{(k_1,\ldots,k_d)}$ coincide with $\widetilde{x}^{(k_1,\ldots,k_d)}$, i.e., the integer $m_d \geq 2$ satisfies

$$m_d \leq \min_{\substack{x^n \in \mathcal{A}, \\ 1 \leq k_1 < \ldots < k_d \leq n}} \Big| \Big\{ y^n \in \mathcal{A} : \widetilde{y}^{(k_1,\ldots,k_d)} = \widetilde{x}^{(k_1,\ldots,k_d)}, \ \overline{x}^{(k_1,\ldots,k_d)} \in \mathcal{A} \Big\} \Big|. \qquad (92)$$

By definition, the integer m_d always exists, and

$$2 \leq m_d \leq \min\{2^d, |\mathcal{A}|\}. \qquad (93)$$

If no information is available about the value of m_d, then it can be taken by default to be equal to 2 (since by assumption the two vectors $x^n \in \mathcal{A}$ and $y^n \triangleq \overline{x}^{(k_1,\ldots,k_d)} \in \mathcal{A}$ satisfy the equality $\widetilde{y}^{(k_1,\ldots,k_d)} = \widetilde{x}^{(k_1,\ldots,k_d)}$).

(b) If $x^n \in \mathcal{A}$ and $\overline{x}^{(k_1,\ldots,k_d)} \notin \mathcal{A}$ for any $(k_1, \ldots, k_d)$ such that $1 \leq k_1 < \ldots < k_d \leq n$, then there are at least $\ell_d \triangleq \ell_d(\mathcal{A})$ vectors $y^n \in \mathcal{A}$ whose subvectors $\widetilde{y}^{(k_1,\ldots,k_d)}$ coincide with $\widetilde{x}^{(k_1,\ldots,k_d)}$, i.e., the integer $\ell_d \geq 1$ satisfies

$$\ell_d \leq \min_{\substack{x^n \in \mathcal{A}, \\ 1 \leq k_1 < \ldots < k_d \leq n}} \Big| \Big\{ y^n \in \mathcal{A} : \widetilde{y}^{(k_1,\ldots,k_d)} = \widetilde{x}^{(k_1,\ldots,k_d)}, \ \overline{x}^{(k_1,\ldots,k_d)} \notin \mathcal{A} \Big\} \Big|. \qquad (94)$$

By definition, the integer ℓ_d always exists, and

$$1 \leq \ell_d \leq \min\{2^d - 1, |\mathcal{A}| - 1\}. \tag{95}$$

Likewise, if no information is available about the value of ℓ_d, then it can be taken by default to be equal to 1 (since $x^n \in \mathcal{A}$ satisfies the requirement about its subvector $\widetilde{x}^{(k_1,\ldots,k_d)}$ in (94)).

In general, it would be preferable to have the largest possible values of m_d and ℓ_d (i.e., those satisfying inequalities (92) and (94) with equalities, for obtaining a better upper bound on the size of G (this point will be clarified in the sequel). If $d = 1$, then $m_d = 2$ and $\ell_d = 1$ are the best possible constants (this holds by the definitions in (92) and (94), which can be also verified by the coincidence of the upper and lower bounds in (93) for $d = 1$, as well as those in (95)).

If $x^n \in \mathcal{A}$, then we distinguish between the following two cases:

- If $\overline{x}^{(k_1,\ldots,k_d)} \in \mathcal{A}$, then

$$P_{X_{k_1},\ldots,X_{k_d} \mid \widetilde{X}^{(k_1,\ldots,k_d)}}(x_{k_1},\ldots,x_{k_d} \mid \widetilde{x}^{(k_1,\ldots,k_d)}) \leq \frac{1}{m_d}, \tag{96}$$

which holds by the way that m_d is defined in (92), and since X^n is randomly selected to be equiprobable in the set $\mathcal{A}$.

- If $\overline{x}^{(k_1,\ldots,k_d)} \notin \mathcal{A}$, then

$$P_{X_{k_1},\ldots,X_{k_d} \mid \widetilde{X}^{(k_1,\ldots,k_d)}}(x_{k_1},\ldots,x_{k_d} \mid \widetilde{x}^{(k_1,\ldots,k_d)}) \leq \frac{1}{\ell_d}, \tag{97}$$

which holds by the way that ℓ_d is defined in (94), and since X^n is equiprobable on $\mathcal{A}$.

For $d \in [\tau]$ and $1 \leq k_1 < \ldots < k_d \leq n$, it follows from (90), (96) and (97) that

$$H(X^n) - H(\widetilde{X}^{(k_1,\ldots,k_d)}) \geq \frac{\log m_d}{|\mathcal{A}|} \sum_{x^n} \mathbb{1}\{x^n \in \mathcal{A}, \overline{x}^{(k_1,\ldots,k_d)} \in \mathcal{A}\}$$
$$+ \frac{\log \ell_d}{|\mathcal{A}|} \sum_{x^n} \mathbb{1}\{x^n \in \mathcal{A}, \overline{x}^{(k_1,\ldots,k_d)} \notin \mathcal{A}\}, \tag{98}$$

which, by summing on both sides of inequality (98) over all integers $k_1, \ldots, k_d$ such that $1 \leq k_1 < \ldots < k_d \leq n$, yields

$$\sum_{\substack{(k_1,\ldots,k_d): \\ 1 \leq k_1 < \ldots < k_d \leq n}} \left(H(X^n) - H(\widetilde{X}^{(k_1,\ldots,k_d)}) \right)$$
$$\geq \frac{\log m_d}{|\mathcal{A}|} \sum_{\substack{(k_1,\ldots,k_d): \\ 1 \leq k_1 < \ldots < k_d \leq n}} \sum_{x^n} \mathbb{1}\{x^n \in \mathcal{A}, \overline{x}^{(k_1,\ldots,k_d)} \in \mathcal{A}\}$$
$$+ \frac{\log \ell_d}{|\mathcal{A}|} \sum_{\substack{(k_1,\ldots,k_d): \\ 1 \leq k_1 < \ldots < k_d \leq n}} \sum_{x^n} \mathbb{1}\{x^n \in \mathcal{A}, \overline{x}^{(k_1,\ldots,k_d)} \notin \mathcal{A}\}. \tag{99}$$

Equality holds in (99) if the minima on the RHS of (92) and (94) are attained by any element in these sets, and if (92) and (94) are satisfied with equalities (i.e., m_d and ℓ_d are the maximal integers to satisfy inequalities (92) and (94) for the given set $\mathcal{A}$). Hence, this equality holds in particular for $d = 1$, with the constants $m_d = 2$ and $\ell_d = 1$.

The double sum in the first term on the RHS of (99) is equal to

$$\sum_{\substack{(k_1,\ldots,k_d):\\1\leq k_1<\ldots<k_d\leq n}} \sum_{x^n} \mathbb{1}\{x^n \in \mathcal{A},\, \overline{x}^{(k_1,\ldots,k_d)} \in \mathcal{A}\} = 2|\mathsf{E}_d(G)|, \qquad (100)$$

since every pair of adjacent vertices in $\mathcal{G}$ that refer to vectors in $\mathcal{A}$ whose Hamming distance is equal to d is of the form $x^n \in \mathcal{A}$ and $\overline{x}^{(k_1,\ldots,k_d)} \in \mathcal{A}$, and vice versa, and every edge $\{x^n, \overline{x}^{(k_1,\ldots,k_d)}\} \in \mathsf{E}_d(G)$ is counted twice in the double summation on the LHS of (100). For calculating the double sum in the second term on the RHS of (99), we first calculate the sum of these two double summations:

$$\sum_{\substack{(k_1,\ldots,k_d):\\1\leq k_1<\ldots<k_d\leq n}} \sum_{x^n} \mathbb{1}\{x^n \in \mathcal{A},\, \overline{x}^{(k_1,\ldots,k_d)} \in \mathcal{A}\} + \sum_{\substack{(k_1,\ldots,k_d):\\1\leq k_1<\ldots<k_d\leq n}} \sum_{x^n} \mathbb{1}\{x^n \in \mathcal{A},\, \overline{x}^{(k_1,\ldots,k_d)} \notin \mathcal{A}\}$$

$$= \sum_{\substack{(k_1,\ldots,k_d):\\1\leq k_1<\ldots<k_d\leq n}} \sum_{x^n} \Big\{\mathbb{1}\{x^n \in \mathcal{A},\, \overline{x}^{(k_1,\ldots,k_d)} \in \mathcal{A}\} + \mathbb{1}\{x^n \in \mathcal{A},\, \overline{x}^{(k_1,\ldots,k_d)} \notin \mathcal{A}\}\Big\} \qquad (101a)$$

$$= \sum_{\substack{(k_1,\ldots,k_d):\\1\leq k_1<\ldots<k_d\leq n}} \sum_{x^n} \mathbb{1}\{x^n \in \mathcal{A}\} \qquad (101b)$$

$$= \sum_{\substack{(k_1,\ldots,k_d):\\1\leq k_1<\ldots<k_d\leq n}} |\mathcal{A}| \qquad (101c)$$

$$= \binom{n}{d}|\mathcal{A}|, \qquad (101d)$$

so, subtracting (100) from (101d) gives that

$$\sum_{\substack{(k_1,\ldots,k_d):\\1\leq k_1<\ldots<k_d\leq n}} \sum_{x^n} \mathbb{1}\{x^n \in \mathcal{A},\, \overline{x}^{(k_1,\ldots,k_d)} \notin \mathcal{A}\} = \binom{n}{d}|\mathcal{A}| - 2|\mathsf{E}_d(G)|. \qquad (102)$$

Substituting (100) and (102) into the RHS of (99) gives that, for all $d \in [\tau]$,

$$\sum_{\substack{(k_1,\ldots,k_d):\\1\leq k_1<\ldots<k_d\leq n}} \Big(\mathrm{H}(X^n) - \mathrm{H}\big(\widetilde{X}^{(k_1,\ldots,k_d)}\big)\Big)$$

$$\geq \frac{2|\mathsf{E}_d(G)|\log m_d}{|\mathcal{A}|} + \frac{\log \ell_d}{|\mathcal{A}|}\bigg[\binom{n}{d}|\mathcal{A}| - 2|\mathsf{E}_d(G)|\bigg] \qquad (103a)$$

$$= \binom{n}{d}\log \ell_d + \frac{2|\mathsf{E}_d(G)|}{|\mathcal{A}|}\log \frac{m_d}{\ell_d}, \qquad (103b)$$

with the same necessary and sufficient condition for equality in (103a) as in (99). (Recall that it is in particular an equality for $d = 1$, where in this case $m_1 = 2$ and $\ell_1 = 1$.)

By the generalized Han's inequality in (28),

$$\sum_{\substack{(k_1,\ldots,k_d):\\1\leq k_1<\ldots<k_d\leq n}} \Big(\mathrm{H}(X^n) - \mathrm{H}\big(\widetilde{X}^{(k_1,\ldots,k_d)}\big)\Big) \leq \binom{n-1}{d-1}\mathrm{H}(X^n) \qquad (104a)$$

$$= \binom{n-1}{d-1}\log|\mathcal{A}|, \qquad (104b)$$

where equality (104b) holds by (87). Combining (103) and (104) yields

$$\binom{n-1}{d-1} \log |\mathcal{A}| \geq \binom{n}{d} \log \ell_d + \frac{2|\mathsf{E}_d(G)|}{|\mathcal{A}|} \log \frac{m_d}{\ell_d}, \tag{105}$$

and, by the identity $\binom{n}{d} = \frac{n}{d}\binom{n-1}{d-1}$, we get

$$|\mathsf{E}_d(G)| \leq \frac{\binom{n-1}{d-1}|\mathcal{A}|\left(\log|\mathcal{A}| - \frac{n}{d}\log \ell_d\right)}{2\log \frac{m_d}{\ell_d}}. \tag{106}$$

This upper bound is specialized, for $d=1$, to Theorem 4.2 of [6] (where, by definition, $m_1 = 2$ and $\ell_1 = 1$). This gives that the number of edges in G, connecting pairs of vertices which refer to binary vectors in $\mathcal{A}$ whose Hamming distance is 1 from each other, satisfies

$$|\mathsf{E}_1(G)| \leq \tfrac{1}{2}|\mathcal{A}| \log_2 |\mathcal{A}|. \tag{107}$$

It is possible to select, by default, the values of the integers m_d and ℓ_d to be equal to 2 and 1, respectively, independently of the value of $d \in [\tau]$. It therefore follows that the upper bound in (106) can be loosened to

$$|\mathsf{E}_d(G)| \leq \tfrac{1}{2}\binom{n-1}{d-1}|\mathcal{A}| \log_2 |\mathcal{A}|. \tag{108}$$

This shows that the bound in (108) generalizes the result in Theorem 4.2 of [6], based only on the knowledge of the cardinality of $\mathcal{A}$. Furthermore, the bound (108) can be tightened by the refined bound (106) if the characterization of the set $\mathcal{A}$ allows one to assert values for m_d and ℓ_d that are larger than the trivial values of 2 and 1, respectively.

In light of (88) and (108), the number of edges in the graph G satisfies

$$|\mathsf{E}(G)| \leq \tfrac{1}{2} \sum_{d=1}^{\tau} \binom{n-1}{d-1} |\mathcal{A}| \log_2 |\mathcal{A}|, \tag{109}$$

and if $\tau \leq \frac{n+1}{2}$, then it follows that

$$|\mathsf{E}(G)| \leq \tfrac{1}{2} \exp\left((n-1)\,\mathsf{H}_\mathsf{b}\!\left(\frac{\tau-1}{n-1}\right)\right) |\mathcal{A}| \log_2 |\mathcal{A}|. \tag{110}$$

Indeed, the transition from (109) to (110) holds by the inequality

$$\sum_{k=0}^{n\theta} \binom{n}{k} \leq \exp(n\mathsf{H}_\mathsf{b}(\theta)), \quad \theta \in [0, \tfrac{1}{2}], \tag{111}$$

where the latter bound is asymptotically tight in the exponent of n (for sufficiently large values of n).

5.4. Comparison of Bounds

We next consider the tightness of the refined bound (106) and the loosened bound (108). Since $\mathcal{A}$ is a subset of the n-dimensional cube $\{-1,1\}^n$, every point in $\mathcal{A}$ has at most $\binom{n}{d}$ neighbors in $\mathcal{A}$ with Hamming distance d, so

$$|\mathsf{E}_d(G)| \leq \tfrac{1}{2}\binom{n}{d}|\mathcal{A}|. \tag{112}$$

Comparing the bound on the RHS of (106) with the trivial bound in (112) shows that the former bound is useful if and only if

$$\frac{\log|\mathcal{A}| - \frac{n}{d}\log \ell_d}{\log \frac{m_d}{\ell_d}} \leq \frac{n}{d}, \tag{113}$$

which is obtained by relying on the identity $\binom{n}{d} = \frac{n}{d}\binom{n-1}{d-1}$. Rearranging terms in (113) gives the necessary and sufficient condition

$$|\mathcal{A}| \leq (m_d)^{\frac{n}{d}}, \tag{114}$$

which is independent of the value of ℓ_d. Since, by definition, $m_d \geq 2$, inequality (114) is automatically satisfied if the stronger condition

$$|\mathcal{A}| \leq 2^{\frac{n}{d}} \tag{115}$$

is imposed. The latter also forms a necessary and sufficient condition for the usefulness of the looser bound on the RHS of (108) in comparison to (112).

Example 1. *Suppose that the set $\mathcal{A} \subseteq \{-1,1\}^n$ is characterized by the property that for all $d \in [\tau]$, with a fixed integer $\tau \in [n]$, if $x^n \in \mathcal{A}$ and $\overline{x}^{(k_1,\ldots,k_d)} \in \mathcal{A}$ then all vectors $y^n \in \{-1,1\}^n$ which coincide with x^n and $\overline{x}^{(k_1,\ldots,k_d)}$ in their $(n-d)$ agreed positions are also included in the set $\mathcal{A}$. Then, for all $d \in [\tau]$, we get by definition that $m_d = 2^d$, which yields $\tau \leq \lfloor \log_2 |\mathcal{A}| \rfloor$. Setting $m_d = 2^d$ and the default value $\ell_d = 1$ on the RHS of (106) gives*

$$|\mathsf{E}_d(G)| \leq \frac{\binom{n-1}{d-1}|\mathcal{A}|\left(\log|\mathcal{A}| - \frac{n}{d}\log \ell_d\right)}{2\log \frac{m_d}{\ell_d}} \tag{116a}$$

$$= \frac{\binom{n-1}{d-1}|\mathcal{A}|\log|\mathcal{A}|}{2\log(2^d)} \tag{116b}$$

$$= \frac{1}{2d}\binom{n-1}{d-1}|\mathcal{A}|\log_2|\mathcal{A}| \tag{116c}$$

$$= \frac{1}{2}\binom{n}{d}|\mathcal{A}| \cdot \frac{\log_2|\mathcal{A}|}{n}. \tag{116d}$$

Unless $\mathcal{A} = \{-1,1\}^n$, the upper bound on the RHS of (116d) is strictly smaller than the trivial upper bound on the RHS of (112). This improvement is consistent with the satisfiability of the (necessary and sufficient) condition in (115), which is strictly satisfied since

$$|\mathcal{A}| < 2^n = (2^d)^{\frac{n}{d}} = (m_d)^{\frac{n}{d}}. \tag{117}$$

On the other hand, the looser upper bound on the RHS of (108) gives

$$|\mathsf{E}_d(G)| \leq \frac{1}{2}\binom{n}{d}|\mathcal{A}| \cdot \frac{d\log_2|\mathcal{A}|}{n}, \tag{118}$$

which is d times larger than the refined bound on the RHS of (116d) (since it is based on the exact value of m_d for the set $\mathcal{A}$, rather than taking the default value of 2), and it is worse than the trivial bound if and only if $|\mathcal{A}| > 2^{\frac{n}{d}}$. The latter finding is consistent with (115).

This exemplifies the utility of the refined upper bound on the RHS of (106) in comparison to the bound on the RHS of (108), where the latter generalizes Theorem 4.2 of [6] from the case where $d = 1$ to all $d \in [n]$. As it is explained above, this refinement is irrelevant in the special case where $d = 1$, though it proves to be useful in general for $d \in [2:n]$ (as it is exemplified here).

The following theorem introduces the results of our analysis (so far) in the present section.

Theorem 2. *Let $\mathcal{A} \subseteq \{-1,1\}^n$, with $n \in \mathbb{N}$, and let $\tau \in [n]$. Let $G = (V(G), E(G))$ be an un-directed, simple graph with vertex set $V(G) = \mathcal{A}$, and edges connecting pairs of vertices in G which are represented by vectors in $\mathcal{A}$ whose Hamming distance is less than or equal to τ. For $d \in [\tau]$, let $E_d(G)$ be the set of edges in G which connect all pairs of vertices that are represented by vectors in $\mathcal{A}$ whose Hamming distance is equal to d (i.e., $|E(G)| = \sum_{d=1}^{\tau} |E_d(G)|$).*

(a) *For $d \in [\tau]$, let the integers $m_d \in [2 : \min\{2^d, |\mathcal{A}|\}]$ and $\ell_d \in [\min\{2^d - 1, |\mathcal{A}| - 1\}]$ (be, preferably, the maximal possible values to) satisfy the requirements in (92) and (94), respectively. Then,*

$$|E_d(G)| \leq \frac{\binom{n-1}{d-1} |\mathcal{A}| \left(\log |\mathcal{A}| - \frac{n}{d} \log \ell_d\right)}{2 \log \frac{m_d}{\ell_d}}. \tag{119}$$

(b) *A loosened bound, which only depends on the cardinality of the set $\mathcal{A}$, is obtained by setting the default values $m_d = 2$ and $\ell_d = 1$. It is then given by*

$$|E_d(G)| \leq \tfrac{1}{2} \binom{n-1}{d-1} |\mathcal{A}| \log_2 |\mathcal{A}|, \quad d \in [\tau], \tag{120}$$

and, if $\tau \leq \frac{n+1}{2}$, then the (overall) number of edges in G satisfies

$$|E(G)| \leq \tfrac{1}{2} \exp\left((n-1) \operatorname{H_b}\left(\frac{\tau-1}{n-1}\right)\right) |\mathcal{A}| \log_2 |\mathcal{A}|. \tag{121}$$

(c) *The refined upper bound on the RHS of (119) and the loosened upper bound on the RHS of (120) improve the trivial bound $\tfrac{1}{2}\binom{n}{d}|\mathcal{A}|$, if and only if $|\mathcal{A}| < (m_d)^{\frac{n}{d}}$ or $|\mathcal{A}| < 2^{\frac{n}{d}}$, respectively (see Example 1).*

5.5. Influence of Fixed-Size Subsets of Bits

The result in Theorem 4.2 of [6], which is generalized and refined in Theorem 2 here, is turned to study the total influence of the n variables of an equiprobable random vector $X^n \in \{-1,1\}^n$ on a subset $\mathcal{A} \subset \{-1,1\}^n$. To this end, let $\overline{X}^{(i)}$ denote the vector where the bit at the i-th position of X^n is flipped, so $\overline{X}^{(i)} \triangleq (X_1, \ldots, X_{i-1}, -X_i, X_{i+1}, \ldots, X_n)$ for all $i \in [n]$. Then, the influence of the i-th variable is defined as

$$I_i(\mathcal{A}) \triangleq \Pr\left[\mathbb{1}\{X^n \in \mathcal{A}\} \neq \mathbb{1}\{\overline{X}^{(i)} \in \mathcal{A}\}\right], \quad i \in [n], \tag{122}$$

and their total influence is defined to be the sum

$$I(\mathcal{A}) \triangleq \sum_{i=1}^{n} I_i(\mathcal{A}). \tag{123}$$

As it is shown in Chapters 9 and 10 of [6], influences of subsets of the binary hypercube have far reaching consequences in the study of threshold phenomena, and many other areas. As a corollary of (107), it is obtained in Theorem 4.3 of [6] that, for every subset $\mathcal{A} \subset \{-1,1\}^n$,

$$I(\mathcal{A}) \geq 2 \Pr(\mathcal{A}) \log_2 \frac{1}{\Pr(\mathcal{A})}, \tag{124}$$

where $\Pr(\mathcal{A}) \triangleq \mathbb{P}[X^n \in \mathcal{A}] = \frac{|\mathcal{A}|}{2^n}$ by the equiprobable distribution of X^n over $\{-1,1\}^n$.

In light of Theorem 2, the same approach which is used in Section 4.4 of [6] for the transition from (107) to (124) can be also used to obtain, as a corollary, a lower bound on the average total influence over all subsets of d variables. To this end, let $k_1, \ldots, k_d$ be integers such that $1 \leq k_1 < \ldots < k_d \leq n$, and the influence of the variables in positions $k_1, \ldots, k_d$ be given by

$$I_{(k_1,\ldots,k_d)}(\mathcal{A}) \triangleq \Pr\left[\mathbb{1}\{X^n \in \mathcal{A}\} \neq \mathbb{1}\{\overline{X}^{(k_1,\ldots,k_d)} \in \mathcal{A}\}\right]. \tag{125}$$

Then, let the average influence of subsets of d variables be defined as

$$I^{(n,d)}(\mathcal{A}) \triangleq \frac{1}{\binom{n}{d}} \sum_{\substack{(k_1,\ldots,k_d):\\ 1 \leq k_1 < \ldots < k_d \leq n}} I_{(k_1,\ldots,k_d)}(\mathcal{A}). \tag{126}$$

Hence, by (123) and (126), $I^{(n,1)}(\mathcal{A}) = \frac{1}{n} I(\mathcal{A})$ for every subset $\mathcal{A} \subset \{-1,1\}^n$. Let

$$\mathcal{B}^{(n,d)}(\mathcal{A}) \triangleq \{(x^n, y^n) : x^n \in \mathcal{A}, \ y^n \in \{-1,1\}^n \setminus \mathcal{A}, \ d_H(x^n, y^n) = d\}, \tag{127}$$

be the set of ordered pairs of sequences (x^n, y^n), where $x^n, y^n \in \{-1,1\}^n$ are of Hamming distance d from each other, with $x^n \in \mathcal{A}$ and $y^n \notin \mathcal{A}$. By the equiprobable distribution of X^n on $\{-1,1\}^n$, we get

$$I^{(n,d)}(\mathcal{A}) = \frac{1}{\binom{n}{d}} \sum_{\substack{(k_1,\ldots,k_d):\\ 1 \leq k_1 < \ldots < k_d \leq n}} \Pr\left[\mathbb{1}\{X^n \in \mathcal{A}\} \neq \mathbb{1}\{\overline{X}^{(k_1,\ldots,k_d)} \in \mathcal{A}\}\right] \tag{128a}$$

$$= \frac{2}{\binom{n}{d}} \sum_{\substack{(k_1,\ldots,k_d):\\ 1 \leq k_1 < \ldots < k_d \leq n}} \Pr\left[X^n \in \mathcal{A}, \ \overline{X}^{(k_1,\ldots,k_d)} \notin \mathcal{A}\right] \tag{128b}$$

$$= \frac{2}{\binom{n}{d}} \cdot \frac{|\mathcal{B}^{(n,d)}(\mathcal{A})|}{2^n} \tag{128c}$$

$$= \frac{|\mathcal{B}^{(n,d)}(\mathcal{A})|}{2^{n-1} \binom{n}{d}}. \tag{128d}$$

Since every point in $\mathcal{A}$ has $\binom{n}{d}$ neighbors of Hamming distance d in the set $\{-1,1\}^n$, it follows that

$$\binom{n}{d} |\mathcal{A}| = 2 |\mathsf{E}_d(G)| + |\mathcal{B}^{(n,d)}(\mathcal{A})|, \tag{129}$$

where G is introduced in Theorem 2, and $\mathsf{E}_d(G)$ is the set of edges connecting pairs of vertices in G which are represented by vectors in $\mathcal{A}$ of Hamming distance d. The multiplication by 2 on the RHS of (129) is because every edge whose two endpoints are in the set $\mathcal{A}$ is counted twice. Hence, by (106) and (129),

$$|\mathcal{B}^{(n,d)}(\mathcal{A})| = \binom{n}{d} |\mathcal{A}| - 2 |\mathsf{E}_d(G)| \tag{130a}$$

$$\geq \binom{n}{d} |\mathcal{A}| - \frac{\binom{n-1}{d-1} |\mathcal{A}| \left(\log |\mathcal{A}| - \frac{n}{d} \log \ell_d\right)}{\log \frac{m_d}{\ell_d}} \tag{130b}$$

$$= \binom{n}{d} |\mathcal{A}| \left(1 - \frac{\frac{d}{n} \log |\mathcal{A}| - \log \ell_d}{\log \frac{m_d}{\ell_d}}\right) \tag{130c}$$

$$= \binom{n}{d} |\mathcal{A}| \left(\frac{\log m_d - \frac{d}{n} \log |\mathcal{A}|}{\log \frac{m_d}{\ell_d}}\right), \tag{130d}$$

and the lower bound on the RHS of (130d) is positive if and only if $|\mathcal{A}| < (m_d)^{\frac{n}{d}}$ (see also (114)). This gives from (128) that the average influence of subsets of d variables satisfies

$$I^{(n,d)}(\mathcal{A}) \geq \frac{|\mathcal{A}|}{2^{n-1}} \left(\frac{\log m_d - \frac{d}{n} \log |\mathcal{A}|}{\log \frac{m_d}{\ell_d}} \right) \tag{131a}$$

$$= 2 \Pr(\mathcal{A}) \left(\frac{\log m_d - \frac{d}{n} \log(2^n \Pr(\mathcal{A}))}{\log \frac{m_d}{\ell_d}} \right) \tag{131b}$$

$$= 2 \Pr(\mathcal{A}) \left(\frac{\frac{d}{n} \log \frac{1}{\Pr(\mathcal{A})} - \log \frac{2^d}{m_d}}{\log \frac{m_d}{\ell_d}} \right). \tag{131c}$$

Note that by setting $d = 1$, and the default values $m_d = 2$ and $\ell_d = 1$ on the RHS of (131c) gives the total influence of the n variables satisfies, for all $\mathcal{A} \subseteq \{-1,1\}^n$,

$$I(\mathcal{A}) = n I^{(n,1)}(\mathcal{A}) \tag{132a}$$

$$\geq 2 \Pr(\mathcal{A}) \log_2 \frac{1}{\Pr(\mathcal{A})}, \tag{132b}$$

which is then specialized to the result in (Theorem 4.3 of [6], see (124)). This gives the following result.

Theorem 3. *Let X^n be an equiprobable random vector over the set $\{-1,1\}^n$, let $d \in [n]$ and $\mathcal{A} \subset \{-1,1\}^n$. Then, the average influence of subsets of d variables of X^n, as it is defined in (126), is lower bounded as follows:*

$$I^{(n,d)}(\mathcal{A}) \geq 2 \Pr(\mathcal{A}) \left(\frac{\frac{d}{n} \log \frac{1}{\Pr(\mathcal{A})} - \log \frac{2^d}{m_d}}{\log \frac{m_d}{\ell_d}} \right), \tag{133}$$

where $\Pr(\mathcal{A}) \triangleq \mathbb{P}[X^n \in \mathcal{A}] = \frac{|\mathcal{A}|}{2^n}$, and the integers m_d and ℓ_d are introduced in Theorem 2. Similarly to the refined upper bound in Theorem 2, the lower bound on the RHS of (133) is informative (i.e., positive) if and only if $|\mathcal{A}| < (m_d)^{\frac{n}{d}}$. The lower bound on the RHS of (133) can be loosened (by setting the default values $m_d = 2$ and $\ell_d = 1$) to

$$I^{(n,d)}(\mathcal{A}) \geq 2 \Pr(\mathcal{A}) \left(\frac{d}{n} \log_2 \frac{1}{\Pr(\mathcal{A})} + 1 - d \right). \tag{134}$$

Funding: This research received no external funding.

Institutional Review Board Statement: Not applicable.

Informed Consent Statement: Not applicable.

Data Availability Statement: Not applicable.

Conflicts of Interest: The author declares no conflict of interest.

Appendix A. Proof of Proposition 1

For completeness, we prove Proposition 1 which introduces results from [25,28,37].

Let Ω be a non-empty finite set, and let $\{X_\omega\}_{\omega \in \Omega}$ be a collection of discrete random variables. We first prove Item (a), showing that the entropy set function $f \colon 2^\Omega \to \mathbb{R}$ in (15) is a rank function.

- $f(\varnothing) = 0$.

- Submodularity: If $\mathcal{S}, \mathcal{T} \subseteq \Omega$, then

$$
\begin{align}
f(\mathcal{T} \cup \mathcal{S}) &+ f(\mathcal{T} \cap \mathcal{S}) \notag \\
&= H(X_{\mathcal{T} \cup \mathcal{S}}) + H(X_{\mathcal{T} \cap \mathcal{S}}) \tag{A1a} \\
&= H(X_{\mathcal{T} \setminus \mathcal{S}}, X_{\mathcal{T} \cap \mathcal{S}}, X_{\mathcal{S} \setminus \mathcal{T}}) + H(X_{\mathcal{T} \cap \mathcal{S}}) \tag{A1b} \\
&= H(X_{\mathcal{T} \setminus \mathcal{S}}, X_{\mathcal{S} \setminus \mathcal{T}} | X_{\mathcal{T} \cap \mathcal{S}}) + 2 H(X_{\mathcal{T} \cap \mathcal{S}}) \tag{A1c} \\
&= \left[H(X_{\mathcal{T} \setminus \mathcal{S}} | X_{\mathcal{T} \cap \mathcal{S}}) + H(X_{\mathcal{S} \setminus \mathcal{T}} | X_{\mathcal{T} \cap \mathcal{S}}) - I(X_{\mathcal{T} \setminus \mathcal{S}}; X_{\mathcal{S} \setminus \mathcal{T}} | X_{\mathcal{T} \cap \mathcal{S}}) \right] \notag \\
&\quad + 2 H(X_{\mathcal{T} \cap \mathcal{S}}) \tag{A1d} \\
&= \left[H(X_{\mathcal{T} \setminus \mathcal{S}} | X_{\mathcal{T} \cap \mathcal{S}}) + H(X_{\mathcal{T} \cap \mathcal{S}}) \right] + \left[H(X_{\mathcal{S} \setminus \mathcal{T}} | X_{\mathcal{T} \cap \mathcal{S}}) + H(X_{\mathcal{T} \cap \mathcal{S}}) \right] \notag \\
&\quad - I(X_{\mathcal{T} \setminus \mathcal{S}}; X_{\mathcal{S} \setminus \mathcal{T}} | X_{\mathcal{T} \cap \mathcal{S}}) \tag{A1e} \\
&= H(X_{\mathcal{T} \setminus \mathcal{S}}, X_{\mathcal{T} \cap \mathcal{S}}) + H(X_{\mathcal{S} \setminus \mathcal{T}}, X_{\mathcal{T} \cap \mathcal{S}}) - I(X_{\mathcal{T} \setminus \mathcal{S}}; X_{\mathcal{S} \setminus \mathcal{T}} | X_{\mathcal{T} \cap \mathcal{S}}) \tag{A1f} \\
&= H(X_{\mathcal{T}}) + H(X_{\mathcal{S}}) - I(X_{\mathcal{T} \setminus \mathcal{S}}; X_{\mathcal{S} \setminus \mathcal{T}} | X_{\mathcal{T} \cap \mathcal{S}}) \tag{A1g} \\
&= f(\mathcal{T}) + f(\mathcal{S}) - I(X_{\mathcal{T} \setminus \mathcal{S}}; X_{\mathcal{S} \setminus \mathcal{T}} | X_{\mathcal{T} \cap \mathcal{S}}), \tag{A1h}
\end{align}
$$

which gives

$$
f(\mathcal{T}) + f(\mathcal{S}) - \left[f(\mathcal{T} \cup \mathcal{S}) + f(\mathcal{T} \cap \mathcal{S}) \right] = I(X_{\mathcal{T} \setminus \mathcal{S}}; X_{\mathcal{S} \setminus \mathcal{T}} | X_{\mathcal{T} \cap \mathcal{S}}) \geq 0. \tag{A2}
$$

This proves the submodularity of f, while also showing that

$$
f(\mathcal{T}) + f(\mathcal{S}) = f(\mathcal{T} \cup \mathcal{S}) + f(\mathcal{T} \cap \mathcal{S}) \iff X_{\mathcal{T} \setminus \mathcal{S}} \perp\!\!\!\perp X_{\mathcal{S} \setminus \mathcal{T}} | X_{\mathcal{T} \cap \mathcal{S}}, \tag{A3}
$$

i.e., the rightmost side of (A2) holds with equality if and only if $X_{\mathcal{T} \setminus \mathcal{S}}$ and $X_{\mathcal{S} \setminus \mathcal{T}}$ are conditionally independent given $X_{\mathcal{T} \cap \mathcal{S}}$.

- Monotonicity: If $\mathcal{S} \subseteq \mathcal{T} \subseteq \Omega$, then

$$
\begin{align}
f(\mathcal{S}) &= H(X_{\mathcal{S}}) \tag{A4a} \\
&\leq H(X_{\mathcal{S}}) + H(X_{\mathcal{T}} | X_{\mathcal{S}}) \tag{A4b} \\
&= H(X_{\mathcal{T}}) \tag{A4c} \\
&= f(\mathcal{T}), \tag{A4d}
\end{align}
$$

so f is monotonically increasing.

We next prove Item (b). Consider the set function f in (16).

- $f(\varnothing) = 0$, and $f(\Omega) = H(X_\Omega)$.
- Supermodularity: If $\mathcal{S}, \mathcal{T} \subseteq \Omega$, then

$$
\begin{align}
f(\mathcal{T} \cup \mathcal{S}) + f(\mathcal{T} \cap \mathcal{S}) &= H(X_{\mathcal{T} \cup \mathcal{S}} | X_{\mathcal{T}^c \cap \mathcal{S}^c}) + H(X_{\mathcal{T} \cap \mathcal{S}} | X_{\mathcal{T}^c \cup \mathcal{S}^c}) \tag{A5a} \\
&= \left[H(X_\Omega) - H(X_{\mathcal{T}^c \cap \mathcal{S}^c}) \right] + \left[H(X_\Omega) - H(X_{\mathcal{T}^c \cup \mathcal{S}^c}) \right] \tag{A5b} \\
&= 2 H(X_\Omega) - \left[H(X_{\mathcal{T}^c \cup \mathcal{S}^c}) + H(X_{\mathcal{T}^c \cap \mathcal{S}^c}) \right] \tag{A5c} \\
&\geq 2 H(X_\Omega) - \left[H(X_{\mathcal{T}^c}) + H(X_{\mathcal{S}^c}) \right] \tag{A5d} \\
&= \left[H(X_\Omega) - H(X_{\mathcal{T}^c}) \right] + \left[H(X_\Omega) - H(X_{\mathcal{S}^c}) \right] \tag{A5e} \\
&= H(X_{\mathcal{T}} | X_{\mathcal{T}^c}) + H(X_{\mathcal{S}} | X_{\mathcal{S}^c}) \tag{A5f} \\
&= f(\mathcal{T}) + f(\mathcal{S}), \tag{A5g}
\end{align}
$$

where inequality (A5d) holds since the entropy function in (15) is submodular (by Item (a)).

- Monotonicity: If $\mathcal{S} \subseteq \mathcal{T} \subseteq \Omega$, then

$$f(\mathcal{S}) = H(X_\mathcal{S} | X_{\mathcal{S}^c}) \tag{A6a}$$

$$\leq H(X_\mathcal{S} | X_{\mathcal{T}^c}) \quad (\mathcal{T}^c \subseteq \mathcal{S}^c) \tag{A6b}$$

$$\leq H(X_\mathcal{T} | X_{\mathcal{T}^c}) \tag{A6c}$$

$$= f(\mathcal{T}), \tag{A6d}$$

so f is monotonically increasing.

Item (c) follows easily from Items (a) and (b). Consider the set function $f: 2^\Omega \to \mathbb{R}$ in (17). Then, for all $\mathcal{T} \in \Omega$, $f(\mathcal{T}) = I(X_\mathcal{T}; X_{\mathcal{T}^c}) = H(X_\mathcal{T}) - H(X_\mathcal{T} | X_{\mathcal{T}^c})$, so f is expressed as a difference of a submodular function and a supermodular function, which gives a submodular function. Furthermore, $f(\varnothing) = 0$; by the symmetry of the mutual information, $f(\mathcal{T}) = f(\mathcal{T}^c)$ for all $\mathcal{T} \subseteq \Omega$, so f is not monotonic.

We next prove Item (d). Consider the set function $f: 2^\mathcal{V} \to \mathbb{R}$ in (18), and we need to prove that f is submodular under the conditions in Item (d) where $\mathcal{U}, \mathcal{V} \subseteq \Omega$ are disjoint subsets, and the entries of the random vector $X_\mathcal{V}$ are conditionally independent given $X_\mathcal{U}$.

- $f(\varnothing) = I(X_\mathcal{U}; X_\varnothing) = 0$.
- Submodularity: If $\mathcal{S}, \mathcal{T} \subseteq \mathcal{V}$, then

$$f(\mathcal{T} \cup \mathcal{S}) + f(\mathcal{T} \cap \mathcal{S})$$

$$= I(X_\mathcal{U}; X_{\mathcal{T} \cup \mathcal{S}}) + I(X_\mathcal{U}; X_{\mathcal{T} \cap \mathcal{S}}) \tag{A7a}$$

$$= [H(X_{\mathcal{T} \cup \mathcal{S}}) - H(X_{\mathcal{T} \cup \mathcal{S}} | X_\mathcal{U})] + [H(X_{\mathcal{T} \cap \mathcal{S}}) - H(X_{\mathcal{T} \cap \mathcal{S}} | X_\mathcal{U})] \tag{A7b}$$

$$= [H(X_{\mathcal{T} \cup \mathcal{S}}) + H(X_{\mathcal{T} \cap \mathcal{S}})] - [H(X_{\mathcal{T} \cup \mathcal{S}} | X_\mathcal{U}) + H(X_{\mathcal{T} \cap \mathcal{S}} | X_\mathcal{U})] \tag{A7c}$$

$$= [H(X_\mathcal{T}) + H(X_\mathcal{S}) - I(X_{\mathcal{T} \setminus \mathcal{S}}; X_{\mathcal{S} \setminus \mathcal{T}} | X_{\mathcal{T} \cap \mathcal{S}})]$$
$$- [H(X_{\mathcal{T} \cup \mathcal{S}} | X_\mathcal{U}) + H(X_{\mathcal{T} \cap \mathcal{S}} | X_\mathcal{U})], \tag{A7d}$$

where equality (A7d) holds by the proof of Item (a) (see (A2)). By the assumption on the conditional independence of the random variables $\{X_v\}_{v \in \mathcal{V}}$ given $X_\mathcal{U}$, we get

$$H(X_{\mathcal{T} \cup \mathcal{S}} | X_\mathcal{U}) + H(X_{\mathcal{T} \cap \mathcal{S}} | X_\mathcal{U}) = \sum_{\omega \in \mathcal{T} \cup \mathcal{S}} H(X_\omega | X_\mathcal{U}) + \sum_{\omega \in \mathcal{T} \cap \mathcal{S}} H(X_\omega | X_\mathcal{U}) \tag{A8a}$$

$$= \sum_{\omega \in \mathcal{T}} H(X_\omega | X_\mathcal{U}) + \sum_{\omega \in \mathcal{S}} H(X_\omega | X_\mathcal{U}) \tag{A8b}$$

$$= H(X_\mathcal{T} | X_\mathcal{U}) + H(X_\mathcal{S} | X_\mathcal{U}). \tag{A8c}$$

Consequently, combining (A7) and (A8) gives

$$f(\mathcal{T} \cup \mathcal{S}) + f(\mathcal{T} \cap \mathcal{S}) = [H(X_\mathcal{T}) + H(X_\mathcal{S}) - I(X_{\mathcal{T} \setminus \mathcal{S}}; X_{\mathcal{S} \setminus \mathcal{T}} | X_{\mathcal{T} \cap \mathcal{S}})]$$
$$- [H(X_\mathcal{T} | X_\mathcal{U}) + H(X_\mathcal{S} | X_\mathcal{U})] \tag{A9a}$$

$$= [H(X_\mathcal{T}) - H(X_\mathcal{T} | X_\mathcal{U})] + [H(X_\mathcal{S}) - H(X_\mathcal{S} | X_\mathcal{U})]$$
$$- I(X_{\mathcal{T} \setminus \mathcal{S}}; X_{\mathcal{S} \setminus \mathcal{T}} | X_{\mathcal{T} \cap \mathcal{S}}) \tag{A9b}$$

$$= I(X_\mathcal{T}; X_\mathcal{U}) + I(X_\mathcal{S}; X_\mathcal{U}) - I(X_{\mathcal{T} \setminus \mathcal{S}}; X_{\mathcal{S} \setminus \mathcal{T}} | X_{\mathcal{T} \cap \mathcal{S}}) \tag{A9c}$$

$$= f(\mathcal{T}) + f(\mathcal{S}) - I(X_{\mathcal{T} \setminus \mathcal{S}}; X_{\mathcal{S} \setminus \mathcal{T}} | X_{\mathcal{T} \cap \mathcal{S}}) \tag{A9d}$$

$$\leq f(\mathcal{T}) + f(\mathcal{S}), \tag{A9e}$$

where the inequality (A9e) holds with equality if and only if $X_{\mathcal{T} \setminus \mathcal{S}}$ and $X_{\mathcal{S} \setminus \mathcal{T}}$ are conditionally independent given $X_{\mathcal{T} \cap \mathcal{S}}$.

- Monotonicity: If $\mathcal{S} \subseteq \mathcal{T} \subseteq \mathcal{V}$, then

$$f(\mathcal{S}) = I(X_{\mathcal{U}}; X_{\mathcal{S}}) \leq I(X_{\mathcal{U}}; X_{\mathcal{T}}) = f(\mathcal{T}), \tag{A10}$$

so f is monotonically increasing.

We finally prove Item (e), where it is needed to show that the entropy of a sum of independent random variables is a rank function. Let $f \colon 2^{\Omega} \to \mathbb{R}$ be the set function as given in (19).

- $f(\emptyset) = 0$.
- Submodularity: Let $\mathcal{S}, \mathcal{T} \subseteq \Omega$. Define

$$U \triangleq \sum_{\omega \in \mathcal{T} \cap \mathcal{S}} X_{\omega}, \quad V \triangleq \sum_{\omega \in \mathcal{S} \setminus \mathcal{T}} X_{\omega}, \quad W \triangleq \sum_{\omega \in \mathcal{T} \setminus \mathcal{S}} X_{\omega}. \tag{A11}$$

From the independence of the random variables $\{X_{\omega}\}_{\omega \in \Omega}$, it follows that U, V and W are independent. Hence, we get

$$\begin{aligned}
&[f(\mathcal{T}) + f(\mathcal{S})] - [f(\mathcal{T} \cup \mathcal{S}) + f(\mathcal{T} \cap \mathcal{S})] \\
&= [f(\mathcal{T}) - f(\mathcal{T} \cap \mathcal{S})] - [f(\mathcal{T} \cup \mathcal{S}) - f(\mathcal{S})] & \text{(A12a)} \\
&= [H(U + W) - H(U)] - [H(U + V + W) - H(U + V)] & \text{(A12b)} \\
&= [H(U + W) - H(U + W|W)] - [H(U + V + W) - H(U + V)] & \text{(A12c)} \\
&= [H(U + W) - H(U + W|W)] - [H(U + V + W) - H(U + V + W|W)] & \text{(A12d)} \\
&= I(U + W; W) - I(U + V + W; W) & \text{(A12e)} \\
&\geq I(U + W; W) - I(U + W, V; W), & \text{(A12f)}
\end{aligned}$$

and

$$\begin{aligned}
I(U + W, V; W) &= I(V; W) + I(U + W; W | V) & \text{(A13a)} \\
&= I(U + W; W | V) & \text{(A13b)} \\
&= I(U + W; W). & \text{(A13c)}
\end{aligned}$$

Combining (A12) and (A13) gives (11).

- Monotonicity: If $\mathcal{S} \subseteq \mathcal{T} \subseteq \Omega$, then since $\{X_{\omega}\}_{\omega \in \Omega}$ are independent random variables, (A11) implies that U and W are independent and $V = 0$. Hence,

$$\begin{aligned}
f(\mathcal{T}) - f(\mathcal{S}) &= H(U + W) - H(U) & \text{(A14a)} \\
&= H(U + W) - H(U + W | W) & \text{(A14b)} \\
&= I(U + W; W) \geq 0. & \text{(A14c)}
\end{aligned}$$

This completes the proof of Proposition 1.

Appendix B. Proof of Proposition 4

Lemma A1. *Let $\{\mathcal{B}_j\}_{j=1}^{\ell}$ (with $\ell \geq 2$) be a sequence of sets that is not a chain (i.e., there is no permutation $\pi \colon [\ell] \to [\ell]$ such that $\mathcal{B}_{\pi(1)} \subseteq \mathcal{B}_{\pi(2)} \subseteq \ldots \subseteq \mathcal{B}_{\pi(\ell)}$). Consider a recursive process where, at each step, a pair of sets that are not related by inclusion is replaced with their intersection and union. Then, there exists such a recursive process that leads to a chain in a finite number of steps.*

Proof. The lemma is proved by mathematical induction on ℓ. It holds for $\ell = 2$ since $\mathcal{B}_1 \cap \mathcal{B}_2 \subseteq \mathcal{B}_1 \cup \mathcal{B}_2$, and the process halts in a single step. Suppose that the lemma holds with a fixed $\ell \geq 2$, and for an arbitrary sequence of ℓ sets which is not a chain. We aim to show that it also holds for every sequence of $\ell + 1$ sets which is not a chain. Let $\{\mathcal{B}_j\}_{j=1}^{\ell+1}$

be such an arbitrary sequence of sets, and consider the subsequence of the first ℓ sets $\mathcal{B}_1, \ldots, \mathcal{B}_\ell$. If it is not a chain, then (by the induction hypothesis) there exists a recursive process as above which enables to transform it into a chain in a finite number of steps, i.e., we get a chain $\mathcal{B}'_1 \subseteq \mathcal{B}'_2 \subseteq \ldots \subseteq \mathcal{B}'_\ell$. If $\mathcal{B}'_\ell \subseteq \mathcal{B}_{\ell+1}$ or $\mathcal{B}_{\ell+1} \subseteq \mathcal{B}'_1$, then we get a chain of $\ell+1$ sets. Otherwise, by proceeding with the recursive process where $\mathcal{B}'_\ell$ and $\mathcal{B}_{\ell+1}$ are replaced with their intersection and union, consider the sequence

$$\mathcal{B}'_1, \ldots, \mathcal{B}'_{\ell-1}, \mathcal{B}'_\ell \cap \mathcal{B}_{\ell+1}, \mathcal{B}'_\ell \cup \mathcal{B}_{\ell+1}. \tag{A15}$$

By the induction hypothesis, the first ℓ sets in this sequence can be transformed into a chain (in a finite number of steps) by a recursive process as above; this gives a chain of the form $\mathcal{B}''_1 \subseteq \mathcal{B}''_2 \ldots \subseteq \mathcal{B}''_{\ell-1} \subseteq \mathcal{B}''_\ell$. The first ℓ sets in (A15) are all included in $\mathcal{B}'_\ell$, so every combination of unions and intersections of these ℓ sets is also included in $\mathcal{B}'_\ell$. Hence, the considered recursive process leads to a chain of the form

$$\mathcal{B}''_1 \subseteq \mathcal{B}''_2 \ldots \subseteq \mathcal{B}''_{\ell-1} \subseteq \mathcal{B}''_\ell \subseteq \mathcal{B}'_\ell \cup \mathcal{B}_{\ell+1}, \tag{A16}$$

where the last inclusion in (A16) holds since $\mathcal{B}''_\ell \subseteq \mathcal{B}'_\ell$. The claim thus holds for $\ell+1$ if it holds for a given ℓ, and it holds for $\ell = 2$, it therefore holds by mathematical induction for all integers $\ell \geq 2$. □

We first prove Proposition 4a. Suppose that there is a permutation $\pi \colon [M] \to [M]$ such that $\mathcal{S}_{\pi(1)} \subseteq \mathcal{S}_{\pi(2)} \subseteq \ldots \subseteq \mathcal{S}_{\pi(M)}$ is a chain. Since every element in Ω is included in at least d of these subsets, then it should be included in (at least) the d largest sets of this chain, so $\mathcal{S}_{\pi(j)} = \Omega$ for every $j \in [M-d+1 : M]$. Due to the non-negativity of f, it follows that

$$\sum_{j=1}^{M} f(\mathcal{S}_j) \geq \sum_{j=M-d+1}^{M} f(\mathcal{S}_{\pi(j)}) \tag{A17a}$$

$$= d\, f(\Omega). \tag{A17b}$$

Otherwise, if we cannot get a chain by possibly permuting the subsets in the sequence $\{\mathcal{S}_j\}_{j=1}^M$, consider a pair of subsets $\mathcal{S}_n$ and $\mathcal{S}_m$ that are not related by inclusion, and replace them with their intersection and union. By the submodularity of f,

$$\sum_{j=1}^{M} f(\mathcal{S}_j) = \sum_{j \neq n,m} f(\mathcal{S}_j) + f(\mathcal{S}_n) + f(\mathcal{S}_m) \tag{A18a}$$

$$\geq \sum_{j \neq n,m} f(\mathcal{S}_j) + f(\mathcal{S}_n \cap \mathcal{S}_m) + f(\mathcal{S}_n \cup \mathcal{S}_m). \tag{A18b}$$

For all $\omega \in \Omega$, let $\deg(\omega)$ be the number of indices $j \in [M]$ such that $\omega \in \mathcal{S}_j$. By replacing $\mathcal{S}_n$ and $\mathcal{S}_m$ with $\mathcal{S}_n \cap \mathcal{S}_m$ and $\mathcal{S}_n \cup \mathcal{S}_m$, the set of values $\{\deg(\omega)\}_{\omega \in \Omega}$ stays unaffected (indeed, if $\omega \in \mathcal{S}_n$ and $\omega \in \mathcal{S}_m$, then it belongs to their intersection and union; if ω belongs to only one of the sets $\mathcal{S}_n$ and $\mathcal{S}_m$, then $\omega \notin \mathcal{S}_n \cap \mathcal{S}_m$ and $\omega \in \mathcal{S}_n \cup \mathcal{S}_m$; finally, if $\omega \notin \mathcal{S}_n$ and $\omega \notin \mathcal{S}_m$, then it does not belong to their intersection and union). Now, consider the recursive process in Lemma A1. Since the profile of the number of inclusions of the elements in Ω is preserved in each step of the recursive process in Lemma A1, it follows that every element in Ω stays to belong to at least d sets in the chain which is obtained at the end of this recursive process. Moreover, in light of (A18), in every step of the recursive process in Lemma A1, the sum in the LHS of (A18) cannot increase. Inequality (45) therefore finally follows from the earlier part of the proof for a chain (see (A17)).

We next prove Proposition 4b. Let $\mathcal{A} \subset \Omega$, and suppose that every element in $\mathcal{A}$ is included in at least $d \geq 1$ of the subsets $\{\mathcal{S}_j\}_{j=1}^M$. For all $j \in [M]$, define $\mathcal{S}'_j \triangleq \mathcal{S}_j \cap \mathcal{A}$, and consider the sequence $\{\mathcal{S}'_j\}_{j=1}^M$ of subsets of $\mathcal{A}$. If f is a rank function, then it is monotonically increasing, which yields

$$f(\mathcal{S}'_j) \leq f(\mathcal{S}_j), \qquad j \in [M]. \tag{A19}$$

Each element of $\mathcal{A}$ is also included in at least d of the subsets $\{\mathcal{S}'_j\}_{j=1}^M$ (by construction, and since (by assumption) each element in $\mathcal{A}$ is included in at least d of the subsets $\{\mathcal{S}_j\}_{j=1}^M$). By the non-negativity and submodularity of f, Proposition 4a gives

$$\sum_{j=1}^M f(\mathcal{S}'_j) \geq d\, f(\mathcal{A}). \tag{A20}$$

Combining (A19) and (A20) yields (46). This completes the proof of Proposition 4.

Remark A1. *Lemma A1 is weaker than a claim that, in every recursive process as in Lemma A1, the number of pairs of sets that are not related by inclusion is strictly decreasing at each step. Lemma A1 is, however, sufficient for our proof of Proposition 4a.*

References

1. Cover, T.M.; Thomas, J.A. *Elements of Information Theory*, 2nd ed.; John Wiley & Sons: Hoboken, NJ, USA, 2006. [CrossRef]
2. Dembo, A.; Cover, T.M.; Thomas, J.A. Information theoretic inequalities. *IEEE Trans. Inf. Theory* **1991**, *37*, 1501–1518. [CrossRef]
3. Chan, T. Recent progresses in characterising information inequalities. *Entropy* **2011**, *13*, 379–401. [CrossRef] [CrossRef]
4. Martin, S.; Padró, C.; Yang, A. Secret sharing, rank inequalities, and information inequalities. *IEEE Trans. Inf. Theory* **2016**, *62*, 599–610. [CrossRef]
5. Babu, S.A.; Radhakrishnan, J. An entropy-based proof for the Moore bound for irregular graphs. In *Perspectives on Computational Complexity*; Agrawal, M., Arvind, V., Eds.; Birkhäuser: Cham, Switzerland, 2014; pp. 173–182.
6. Boucheron, S.; Lugosi, G.; Massart, P. *Concentration Inequalities - A Nonasymptotic Theory of Independence*; Oxford University Press: Oxford, UK, 2013.
7. Chung, F.R.K.; Graham, L.R.; Frankl, P.; Shearer, J.B. Some intersection theorems for ordered sets and graphs. *J. Comb. Theory Ser. A* **1986**, *43*, 23–37. [CrossRef]
8. Erdős, P.; Rényi, A. On two problems of information theory. *Publ. Math. Inst. Hung. Acad. Sci.* **1963**, *8*, 241–254.
9. Friedgut, E. Hypergraphs, entropy and inequalities. *Am. Math. Mon.* **2004**, *111*, 749–760. [CrossRef]
10. Jukna, S. *Extremal Combinatorics with Applications in Computer Science*, 2nd ed.; Springer: Berlin/Heidelberg, Germany, 2011.
11. Kaced, T.; Romashchenko, A.; Vereshchagin, N. A conditional information inequality and its combinatorial applications. *IEEE Trans. Inf. Theory* **2018**, *64*, 3610–3615. [CrossRef]
12. Kahn, J. An entropy approach to the hard-core model on bipartite graphs. *Comb. Comput.* **2001**, *10*, 219–237. [CrossRef]
13. Kahn, J. Entropy, independent sets and antichains: A new approach to Dedekind's problem. *Proc. Am. Math. Soc.* **2001**, *130*, 371–378. [CrossRef]
14. Madiman, M.; Marcus, A.W.; Tetali, P. Entropy and set cardinality inequalities for partition-determined functions. *Random Struct. Algorithms* **2012**, *40*, 399–424. [CrossRef]
15. Madiman, M.; Marcus, A.W.; Tetali, P. Information–theoretic inequalities in additive combinatorics. In Proceedings of the 2010 IEEE Information Theory Workshop, Cairo, Egypt, 6–8 January 2010. [CrossRef]
16. Pippenger, N. An information–theoretic method in combinatorial theory. *J. Comb. Ser. A* **1977**, *23*, 99–104. [CrossRef]
17. Pippenger, N. Entropy and enumeration of boolean functions. *IEEE Trans. Inf. Theory* **1999**, *45*, 2096–2100. [CrossRef]
18. Radhakrishnan, J. An entropy proof of Bregman's theorem. *J. Comb. Theory Ser. A* **1997**, *77*, 161–164. [CrossRef]
19. Radhakrishnan, J. Entropy and counting. In *Computational Mathematics, Modelling and Algorithms*; Narosa Publishers: New Delhi, India, 2001; pp. 1–25.
20. Sason, I. A generalized information–theoretic approach for bounding the number of independent sets in bipartite graphs. *Entropy* **2021**, *23*, 270. [CrossRef]
21. Sason, I. Entropy-based proofs of combinatorial results on bipartite graphs. In Proceedings of the 2021 IEEE International Symposium on Information Theory, Melbourne, Australia, 12–20 July 2021; pp. 3225–3230. [CrossRef]
22. Madiman, M.; Tetali, P. Information inequalities for joint distributions, interpretations and applications. *IEEE Trans. Inf. Theory* **2010**, *56*, 2699–2713. [CrossRef]
23. Bach, F. Learning with submodular functions: A convex optimization perspective. *Found. Trends Mach. Learn.* **2013**, *6*, 145–373. [CrossRef]
24. Chen, Q.; Cheng, M.; Bai, B. Matroidal entropy functions: A quartet of theories of information, matroid, design and coding. *Entropy* **2021**, *23*, 323. [CrossRef]

25. Fujishige, S. Polymatroidal dependence structure of a set of random variables. *Inf. Control.* **1978**, *39*, 55–72. [CrossRef]
26. Fujishige, S. *Submodular Functions and Optimization*, 2nd ed.; Annals of Discrete Mathematics Series; Elsevier: Amsterdam, The Netherlands, 2005; Volume 58.
27. Iyer, R.; Khargonkar, N.; Bilems, J.; Asnani, H. Generalized submodular information measures: Theoretical properties, examples, optimization algorithms, and applications. *IEEE Trans. Inf. Theory* **2022**, *68*, 752–781. [CrossRef]
28. Krause, A.; Guestrin, C. Near-optimal nonmyopic value of information in graphical models. In Proceedings of the Twenty-First Conference on Uncertainty in Artificial Intelligence (UAI 2005), Edinburgh, Scotland, UK, 26–29 July 2005; pp. 324–331. [CrossRef]
29. Lovász, L. Submodular functions and convexity. In *Mathematical Programming The State of the Art*; Bachem, A.; Korte, B.; Grotschel, M., Eds.; Springer: Berlin/Heidelberg, Germany, 1983; pp. 235–257. [CrossRef]
30. Tian, C. Inequalities for entropies of sets of subsets of random variables. In Proceedings of the 2011 IEEE International Symposium on Information Theory, Saint Petersburg, Russia, 31 July–5 August 2011; pp. 1950–1954. [CrossRef]
31. Kishi, Y.; Ochiumi, N.; Yanagida, M. Entropy inequalities for sums over several subsets and their applications to average entropy. In Proceedings of the 2014 IEEE International Symposium on Information Theory (ISIT 2014), Honolulu, HI, USA, 30 June–4 July 2014; pp. 2824–2828. [CrossRef]
32. Shannon, C.E. A Mathematical Theory of Communication. *Bell Syst. Tech. J.* **1948**, *27*, 379–423. 623–656. [CrossRef]
33. Madiman, M.; Mellbourne, J.; Xeng, P. Forward and reverse entropy power inequalities in convex geometry. In *Convexity and Concentration*; Carlen, E.; Madiman, M.; Werner, E.M., Eds.; IMA Volumes in Mathematics and Its Applications; Springer: Berlin/Heidelberg, Germany, 2017; Volume 161; pp. 427–485.
34. Han, T.S. Nonnegative entropy measures of multivariate symmetric correlations. *Inf. Control.* **1978**, *36*, 133–156. [CrossRef]
35. Polyanskiy, Y.; Wu, Y. Lecture Notes on Information Theory, version 5. Available online: http://people.lids.mit.edu/yp/homepage/data/itlectures_v5.pdf (accessed on May 15, 2019).
36. Bollobás, B. *Extremal Graph Theory*; Academic Press: Cambridge, MA, USA, 1978.
37. Madiman, M. On the entropy of sums. In Proceedings of the 2008 IEEE Information Theory Workshop, Porto, Portugal, 5–9 May 2008. [CrossRef]
38. Tao, T. Sumset and inverse sumset theory for Shannon entropy. *Comb. Comput.* **2010**, *19*, 603–639. [CrossRef]
39. Kontoyiannis, I.; Madiman, M. Sumset and inverse sumset inequalities for differential entropy and mutual information. *IEEE Trans. Inf. Theory* **2014**, *60*, 4503–4514. [CrossRef]
40. Artstein, S.; Ball, K.M.; Barthe, F.; Naor, A. Solution of Shannon's problem on the monotonicity of entropy. *J. Am. Soc.* **2004**, *17*, 975–982. [CrossRef]
41. Madiman, M.; Barron, A. Generalized entropy power inequalities and monotonicity properties of information. *IEEE Trans. Inf. Theory* **2007**, *53*, 2317–2329. [CrossRef]

Article

A Skew Logistic Distribution for Modelling COVID-19 Waves and Its Evaluation Using the Empirical Survival Jensen–Shannon Divergence

Mark Levene

Department of Computer Science and Information Systems, Birkbeck, University of London, London WC1E 7HX, UK; mlevene@dcs.bbk.ac.uk

Abstract: A novel yet simple extension of the symmetric logistic distribution is proposed by introducing a skewness parameter. It is shown how the three parameters of the ensuing skew logistic distribution may be estimated using maximum likelihood. The skew logistic distribution is then extended to the skew bi-logistic distribution to allow the modelling of multiple waves in epidemic time series data. The proposed skew-logistic model is validated on COVID-19 data from the UK, and is evaluated for goodness-of-fit against the logistic and normal distributions using the recently formulated empirical survival Jensen–Shannon divergence ($\mathcal{ESJS}$) and the Kolmogorov–Smirnov two-sample test statistic ($KS2$). We employ 95% bootstrap confidence intervals to assess the improvement in goodness-of-fit of the skew logistic distribution over the other distributions. The obtained confidence intervals for the $\mathcal{ESJS}$ are narrower than those for the $KS2$ on using this dataset, implying that the $\mathcal{ESJS}$ is more powerful than the $KS2$.

Keywords: empirical survival Jensen–Shannon divergence; Kolmogorov–Smirnov two-sample test; skew logistic distribution; bi-logistic growth; epidemic waves; COVID-19 data

1. Introduction

In exponential growth, the population grows at a rate proportional to its current size. This is unrealistic, since in reality, growth will not exceed some maximum, called its carrying capacity. The logistic equation [1] (Chapter 6) deals with this problem by ensuring that the growth rate of the population decreases once the population reaches its carrying capacity [2]. Statistical modelling of the logistic equation's growth and decay is accomplished with the *logistic distribution* [3] and [4] (Chapter 22), noting that the tails of the logistic distribution are heavier than those of the ubiquitous normal distribution. The normal and logistic distributions are both symmetric, however, real data often exhibits skewness [5], which has given rise to extensions of the normal distribution to accommodate for skewness, as in the skew normal [6] and epsilon skew normal [7] distributions. Subsequently, skew logistic distributions were also devised, as in [8,9].

Epidemics, such as COVID-19, are traditionally modelled by compartmental models such as the SIR (Susceptible-Infected-Removed) model and its extension, the SEIR (Susceptible-Exposed-Infected-Removed) model, which estimate the trajectory of an epidemic [10]. These models typically rely on assumptions on how the disease is transmitted and progresses [11], and are routinely used to understand the consequences of policies such as mask wearing and social distancing [12]. Time series models [13], on the other hand, employ historical data to make forecasts about the future, are generally simpler than compartmental models, and are able to make forecasts on, for example, number of cases, hospitalisations and deaths. The SIR model can be interpreted as a logistic growth model [14,15]. However, as the data is inherently skewed, a skewed logistic statistical model would be a natural choice, although, as such, it does not rely on biological assumptions in its forecasts [16].

Herein, we present a novel yet simple (one may argue the simplest), three parameter skewed extension to the logistic distribution to allow for asymmetry; c.f. [16]. Nevertheless, if instead of our extension we deploy one of the other skew logistic distributions (such as the one described in [8]) the results would no doubt be comparable to the results we obtain herein; however, we pursue our simpler extension, detailing its statistical properties.

In the context of analysing epidemics, the logistic distribution is normally preferred, as it is a natural distribution to use in modelling population growth and decay. However, we still briefly mention a comparison of the results we obtain in modelling COVID-19 waves with the skew logistic distribution, to one which, instead, employs a skew normal distribution (more specifically we choose the, flexible, epsilon skew normal distribution [7]). The result of this comparison implies that utilising the epsilon skew normal distribution leads, overall, to results which are comparable to those when utilising the skew logistic distribution. However, in practice, it is still preferable to make use of the skew logistic distribution as it is the natural model to deploy in this context [17], since, on the whole, it is more consistent with the data as its tails are heavier than those of a skew normal distribution.

Epidemics are said to come in "waves". The precise definition of a wave is somewhat elusive [18], but it is generally accepted that, assuming we have a time series of the number of, say, daily hospitalisations, a wave will span over a period from one valley (minima) in the time series to another valley, with a peak (maxima) in between them. There is no strict requirement that waves do not overlap, although, for simplicity we will not consider any overlap as such; see [18], for an attempt to give an operational definition of the concept of epidemic wave. In order to combine waves, we make use of the concept of *bi-logistic growth* [19,20], or more generally, multi-logistic growth, which allows us to sum two or more instances of logistic growth when the time series spans over more than a single wave.

To fit the skew logistic distribution to the time series data we employ maximum likelihood, and to evaluate the goodness-of-fit we make use of the recently formulated *empirical survival Jensen–Shannon divergence* ($\mathcal{ESJS}$) [21,22] and the well-established *Kolmogorov–Smirnov two-sample test statistic* ($KS2$) [23] (Section 6.3). The $\mathcal{ESJS}$ is an information-theoretic goodness-of-fit measure of a fitted parametric continuous distribution, which overcomes the inadequacy of the *coefficient of determination*, R^2, as a goodness-of-fit measure for non-linear models [24]. The $KS2$ statistic also satisfies this criteria regarding R^2; however, we observe that the 95% bootstrap confidence intervals [25] we obtain for the $\mathcal{ESJS}$ are narrower than those for the $KS2$, suggesting that the $\mathcal{ESJS}$ is more powerful [26] than the $KS2$. Another well-known limitation of the $KS2$ statistic is that it is less sensitive to discrepancies at the tails of the distribution than the $\mathcal{ESJS}$ statistic is, in the sense that as opposed to $\mathcal{ESJS}$ it is "local", i.e., its value is determined by a single point [27].

The rest of the paper is organised as follows. In Section 2, we introduce a skew logistic distribution, which is a simple extension of the standard, symmetric, logistic distribution obtained by adding to it a single skew parameter and derive some of its properties. In Section 3, we formulate the solution to the maximum likelihood estimation of the parameters of the skew logistic distribution. In Section 4, we make use of an extension of the skew logistic distribution to the bi-skew logistic distribution to model a time series of COVID-19 data items having more than a single wave. In Section 5, we provide analysis of daily COVID-19 deaths in the UK from 30 January 2020 to 30 July 2021, assuming the skew logistic distribution as an underlying model of the data. The evaluation of goodness-of-fit of the skew logistic distribution to the data makes use of the recently formulated $\mathcal{ESJS}$, and compares the results to those when employing the $KS2$ instead. We observe that the same technique, which we applied to the analysis of COVID-19 deaths, can be used to model new cases and hospitalisations. Finally, in Section 6, we present our concluding remarks. It is worth noting that in the more general setting of information modelling, being able to detect epidemic waves may help supply chains in planning increased resistance to such adverse events [28]. We note that all computations were carried out using the Matlab software package.

2. A Skew Logistic Distribution

Here, we introduce a novel *skew logistic distribution*, which extends, in straightforward manner, the standard two parameter logistic distribution [3] and [4] (Chapter 22) by adding to it a skew parameter. The rationale for introducing the distribution is that, apart from its simple formulation, we believe that the maximum likelihood solution presented below is also simpler than those derived for other skew logistic distributions, such as the ones investigated in [8,9]. This point provides further justification for our skew logistic distribution when introducing the bi-skew logistic distribution in Section 4.

Now, let μ be a location parameter, s be a scale parameter and λ be a skew parameter, where $s > 0$ and $0 < \lambda < 2$. Then, the probability density function of the skew logistic distribution at a value x of the random variable X, denoted as $f(x; \lambda, \mu, s)$, is given by:

$$f(x; \lambda, \mu, s) = \kappa_\lambda \frac{\exp\left(-\lambda \frac{x-\mu}{s}\right)}{s\left(1 + \exp\left(-\frac{x-\mu}{s}\right)\right)^2}, \tag{1}$$

noting that for clarity we write $x - \mu$ above as a shorthand for $(x - \mu)$, and κ_λ is a normalisation constant, which depends on λ.

When $\lambda = 1$, the skew logistic distribution reduces to the standard logistic distribution as in [3] and [4] (Chapter 22), which is symmetric. On the other hand, when $0 < \lambda < 1$, the skew logistic distribution is positively skewed, and when $1 < \lambda < 2$, it is negatively skewed. So, when $\lambda = 1$, $\kappa_\lambda = 1$, and, for example, when $\lambda = 0.5$ or 1.5, $\kappa_\lambda = 2/\pi$. For simplicity, from now on, unless necessary, we will omit to mention the constant κ_λ as it will not effect any of the results.

The *skewness* of a random variable X [4,5], is defined as:

$$\mathrm{E}\left[\left(\frac{X-\mu}{s}\right)^3\right],$$

and thus, assuming for simplicity of exposition (due the linearity of expectations [5]) that $\mu = 0$ and $s = 1$, the skewness of the skew logistic distribution, denoted by $\gamma(\lambda)$, is given by:

$$\gamma(\lambda) = \int_{-\infty}^{\infty} x^3 \frac{\exp(-\lambda x)}{s(1 + \exp(-x))^2} \, dx. \tag{2}$$

First, we will show that letting $\lambda_1 = \lambda$, with $0 < \lambda_1 < 1$, we have $\gamma(\lambda_1) > 0$, that is $f(x; \lambda_1, 0, 1)$ is positively skewed. We can split the integral in (2) into two integrals for the negative part from $-\infty$ to 0 and the positive part from 0 to ∞, noting that when $x = 0$, the expression to the right of the integral is equal to 0. Then, on setting $y = -x$ for the negative part, and $y = x$ for the positive part, the result follows, as by algebraic manipulation it can be shown that:

$$\frac{\exp(-\lambda_1 y)}{(1 + \exp(-y))^2} > \frac{\exp(\lambda_1 y)}{(1 + \exp(y))^2}, \tag{3}$$

implying that $\gamma(\lambda_1) > 0$ as required.

Second, in a similar fashion to above, on letting $\lambda_2 = \lambda_1 + 1 = \lambda$, with $1 < \lambda_2 < 2$, it follows that $\gamma(\lambda_2) < 0$, that is $f(x; \lambda_2, 0, 1)$ is negatively skewed. In particular, by algebraic manipulation we have that:

$$\frac{\exp(-\lambda_2 y)}{(1 + \exp(-y))^2} < \frac{\exp(\lambda_2 y)}{(1 + \exp(y))^2}, \tag{4}$$

implying that $\gamma(\lambda_2) < 0$ as required.

The cumulative distribution function of the skew logistic distribution at a value x of the random variable X is obtained by integrating $f(x; \lambda, \mu, s)$, to obtain $F(x; \mu, s, \lambda)$, which is given by:

$$F(x; \lambda, \mu, s) = \kappa_\lambda \exp\left(-(\lambda - 2)\frac{x-\mu}{s}\right)\left(\frac{1}{\left(1+\exp\left(\frac{x-\mu}{s}\right)\right)} - \frac{\lambda-1}{\lambda-2}\,{}_2F_1\left(1, 2-\lambda; 3-\lambda; -\exp\left(\frac{x-\mu}{s}\right)\right)\right), \tag{5}$$

where ${}_2F_1(a, b; c; z)$ is the *Gauss hypergemoetric function* [29] (Chapter 15); we assume a, b and c are positive real numbers, and that z is a real number extended outside the unit disk by analytic continuation [30].

The hypergeometric function has the following integral representation [29] (Chapter 15),

$$\frac{\Gamma(c)}{\Gamma(b)\Gamma(c-b)}\int_0^1 \frac{t^{b-1}(1-t)^{c-b-1}}{(1-tz)^a}\,dt, \tag{6}$$

where $c > b$. Now, assuming without loss of generality that $\mu = 0$ and $s = 1$, we have that:

$$ {}_2F_1(1, 2-\lambda; 3-\lambda; -\exp(x)) = (2-\lambda)\int_0^1 \frac{t^{1-\lambda}}{(1+t\,\exp(x))}\,dt, \tag{7}$$

where x is a real number.

Therefore, from (7) it can be verified that: (i) ${}_2F_1(1, 2-\lambda; 3-\lambda; -\exp(x))$ is monotonically decreasing with x, (ii) as x tends to plus infinity, ${}_2F_1(1, 2-\lambda; 3-\lambda; -\exp(x))$ tends to 0 and (iii) as x tends to minus infinity, ${}_2F_1(1, 2-\lambda; 3-\lambda; -\exp(x))$ tends to 1, since:

$$(2-\lambda)\int_0^1 t^{1-\lambda}\,dt = 1.$$

3. Maximum Likelihood Estimation for the Skew Logistic Distribution

We now formulate the maximum likelihood estimation [31] of the parameters μ, s and λ of the skew logistic distribution. Let $\{x_1, x_2, \ldots, x_n\}$ be a random sample of n values from the density function of the skew logistic distribution in (1). Then, the log likelihood function of its three parameters is given by:

$$\ln L(\lambda, \mu, s) = -n\ln(s) - \frac{\lambda}{s}\sum_{i=1}^n (x_i - \mu) - 2\sum_{i=1}^n \ln\left(1+\exp\left(-\frac{x_i-\mu}{s}\right)\right). \tag{8}$$

In order to solve the log likelihood function, we first partially differentiate $\ln L(\lambda, \mu, s)$ as follows:

$$\frac{\partial \ln L(\lambda, \mu, s)}{\partial \lambda} = \sum_{i=1}^n \frac{\mu - x_i}{s},$$

$$\frac{\partial \ln L(\lambda, \mu, s)}{\partial \mu} = \frac{\lambda n}{s} - \frac{2}{s}\sum_{i=1}^n \frac{1}{1+\exp\left(\frac{x_i-\mu}{s}\right)} \quad \text{and}$$

$$\frac{\partial \ln L(\lambda, \mu, s)}{\partial s} = -\frac{n}{s} + \frac{1}{s^2}\sum_{i=1}^n (x_i - \mu)\left(\lambda - \frac{2}{1+\exp\left(\frac{x_i-\mu}{s}\right)}\right). \tag{9}$$

It is therefore implied that the maximum likelihood estimators are the solutions to the following three equations:

$$\mu = \frac{\sum_{i=1}^{n} x_i}{n},$$

$$\lambda = \frac{2}{n} \sum_{i=1}^{n} \frac{1}{1 + \exp\left(\frac{x_i - \mu}{s}\right)} \quad \text{and}$$

$$s = \frac{1}{n} \sum_{i=1}^{n} (x_i - \mu)\left(\lambda - \frac{2}{1 + \exp\left(\frac{x_i - \mu}{s}\right)}\right), \tag{10}$$

which can be solved numerically.

We observe that the equation for μ in (10) does not contribute to solving the maximum likelihood, since the location parameter μ is equal to the mean only when $\lambda = 1$. We thus look at an alternative equation for μ, which involves the mode of the skew logistic distribution.

To derive the mode of the skew logistic distribution we solve the equation,

$$\frac{\partial}{\partial x} \frac{\exp\left(-\lambda \frac{x-\mu}{s}\right)}{s\left(1 + \exp\left(-\frac{x-\mu}{s}\right)\right)^2} = 0, \tag{11}$$

to obtain:

$$\mu = x - s \log\left(-\frac{\lambda - 2}{\lambda}\right). \tag{12}$$

Thus, motivated by (12) we replace the equation for μ in (10) with:

$$\mu = m - s \log\left(-\frac{\lambda - 2}{\lambda}\right), \tag{13}$$

where m is the mode of the random sample.

4. The Bi-Skew Logistic Distribution for Modelling Epidemic Waves

We start by defining the bi-skew logistic distribution, which will enable us to model more than one wave of infections at a time. We then discuss how we partition the data into single waves, in a way that we can apply the maximum likelihood from the previous section to the data in a consistent manner.

We present the *bi-skew logistic distribution*, which is described by the sum,

$$f(x; \lambda_1, \mu_1, s_1) + f(x; \lambda_2, \mu_2, s_2),$$

of two skew logistic distributions. It is given in full as:

$$\frac{\exp\left(-\lambda_1 \frac{x-\mu_1}{s_1}\right)}{s_1\left(1 + \exp\left(-\frac{x-\mu_1}{s_1}\right)\right)^2} + \frac{\exp\left(-\lambda_2 \frac{x-\mu_2}{s_2}\right)}{s_2\left(1 + \exp\left(-\frac{x-\mu_2}{s_2}\right)\right)^2}, \tag{14}$$

which characterises two distinct phases of logistic growth (c.f. [19,32]). We note that (14) can be readily extended to the general case of the sum of multiple skew logistic distributions; however, for simplicity, we only present the formula for the bi-skew logistic case. Thus, while the (single) skew logistic distribution can only model one wave of infected cases (or deaths, or hospitalisations), the bi-skew logistic distribution can model two waves of infections, and in the general cases, any number of waves.

In the presence of two waves, the maximum likelihood solution to (14), would give us access to the necessary model parameters, and solving the general case in the presence of multiple waves, when the sum in (14) may have two or more skew logistic distributions, is evidently even more challenging. Thus, we simplify the solution for the multiple wave case, and concentrate on an approximation assuming a sequential time series when one wave strictly follows the next. More specifically, we assume that each wave is modelled by a single skewed logistic distribution describing the growth phase until a peak is reached, followed by a decline phase; see [33] who consider epidemic waves in the context of the standard logistic distribution. Thus, a wave is represented by a temporal pattern of growth and decline, and the time series as a whole describes several waves as they evolve.

To provide further clarification of the model, we mention that the skew-bi logistic distribution is *not* a *mixture model* per se, in which case there is a mixture weight for each distribution in the sum, as in, say, a Gaussian mixture [34] (Chapter 9). In the bi-skew logistic distribution case we do not have mixture weights, rather, we have two phases in our context waves, which are sequential in nature, possibly with some overlap, as can be seen in Figure 1 (c.f. [19,32]). Strictly speaking, the bi-skew logistic distribution can be viewed as a mixture model where the mixture weights are each 0.5 and a scaling factor of 2 is applied. Thus, as an approximation, we add a preprocessing step where we segment the time series into distinct waves, resulting in a considerable reduction to the complexity of the maximum likelihood estimation. We do, however, remark that the maximum likelihood estimation for the bi-skew logistic distribution is much simpler than that of a corresponding mixture model, due to the absence of mixture weights. In particular, although we could, in principle, make use of the EM (expectation-maximisation) algorithm [34] (Chapter 9) and [35] to approximate the maximum likelihood estimates of the parameters, this would not be strictly necessary in the bi-skew logistic case, cf. [36]. The only caveat, which holds independently of whether the EM algorithm is deployed or not, is the additional number of parameters present in the equations being solved. We leave this investigation as future work, and focus on our approximation, which does not require the solution to the maximum likelihood of (14); the details of the preprocessing heuristic we apply are given in the following section.

5. Data Analysis of COVID-19 Deaths in the UK

Here, we provide a full analysis of COVID-19 deaths in the UK from 30 January 2020 to 30 July 2021, employing the $\mathcal{ESJS}$ goodness-of-fit statistic and comparing it to the $KS2$ statistic. The daily UK COVID-19 data we used was obtained from [37].

As a proof of concept of the modelling capability of the skew logistic distribution, we now provide a detailed analysis of the time series of COVID-19 deaths in the UK from 30 January 2020 to 30 July 2021.

To separate the waves, we first smoothed the raw data using a moving average with a centred sliding window of 7 days. We then applied a simple heuristic, where we identified all the minima in the time series and defined a wave as a consecutive portion of the time, of at least 72 days, with the endpoints of each wave being local minima apart from the first wave, which starts from day 0. The resulting four waves in the time series are shown in Figure 1; see last column of Table 1 for the endpoints of the four waves. It would be worthwhile, as future work, to investigate other heuristics, which may, for example, allow overlap between the waves to obtain more accurate start and end points and to distribute the number of cases between the waves when there is overlap between them.

In Table 1, we show the parameters resulting from maximum likelihood fits of the skew logistic distribution to the four waves. Figure 2 shows histograms of the four COVID-19 waves, each overlaid with the curve of the maximum likelihood fit of the skew logistic distribution to the data. Pearson's moment and median skewness coefficients [38] for the four waves are recorded in Table 2. It can be seen that the correlation between these and $1 - \lambda$ is close to 1, as we would expect.

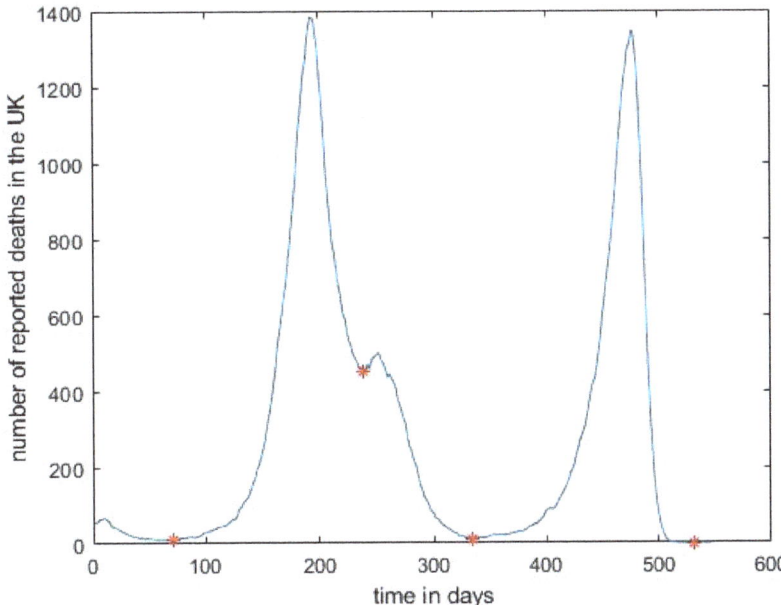

Figure 1. Reported daily COVID-19 deaths from 30 January 2020 to 30 July 2021 and their minima labelled '*', resulting in four distinct waves; a moving average with a centred sliding window of 7 days was applied to the raw data.

Table 1. Parameters from maximum likelihood fits of the skew logistic distribution to the four waves, and the day of the local minimum (End), which is the end point of the wave.

Fitted Parameters for the Skew Logistic Distribution				
Wave	λ	μ	s	End
1	0.2150	3.5137	3.8443	71
2	1.0741	196.5157	14.4323	239
3	0.2297	243.0709	4.5882	334
4	1.7306	502.2758	7.0195	532

Table 2. Pearson's moment and median skewness coefficients for the four waves, and the correlation between $1 - \lambda$ and these coefficients.

	Skewness		
Wave	$1 - \lambda$	Moment	Median
1	0.7850	0.9314	0.2939
2	−0.0741	−0.7758	−0.0797
3	0.7703	0.9265	0.1939
4	−0.7306	−1.5555	−0.2413
Correlation		0.9931	0.9826

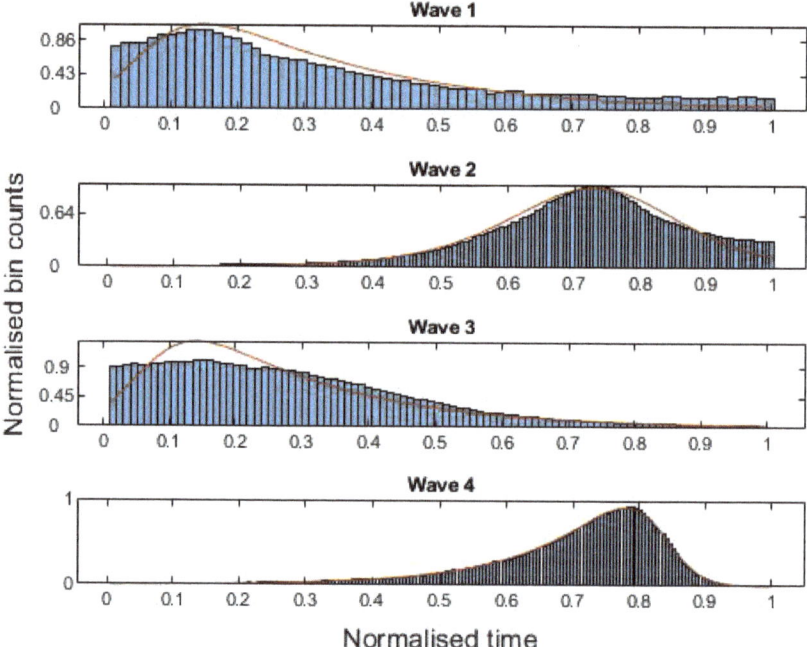

Figure 2. Histograms for the four waves of COVID-19 deaths from 30 January 2020 to 30 July 2021, each overlaid with the curve of the maximum likelihood fit of the skew logistic distribution to the data.

We now turn to the evaluation of goodness-of-fit using the $\mathcal{ESJS}$ (empirical survival Jensen–Shannon divergence) [21,22], which generalises the Jensen–Shannon divergence [39] to survival functions, and the well-known $KS2$ (Kolmogorov–Smirnov two-sample test statistic) [23] (Section 6.3). We will also employ 95% bootstrap confidence intervals [25] to measure the improvement in the $\mathcal{ESJS}$ and $KS2$, goodness-of-fit measures, of the skew-logistic over the logistic and normal distributions, respectively. For completeness, we formally define the $\mathcal{ESJS}$ and $KS2$.

To set the scene, we assume a time series [40], $\mathbf{x} = \{x_1, x_2, \ldots, x_n\}$, where x_t, for $t = 1, 2, \ldots, n$ is a value indexed by time, t, in our case modelling the number of daily COVID-19 deaths. We are, in particular, interested in the marginal distribution of $\mathbf{x}$, which we suppose comes from an underlying parametric continuous distribution D.

The *empirical survival function* of a value z for the time series $\mathbf{x}$, denoted by $\widehat{S}(\mathbf{x})[z]$, is given by:

$$\widehat{S}(\mathbf{x})[z] = \frac{1}{n} \sum_{i=1}^{n} I_{\{x_i > z\}}, \quad (15)$$

where I is the indicator function. In the following, we will let $\widehat{P}(z) = \widehat{S}(\mathbf{x})[z]$ stand for the empirical survival function $\widehat{S}(\mathbf{x})[z]$, where the time series $\mathbf{x}$ is assumed to be understood from context. We will generally be interested in the empirical survival function $\widehat{P}$, which we suppose arises from the survival function P of the parametric continuous distribution D, mentioned above.

The *empirical survival Jensen–Shannon divergence* ($\mathcal{ESJS}$) between two empirical survival functions, $\widehat{Q}_1$ and $\widehat{Q}_2$ arising from the survival functions Q_1 and Q_2, is given by:

$$\mathcal{ESJS}(\widehat{Q}_1, \widehat{Q}_2) = \frac{1}{2} \int_0^\infty \widehat{Q}_1(z) \log\left(\frac{\widehat{Q}_1(z)}{\widehat{M}(z)}\right) + \widehat{Q}_2(z) \log\left(\frac{\widehat{Q}_2(z)}{\widehat{M}(z)}\right) dz, \quad (16)$$

where:

$$\widehat{M}(z) = \frac{1}{2}\left(\widehat{Q}_1(z) + \widehat{Q}_2(z)\right).$$

We note that the $\mathcal{ESJS}$ is bounded and can thus be normalised, so it is natural to assume its values are between 0 and 1; in particular, when $\widehat{Q}_1 = \widehat{Q}_2$ its value is zero. Moreover, its square root is a metric [41], cf. [21].

The *Kolmogorov–Smirnov* two-sample test statistic between $\widehat{Q}_1$ and $\widehat{Q}_2$ as above, is given by:

$$KS2(\widehat{Q}_1, \widehat{Q}_2) = \max_z |\widehat{Q}_1(z) - \widehat{Q}_2(z)|, \quad (17)$$

where *max* is the maximum function, and $|v|$ is the absolute value of a number v. We note that $KS2$ is bounded between 0 and 1, and is also a metric.

For a parametric continuous distribution D, we let $\phi = \phi(D, \widehat{P})$ be the parameters that are obtained from fitting D to the empirical survival function, $\widehat{P}$, using maximum likelihood estimation. In addition, we let $P_\phi = S_\phi(\mathbf{x})$ be the survival function of $\mathbf{x}$, for D with parameters ϕ. Thus, the empirical survival Jensen–Shannon divergence and the Kolmogorov–Smirnov two-sample test statistic, between $\widehat{P}$ and P_ϕ, are given by $\mathcal{ESJS}(\widehat{P}, P_\phi)$ and $KS2(\widehat{P}, P_\phi)$, respectively, where $\widehat{P}$ and P_ϕ are omitted below as they will be understood from context. These values provide us with two measures of goodness-of-fit for how well D with parameters ϕ is fitted to $\mathbf{x}$ [22].

We are now ready to present the results of the evaluation. In Table 3, we show the $\mathcal{ESJS}$ values for the four waves and the said improvements, while in Table 4, we show the corresponding $KS2$ values and improvements. In all cases, the skew logistic is a preferred model over both the logistic and normal distributions, justifying the addition of a skewness parameter as can be see in Figure 2. Moreover, in all but one case the logistic distribution was preferred over the normal distribution—wave 3, where the $KS2$ statistic of the normal distribution was smaller than that of the logistic distribution. We observe that, for the second wave, the $\mathcal{ESJS}$ and $KS2$ values for the skew logistic and logistic distribution were the closest, since, as can be seen from Table 1, the second wave was more or less symmetric, in which case the skew logistic distribution reduces to the logistic distribution.

Table 3. $\mathcal{ESJS}$ values for the skew logistic (SL), logistic (Logit) and normal (Norm) distributions, and the improvement percentage of the skew logistic over the logistic (SL-Logit) and normal (SL-Norm) distributions, respectively.

	$\mathcal{ESJS}$ Values for SL, Logit and Norm Distributions				
Wave	SL	Logit	SL-Logit	Norm	SL-Norm
1	0.0419	0.0583	28.25%	0.0649	35.54%
2	0.0392	0.0448	12.52%	0.0613	36.17%
3	0.0316	0.0387	18.38%	0.0423	25.38%
4	0.0237	0.0927	74.47%	0.0939	74.79%

In Tables 5 and 6, we present the bootstrap 95% confidence intervals of the $\mathcal{ESJS}$ and $KS2$ improvements, respectively, using the *percentile* method, while in Tables 7 and 8, we provide the 95% confidence intervals of the $\mathcal{ESJS}$ and $KS2$ improvements, respectively, using the *bias-corrected and accelerated* (BCa) method [25], which adjusts the confidence intervals for bias and skewness in the empirical bootstrap distribution. In all cases, the mean of the bootstrap samples is above zero with a very tight standard deviation. As noted above, the second wave is more or less symmetric, so we expect that the standard logistic distribution will provide a fit to the data, which is as good as the skew logistic fit. It is thus not surprising that in this case the improvement percentages are, generally, not significant. In addition, the improvements for the third wave are also, generally, not significant, which may be due to the starting point of the third wave, given our heuristic, being close to its peak; see Figure 1. We observe that, for this dataset, it is not clear whether deploying the BCa method yields a significant advantage over simply deploying the percentile method.

Table 4. $KS2$ values for the skew logistic (SL), logistic (Logit) and normal (Norm) distributions, and the improvement percentage of the skew logistic over the logistic (SL-Logit) and normal (SL-Norm) distributions, respectively.

	$KS2$ Values for SL, Logit and Norm Distributions				
Wave	SL	Logit	SL-Logit	Norm	SL-Norm
1	0.0621	0.1245	50.14%	0.1280	51.50%
2	0.0357	0.0391	8.57%	0.0420	15.01%
3	0.0571	0.0930	38.66%	0.0854	33.18%
4	0.0098	0.0817	87.98%	0.1046	90.61%

In Table 9, we show the mean and standard deviation statistics of the confidence interval widths, of the metrics we used to compare the distributions, implying that, in general, the $\mathcal{E}SJS$ goodness-of-fit measure is more powerful than the $KS2$ goodness-of-fit measure. This is based on the known result that statistical tests using measures resulting in smaller confidence intervals are normally considered to be more powerful, implying that a smaller sample size may be deployed [42].

Table 5. Results from the percentile method for the confidence interval of the difference of the $\mathcal{E}SJS$ between the logistic (Logit) and skew logistic (SL), and between the normal (Norm) and skew logistic (SL) distributions, respectively; Diff, LB, UB, CI, Mean and STD stand for difference, lower bound, upper bound, confidence interval, mean of samples and standard deviation of samples, respectively.

	Percentile Confidence Intervals for $\mathcal{E}SJS$ Improvement				
Wave/Diff	LB of CI	UB of CI	Width of CI	Mean	STD
1/SL-Logit	0.0093	0.0317	0.0224	0.0211	0.0063
1/SL-Norm	0.0170	0.0382	0.0212	0.0278	0.0063
2/SL-Logit	−0.0010	0.0066	0.0076	0.0034	0.0049
2/SL-Norm	0.0154	0.0232	0.0078	0.0201	0.0051
3/SL-Logit	−0.0028	0.0112	0.0140	0.0083	0.0022
3/SL-Norm	0.0021	0.0149	0.0128	0.0120	0.0022
4/SL-Logit	0.0549	0.0810	0.0261	0.0714	0.0068
4/SL-Norm	0.0560	0.0821	0.0261	0.0722	0.0070

As mentioned in the introduction, we obtained comparable results to the above when modelling epidemic waves with the epsilon skew normal distribution [7] as opposed to using the skew logistic distribution; see also [43] for a comparison of a skew logistic and skew normal distribution in the context of insurance loss data, showing that the skew logistic performed better than the skew normal distribution for fitting the datasets tested. Further to the note in the introduction that the skew logistic distribution is a more natural one to deploy in this case due to its heavier tails, we observe that in an epidemic scenario, the number of cases counted can only be non-negative, while the epsilon skew normal also supports negative values.

Table 6. Results from the percentile method for the confidence interval of the difference of the $KS2$ between the logistic (Logit) and skew logistic (SL), and between the normal (Norm) and skew logistic (SL) distributions, respectively; Diff, LB, UB, CI, Mean and STD stand for difference, lower bound, upper bound, confidence interval, mean of samples and standard deviation of samples, respectively.

Percentile Confidence Intervals for $KS2$ Improvement					
Wave/Diff	LB of CI	UB of CI	Width of CI	Mean	STD
1/SL-Logit	0.0438	0.0760	0.0322	0.0621	0.0073
1/SL-Norm	0.0411	0.0821	0.0410	0.0684	0.0078
2/SL-Logit	0.0003	0.0047	0.0044	0.0033	0.0009
2/SL-Norm	0.0007	0.0092	0.0085	0.0065	0.0017
3/SL-Logit	−0.0073	0.0441	0.0514	0.0343	0.0082
3/SL-Norm	−0.0142	0.0365	0.0507	0.0267	0.0080
4/SL-Logit	0.0474	0.0728	0.0254	0.0680	0.0046
4/SL-Norm	0.0710	0.0962	0.0252	0.0905	0.0048

Table 7. Results from the BCa method for the confidence interval of the difference of the $\mathcal{ESJS}$ between the logistic (Logit) and skew logistic (SL), and between the normal (Norm) and skew logistic (SL) distributions, respectively; Diff, LB, UB, CI, Mean and STD stand for difference, lower bound, upper bound, confidence interval, mean of samples and standard deviation of samples, respectively.

BCa Confidence Intervals for $\mathcal{ESJS}$ Improvement					
Wave/Diff	LB of CI	UB of CI	Width of CI	Mean	STD
1/SL-Logit	0.0087	0.0260	0.0173	0.0210	0.0062
1/SL-Norm	0.0165	0.0333	0.0168	0.0275	0.0063
2/SL-Logit	−0.0009	0.0258	0.0267	0.0036	0.0053
2/SL-Norm	0.0153	0.0425	0.0272	0.0201	0.0050
3/SL-Logit	−0.0024	0.0095	0.0119	0.0084	0.0023
3/SL-Norm	−0.0027	0.0135	0.0162	0.0119	0.0024
4/SL-Logit	0.0308	0.0703	0.0395	0.0708	0.0074
4/SL-Norm	0.0554	0.0713	0.0159	0.0726	0.0069

Table 8. Results from the BCa method for the confidence interval of the difference of the $KS2$ between the logistic (Logit) and skew logistic (SL), and between the normal (Norm) and skew logistic (SL) distributions, respectively; Diff, LB, UB, CI, Mean and STD stand for difference, lower bound, upper bound, confidence interval, mean of samples and standard deviation of samples, respectively.

BCa Confidence Intervals for $KS2$ Improvement					
Wave/Diff	LB of CI	UB of CI	Width of CI	Mean	STD
1/SL-Logit	0.0428	0.0801	0.0373	0.0624	0.0074
1/SL-Norm	0.0444	0.0777	0.0333	0.0683	0.0078
2/SL-Logit	0.0005	0.0047	0.0042	0.0033	0.0008
2/SL-Norm	0.0001	0.0089	0.0088	0.0064	0.0017
3/SL-Logit	0.0013	0.0445	0.0432	0.0346	0.0077
3/SL-Norm	−0.0111	0.0368	0.0479	0.0263	0.0082
4/SL-Logit	0.0491	0.0739	0.0248	0.0676	0.0047
4/SL-Norm	0.0685	0.0985	0.0300	0.0908	0.0046

Table 9. Mean and standard deviation (STD) statistics for the confidence interval (CI) widths using the percentile (P) and BCa methods.

Statistic	Summary Statistics for the CI Widths			
	$\mathcal{E}SJS$-P	KS2-P	$\mathcal{E}SJS$-BCa	KS2-BCa
Mean	0.0172	0.0298	0.0214	0.0287
STD	0.0077	0.0176	0.0091	0.0155

6. Concluding Remarks

We have proposed the skew-logistic and bi-logistic distributions as models for single and multiple epidemic waves, respectively. The model is a simple extension of the symmetric logistic distribution, which can readily be deployed in the presence of skewed data that exhibits growth and decay. We provided validation for the proposed model using the $\mathcal{E}SJS$ as a goodness-of-fit statistic, showing that it is a good fit to COVID-19 data in UK and more powerful than the alternative $KS2$ statistic. As future work, we could use the model to compare the progression of multiple waves across different countries, extending the work of [16].

Funding: This research received no external funding.

Institutional Review Board Statement: Not applicable.

Informed Consent Statement: Not applicable.

Data Availability Statement: Publicly available datasets were analysed in this study. This data can be found here: https://coronavirus.data.gov.uk/details/download, accessed on 20 March 2022.

Conflicts of Interest: The author declares no conflicts of interest.

References

1. Bacaër, N. *A Short History of Mathematical Population Dynamics*; Springer: London, UK, 2011.
2. Panik, M. *Growth Curve Modeling: Theory and Applications*; John Wiley & Sons: Hoboken, NJ, USA, 2014.
3. Johnson, N.; Kotz, S.; Balkrishnan, N. *Continuous Univariate Distributions, Volume 2*; Wiley Series in Probability and Mathematical Statistics; John Wiley & Sons: New York, NY, USA, 1995; Chapter 23 Logistic Distribution, pp. 113–163.
4. Krishnamoorthy, K. *Handbook of Statistical Distributions with Applications*, 2nd ed.; CRC Press: Boca Raton, FL, USA, 2015.
5. DasGupta, A. *Fundamentals of Probability: A First Course*; Springer Texts in Statistics; Springer Science+Business Media: New York, NY, USA, 2010.
6. Azzalini, A.; Capitanio, A. *The Skew-Normal and Related Families*; Institute Of Mathematical Statistics Monographs, Cambridge University Press: Cambridge, UK, 2014.
7. Mudholkar, G.; Hutson, A. The epsilon–skew–normal distribution for analyzing near-normal data. *J. Stat. Plan. Inference* **2000**, *83*, 291–309. [CrossRef]
8. Nadarajah, S. The skew logistic distribution. *AStA Adv. Stat. Anal.* **2009**, *93*, 187–203. [CrossRef]
9. Sastry, D.; Bhati, D. A new skew logistic distribution: Properties and applications. *Braz. J. Probab. Stat.* **2016**, *30*, 248–271. [CrossRef]
10. Li, M. *An Introduction to Mathematical Modeling of Infectious Diseases*; Mathematics of Planet Earth, Springer Nature: Cham, Switzerland, 2018.
11. Ioannidis, J.; Cripps, S.; Tanner, M. Forecasting for COVID-19 has failed. *Int. J. Forecast.* **2022**, *38*, 423–438. [CrossRef]
12. Davies, N.; Kucharski, A.; Eggo, R.; Gimma, A.; Edmunds, W. Effects of non-pharmaceutical interventions on COVID-19 cases, deaths, and demand for hospital services in the UK: A modelling study. *LANCET Public Health* **2020**, *5*, e375–e385. [CrossRef]
13. Harvey, A.; Kattuman, P.; Thamotheram, C. Tracking the mutant: Forecasting and nowcasting COVID-19 in the UK in 2021. *Natl. Inst. Econ. Rev.* **2021**, *256*, 110–126. [CrossRef]
14. De la Sen, M.; Ibeas, A. On an Sir epidemic model for the COVID-19 Pandemic and the logistic equation. *Discret. Dyn. Nat. Soc.* **2020**, *2020*, 1382870. [CrossRef]
15. Postnikov, E. Estimation of COVID-19 dynamics "on a back-of-envelope": Does the simplest SIR model provide quantitative parameters and predictions? *Chaos Solitons Fractals* **2020**, *135*, 109841-1–109841-6. [CrossRef]
16. Dye, C.; Cheng, R.; Dagpunar, J.; Williams, B. The scale and dynamics of COVID-19 epidemics across Europe. *R. Soc. Open Sci.* **2020**, *7*, 201726-1–201726-8. [CrossRef]
17. Pelinovsky, E.; Kurkin, A.; Kurkina, O.; Kokoulina, M.; Epifanova, A. Logistic equation and COVID-19. *Chaos Solitons Fractals* **2020**, *140*, 110241-1–110241-13. [CrossRef]

18. Zhang, S.; Marioli, F.; Gao, R. A second wave? What do people mean by COVID waves?—A working definition of epidemic waves. *Risk Manag. Healthc. Policy* **2021**, *14*, 3775–3782. [CrossRef]
19. Meyer, P. Bi-logistic growth. *Technol. Forecast. Soc. Chang.* **1994**, *47*, 89–102. [CrossRef]
20. Fenner, T.; Levene, M.; Loizou, G. A bi-logistic growth model for conference registration with an early bird deadline. *Cent. Eur. J. Phys.* **2013**, *11*, 904–909. [CrossRef]
21. Levene, M.; Kononovicius, A. Empirical survival Jensen-Shannon divergence as a goodness-of-fit measure for maximum likelihood estimation and curve fitting. *Commun. Stat.-Simul. Comput.* **2021**, *50*, 3751–3767. [CrossRef]
22. Levene, M. A hypothesis test for the goodness-of-fit of the marginal distribution of a time series with application to stablecoin data. *Eng. Proc.* **2021**, *5*, 10.
23. Gibbons, J.; Chakraborti, S. *Nonparametric Statistical Inference*, 6th ed.; Marcel Dekker: New York, NY, USA, 2021.
24. Spiess, A.N.; Neumeyer, N. An evaluation of R^2 as an inadequate measure for nonlinear models in pharmacological and biochemical research: A Monte Carlo approach. *BMC Pharmacol.* **2010**, *10*, 6. [CrossRef] [PubMed]
25. Efron, B.; Tibshirani, R. *An Introduction to the Bootstrap*; Monographs on Statistics and Applied Probability 57; Springer Science+Business Media: New York, NY, USA, 1993.
26. Colegrave, N.; Ruxton, G. *Power Analysis: An Introduction for the Life Sciences*; Oxford Biology Primers; Oxford University Press: Oxford, UK, 2019.
27. Ben-David, A.; Liu, H.; Jackson, A. The Kullback-Leibler divergence as an estimator of the statistical properties of CMB maps. *J. Cosmol. Astropart. Phys.* **2015**, *2015*, JCAP06051. [CrossRef]
28. Semenov, I.; Jacyna, M. The synthesis model as a planning tool for effective supply chains resistant to adverse events. *Maint. Reliab.* **2022**, *24*, 140–152. [CrossRef]
29. Abramowitz, M.; Stegun, I. (Eds.) *Handbook of Mathematical Functions with Formulas, Graphs and Mathematical Tables*; Dover: New York, NY, USA, 1972.
30. Pearson, J.; Olver, S.; Porter, M. Numerical methods for the computation of the confluent and Gauss hypergeometric functions. *Numer. Algorithms* **2017**, *74*, 821–866. [CrossRef]
31. Ward, M.; Ahlquist, J. *Maximum Likelihood for Social Science: Strategies for Analysis*; Analytical Methods for Social Research; Cambridge University Press: Cambridge, UK, 2018.
32. Sheehy, J.; Mitchell, P.; Ferrer, A. Bi-phasic growth patterns in rice. *Ann. Bot.* **2004**, *94*, 811–817. [CrossRef]
33. Cliff, A.; Haggett, P. Methods for the measurement of epidemic velocity from time-series data. *Int. J. Epidemiol.* **1982**, *11*, 82–89. [CrossRef] [PubMed]
34. Bishop, C. *Pattern Recognition and Machine Learning*; Information Science and Statistics; Springer Science+Business Media: New York, NY, USA, 2006.
35. Redner, R.; Walker, H. Mixture densities, maximum likelihood and the Em algorithm. *SIAM Rev.* **1984**, *26*, 195–239. [CrossRef]
36. MacDonald, I. Is EM really necessary here? Examples where it seems simpler not to use EM. *AStA Adv. Stat. Anal.* **2021**, *105*, 629–647. [CrossRef]
37. GOV.UK. Coronavirus (COVID-19) in the UK, Download Data. 2021. Available online: https://coronavirus.data.gov.uk/details/download (accessed on 18 August 2021).
38. Doane, D.; Seward, L. Measuring skewness A forgotten statistic? *J. Stat. Educ.* **2011**, *19*, 1–19. [CrossRef]
39. Lin, J. Divergence measures based on the Shannon entropy. *IEEE Trans. Inf. Theory* **1991**, *37*, 145–151. [CrossRef]
40. Chatfield, C.; Xing, H. *The Analysis of Time Series: An Introduction with R*, 7th ed.; Text in Statistical Science; Chapman & Hall: London, UK, 2019.
41. Nguyen, H.; Vreeken, J. Non-parametric Jensen-Shannon divergence. In Proceedings of the European Conference on Machine Learning and Principles and Practice of Knowledge Discovery in Databases (ECML PKDD), Porto, Portugal, 7–11 September 2015; pp. 173–189.
42. Liu, X. Comparing sample size requirements for significance tests and confidence intervals. *Couns. Outcome Res. Eval.* **2013**, *4*, 3–12. [CrossRef]
43. Kazemi, R.; Noorizadeh, M. A comparison between skew-logistic and skew-normal distributions. *Matematika* **2015**, *31*, 15–24.

Article

Robust Test Statistics Based on Restricted Minimum Rényi's Pseudodistance Estimators

María Jaenada [†], Pedro Miranda [†] and Leandro Pardo [*,†]

Department of Statistics and Operation Research, Faculty of Mathematics, Interdisciplinary Mathematical Insititute, Complutense University of Madrid, Plaza Ciencias, 3, 28040 Madrid, Spain; mjaenada@ucm.es (M.J.); pmiranda@mat.ucm.es (P.M.)
* Correspondence: lpardo@mat.ucm.es
† These authors contributed equally to this work.

Abstract: The Rao's score, Wald and likelihood ratio tests are the most common procedures for testing hypotheses in parametric models. None of the three test statistics is uniformly superior to the other two in relation with the power function, and moreover, they are first-order equivalent and asymptotically optimal. Conversely, these three classical tests present serious robustness problems, as they are based on the maximum likelihood estimator, which is highly non-robust. To overcome this drawback, some test statistics have been introduced in the literature based on robust estimators, such as robust generalized Wald-type and Rao-type tests based on minimum divergence estimators. In this paper, restricted minimum Rényi's pseudodistance estimators are defined, and their asymptotic distribution and influence function are derived. Further, robust Rao-type and divergence-based tests based on minimum Rényi's pseudodistance and restricted minimum Rényi's pseudodistance estimators are considered, and the asymptotic properties of the new families of tests statistics are obtained. Finally, the robustness of the proposed estimators and test statistics is empirically examined through a simulation study, and illustrative applications in real-life data are analyzed.

Keywords: Rényi's pseudodistance; minimum Rényi's pseudodistance estimators; restricted minimum Rényi's pseudodistance estimators; Rao-type tests; divergence-based tests

1. Introduction

Let $(\mathcal{X}, \beta_\mathcal{X}, P_\theta)_{\theta \in \Theta}$ be the statistical space associated with the random variable X, where $\beta_\mathcal{X}$ is the σ-field of Borel subsets $A \subset \mathcal{X}$ and $\{P_\theta\}_{\theta \in \Theta}$ is a family of probability distributions defined on the measurable space $(\mathcal{X}, \beta_\mathcal{X})$, whit Θ an open subset of $\mathbb{R}^p$ and $p \geq 1$. We assume that the probability measures P_θ are described by densities $f_\theta(x) = dP_\theta/d\mu(x)$, where μ is a σ-finite measure on $(\mathcal{X}, \beta_\mathcal{X})$. Given a random sample $X_1, \ldots, X_n$, of the random variable X with density belonging to the parametric family P_θ, the most popular estimator for the model parameter θ is the maximum likelihood estimator (MLE), which maximizes the likelihood function of the assumed model. The MLE has been widely studied in the literature for general statistical models, and it has been shown that, under certain regularity conditions, the sequence of MLEs of θ, $\widehat{\theta}_n$, is asymptotically normal and it satisfies some desirable properties, such as consistency and asymptotic efficiency. That is, the MLE is the BAN (best asymptotically normal) estimator. However, in many popular statistical models, the MLE is markedly non-robust against deviations, even very small ones, from the parametric conditions.

To overcome the lack of robustness, minimum distance (or minimum divergence) estimators (MDEs) have been developed. MDEs have received growing attention in statistical inference because of their ability to conciliate efficiency and robustness. In parametric estimation, the role of divergence or distance measures is very intuitive: the estimates of the unknown parameters are obtained by minimizing a suitable divergence measure between the estimated from data and the assumed model distributions. There is a growing body of literature that recognizes the importance of MDEs in terms of robustness, without a significant loss of efficiency, with respect to the MLE. See, for instance, the works of Beran [1], Tamura and Boes [2], Simpson [3,4], Lindsay [5], Pardo [6], and Basu et al. [7] and the references therein.

Let G denote the unknown distribution function, with associated density g, underlying the data. The minimum divergence (distance) functional evaluated at G, $T(G)$, is defined as

$$d(g, f_{T(G)}) = \min_{\theta \in \Theta} d(g, f_\theta), \tag{1}$$

with $d(g, f_\theta)$ being a distance or divergence measure between the densities g and f_θ. As the true distribution underlying the data is unknown, given a random sample, we could estimate the model parameter θ, substituting in the previous expression the true distribution G by its empirical estimation G_n. Therefore, the MDE of θ is given by

$$\widehat{\theta}_n = T(G_n), \tag{2}$$

When dealing with continuous models, it is convenient to consider families of divergence measures for which non-parametric estimators of the unknown density function are not needed. From this perspective, the density power divergence (DPD) family, leading to the minimum density power divergence estimators (MDPDEs) (see Basu et al. [7]), as well as the Rényi's pseudodistance (RP), leading to the minimum Rényi's pseudodistance estimators (MRPE) (see Broniatowski et al. [8]) between others, play an important role. The results presented in Broniatowski et al. [8] in the context of independent and identically distributed random variables were extended for the case of independent but not identically distributed random variables by Castilla et al. [9].

In many situations we have additional knowledge about the true parameter value, as it must satisfy certain constraints. Then, the restricted parameter space has the form

$$\{\theta \in \Theta / \, g(\theta) = 0_r\}, \tag{3}$$

where 0_r denotes the null vector of dimension r, and $g : \mathbb{R}^p \to \mathbb{R}^r$ is a vector-valued function such that the $p \times r$ matrix

$$G(\theta) = \frac{\partial g^T(\theta)}{\partial \theta} \tag{4}$$

exists and is continuous in θ, and $\text{rank}(G(\theta)) = r$. Here, superscript T represents the transpose of the matrix. In the following, the restricted parameter space given in (3) is denoted by Θ_0, as in most situations, it will represent a composite null hypothesis.

The most popular estimator of θ under the non-linear constraint given in (3) is the restricted MLE (RMLE) that maximizes the likelihood function subject to the constraint $g(\theta) = 0_r$ (see Silvey [10]). The RMLE encounters similar robustness problems to the MLE. To overcome such deficiency, the restricted MDPDEs (RMDPDEs) were introduced in Basu et al. [11] and their theoretical robustness properties were later studied in Ghosh [12].

The main purpose in this paper is extending the theory developed for the MRPE to the restricted parameter space setting, yielding to the restricted MRPE (RMPRE), where the parameter space has the form (3). The rest of the paper is as follows: In Section 2, MRPE is introduced. Section 3 presents RMPRE, and its asymptotic distribution as well as its influence function are obtained. In Section 4, two different test statistics for testing composite null hypothesis, based on the RMRPE, are developed, and explicit expressions of the statistics are presented for testing in normal populations. Section 5 presents a simulation study, where the robustness of the proposed estimators and test statistics is empirically shown. Section 6 deals with real-data situations. Finally, some conclusions are presented in Section 7.

2. Minimum Rényi Pseudodistance Estimators

In this section, we introduce the MRPE. We derive the estimating equations of the MRPE and recall its asymptotic distribution.

Let $X_1, \ldots, X_n$ be a random sample of size n from a population having true and unknown density function g, modeled by a parametric family of densities f_θ with $\theta \in \Theta \subset \mathbb{R}^p$. The RP between the densities f_θ and g is given, for $\tau > 0$, by

$$R_\tau(f_\theta, g) = \frac{1}{\tau+1} \log\left(\int f_\theta(x)^{\tau+1} dx\right) + \frac{1}{\tau(\tau+1)} \log\left(\int g(x)^{\tau+1} dx\right)$$
$$- \frac{1}{\tau} \log\left(\int f_\theta(x)^\tau g(x) dx\right).$$

The RP can be defined for $\tau = 0$ taking continuous limits, yielding the expression

$$R_0(f_\theta, g) = \lim_{\tau \downarrow 0} R_\tau(f_\theta, g) = \int g(x) \log \frac{g(x)}{f_\theta(x)} dx.$$

Then, the RP coincides with the Kullback–Leibler divergence (KL) between g and f_θ, at $\tau = 0$ (see Pardo, 2006).

The RP was considered for the first time by Jones et al. [13]. Later Broniatowski et al. [8] established some useful properties of the divergence, such as the positivity of the RP for any two densities and for all values of the parameter τ, $R_\tau(f_\theta, g) \geq 0$ and uniqueness of the minimum RP within a parametric family, that is, $R_\tau(f_\theta, g) = 0$ if and only if $f_\theta = g$. The last property justifies the definition of the MRPEs as the minimizer of the RP between the assumed distribution and the empirical distribution of the data. It is interesting to note that the so-called RP by Broniatowski et al. [8] had been previously considered by Fujisawa and Eguchi [14] under the name of γ-cross entropy. In that paper, some appealing robustness properties of the estimators based on such entropy are shown.

Given a sample $X_1, \ldots, X_n$, from Broniatowski et al. [8] it can be seen that minimizing $R_\tau(f_\theta, g)$ leads to the following definition.

Definition 1. *Let $(\mathcal{X}, \beta_{\mathcal{X}}, f_\theta)_{\theta \in \Theta \subset \mathbb{R}^p}$ be a statistical space. The MRPE based on the random sample $X_1, \ldots, X_n$ for the unknown parameter θ is given, for $\tau > 0$, by*

$$\widehat{\theta}_\tau(X_1, \ldots, X_n) = \arg\sup_{\theta \in \Theta} \sum_{i=1}^n \frac{f_\theta(X_i)^\tau}{C_\tau(\theta)}, \tag{5}$$

where

$$C_\tau(\theta) = \left(\int f_\theta(x)^{\tau+1} dx\right)^{\frac{\tau}{\tau+1}}.$$

Further, at $\tau = 0$, $\widehat{\theta}_0(X_1, \ldots, X_n)$ minimizes the KL divergence, and thus the MRPE coincides with the MLE for $\tau = 0$. Based on the previous definition (5), differentiating, we obtain that the estimating equations of the MRPE are given by

$$\sum_{i=1}^n \Psi_\tau(x_i; \theta) = \mathbf{0}_p, \tag{6}$$

with

$$\Psi_\tau(x; \theta) = f_\theta(x)^\tau (u_\theta(x) - c_\tau(\theta)),$$
$$u_\theta(x) = \left(u_{\theta_1}(x), \ldots, u_{\theta_p}(x)\right)^T, \quad u_{\theta_i}(x) = \frac{\partial}{\partial \theta_i} \log f_\theta(x),$$
$$\frac{\partial C_\tau(\theta)}{\partial \theta} = C_\tau(\theta) c_\tau(\theta) \tau, \tag{7}$$

being

$$c_\tau(\theta) = \frac{1}{\kappa_\tau(\theta)} \xi_\tau(\theta) = \left(c_{\tau,1}(\theta), \ldots, c_{\tau,p}(\theta)\right)^T, \tag{8}$$

$$\xi_\tau(\theta) = \int f_\theta(x)^{\tau+1} u_\theta(x) dx, \tag{9}$$

$$\kappa_\tau(\theta) = \int f_\theta(x)^{\tau+1} dx. \tag{10}$$

The MRPE is an M-estimator and thus its asymptotic distribution and influence function (IF) can be obtained based on the asymptotic theory of the M-estimators. Broniatowski et al. [8] studied the asymptotic properties and robustness of the MRPEs. The next result recalls the asymptotic distribution of the MRPEs.

Theorem 1. *Let θ_0 be the true unknown value of θ. Then,*

$$\sqrt{n}(\hat{\theta}_\tau - \theta_0) \xrightarrow[n \to \infty]{\mathcal{L}} \mathcal{N}(0_p, V_\tau(\theta_0)) \tag{11}$$

where

$$V_\tau(\theta) = S_\tau(\theta)^{-1} K_\tau(\theta) S_\tau(\theta)^{-1} \tag{12}$$

with

$$S_\tau(\theta) = -\mathrm{E}\left[\frac{\partial \Psi_\tau(X;\theta)^T}{\partial \theta}\right], \tag{13}$$

$$K_\tau(\theta) = \mathrm{E}\left[\Psi_\tau(X;\theta) \Psi_\tau^T(X;\theta)\right]. \tag{14}$$

Castilla et al. [15] introduced useful notation for the computation of $V_\tau(\theta)$.

$$S_\tau(\theta) = J_\tau(\theta) - \frac{1}{\kappa_\tau(\theta)} \xi_\tau(\theta) \xi_\tau(\theta)^T, \tag{15}$$

$$K_\tau(\theta) = J_{2\tau}(\theta) + \frac{1}{\kappa_\tau(\theta)} \left(\frac{\kappa_{2\tau}(\theta)}{\kappa_\tau(\theta)} \xi_\tau(\theta) \xi_\tau(\theta)^T - \xi_\tau(\theta) \xi_{2\tau}(\theta)^T - \xi_{2\tau}(\theta) \xi_\tau(\theta)^T\right), \tag{16}$$

where

$$J_\tau(\theta) = \int f_\theta(x)^{\tau+1} u_\theta(x) u_\theta(x)^T dx, \tag{17}$$

and $\kappa_\tau(\theta)$ and $\xi_\tau(\theta)$ are as in (9) and (10), respectively.

Toma and Leoni-Aubin [16] defined new robust and efficient measures based on the RP. Later, Toma et al. [17] considered the MRPE for general parametric models and developed a model selection criterion for regression models. Broniatowski et al. [8] applied the method to the multiple regression model (MRM) with random covariates. Subsequently, Castilla et al. [18] developed Wald-type tests based on MRPE for the MRM, and Castilla et al. [19] studied the MRPE for the MRM in the ultra-high dimensional set-up. Further, Jaenada and Pardo [20,21] considered the MRPE and Wald-type test statistics for generalized linear models (GLM). Despite Wald-type test statistics, there exist others relevant test statistics having an important role in the statistical literature: the likelihood-ratio and Rao (or score) tests, which are based on restricted estimators, usually the RMLE. Then, it makes sense to develop robust versions of these popular statistics based on the RMRPE.

3. The Restricted Minimum Rényi Pseudodistance Estimator: Asymptotic Distribution and Influence Function of RMRPE

In this section, we introduce the RMRPE and we derive its asymptotic distribution. Moreover, we study its robustness properties through its influence function (IF).

Definition 2. *The RMRPE functional $\widetilde{T}_\tau(G)$ evaluated at the distribution G is defined by*

$$R_\tau(g, f_{\widetilde{T}_\tau(G)}) = \min_{\theta \in \Theta_0} R_\tau(g, f_\theta),$$

given that such a minimum exists.

Accordingly, given random sample $X_1, \ldots, X_n$ from the distribution G, the RMRPE of θ is defined as

$$\widetilde{\theta}_\tau = \arg\sup_{\theta \in \Theta_0} \sum_{i=1}^n \frac{f_\theta(X_i)^\tau}{C_\tau(\theta)}.$$

Next, the result states the asymptotic distribution of the RMRPE, $\widetilde{\theta}_\tau = \widetilde{T}_\tau(G)$.

Theorem 2. *Suppose that the true distribution satisfies the conditions of the model and let us denote by $\theta_0 \in \Theta_0$ the true parameter. Then, the RMRPE $\widetilde{\theta}_\tau$ of θ obtained under the constraints $g(\theta) = 0_r$ has distribution*

$$n^{1/2}(\widetilde{\theta}_\tau - \theta_0) \xrightarrow[n \to \infty]{\mathcal{L}} \mathcal{N}(0_p, \Sigma_\tau(\theta_0))$$

where

$$\Sigma_\tau(\theta_0) = P_\tau^*(\theta_0) K_\tau(\theta_0) P_\tau^*(\theta_0)^T,$$

$$P_\tau^*(\theta_0) = S_\tau(\theta_0)^{-1} - Q_\tau(\theta_0) G(\theta_0)^T S_\tau(\theta_0)^{-1}, \tag{18}$$

$$Q_\tau(\theta_0) = S_\tau(\theta_0)^{-1} G(\theta_0) \left[G(\theta_0)^T S_\tau(\theta_0)^{-1} G(\theta_0) \right]^{-1}. \tag{19}$$

and $S_\tau(\theta_0)$ is defined in (13), evaluated at $\theta = \theta_0$.

Proof. See Appendix A. □

To analyze the robustness of an estimator, Hampel et al. [22] introduced the concept of the influence function (IF). Since then, the IF has been widely used in statistical literature to measure robustness in different statistical contexts. Intuitively, the IF describes the effect of an infinitesimal contamination of the model on the estimate. Then, IFs associated to locally robust (B-robust) estimators should be bounded. Let us now obtain the IF of RMRPE and analyze its boundedness to asses the robustness of the proposed estimators. We consider the contaminated model $g_\varepsilon(x) = (1-\varepsilon) f_\theta(x) + \varepsilon \Delta_x$, with Δ_x the indicator function in x, and we denote $\widetilde{\theta}_{\tau,\varepsilon} = \widetilde{T}_\tau(G_\varepsilon)$, being G_ε the distribution function associated to g_ε. By definition, $\widetilde{\theta}_{\tau,\varepsilon}$ is the minimizer of $R_\tau(g, f_\theta)$ subject to $g(\widetilde{\theta}_{\tau,\varepsilon}) = 0$. Following the same steps as in Theorem 5 in Broniatowski et al. [8], it can be seen that the influence function of $\widetilde{T}_\tau$ in f_θ is given by

$$IF(x, \widetilde{T}_\tau, \theta) = M_\tau(\theta)^{-1} [f_\theta(x)^\tau u_\theta(x) - c_\tau(\theta) f_\theta(x)^\tau], \tag{20}$$

where $c_\tau(\theta)$ was defined in (8) and

$$M_\tau(\theta) = \frac{1}{\int f_\theta(x)^{\tau+1} dx} \left[\int f_\theta(x)^{\tau+1} dx \int f_\theta(x)^{\tau+1} u_\theta(x) u_\theta(x)^T dx \right.$$
$$\left. - \left(\int f_\theta(x)^{\tau+1} u_\theta(x) dx \right) \left(\int f_\theta(x)^{\tau+1} u_\theta(x) dx \right)^T \right],$$

with the additional condition that $g(\widetilde{\theta}_{\tau,\varepsilon}) = 0$. Note that expression (20) corresponds to the IF of the unrestricted MRPE. Differentiating this last equation gives, at $\varepsilon = 0$,

$$G(\theta)^T IF(x, \widetilde{T}_\tau, \theta) = 0. \tag{21}$$

Based on (20) and (21) we have

$$\begin{pmatrix} M_\tau(\theta) \\ G(\theta)^T \end{pmatrix} IF(x, \widetilde{T}_\tau, \theta) = \begin{pmatrix} [f_\theta(x)^\tau u_\theta(x) - c_\tau(\theta) f_\theta(x)^\tau] \\ 0 \end{pmatrix}.$$

Therefore,

$$\begin{pmatrix} M_\tau(\theta)^T & G(\theta) \end{pmatrix} \begin{pmatrix} M_\tau(\theta) \\ G(\theta)^T \end{pmatrix} IF(x, \widetilde{T}_\tau, \theta) = M_\tau(\theta)^T [f_\theta(x)^\tau u_\theta(x) - c_\tau(\theta) f_\theta(x)^\tau]$$

and

$$IF(x, \widetilde{T}_\tau, \theta) = \left(M_\tau(\theta)^T M_\tau(\theta) + G(\theta) G(\theta)^T\right)^{-1} M_\tau(\theta)^T [f_\theta(x)^\tau u_\theta(x) - c_\tau(\theta) f_\theta(x)^\tau]. \tag{22}$$

Note that matrices $M_\tau(\theta)$ and $G(\theta)$ involved in the expression (22) are defined except for the model and tuning parameters θ and τ, and so the boundedness of the IF of the RMRPE depends, therefore, on the boundedness of the factor

$$[f_\theta(x)^\tau u_\theta(x) - c_\tau(\theta) f_\theta(x)^\tau].$$

Therefore, the boundedness of the IF of the RMRPE depends directly on the boundedness of IF of the MRPE, stated in (20). The IF of the MRPE has been widely studied for general statistical models, concluding that the MRPEs are robust for positive values of τ, and that such robustness increases with the tuning parameter. A whole discussion can be found in the work of Broniatowski et al. [8]. Hence, the same properties hold for RMRPEs.

4. Robust Test Statistics Based on RMRPEs

In this section, we develop two statistics based on the RMRPEs for testing composite null hypothesis, and their asymptotic distributions are obtained. Both procedures are particularized to standard deviation testing (with unknown mean) under normal populations, and explicit expressions of the test statistics are obtained.

4.1. Testing Based on Divergence Measures

In this section, we present the family of Rényi's pseudodistance test statistics (RPTS) for testing the null hypothesis given in (3). This family of test statistics is given by

$$T_\gamma(\widehat{\theta}_\tau, \widetilde{\theta}_\tau) = 2n R_\gamma(f_{\widehat{\theta}_\tau}, f_{\widetilde{\theta}_\tau}). \tag{23}$$

The RPTS, $T_\gamma(\widehat{\theta}_\tau, \widetilde{\theta}_\tau)$, can be understood as a measure between the best unrestricted estimator of the model parameter, and the best estimator satisfying the null hypothesis. Large values of the RPTS indicate that the model densities associated with the restricted and unrestricted estimators are far away one from the other, and so the null hypothesis is not supported by the observed data. Hence, we should reject H_0 for large enough $T_\gamma(\widehat{\theta}_\tau, \widetilde{\theta}_\tau)$. We can observe that the family of RPTS defined in (23) depends on two tuning parameters, τ and γ. The first is used for estimating the unknown parameters, while the second is applied to obtain the family of test statistics. The following theorem presents the asymptotic distribution of the family of RPTS defined in (23).

Theorem 3. *The asymptotic distribution of $T_\gamma(\widehat{\theta}_\tau, \widetilde{\theta}_\tau)$ defined in (23) coincides, under the null hypothesis H_0 given in (3), with the distribution of the random variable*

$$\sum_{i=1}^r \lambda_i^{\tau,\gamma}(\theta_0) Z_i^2,$$

where $Z_1, \ldots, Z_r$ are independent standard normal variables, $\lambda_1^{\tau,\gamma}(\theta_0), \ldots, \lambda_r^{\tau,\gamma}(\theta_0)$ are the nonzero eigenvalues of $M_{\gamma,\tau}(\theta_0) = A_\gamma(\theta_0) B_\tau(\theta_0) K_\tau(\theta_0) B_\tau(\theta_0)$ and $k = r$. The matrices $A_\gamma(\theta_0)$ and $B_\tau(\theta_0)$ are given by,

$$A_\gamma(\theta_0) = \frac{S_\gamma(\theta_0)}{K_\tau(\theta_0)}, \tag{24}$$

$$B_\tau(\theta_0) = Q_\tau(\theta_0) G(\theta_0)^T S_\tau(\theta_0)^{-1}. \tag{25}$$

Proof. See Appendix A. □

Rényi's Pseudodistance Test Statistics for Normal Populations

Under the $\mathcal{N}(\mu, \sigma^2)$ model, consider the problem of testing

$$H_0 : \sigma = \sigma_0 \text{ versus } H_1 : \sigma \neq \sigma_0 \tag{26}$$

where μ is an unknown nuisance parameter. In this case, the unrestricted and null parameter spaces are given by $\Theta = \{(\mu, \sigma^2) \in \mathbb{R}^2 | \mu \in \mathbb{R}, \sigma^2 \in \mathbb{R}^+\}$ and $\Theta_0 = \{(\mu, \sigma) \in \mathbb{R}^2 | \sigma = \sigma_0, \mu \in \mathbb{R}\}$, respectively. If we consider the function $g(\theta) = \sigma - \sigma_0$, with $\theta = (\mu, \sigma)^T$, the null hypothesis H_0 can be written as

$$H_0 : g(\theta) = 0$$

and we are in the situation considered in (26). We can observe that in our case $G(\theta) = (0, 1)^T$. Based on (6) and taking into account the fact that $f_\theta(x)$ is the normal density with mean μ and variance σ^2, the MRPE $\widehat{\theta}_\tau = (\widehat{\mu}_\tau, \widehat{\sigma}_\tau)^T$ of $\theta = (\mu, \sigma)^T$ is the solution of the system of nonlinear equations

$$\begin{cases} \sum_{i=1}^n (X_i - \mu) \exp\left\{-\frac{\tau}{2}\left(\frac{X_i - \mu}{\sigma}\right)^2\right\} = 0 \\ \sum_{i=1}^n \left\{\left(\frac{X_i - \mu}{\sigma}\right)^2 - \frac{1}{1+\tau}\right\} \exp\left\{-\frac{\tau}{2}\left(\frac{X_i - \mu}{\sigma}\right)^2\right\} = 0 \end{cases}$$

while the RMRPE $\widetilde{\theta}_\beta = (\widetilde{\mu}_\tau, \sigma_0)^T$, when $\sigma = \sigma_0$ is the solution of the nonlinear equation

$$\sum_{i=1}^n \left\{\left(\frac{X_i - \mu}{\sigma_0}\right)^2 - \frac{1}{1+\tau}\right\} \exp\left\{-\frac{\tau}{2}\left(\frac{X_i - \mu}{\sigma_0}\right)^2\right\} = 0.$$

After some algebra (see the Appendix A) we obtain that the RPTS for testing (26) under normal populations can be expressed as

$$T_\gamma(\widehat{\theta}_\tau, \widetilde{\theta}_\tau) = 2n R_\gamma\left(\mathcal{N}(\widehat{\mu}_\tau, \widehat{\sigma}_\tau^2), \mathcal{N}(\widetilde{\mu}_\tau, \sigma_0)\right) \tag{27}$$

$$= \frac{2n}{\gamma(\gamma+1)} \log\left[\frac{1}{\widehat{\sigma}_\tau \sigma_0^\gamma}\left(\frac{\sqrt{\widehat{\sigma}_\tau^2 + \gamma \sigma_0^2}}{\sqrt{\gamma+1}}\right)^{\gamma+1}\right] + n \frac{(\widehat{\mu}_\tau - \widetilde{\mu}_\tau)^2}{(\gamma \sigma_0^2 + \widehat{\sigma}_\tau^2)}$$

Based in (27), and taking into account that the eigenvalue of the matrix $A_\gamma(\theta) B_\tau(\theta) K_\tau(\theta) B_\tau(\theta)$ is given by (see Appendix A)

$$l_{\tau,\gamma}(\sigma) = \frac{1}{2} \frac{(\tau+1)^3}{(\gamma+1)^2 (2\tau+1)^{\frac{5}{2}}} \left(3\tau^2 + 4\tau + 2\right),$$

we apply Theorem 3 such that

$$l_{\tau,\gamma}(\sigma_0)^{-1} \left(\frac{2n}{\gamma(\gamma+1)} \log\left[\frac{1}{\widehat{\sigma}_\tau \sigma_0^\gamma}\left(\frac{\sqrt{\widehat{\sigma}_\tau^2 + \gamma \sigma_0^2}}{\sqrt{\gamma+1}}\right)^{\gamma+1}\right] + n \frac{(\widehat{\mu}_\tau - \widetilde{\mu}_\tau)^2}{(\gamma \sigma_0^2 + \widehat{\sigma}_\tau^2)}\right) \xrightarrow[n \to \infty]{L} \chi_1^2.$$

Note that the RPTS is indexed by two tuning parameters, γ and τ, the first controlling the robustness of the pseudodistance and the second controlling the robustness on the estimation. For simplicity, we use $\gamma = \tau$ for the normal population application.

Remark 1. *For $\tau = \gamma = 0$, the RPTS coincides with the asymptotic likelihood ratio test for testing* (26). *Indeed, for $\tau = 0$, we have that the MLE and RMLE are given, respectively, by*

$$\widehat{\boldsymbol{\theta}} = (\overline{X}, \widehat{\sigma}_n^2 = \frac{1}{n}\sum_{i=1}^n (X_i - \overline{X})^2) \text{ and } \widetilde{\boldsymbol{\theta}} = (\overline{X}, \sigma_0^2).$$

Now, the expression of the Kullback–Leibler divergence (the RP for $\gamma = 0$) between two normal densities, $\mathcal{N}(\mu_1, \sigma_1)$ and $\mathcal{N}(\mu_2, \sigma_2)$, is given by

$$\lim_{\gamma \to 0} R_\gamma(\mathcal{N}(\mu_1,\sigma_1), \mathcal{N}(\mu_2,\sigma_2)) = \frac{\sigma_2^2 - \sigma_1^2}{2\sigma_1^2} + \ln\frac{\sigma_1}{\sigma_2} + \frac{1}{2}\frac{(\mu_1 - \mu_2)^2}{\sigma_1^2}. \tag{28}$$

and thus the RPTS for $\gamma = \tau = 0$ is

$$T_0(\widehat{\boldsymbol{\theta}}, \widetilde{\boldsymbol{\theta}}) = n\frac{\sigma_0^2}{\widehat{\sigma}_n^2} - n + 2n\ln\frac{\widehat{\sigma}_n}{\sigma_0}.$$

On the other hand, the likelihood ratio for testing (26) *is given by*

$$\lambda(X_1, \ldots, X_n) = \left(\frac{\widehat{\sigma}_n}{\sigma_0}\right)^{n/2} e^{-n\frac{\widehat{\sigma}_n^2}{2\sigma_0^2}} e^{n/2},$$

and so, both expressions are related through

$$-2\ln\lambda(X_1, \ldots, X_n) = T_0(\widehat{\boldsymbol{\theta}}, \widetilde{\boldsymbol{\theta}}).$$

4.2. Rao's-Type Tests Based on RMRPE

Rao test statistics are one of the most popular score test statistics for testing a simple and composite null hypothesis in general statistical models. For the simple null hypothesis testing, it requires no parameter estimation, but for composite ones, the classical Rao test is based on the likelihood score function associated with the restricted MLE (see Rao [23]). Basu et al. [24] generalized Rao's procedure by using score functions associated with RMDPDEs, bringing in a considerable gain of robustness of the Rao-type test obtained. In this section, we develop Rao-type test statistics based on the score function associated to RMRPEs.

Let us consider the τ-score function associated to the RMRPE,

$$\boldsymbol{\psi}_\tau(x; \boldsymbol{\theta}) = f_{\boldsymbol{\theta}}(x)^\tau (\boldsymbol{u}_{\boldsymbol{\theta}}(x) - \boldsymbol{c}_\tau(\boldsymbol{\theta})),$$

so the estimating equations for the MRPE are given by

$$\sum_{i=1}^n \boldsymbol{\psi}_\tau(x_i; \boldsymbol{\theta}) = \boldsymbol{0}_p.$$

Then, the τ-score statistic can be defined as

$$\boldsymbol{\Psi}_\tau(\boldsymbol{\theta}) = \sum_{i=1}^n \boldsymbol{\psi}_\tau(x_i; \boldsymbol{\theta}) = \left(\sum_{i=1}^n \psi_\tau^1(x_i; \boldsymbol{\theta}), \ldots, \sum_{i=1}^n \psi_\tau^k(x_i; \boldsymbol{\theta})\right)^T.$$

However, taking expectations in the corresponding quantities, it is not difficult to show that

$$E\left[\left(\frac{\tau}{C_\tau(\boldsymbol{\theta})}f_{\boldsymbol{\theta}}(X)^\tau(u_{\boldsymbol{\theta}}(X)-c_\tau(\boldsymbol{\theta}))\right)_{\boldsymbol{\theta}=\boldsymbol{\theta}_0}\right]=\mathbf{0}_p$$

$$E\left[\left(f_{\boldsymbol{\theta}}(X)^{2\tau}(u_{\boldsymbol{\theta}}(X)-c_\tau(\boldsymbol{\theta}))(u_{\boldsymbol{\theta}}(X)-c_\tau(\boldsymbol{\theta}))^T\right)_{\boldsymbol{\theta}=\boldsymbol{\theta}_0}\right]=\boldsymbol{K}_\tau(\boldsymbol{\theta}_0),$$

where $\boldsymbol{K}_\tau(\boldsymbol{\theta})$ is defined in (16), and so, by the central limit theorem, the τ-score statistic is asymptotically normal,

$$\frac{1}{\sqrt{n}}\boldsymbol{\Psi}_\tau(\boldsymbol{\theta})\xrightarrow[n\to\infty]{L}\mathcal{N}(\mathbf{0}_p,\boldsymbol{K}_\tau(\boldsymbol{\theta})). \tag{29}$$

The previous convergence motivates the definition of the Rao-type test statistics.

4.2.1. Rao-Type Test Statistics for Testing Simple Null Hypothesis

We first consider the simple null hypothesis test

$$H_0:\boldsymbol{\theta}=\boldsymbol{\theta}_0 \text{ vs. } H_1:\boldsymbol{\theta}\neq\boldsymbol{\theta}_0. \tag{30}$$

Then, the Rao-type test statistics $R_\tau(\boldsymbol{\theta}_0)$ for testing (30) is defined as

$$R_\tau(\boldsymbol{\theta}_0)=\frac{1}{n}\boldsymbol{\Psi}_\tau(\boldsymbol{\theta}_0)^T\boldsymbol{K}_\tau(\boldsymbol{\theta}_0)^{-1}\boldsymbol{\Psi}_\tau(\boldsymbol{\theta}_0).$$

Note that here the last test statistics depend on τ through the matrices $\boldsymbol{\Psi}_\tau(\boldsymbol{\theta}_0)$ and $\boldsymbol{K}_\tau(\boldsymbol{\theta}_0)$ involved in the definition, and again, the robustness of the statistics increases with τ. Moreover, the last matrix may have an explicit expression for certain statistical models, but otherwise it would have to be estimated from the sample.

Further, from (29), we have that, under the null hypothesis,

$$R_\tau(\boldsymbol{\theta}_0)\xrightarrow[n\to\infty]{L}\chi_p^2$$

with p being the dimension of the parameter space. Then, the null hypothesis is rejected if $R_\tau(\boldsymbol{\theta}_0)>\chi_{p,\alpha}^2$, where $\chi_{p,\alpha}^2$ denotes the upper α-quantile of a chi-square distribution with p degrees of freedom.

4.2.2. Rao-Type Test Statistics for Testing Composite Null Hypothesis

Next, let us consider composite null hypothesis of the form

$$H_0:\mathbf{g}(\boldsymbol{\theta})=\mathbf{0}_r \text{ vs. } H_1:\mathbf{g}(\boldsymbol{\theta})\neq\mathbf{0}_r, \tag{31}$$

where the function $\mathbf{g}:\mathbb{R}^p\to\mathbb{R}^r$ is a differentiable vector-valued function. Then, any vector $\boldsymbol{\theta}$ satisfying the null hypothesis belongs to a restricted parameter space given in (3). The generalized Rao-type test statistic associated to the RMRPE with tuning parameter τ, $\widetilde{\boldsymbol{\theta}}_\tau$, for testing (31) is given by

$$R_\tau\left(\widetilde{\boldsymbol{\theta}}_\tau\right)=\frac{1}{n}\boldsymbol{\Psi}_\tau(\widetilde{\boldsymbol{\theta}}_\tau)^T\boldsymbol{Q}_\tau(\widetilde{\boldsymbol{\theta}}_\tau)\left[\boldsymbol{Q}_\tau(\widetilde{\boldsymbol{\theta}}_\tau)^T\boldsymbol{K}_\tau(\widetilde{\boldsymbol{\theta}}_\tau)\boldsymbol{Q}_\tau(\widetilde{\boldsymbol{\theta}}_\tau)\right]^{-1}\boldsymbol{Q}_\tau(\widetilde{\boldsymbol{\theta}}_\tau)^T\boldsymbol{\Psi}_\tau(\widetilde{\boldsymbol{\theta}}_\tau). \tag{32}$$

Using similar arguments to Basu et al. [24], it is possible to show that, under general regularity conditions, the Rao-type test statistics $R_\tau\left(\widetilde{\boldsymbol{\theta}}_\tau\right)$ have an asymptotic chi-square distribution with r degrees of freedom under the null hypothesis given in (31). Therefore, the rejection region of the test is given by

$$\{X_1,\ldots,X_n:R_\tau(\widetilde{\boldsymbol{\theta}}_\tau)>\chi_{r,\alpha}^2\}.$$

Again, the tuning parameter τ controls the trade-off between efficiency and robustness of the test. Indeed, for $\tau=0$, the generalized Rao type test statistic $R_{\tau=0}\left(\widetilde{\boldsymbol{\theta}}_0\right)$ coincides with the classical Rao test for composite null hypothesis.

4.2.3. Rao Test for Normal Populations

Consider the test defined in (26) for testing the standard deviation value of a normal population with unknown mean. The explicit expression of the main matrices involved in the definition (32) for such testing procedure and assumed parametric model is given by

$$\boldsymbol{\psi}_\tau(X;(\mu,\sigma)) = \left(\frac{X-\mu}{\sigma^2} \frac{1}{\left(\sigma\sqrt{2\pi}\right)^\tau} e^{-\frac{\tau}{2}\left(\frac{X-\mu}{\sigma}\right)^2}, \left(\left(\frac{X-\mu}{\sigma}\right)^2 - \frac{1}{1+\tau} \right) \frac{1}{\sigma} \frac{1}{\left(\sigma\sqrt{2\pi}\right)^\tau} e^{-\frac{\tau}{2}\left(\frac{X-\mu}{\sigma}\right)^2} \right)^T,$$

$$\boldsymbol{K}_\tau((\mu,\sigma)) = \frac{1}{\sigma^2} \frac{1}{\left(\sigma\sqrt{2\pi}\right)^{2\tau}(1+2\tau)^{3/2}} \begin{pmatrix} 1 & 0 \\ 0 & \frac{3\tau^2+2+4\tau}{(1+\tau)^2(1+2\tau)} \end{pmatrix},$$

$$\boldsymbol{Q}_\tau((\mu,\sigma)) = \begin{pmatrix} 0 \\ 1 \end{pmatrix}.$$

The step-by-step calculation of such values are detailed in the Appendix A. Then, the Rao-type test for composite null hypothesis of the form (31) is given by

$$R_\tau(\widetilde{\mu}) = \frac{1}{n} \frac{(1+2\tau)^{3/2}(1+\tau)^2(1+2\tau)}{3\tau^2+4\tau+2} \left[\sum_{i=1}^n \left(\left(\frac{x_i-\widetilde{\mu}}{\sigma_0}\right)^2 - \frac{1}{\tau+1} \right) e^{-\frac{\tau}{2}\left(\frac{x_i-\widetilde{\mu}}{\sigma_0}\right)^2} \right]^2$$

where $(\widetilde{\mu}_\tau, \sigma_0)$ denotes the RMRPE with tuning parameter τ. Note that, for $\tau = 0$, $\widetilde{\mu}_{\tau=0} = \overline{X}$. Then, the Rao-type test statistic based on RMRPE with $\tau = 0$ (the restricted MLE) coincides with the classical Rao test.

5. Simulation Study: Application to Normal Populations

In this section, we empirically analyze the performance of the proposed estimators under the normal parametric model and RPTS and Rao-type test statistics for the problem of testing (26) in terms of efficiency and robustness. We examine the accuracy of the RMRPEs, and we further examine the robustness properties of both families of estimators under different contamination scenarios. Further, we investigate the empirical level and power of the proposed test statistics under different sample sizes and contamination scenarios.

Let us consider a univariate normal model with true parameter value $\theta_0 = (\mu = 0, \sigma = 1)$, and the problem of testing

$$H_0 : \sigma = 1 \text{ vs. } H_1 : \sigma \neq 1. \tag{33}$$

The restricted parameter space is then given by

$$\Theta_0 = \{(\mu, 1) : \mu \in \mathbb{R}\}.$$

In order to evaluate the robustness properties of the estimators and test statistics, we introduce contamination in data by replacing a $\varepsilon\%$ of the observations by a contaminated sample, where ε denotes the contamination level. We generate five different scenarios of contamination:

- Pure data.
- Scenario 1: Slightly contaminated data. We replace a $\varepsilon\%$ of the samples by a contaminated sample from a normal distribution, $\mathcal{N}(0, \sqrt{3})$.
- Scenario 2: Heavily contaminated data. We replace a $\varepsilon\%$ of the samples by a contaminated sample from a normal distribution, $\mathcal{N}(0, \sqrt{5})$.

Further, in order to evaluate the power of the test, we consider an alternative true parameter value $\theta_1 = (0, 0.7)$ which does not satisfy the null hypothesis (33) (or equivalently the restrictions of the parameter space). In this scenario, contaminated parameters are set $\theta_1 = (0, 1.2)$ for slightly and $\theta_1 = (0, 1.5)$ for heavily contamination.

Figure 1 shows the root mean square error (RMSE) of the RMRPE of the scale parameter σ, for different values of the tuning parameter $\tau = 0, 0.2, 0.4, 0.6$ and $\tau = 0.8$ over $R = 10{,}000$ replications. As expected, large values of the tuning parameter produce more robust estimators, which is particularly advantageous for the heavily contaminated scenario. Furthermore, even when introducing very low levels of contamination in data, $\varepsilon = 5\%$, the RMRPE with moderate value of the tuning parameter outperforms the classical MLE, without a significant loss of efficiency in the absence of contamination.

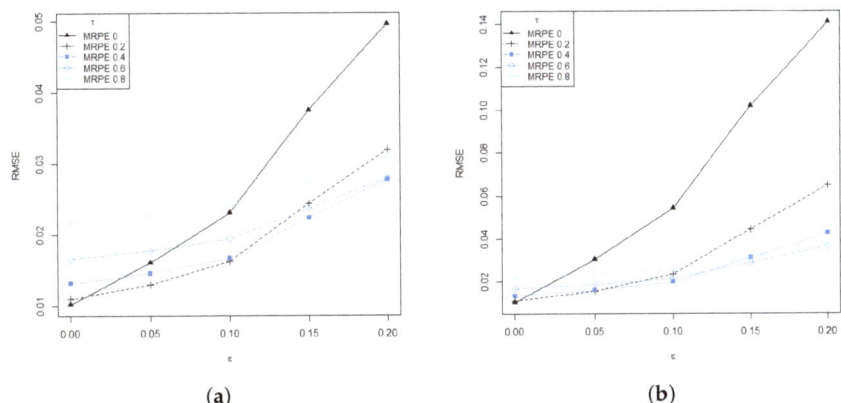

Figure 1. RMSE of the RMRPE under increasing contamination levels (slightly contaminated at left and heavily contaminated at right) for different values of the tuning parameter τ over $R = 10{,}000$ replications. (**a**) Scenario 1, (**b**) Scenario 2.

On the other hand, Figure 2 presents the empirical level and power of both RPTS and Rao-type test statistics based on RMRPEs for different values of the tuning parameter, $\tau = 0, 0.2, 0.4, 0.6, 0.8$, under increasing contamination levels. The empirical level and power are computed as the mean number of rejections over $R = 10{,}000$ replications. The empirical level produced by the classical ratio and Rao-type tests rapidly increases and separates from levels obtained with any robust test. Regarding the empirical power, all robust tests with moderate and large values of the tuning parameter outperform the classical estimator within their family under contaminated scenarios, but Rao-type test statistics based on RMRPEs are more conservative than RPTSs, thus exhibiting lower levels and powers. Then, the proposed test statistics provides an appealing alternative to classical likelihood ratio and Rao tests, with a small loss of efficiency in favor of a clear gain in terms of robustness.

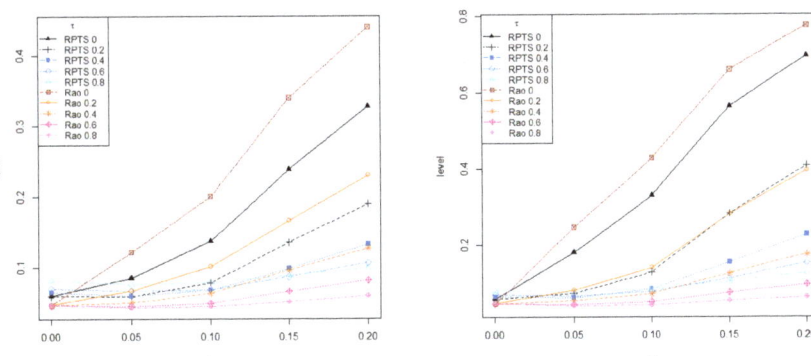

Figure 2. *Cont.*

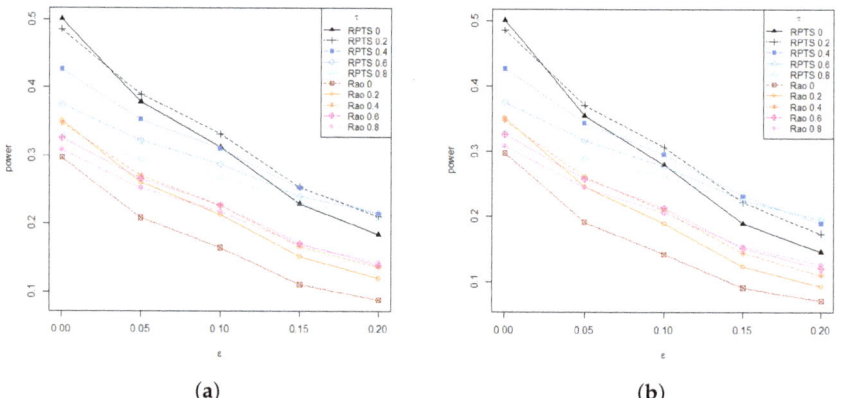

Figure 2. Empirical level and power under increasing contamination (slightly contaminated at left and heavily contaminated at right) over $R = 10{,}000$ repetitions. (**a**) Scenario 1, (**b**) Scenario 2.

On the other hand, the sample size could play a crucial role in the performance of the tests, even more accentuated when there exists data contamination. Figure 3 shows the sample size effect on the performance of the tests in terms of empirical level, under a 10% of contamination level in data. As discussed, Rao-type test statistics based on RMRPEs is more conservative and so tests based on RMRPEs with positive values of the tuning parameter produce lower empirical levels. Here, it outperforms the poor performance of the classical Rao-type test statistics with respect to any other. Moreover, when the sample size increases, the performance gap between non-robust and robust methods is widening.

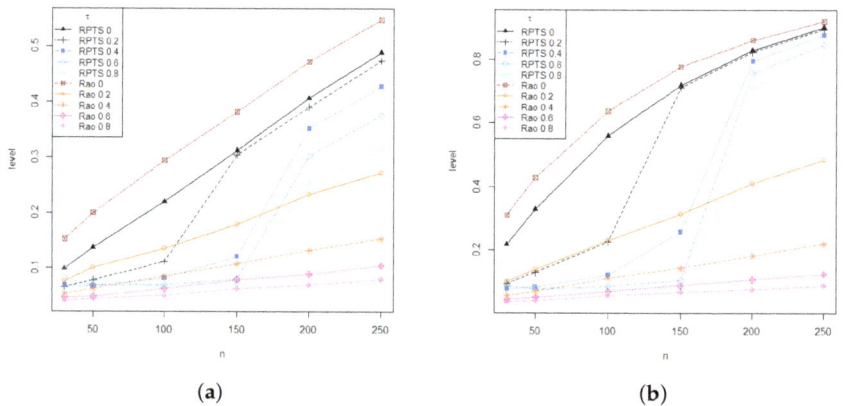

Figure 3. Empirical level under increasing sample sizes for 10% of contamination level (slightly contaminated at left and heavily contaminated at right) over $R = 10{,}000$ repetitions. (**a**) Scenario 1, (**b**) Scenario 2.

Following the discussions in the preceding sections, larger values of the tuning parameter produce more robust but less efficient estimators. Therefore, the optimal value of τ should obtain the best trade-off between efficiency and robustness. Warwick and Jones [25] first introduced a useful data-based procedure for the choice of the tuning parameter for the MDPDE based on minimizing the asymptotic MSE of the estimator. However, this method depends on the choice of a pilot estimator, and Basak et al. [26] improved the method by removing the dependency on an initial estimator. The proposed algorithm was developed ad hoc for the MDPDE, but it can be easily adapted to the MRPE and RMRPE by simply substituting the expression of the variance of the MDPDE by the variance of the MRPPE or the RMRPE, respectively.

6. Real Data Application

Finally, we illustrate the outperformance of the proposed test statistics in two real data applications, where the gathered information contains some outlying observations. Both real dataset are modeled under the normal model, and hypothesis tests on the standard deviation of the population are performed.

6.1. Telephone-Fault Data

We consider the data on telephone line faults presented and analyzed by Welch [27] and Simpson [4]. The dataset consist of $n = 14$ ordered differences between the inverse test rates and the inverse control rates in matched pairs of areas,

$$-988, -135, -78, 3, 59, 83, 93, 110, 189, 197, 204, 229, 289, 310.$$

Basu et al. ([24,28]) modeled these differences as a normal random variable and pointed out that the first observation is a clear outlier, as its value is distant from the rest of the data. They tested simple and composite null hypotheses for the mean under the normal model, as well as a simple null hypothesis assuming a known mean. Here, we propose to test for the standard deviation of the normal distribution. Note that, computing the MLE of the sample with full and clean data (after removing the outlying observation), we obtain $(\hat{\mu}, \hat{\sigma}) = (40.36, 323.08)$, and $(\hat{\mu}, \hat{\sigma}) = (119.46, 134.82)$, respectively. Accordingly, the outlier clearly influences the model parameter estimates, playing a crucial role on the rejection of any null hypothesis. We consider the composite null hypothesis

$$H_0 : \sigma = 135 \text{ vs. } H_1 : \sigma \neq 135, \tag{34}$$

where the value $\sigma = 135$ has been chosen according to the estimation with clean data.

Figure 4 presents the RPTS (top) and Rao (bottom) test statistics (left) and p-values (right) for the telephone data against increasing tuning parameters. While it is clearly seen that both classical tests fail to not reject the null hypothesis when fitting the model with the original data, the decision turns around sharply as the tuning parameter τ crosses and goes beyond 0.2 for the RPTS and 0.15 for Rao-type test statistics based on MRPEs. On the other hand, the decision of not rejecting is agreed by all statistics when fitting the model with clean data. This example illustrates the great applicability of the robust methods, which are not too affected by a such outlying observation, and the good performance of the proposed statistics under contaminated observations, which stay stable.

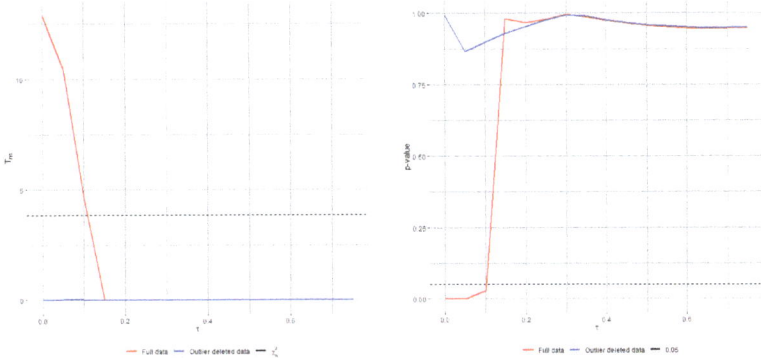

Figure 4. *Cont.*

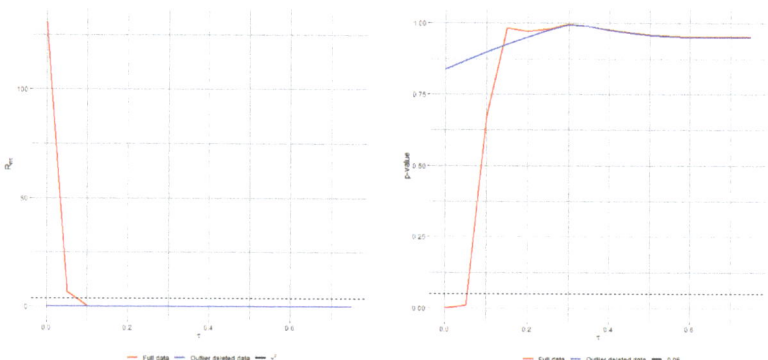

Figure 4. RPTS (**top**) and Rao-type test statistics (**bottom**), jointly with their associated *p*-valuess (right), for testing (34) with original and cleaned (after outliers removal) telephone-fault data.

6.2. Darwin's Plant Fertilization Data

Darwin [29] performed an experiment to determine whether self-fertilized plants and cross-fertilized plants have different growth rates. He sowed in pots pairs of *Zea mays* plants, one self-fertilized and the other cross-fertilized, and after a specific time period, the height of each plant was measured. A particular sample of $n = 15$ pairs of plants led to the following paired differences (cross-fertilized minus self-fertilized).

$$-67, -48, 6, 8, 14, 16, 23, 24, 28, 29, 41, 49, 56, 60, 75$$

A parametric approach to analyze the data as a random sample from a normal distribution with unknown mean and standard deviation was developed by Basu et al. [24]. Here, there is not any huge outlying observation, but the first two observations seem to be distant from the rest of the sample, influencing the model parameter estimates and test decisions. Indeed, the MLE, computing with original data, is $(\widehat{\mu}, \widehat{\sigma}) = (20.93, 37.74)$, while the MLE, when removing the two first observations, switches to $(\widehat{\mu}, \widehat{\sigma}) = (33, 21.54)$. Therefore, removing influential observations may alter the decision of a test. According to these results, we consider the testing problem

$$H_0 : \sigma = 23 \text{ vs. } H_1 : \sigma \neq 23. \tag{35}$$

Figure 5 shows the test statistics (left) and corresponding *p*-values (right) for the two families of statistics considered, the RPTS (top) and Rao-type test statistics (bottom) against the tuning parameter value τ. Again, test statistics based on RMRPE with large enough tuning parameters do not reject the null hypothesis, unlike tests based on low values of $\tau = 0$, including the RMLE. The disagreement departs when using the clean data, as all tests agree on not rejecting the null hypothesis.

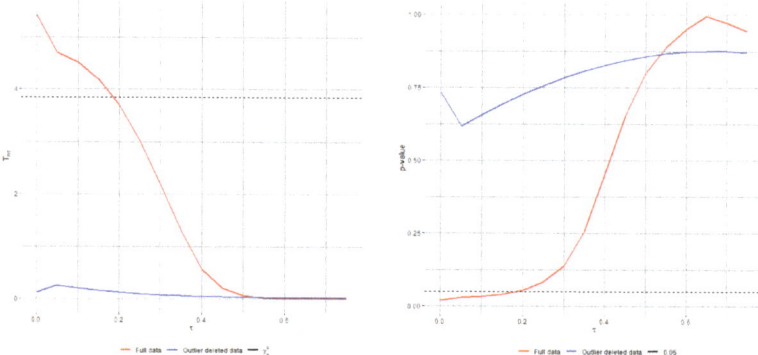

Figure 5. *Cont.*

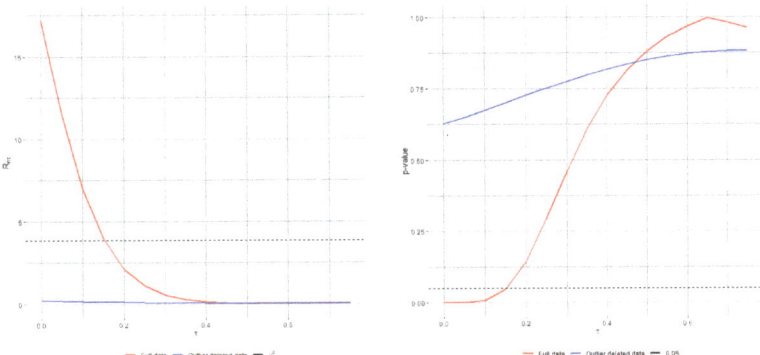

Figure 5. RPTS (**top**) and Rao-type test statistics (**bottom**), jointly with their associated p-values (right), for testing (35) with original and cleaned (after outliers removal) Darwing data.

7. Concluding Remarks

In this paper, we presented for the first time the family of RMRPEs. We derived their asymptotic distribution, and proved some suitable properties as consistency under the parameter restriction and robustness against data contamination. Further, based on these RMRPEs, we generalized two important families of statistics, namely RPTS and Rao-type tests, for testing a composite null hypothesis. Moreover, we obtained some explicit expressions of the RMRPEs, RPTS and Rao-type test statistics for testing the variance under a normal population with an unknown mean. It was empirically shown that the proposed RPTS and Rao-type test statistics are robust, unlike classical tests based on the MLE, under normal populations. Indeed, the robustness of the tests is controlled by a tuning parameter τ, and so larger values of τ produce more robust estimators (although less efficient). Finally, some classical numerical examples illustrate the theoretical properties and applicability of the proposed methods.

Author Contributions: Conceptualization, M.J., P.M. and L.P.; methodology, M.J., P.M. and L.P.; software, M.J., P.M. and L.P.; validation, M.J., P.M. and L.P.; formal analysis, M.J., P.M. and L.P.; investigation, M.J., P.M. and L.P.; resources, M.J., P.M. and L.P.; data curation, M.J., P.M. and L.P.; writing—original draft preparation, M.J., P.M. and L.P.; writing—review and editing, M.J., P.M. and L.P.; visualization, M.J., P.M. and L.P.; supervision, M.J., P.M. and L.P.; project administration, M.J., P.M. and L.P.; funding acquisition, M.J., P.M. and L.P. All authors have read and agreed to the published version of the manuscript.

Funding: This research is supported by the Spanish Grants PGC2018-095 194-B-100 (M. Jaenada, P. Miranda and L. Pardo) and FPU 19/01824 (M.Jaenada). The three authors are members of the Interdisciplinary Mathematics Institute (IMI).

Institutional Review Board Statement: Not applicable.

Informed Consent Statement: Not applicable.

Data Availability Statement: Not applicable.

Acknowledgments: We are very grateful to the referees and associate editor for their helpful comments and suggestions.

Conflicts of Interest: The authors declare no conflict of interest. The funders had no role in the design of the study; in the collection, analyses, or interpretation of data; in the writing of the manuscript, or in the decision to publish the results.

Abbreviations

The following abbreviations are used in this manuscript:

DPD	Density Power Divergence
IF	Influence Function
KL	Kullback–Leibler
LRM	Linear Regression Model
MLE	Maximum Likelihood Estimator
MDPDE	Minimum Density Power Divergence Estimator
MRPE	Minimum Rényi Pseudodistance Estimator
RMRPE	Restricted minimum Rényi Pseudodistance Estimator
RP	Rényi Pseudodistance
RPTS	Rényi Pseudodistance test statistic

Appendix A

Appendix A.1. Proof of Theorem 2

We denote

$$h_n(\boldsymbol{\theta}) = \frac{1}{n}\sum_{i=1}^{n} \frac{f_{\boldsymbol{\theta}}(X_i)^\tau}{C_\tau(\boldsymbol{\theta})}.$$

Differentiating both sides of the equality, we have

$$\frac{\partial h_n(\boldsymbol{\theta})}{\partial \boldsymbol{\theta}} = \frac{\tau}{C_\tau(\boldsymbol{\theta})}\frac{1}{n}\sum_{i=1}^{n} f_{\boldsymbol{\theta}}(X_i)^\tau (\boldsymbol{u}_{\boldsymbol{\theta}}(X_i) - \boldsymbol{c}_\tau(\boldsymbol{\theta})).$$

Now we establish that

$$\left(\frac{\partial^2 h_n(\boldsymbol{\theta})}{\partial \boldsymbol{\theta} \partial \boldsymbol{\theta}^T}\right)_{\boldsymbol{\theta}=\boldsymbol{\theta}_0} \xrightarrow[n\to\infty]{P} -\frac{\tau}{C_\tau(\boldsymbol{\theta})}\boldsymbol{S}_\tau(\boldsymbol{\theta}_0).$$

We have

$$\begin{aligned}\frac{\partial^2 h_n(\boldsymbol{\theta})}{\partial \boldsymbol{\theta} \partial \boldsymbol{\theta}^T} &= \frac{1}{C_\tau(\boldsymbol{\theta})^2}\left\{\frac{1}{n}\sum_{i=1}^{n}\left[\left(\tau^2 f_{\boldsymbol{\theta}}(X_i)^\tau \boldsymbol{u}_{\boldsymbol{\theta}}(X_i)\boldsymbol{u}_{\boldsymbol{\theta}}(X_i)^T + \tau f_{\boldsymbol{\theta}}(X_i)^\tau \frac{\partial \boldsymbol{u}_{\boldsymbol{\theta}}(X_i)}{\partial \boldsymbol{\theta}^T}\right)C_\tau(\boldsymbol{\theta})\right.\right.\\ &\qquad\left.\left. -\tau C_\tau(\boldsymbol{\theta})\boldsymbol{c}_\tau(\boldsymbol{\theta})\tau f_{\boldsymbol{\theta}}(X_i)^\tau \boldsymbol{u}_{\boldsymbol{\theta}}(X_i)^T\right]\right\}\\ &\quad -\frac{1}{C_\tau(\boldsymbol{\theta})^2}\left\{\frac{1}{n}\sum_{i=1}^{n}\left[\left(\tau\frac{\partial \boldsymbol{c}_\tau(\boldsymbol{\theta})}{\partial \boldsymbol{\theta}^T}f_{\boldsymbol{\theta}}(X_i)^\tau + \tau^2 f_{\boldsymbol{\theta}}(X_i)^\tau \boldsymbol{c}_\tau(\boldsymbol{\theta})\boldsymbol{u}_{\boldsymbol{\theta}}(X_i)^T\right)C_\tau(\boldsymbol{\theta})\right.\right.\\ &\qquad\left.\left.-\tau C_\tau(\boldsymbol{\theta})\boldsymbol{c}_\tau(\boldsymbol{\theta})\tau \boldsymbol{c}_\tau(\boldsymbol{\theta})^T f_{\boldsymbol{\theta}}(X_i)^\tau\right]\right\}\\ &= \frac{1}{C_\tau(\boldsymbol{\theta})}\left\{\frac{1}{n}\sum_{i=1}^{n}\left[\tau^2 f_{\boldsymbol{\theta}}(X_i)^\tau \boldsymbol{u}_{\boldsymbol{\theta}}(X_i)\boldsymbol{u}_{\boldsymbol{\theta}}(X_i)^T + \tau f_{\boldsymbol{\theta}}(X_i)^\tau \frac{\partial \boldsymbol{u}_{\boldsymbol{\theta}}(X_i)}{\partial \boldsymbol{\theta}^T}\right.\right.\\ &\qquad -\tau^2 \boldsymbol{c}_\tau(\boldsymbol{\theta})^T f_{\boldsymbol{\theta}}(X_i)^\tau \boldsymbol{u}_{\boldsymbol{\theta}}(X_i)^T - \tau\frac{\partial \boldsymbol{c}_\tau(\boldsymbol{\theta})}{\partial \boldsymbol{\theta}^T}f_{\boldsymbol{\theta}}(X_i)^\tau\\ &\qquad\left.\left. -\tau^2 \boldsymbol{c}_\tau(\boldsymbol{\theta})f_{\boldsymbol{\theta}}(X_i)^\tau \boldsymbol{u}_{\boldsymbol{\theta}}(X_i)^T - \tau^2 \boldsymbol{c}_\tau(\boldsymbol{\theta})\boldsymbol{c}_\tau(\boldsymbol{\theta})^T f_{\boldsymbol{\theta}}(X_i)^\tau\right]\right\}.\end{aligned}$$

As $n \to \infty$, we have

$$\left(\frac{\partial^2 h_n(\boldsymbol{\theta})}{\partial \boldsymbol{\theta} \partial \boldsymbol{\theta}^T}\right)_{\boldsymbol{\theta}=\boldsymbol{\theta}_0} \xrightarrow[n\to\infty]{P} \boldsymbol{T}(\boldsymbol{\theta}_0)$$

with $\boldsymbol{T}(\boldsymbol{\theta}_0)$ being the matrix given by

$$\begin{aligned}\boldsymbol{T}(\boldsymbol{\theta}_0) &= \frac{1}{C_\tau(\boldsymbol{\theta})}\left\{\tau^2\int f_{\boldsymbol{\theta}}(x)^{\tau+1}\boldsymbol{u}_{\boldsymbol{\theta}}(x)\boldsymbol{u}_{\boldsymbol{\theta}}(x)^T dx + \tau\int f_{\boldsymbol{\theta}}(x)^{\tau+1}\frac{\partial \boldsymbol{u}_{\boldsymbol{\theta}}(x)}{\partial \boldsymbol{\theta}^T}dx\right.\\ &\qquad -\tau^2 \boldsymbol{c}_\tau(\boldsymbol{\theta})\int f_{\boldsymbol{\theta}}(x)^{\tau+1}\boldsymbol{u}_{\boldsymbol{\theta}}(x)^T dx - \tau\frac{\partial \boldsymbol{c}_\tau(\boldsymbol{\theta})}{\partial \boldsymbol{\theta}^T}\int f_{\boldsymbol{\theta}}(x)^{\tau+1}dx\\ &\qquad\left. +\tau^2 \boldsymbol{c}_\tau(\boldsymbol{\theta})\int f_{\boldsymbol{\theta}}(x)^{\tau+1}\boldsymbol{u}_{\boldsymbol{\theta}}(x)^T dx - \tau^2 \boldsymbol{c}_\tau(\boldsymbol{\theta})\boldsymbol{c}_\tau(\boldsymbol{\theta})^T\int f_{\boldsymbol{\theta}}(x)^{\tau+1}dx\right\}.\end{aligned}$$

From the above, after some algebra, we obtain

$$T(\theta_0) = \frac{1}{C_\tau(\theta)}\left\{\tau^2\int f_\theta(x)^{\tau+1}u_\theta(x)u_\theta(x)^T dx + \tau\int f_\theta(x)^{\tau+1}\frac{\partial u_\theta(x)}{\partial \theta^T}dx\right.$$
$$\left. -\tau\frac{\partial c_\tau(\theta)}{\partial \theta^T}\int f_\theta(x)^{\tau+1}dx - \tau^2 c_\tau(\theta)^T c_\tau(\theta)\int f_\theta(x)^{\tau+1}dx\right\}.$$

On the other hand, it not difficult to establish that

$$\frac{\partial c_\tau(\theta)}{\partial \theta^T} = (\tau+1)\frac{\int f_\theta(x)^{\tau+1}u_\theta(x)u_\theta(x)^T dx}{\int f_\theta(x)^{\tau+1}dx} + \frac{\int f_\theta(x)^{\tau+1}\frac{\partial u_\theta(x)}{\partial \theta^T}dx}{\int f_\theta(x)^{\tau+1}dx}$$
$$-(\tau+1)\frac{\int f_\theta(x)^{\tau+1}u_\theta(x)dx \int f_\theta(x)^{\tau+1}u_\theta(x)^T dx}{\left(\int f_\theta(x)^{\tau+1}dx\right)^2}.$$

Therefore we have

$$-\tau\frac{\partial c_\tau(\theta)}{\partial \theta^T}\int f_\theta(x)^{\tau+1}dx = -\tau(\tau+1)\int f_\theta(x)^{\tau+1}u_\theta(x)u_\theta(x)^T dx - \tau\int f_\theta(x)^{\tau+1}\frac{\partial u_\theta(x)}{\partial \theta^T}$$
$$+\tau(\tau+1)\frac{\int f_\theta(x)^{\tau+1}u_\theta(x)dx \int f_\theta(x)^{\tau+1}u_\theta(x)^T dx}{\int f_\theta(x)^{\tau+1}dx}.$$

Finally,

$$T(\theta_0) = \frac{1}{C_\tau(\theta)}\left\{\tau^2\int f_\theta(x)^{\tau+1}u_\theta(x)u_\theta(x)^T dx + \tau\int f_\theta(x)^{\tau+1}\frac{\partial u_\theta(x)}{\partial \theta^T}dx\right.$$
$$-\tau(\tau+1)\int f_\theta(x)^{\tau+1}u_\theta(x)u_\theta(x)^T dx - \tau\int f_\theta(x)^{\tau+1}\frac{\partial u_\theta(x)}{\partial \theta^T}$$
$$\left.+\tau(\tau+1)\frac{\int f_\theta(x)^{\tau+1}u_\theta(x)dx \int f_\theta(x)^{\tau+1}u_\theta(x)^T dx}{\int f_\theta(x)^{\tau+1}dx} - \tau^2 c_\tau(\theta)c_\tau(\theta)^T\int f_\theta(x)^{\tau+1}dx\right\}$$
$$= \frac{1}{C_\tau(\theta)}\left\{-\tau\int f_\theta(x)^{\tau+1}u_\theta(x)u_\theta(x)^T dx + \tau\frac{\int f_\theta(x)^{\tau+1}u_\theta(x)dx \int f_\theta(x)^{\tau+1}u_\theta(x)^T dx}{\int f_\theta(x)^{\tau+1}dx}\right\}$$
$$= -\frac{\tau}{C_\tau(\theta)}S(\theta_0).$$

On the other hand,

$$\sqrt{n}\frac{\partial h_n(\theta)}{\partial \theta} = \frac{\tau}{C_\tau(\theta)}\frac{1}{\sqrt{n}}\sum_{i=1}^n f_\theta(X_i)^\tau(u_\theta(X_i) - c_\tau(\theta)) \xrightarrow[n\to\infty]{L} \mathcal{N}\left(0_p, \left(\frac{\tau}{C_\tau(\theta)}\right)^2 K_\tau(\theta_0)\right),$$

as

$$E\left[\left(\frac{\tau}{C_\tau(\theta)}f_\theta(X)^\tau(u_\theta(X) - c_\tau(\theta))\right)_{\theta=\theta_0}\right] = 0_p$$

and

$$Cov\left[\left(\frac{\tau}{C_\tau(\theta)}f_\theta(X)^\tau(u_\theta(X) - c_\tau(\theta))\right)_{\theta=\theta_0}\right] = \left(\frac{\tau}{C_\tau(\theta_0)}\right)^2 K_\tau(\theta_0)$$

Then, the RMRPE estimator of θ, $\widetilde{\theta}_\tau$, must satisfy

$$\begin{cases} \frac{\partial}{\partial \theta}h_n(\theta)|_{\theta=\widetilde{\theta}_\tau} + G(\widetilde{\theta}_\tau)\lambda_n = 0_p, \\ g(\widetilde{\theta}_\tau) = 0_r, \end{cases} \tag{A1}$$

where λ_n is a vector of Lagrangian multipliers. Now we consider $\theta_n = \theta_0 + mn^{-1/2}$, with $||m|| < k$, for $0 < k < \infty$. We have,

$$\frac{\partial}{\partial \theta} h_n(\theta)|_{\theta=\theta_n} = \frac{\partial}{\partial \theta} h_n(\theta)|_{\theta=\theta_0} + \frac{\partial}{\partial \theta^T}\frac{\partial}{\partial \theta} h_n(\theta)|_{\theta=\theta_0}(\theta_n - \theta_0) + o(||\theta_n - \theta_0||^2)$$

and

$$n^{1/2}\frac{\partial}{\partial \theta} h_n(\theta)\bigg|_{\theta=\theta_n} = n^{1/2}\frac{\partial}{\partial \theta} h_n(\theta)|_{\theta=\theta_0} - \frac{\partial}{\partial \theta^T}\frac{\partial}{\partial \theta} h_n(\theta)|_{\theta=\theta_0} n^{1/2}(\theta_n - \theta_0) + o(n^{1/2}||\theta_n - \theta_0||^2). \quad (A2)$$

However,

$$o(n^{1/2}||\theta_n - \theta_0||^2) = o(n^{1/2}||m||^2/n) = o(n^{-1/2}||m||^2) = o(O_p(1)) = o_p(1).$$

Since

$$\lim_{n\to\infty} \frac{\partial}{\partial \theta^T}\frac{\partial}{\partial \theta} h_n(\theta)|_{\theta=\theta_0} = -\frac{\tau}{C_\tau(\theta)} S_\tau(\theta_0)$$

we obtain

$$n^{1/2}\frac{\partial}{\partial \theta} h_n(\theta)\bigg|_{\theta=\theta_n} = n^{1/2}\frac{\partial}{\partial \theta} h_n(\theta)|_{\theta=\theta_0} + \frac{\tau}{C_\tau(\theta)} S_\tau(\theta_0) n^{1/2}(\theta_n - \theta_0) + o_p(1). \quad (A3)$$

Now, we know that

$$n^{1/2} g(\theta_n) = G(\theta_0)^T n^{1/2}(\theta_n - \theta_0) + o_p(1). \quad (A4)$$

Further, the RMRPE $\tilde{\theta}_\tau$ must satisfy the conditions in (A1), and in view of (A3) and (A4) we have

$$n^{1/2}\frac{\partial}{\partial \theta} h_n(\theta)|_{\theta=\theta_0} + \frac{\tau}{C_\tau(\theta)} S_\tau(\theta_0) n^{1/2}(\tilde{\theta}_\tau - \theta_0) + G(\theta_0) n^{1/2} \lambda_n + o_p(1) = 0_p. \quad (A5)$$

From (A4) it follows that

$$G(\theta_0)^T n^{1/2}(\tilde{\theta}_\tau - \theta_0) + o_p(1) = 0_r. \quad (A6)$$

Now we can express equations (A5) and (A6) in matrix form as

$$\begin{pmatrix} \frac{\tau}{C_\tau(\theta_0)} S_\tau(\theta_0) & G(\theta_0) \\ G(\theta_0)^T & 0_{r\times r} \end{pmatrix} \begin{pmatrix} n^{1/2}(\tilde{\theta}_\tau - \theta_0) \\ n^{1/2}\lambda_n \end{pmatrix} = \begin{pmatrix} -n^{1/2}\frac{\partial}{\partial \theta} h_n(\theta)|_{\theta=\theta_0} \\ 0_r \end{pmatrix} + o_p(1).$$

Therefore

$$\begin{pmatrix} n^{1/2}(\tilde{\theta}_\tau - \theta_0) \\ n^{1/2}\lambda_n \end{pmatrix} = \begin{pmatrix} \frac{\tau}{C_\tau(\theta_0)} S_\tau(\theta_0) & G(\theta_0) \\ G(\theta_0)^T & 0_{r\times r} \end{pmatrix}^{-1} \begin{pmatrix} -n^{1/2}\frac{\partial}{\partial \theta} h_n(\theta)|_{\theta=\theta_0} \\ 0_r \end{pmatrix} + o_p(1).$$

However,

$$\begin{pmatrix} \frac{\tau}{C_\tau(\theta_0)} S_\tau(\theta_0) & G(\theta_0) \\ G(\theta_0)^T & 0 \end{pmatrix}^{-1} = \begin{pmatrix} \left(\frac{\tau}{C_\tau(\theta_0)}\right)^{-1} P_\tau^*(\theta_0) & Q_\tau(\theta_0) \\ Q_\tau(\theta_0)^T & R_\tau(\theta_0) \end{pmatrix},$$

where $P_\tau^*(\theta_0)$ and $Q_\tau(\theta_0)$ are defined in (18) and (19), respectively. The matrix $R_\tau(\theta_0)$ is the quantity needed to make the right hand side of the above equation equal to the indicated inverse. Then,

$$n^{1/2}(\tilde{\theta}_\tau - \theta_0) = -\left(\frac{\tau}{C_\tau(\theta)}\right)^{-1} P_\tau^*(\theta_0) n^{1/2}\frac{\partial}{\partial \theta} h_n(\theta)|_{\theta=\theta_0} + o_p(1), \quad (A7)$$

and we know
$$n^{1/2}\frac{\partial}{\partial\theta}h_n(\theta)|_{\theta=\theta_0} \xrightarrow[n\to\infty]{\mathcal{L}} \mathcal{N}\left(0, \left(\frac{\tau}{C_\tau(\theta_0)}\right)^2 K_\tau(\theta_0)\right). \tag{A8}$$

Now by (A7) and (A8), we have the desired result.

Appendix A.2. Proof of Theorem 3

Consider the expression $R_\gamma(f_\theta, f_{\tilde{\theta}_\tau})$. A Taylor expansion for an arbitrary $\theta \in \Theta$, around $\tilde{\theta}_\tau$ leads to the relation

$$R_\gamma(f_\theta, f_{\tilde{\theta}_\tau}) = R_\gamma(f_{\tilde{\theta}_\tau}, f_{\tilde{\theta}_\tau}) + \left(\frac{\partial R_\gamma(f_\theta, f_{\tilde{\theta}_\tau})}{\partial\theta}\right)_{\theta=\tilde{\theta}_\tau} (\theta - \tilde{\theta}_\tau)$$
$$+ \frac{1}{2}(\theta - \tilde{\theta}_\tau)\left(\frac{\partial^2 R_\gamma(f_\theta, f_{\tilde{\theta}_\tau})}{\partial\theta\partial\theta^T}\right)_{\theta=\tilde{\theta}_\tau}(\theta - \tilde{\theta}_\tau)^T + o\left(\|\theta - \tilde{\theta}_\tau\|^2\right).$$

It is clear that $R_\gamma(f_{\tilde{\theta}_\tau}, f_{\tilde{\theta}_\tau}) = 0$ and

$$\frac{\partial R_\gamma(f_\theta, f_{\tilde{\theta}_\tau})}{\partial\theta} = \frac{\partial L_\gamma^1(\theta)}{\partial\theta} - \frac{\partial L_\gamma^2(\theta)}{\partial\theta},$$

being

$$L_\gamma^1(\theta) = \frac{1}{\gamma+1}\log\left(\int f_\theta(x)^{\gamma+1}dx\right)$$

and

$$L_\gamma^2(\theta) = \frac{1}{\gamma}\log\left(\int f_\theta(x)^\gamma f_{\tilde{\theta}_\tau}(x)dx\right).$$

Then,

$$\frac{\partial L_\gamma^1(\theta)}{\partial\theta} = \frac{\int f_\theta(x)^{\gamma+1}u_\theta(x)dx}{\int f_\theta(x)^{\gamma+1}dx} \quad \text{and} \quad \frac{\partial L_\gamma^2(\theta)}{\partial\theta} = \frac{\int f_\theta(x)^\gamma u_\theta(x)f_{\tilde{\theta}_\tau}(x)dx}{\int f_\theta(x)^\gamma f_{\tilde{\theta}_\tau}(x)dx}.$$

Therefore,

$$\left(\frac{\partial R_\gamma(f_\theta, f_{\tilde{\theta}_\tau})}{\partial\theta}\right)_{\theta=\tilde{\theta}_\tau} = 0.$$

Regarding the second derivatives, we have

$$\frac{\partial^2 L_\gamma^1(\theta)}{\partial\theta\partial\theta^T} = (\gamma+1)\frac{\int f_\theta(x)^{\gamma+1}u_\theta(x)u_\theta(x)^T dx}{\int f_\theta(x)^{\gamma+1}dx} + \frac{\int f_\theta(x)^{\gamma+1}\frac{\partial u_\theta(x)}{\partial\theta^T}dx}{\int f_\theta(x)^{\gamma+1}dx}$$
$$-(\gamma+1)\frac{\int f_\theta(x)^{\gamma+1}u_\theta(x)dx \int f_\theta(x)^{\gamma+1}u_\theta(x)^T dx}{\left(\int f_\theta(x)^{\gamma+1}dx\right)^2}$$

and

$$\frac{\partial^2 L_\gamma^2(\theta)}{\partial\theta\partial\theta^T} = \gamma\frac{\int f_\theta(x)^\gamma u_\theta(x)u_\theta(x)^T f_{\tilde{\theta}_\tau}(x)dx}{\int f_\theta(x)^\gamma f_{\tilde{\theta}_\tau}(x)dx} + \frac{\int f_\theta(x)^\gamma \frac{\partial u_\theta(x)}{\partial\theta^T}f_{\tilde{\theta}_\tau}(x)dx}{\int f_\theta(x)^\gamma f_{\tilde{\theta}_\tau}(x)dx}$$
$$-\gamma\frac{\int f_\theta(x)^\gamma f_{\tilde{\theta}_\tau}(x)u_\theta(x)dx \int f_\theta(x)^\gamma f_{\tilde{\theta}_\tau}(x)u_\theta(x)^T dx}{\left(\int f_\theta(x)^\gamma f_{\tilde{\theta}_\tau}(x)dx\right)^2}.$$

and so

$$\left(\frac{\partial^2 R_\gamma(f_\theta, f_{\tilde{\theta}_\tau})}{\partial\theta\partial\theta^T}\right)_{\theta=\tilde{\theta}_\tau} = \frac{S_\gamma(\tilde{\theta}_\tau)}{K_\gamma(\tilde{\theta}_\tau)}.$$

Therefore,

$$T_\gamma(\hat{\theta}_\tau, \tilde{\theta}_\tau) = 2nR_\gamma(f_{\hat{\theta}_\tau}, f_{\tilde{\theta}_\tau}) = n^{1/2}(\hat{\theta}_\tau - \tilde{\theta}_\tau)^T \frac{S_\gamma(\tilde{\theta}_\tau)}{\kappa_\gamma(\tilde{\theta}_\tau)} n^{1/2}(\hat{\theta}_\tau - \tilde{\theta}_\tau) + n \times o\left(\left\|\hat{\theta}_\tau - \tilde{\theta}_\tau\right\|^2\right).$$

Under $\theta_0 \in \Theta_0$,

$$\frac{S_\gamma(\tilde{\theta}_\tau)}{\kappa_\gamma(\tilde{\theta}_\tau)} \xrightarrow[n \to \infty]{\mathcal{P}} \frac{S_\gamma(\theta_0)}{\kappa_\tau(\theta_0)}.$$

Based on $\hat{\theta}_\tau$ and using by (A4) and (A5), we have that

$$n^{1/2} \frac{\partial}{\partial \theta} h_n(\theta)|_{\theta=\theta_0} = -\frac{\tau}{C_\tau(\theta_0)} n^{1/2} S_\tau(\theta_0)(\hat{\theta}_\tau - \theta_0) + o_p(1),$$

and using (A7), we obtain

$$n^{1/2}(\tilde{\theta}_\tau - \theta_0) = P_\tau^*(\theta_0) n^{1/2} S_\tau(\theta_0)(\hat{\theta}_\tau - \theta_0) + o_p(1)$$
$$= n^{1/2}(\hat{\theta}_\tau - \theta_0) - Q_\tau(\theta_0) G(\theta_0)^T n^{1/2}(\hat{\theta}_\tau - \theta_0) + o_p(1).$$

Therefore,

$$n^{1/2}(\hat{\theta}_\tau - \tilde{\theta}_\tau) = Q_\tau(\theta_0) G(\theta_0)^T n^{1/2}(\hat{\theta}_\tau - \theta_0) + o_p(1). \quad (A9)$$

On the other hand, we know that

$$n^{1/2}(\hat{\theta}_\tau - \theta_0) \xrightarrow[n \to \infty]{\mathcal{L}} \mathcal{N}(0, S_\tau(\theta_0)^{-1} K_\tau(\theta_0) S_\tau(\theta_0)^{-1}).$$

From equations (19) and (25), we can establish that

$$B_\tau(\theta_0) = S_\tau(\theta_0)^{-1} G(\theta_0) \left[G(\theta_0)^T S_\tau(\theta_0)^{-1} G(\theta_0)\right]^{-1} G(\theta_0)^T S_\tau(\theta_0)^{-1}$$
$$= Q_\tau(\theta_0) G(\theta_0)^{-1} S_\tau(\theta_0)^{-1}.$$

Therefore, it follows that

$$n^{1/2}(\hat{\theta}_\tau - \tilde{\theta}_\tau) \xrightarrow[n \to \infty]{\mathcal{L}} \mathcal{N}(0, B_\tau(\theta_0) K_\tau(\theta_0) B_\tau(\theta_0)^T).$$

Now, observe from the definition that $B_\tau(\theta_0) = B_\tau(\theta_0)^T$.
Then, the asymptotic distribution of the random variables

$$T_\gamma(\hat{\theta}_\tau, \tilde{\theta}_\tau) = 2nR_\gamma(f_{\hat{\theta}_\tau}, f_{\tilde{\theta}_\tau})$$

and

$$n^{1/2}(\hat{\theta}_\tau - \tilde{\theta}_\tau)^T \frac{S_\gamma(\theta_0)}{\kappa_\gamma(\theta_0)} n^{1/2}(\hat{\theta}_\tau - \tilde{\theta}_\tau)$$

are the same, as we have established that

$$n \times o\left(\left\|\hat{\theta}_\tau - \tilde{\theta}_\tau\right\|^2\right) = o_p(1).$$

Next, we apply Corollary 2.1 in Dik and Gunst [30], which states: "Let X be a q-variate normal random variable with mean vector 0 and variance-covariance matrix Σ. Let M be a real symmetric matrix of order q. Let $k = \text{rank}(\Sigma M \Sigma)$, $k \geq 1$ and let $\lambda_1, \ldots, \lambda_k$, be the nonzero eigenvalues of $M\Sigma$. Then, the distribution of the quadratic form $X^T M X$ coincides with the distribution of the random variable $\sum_{i=1}^{k} \lambda_i Z_i^2$, where $Z_1, \ldots, Z_k$ are independent, each having a standard normal variable". In our case, the asymptotic distribution of $T_\gamma(\hat{\theta}_\tau, \tilde{\theta}_\tau)$ coincides with the distribution of the random variable $\sum_{i=1}^{k} \lambda_i^{\tau,\gamma}(\theta_0) Z_i^2$ where $\lambda_1^{\tau,\gamma}(\theta_0), \ldots, \lambda_k^{\tau,\gamma}(\theta_0)$, are the nonzero eigenvalues of $A_\gamma(\theta_0) B_\tau(\theta_0) K_\tau(\theta_0) B_\tau(\theta_0)$ and

$$k = \min\{r, rank(B_\tau(\theta_0)K_\tau(\theta_0)B_\tau(\theta_0)A_\gamma(\theta_0)B_\tau(\theta_0)K_\tau(\theta_0)B_\tau(\theta_0))\}. \quad (A10)$$

We now establish that $k = r$. The matrix,

$$N_\tau(\theta_0) = B_\tau(\theta_0)K_\tau(\theta_0)B_\tau(\theta_0)$$

is given by

$$\begin{aligned}
N_\tau(\theta_0) &= S_\tau(\theta_0)^{-1}G(\theta_0)\left[G(\theta_0)^T S_\tau(\theta_0)^{-1}G(\theta_0)\right]^{-1}G(\theta_0)^T S_\tau(\theta_0)^{-1} \\
&\quad K_\tau(\theta_0)S_\tau(\theta_0)^{-1}G(\theta_0)\left[G(\theta_0)^T S_\tau(\theta_0)^{-1}G(\theta_0)\right]^{-1}G(\theta_0)^T S_\tau(\theta_0)^{-1}.
\end{aligned}$$

Corollary 14.11.3 in Harville [31] (p. 259) establishes the following: "For any $m \times n$ matrix A and any $m \times m$ symmetric positive definite matrix W, $rank(A^T W A) = rank(A)$". Based on this Corollary we have that $rank(N_\tau(\theta_0))$ coincides with $rank(N_\tau(\theta_0)S_\gamma(\theta_0)N_\tau(\theta_0))$. On the other hand, we know the following additional properties:

(a) $rank(AB) = rank(A)$ if B is full rank (Corollary b.3.3 in Harville [31] (p. 83)).

(b) $rank(AB) = rank(BA)$ if dimension of A coincides with dimension of B^T.

Matrix $K_\tau(\theta_0)$ should be "full rank"; in fact, if $K_\tau(\theta_0)$ were not full rank, the variance–covariance matrix of $\widehat{\theta}_\beta$ and $\widetilde{\theta}_\beta$ would not be full rank (there were redundant components in θ and this is not true).

Therefore, we have

$$\begin{aligned}
rank(N_\tau(\theta_0)) &=_{(a)} rank\Big(S_\tau(\theta_0)^{-\frac{1}{2}}G(\theta_0)\left[G(\theta_0)^T S_\tau(\theta_0)^{-1}G(\theta_0)\right]^{-1} \\
&\quad G(\theta_0)^T S_\tau(\theta_0)^{-1}K_\tau(\theta_0)S_\tau(\theta_0)^{-1}G(\theta_0) \\
&\quad \left[G(\theta_0)^{-1}S_\tau(\theta_0)^{-1}G(\theta_0)\right]^{-1}G(\theta_0)^T S_\tau(\theta_0)^{-\frac{1}{2}}\Big) \\
&=_{(b)} rank\Big(G(\theta_0)^T S_\tau(\theta_0)^{-1}K_\tau(\theta_0)S_\tau(\theta_0)^{-1}G(\theta_0)\left[G(\theta_0)^T S_\tau(\theta_0)^{-1}G(\theta_0)\right]^{-1}\Big) \\
&=_{(a)} ran\Big(G(\theta_0)^T S_\tau(\theta_0)^{-1}K_\tau(\theta_0)S_\tau(\theta_0)^{-1}G(\theta_0)\Big) \\
&=_{Corollary\,14.11.3} rank\Big(S_\tau(\theta_0)^{-1}G(\theta_0)\Big) \\
&=_{(a)} rank(G(\theta_0)) = r.
\end{aligned}$$

Appendix A.3. Rényi's Pseudodistance between Normal Populations

Here, we compute the expression of the RP between densities belonging to the normal model with parameters (μ_1, σ_1) and (μ_2, σ_2), respectively. The RP between $\mathcal{N}(\mu_1, \sigma_1)$ and $\mathcal{N}(\mu_2, \sigma_2)$ is given by

$$\begin{aligned}
R_\gamma(\mathcal{N}(\mu_1,\sigma_1),\mathcal{N}(\mu_2,\sigma_2)) &= \frac{1}{\gamma+1}\log\int \mathcal{N}(\mu_1,\sigma_1)^{\gamma+1}dx \\
&\quad + \frac{1}{\gamma(\gamma+1)}\log\int \mathcal{N}(\mu_2,\sigma_2)^{\gamma+1}dx - \frac{1}{\gamma}\log\int \mathcal{N}(\mu_1,\sigma_1)^\gamma \mathcal{N}(\mu_2,\sigma_2)dx \\
&= \frac{1}{\gamma+1}\log L_1 + \frac{1}{\gamma(\gamma+1)}\log L_2 - \frac{1}{\gamma}\log L_3.
\end{aligned}$$

We first compute

$$\int \mathcal{N}(\mu,\sigma)^\beta dx$$

for the seek of simplicity in later calculations.

$$\int \mathcal{N}(\mu,\sigma)^\beta dx = \int \left(\frac{1}{\sigma\sqrt{2\pi}}e^{-\frac{1}{2}\left(\frac{x-\mu}{\sigma}\right)^2}\right)^\beta dx$$

$$= \frac{1}{\sigma^{\beta-1}\left(\sqrt{2\pi}\right)^{\beta-1}}\frac{1}{\sqrt{\beta}}\int \frac{1}{\frac{\sigma}{\sqrt{\beta}}\sqrt{2\pi}}e^{-\frac{1}{2}\left(\frac{x-\mu}{\frac{\sigma}{\sqrt{\beta}}}\right)^2}dx$$

$$= \frac{1}{\sigma^{\beta-1}\left(\sqrt{2\pi}\right)^{\beta-1}}\frac{1}{\sqrt{\beta}}.$$

Therefore,

$$L_1 = \frac{1}{\sigma_1^\gamma \left(\sqrt{2\pi}\right)^\gamma}\frac{1}{\sqrt{\gamma+1}} \text{ and } L_2 = \frac{1}{\sigma_2^\gamma \left(\sqrt{2\pi}\right)^\gamma}\frac{1}{\sqrt{\gamma+1}}.$$

In relation with L_3 we have,

$$L_3 = \int \mathcal{N}(\mu_1,\sigma_1)^\gamma \mathcal{N}(\mu_2,\sigma_2) dx$$

$$= \int \frac{1}{\sigma_1^\gamma \left(\sqrt{2\pi}\right)^\gamma}e^{-\frac{1}{2}\left(\frac{x-\mu_1}{\frac{\sigma_1}{\sqrt{\gamma}}}\right)^2}\frac{1}{\sigma_2\sqrt{2\pi}}e^{-\frac{1}{2}\left(\frac{x-\mu_2}{\sigma_2}\right)^2}$$

$$= \frac{1}{\sigma_1^\gamma \left(\sqrt{2\pi}\right)^\gamma}\frac{1}{\sigma_2\sqrt{2\pi}} \times$$

$$\times \int \exp\left\{-\frac{1}{2}\left[x^2\left(\frac{1}{\left(\frac{\sigma_1}{\sqrt{\gamma}}\right)^2}+\frac{1}{\sigma_2^2}\right)-2x\left(\frac{\mu_1}{\left(\frac{\sigma_1}{\sqrt{\gamma}}\right)^2}+\frac{\mu_2}{\sigma_2^2}\right)+\frac{\mu_1^2}{\left(\frac{\sigma_1}{\sqrt{\gamma}}\right)^2}+\frac{\mu_2^2}{\sigma_2^2}\right]\right\}dx$$

$$= \frac{1}{\sigma_1^\gamma \left(\sqrt{2\pi}\right)^\gamma}\frac{1}{\sigma_2\sqrt{2\pi}}\exp\left\{-\frac{1}{2}\left[\frac{\mu_1^2}{\left(\frac{\sigma_1}{\sqrt{\gamma}}\right)^2}+\frac{\mu_2^2}{\sigma_2^2}\right]\right\} \times$$

$$\times \int \exp\left\{-\frac{1}{2}\left[x^2\left(\frac{1}{\left(\frac{\sigma_1}{\sqrt{\gamma}}\right)^2}+\frac{1}{\sigma_2^2}\right)-2x\left(\frac{\mu_1}{\left(\frac{\sigma_1}{\sqrt{\gamma}}\right)^2}+\frac{\mu_2}{\sigma_2^2}\right)\right]\right\}dx$$

$$= \frac{1}{\sigma_1^\gamma \left(\sqrt{2\pi}\right)^\gamma}\frac{1}{\sigma_2\sqrt{2\pi}}\exp\left\{-\frac{1}{2}\left[\frac{\mu_1^2}{\left(\frac{\sigma_1}{\sqrt{\gamma}}\right)^2}+\frac{\mu_2^2}{\sigma_2^2}\right]\right\}\exp\left\{\frac{1}{2}\frac{A^2}{B^2}\right\}B\sqrt{2\pi}\times$$

$$\times \int \frac{1}{\sqrt{2\pi}B}\exp\left\{-\frac{1}{2}\left(\frac{x-A}{B}\right)^2\right\}dx$$

$$= \frac{1}{\sigma_1^\gamma \left(\sqrt{2\pi}\right)^\gamma}\frac{1}{\sigma_2\sqrt{2\pi}}\exp\left\{-\frac{1}{2}\left[\frac{\mu_1^2}{\left(\frac{\sigma_1}{\sqrt{\gamma}}\right)^2}+\frac{\mu_2^2}{\sigma_2^2}\right]\right\}\exp\left\{\frac{1}{2}\frac{A^2}{B^2}\right\}B\sqrt{2\pi}.$$

Now it is necessary to obtain A and B. However, for this, we have,

$$\begin{cases} \frac{1}{B^2} = \frac{1}{\left(\frac{\sigma_1}{\sqrt{\gamma}}\right)^2}+\frac{1}{\sigma_2^2} \\ \frac{A}{B^2} = \left(\frac{\mu_1}{\left(\frac{\sigma_1}{\sqrt{\gamma}}\right)^2}+\frac{\mu_2}{\sigma_2^2}\right) \end{cases}.$$

Then,
$$A\left(\frac{1}{\left(\frac{\sigma_1}{\sqrt{\gamma}}\right)^2}+\frac{1}{\sigma_2^2}\right)=\frac{\mu_1}{\left(\frac{\sigma_1}{\sqrt{\gamma}}\right)^2}+\frac{\mu_2}{\sigma_2^2}$$

and
$$A=\frac{\frac{\mu_1}{\left(\frac{\sigma_1}{\sqrt{\gamma}}\right)^2}+\frac{\mu_2}{\sigma_2^2}}{\frac{1}{\left(\frac{\sigma_1}{\sqrt{\gamma}}\right)^2}+\frac{1}{\sigma_2^2}}=\frac{\frac{\sigma_2^2\mu_1+\mu_2\left(\frac{\sigma_1}{\sqrt{\gamma}}\right)^2}{\sigma_2^2\left(\frac{\sigma_1}{\sqrt{\gamma}}\right)^2}}{\frac{\sigma_2^2+\left(\frac{\sigma_1}{\sqrt{\gamma}}\right)^2}{\sigma_2^2\left(\frac{\sigma_1}{\sqrt{\gamma}}\right)^2}}=\frac{\sigma_2^2\mu_1+\mu_2\frac{\sigma_1^2}{\gamma}}{\sigma_2^2+\frac{\sigma_1^2}{\gamma}}=\frac{\gamma\sigma_2^2\mu_1+\mu_2\sigma_1^2}{\gamma\sigma_2^2+\sigma_1^2}.$$

We have,
$$\frac{1}{B^2}=\frac{1}{\left(\frac{\sigma_1}{\sqrt{\gamma}}\right)^2}+\frac{1}{\sigma_2^2}=\frac{\gamma}{\sigma_1^2}+\frac{1}{\sigma_2^2}=\frac{\sigma_2^2\gamma+\sigma_1^2}{\sigma_1^2\sigma_2^2}$$

Therefore,
$$B=\frac{\sigma_1\sigma_2}{\sqrt{\sigma_2^2\gamma+\sigma_1^2}}.$$

On the other hand,
$$\frac{A^2}{B^2}=\left(\frac{\gamma\sigma_2^2\mu_1+\mu_2\sigma_1^2}{\gamma\sigma_2^2+\sigma_1^2}\right)^2\frac{\sigma_2^2\gamma+\sigma_1^2}{\sigma_1^2\sigma_2^2}=\frac{(\gamma\sigma_2^2\mu_1+\mu_2\sigma_1^2)^2}{(\gamma\sigma_2^2+\sigma_1^2)\sigma_1^2\sigma_2^2}$$

and
$$\begin{aligned}L_3&=\frac{1}{\sigma_1^\gamma\left(\sqrt{2\pi}\right)^\gamma}\frac{1}{\sigma_2\sqrt{2\pi}}\exp\left\{-\frac{1}{2}\left[\frac{\mu_1^2}{\left(\frac{\sigma_1}{\sqrt{\gamma}}\right)^2}+\frac{\mu_2^2}{\sigma_2^2}\right]\right\}\exp\left\{\frac{1}{2}\frac{A^2}{B^2}\right\}B\sqrt{2\pi}\\&=\frac{1}{\sigma_1^\gamma\left(\sqrt{2\pi}\right)^\gamma}\frac{1}{\sigma_2}\exp\left\{-\frac{1}{2}\left[\frac{\mu_1^2}{\left(\frac{\sigma_1}{\sqrt{\gamma}}\right)^2}+\frac{\mu_2^2}{\sigma_2^2}\right]\right\}\exp\left\{\frac{1}{2}\frac{(\gamma\sigma_2^2\mu_1+\mu_2\sigma_1^2)^2}{(\gamma\sigma_2^2+\sigma_1^2)\sigma_1^2\sigma_2^2}\right\}\frac{\sigma_1\sigma_2}{\sqrt{\sigma_2^2\gamma+\sigma_1^2}}\\&=\frac{\sigma_1\sigma_2}{\sqrt{\sigma_2^2\gamma+\sigma_1^2}}\frac{1}{\sigma_1^\gamma\left(\sqrt{2\pi}\right)^\gamma}\frac{1}{\sigma_2}\exp\left\{\frac{1}{2}\left[\frac{(\gamma\sigma_2^2\mu_1+\mu_2\sigma_1^2)^2}{(\gamma\sigma_2^2+\sigma_1^2)\sigma_1^2\sigma_2^2}-\frac{\gamma\mu_1^2\sigma_2^2+\sigma_1^2\mu_2^2}{\sigma_2^2\sigma_1^2}\right]\right\}.\end{aligned}$$

However,
$$\begin{aligned}\frac{(\gamma\sigma_2^2\mu_1+\mu_2\sigma_1^2)^2}{(\gamma\sigma_2^2+\sigma_1^2)\sigma_1^2\sigma_2^2}-\frac{\gamma\mu_1^2\sigma_2^2+\sigma_1^2\mu_2^2}{\sigma_2^2\sigma_1^2}&=\frac{(\gamma\sigma_2^2\mu_1+\mu_2\sigma_1^2)^2-(\gamma\mu_1^2\sigma_2^2+\sigma_1^2\mu_2^2)(\gamma\sigma_2^2+\sigma_1^2)}{(\gamma\sigma_2^2+\sigma_1^2)\sigma_1^2\sigma_2^2}\\&=\frac{\gamma^2\sigma_2^4\mu_1^2+\mu_2^2\sigma_1^4+2\gamma\sigma_2^2\mu_1\mu_2\sigma_1^2}{(\gamma\sigma_2^2+\sigma_1^2)\sigma_1^2\sigma_2^2}\\&\quad-\frac{\gamma^2\mu_1^2\sigma_2^4+\gamma\mu_1^2\sigma_2^2\sigma_1^2+\mu_2^2\gamma\sigma_2^2\sigma_1^2+\mu_2^2\sigma_1^4}{(\gamma\sigma_2^2+\sigma_1^2)\sigma_1^2\sigma_2^2}\\&=\frac{2\gamma\sigma_2^2\mu_1\mu_2\sigma_1^2-\gamma\mu_1^2\sigma_2^2\sigma_1^2-\mu_2^2\gamma\sigma_2^2\sigma_1^2}{(\gamma\sigma_2^2+\sigma_1^2)\sigma_1^2\sigma_2^2}\\&=\frac{\sigma_2^2\sigma_1^2\gamma(2\mu_1\mu_2-\mu_1^2-\mu_2^2)}{(\gamma\sigma_2^2+\sigma_1^2)\sigma_1^2\sigma_2^2}\\&=-\frac{\gamma(\mu_1-\mu_2)^2}{(\gamma\sigma_2^2+\sigma_1^2)}\end{aligned}$$

Therefore,
$$L_3 = \frac{1}{\sigma_1^{\gamma-1}\sqrt{\sigma_2^2\gamma+\sigma_1^2}}\frac{1}{\left(\sqrt{2\pi}\right)^\gamma}\exp\left\{-\frac{1}{2}\frac{\gamma(\mu_1-\mu_2)^2}{(\gamma\sigma_2^2+\sigma_1^2)}\right\}.$$

Then,

$$\begin{aligned}
R_\gamma(\mathcal{N}(\mu_1,\sigma_1),\mathcal{N}(\mu_2,\sigma_2)) &= \frac{1}{\gamma+1}\ln L_1 + \frac{1}{\gamma(\gamma+1)}\ln L_2 - \frac{1}{\gamma}\ln L_3\\
&= \frac{1}{\gamma+1}\ln\frac{1}{\sigma_1^\gamma\left(\sqrt{2\pi}\right)^\gamma}\frac{1}{\sqrt{\gamma+1}} + \frac{1}{\gamma(\gamma+1)}\ln\frac{1}{\sigma_2^\gamma\left(\sqrt{2\pi}\right)^\gamma}\frac{1}{\sqrt{\gamma+1}}\\
&\quad -\frac{1}{\gamma}\ln\frac{1}{\sigma_1^{\gamma-1}\sqrt{\sigma_2^2\gamma+\sigma_1^2}\left(\sqrt{2\pi}\right)^\gamma} + \frac{1}{2}\frac{\gamma(\mu_1-\mu_2)^2}{\gamma(\gamma\sigma_2^2+\sigma_1^2)}\\
&= \frac{1}{\gamma(\gamma+1)}\left(\ln\frac{\sigma_1^{\gamma-1}}{\sigma_2^\gamma\sqrt{\gamma+1}}\sqrt{\sigma_1^2+\gamma\sigma_2^2} + \gamma\ln\frac{1}{\sigma_1\sqrt{\gamma+1}}\sqrt{\sigma_1^2+\gamma\sigma_2^2}\right)\\
&\quad +\frac{1}{2}\frac{\gamma(\mu_1-\mu_2)^2}{\gamma(\gamma\sigma_2^2+\sigma_1^2)}\\
&= \frac{1}{\gamma(\gamma+1)}\ln\frac{1}{\sigma_1\sigma_2^\gamma}\left(\frac{\sqrt{\sigma_1^2+\gamma\sigma_2^2}}{\sqrt{\gamma+1}}\right)^{\gamma+1} + \frac{1}{2}\frac{(\mu_1-\mu_2)^2}{(\gamma\sigma_2^2+\sigma_1^2)}
\end{aligned}$$

For $\gamma \to 0$ we have,

$$\lim_{\gamma\to 0} R_\gamma(\mathcal{N}(\mu_1,\sigma_1),\mathcal{N}(\mu_2,\sigma_2)) = \frac{\sigma_2^2-\sigma_1^2}{2\sigma_1^2} + \ln\frac{\sigma_1}{\sigma_2} + \frac{1}{2}\frac{(\mu_1-\mu_2)^2}{\sigma_1^2}. \quad (A11)$$

Appendix A.4. Computation of the Nonzero Eigenvalues of $A_\gamma(\theta_0)B_\tau(\theta_0)K_\tau(\theta_0)B_\tau(\theta_0)$

We know that the matrix $\xi(\theta)$ can be expressed as

$$\xi(\theta) = c_\tau(\theta)\kappa(\theta)$$

with

$$\kappa(\theta) = \int f_\theta(x)^{\tau+1}dx = \frac{1}{\sigma^\tau\left(\sqrt{2\pi}\right)^\tau\sqrt{1+\tau}}.$$

Then,

$$\xi(\theta) = \frac{1}{\sigma^\tau\left(\sqrt{2\pi}\right)^\tau\sqrt{1+\tau}}\left(0, -\frac{\tau}{(\tau+1)}\frac{1}{\sigma}\right)^T.$$

Therefore,

$$c_\tau(\theta) = \frac{\xi(\theta)}{\kappa(\theta)} = \left(0, -\frac{\tau}{(\tau+1)}\frac{1}{\sigma}\right).$$

On the other hand

$$\frac{\partial \log f_{\mu,\sigma}(X_i)}{\partial \mu} = \frac{X_i-\mu}{\sigma^2} \text{ and } \frac{\partial \log f_{\mu,\sigma}(X_i)}{\partial \sigma} = -\frac{1}{\sigma}+\frac{1}{\sigma^3}(X_i-\mu)^2$$

and

$$u_\theta(X_i) = \left(\frac{X_i-\mu}{\sigma^2}, -\frac{1}{\sigma}+\frac{1}{\sigma^3}(X_i-\mu)^2\right).$$

Then,
$$\boldsymbol{\Psi}_\tau(X;\theta) = \left(\Psi_\tau^1(X;\theta), \Psi_\tau^2(X;\theta)\right)$$
is given by
$$\boldsymbol{\Psi}_\tau(X;\theta) = \left(\frac{X-\mu}{\sigma^2}\frac{1}{(\sigma\sqrt{2\pi})^\tau}e^{-\frac{\tau}{2}\left(\frac{X-\mu}{\sigma}\right)^2}, \left(\left(\frac{X-\mu}{\sigma}\right)^2 - \frac{1}{1+\tau}\right)\frac{1}{\sigma}\frac{1}{(\sigma\sqrt{2\pi})^\tau}e^{-\frac{\tau}{2}\left(\frac{X-\mu}{\sigma}\right)^2}\right)$$
and
$$K_\tau(\theta) = E\left[\boldsymbol{\Psi}_\tau(X;\theta)\boldsymbol{\Psi}_\tau(X;\theta)^T\right].$$

Now we obtain the elements of that matrix,

$$\begin{aligned}
K_\tau^{11}(\theta) &= E\left[\left(\frac{X-\mu}{\sigma^2}\right)^2 \frac{1}{(\sigma\sqrt{2\pi})^{2\tau}} e^{-\frac{2\tau}{2}\left(\frac{X-\mu}{\sigma}\right)^2}\right] \\
&= \frac{1}{(\sigma\sqrt{2\pi})^{2\tau}(1+2\tau)^{3/2}}\frac{1}{\sigma^2}
\end{aligned}$$

$$\begin{aligned}
K_\tau^{12}(\theta) &= K_\tau^{21}(\theta) = E\left[\left(\frac{X-\mu}{\sigma^2}\right)\left(\left(\frac{X-\mu}{\sigma}\right)^2 - \frac{1}{1+\tau}\right)\frac{1}{\sigma}\frac{1}{(\sigma\sqrt{2\pi})^{2\tau}}e^{-\frac{2\tau}{2}\left(\frac{X-\mu}{\sigma}\right)^2}\right] \\
&= 0
\end{aligned}$$

and

$$\begin{aligned}
K_\tau^{22}(\theta) &= E\left[\left(\left(\frac{X-\mu}{\sigma}\right)^2 - \frac{1}{1+\tau}\right)^2 \frac{1}{\sigma^2}\frac{1}{(\sigma\sqrt{2\pi})^{2\tau}}e^{-\frac{2\tau}{2}\left(\frac{X-\mu}{\sigma}\right)^2}\right] \\
&= \frac{1}{\sigma^2}\frac{3\tau^2+2+4\tau}{(\sigma\sqrt{2\pi})^{2\tau}(1+2\tau)^{5/2}(1+\tau)^2}
\end{aligned}$$

and

$$\begin{aligned}
K_\tau(\theta) &= \begin{pmatrix} \frac{1}{(\sigma\sqrt{2\pi})^{2\tau}(1+2\tau)^{3/2}}\frac{1}{\sigma^2} & 0 \\ 0 & \frac{1}{\sigma^2}\frac{3\tau^2+2+4\tau}{(\sigma\sqrt{2\pi})^{2\tau}(1+2\tau)^{5/2}(1+\tau)^2} \end{pmatrix} \\
&= \frac{1}{\sigma^2}\frac{1}{(\sigma\sqrt{2\pi})^{2\tau}(1+2\tau)^{3/2}}\begin{pmatrix} 1 & 0 \\ 0 & \frac{3\tau^2+2+4\tau}{(1+\tau)^2(1+2\tau)} \end{pmatrix}.
\end{aligned}$$

Now we obtain the matrix $S_\tau(\theta)$. We have
$$\xi(\theta) = c_\tau(\theta)\kappa(\theta)$$
with
$$\kappa(\theta) = \int f_\theta(x)^{\tau+1}dx = \frac{1}{\sigma^\tau\left(\sqrt{2\pi}\right)^\tau\sqrt{1+\tau}}.$$

Then,
$$\xi(\theta) = \frac{1}{\sigma^\tau \left(\sqrt{2\pi}\right)^\tau \sqrt{1+\tau}} \left(0, -\frac{\tau}{(\tau+1)}\frac{1}{\sigma}\right)^T$$

and
$$\frac{1}{\kappa(\theta)}\xi(\theta)\xi(\theta)^T = \frac{1}{\sigma^{\tau+2}\left(\sqrt{2\pi}\right)^\tau \sqrt{1+\tau}} \begin{pmatrix} 0 & 0 \\ 0 & \frac{\tau^2}{(\tau+1)^2} \end{pmatrix}.$$

On the other hand

$$J_\tau(\theta) = E\left[\begin{pmatrix} \frac{1}{\sigma^4}(X-\mu)^2 & \frac{1}{\sigma^2}\left(\frac{1}{\sigma} - \frac{1}{\sigma^3}(X-\mu)^2\right)(X-\mu) \\ \frac{1}{\sigma^2}\left(\frac{1}{\sigma} - \frac{1}{\sigma^3}(X-\mu)^2\right)(X-\mu) & \left(\frac{1}{\sigma} - \frac{1}{\sigma^3}(X-\mu)^2\right)^2 \end{pmatrix} \frac{1}{\left(\sigma\sqrt{2\pi}\right)^\tau}e^{-\frac{\tau}{2}\left(\frac{X-\mu}{\sigma}\right)^2}\right]$$

$$J_\tau^{11}(\theta) = E\left[\frac{1}{\sigma^4}(\mu-X)^2 \frac{1}{\left(\sigma\sqrt{2\pi}\right)^\tau}e^{-\frac{\tau}{2}\left(\frac{X-\mu}{\sigma}\right)^2}\right] = \frac{1}{\sigma^{\tau+2}}\frac{1}{(\tau+1)^{3/2}}\frac{1}{\left(\sqrt{2\pi}\right)^\tau}$$

$$J_\tau^{12}(\theta) = J_\tau^{21}(\theta) = 0$$

$$J_\tau^{22}(\theta) = E\left[\left(\frac{1}{\sigma} - \frac{1}{\sigma^3}(\mu-X)^2\right)^2 \frac{1}{\left(\sigma\sqrt{2\pi}\right)^\tau}e^{-\frac{\tau}{2}\left(\frac{X-\mu}{\sigma}\right)^2}\right] = \frac{1}{\sigma^{\tau+2}}\frac{1}{\left(\sqrt{2\pi}\right)^\tau}\frac{1}{\sqrt{1+\tau}}\frac{2+\tau^2}{(1+\tau)^2}$$

Therefore
$$J_\tau(\theta) = \frac{1}{\sigma^{\tau+2}}\frac{1}{\left(\sqrt{2\pi}\right)^\tau}\frac{1}{\sqrt{1+\tau}}\begin{pmatrix} \frac{1}{1+\tau} & 0 \\ 0 & \frac{2+\tau^2}{(1+\tau)^2} \end{pmatrix}$$

$$S_\tau(\theta) = J_\tau(\theta) - \frac{1}{\kappa(\theta)}\xi(\theta)\xi(\theta)^T$$

$$= \frac{1}{\sigma^{\tau+2}}\frac{1}{\left(\sqrt{2\pi}\right)^\tau}\frac{1}{\sqrt{1+\tau}}\left(\begin{pmatrix} \frac{1}{1+\tau} & 0 \\ 0 & \frac{2+\tau^2}{(1+\tau)^2} \end{pmatrix} - \begin{pmatrix} 0 & 0 \\ 0 & \frac{\tau^2}{(\tau+1)^2} \end{pmatrix}\right)$$

$$= \frac{1}{\sigma^{\tau+2}}\frac{1}{\left(\sqrt{2\pi}\right)^\tau}\frac{1}{\sqrt{1+\tau}}\begin{pmatrix} \frac{1}{1+\tau} & 0 \\ 0 & \frac{2}{(\tau+1)^2} \end{pmatrix}$$

Now we have,
- The matrix $\left[G(\theta_0)^T S_\tau(\theta_0)^{-1} G(\theta_0)\right]^{-1}$ $(G(\theta) = (0,1)^T)$

$$G(\theta_0)^T S_\tau(\theta_0)^{-1} G(\theta_0) = (0\ 1)\left(\frac{1}{\sigma^{\tau+2}}\frac{1}{\left(\sqrt{2\pi}\right)^\tau}\frac{1}{\sqrt{1+\tau}}\begin{pmatrix} \frac{1}{1+\tau} & 0 \\ 0 & \frac{2}{(\tau+1)^2} \end{pmatrix}\right)^{-1}\begin{pmatrix} 0 \\ 1 \end{pmatrix}$$

$$= \frac{1}{2}\sigma^2\sigma^\tau(\tau+1)^{\frac{5}{2}}\left(\sqrt{2\sqrt{\pi}}\right)^\tau$$

- The matrix $Q_\tau(\theta_0) = S_\tau^{-1}(\theta_0)G(\theta_0)\left[G^T(\theta_0)S_\tau^{-1}(\theta_0)G(\theta_0)\right]^{-1}$

$$Q_\tau(\theta_0) = \left(\frac{1}{\sigma^{\tau+2}}\frac{1}{\left(\sqrt{2\pi}\right)^\tau}\frac{1}{\sqrt{1+\tau}}\begin{pmatrix}\frac{1}{1+\tau} & 0 \\ 0 & \frac{2}{(\tau+1)^2}\end{pmatrix}\right)^{-1}\begin{pmatrix}0 \\ 1\end{pmatrix}\left(\frac{1}{2}\sigma^2\sigma^\tau(\tau+1)^{\frac{5}{2}}\left(\sqrt{2}\sqrt{\pi}\right)^\tau\right)^{-1}$$

$$= \begin{pmatrix}0 \\ 1\end{pmatrix}$$

- The matrix $B_\tau(\theta_0) = S_\tau(\theta_0)^{-1}G(\theta_0)\left[G(\theta_0)^T S_\tau(\theta_0)^{-1}G(\theta_0)\right]^{-1}G(\theta_0)^T S_\tau(\theta_0)^{-1} = Q_\tau(\theta_0)G(\theta_0)^T S_\tau(\theta_0)^{-1}$

$$B_\tau(\theta_0) = Q_\tau(\theta_0)G^T(\theta_0)S_\tau^{-1}(\theta_0) = \begin{pmatrix}0 \\ 1\end{pmatrix}\begin{pmatrix}0 & 1\end{pmatrix}\frac{1}{\sigma^{\tau+2}}\frac{1}{\left(\sqrt{2\pi}\right)^\tau}\frac{1}{\sqrt{1+\tau}}\begin{pmatrix}\frac{1}{1+\tau} & 0 \\ 0 & \frac{2}{(\tau+1)^2}\end{pmatrix}^{-1}$$

$$= \begin{pmatrix}0 & 0 \\ 0 & \frac{1}{2}\sigma^2\sigma^\tau(\tau+1)^{\frac{5}{2}}\left(\sqrt{2}\sqrt{\pi}\right)^\tau\end{pmatrix}$$

- The matrix $M_{\gamma,\tau}(\theta_0) = \frac{S_\gamma(\theta_0)}{\kappa_\gamma(\theta_0)}B_\tau(\theta_0)K_\tau(\theta_0)B_\tau(\theta_0)$

$$M_{\gamma,\tau}(\theta_0) = \frac{\sigma^\gamma\left(\sqrt{2\pi}\right)^\gamma\sqrt{1+\gamma}}{\sigma^{\gamma+2}}\frac{1}{\left(\sqrt{2\pi}\right)^\gamma}\frac{1}{\sqrt{1+\gamma}}\begin{pmatrix}\frac{1}{1+\gamma} & 0 \\ 0 & \frac{2}{(\gamma+1)^2}\end{pmatrix}$$

$$\times \begin{pmatrix}0 & 0 \\ 0 & \frac{1}{2}\sigma^2\sigma^\tau(\tau+1)^{\frac{5}{2}}\left(\sqrt{2}\sqrt{\pi}\right)^\tau\end{pmatrix}$$

$$\times \frac{1}{\sigma^2}\frac{1}{\left(\sigma\sqrt{2\pi}\right)^{2\tau}}\frac{1}{(1+2\tau)^{3/2}}\begin{pmatrix}1 & 0 \\ 0 & \frac{3\tau^2+2+4\tau}{(1+\tau)^2(1+2\tau)}\end{pmatrix}$$

$$\times \begin{pmatrix}0 & 0 \\ 0 & \frac{1}{2}\sigma^2\sigma^\tau(\tau+1)^{\frac{5}{2}}\left(\sqrt{2}\sqrt{\pi}\right)^\tau\end{pmatrix}$$

$$= \begin{pmatrix}0 & 0 \\ 0 & \frac{1}{2}\frac{(\tau+1)^3}{(\gamma+1)^2(2\tau+1)^{\frac{5}{2}}}(3\tau^2+4\tau+2)\end{pmatrix}.$$

References

1. Beran, R. Minimum Hellinger distance estimates for parametric models. *Ann. Stat.* **1977**, *5*, 445–463. [CrossRef]
2. Tamura, R.N.; Boos, D.D. Minimum Hellinger distance estimation for multivariate location and covariance. *J. Am. Stat. Assoc.* **1986**, *81*, 223–229. [CrossRef]
3. Simpson, D.G. Minimum Hellinger distance estimation for the analysis of count data. *J. Am. Stat. Assoc.* **1987**, *82*, 802–807. [CrossRef]
4. Simpson, D.G. Hellinger deviance tests: Efficiency, breakdown points, and examples. *J. Am. Stat. Assoc.* **1989**, *84*, 107–113. [CrossRef]
5. Lindsay, B.G. Efficiency versus robustness: The case for minimum Hellinger distance and related methods. *Ann. Stat.* **1994**, *22*, 1081–1114. [CrossRef]
6. Pardo, L. *Statistical Inference Based on Divergence Measures*; Chapman & Hall/CRC: Boca Raton, FL, USA, 2006.
7. Basu, A.; Shioya, H.; Park, C. *Statistical Inference: The minimum Distance Approach*; Chapman & Hall/CRC Press: Boca de Raton, FL, USA, 2011.
8. Broniatowski, M.; Toma, A.; Vajda, I. Decomposable pseudodistances and applications in statistical estimation. *J. Stat. Plan. Inference* **2012**, *142*, 2574–2585. [CrossRef]
9. Castilla, E.; Jaenada, M.; Pardo, L. Estimation and testing on independent not identically distributed observations based on Rényi's pseudodistances. *IEEE Trans. Inf. Theory* **2022**, in press. [CrossRef]
10. Silvey, S.D. *Reprinting, Monographs on Statistical Subjects*; Chapman and Hall: London, UK, 1975.

11. Basu, A.; Mandal, A.; Martin, N.; Pardo, L. Testing Composite Hypothesis Based on the Density Power Divergence. *Sankhya B Indian J. Stat.* **2018**, *80*, 222–262. [CrossRef]
12. Ghosh, A. Influence function analysis of the restricted minimum divergence estimators: A general form. *Electron. J. Stat.* **2015**, *9*, 1017–1040. [CrossRef]
13. Jones, M.C.; Hjort, N.L.; Harris, I.R.; Basu, A. A comparison of related density-based minimum divergence estimators. *Biometrika* **2001**, *88*, 865–873. [CrossRef]
14. Fujisawa, H.; Eguchi, S. Robust parameter estimation with a small bias against heavy contamination. *J. Multivariante Anal.* **2008**, *99*, 2053–2081. [CrossRef]
15. Castilla, E.; Jaenada, M.; Martin, N.; Pardo, L. Robust approach for comparing two dependent normal populations through Wald-type tests based on Rényi's pseudodistance estimators. *arXiv* **2022**, arXiv:2202.00982.
16. Toma, A.; Leoni-Aubin, S. Robust tests based on dual divergence estimators and saddlepoint approximations. *J. Multivariante Anal.* **2010**, *101*, 1143–1155. [CrossRef]
17. Toma, A.; Karagrigoriou, A.; Trentou, P. Robust model selection criteria based on pseudodistances. *Entropy* **2020**, *22*, 304. [CrossRef] [PubMed]
18. Castilla, E.; Martin, N.; Muñoz, S.; Pardo, L. Robust Wald-type tests based on Minimum Rényi Pseudodistance Estimators for the Multiple Regression Model. *J. Stat. Comput. Simul.* **2020**, *14*, 2592–2613. [CrossRef]
19. Castilla, E.; Ghosh, A.; Jaenada, M.; Pardo, L. On regularization methods based on Rényi's pseudodistances for sparse high-dimensional linear regression models. *arXiv* **2022**, arXiv:2202.00982.
20. Jaenada, M.; Pardo, L. The minimum Renyi's Pseudodistances estimators for Generalized Linear Models. In *Data Analysis and Related Applications: Theory and Practice*; Proceeding of the ASMDA; Wiley: Athens, Greece, 2021.
21. Jaenada, M.; Pardo, L. Robust Statistical Inference in Generalized Linear Models Based on Minimum Renyi's Pseudodistance Estimators. *Entropy* **2022**, *24*, 123. [CrossRef]
22. Hampel, F.R.; Ronchetti, E.; Rousseauw, P.J.; Stahel, W. *Robust Statistics: The Approach Based on Influence Functions*; John Wiley & Sons: Hoboken, NJ, USA, 1986.
23. Rao, C.R. Score test: Historical review and recent developments. In *Advances in Ranking and Selection, Multiple Comparisons, and Reliability*; Birkhäuser: Boston, MA, USA, 2005; pp. 3–20.
24. Basu, A.; Ghosh, A.; Martin, N.; Pardo, L. A Robust Generalization of the Rao Test. *J. Bus. Econ. Stat.* **2021**, *40*, 868–879. [CrossRef]
25. Warwick, J.; Jones, M.C. Choosing a robustness tuning parameter. *J. Stat. Comput. Simul.* **2005**, *75*, 581–588. [CrossRef]
26. Basak, S.; Basu, A.; Jones, M.C. On the optimal density power divergence tuning parameter. *J. Appl. Stat.* **2021**, *48*, 536–556. [CrossRef]
27. Welch, W.J. Rerandomizing the median in matched-pairs designs. *Biometrika* **1987**, *74*, 609–614. [CrossRef]
28. Basu, A.; Mandal, A.; Martin, N.; Pardo, L. Testing statistical hypotheses based on the density power divergence. *Ann. Inst. Stat. Math.* **2013**, *65*, 319–348. [CrossRef]
29. Darwin, C. *The Effects of Cross and Self Fertilisation in the Vegetable Kingdom*; AMS Press Inc.: New York, NY, USA, 1877.
30. Dik, J.J.; de Gunst, M.C.M. The Distribution of General Quadratic Forms in Norma. *Stat. Neerl.* **1985**, *39*, 14–26. [CrossRef]
31. Harville, D.A. *Matrix Algebra from a Statistician's Perspective*; Springer: New York, NY, USA, 2008.

Article

A Generic Formula and Some Special Cases for the Kullback–Leibler Divergence between Central Multivariate Cauchy Distributions

Nizar Bouhlel [1,*] and David Rousseau [2]

1. ImhorPhen Unit, UMR INRAe IRHS, Institut Agro Rennes-Angers, Université d'Angers, 42 Rue Georges Morel, 49070 Beaucouzé, France
2. LARIS, UMR INRAe IRHS, Université d'Angers, 62 Avenue Notre Dame du Lac, 49000 Angers, France; david.rousseau@univ-angers.fr
* Correspondence: nizar.bouhlel@agrocampus-ouest.fr

Abstract: This paper introduces a closed-form expression for the Kullback–Leibler divergence (KLD) between two central multivariate Cauchy distributions (MCDs) which have been recently used in different signal and image processing applications where non-Gaussian models are needed. In this overview, the MCDs are surveyed and some new results and properties are derived and discussed for the KLD. In addition, the KLD for MCDs is showed to be written as a function of Lauricella D-hypergeometric series $F_D^{(p)}$. Finally, a comparison is made between the Monte Carlo sampling method to approximate the KLD and the numerical value of the closed-form expression of the latter. The approximation of the KLD by Monte Carlo sampling method are shown to converge to its theoretical value when the number of samples goes to the infinity.

Keywords: Multivariate Cauchy distribution (MCD); Kullback–Leibler divergence (KLD); multiple power series; Lauricella D-hypergeometric series

Citation: Bouhlel, N.; Rousseau, D. A Generic Formula and Some Special Cases for the Kullback–Leibler Divergence between Central Multivariate Cauchy Distributions. *Entropy* **2022**, *24*, 838. https://doi.org/10.3390/e24060838

Academic Editors: Karagrigoriou Alexandros and Makrides Andreas

Received: 22 May 2022
Accepted: 15 June 2022
Published: 17 June 2022

Publisher's Note: MDPI stays neutral with regard to jurisdictional claims in published maps and institutional affiliations.

Copyright: © 2022 by the authors. Licensee MDPI, Basel, Switzerland. This article is an open access article distributed under the terms and conditions of the Creative Commons Attribution (CC BY) license (https://creativecommons.org/licenses/by/4.0/).

1. Introduction

Multivariate Cauchy distribution (MCD) belongs to the elliptical symmetric distributions [1] and is a special case of the multivariate t-distribution [2] and the multivariate stable distribution [3]. MCD has been recently used in several signal and image processing applications for which non-Gaussian models are needed. To name a few of them, in speckle denoizing, color image denoizing, watermarking, speech enhancement, among others. Sahu et al. in [4] presented a denoizing method for speckle noise removal applied to a retinal optical coherence tomography (OCT) image. The method was based on the wavelet transform where the sub-bands coefficients were modeled using a Cauchy distribution. In [5], a dual tree complex wavelet transform (DTCWT)-based despeckling algorithm was proposed for synthetic aperture radar (SAR) images, where the DTCWT coefficients in each subband were modeled with a multivariate Cauchy distribution. In [6], a new color image denoizing method in the contourlet domain was suggested for reducing noise in images corrupted by Gaussian noise where the contourlet subband coefficients were described by the heavy-tailed MCD. Sadreazami et al. in [7] put forward a novel multiplicative watermarking scheme in the contourlet domain where the watermark detector was based on the bivariate Cauchy distribution and designed to capture the across scale dependencies of the contourlet coefficients. Fontaine et al. in [8] proposed a semi-supervised multichannel speech enhancement system where both speech and noise follow the heavy-tailed multi-variate complex Cauchy distribution.

Kullback–Leibler divergence (KLD), also called relative entropy, is one of the most fundamental and important measures in information theory and statistics [9,10]. KLD was first introduced and studied by Kullback and Leibler [11] and Kullback [12] to measure the divergence between two probability mass functions in the case of discrete random variables and between two univariate or multivariate probability density functions in the case of continuous random variables. In the literature, numerous entropy and divergence measures have been suggested for measuring the similarity between probability distributions, such as Rényi [13] divergence, Sharma and Mittal [14] divergence, Bhattacharyya [15,16] divergence and Hellinger divergence measures [17]. Other general divergence families have been also introduced and studied like the ϕ-divergence family of divergence measures defined simultaneously by Csiszár [18] and Ali and Silvey [19] where the KLD measure is a special case, the Bregman family divergence [20], the R-divergences introduced by Burbea and Rao [21–23], the statistical f-divergences [24,25] and recently the new family of a generalized divergence called the (h, ϕ)-divergence measures introduced and studied in Menéndez et al. [26]. Readers are referred to [10] for details about these divergence family measures.

KLD has a specific interpretation in coding theory [27] and is therefore the most popular and widely used as well. Since information theoretic divergence and KLD in particular are ubiquitous in information sciences [28,29], it is therefore important to establish closed-form expressions of such divergence [30]. An analytical expression of the KLD between two univariate Cauchy distributions was presented in [31,32]. To date, the KLD of MCDs has no known explicit form, and it is in practice either estimated using expensive Monte Carlo stochastic integration or approximated. Monte Carlo sampling can efficiently estimate the KLD provided that a large number of independent and identically distributed samples is provided. Nevertheless, Monte Carlo integration is a too slow process to be useful in many applications. The main contribution of this paper is to derive a closed-form expression for the KLD between two central MCDs in a general case to benchmark future approaches while avoiding approximation using expensive Monte Carlo (MC) estimation techniques. The paper is organized as follows. Section 2 introduces the MCD and the KLD. Section 3 gives some definitions and propositions related to a multiple power series used to compute the closed-form expression of the KLD between two central MCDs. In Sections 4 and 5, expressions of some expectations related to the KLD are developed by exploiting the propositions presented in the previous section. Section 6 demonstrates some final results on the KLD computed for the central MCD. Section 7 presents some particular results such as the KLD for the univariate and the bivariate Cauchy distribution. Section 8 presents the implementation procedure of the KLD and a comparison with Monte Carlo sampling method. A summary and some conclusions are provided in the final section.

2. Multivariate Cauchy Distribution and Kullback–Leibler Divergence

Let $\mathbf{X}$ be a random vector of $\mathbb{R}^p$ which follows the MCD, characterized by the following probability density function (pdf) given as follows [2]

$$f_{\mathbf{X}}(x|\boldsymbol{\mu}, \boldsymbol{\Sigma}, p) = \frac{\Gamma(\frac{1+p}{2})}{\pi^{\frac{p}{2}}\Gamma(\frac{1}{2})} \frac{1}{|\boldsymbol{\Sigma}|^{\frac{1}{2}}} \frac{1}{[1 + (x-\boldsymbol{\mu})^T \boldsymbol{\Sigma}^{-1}(x-\boldsymbol{\mu})]^{\frac{1+p}{2}}}. \tag{1}$$

This is for any $x \in \mathbb{R}^p$, where p is the dimensionality of the sample space, $\boldsymbol{\mu}$ is the location vector, $\boldsymbol{\Sigma}$ is a symmetric, positive definite $(p \times p)$ scale matrix and $\Gamma(.)$ is the Gamma function. Let $\mathbf{X}^1$ and $\mathbf{X}^2$ be two random vectors that follow central MCDs with pdfs $f_{\mathbf{X}^1}(x|\boldsymbol{\Sigma}_1, p) = f_{\mathbf{X}^1}(x|0, \boldsymbol{\Sigma}_1, p)$ and $f_{\mathbf{X}^2}(x|\boldsymbol{\Sigma}_2, p) = f_{\mathbf{X}^2}(x|0, \boldsymbol{\Sigma}_2, p)$ given by (1). KLD provides an asymmetric measure of the similarity of the two pdfs. Indeed, the KLD between the two central MCDs is given by

$$\mathrm{KL}(\mathbf{X}^1 || \mathbf{X}^2) = \int_{\mathbb{R}^p} \ln\left(\frac{f_{\mathbf{X}^1}(x|\boldsymbol{\Sigma}_1, p)}{f_{\mathbf{X}^2}(x|\boldsymbol{\Sigma}_2, p)}\right) f_{\mathbf{X}^1}(x|\boldsymbol{\Sigma}_1, p) dx \tag{2}$$

$$= E_{\mathbf{X}^1}\{\ln f_{\mathbf{X}^1}(\mathbf{X})\} - E_{\mathbf{X}^1}\{\ln f_{\mathbf{X}^2}(\mathbf{X})\}. \tag{3}$$

Since the KLD is the relative entropy defined as the difference between the cross-entropy and the entropy, we have the following relation:

$$\mathrm{KL}(\mathbf{X}^1||\mathbf{X}^2) = H(f_{\mathbf{X}^1}, f_{\mathbf{X}^2}) - H(f_{\mathbf{X}^1}) \tag{4}$$

where $H(f_{\mathbf{X}^1}, f_{\mathbf{X}^2}) = -E_{\mathbf{X}^1}\{\ln f_{\mathbf{X}^2}(\mathbf{X})\}$ denotes the cross-entropy and $H(f_{\mathbf{X}^1}) = -E_{\mathbf{X}^1}\{\ln f_{\mathbf{X}^1}(\mathbf{X})\}$ the entropy. Therefore, the determination of KLD requires the expression of the entropy and the cross-entropy. It should be noted that the smaller $\mathrm{KL}(\mathbf{X}^1||\mathbf{X}^2)$, the more similar are $f_{\mathbf{X}^1}(x|\mathbf{\Sigma}_1, p)$ and $f_{\mathbf{X}^2}(x|\mathbf{\Sigma}_2, p)$. The symmetric KL similarity measure between $\mathbf{X}^1$ and $\mathbf{X}^2$ is $d_{\mathrm{KL}}(\mathbf{X}^1, \mathbf{X}^2) = \mathrm{KL}(\mathbf{X}^1||\mathbf{X}^2) + \mathrm{KL}(\mathbf{X}^2||\mathbf{X}^1)$. In order to compute the KLD, we have to derive the analytical expressions of $E_{\mathbf{X}^1}\{\ln f_{\mathbf{X}^1}(\mathbf{X})\}$ and $E_{\mathbf{X}^1}\{\ln f_{\mathbf{X}^2}(\mathbf{X})\}$ which depend, respectively, on $E_{\mathbf{X}^1}\{\ln[1 + \mathbf{X}^T \mathbf{\Sigma}_1^{-1} \mathbf{X}]\}$ and $E_{\mathbf{X}^1}\{\ln[1 + \mathbf{X}^T \mathbf{\Sigma}_2^{-1} \mathbf{X}]\}$. Consequently, the closed-form expression of the KLD between two zero-mean MCDs is given by

$$\mathrm{KL}(\mathbf{X}^1||\mathbf{X}^2) = \frac{1}{2} \log \frac{|\mathbf{\Sigma}_2|}{|\mathbf{\Sigma}_1|} - \frac{1+p}{2} \left(E_{\mathbf{X}^1}\{\ln[1 + \mathbf{X}^T \mathbf{\Sigma}_1^{-1} \mathbf{X}]\} - E_{\mathbf{X}^1}\{\ln[1 + \mathbf{X}^T \mathbf{\Sigma}_2^{-1} \mathbf{X}]\} \right). \tag{5}$$

To provide the expression of these two expectations, some tools based on the multiple power series are required. The next section presents some definitions and propositions used for this goal.

3. Definitions and Propositions

This section presents some definitions and exposes some propositions related to the multiple power series used to derive the closed-form expression of the expectation $E_{\mathbf{X}^1}\{\ln[1 + \mathbf{X}^T \mathbf{\Sigma}_1^{-1} \mathbf{X}]\}$ and $E_{\mathbf{X}^1}\{\ln[1 + \mathbf{X}^T \mathbf{\Sigma}_2^{-1} \mathbf{X}]\}$, and as a consequence the KLD between two central MCDs.

Definition 1. *The Humbert series of n variables, denoted $\Phi_2^{(n)}$, is defined for all $x_i \in \mathbb{C}$, $i = 1, \ldots, n$, by the following multiple power series (Section 1.4 in [33])*

$$\Phi_2^{(n)}(b_1, \ldots, b_n; c; x_1, \ldots, x_n) = \sum_{m_1=0}^{\infty} \cdots \sum_{m_n=0}^{\infty} \frac{(b_1)_{m_1} \cdots (b_n)_{m_n}}{(c)_{\sum_{i=1}^n m_i}} \prod_{i=1}^n \frac{x_i^{m_i}}{m_i!}. \tag{6}$$

The Pochhammer symbol $(q)_i$ indicates the i-th rising factorial of q, i.e., for an integer $i > 0$

$$(q)_i = q(q+1)\ldots(q+i-1) = \prod_{k=0}^{i-1}(q+k) = \frac{\Gamma(q+i)}{\Gamma(q)} \tag{7}$$

3.1. Integral Representation for $\Phi_2^{(n)}$

Proposition 1. *The following integral representation is true for $\mathrm{Real}\{c\} > \mathrm{Real}\{\sum_{i=1}^n b_i\} > 0$ and $\mathrm{Real}\{b_i\} > 0$ where $\mathrm{Real}\{.\}$ denotes the real part of the complex coefficients*

$$\int \cdots \int_\Delta \left(1 - \sum_{i=1}^n u_i\right)^{c - \sum_{i=1}^n b_i - 1} \prod_{i=1}^n u_i^{b_i - 1} e^{x_i u_i} du_i = B\left(b_1, \ldots, b_n, c - \sum_{i=1}^n b_i\right) \Phi_2^{(n)}(b_1, \ldots, b_n; c; x_1, \ldots, x_n) \tag{8}$$

where $\Delta = \{(u_1, \ldots, u_n) | 0 \leq u_i \leq 1, i = 1, \ldots, n; 0 \leq u_1 + \ldots + u_n \leq 1\}$ and the multivariate beta function B is the extension of beta function to more than two arguments (called also Dirichlet function) defined as (Section 1.6.1 in [34])

$$B(b_1, \ldots, b_n, b_{n+1}) = \frac{\prod_{i=1}^{n+1} \Gamma(b_i)}{\Gamma(\sum_{i=1}^{n+1} b_i)}. \tag{9}$$

Proof. The power series of exponential function is given by

$$e^{x_i u_i} = \sum_{m_i=0}^{\infty} \frac{x_i^{m_i}}{m_i!} u_i^{m_i}. \tag{10}$$

By substituting the expression of the exponential into the multiple integrals we have

$$\int \cdots \int_\Delta \left(1 - \sum_{i=1}^n u_i\right)^{c-\sum_{i=1}^n b_i - 1} \prod_{i=1}^n u_i^{b_i-1} e^{x_i u_i} du_i$$

$$= \int \cdots \int_\Delta \left(1 - \sum_{i=1}^n u_i\right)^{c-\sum_{i=1}^n b_i - 1} \left(\prod_{i=1}^n \sum_{m_i=0}^{\infty} \frac{x_i^{m_i}}{m_i!} u_i^{m_i+b_i-1} du_i\right) \tag{11}$$

$$= \sum_{m_1=0}^{\infty} \cdots \sum_{m_n=0}^{\infty} \left(\prod_{i=1}^n \frac{x_i^{m_i}}{m_i!}\right) \times \mathbf{I}_D$$

where the multivariate integral $\mathbf{I}_D$, which is a generalization of a beta integral, is the type-1 Dirichlet integral (Section 1.6.1 in [34]) given by

$$\mathbf{I}_D = \int \cdots \int_\Delta \left(1 - \sum_{i=1}^n u_i\right)^{c-\sum_{i=1}^n b_i - 1} \prod_{i=1}^n u_i^{m_i+b_i-1} du_i$$

$$= \frac{\prod_{i=1}^n \Gamma(b_i+m_i)\Gamma(c-\sum_{i=1}^n b_i)}{\Gamma(c+\sum_{i=1}^n m_i)}. \tag{12}$$

Knowing that $\Gamma(b_i + m_i) = \Gamma(b_i)(b_i)_{m_i}$, the expression of $\mathbf{I}_D$ can be written otherwise

$$\mathbf{I}_D = \frac{\prod_{i=1}^n \Gamma(b_i)\Gamma(c-\sum_{i=1}^n b_i)}{\Gamma(c)} \frac{\prod_{i=1}^n (b_i)_{m_i}}{(c)_{\sum_{i=1}^n m_i}}. \tag{13}$$

Finally, plugging (13) back into (12) leads to the final result

$$\frac{\Gamma(c - \sum_{i=1}^n b_i) \prod_{i=1}^n \Gamma(b_i)}{\Gamma(c)} \sum_{\substack{m_1, \ldots, \\ m_n = 0}}^{+\infty} \frac{\prod_{i=1}^n (b_i)_{m_i}}{(c)_{\sum_{i=1}^n m_i}} \prod_{i=1}^n \frac{x_i^{m_i}}{m_i!} = B\left(b_1, \ldots, b_n, c - \sum_{i=1}^n b_i\right) \Phi_2^{(n)}(b_1, \ldots, b_n; c; x_1, \ldots, x_n) \tag{14}$$

□

Given Proposition 1, we consider the particular cases $n = \{1, 2\}$ one by one as follows:
Case $n = 1$

$$\frac{1}{B(b_1, c - b_1)} \int_0^1 u_1^{b_1-1} e^{x_1 u_1} (1 - u_1)^{c-b_1-1} du_1 = \sum_{m_1=0}^{\infty} \frac{(b_1)_{m_1}}{(c)_{m_1}} \frac{x_1^{m_1}}{m_1!} = \Phi_2^{(1)}(b_1; c; x_1) = {}_1F_1(b_1, c; x_1) \tag{15}$$

where ${}_1F_1(.)$ is the confluent hypergeometric function of the first kind (Section 9.21 in [35]).
Case $n = 2$

$$\frac{1}{B(b_1, b_2, c - b_1 - b_2)} \iint_{\substack{u_1 \geq 0, u_2 \geq 0, \\ u_1+u_2 \leq 1}} u_1^{b_1-1} u_2^{b_2-1} e^{x_1 u_1 + x_2 u_2} (1 - u_1 - u_2)^{c-b_1-b_2-1} du_1 du_2$$

$$= \sum_{m_1=0}^{\infty} \sum_{m_2=0}^{\infty} \frac{(b_1)_{m_1}(b_2)_{m_2}}{(c)_{m_1+m_2}} \frac{x_1^{m_1}}{m_1!} \frac{x_2^{m_2}}{m_2!} = \Phi_2^{(2)}(b_1, b_2; c; x_1, x_2) = \Phi_2(b_1, b_2; c; x_1, x_2) \tag{16}$$

where the double series Φ_2 is one of the components of the Humbert series of two variables [36] that generalize Kummer's confluent hypergeometric series ${}_1F_1$ of one variable. The double series Φ_2 converges absolutely at any $x_1, x_2 \in \mathbb{C}$.

3.2. Multiple Power Series $F_N^{(n)}$

Definition 2. *We define a new multiple power series, denoted by $F_N^{(n)}$ and given by*

$$F_N^{(n)}(a; b_1, \ldots, b_n; c, c_n; x_1, \ldots, x_n)$$
$$= x_n^{-a} \sum_{\substack{m_1, \ldots, \\ m_n = 0}}^{+\infty} \frac{(a)_{\sum_{i=1}^n m_i}(a - c_n + 1)_{\sum_{i=1}^{n-1} m_i} \prod_{i=1}^{n-1}(b_i)_{m_i}}{(a + b_n - c_n + 1)_{\sum_{i=1}^n m_i}(c)_{\sum_{i=1}^{n-1} m_i}} \prod_{i=1}^{n-1} \left(\frac{x_i}{x_n}\right)^{m_i} \frac{1}{m_i!} \frac{(1 - x_n^{-1})^{m_n}}{m_n!}. \quad (17)$$

The multiple power series (17) is absolutely convergent on the region $|x_i x_n^{-1}| + |1 - x_n^{-1}| < 1$ in $\mathbb{C}^n$, $\forall\, i \in \{1, \ldots, n-1\}$.

The multiple power series $F_N^{(n)}(.)$ can also be transformed into two other expressions as follows

$$F_N^{(n)}(a; b_1, \ldots, b_n; c, c_n; x_1, \ldots, x_n)$$
$$= \sum_{\substack{m_1, \ldots, \\ m_n = 0}}^{+\infty} \frac{(a - c_n + 1)_{\sum_{i=1}^{n-1} m_i}(b_n)_{m_n}(a)_{\sum_{i=1}^n m_i} \prod_{i=1}^{n-1}(b_i)_{m_i}}{(a + b_n - c_n + 1)_{\sum_{i=1}^n m_i}(c)_{\sum_{i=1}^{n-1} m_i}} \prod_{i=1}^{n-1} \frac{x_i^{m_i}}{m_i!} \frac{(1 - x_n)^{m_n}}{m_n!}, \quad (18)$$

$$= x_n^{1-c_n} \sum_{\substack{m_1, \ldots, \\ m_n = 0}}^{+\infty} \frac{(a - c_n + 1)_{\sum_{i=1}^n m_i}(b_n - c_n + 1)_{m_n}(a)_{\sum_{i=1}^{n-1} m_i} \prod_{i=1}^{n-1}(b_i)_{m_i}}{(a + b_n - c_n + 1)_{\sum_{i=1}^n m_i}(c)_{\sum_{i=1}^{n-1} m_i}} \prod_{i=1}^{n-1} \frac{x_i^{m_i}}{m_i!} \frac{(1 - x_n)^{m_n}}{m_n!}. \quad (19)$$

By Horn's rule for the determination of the convergence region (see [37], Section 5.7.2), the multiple power series (18) and (19) are absolutely convergent on region $|x_i| < 1$, $\forall\, i \in \{1, \ldots, n-1\}$, $|1 - x_n| < 1$ in $\mathbb{C}^n$.

Equation (18) can then be deduced from (17) by using the following development where the $F_N^{(p)}$ function can be written as

$$F_N^{(n)}(a; b_1, \ldots, b_n; c, c_n; x_1, \ldots, x_n) = x_n^{-a} \sum_{\substack{m_1, \ldots, \\ m_{n-1} = 0}}^{+\infty} \frac{(a)_{\sum_{i=1}^{n-1} m_i}(a - c_n + 1)_{\sum_{i=1}^{n-1} m_i} \prod_{i=1}^{n-1}(b_i)_{m_i}}{(a + b_n - c_n + 1)_{\sum_{i=1}^{n-1} m_i}(c)_{\sum_{i=1}^{n-1} m_i}}$$
$$\times \prod_{i=1}^{n-1} \left(\frac{x_i}{x_n}\right)^{m_i} \frac{1}{m_i!} \sum_{m_n = 0}^{\infty} \frac{(\alpha)_{m_n}(\alpha - c_n + 1)_{m_n}}{(\alpha + b_n - c_n + 1)_{m_n}} \frac{(1 - x_n^{-1})^{m_n}}{m_n!} \quad (20)$$

and $\alpha = a + \sum_{i=1}^{n-1} m_i$ is used here to alleviate writing equations. Using the definition of Gauss' hypergeometric series $_2F_1(.)$ [34] and the Pfaff transformation [38], we can write

$$\sum_{m_n = 0}^{\infty} \frac{(\alpha)_{m_n}(\alpha - c_n + 1)_{m_n}}{(\alpha + b_n - c_n + 1)_{m_n}} \frac{(1 - x_n^{-1})^{m_n}}{m_n!} = {}_2F_1\left(\alpha, \alpha - c_n + 1; \alpha + b_n - c_n + 1; 1 - x_n^{-1}\right) \quad (21)$$

$$= x_n^{\alpha} \, {}_2F_1\left(\alpha, b_n; \alpha + b_n - c_n + 1; 1 - x_n\right) \quad (22)$$

$$= x_n^{\alpha} \sum_{m_p = 0}^{\infty} \frac{(\alpha)_{m_n}(b_n)_{m_n}}{(\alpha + b_n - c_n + 1)_{m_n}} \frac{(1 - x_n)^{m_n}}{m_n!}. \quad (23)$$

By substituting (23) into (20), and using the following two relations:

$$(a)_{\sum_{i=1}^{n-1} m_i}(\alpha)_{m_n} = (a)_{\sum_{i=1}^n m_i}, \quad (24)$$

$$(a + b_n - c_n + 1)_{\sum_{i=1}^{n-1} m_i}(\alpha + b_n - c_n + 1)_{m_n} = (a + b_n - c_n + 1)_{\sum_{i=1}^n m_i} \quad (25)$$

we can get (18).

The second transformation is given as follows

$$_2F_1\left(\alpha, \alpha - c_n + 1; b_n - c_n + \alpha + 1; 1 - x_n^{-1}\right)$$
$$= x_n^{\alpha - c_n + 1} \, _2F_1\left(b_n - c_n + 1, \alpha - c_n + 1; \alpha + b_n - c_n + 1; 1 - x_n\right) \qquad (26)$$
$$= x_n^{\alpha - c_n + 1} \sum_{m_n=0}^{\infty} \frac{(\alpha - c_n + 1)_{m_n}(b_n - c_n + 1)_{m_n}}{(\alpha + b_n - c_n + 1)_{m_n}} \frac{(1 - x_n)^{m_n}}{m_n!}. \qquad (27)$$

By substituting (27) into (20), we get (19).

Lemma 1. *The multiple power series $F_N^{(n)}$ is equal to the Lauricella D-hypergeometric function $F_D^{(n)}$ (see Appendix A) [39] when $a - c_n + 1 = c$ and is given as follows*

$$F_N^{(n)}(a; b_1, \ldots, b_n; c, c_n; x_1, \ldots, x_n) = \sum_{\substack{m_1, \ldots, \\ m_n = 0}}^{+\infty} \frac{(a)_{\sum_{i=1}^n m_i} \prod_{i=1}^n (b_i)_{m_i}}{(a + b_n - c_n + 1)_{\sum_{i=1}^n m_i}} \prod_{i=1}^{n-1} \frac{x_i^{m_i}}{m_i!} \frac{(1 - x_n)^{m_n}}{m_n!} \qquad (28)$$

$$= F_D^{(n)}(a, b_1, \ldots, b_n; a + b_n - c_n + 1; x_1, \ldots, x_{n-1}, 1 - x_n) \qquad (29)$$

Proof. By using Equation (18) of the multiple power series $F_N^{(n)}$ and after having simplified $(a - c_n + 1)_{\sum_{i=1}^{n-1} m_i}$ to the numerator and $(c)_{\sum_{i=1}^{n-1} m_i}$ to the denominator, we can get the result. □

3.3. Integral Representation for $F_N^{(n+1)}$

Proposition 2. *The following integral representation is true for $\text{Real}\{a\} > 0, \text{Real}\{a - c_{n+1} + 1\} > 0$, and $\text{Real}\{a - c_{n+1} + b_{n+1} + 1\} > 0$*

$$\frac{\Gamma(a)\Gamma(a - c_{n+1} + 1)}{\Gamma(a - c_{n+1} + b_{n+1} + 1)} F_N^{(n+1)}(a; b_1, \ldots, b_{n+1}; c, c_{n+1}; x_1, \ldots, x_{n+1})$$
$$= \int_0^\infty e^{-r} r^{a-1} \Phi_2^{(n)}(b_1, \ldots, b_n; c; rx_1, \ldots, rx_n) U(b_{n+1}, c_{n+1}; rx_{n+1}) dr \qquad (30)$$

where $U(\cdot)$ is the confluent hypergeometric function of the second kind (Section 9.21 in [35]) defined for $\text{Real}\{b\} > 0, \text{Real}\{z\} > 0$ by the following integral representation

$$U(b, c; z) = \frac{1}{\Gamma(b)} \int_0^\infty e^{-zt} t^{b-1} (1 + t)^{c-b-1} dt \qquad (31)$$

and $\Phi_2^{(n)}(\cdot)$ is defined by Equation (6).

Proof. The multiple power series $\Phi_2^{(n)}$ and the confluent hypergeometric function $U(\cdot)$ are absolutely convergent on $[0, +\infty]$. Using these functions in the above integral and changing the order of integration and summation, which is easily justified by absolute convergence, we get

$$\int_0^\infty e^{-r} r^{a-1} \Phi_2^{(n)}(b_1, \ldots, b_n; c; rx_1, \ldots, rx_n) U(b_{n+1}, c_{n+1}; rx_{n+1}) dr$$
$$= \sum_{m_1=0}^\infty \cdots \sum_{m_n=0}^\infty \frac{(b_1)_{m_1} \cdots (b_n)_{m_n}}{(c)_{\sum_{i=1}^n m_i}} \left(\prod_{i=1}^n \frac{x_i^{m_i}}{m_i!}\right) \mathbf{I} \qquad (32)$$

where integral $\mathbf{I}$ is defined as follows

$$\mathbf{I} = \int_0^\infty e^{-r} r^{a - 1 + \sum_{i=1}^n m_i} U(b_{n+1}, c_{n+1}; rx_{n+1}) dr. \qquad (33)$$

Substituting the integral expression of $U(\cdot)$ in the previous equation and replacing $\alpha = a + \sum_{i=1}^{n} m_i$ to alleviate writing equations, we have

$$\mathbf{I} = \frac{1}{\Gamma(b_{n+1})} \int_0^\infty \int_0^\infty \frac{e^{-(1+x_{n+1}t)r} r^{\alpha-1} t^{b_{n+1}-1}}{(1+t)^{-(c_{n+1}-b_{n+1}-1)}} dr dt. \tag{34}$$

Knowing that [35]

$$\int_0^\infty e^{-(1+x_{n+1}t)r} r^{\alpha-1} dr = \frac{\Gamma(\alpha)}{(1+x_{n+1}t)^\alpha} \tag{35}$$

and

$$\int_0^\infty \frac{t^{b_{n+1}-1}(1+t)^{c_{n+1}-b_{n+1}-1}}{(1+x_{n+1}t)^\alpha} dt = \frac{\Gamma(b_{n+1})\Gamma(\alpha - c_{n+1} + 1)}{\Gamma(\alpha + b_{n+1} - c_{n+1} + 1)} \,_2F_1(\alpha, b_{n+1}; \alpha + b_{n+1} - c_{n+1} + 1; 1 - x_{n+1}) \tag{36}$$

the new expression of **I** is then given by

$$\mathbf{I} = \frac{\Gamma(\alpha)\Gamma(\alpha - c_{n+1} + 1)}{\Gamma(\alpha + b_{n+1} - c_{n+1} + 1)} \sum_{m_{n+1}=0}^{+\infty} \frac{(\alpha)_{m_{n+1}}(b_{n+1})_{m_{n+1}}}{(\alpha + b_{n+1} - c_{n+1} + 1)_{m_{n+1}}} \frac{(1 - x_{n+1})^{m_{n+1}}}{m_{n+1}!}. \tag{37}$$

Using the fact that $\Gamma(\alpha) = \Gamma(a)(a)_{\sum_{i=1}^{n} m_i}$ and $(a)_{\sum_{i=1}^{n} m_i} (\alpha)_{m_{n+1}} = (a)_{\sum_{i=1}^{n+1} m_i}$, and developing the same method to $\Gamma(\alpha + b_{n+1} - c_{n+1} + 1)$, the final complete expression of the integral is then given by

$$\frac{\Gamma(a)\Gamma(a - c_{n+1} + 1)}{\Gamma(a + b_{n+1} - c_{n+1} + 1)} \sum_{m_1=0}^{\infty} \cdots \sum_{m_{n+1}=0}^{\infty} \frac{(b_1)_{m_1} \cdots (b_n)_{m_n}}{(c)_{\sum_{i=1}^{n} m_i}} \frac{(a - c_{n+1} + 1)_{\sum_{i=1}^{n} m_i}(b_{n+1})_{m_{n+1}}(a)_{\sum_{i=1}^{n+1} m_i}}{(a + b_{n+1} - c_{n+1} + 1)_{\sum_{i=1}^{n+1} m_i}} \prod_{i=1}^{n} \frac{x_i^{m_i}}{m_i!}$$

$$\times \frac{(1 - x_{n+1})^{m_{n+1}}}{m_{n+1}!} = \frac{\Gamma(a)\Gamma(a - c_{n+1} + 1)}{\Gamma(a - c_{n+1} + b_{n+1} + 1)} F_N^{(n+1)}(a; b_1, \ldots, b_{n+1}; c, c_{n+1}; x_1, \ldots, x_{n+1}). \tag{38}$$

□

4. Expression of $E_{\mathbf{X}^1}\{\ln[1 + \mathbf{X}^T \mathbf{\Sigma}_1^{-1} \mathbf{X}]\}$

Proposition 3. *Let $\mathbf{X}^1$ be a random vector that follows a central MCD with pdf given by $f_{\mathbf{X}^1}(x|\mathbf{\Sigma}_1, p)$. Expectation $E_{\mathbf{X}^1}\{\ln[1 + \mathbf{X}^T \mathbf{\Sigma}_1^{-1} \mathbf{X}]\}$ is given as follows*

$$E_{\mathbf{X}^1}\{\ln[1 + \mathbf{X}^T \mathbf{\Sigma}_1^{-1} \mathbf{X}]\} = \psi\left(\frac{1+p}{2}\right) - \psi\left(\frac{1}{2}\right) \tag{39}$$

where $\psi(.)$ is the digamma function defined as the logarithmic derivative of the Gamma function (Section 8.36 in [35]).

Proof. Expectation $E_{\mathbf{X}^1}\{\ln[1 + \mathbf{X}^T \mathbf{\Sigma}_1^{-1} \mathbf{X}]\}$ is developed as follows

$$E_{\mathbf{X}^1}\{\ln[1 + \mathbf{X}^T \mathbf{\Sigma}_1^{-1} \mathbf{X}]\} = \frac{A}{|\mathbf{\Sigma}_1|^{\frac{1}{2}}} \int_{\mathbb{R}^p} \frac{\ln[1 + x^T \mathbf{\Sigma}_1^{-1} x]}{[1 + x^T \mathbf{\Sigma}_1^{-1} x]^{\frac{1+p}{2}}} dx \tag{40}$$

where $A = \Gamma(\frac{1+p}{2})\pi^{-\frac{1+p}{2}}$. Utilizing the following property $\int \log(x) f(x) dx = \frac{\partial}{\partial a} \int x^a f(x) dx\big|_{a=0}$, as a consequence the expectation is given as follows

$$E_{\mathbf{X}^1}\{\ln[1 + \mathbf{X}^T \mathbf{\Sigma}_1^{-1} \mathbf{X}]\} = \frac{A}{|\mathbf{\Sigma}_1|^{\frac{1}{2}}} \frac{\partial}{\partial a} \int_{\mathbb{R}^p} [1 + x^T \mathbf{\Sigma}_1^{-1} x]^{a - \frac{1+p}{2}} dx \bigg|_{a=0} \tag{41}$$

Consider the transformation $\mathbf{y} = \mathbf{\Sigma}_1^{-1/2} x$ where $\mathbf{y} = [y_1, y_2, \ldots, y_p]^T$. The Jacobian determinant is given by $d\mathbf{y} = |\mathbf{\Sigma}_1|^{-1/2} dx$ (Theorem 1.12 in [40]). The new expression of the expectation is given by

$$E_{\mathbf{X}^1}\{\ln[1+\mathbf{X}^T\mathbf{\Sigma}_1^{-1}\mathbf{X}]\} = A\frac{\partial}{\partial a}\int_{\mathbb{R}^p}[1+\mathbf{y}^T\mathbf{y}]^{a-\frac{1+p}{2}}d\mathbf{y}\bigg|_{a=0}. \tag{42}$$

Let $u = \mathbf{y}^T\mathbf{y}$ be a transformation where the Jacobian determinant is given by (Lemma 13.3.1 in [41])

$$d\mathbf{y} = \frac{\pi^{\frac{p}{2}}}{\Gamma(\frac{p}{2})}u^{\frac{p}{2}-1}du. \tag{43}$$

The new expectation is as follows

$$E_{\mathbf{X}^1}\{\ln[1+\mathbf{X}^T\mathbf{\Sigma}_1^{-1}\mathbf{X}]\} = \frac{\Gamma(\frac{1+p}{2})}{\pi^{1/2}\Gamma(\frac{p}{2})}\frac{\partial}{\partial a}\int_0^{+\infty}u^{\frac{p}{2}-1}(1+u)^{a-\frac{1+p}{2}}du\bigg|_{a=0} \tag{44}$$

Using the definition of beta function, we can write that

$$\int_0^{+\infty}u^{\frac{p}{2}-1}(1+u)^{a-\frac{1+p}{2}}du = \frac{\Gamma(\frac{p}{2})\Gamma(\frac{1}{2}-a)}{\Gamma(\frac{1+p}{2}-a)}. \tag{45}$$

The derivative of the last integral w.r.t a is given by

$$\frac{\partial}{\partial a}\int_0^{+\infty}u^{\frac{p}{2}-1}(1+u)^{a-\frac{1+p}{2}}du\bigg|_{a=0} = \frac{\Gamma(\frac{p}{2})\Gamma(\frac{1}{2})}{\Gamma(\frac{1+p}{2})}\left[\psi(\frac{1+p}{2})-\psi(\frac{1}{2})\right] \tag{46}$$

Finally, the expression of $E_{\mathbf{X}^1}\{\ln[1+\mathbf{X}^T\mathbf{\Sigma}_1^{-1}\mathbf{X}]\}$ is given by

$$E_{\mathbf{X}^1}\{\ln[1+\mathbf{X}^T\mathbf{\Sigma}_1^{-1}\mathbf{X}]\} = \psi\left(\frac{1+p}{2}\right) - \psi\left(\frac{1}{2}\right). \tag{47}$$

□

5. Expression of $E_{\mathbf{X}^1}\{\ln[1+\mathbf{X}^T\mathbf{\Sigma}_2^{-1}\mathbf{X}]\}$

Proposition 4. *Let $\mathbf{X}^1$ and $\mathbf{X}^2$ be two random vectors that follow central MCDs with pdfs given, respectively, by $f_{\mathbf{X}^1}(\mathbf{x}|\mathbf{\Sigma}_1,p)$ and $f_{\mathbf{X}^2}(\mathbf{x}|\mathbf{\Sigma}_2,p)$. Expectation $E_{\mathbf{X}^1}\{\ln[1+\mathbf{X}^T\mathbf{\Sigma}_2^{-1}\mathbf{X}]\}$ is given as follows*

$$E_{\mathbf{X}^1}\{\ln[1+\mathbf{X}^T\mathbf{\Sigma}_2^{-1}\mathbf{X}]\} = \psi\left(\frac{1+p}{2}\right) - \psi\left(\frac{1}{2}\right) + \ln\lambda_p$$
$$- \frac{\partial}{\partial a}\left\{F_D^{(p)}\left(a,\underbrace{\frac{1}{2},\frac{1}{2},\ldots,\frac{1}{2}}_{p},a+\frac{1}{2};a+\frac{1+p}{2};1-\frac{\lambda_1}{\lambda_p},\ldots,1-\frac{\lambda_{p-1}}{\lambda_p},1-\frac{1}{\lambda_p}\right)\right\}\bigg|_{a=0}. \tag{48}$$

where $\lambda_1,\ldots,\lambda_p$ are the eigenvalues of the real matrix $\mathbf{\Sigma}_1\mathbf{\Sigma}_2^{-1}$, and $F_D^{(p)}(.)$ represents the Lauricella D-hypergeometric function defined for p variables.

Proof. To prove Proposition 4, different steps are necessary. They are described in the following:

5.1. First Step: Eigenvalue Expression

Expectation $E_{\mathbf{X}^1}\{\ln[1+\mathbf{X}^T\mathbf{\Sigma}_2^{-1}\mathbf{X}]\}$ is computed as follows

$$E_{\mathbf{X}^1}\{\ln[1+\mathbf{X}^T\mathbf{\Sigma}_2^{-1}\mathbf{X}]\} = \frac{A}{|\mathbf{\Sigma}_1|^{\frac{1}{2}}}\int_{\mathbb{R}^p}\frac{\ln[1+\mathbf{x}^T\mathbf{\Sigma}_2^{-1}\mathbf{x}]}{[1+\mathbf{x}^T\mathbf{\Sigma}_1^{-1}\mathbf{x}]^{\frac{1+p}{2}}}d\mathbf{x} \tag{49}$$

where $A = \Gamma(\frac{1+p}{2})\pi^{-\frac{1+p}{2}}$. Consider transformation $y = \Sigma_1^{-1/2}x$ where $y = [y_1, y_2, \ldots, y_p]^T$. The Jacobian determinant is given by $dy = |\Sigma_1|^{-1/2}dx$ (Theorem 1.12 in [40]) and matrix $\Sigma = \Sigma_1^{\frac{1}{2}}\Sigma_2^{-1}\Sigma_1^{\frac{1}{2}}$ is a real symmetric matrix since Σ_1 and Σ_2 are real symmetric matrixes. Then, the expectation is evaluated as follows

$$E_{X^1}\{\ln[1 + X^T\Sigma_2^{-1}X]\} = A\int_{\mathbb{R}^p} \frac{\ln[1 + y^T\Sigma y]}{[1 + y^Ty]^{\frac{1+p}{2}}} dy. \tag{50}$$

Matrix Σ can be diagonalized by an orthogonal matrix P with $P^{-1} = P^T$ and $\Sigma = PDP^{-1}$ where D is a diagonal matrix composed of the eigenvalues of Σ. Considering that $y^T\Sigma y = \text{tr}(\Sigma yy^T) = \text{tr}(PDP^Tyy^T) = \text{tr}(DP^Tyy^TP)$, the expectation can be written as

$$E_{X^1}\{\ln[1 + X^T\Sigma_2^{-1}X]\} = A\int_{\mathbb{R}^p} \frac{\ln[1 + \text{tr}(DP^Tyy^TP)]}{[1 + y^Ty]^{\frac{1+p}{2}}} dy. \tag{51}$$

Let $z = P^Ty$ with $z = [z_1, z_2, \ldots, z_p]^T$ be a transformation where the Jacobian determinant is given by $dz = |P^T|dy = dy$. Using the fact that $\text{tr}(DP^Tyy^TP) = \text{tr}(Dzz^T) = z^TDz$ and $y^Ty = z^TP^TPz = z^Tz$, then the previous expectation (51) is given as follows

$$E_{X^1}\{\ln[1 + X^T\Sigma_2^{-1}X]\} = A\int_{\mathbb{R}^p} \frac{\ln[1 + z^TDz]}{[1 + z^Tz]^{\frac{1+p}{2}}} dz \tag{52}$$

$$= A\int_{\mathbb{R}} .. \int_{\mathbb{R}} \frac{\ln[1 + \sum_{i=1}^{p}\lambda_i z_i^2]}{[1 + \sum_{i=1}^{p} z_i^2]^{\frac{1+p}{2}}} dz_1 \ldots dz_p \tag{53}$$

where $\lambda_1, \ldots, \lambda_p$ are the eigenvalues of $\Sigma_1\Sigma_2^{-1}$.

5.2. Second Step: Polar Decomposition

Let the independent real variables $z_1, \ldots, z_p$ be transformed to the general polar coordinates $r, \theta_1, \ldots, \theta_{p-1}$ as follows, where $r > 0, -\pi/2 < \theta_j \leq \pi/2, j = 1, \ldots, p-2, -\pi < \theta_{p-1} \leq \pi$ [40],

$$z_1 = r\sin\theta_1 \tag{54}$$
$$z_2 = r\cos\theta_1\sin\theta_2 \tag{55}$$
$$z_j = r\cos\theta_1\cos\theta_2 \ldots \cos\theta_{j-1}\sin\theta_j, \quad j = 2, 3, \ldots, p-1 \tag{56}$$
$$z_p = r\cos\theta_1\cos\theta_2 \ldots \cos\theta_{p-1}. \tag{57}$$

The Jacobian determinant according to theorem (1.24) in [40] is

$$dz_1 \ldots dz_p = r^{p-1}\prod_{j=1}^{p-1}|\cos\theta_j|^{p-j-1} dr d\theta_j. \tag{58}$$

It is clear that with the last transformations, we get $\sum_{i=1}^{p} z_i^2 = r^2$ and the multiple integral in (53) is then given as follows

$$E_{X^1}\{\ln[1 + X^T\Sigma_2^{-1}X]\} = A\int_0^{+\infty} \frac{r^{p-1}}{[1+r^2]^{\frac{1+p}{2}}} \int_{-\pi/2}^{\pi/2} .. \int_{-\pi}^{\pi} \left(\prod_{j=1}^{p-1}|\cos\theta_j|^{p-j-1}\right) \times$$

$$\ln\left[1 + r^2(\lambda_1\sin^2\theta_1 + \ldots + \lambda_p\cos^2\theta_1 \ldots \cos^2\theta_{p-1})\right] dr \prod_{j=1}^{p-1} d\theta_j. \tag{59}$$

By replacing the expression of $\sin^2\theta_j$ by $1 - \cos^2\theta_j$, for $j = 1, \ldots, p-1$, we have the following expression

$$\lambda_1 \sin^2 \theta_1 + \ldots + \lambda_p \cos^2 \theta_1 \ldots \cos^2 \theta_{p-1} = \lambda_1 + (\lambda_2 - \lambda_1) \cos^2 \theta_1$$
$$+ \ldots + (\lambda_p - \lambda_{p-1}) \cos^2 \theta_1 \cos^2 \theta_2 \ldots \cos^2 \theta_{p-1}. \tag{60}$$

Let $x_i = \cos^2 \theta_i$ be a transformation to use where $dx_i = 2x_i^{1/2}(1-x_i)^{1/2} d\theta_i$. Then the expectation given by the multiple integral over all θ_j, $j = 1, \ldots, p-1$ is as follows

$$2A \int_0^{+\infty} \frac{r^{p-1}}{[1+r^2]^{\frac{1+p}{2}}} \int_0^1 \ldots \int_0^1 \left(\prod_{j=1}^{p-1} x_j^{\frac{p-j}{2}-1} (1-x_j)^{-\frac{1}{2}} \right) \ln[1 + r^2 B_p(x_1, \ldots, x_{p-1})] dr dx_1 \ldots dx_{p-1} \tag{61}$$

where $B_p(x_1, \ldots, x_{p-1}) = \lambda_1 + (\lambda_2 - \lambda_1)x_1 + \ldots + (\lambda_p - \lambda_{p-1})x_1 x_2 \ldots x_{p-1}$, $p \geq 1$ and $B_1 = \lambda_1$. In the following, we use the notation B_p instead of $B_p(x_1, \ldots, x_{p-1})$ to alleviate writing equations.

Let $t = r^2$ be transformation to use. Then, one can write

$$= A \int_0^{+\infty} \frac{t^{\frac{p}{2}-1}}{[1+t]^{\frac{1+p}{2}}} \int_0^1 \ldots \int_0^1 \left(\prod_{j=1}^{p-1} x_j^{\frac{p-j}{2}-1} (1-x_j)^{-\frac{1}{2}} \right) \ln[1 + t B_p] dt dx_1 \ldots dx_{p-1}. \tag{62}$$

In order to solve the integral in (62), we consider the following property given by $\int \log(x) f(x) dx = -\frac{\partial}{\partial a} \int x^{-a} f(x) dx \big|_{a=0}$ and the following equation given as follows

$$(1 + B_p t)^{-a} = \frac{1}{\Gamma(a)} \int_0^{+\infty} y^{a-1} e^{-(1+B_p t)y} dy. \tag{63}$$

Making use of the above equation, we obtain a new expression of (62) given as follows

$$E_{\mathbf{X}^1}\{\ln[1 + \mathbf{X}^T \mathbf{\Sigma}_2^{-1} \mathbf{X}]\}$$
$$= -\frac{\partial}{\partial a} \left\{ \frac{A}{\Gamma(a)} \int_0^{+\infty} \frac{t^{\frac{p}{2}-1}}{[1+t]^{\frac{1+p}{2}}} \int_0^{+\infty} y^{a-1} e^{-(1+B_p t)y} \int_0^1 \ldots \int_0^1 \prod_{j=1}^{p-1} x_j^{\frac{p-j}{2}-1} (1-x_j)^{-\frac{1}{2}} dx_j dy dt \right\} \bigg|_{a=0} \tag{64}$$
$$= -\frac{\partial}{\partial a} \left\{ \frac{A}{\Gamma(a)} \int_0^{+\infty} \frac{t^{\frac{p}{2}-1}}{[1+t]^{\frac{1+p}{2}}} \int_0^{+\infty} y^{a-1} e^{-y} \mathbf{H}(t,y) dy dt \right\} \bigg|_{a=0} \tag{65}$$

where $\mathbf{H}(t,y)$ is defined as

$$\mathbf{H}(t,y) = \int_0^1 \ldots \int_0^1 e^{-B_p t y} \prod_{j=1}^{p-1} x_j^{\frac{p-j}{2}-1} (1-x_j)^{-\frac{1}{2}} dx_j. \tag{66}$$

5.3. Third Step: Expression for H(t,y) by Humbert and Beta Functions

Let $x'_i = 1 - x_i$, $i = 1, \ldots, p-1$ be transformations to use. Then

$$(\lambda_2 - \lambda_1) x_1 = (\lambda_2 - \lambda_1)(1 - x'_1) \tag{67}$$
$$(\lambda_3 - \lambda_2) x_1 x_2 = (\lambda_3 - \lambda_2)(1 - x'_1)[1 - x'_2] \tag{68}$$
$$(\lambda_4 - \lambda_3) x_1 x_2 x_3 = (\lambda_4 - \lambda_3)(1 - x'_1)(1 - x'_2)[1 - x'_3] \tag{69}$$
$$\vdots = \vdots$$
$$(\lambda_p - \lambda_{p-1}) \prod_{i=1}^{p-1} x_i = (\lambda_p - \lambda_{p-1}) \prod_{i=1}^{p-1} (1 - x'_i). \tag{70}$$

Adding equations from (67) to (70), we can state that the new expression of the function B_p becomes

$$B_p = \lambda_p - (\lambda_p - \lambda_1)x'_1 - (\lambda_p - \lambda_2)(1 - x'_1)x'_2 - (\lambda_p - \lambda_3)(1 - x'_1)(1 - x'_2)x'_3$$
$$- \ldots - (\lambda_p - \lambda_{p-1})(1 - x'_1)\ldots(1 - x'_{p-2})x'_{p-1}. \tag{71}$$

Then, the multiple integral $\mathbf{H}(t,y)$ given by (66) can be written otherwise

$$\mathbf{H}(t,y) = \int_0^1 \ldots \int_0^1 e^{-B_p t y} \prod_{j=1}^{p-1} (1 - x'_j)^{\frac{p-j}{2} - 1} x'_j{}^{-\frac{1}{2}} dx'_1 \ldots dx'_{p-1}. \tag{72}$$

Let the real variables $x'_1, x'_2, \ldots, x'_{p-1}$ be transformed to the real variables $u_1, u_2, \ldots, u_{p-1}$ as follows

$$u_1 = x'_1 \tag{73}$$
$$u_2 = (1 - x'_1)x'_2 = (1 - u_1)x'_2 \tag{74}$$
$$u_3 = (1 - x'_1)(1 - x'_2)x'_3 = (1 - u_1 - u_2)x'_3 \tag{75}$$
$$\vdots$$
$$u_{p-1} = \prod_{i=1}^{p-2}(1 - x'_i)x'_{p-1} = (1 - \sum_{i=1}^{p-2} u_i)x'_{p-1}. \tag{76}$$

The Jacobian determinant is given by

$$du_1 \ldots du_{p-1} = \prod_{j=1}^{p-1}\left(1 - \sum_{i=1}^{j-1} u_i\right) dx'_1 \ldots dx'_{p-1}. \tag{77}$$

Accordingly, the new expression of B_p becomes

$$B_p = \lambda_p - \sum_{i=1}^{p-1}(\lambda_p - \lambda_i)u_i. \tag{78}$$

As a consequence, the new domain of the multiple integral (72) is $\Delta = \{(u_1, u_2, \ldots, u_{p-1}) \in \mathbb{R}^{p-1}; 0 \leq u_1 \leq 1, 0 \leq u_2 \leq 1 - u_1, 0 \leq u_3 \leq 1 - u_1 - u_2, \ldots,$ and $0 \leq u_{p-1} \leq 1 - u_1 - u_2 \ldots - u_{p-2}\}$, and the expression of $\mathbf{H}(t,y)$ is given as follows

$$\mathbf{H}(t,y) = \int \ldots \int_\Delta e^{-B_p t y} \prod_{j=1}^{p-1}\left(1 - \sum_{i=1}^{j-1} u_i\right)^{-1} \left(\frac{u_j}{1 - \sum_{i=1}^{j-1} u_i}\right)^{-\frac{1}{2}} \prod_{j=1}^{p-1}\left(1 - \frac{u_j}{1 - \sum_{i=1}^{j-1} u_i}\right)^{\frac{p-j}{2} - 1} du_j \tag{79}$$

$$= \int \ldots \int_\Delta e^{-B_p t y} \prod_{j=1}^{p-1} u_j^{-\frac{1}{2}} \left(1 - \sum_{i=1}^{j} u_i\right)^{\frac{p-j}{2} - 1} \left(1 - \sum_{i=1}^{j-1} u_i\right)^{\frac{1}{2} - \frac{p-j}{2}} du_1 \ldots du_{p-1} \tag{80}$$

$$= \int \ldots \int_\Delta e^{-B_p t y} \left(1 - \sum_{i=1}^{p-1} u_i\right)^{\frac{p}{2} - \frac{p-1}{2} - 1} \prod_{j=1}^{p-1} u_j^{-\frac{1}{2}} du_j \tag{81}$$

$$= e^{-\lambda_p t y} \int \ldots \int_\Delta \left(1 - \sum_{i=1}^{p-1} u_i\right)^{-\frac{1}{2}} \prod_{i=1}^{p-1} u_i^{-\frac{1}{2}} e^{(\lambda_p - \lambda_i) u_i t y} du_i. \tag{82}$$

Using Proposition 1, we subsequently find that

$$\mathbf{H}(t,y) = e^{-\lambda_p t y} B\underbrace{\left(\frac{1}{2}, \ldots, \frac{1}{2}\right)}_{p} \Phi_2^{(p-1)}\underbrace{\left(\frac{1}{2}, \ldots, \frac{1}{2}; \frac{p}{2}; (\lambda_p - \lambda_1)ty, (\lambda_p - \lambda_2)ty, \ldots, (\lambda_p - \lambda_{p-1})ty\right)}_{p-1}. \tag{83}$$

where $\Phi_2^{(p-1)}(.)$ is the Humbert series of $p-1$ variables and $B(\frac{1}{2},\ldots,\frac{1}{2})$ is the multivariate beta function. Applying the following successive two transformations $r = ty$ ($dr = tdy$) and $u = 1/t$ ($du = -u^2 dt$), the new expression of the expectation given by (65) is written as follows

$$E_{\mathbf{X}^1}\{\ln[1+\mathbf{X}^T\mathbf{\Sigma}_2^{-1}\mathbf{X}]\} = -\frac{\partial}{\partial a}\left\{\frac{A}{\Gamma(a)}B\underbrace{\left(\frac{1}{2},\ldots,\frac{1}{2}\right)}_{p}\int_0^{+\infty} r^{a-1}e^{-\lambda_p r}\right.$$

$$\left.\times \Phi_2^{(p-1)}\underbrace{\left(\frac{1}{2},\ldots,\frac{1}{2};\frac{p}{2};(\lambda_p-\lambda_1)r,\ldots,(\lambda_p-\lambda_{p-1})r\right)}_{p-1}\left(\int_0^{+\infty} u^{a-\frac{1}{2}}(1+u)^{-\frac{1+p}{2}}e^{-ru}du\right)dr\right\}\bigg|_{a=0}. \quad (84)$$

5.4. Final Step

The last integral is related to the confluent hypergeometric function of the second kind $U(.)$ as follows

$$\int_0^{+\infty} u^{a-\frac{1}{2}}(1+u)^{-\frac{1+p}{2}}e^{-ru}du = \Gamma(a+\frac{1}{2})U(a+\frac{1}{2},a+1-\frac{p}{2},r). \quad (85)$$

As a consequence, the new expression is

$$E_{\mathbf{X}^1}\{\ln[1+\mathbf{X}^T\mathbf{\Sigma}_2^{-1}\mathbf{X}]\} = -\frac{\partial}{\partial a}\left\{A\frac{\Gamma(a+\frac{1}{2})}{\Gamma(a)}B\left(\frac{1}{2},\ldots,\frac{1}{2}\right)\right.$$

$$\left.\times \int_0^{+\infty} r^{a-1}e^{-\lambda_p r}\Phi_2^{(p-1)}\left(\frac{1}{2},\ldots,\frac{1}{2};\frac{p}{2};1;(\lambda_p-\lambda_1)r,\ldots,(\lambda_p-\lambda_{p-1})r\right)U(a+\frac{1}{2},a+1-\frac{p}{2},r)dr\right\}\bigg|_{a=0}. \quad (86)$$

Using the transformation $r' = \lambda_p r$ and the Proposition 2, and taking into account the expression of A, the new expression becomes

$$E_{\mathbf{X}^1}\{\ln[1+\mathbf{X}^T\mathbf{\Sigma}_2^{-1}\mathbf{X}]\} = -\frac{\partial}{\partial a}\left\{\frac{B(a+\frac{1}{2},\frac{p}{2})}{B(\frac{1}{2},\frac{p}{2})}\lambda_p^{-a}\right.$$

$$\left.\times F_N^{(p)}\left(a;\underbrace{\frac{1}{2},\ldots,\frac{1}{2}}_{p},a+\frac{1}{2};\frac{p}{2},a-\frac{p}{2}+1;1-\frac{\lambda_1}{\lambda_p},\ldots,1-\frac{\lambda_{p-1}}{\lambda_p},\lambda_p^{-1}\right)\right\}\bigg|_{a=0} \quad (87)$$

Knowing that

$$\frac{\partial}{\partial a}\left\{\frac{B(\frac{p}{2},a+\frac{1}{2})}{B(\frac{p}{2},\frac{1}{2})}\right\}\bigg|_{a=0} = \psi\left(\frac{1}{2}\right) - \psi\left(\frac{1+p}{2}\right), \text{ and} \quad (88)$$

$$F_N^{(p)}\left(a;\frac{1}{2},\ldots,\frac{1}{2},a+\frac{1}{2};\frac{p}{2},a-\frac{p}{2}+1;1-\frac{\lambda_1}{\lambda_p},\ldots,1-\frac{\lambda_{p-1}}{\lambda_p},\lambda_p^{-1}\right)\bigg|_{a=0} = 1, \quad (89)$$

the new expression of $E_{\mathbf{X}^1}\{\ln[1+\mathbf{X}^T\mathbf{\Sigma}_2^{-1}\mathbf{X}]\}$ becomes

$$E_{\mathbf{X}^1}\{\ln[1+\mathbf{X}^T\mathbf{\Sigma}_2^{-1}\mathbf{X}]\} = \psi\left(\frac{1+p}{2}\right) - \psi\left(\frac{1}{2}\right)$$

$$-\frac{\partial}{\partial a}\left\{\lambda_p^{-a}F_N^{(p)}\left(a;\underbrace{\frac{1}{2},\ldots,\frac{1}{2}}_{p},a+\frac{1}{2};\frac{p}{2},a-\frac{p}{2}+1;1-\frac{\lambda_1}{\lambda_p},\ldots,1-\frac{\lambda_{p-1}}{\lambda_p},\lambda_p^{-1}\right)\right\}\bigg|_{a=0}. \quad (90)$$

Applying the expression given by (18) of Definition 2 and relying on Lemma 1, the final result corresponds to the D-hypergeometric function of Lauricella $F_D^{(p)}(.)$ given by

$$E_{\mathbf{X}^1}\{\ln[1+\mathbf{X}^T\mathbf{\Sigma}_2^{-1}\mathbf{X}]\} = \psi\left(\frac{1+p}{2}\right) - \psi\left(\frac{1}{2}\right)$$

$$-\frac{\partial}{\partial a}\left\{\lambda_p^{-a}\sum_{\substack{m_1,\ldots,\\m_p=0}}^{+\infty}\frac{(a)_{\sum_{i=1}^p m_i}(a+\frac{1}{2})_{m_p}\prod_{i=1}^{p-1}(\frac{1}{2})_{m_i}}{(a+\frac{1+p}{2})_{\sum_{i=1}^p m_i}}\prod_{i=1}^{p-1}\left(1-\frac{\lambda_i}{\lambda_p}\right)^{m_i}\frac{1}{m_i!}\frac{(1-\lambda_p^{-1})^{m_p}}{m_p!}\right\}\bigg|_{a=0} \quad (91)$$

$$= \psi\left(\frac{1+p}{2}\right) - \psi\left(\frac{1}{2}\right) - \frac{\partial}{\partial a}\left\{\lambda_p^{-a}F_D^{(p)}\left(a,\underbrace{\frac{1}{2},\ldots,\frac{1}{2}}_{p},a+\frac{1}{2};a+\frac{1+p}{2};1-\frac{\lambda_1}{\lambda_p},\ldots,1-\frac{\lambda_{p-1}}{\lambda_p},1-\frac{1}{\lambda_p}\right)\right\}\bigg|_{a=0}. \quad (92)$$

The final development of the previous expression is as follows

$$E_{\mathbf{X}^1}\{\ln[1+\mathbf{X}^T\mathbf{\Sigma}_2^{-1}\mathbf{X}]\} = \psi\left(\frac{1+p}{2}\right) - \psi\left(\frac{1}{2}\right) + \ln\lambda_p$$

$$- \frac{\partial}{\partial a}\left\{F_D^{(p)}\left(a,\underbrace{\frac{1}{2},\frac{1}{2},\ldots,\frac{1}{2}}_{p},a+\frac{1}{2};a+\frac{1+p}{2};1-\frac{\lambda_1}{\lambda_p},\ldots,1-\frac{\lambda_{p-1}}{\lambda_p},1-\frac{1}{\lambda_p}\right)\right\}\bigg|_{a=0}. \quad (93)$$

□

In this section, we presented the exact expression of $E_{\mathbf{X}^1}\{\ln[1+\mathbf{X}^T\mathbf{\Sigma}_2^{-1}\mathbf{X}]\}$. In addition, the multiple power series $F_D^{(p)}$ which appears to be a special case of $F_N^{(p)}$ provides many properties and numerous transformations (see Appendix A) that make easier the convergence of the multiple power series. In the next section, we establish the KLD closed-form expression based on the expression of the latter expectation.

6. KLD between Two Central MCDs

Plugging (39) and (93) into (5) yields the closed-form expression of the KLD between two central MCDs with pdfs $f_{\mathbf{X}^1}(x|\mathbf{\Sigma}_1,p)$ and $f_{\mathbf{X}^2}(x|\mathbf{\Sigma}_2,p)$. This result is presented in the following theorem.

Theorem 1. *Let $\mathbf{X}^1$ and $\mathbf{X}^2$ be two random vectors that follow central MCDs with pdfs given, respectively, by $f_{\mathbf{X}^1}(x|\mathbf{\Sigma}_1,p)$ and $f_{\mathbf{X}^2}(x|\mathbf{\Sigma}_2,p)$. The Kullback–Leibler divergence between central MCDs is*

$$KL(\mathbf{X}^1||\mathbf{X}^2) = -\frac{1}{2}\log\prod_{i=1}^p \lambda_i + \frac{1+p}{2}\bigg[\log\lambda_p$$

$$- \frac{\partial}{\partial a}\left\{F_D^{(p)}\left(a,\underbrace{\frac{1}{2},\ldots,\frac{1}{2}}_{p},a+\frac{1}{2};a+\frac{1+p}{2};1-\frac{\lambda_1}{\lambda_p},\ldots,1-\frac{\lambda_{p-1}}{\lambda_p},1-\frac{1}{\lambda_p}\right)\right\}\bigg|_{a=0}\bigg] \quad (94)$$

where $\lambda_1,\ldots,\lambda_p$ are the eigenvalues of the real matrix $\mathbf{\Sigma}_1\mathbf{\Sigma}_2^{-1}$, and $F_D^{(p)}(.)$ represents the Lauricella D-hypergeometric function defined for p variables.

Lauricella [39] gave several transformation formulas (see Appendix A), whose relations (A5)–(A7), and (A9) are applied to $F_D^{(p)}(.)$ in (94). The results of transformation are as follows

$$F_D^{(p)}\left(a, \frac{1}{2}, \ldots, \frac{1}{2}, a+\frac{1}{2}; a+\frac{1+p}{2}; 1-\frac{\lambda_1}{\lambda_p}, \ldots, 1-\frac{\lambda_{p-1}}{\lambda_p}, 1-\frac{1}{\lambda_p}\right)$$

$$= \lambda_p^{a+\frac{p}{2}} \prod_{i=1}^{p-1} \lambda_i^{-\frac{1}{2}} F_D^{(p)}\left(\frac{1+p}{2}, \frac{1}{2}, \ldots, \frac{1}{2}, a+\frac{1}{2}; a+\frac{1+p}{2}; 1-\frac{\lambda_p}{\lambda_1}, \ldots, 1-\frac{\lambda_p}{\lambda_{p-1}}, 1-\lambda_p\right) \quad (95)$$

$$= \left(\frac{\lambda_1}{\lambda_p}\right)^{-a} F_D^{(p)}\left(a, \frac{1}{2}, \ldots, \frac{1}{2}, a+\frac{1}{2}; a+\frac{1+p}{2}; 1-\frac{\lambda_p}{\lambda_1}, \ldots, 1-\frac{\lambda_2}{\lambda_1}, 1-\frac{1}{\lambda_1}\right) \quad (96)$$

$$= \lambda_p^a F_D^{(p)}\left(a, \frac{1}{2}, \ldots, \frac{1}{2}; a+\frac{1+p}{2}; 1-\lambda_1, 1-\lambda_2, \ldots, 1-\lambda_p\right) \quad (97)$$

$$= \lambda_p^a \prod_{i=1}^{p} \lambda_i^{-\frac{1}{2}} F_D^{(p)}\left(\frac{1+p}{2}, \frac{1}{2}, \ldots, \frac{1}{2}; a+\frac{1+p}{2}; 1-\frac{1}{\lambda_1}, 1-\frac{1}{\lambda_2}, \ldots, 1-\frac{1}{\lambda_p}\right). \quad (98)$$

Considering the above equations, it is easy to provide different expressions of $KL(\mathbf{X}^1||\mathbf{X}^2)$ shown in Table 1. The derivative of the Lauricella D-hypergeometric series with respect to a goes through the derivation of the following expression

$$\frac{\partial}{\partial a}\left\{F_D^{(p)}\left(a, \frac{1}{2}, \frac{1}{2}, \ldots, \frac{1}{2}, a+\frac{1}{2}; a+\frac{1+p}{2}; 1-\frac{\lambda_1}{\lambda_p}, \ldots, 1-\frac{\lambda_{p-1}}{\lambda_p}, 1-\frac{1}{\lambda_p}\right)\right\}\bigg|_{a=0} \quad (99)$$

$$= \sum_{m_1,\ldots,m_p=0}^{+\infty} \frac{\partial}{\partial a}\left\{\frac{(a)_{\sum_{i=1}^{p} m_i}(a+\frac{1}{2})_{m_p}}{(a+\frac{1+p}{2})_{\sum_{i=1}^{p} m_i}}\right\}\bigg|_{a=0} \prod_{i=1}^{p-1}\left(\frac{1}{2}\right)_{m_i}\left(1-\frac{\lambda_i}{\lambda_p}\right)^{m_i} \frac{1}{m_i!} \frac{(1-\lambda_p^{-1})^{m_p}}{m_p!} \quad (100)$$

The derivative with respect to a of the Lauricella D-hypergeometric series and its transformations goes through the following expressions (see Appendix B for demonstration)

$$\frac{\partial}{\partial a}\left\{\frac{(a)_{\sum_{i=1}^{p} m_i}(a+\frac{1}{2})_{m_p}}{(a+\frac{1+p}{2})_{\sum_{i=1}^{p} m_i}}\right\}\bigg|_{a=0} = \frac{(\frac{1}{2})_{m_p}(1)_{\sum_{i=1}^{p} m_i}}{(\frac{1+p}{2})_{\sum_{i=1}^{p} m_i}(\sum_{i=1}^{p} m_i)}, \quad (101)$$

$$\frac{\partial}{\partial a}\left\{\frac{(a)_{\sum_{i=1}^{p} m_i}}{(a+\frac{1+p}{2})_{\sum_{i=1}^{p} m_i}}\right\}\bigg|_{a=0} = \frac{(1)_{\sum_{i=1}^{p} m_i}}{(\frac{1+p}{2})_{\sum_{i=1}^{p} m_i}(\sum_{i=1}^{p} m_i)}, \quad (102)$$

$$\frac{\partial}{\partial a}\left\{\frac{(a+\frac{1}{2})_{m_p}}{(a+\frac{1+p}{2})_{\sum_{i=1}^{p} m_i}}\right\}\bigg|_{a=0} = \frac{(\frac{1}{2})_{m_p}}{(\frac{1+p}{2})_{\sum_{i=1}^{p} m_i}}\left[\sum_{k=0}^{m_p-1}\frac{1}{k+\frac{1}{2}} - \sum_{k=0}^{\sum_{i=1}^{p} m_i - 1}\frac{1}{k+\frac{1+p}{2}}\right], \quad (103)$$

$$\frac{\partial}{\partial a}\left\{\frac{1}{(a+\frac{1+p}{2})_{\sum_{i=1}^{p} m_i}}\right\}\bigg|_{a=0} = \frac{-1}{(\frac{1+p}{2})_{\sum_{i=1}^{p} m_i}} \sum_{k=0}^{\sum_{i=1}^{p} m_i - 1} \frac{1}{k+\frac{1+p}{2}}. \quad (104)$$

To derive the closed-form expression of $d_{KL}(\mathbf{X}^1, \mathbf{X}^2)$ we have to evaluate the expression of $KL(\mathbf{X}^2||\mathbf{X}^1)$. The latter can be easily deduced from $KL(\mathbf{X}^1||\mathbf{X}^2)$ as follows

$$KL(\mathbf{X}^2||\mathbf{X}^1) = \frac{1}{2}\log\prod_{i=1}^{p}\lambda_i - \frac{1+p}{2}\left[\log\lambda_p \right.$$
$$\left. + \frac{\partial}{\partial a}\left\{F_D^{(p)}\left(a, \frac{1}{2}, \ldots, \frac{1}{2}, a+\frac{1}{2}; a+\frac{1+p}{2}; 1-\frac{\lambda_p}{\lambda_1}, \ldots, 1-\frac{\lambda_p}{\lambda_{p-1}}, 1-\lambda_p\right)\right\}\bigg|_{a=0}\right]. \quad (105)$$

Proceeding in the same way by using Lauricella transformations, different expressions of $KL(\mathbf{X}^2||\mathbf{X}^1)$ are provided in Table 1. Finally, given the above results, it is straightforward to compute the symmetric KL similarity measure $d_{KL}(\mathbf{X}^1, \mathbf{X}^2)$ between $\mathbf{X}^1$ and $\mathbf{X}^2$. Technically, any combination of the $KL(\mathbf{X}^1||\mathbf{X}^2)$ and $KL(\mathbf{X}^2||\mathbf{X}^1)$ expressions is possible to compute $d_{KL}(\mathbf{X}^1, \mathbf{X}^2)$. However, we choose the same convergence region for the two divergences for the calculation of the distance. Some expressions of $d_{KL}(\mathbf{X}^1, \mathbf{X}^2)$ are given in Table 1.

Table 1. KLD and KL distance computed when $\mathbf{X}^1$ and $\mathbf{X}^2$ are two random vectors following central MCDs with pdfs $f_{\mathbf{X}^1}(x|\Sigma_1, p)$ and $f_{\mathbf{X}^2}(x|\Sigma_2, p)$.

$\mathrm{KL}(\mathbf{X}^1 \| \mathbf{X}^2)$

$$= -\frac{1}{2}\log \prod_{i=1}^{p}\lambda_i + \frac{1+p}{2}\left[\log \lambda_p - \frac{\partial}{\partial a}\left\{F_D^{(p)}\left(a, \frac{1}{2},\ldots,\frac{1}{2},a+\frac{1}{2}; a+\frac{1+p}{2}; 1-\frac{\lambda_1}{\lambda_p},\ldots,1-\frac{\lambda_{p-1}}{\lambda_p},1-\frac{1}{\lambda_p}\right)\right\}\bigg|_{a=0}\right] \quad (106)$$

$$= -\frac{1}{2}\log \prod_{i=1}^{p}\lambda_i - \frac{1+p}{2}\lambda_p^{\frac{p}{2}}\prod_{i=1}^{p-1}\lambda_i^{-\frac{1}{2}}\frac{\partial}{\partial a}\left\{F_D^{(p)}\left(\frac{1+p}{2}, \frac{1}{2},\ldots,\frac{1}{2},a+\frac{1}{2}; a+\frac{1+p}{2}; 1-\frac{\lambda_p}{\lambda_1},\ldots,1-\frac{\lambda_p}{\lambda_{p-1}},1-\lambda_p\right)\right\}\bigg|_{a=0} \quad (107)$$

$$= -\frac{1}{2}\log \prod_{i=1}^{p}\lambda_i + \frac{1+p}{2}\left[\log \lambda_1 - \frac{\partial}{\partial a}\left\{F_D^{(p)}\left(a, \frac{1}{2},\ldots,\frac{1}{2},a+\frac{1}{2}; a+\frac{1+p}{2}; 1-\frac{\lambda_p}{\lambda_1},\ldots,1-\frac{\lambda_2}{\lambda_1},1-\frac{1}{\lambda_1}\right)\right\}\bigg|_{a=0}\right] \quad (108)$$

$$= -\frac{1}{2}\log \prod_{i=1}^{p}\lambda_i - \frac{1+p}{2}\frac{\partial}{\partial a}\left\{F_D^{(p)}\left(a, \frac{1}{2},\ldots,\frac{1}{2}; a+\frac{1+p}{2}; 1-\lambda_1,\ldots,1-\lambda_p\right)\right\}\bigg|_{a=0} \quad (109)$$

$$= -\frac{1}{2}\log \prod_{i=1}^{p}\lambda_i - \frac{1+p}{2}\prod_{i=1}^{p}\lambda_i^{-\frac{1}{2}}\frac{\partial}{\partial a}\left\{F_D^{(p)}\left(\frac{1+p}{2}, \frac{1}{2},\ldots,\frac{1}{2}; a+\frac{1+p}{2}; 1-\frac{1}{\lambda_1},\ldots,1-\frac{1}{\lambda_p}\right)\right\}\bigg|_{a=0} \quad (110)$$

$\mathrm{KL}(\mathbf{X}^2 \| \mathbf{X}^1)$

$$= \frac{1}{2}\log \prod_{i=1}^{p}\lambda_i - \frac{1+p}{2}\left[\log \lambda_p + \frac{\partial}{\partial a}\left\{F_D^{(p)}\left(a, \frac{1}{2},\ldots,\frac{1}{2},a+\frac{1}{2}; a+\frac{1+p}{2}; 1-\frac{\lambda_p}{\lambda_1},\ldots,1-\frac{\lambda_p}{\lambda_{p-1}},1-\lambda_p\right)\right\}\bigg|_{a=0}\right] \quad (111)$$

$$= \frac{1}{2}\log \prod_{i=1}^{p}\lambda_i - \frac{1+p}{2}\lambda_p^{-\frac{p}{2}}\prod_{i=1}^{p-1}\lambda_i^{\frac{1}{2}}\frac{\partial}{\partial a}\left\{F_D^{(p)}\left(\frac{1+p}{2}, \frac{1}{2},\ldots,\frac{1}{2},a+\frac{1}{2}; a+\frac{1+p}{2}; 1-\frac{\lambda_1}{\lambda_p},\ldots,1-\frac{\lambda_{p-1}}{\lambda_p},1-\frac{1}{\lambda_p}\right)\right\}\bigg|_{a=0} \quad (112)$$

$$= \frac{1}{2}\log \prod_{i=1}^{p}\lambda_i - \frac{1+p}{2}\left[\log \lambda_1 + \frac{\partial}{\partial a}\left\{F_D^{(p)}\left(a, \frac{1}{2},\ldots,\frac{1}{2},a+\frac{1}{2}; a+\frac{1+p}{2}; 1-\frac{\lambda_1}{\lambda_p},\ldots,1-\frac{\lambda_1}{\lambda_2},1-\lambda_1\right)\right\}\bigg|_{a=0}\right] \quad (113)$$

$$= \frac{1}{2}\log \prod_{i=1}^{p}\lambda_i - \frac{1+p}{2}\frac{\partial}{\partial a}\left\{F_D^{(p)}\left(a, \frac{1}{2},\ldots,\frac{1}{2}; a+\frac{1+p}{2}; 1-\frac{1}{\lambda_1},\ldots,1-\frac{1}{\lambda_p}\right)\right\}\bigg|_{a=0} \quad (114)$$

$$= \frac{1}{2}\log \prod_{i=1}^{p}\lambda_i - \frac{1+p}{2}\prod_{i=1}^{p}\lambda_i^{\frac{1}{2}}\frac{\partial}{\partial a}\left\{F_D^{(p)}\left(\frac{1+p}{2}, \frac{1}{2},\ldots,\frac{1}{2}; a+\frac{1+p}{2}; 1-\lambda_1,\ldots,1-\lambda_p\right)\right\}\bigg|_{a=0} \quad (115)$$

$d_{\mathrm{KL}}(\mathbf{X}^1, \mathbf{X}^2)$

$$= \frac{1+p}{2}\left[\log \lambda_p - \frac{\partial}{\partial a}\left\{F_D^{(p)}\left(a, \frac{1}{2},\ldots,\frac{1}{2},a+\frac{1}{2}; a+\frac{1+p}{2}; 1-\frac{\lambda_1}{\lambda_p},\ldots,1-\frac{\lambda_{p-1}}{\lambda_p},1-\frac{1}{\lambda_p}\right)\right\}\bigg|_{a=0} - \lambda_p^{-\frac{p}{2}}\prod_{i=1}^{p-1}\lambda_i^{\frac{1}{2}} \right.$$
$$\left. \times \frac{\partial}{\partial a}\left\{F_D^{(p)}\left(\frac{1+p}{2}, \frac{1}{2},\ldots,\frac{1}{2},a+\frac{1}{2}; a+\frac{1+p}{2}; 1-\frac{\lambda_1}{\lambda_p},\ldots,1-\frac{\lambda_{p-1}}{\lambda_p},1-\frac{1}{\lambda_p}\right)\right\}\bigg|_{a=0}\right] \quad (116)$$

$$= -\frac{1+p}{2}\left[\frac{\partial}{\partial a}\left\{F_D^{(p)}\left(a, \frac{1}{2},\ldots,\frac{1}{2}; a+\frac{1+p}{2}; 1-\lambda_1,\ldots,1-\lambda_p\right)\right\}\bigg|_{a=0} + \prod_{i=1}^{p}\lambda_i^{\frac{1}{2}}\frac{\partial}{\partial a}\left\{F_D^{(p)}\left(\frac{1+p}{2}, \frac{1}{2},\ldots,\frac{1}{2}; a+\frac{1+p}{2};\right.\right.\right.$$
$$\left.\left.\left. 1-\lambda_1,\ldots,1-\lambda_p\right)\right\}\bigg|_{a=0}\right] \quad (117)$$

$$= -\frac{1+p}{2}\left[\prod_{i=1}^{p}\lambda_i^{-\frac{1}{2}}\frac{\partial}{\partial a}\left\{F_D^{(p)}\left(\frac{1+p}{2}, \frac{1}{2},\ldots,\frac{1}{2}; a+\frac{1+p}{2}; 1-\frac{1}{\lambda_1},\ldots,1-\frac{1}{\lambda_p}\right)\right\}\bigg|_{a=0} + \frac{\partial}{\partial a}\left\{F_D^{(p)}\left(a, \frac{1}{2},\ldots,\frac{1}{2}; a+\frac{1+p}{2};\right.\right.\right.$$
$$\left.\left.\left. 1-\frac{1}{\lambda_1},\ldots,1-\frac{1}{\lambda_p}\right)\right\}\bigg|_{a=0}\right] \quad (118)$$

7. Particular Cases: Univariate and Bivariate Cauchy Distribution

7.1. Case of $p = 1$

This case corresponds to the univariate Cauchy distribution. The KLD is given by

$$\mathrm{KL}(X^1||X^2) = -\frac{1}{2}\log\lambda - \frac{\partial}{\partial a}\left\{{}_2F_1(a, \frac{1}{2}; a+1; 1-\lambda)\right\}\bigg|_{a=0} \quad (119)$$

where ${}_2F_1$ is the Gauss's hypergeometric function. The expression of the derivative of ${}_2F_1$ is given as follows (see Appendix C.1 for details of computation)

$$\frac{\partial}{\partial a}\left\{{}_2F_1(a, \frac{1}{2}; a+1; 1-\lambda)\right\}\bigg|_{a=0} = \sum_{n=1}^{\infty}\left(\frac{1}{2}\right)_n \frac{1}{n}\frac{(1-\lambda)^n}{n!}$$

$$= -2\ln\left(\frac{1+\lambda^{1/2}}{2}\right). \quad (120)$$

Accordingly, the KLD is then expressed as

$$\mathrm{KL}(X^1||X^2) = \log\frac{(1+\lambda^{\frac{1}{2}})^2}{4\lambda^{\frac{1}{2}}} \quad (121)$$

$$= \log\frac{(1+\lambda^{-\frac{1}{2}})^2}{4\lambda^{-\frac{1}{2}}} = \mathrm{KL}(X^2||X^1). \quad (122)$$

We conclude that KLD between Cauchy densities is always symmetric. Interestingly, this is consistent with the result presented in [31].

7.2. Case of $p = 2$

This case corresponds to the Bivariate Cauchy distribution. The KLD is then given by

$$\mathrm{KL}(\mathbf{X}^1||\mathbf{X}^2) = -\frac{1}{2}\log\lambda_1\lambda_2 - \frac{3}{2}\frac{\partial}{\partial a}\left\{F_1(a, \frac{1}{2}, \frac{1}{2}; a+\frac{3}{2}; 1-\lambda_1, 1-\lambda_2)\right\}\bigg|_{a=0} \quad (123)$$

where F_1 is the Appell's hypergeometric function (see Appendix A). The expression of the derivative of F_1 can be further developed

$$\frac{\partial}{\partial a}\left\{F_1(a, \frac{1}{2}, \frac{1}{2}; a+\frac{3}{2}; 1-\lambda_1, 1-\lambda_2)\right\}\bigg|_{a=0}$$

$$= \sum_{n,m=0}^{+\infty}\frac{(1)_{m+n}(\frac{1}{2})_n(\frac{1}{2})_m}{(\frac{3}{2})_{m+n}}\frac{1}{m+n}\frac{(1-\lambda_1)^n}{n!}\frac{(1-\lambda_2)^m}{m!}. \quad (124)$$

In addition, when the eigenvalue λ_i for $i = 1, 2$ takes some particular values, the expression of the KLD becomes very simple. In the following, we show some cases:
$(\lambda_1 = 1, \lambda_2 \neq 1)$ or $(\lambda_2 = 1, \lambda_1 \neq 1)$

For this particular case, we have

$$\frac{\partial}{\partial a}\left\{F_1(a, \frac{1}{2}, \frac{1}{2}; a+\frac{3}{2}; 1-\lambda_i, 0)\right\}\bigg|_{a=0} = \frac{\partial}{\partial a}\left\{{}_2F_1(a, \frac{1}{2}; a+\frac{3}{2}; 1-\lambda_i)\right\}\bigg|_{a=0} \quad (125)$$

$$= -\ln\lambda_i + \frac{1}{\sqrt{1-\lambda_i}}\ln\left(\frac{1-\sqrt{1-\lambda_i}}{1+\sqrt{1-\lambda_i}}\right) + 2. \quad (126)$$

The demonstration of the derivation is shown in Appendix C.2. Then, KLD becomes equal to

$$\mathrm{KL}(\mathbf{X}^1||\mathbf{X}^2) = \ln\lambda_i - \frac{3}{2}\frac{1}{\sqrt{1-\lambda_i}}\ln\left(\frac{1-\sqrt{1-\lambda_i}}{1+\sqrt{1-\lambda_i}}\right) - 3. \quad (127)$$

$\lambda_1 = \lambda_2 = \lambda$

For this particular case, we have

$$\frac{\partial}{\partial a}\left\{F_1\left(a, \frac{1}{2}, \frac{1}{2}; a + \frac{3}{2}; 1 - \lambda, 1 - \lambda\right)\right\}\bigg|_{a=0} = \frac{\partial}{\partial a}\left\{{}_2F_1\left(a, 1; a + \frac{3}{2}; 1 - \lambda\right)\right\}\bigg|_{a=0} \quad (128)$$

$$= -\frac{2}{\sqrt{1 - \lambda^{-1}}}\ln(\sqrt{\lambda} + \sqrt{\lambda - 1}) + 2. \quad (129)$$

For more details about the demonstration see Appendix C.3. The KLD becomes equal to

$$\mathrm{KL}(\mathbf{X}^1||\mathbf{X}^2) = -\ln\lambda + \frac{3}{\sqrt{1 - \lambda^{-1}}}\ln(\sqrt{\lambda} + \sqrt{\lambda - 1}) - 3. \quad (130)$$

It is easy to deduce that

$$\mathrm{KL}(\mathbf{X}^2||\mathbf{X}^1) = \ln\lambda + \frac{3}{\sqrt{1 - \lambda}}\ln(\sqrt{\lambda^{-1}} + \sqrt{\lambda^{-1} - 1}) - 3. \quad (131)$$

This result can be demonstrated using the same process as $\mathrm{KL}(\mathbf{X}^1||\mathbf{X}^2)$. It is worth to notice that $\mathrm{KL}(\mathbf{X}^1||\mathbf{X}^2) \neq \mathrm{KL}(\mathbf{X}^2||\mathbf{X}^1)$ which leads us to conclude that the property of symmetry observed for the univariate case is no longer valid in the multivariate case. Nielsen et al. in [32] gave the same conclusion.

8. Implementation and Comparison with Monte Carlo Technique

In this section, we show how we practically compute the numerical values of the KLD, especially when we have several equivalent expressions which differ in the region of convergence. To reach this goal, the eigenvalues of $\Sigma_1 \Sigma_2^{-1}$ are rearranged in a descending order $\lambda_p > \lambda_{p-1} > \ldots > \lambda_1 > 0$. This operation is justified by Equation (53) where it can be seen that the permutation of the eigenvalues does not affect the expectation result. Three cases can be identified from the expressions of KLD.

8.1. Case $1 > \lambda_p > \lambda_{p-1} > \ldots > \lambda_1 > 0$

The expression of $\mathrm{KL}(\mathbf{X}^1||\mathbf{X}^2)$ is given by Equation (109) and $\mathrm{KL}(\mathbf{X}^2||\mathbf{X}^1)$ is given by (115).

8.2. Case $\lambda_p > \lambda_{p-1} > \ldots > \lambda_1 > 1$

$\mathrm{KL}(\mathbf{X}^1||\mathbf{X}^2)$ is given by the Equation (110) and $\mathrm{KL}(\mathbf{X}^2||\mathbf{X}^1)$ is given by (114).

8.3. Case $\lambda_p > 1$ and $\lambda_1 < 1$

This case guarantees that $0 \leq 1 - \lambda_j/\lambda_p < 1$, $j = 1, \ldots, p-1$ and $0 \leq 1 - 1/\lambda_p < 1$. The expression of the $\mathrm{KL}(\mathbf{X}^1||\mathbf{X}^2)$ is given by Equation (106) and $\mathrm{KL}(\mathbf{X}^2||\mathbf{X}^1)$ is given by (112) or (113). To perform an evaluation of the quality of the numerical approximation of the derivative of the Lauricella series, we consider a case where an exact and simple expression of $\frac{\partial}{\partial a}\{F_D^{(p)}(.)\}|_{a=0}$ is possible. The following case where $\lambda_1 = \ldots = \lambda_p = \lambda$ allows the Lauricella series to be equivalent to the Gauss hypergeometric function given as follows

$$F_D^{(p)}\left(a, \underbrace{\frac{1}{2}, \ldots, \frac{1}{2}}_{p}; a + \frac{1+p}{2}; 1 - \lambda, \ldots, 1 - \lambda\right) = {}_2F_1\left(a, \frac{p}{2}; a + \frac{1+p}{2}; 1 - \lambda\right). \quad (132)$$

This relation allows us to compare the computational accuracy of the approximation of the Lauricella series with respect to the Gauss function. In addition, to compute the numerical value the indices of the series will evolve from 0 to N instead of infinity. The latter is chosen to ensure a good approximation of the Lauricella series. Table 2 shows the computation of the derivative of $F_D^{(p)}(.)$ and ${}_2F_1(.)$, along with the absolute value of error $|\epsilon|$, where

$p = 2, N = \{20, 30, 40\}$. The exact expression of $\frac{\partial}{\partial a}\{_2F_1(.)\}|_{a=0}$ when $p = 2$ is given by Equation (129). We can deduce the following conclusions. First, the error is reasonably low and decreases as the value of N increases. Second, the error increases for values of $1 - \lambda$ close to 1 as expected, which corresponds to the convergence region limit.

Table 2. Computation of $A = \frac{\partial}{\partial a}\{_2F_1(.)\}|_{a=0}$ and $B = \frac{\partial}{\partial a}\{F_D^{(p)}(.)\}|_{a=0}$ when $p = 2$ and $\lambda_1 = \ldots = \lambda_p = \lambda$.

			$N = 20$		$N = 30$		$N = 40$
$1 - \lambda$	A	B	$|\epsilon|$	B	$|\epsilon|$	B	$|\epsilon|$
0.1	0.0694	0.0694	9.1309×10^{-16}	0.0694	9.1309×10^{-16}	0.0694	9.1309×10^{-16}
0.3	0.2291	0.2291	3.7747×10^{-14}	0.2291	1.1102×10^{-16}	0.2291	1.1102×10^{-16}
0.5	0.4292	0.4292	2.6707×10^{-9}	0.4292	1.2458×10^{-12}	0.4292	6.6613×10^{-16}
0.7	0.7022	0.7022	5.9260×10^{-6}	0.7022	8.2678×10^{-8}	0.7022	1.3911×10^{-9}
0.9	1.1673	1.1634	0.0038	1.1665	7.2760×10^{-4}	1.1671	1.6081×10^{-4}
0.99	1.7043	1.5801	0.1241	1.6267	0.0776	1.6514	0.0529

In the following section, we compare the Monte Carlo sampling method to approximate the KLD value with the numerical value of the closed-form expression of the latter. The Monte Carlo method involves sampling a large number of samples and using them to calculate the sum rather than the integral. Here, for each sample size, the experiment is repeated 2000 times. The elements of Σ_1 and Σ_2 are given in Table 3. Figure 1 depicts the absolute value of bias, mean square error (MSE) and box plot of the difference between the symmetric KL approximated value and its theoretical one, given versus the sample sizes. As the sample size increases, the bias and the MSE decrease. Accordingly, the approximated value will be very close to the theoretical KLD when the number of samples is very large. The computation time of the proposed approximation and the classical Monte Carlo sampling method are recorded using Matlab on a 1.6 GHz processor with 16 GB of memory. For the proposed numerical approximation, the computation time is evaluated to 1.56 s with $N = 20$. The value of N can be increased to further improve the accuracy, but it will increase the computation time. For the Monte Carlo sampling method, the mean time values at sample sizes of $\{65{,}536; 131{,}072; 262{,}144\}$ are $\{2.71; 5.46; 10.78\}$ seconds, respectively.

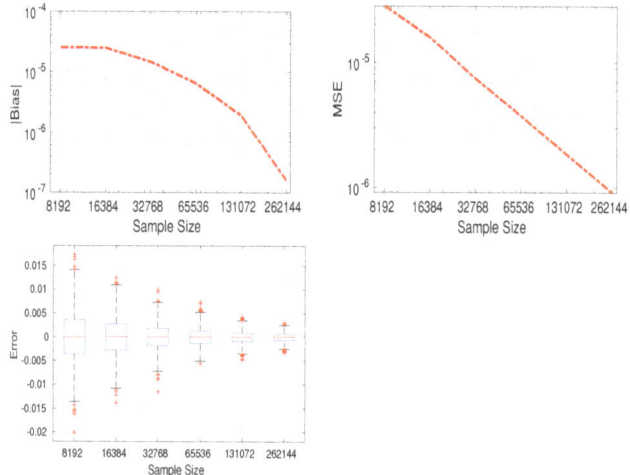

Figure 1. Top row: Bias (**left**) and MSE (**right**) of the difference between the approximated and theoretical symmetric KL for MCD. Bottom row: Box plot of the error. The mean error is the bias. Outliers are larger than $Q_3 + 1.5 \times IQR$ or smaller than $Q_1 - 1.5 \times IQR$, where Q_1, Q_3, and IQR are the 25th, 75th percentiles, and the interquartile range, respectively.

Table 3. Parameters Σ_1 and Σ_2 used to compute KLD for central MCD.

Σ	$\Sigma_{11}, \Sigma_{22}, \Sigma_{33}, \Sigma_{12}, \Sigma_{13}, \Sigma_{23}$
Σ_1	1, 1, 1, 0.6, 0.2, 0.3
Σ_2	1, 1, 1, 0.3, 0.1, 0.4

To further encourage the dissemination of these results, we provide a code available as attached file to this paper. This is given in Matlab with a specific case of $p = 3$. This can be easily extended to any value of p, thanks to the general closed-form expression established in this paper.

```
%*************************************************************************
% Compute the KL divergence and distance between two central multivariate Cauchy
% distribution.
%% Input:
% + Sigma1: Symmetric positive definite (p*p) scale matrix
% + Sigma2: Symmetric positive definite (p*p) scale matrix
% + nb: indices used to compute the KL and dis; nb={20,30,40,etc}.
% Increase nb means increase the precision and also the computation time.
%% Output:
% + KL_12: KL divergence between X1 and X2: KL(X1||X2)
% + KL_21: KL divergence between X2 and X1: KL(X2||X1)
% + Esp_12: expectation E_{X}\{ln[1+ X^T*Sigma2^{-1}*X]\} where X~MCD(Sigma1,p=3)
% + Esp_21: expectation E_{X}\{ln[1+ X^T*Sigma1^{-1}*X]\} where X~MCD(Sigma2,p=3)
% + dis: distance between X1 and X2: dis = KL(X1||X2) + KL(X2||X1)
%% Example:
% Sigma1 = [1 0.6 0.2; 0.6 1 0.3; 0.2 0.3 1];
% Sigma2 = [1 0.3 0.1; 0.3 1 0.4; 0.1 0.4 1];
% [KL_12, KL_21, Esp_12, Esp_21, dis] = fonction_KL_MCD_final(Sigma1,Sigma2,20);
%*************************************************************************
function [KL_12, KL_21, Esp_12, Esp_21, dis] = fonction_KL_MCD_final(Sigma1,Sigma2,nb)
format long;
p = 3;

vpr = real(eig(Sigma1*inv(Sigma2)));
vpr = sort(vpr,'ascend');

nbre = nb;
[N,M,L] = ndgrid(0:nbre,0:nbre,0:nbre);

if vpr(p)< 1
%*************************************************************************
%% Derivative of Fd(a,1/2,1/2,1/2;a+(1+p)/2;1-vpr(1),1-vpr(2),1-vpr(3))| a=0
%*************************************************************************
    H = N+M+L;
    H(H==0)= inf;
    commun = (1-vpr(1)).^N./factorial(N).*(1-vpr(2)).^M./factorial(M).*(1-vpr(3)).^L./factorial(L).*...
        pochhammer(1/2,N).*pochhammer(1/2,M).*pochhammer(1/2,L);
    h1 = commun.* pochhammer(1,N+M+L)./pochhammer((1+p)/2, N+M+L)*1./H;
    derive1 = sum(sum(sum(h1)))     % Eq. (102) and (A1)
%--------------------------------------------------------------------------
    J = N+M+L-1;
    A=[0, cumsum(1./(((p+1)/2 +(0:p*nbre-1)))];
    for i=1:nbre+1
        for j=1:nbre+1
            for l=1:nbre+1
                G(i,j,l)= -A(J(i,j,l)+2);
            end
        end
    end
    h2 = commun.*G;
    derive2 = sum(sum(sum(h2)))     % Eq. (104) and (A1)
%--------------------------------------------------------------------------
    Esp_12 = psi(1/2 + p/2)-psi(1/2) - derive1
    Esp_21 = psi(1/2 + p/2)-psi(1/2) - prod(vpr).^(1/2)*derive2
    KL_12 = -1/2*log(prod(vpr))-(1+p)/2*derive1          % Eq.(109)
```

```
    KL_21 = 1/2*log(prod(vpr))-(1+p)/2*prod(vpr).^(1/2)*derive2    % Eq.(115)

elseif vpr(1) > 1
%*******************************************************************************
%%% Derivative of Fd((1+p)/2,1/2,1/2,1/2;a+(1+p)/2;1-1/vpr(1),1-1/vpr(2),1-1/vpr(3)) | a=0
%*******************************************************************************
    J = N+M+L-1;
    A=[0, cumsum(1./((p+1)/2 +(0:p*nbre-1)))];
    for i=1:nbre+1
        for j=1:nbre+1
            for l=1:nbre+1
                G(i,j,l)= -A(J(i,j,l)+2);
            end
        end
    end
    commun = (1-1/vpr(1)).^N./factorial(N).*(1-1/vpr(2)).^M./factorial(M).*(1-1/vpr(3)).^L./factorial(L).*...
             pochhammer(1/2,N).*pochhammer(1/2,M).*pochhammer(1/2,L);
    h1 = commun.*G;
    derive1 = sum(sum(sum(h1)))    % Eq. (104) and (A1)
    %---------------------------------------------------
    H = N+M+L;
    H(H==0)= inf;
    h2 = commun.*pochhammer(1,N+M+L)./pochhammer((1+p)/2, N+M+L)*1./H;
    derive2 = sum(sum(sum(h2)))    % Eq. (102) and (A1)
    %---------------------------------------------------
    Esp_12 = psi(1/2 + p/2)-psi(1/2) - prod(vpr).^(-1/2)*derive1
    Esp_21 = psi(1/2 + p/2)-psi(1/2) - derive2
    KL_12 = -1/2*log(prod(vpr))-(1+p)/2*prod(vpr).^(-1/2)*derive1    % Eq.(110)
    KL_21 = 1/2*log(prod(vpr))-(1+p)/2*derive2                       % Eq.(114)

else
%*******************************************************************************
%%% Derivative of Fd(a,1/2,1/2,a+1/2;a+(1+p)/2;1-vpr(1)/vpr(3),1-vpr(2)/vpr(3),1-1/vpr(3)) | a=0
%*******************************************************************************
    H = N+M+L;
    H(H==0)= inf;
    commun = (1-vpr(1)/vpr(3)).^N./factorial(N).*(1-vpr(2)/vpr(3)).^M./factorial(M).*...
             (1-1/vpr(3)).^L./factorial(L).*...
             pochhammer(1/2,N).*pochhammer(1/2,M).*pochhammer(1/2,L);
    h1 = commun.*pochhammer(1,N+M+L)./pochhammer((1+p)/2,N+M+L)./H;
    derive1 = sum(sum(sum(h1)))    % Eq.(101) and (A1)
    %---------------------------------------------------
    J = N+M+L-1;
    JJ = L-1;
    A = [0, cumsum(1./((p+1)/2 +(0:p*nbre-1)))];
    B = [0, cumsum(1./(1/2 +(0:nbre-1)))];
    for i=1:nbre+1
        for j=1:nbre+1
            for l=1:nbre+1
                G(i,j,l)= B(JJ(i,j,l)+2) - A(J(i,j,l)+2);
            end
        end
    end
    h2 = commun.*G;
    derive2 = sum(sum(sum(h2)))    % Eq. (103) and (A1)
    %---------------------------------------------------
    Esp_12 = psi(1/2 + p/2)-psi(1/2) + log(vpr(p)) - derive1
    Esp_21 = psi(1/2 + p/2)-psi(1/2) - vpr(p)^(-p/2)*(vpr(1)*vpr(2))^(1/2)*derive2
    KL_12 = -1/2*log(prod(vpr)) -(1+p)/2*(-log(vpr(p)) + derive1)         % Eq. (106)
    KL_21 = 1/2*log(prod(vpr)) -(1+p)/2*vpr(p)^(-p/2)*(vpr(1)*vpr(2))^(1/2)*derive2  % Eq. (112)
end

dis = KL_12 + KL_21
```

9. Conclusions

Since the MCDs have various applications in signal and image processing, the KLD between central MCDs tackles an important problem for future work on statistics, machine learning and other related fields in computer science. In this paper, we derived a closed-form expression of the KLD and distance between two central MCDs. The similarity measure can be expressed as function of the Lauricella D-hypergeometric series $F_D^{(p)}$. We have also proposed a simple scheme to compute easily the Lauricella series and to bypass the convergence constraints of this series. Codes and examples for numerical calculations are presented and explained in detail. Finally, a comparison is made to show how the Monte Carlo sampling method gives approximations close to the KLD theoretical value. As a final note, it is also possible to extend these results on the KLD to the case of the multivariate t-distribution since the MCD is a particular case of this multivariate distribution.

Author Contributions: Conceptualization, N.B.; methodology, N.B.; software, N.B.; writing original draft preparation, N.B.; writing review and editing, N.B. and D.R.; supervision, D.R. All authors have read and agreed to the published version of the manuscript.

Funding: This research received no external funding.

Institutional Review Board Statement: Not applicable.

Informed Consent Statement: Not applicable.

Data Availability Statement: Not applicable.

Acknowledgments: Authors gratefully acknowledge the PHENOTIC platform node of the french national infrastructure on plant phenotyping ANR PHENOME 11-INBS-0012. The authors would like also to thank the anonymous reviewers for their helpful comments valuable comments and suggestions.

Conflicts of Interest: The authors declare no conflict of interest.

Appendix A. Lauricella Function

In 1893, G. Lauricella [39] investigated the properties of four series $F_A^{(n)}, F_B^{(n)}, F_C^{(n)}, F_D^{(n)}$ of n variables. When $n = 2$, these functions coincide with Appell's F_2, F_3, F_4, F_1, respectively. When $n = 1$, they all coincide with Gauss' $_2F_1$. We present here only the Lauricella series $F_D^{(n)}$ given as follows

$$F_D^{(n)}(a, b_1, \ldots, b_n; c; x_1, \ldots, x_n) = \sum_{m_1=0}^{\infty} \cdots \sum_{m_n=0}^{\infty} \frac{(a)_{m_1+\ldots+m_n}(b_1)_{m_1}\cdots(b_n)_{m_n}}{(c)_{m_1+\ldots+m_n}} \frac{x_1^{m_1}}{m_1!}\cdots\frac{x_n^{m_n}}{m_n!} \tag{A1}$$

where $|x_1|, \ldots, |x_n| < 1$. The Pochhammer symbol $(q)_i$ indicates the i-th rising factorial of q, i.e.,

$$(q)_i = q(q+1)\ldots(q+i-1) = \frac{\Gamma(q+i)}{\Gamma(q)} \quad \text{if} \quad i = 1, 2, \ldots \tag{A2}$$

If $i = 0$, $(q)_i = 1$. Function $F_D^{(n)}(.)$ can be expressed in terms of multiple integrals as follows [42]

$$F_D^{(n)}(a, b_1, \ldots, b_n; c; x_1, \ldots, x_n) = \frac{\Gamma(c)}{\Gamma(c - \sum_{i=1}^{n} b_i)\prod_{i=1}^{n}\Gamma(b_i)} \times$$
$$\int_{\Omega}\cdots\int \prod_{i=1}^{n} u_i^{b_i-1}(1 - \sum_{i=1}^{n} u_i)^{c-\sum_{i=1}^{n} b_i - 1}(1 - \sum_{i=1}^{n} x_i u_i)^{-a} \prod_{i=1}^{n} du_i \tag{A3}$$

where $\Omega = \{(u_1, u_2, \ldots, u_n); 0 \le u_i \le 1, i = 1, \ldots, n, \text{and } 0 \le u_1 + u_2 + \ldots + u_n \le 1\}$, $\text{Real}(b_i) > 0$ for $i = 1, \ldots, n$ and $\text{Real}(c - b_1 - \ldots - b_n) > 0$. Lauricella's F_D can be written as a one-dimensional Euler-type integral for any number n of variables. The integral form of $F_D^{(n)}(.)$ is given as follows when $\text{Real}(a) > 0$ and $\text{Real}(c - a) > 0$

$$F_D^{(n)}(a, b_1, \ldots, b_n; c; x_1, \ldots, x_n) = \frac{\Gamma(c)}{\Gamma(a)\Gamma(c - a)} \int_0^1 u^{a-1}(1-u)^{c-a-1}(1 - ux_1)^{-b_1}\ldots(1 - ux_n)^{-b_n} du. \tag{A4}$$

Lauricella has given several transformation formulas, from which we use the two following relationships. More details can be found in Exton's book [43] on hypergeometric equations.

$$F_D^{(n)}(a, b_1, \ldots, b_n; c; x_1, \ldots, x_n)$$

$$= \prod_{i=1}^n (1-x_i)^{-b_i} F_D^{(n)}\left(c-a, b_1, \ldots, b_n; c; \frac{x_1}{x_1-1}, \ldots, \frac{x_n}{x_n-1}\right) \tag{A5}$$

$$= (1-x_1)^{-a} F_D^{(n)}\left(a, c - \sum_{i=1}^n b_i, b_2, \ldots, b_n; c; \frac{x_1}{x_1-1}, \frac{x_1-x_2}{x_1-1}, \ldots, \frac{x_1-x_n}{x_1-1}\right) \tag{A6}$$

$$= (1-x_n)^{-a} F_D^{(n)}\left(a, b_1, \ldots, b_{n-1}, c - \sum_{i=1}^n b_i; c; \frac{x_n-x_1}{x_n-1}, \frac{x_n-x_2}{x_n-1}, \ldots, \frac{x_n-x_{n-1}}{x_n-1}, \frac{x_n}{x_n-1}\right) \tag{A7}$$

$$= (1-x_1)^{c-a} \prod_{i=1}^n (1-x_i)^{-b_i} F_D^{(n)}\left(c-a, c - \sum_{i=1}^n b_i, b_2, \ldots, b_n; c; x_1, \frac{x_2-x_1}{x_2-1}, \ldots, \frac{x_n-x_1}{x_n-1}\right) \tag{A8}$$

$$= (1-x_n)^{c-a} \prod_{i=1}^n (1-x_i)^{-b_i} F_D^{(n)}\left(c-a, b_1, \ldots, b_{n-1}, c - \sum_{i=1}^n b_i; c; \frac{x_1-x_n}{x_1-1}, \ldots, \frac{x_{n-1}-x_n}{x_{n-1}-1}, x_n\right). \tag{A9}$$

Appendix B. Demonstration of Derivative

Appendix B.1. Demonstration

We use the following notation $\alpha = \sum_{i=1}^p m_i$ to alleviate the writing of equations. Knowing that $\frac{\partial}{\partial c}(c)_k = (c)_k(\psi(c+k) - \psi(c))$, $\psi(c+k) - \psi(c) = \sum_{\ell=0}^{k-1} \frac{1}{c+\ell}$ and $(c)_k = \prod_{i=0}^{k-1}(c+i)$ we can state that

$$\frac{\partial}{\partial a}\left\{\frac{(a)_\alpha}{(a+\frac{1+p}{2})_\alpha}\right\} = \frac{(a)_\alpha[\psi(a+\alpha) - \psi(a) - \psi(a+\frac{1+p}{2}+\alpha) + \psi(a+\frac{1+p}{2})]}{(a+\frac{1+p}{2})_\alpha}$$

$$= \frac{\prod_{k=0}^{\alpha-1}(a+k)\left(\sum_{k=0}^{\alpha-1}\frac{1}{a+k} - \frac{1}{a+\frac{1+p}{2}+k}\right)}{(a+\frac{1+p}{2})_\alpha}. \tag{A10}$$

Using the fact that

$$\prod_{k=0}^{\alpha-1}(a+k) \sum_{k=0}^{\alpha-1}\frac{1}{a+k} = \prod_{k=1}^{\alpha-1}(a+k) + \prod_{k=0, k\neq 1}^{\alpha-1}(a+k) + \ldots + \prod_{k=0}^{\alpha-2}(a+k) \tag{A11}$$

we can state that

$$\frac{\partial}{\partial a}\left\{\frac{(a)_\alpha}{(a+\frac{1+p}{2})_\alpha}\right\}\bigg|_{a=0} = \frac{(\alpha-1)!}{(\frac{1+p}{2})_\alpha} = \frac{(1)_\alpha}{(\frac{1+p}{2})_\alpha}\frac{1}{\alpha}. \tag{A12}$$

Appendix B.2. Demonstration

$$\frac{\partial}{\partial a}\left\{\frac{(a)_\alpha(a+\frac{1}{2})_{m_p}}{(a+\frac{1+p}{2})_\alpha}\right\} = \frac{(a+\frac{1}{2})_{m_p}(a)_\alpha[\psi(a+\alpha) - \psi(a) + \psi(a+\frac{1}{2}+m_p) - \psi(a+\frac{1}{2})]}{(a+\frac{1+p}{2})_\alpha} -$$

$$\frac{(a)_\alpha(a+\frac{1}{2})_{m_p}[\psi(a+\frac{1+p}{2}+\alpha) - \psi(a+\frac{1+p}{2})]}{(a+\frac{1+p}{2})_\alpha} \tag{A13}$$

$$= \frac{(a+\frac{1}{2})_{m_p}\prod_{k=0}^{\alpha-1}(a+k)\left[\sum_{k=0}^{\alpha-1}\frac{1}{a+k} - \frac{1}{a+\frac{1+p}{2}+k} + \sum_{k=0}^{m_p-1}\frac{1}{a+\frac{1}{2}+k}\right]}{(a+\frac{1+p}{2})_\alpha}. \tag{A14}$$

By developing the previous expression we can state that

$$\frac{\partial}{\partial a}\left\{\frac{(a)_\alpha(a+\frac{1}{2})_{m_p}}{(a+\frac{1+p}{2})_\alpha}\right\}\bigg|_{a=0} = \frac{(\frac{1}{2})_{m_p}(\alpha-1)!}{(\frac{1+p}{2})_\alpha} = \frac{(\frac{1}{2})_{m_p}(1)_\alpha}{(\frac{1+p}{2})_\alpha}\frac{1}{\alpha}. \tag{A15}$$

Appendix B.3. Demonstration

$$\frac{\partial}{\partial a}\left\{\frac{(a+\frac{1}{2})_{m_p}}{(a+\frac{1+p}{2})_\alpha}\right\} = \frac{(a+\frac{1}{2})_{m_p}}{(a+\frac{1+p}{2})_\alpha}\left[\sum_{k=0}^{m_p-1}\frac{1}{a+\frac{1}{2}+k} - \sum_{k=0}^{\alpha-1}\frac{1}{a+\frac{1+p}{2}+k}\right]. \tag{A16}$$

As a consequence,

$$\frac{\partial}{\partial a}\left\{\frac{(a+\frac{1}{2})_{m_p}}{(a+\frac{1+p}{2})_\alpha}\right\}\bigg|_{a=0} = \frac{(\frac{1}{2})_{m_p}}{(\frac{1+p}{2})_\alpha}\left[\sum_{k=0}^{m_p-1}\frac{1}{\frac{1}{2}+k} - \sum_{k=0}^{\alpha-1}\frac{1}{\frac{1+p}{2}+k}\right]. \tag{A17}$$

Appendix B.4. Demonstration

$$\frac{\partial}{\partial a}\left\{\frac{1}{(a+\frac{1+p}{2})_\alpha}\right\} = -\frac{\psi(a+\frac{1+p}{2}+\alpha)-\psi(a+\frac{1+p}{2})}{(a+\frac{1+p}{2})_\alpha} \tag{A18}$$

$$= \frac{-1}{(a+\frac{1+p}{2})_\alpha}\sum_{k=0}^{\alpha-1}\frac{1}{a+\frac{1+p}{2}+k}. \tag{A19}$$

Finally,

$$\frac{\partial}{\partial a}\left\{\frac{1}{(a+\frac{1+p}{2})_\alpha}\right\}\bigg|_{a=0} = \frac{-1}{(\frac{1+p}{2})_\alpha}\sum_{k=0}^{\alpha-1}\frac{1}{\frac{1+p}{2}+k}. \tag{A20}$$

Appendix C. Computations of Some Equations

Appendix C.1. Computation

Let f be a function of λ defined as follows:

$$f(\lambda) = \sum_{n=1}^{\infty}\left(\frac{1}{2}\right)_n\frac{1}{n}\frac{(1-\lambda)^n}{n!}. \tag{A21}$$

The multiplication of the derivative of f with respect to λ by $(1-\lambda)$ is given as follows

$$(1-\lambda)\frac{\partial}{\partial\lambda}f(\lambda) = -\sum_{n=1}^{\infty}\left(\frac{1}{2}\right)_n\frac{(1-\lambda)^n}{n!} = 1-\lambda^{-1/2}. \tag{A22}$$

As a consequence,

$$\frac{\partial}{\partial\lambda}f(\lambda) = \frac{1-\lambda^{-1/2}}{1-\lambda} = \frac{-\lambda^{-1/2}}{1+\lambda^{1/2}}. \tag{A23}$$

Finally,

$$f(\lambda) = -2\ln\frac{1+\lambda^{1/2}}{2}. \tag{A24}$$

Appendix C.2. Computation

$$\frac{\partial}{\partial a}\left\{{}_2F_1\left(a,\frac{1}{2};a+\frac{3}{2};1-\lambda_i\right)\right\}\bigg|_{a=0} = \sum_{n=1}^{\infty}\frac{(\frac{1}{2})_n(1)_n}{(\frac{3}{2})_n n}\frac{(1-\lambda_i)^n}{n!}$$
$$= f(\lambda_i) \quad (A25)$$

where f is a function of λ_i. The multiplication of the derivative of f with respect to λ_i by $(1-\lambda_i)$ is given as follows

$$(1-\lambda_i)\frac{\partial}{\partial \lambda_i}f(\lambda_i) = -\sum_{n=1}^{\infty}\frac{(\frac{1}{2})_n(1)_n}{(\frac{3}{2})_n}\frac{(1-\lambda_i)^n}{n!} \quad (A26)$$

$$= -{}_2F_1\left(\frac{1}{2},1;\frac{3}{2};1-\lambda_i\right)+1. \quad (A27)$$

Knowing that

$$_2F_1\left(\frac{1}{2},1;\frac{3}{2};1-\lambda_i\right) = \frac{\arctan(\sqrt{\lambda_i-1})}{\sqrt{\lambda_i-1}} \quad (A28)$$

$$= \frac{1}{2\sqrt{1-\lambda_i}}\ln\left(\frac{1+\sqrt{1-\lambda_i}}{1-\sqrt{1-\lambda_i}}\right) \quad (A29)$$

we can deduce an expression of

$$\frac{\partial}{\partial \lambda_i}f(\lambda_i) = \frac{\arctan(\sqrt{\lambda_i-1})}{(\lambda_i-1)^{3/2}} + \frac{1}{1-\lambda_i}. \quad (A30)$$

Accordingly,

$$f(\lambda_i) = -\ln\lambda_i - 2\frac{\arctan(\sqrt{\lambda_i-1})}{\sqrt{\lambda_i-1}} + 2 \quad (A31)$$

$$= -\ln\lambda_i + \frac{1}{\sqrt{1-\lambda_i}}\ln\left(\frac{1-\sqrt{1-\lambda_i}}{1+\sqrt{1-\lambda_i}}\right) + 2. \quad (A32)$$

Appendix C.3. Computation

$$\frac{\partial}{\partial a}\left\{{}_2F_1\left(a,1;a+\frac{3}{2};1-\lambda\right)\right\}\bigg|_{a=0} = \sum_{n=1}^{\infty}\frac{(1)_n(1)_n}{(\frac{3}{2})_n n}\frac{(1-\lambda)^n}{n!}$$
$$= f(\lambda) \quad (A33)$$

where f is a function of λ. The multiplication of the derivative of f with respect to λ by $(1-\lambda)$ is given as follows

$$(1-\lambda)\frac{\partial}{\partial \lambda}f(\lambda) = -\sum_{n=1}^{\infty}\frac{(1)_n(1)_n}{(\frac{3}{2})_n}\frac{(1-\lambda)^n}{n!} \quad (A34)$$

$$= -{}_2F_1\left(1,1;\frac{3}{2};1-\lambda\right)+1. \quad (A35)$$

Knowing that

$$_2F_1\left(1,1;\frac{3}{2};1-\lambda\right) = \frac{1}{\sqrt{\lambda}}\frac{\arcsin(\sqrt{1-\lambda})}{\sqrt{1-\lambda}} \quad (A36)$$

we can state that

$$\frac{\partial}{\partial \lambda}f(\lambda) = -\frac{1}{\sqrt{\lambda}}\frac{\arcsin(\sqrt{1-\lambda})}{(1-\lambda)^{3/2}} + \frac{1}{1-\lambda}. \quad (A37)$$

As a consequence,

$$f(\lambda) = -\frac{2\sqrt{\lambda}\arcsin(\sqrt{1-\lambda})}{\sqrt{1-\lambda}} + 2 \tag{A38}$$

$$= -\frac{2}{\sqrt{1-\lambda^{-1}}}\ln(\sqrt{\lambda}+\sqrt{\lambda-1}) + 2. \tag{A39}$$

References

1. Ollila, E.; Tyler, D.E.; Koivunen, V.; Poor, H.V. Complex Elliptically Symmetric Distributions: Survey, New Results and Applications. *IEEE Trans. Signal Process.* **2012**, *60*, 5597–5625. [CrossRef]
2. Kotz, S.; Nadarajah, S. *Multivariate T-Distributions and Their Applications*; Cambridge University Press: Cambridge, UK, 2004. [CrossRef]
3. Press, S. Multivariate stable distributions. *J. Multivar. Anal.* **1972**, *2*, 444–462. [CrossRef]
4. Sahu, S.; Singh, H.V.; Kumar, B.; Singh, A.K. Statistical modeling and Gaussianization procedure based de-speckling algorithm for retinal OCT images. *J. Ambient. Intell. Humaniz. Comput.* **2018**, 1–14. [CrossRef]
5. Ranjani, J.J.; Thiruvengadam, S.J. Generalized SAR Despeckling Based on DTCWT Exploiting Interscale and Intrascale Dependences. *IEEE Geosci. Remote Sens. Lett.* **2011**, *8*, 552–556. [CrossRef]
6. Sadreazami, H.; Ahmad, M.O.; Swamy, M.N.S. Color image denoising using multivariate cauchy PDF in the contourlet domain. In Proceedings of the 2016 IEEE Canadian Conference on Electrical and Computer Engineering (CCECE), Vancouver, BC, Canada, 15–18 May 2016; pp. 1–4. [CrossRef]
7. Sadreazami, H.; Ahmad, M.O.; Swamy, M.N.S. A Study of Multiplicative Watermark Detection in the Contourlet Domain Using Alpha-Stable Distributions. *IEEE Trans. Image Process.* **2014**, *23*, 4348–4360. [CrossRef]
8. Fontaine, M.; Nugraha, A.A.; Badeau, R.; Yoshii, K.; Liutkus, A. Cauchy Multichannel Speech Enhancement with a Deep Speech Prior. In Proceedings of the 2019 27th European Signal Processing Conference (EUSIPCO), A Coruna, Spain, 2–6 September 2019; pp. 1–5.
9. Cover, T.M.; Thomas, J.A. *Elements of Information Theory (Wiley Series in Telecommunications and Signal Processing)*; Wiley-Interscience: Hoboken, NJ, USA, 2006. [CrossRef]
10. Pardo, L. *Statistical Inference Based on Divergence Measures*; CRC Press: Abingdon, UK, 2005.
11. Kullback, S.; Leibler, R.A. On Information and Sufficiency. *Ann. Math. Stat.* **1951**, *22*, 79–86. [CrossRef]
12. Kullback, S. *Information Theory and Statistics*; Wiley: New York, NY, USA, 1959.
13. Rényi, A. On Measures of Entropy and Information. In *Proceedings of the Fourth Berkeley Symposium on Mathematical Statistics and Probability*; University of California Press: Berkeley, CA, USA, 1961; Volume 1, pp. 547–561.
14. Sharma, B.D.; Mittal, D.P. New non-additive measures of relative information. *J. Comb. Inf. Syst. Sci.* **1977**, *2*, 122–132.
15. Bhattacharyya, A. On a measure of divergence between two statistical populations defined by their probability distributions. *Bull. Calcutta Math. Soc.* **1943**, *35*, 99–109.
16. Kailath, T. The Divergence and Bhattacharyya Distance Measures in Signal Selection. *IEEE Trans. Commun. Technol.* **1967**, *15*, 52–60. [CrossRef]
17. Giet, L.; Lubrano, M. A minimum Hellinger distance estimator for stochastic differential equations: An application to statistical inference for continuous time interest rate models. *Comput. Stat. Data Anal.* **2008**, *52*, 2945–2965. [CrossRef]
18. Csiszár, I. Eine informationstheoretische Ungleichung und ihre Anwendung auf den Beweis der Ergodizität von Markoffschen Ketten. *Publ. Math. Inst. Hung. Acad. Sci. Ser. A* **1963**, *8*, 85–108.
19. Ali, S.M.; Silvey, S.D. A General Class of Coefficients of Divergence of One Distribution from Another. *J. R. Stat. Soc. Ser. B (Methodol.)* **1966**, *28*, 131–142. [CrossRef]
20. Bregman, L. The relaxation method of finding the common point of convex sets and its application to the solution of problems in convex programming. *USSR Comput. Math. Math. Phys.* **1967**, *7*, 200–217. [CrossRef]
21. Burbea, J.; Rao, C. On the convexity of some divergence measures based on entropy functions. *IEEE Trans. Inf. Theory* **1982**, *28*, 489–495. [CrossRef]
22. Burbea, J.; Rao, C. On the convexity of higher order Jensen differences based on entropy functions (Corresp.). *IEEE Trans. Inf. Theory* **1982**, *28*, 961–963. [CrossRef]
23. Burbea, J.; Rao, C. Entropy differential metric, distance and divergence measures in probability spaces: A unified approach. *J. Multivar. Anal.* **1982**, *12*, 575–596. [CrossRef]
24. Csiszar, I. Information-type measures of difference of probability distributions and indirect observation. *Stud. Sci. Math. Hung.* **1967**, *2*, 229–318.
25. Nielsen, F.; Nock, R. On the chi square and higher-order chi distances for approximating f-divergences. *IEEE Signal Process. Lett.* **2014**, *21*, 10–13. [CrossRef]
26. Menéndez, M.L.; Morales, D.; Pardo, L.; Salicrú, M. Asymptotic behaviour and statistical applications of divergence measures in multinomial populations: A unified study. *Stat. Pap.* **1995**, *36*, 1–29. [CrossRef]
27. Cover, T.M.; Thomas, J.A. Information theory and statistics. *Elem. Inf. Theory* **1991**, *1*, 279–335.

28. MacKay, D.J.C. *Information Theory, Inference and Learning Algorithms*; Cambridge University Press: Cambridge, UK, 2003.
29. Ruiz, F.E.; Pérez, P.S.; Bonev, B.I. *Information Theory in Computer Vision and Pattern Recognition*; Springer Science & Business Media: Berlin/Heidelberg, Germany, 2009.
30. Nielsen, F. Statistical Divergences between Densities of Truncated Exponential Families with Nested Supports: Duo Bregman and Duo Jensen Divergences. *Entropy* **2022**, *24*, 421. [CrossRef] [PubMed]
31. Chyzak, F.; Nielsen, F. A closed-form formula for the Kullback–Leibler divergence between Cauchy distributions. *arXiv* **2019**, arXiv:1905.10965.
32. Nielsen, F.; Okamura, K. On f-divergences between Cauchy distributions. *arXiv* **2021**, arXiv:2101.12459.
33. Srivastava, H.; Karlsson, P.W. *Multiple Gaussian Hypergeometric Series*; Ellis Horwood Series in Mathematics and Its Applications Statistics and Operational Research, E; Horwood Halsted Press: Chichester, UK; West Sussex, UK; New York, NY, USA, 1985.
34. Mathai, A.M.; Haubold, H.J. *Special Functions for Applied Scientists*; Springer Science+Business Media: New York, NY, USA, 2008.
35. Gradshteyn, I.; Ryzhik, I. *Table of Integrals, Series, and Products*, 7th ed.; Academic Press is an Imprint of Elsevier: Cambridge, MA, USA, 2007.
36. Humbert, P. The Confluent Hypergeometric Functions of Two Variables. *Proc. R. Soc. Edinb.* **1922**, *41*, 73–96. [CrossRef]
37. Erdélyi, A. *Higher Transcendental Functions*; McGraw-Hill: New York, NY, USA, 1953; Volume I.
38. Koepf, W. *Hypergeometric Summation an Algorithmic Approach to Summation and Special Function Identities*, 2nd ed.; Universitext, Springer: London, UK, 2014.
39. Lauricella, G. Sulle funzioni ipergeometriche a piu variabili. *Rend. Del Circ. Mat. Palermo* **1893**, *7*, 111–158. [CrossRef]
40. Mathai, A.M. *Jacobians of Matrix Transformations and Functions of Matrix Argument*; World Scientific: Singapore, 1997.
41. Anderson, T.W. *An Introduction to Multivariate Statistical Analysis*; John Wiley & Sons: Hoboken, NJ, USA, 2003.
42. Hattori, A.; Kimura, T. On the Euler integral representations of hypergeometric functions in several variables. *J. Math. Soc. Jpn.* **1974**, *26*, 1–16. [CrossRef]
43. Exton, H. *Multiple Hypergeometric Functions and Applications*; Wiley: New York, NY, USA, 1976.

Article

Application of Statistical K-Means Algorithm for University Academic Evaluation

Daohua Yu [1], Xin Zhou [2], Yu Pan [2], Zhendong Niu [1,3,*] and Huafei Sun [2]

1 School of Computer Science and Technology, Beijing Institute of Technology, Beijing 100081, China; yudaohua@bit.edu.cn
2 School of Mathematics and Statistics, Beijing Institute of Technology, Beijing 100081, China; 3120211473@bit.edu.cn (X.Z.); p4nyu@foxmail.com (Y.P.); huafeisun@bit.edu.cn (H.S.)
3 School of Computing and Information, University of Pittsburgh, Pittsburgh, PA 15260, USA
* Correspondence: zniu@bit.edu.cn

Abstract: With the globalization of higher education, academic evaluation is increasingly valued by the scientific and educational circles. Although the number of published papers of academic evaluation methods is increasing, previous research mainly focused on the method of assigning different weights for various indicators, which can be subjective and limited. This paper investigates the evaluation of academic performance by using the statistical K-means (SKM) algorithm to produce clusters. The core idea is mapping the evaluation data from Euclidean space to Riemannian space in which the geometric structure can be used to obtain accurate clustering results. The method can adapt to different indicators and make full use of big data. By using the K-means algorithm based on statistical manifolds, the academic evaluation results of universities can be obtained. Furthermore, through simulation experiments on the top 20 universities of China with the traditional K-means, GMM and SKM algorithms, respectively, we analyze the advantages and disadvantages of different methods. We also test the three algorithms on a UCI ML dataset. The simulation results show the advantages of the SKM algorithm.

Keywords: statistical K-means; academic evaluation; statistical manifold; clustering

1. Introduction

University academic evaluation involves using different indicators and methods to measure the academic level of universities. It has great motivating, guiding and restricting effects on the development of universities, thus gaining more and more attention nowadays [1–4]. In [5], the authors proposed a statistical method of constructing an evaluation system for the transformation of scientific and technological achievements by using Principal Component Analysis (PCA) and the comprehensive indicator method. In [6], the authors used Decision-making Trial and Evaluation Laboratory (DEMATEL) and the entropy-weighting method to give assessments on the research innovation ability of universities in a subjective and objective way. In [7], the authors used the Analytic Hierarchy Process (AHP) method to design the evaluation indicators and give the corresponding weights. However, these works are all based on the specific design of weighted indicators, which cannot avoid the interference of the subjective thoughts of the evaluators and highly depend on the type of universities. In addition, with the development of big data, more and more statistic data are generated yet not properly used, as it is hard to attribute weights for so many indicators. In this paper, we introduce the statistical K-means algorithm to give the academic evaluation results of universities. The idea is mapping the evaluation data together with the clustering problem from Euclidean space to Riemannian space. Specifically, the local statistics are used as parameters to determine a special parameter distribution, which projects all data points into parameter space to obtain a parameter point cloud. This idea has been well applied in many research fields. In [8], the authors take a step forward in image and video coding by extending the well-known Vector of Locally Aggregated Descriptors (VLAD) onto an extensive space of curved Riemannian manifolds. In [9], the authors propose a method which allows us to fuse information from feature representations from both Euclidean and Riemannian spaces by mapping data in a Reproducing Kernel Hilbert Space (RKHS). This method achieves state-of-the-art performance on the problem of pose-based gait recognition. These findings suggest that this idea has great value and significance in the information field. In this paper, our main contributions can be summarized as two points. Firstly, we use statistical manifolds theory to extract features from the origin point cloud, which is capable of processing the high-dimensional data and proves to be a great substitution of the traditional method PCA. Secondly, we use clustering methods to give an evaluation on the academic level of Chinese universities instead of scoring or rating. With the change of the cluster numbers, the underlying relationships of universities in terms of subject development can be found, and the academic level can be assessed by the clustering results subjectively. These two points also provide new research ideas for related problems.

The paper is organized as follows. In Section 2, we introduce some basic knowledge about multivariate normal distribution manifold, difference functions and Gaussian mixture models. In Section 3, we introduce the local statistical methods and statistical K-means (SKM) algorithm. In Section 4, we describe the work of data pre-processing, including the data source and data pre-processing strategies, and we introduce the criteria for assessing the clustering algorithms. In Section 5, we conducted the simulation experiments with the traditional K-means, GMM and SKM algorithm for the top 20 universities of China and analyze their advantages and disadvantages, respectively. A UCI ML dataset is also tested to quantitatively measure the algorithms.

2. Preliminary

2.1. Multivariate Normal Distribution Manifold

Information geometry is used to solve some nonlinear and stochastic problems in the information field, because compared with the treatment in the Euclidean space, the one of Riemannian manifold can often achieve precise results. The statistical manifold is a set of all probability density functions with some regular conditions. In addition, by introducing the Fisher information matrix as a Riemannian metric, the statistical manifold becomes a Riemannian manifold. It is well known that the Kullback–Leibler divergence is a suitable difference function measuring the difference of two points on the statistical manifold, even though it is not a real distance function [10,11]. The manifold of a family of multivariate normal distributions is an important statistical manifold and is widely applied to the researches of signal processing, image processing, neural networks and so on. The K-means algorithm on statistical manifolds introduced in this paper is to transform the data point cloud in Euclidean space into the parameter point cloud on the statistical manifold of a family of multivariate normal distributions, and then, it applies cluster analysis to the parameter point cloud.

Definition 1. *We call a set*

$$S = \{p(x;\theta) \mid \theta \in \Theta \subset \mathbb{R}^n\}$$

an n-dimensional statistical manifold, where $p(x;\theta)$ is the probability density of functions, with some regular conditions.

Since each n multivariate normal distribution density function can be determined by an n-dimensional vector (mean) and an n-order symmetric positive definite matrix (covariance matrix), the manifold that consists of the family of normal distributions is closely related to manifold of the symmetric positive definite matrices [12].

Definition 2. *The manifold of symmetric positive definite matrices* SPD(n) *is defined as*

$$\mathrm{SPD}(n) = \left\{ P \in M(n) \mid P^T = P, \text{and } x^T P x > 0, \forall x \in \mathbb{R}^n - \{0\} \right\},$$

where $M(n)$ is the set of n-order matrices and P^T denotes the transpose of the matrix P. The smooth structure on SPD(n) is induced as the submanifold of the general linear group $GL(n, \mathbb{R})$, which is a set of all non-singular matrices.

Definition 3. *The multivariate normal distribution manifold consists of the probability density functions of all n multivariate normal distributions, which is defined as*

$$\mathcal{N}_n = \left\{ f \middle| f(\mu, \Sigma) = \frac{1}{\sqrt{(2\pi)^n \det(\Sigma)}} \exp\left\{ -\frac{(x-\mu)^T \Sigma^{-1}(x-\mu)}{2} \right\} \right\},$$

where $\mu \in \mathbb{R}^n$ and $\Sigma \in \mathrm{SPD}(n)$ are the mean and the covariance matrix of the distributions, respectively, and (μ, Σ) is called the parameter coordinate of $\mathcal{N}_n$.

It is worth noting that $\mathcal{N}_n$ is topologically homeomorphic in the product space $\mathbb{R}^n \times \mathrm{SPD}(n)$.

2.2. Difference Functions on Multivariate Normal Distribution Manifold

In this paper, we need to consider the difference between the probability density functions of different multivariate normal distributions. We select the Wasserstein distance as the difference function. At the same time, we also use Kullback–Leibler divergence, which is a difference function commonly used in classical information theory. We will introduce these difference functions respectively below [13–15].

2.2.1. Wasserstein Distance

The Wasserstein distance of the probability measure on $\mathbb{R}^n$ describes the energy required to transfer between the two distributions.

In particular, for the multivariate normal distribution, the literature [13] gives a specific expression.

Proposition 1. *The Wasserstein distance between* $P_1, P_2 \in \mathcal{N}_n$ *is*

$$D_W^2(P_1, P_2) = \|\mu_1 - \mu_2\|^2 + \mathrm{tr}\left(\Sigma_1 + \Sigma_2 - 2(\Sigma_1 \Sigma_2)^{\frac{1}{2}} \right), \tag{1}$$

where (μ_1, Σ_1) and (μ_2, Σ_2) correspond to the distribution of P_1 and P_2, respectively.

Unfortunately, there is not a simply explicit expression of the geometric mean of the Wasserstein distance; hence, this paper temporarily replaces the geometric mean with the arithmetic mean in the simulation experiments.

2.2.2. Kullback–Leibler Divergence

Kullback–Leibler (KL) divergence is a non-negative function which measures the difference between any two probability density functions. It is worth noting that KL divergence is not a distance function, since it does not satisfy the symmetry and triangle inequality. In the following, we give its definition and the expression of its geometric mean.

Definition 4. *Let* P_1, P_2 *be two probability density functions. KL divergence is defined as*

$$D_{KL}(P_1 \| P_2) = E_{P_1}\left[\log \frac{P_1}{P_2} \right], \tag{2}$$

and it can be shown that $D_{KL}(P_1 \| P_2) \geq 0$; the equality holds if and only if $P_1 = P_2$.

In particular, for any $P_1, P_2 \in \mathcal{N}_n$ with the parameters (μ_1, Σ_1) and (μ_2, Σ_2), by direct calculation, we can obtain

$$D_{KL}(P_1\|P_2) = \frac{1}{2}\left\{\log\frac{|\Sigma_2|}{|\Sigma_1|} - n + \text{tr}\left(\Sigma_2^{-1}\Sigma_1\right) + (\mu_2 - \mu_1)^T \Sigma_2^{-1}(\mu_2 - \mu_1)\right\}. \quad (3)$$

Under the parameter coordinate (μ, Σ), the expression of the geometric mean $c(C) = \operatorname*{argmin}_{P \in \mathcal{N}_n} \frac{1}{m}\sum_{i=1}^{m} D_{KL}(P_i\|P)$ is very complicated, and it is not convenient to use. In order to overcome the difficulty, we will throughout the equation change the probability density function of $P \in \mathcal{N}_n$ into the form of exponential distribution. In fact, by setting $x_1 = x$, $x_2 = -\frac{1}{2}x^T x$ and $\theta_1 = \Sigma^{-1}\mu, \theta_2 = \Sigma^{-1}$, we can obtain the form of exponential distribution

$$P(x; \mu, \Sigma) = P(x_1, x_2; \theta) = \exp\{\langle \bar{x}, \theta \rangle - \varphi(\theta)\}, \quad (4)$$

where $\bar{x} = (x_1, x_2), \theta = (\theta_1, \theta_2)$ is called the natural parameter, $\langle \bar{x}, \theta \rangle$ is the inner product of $\bar{x}$ and θ, and the function $\varphi(\theta) = \frac{1}{2}\left(\theta_1^T \theta_2^{-1}\theta_1 - \log|\theta_2| - n\log 2\pi\right)$ is called the potential function, which is a convex function.

By using the potential function φ, we can define the generalized KL divergence, namely the Bregman divergence on $\mathcal{N}_n$, as

$$B_\varphi(P_2\|P_1) := \varphi(\theta_2) - \varphi(\theta_1) - \langle \nabla\varphi(\theta_1), \theta_2 - \theta_1\rangle, \quad (5)$$

where θ_1, θ_2 are two parameters of $\mathcal{N}_n$.

Remark 1. *By means of the exponential form for the probability density functions $P_1, P_2 \in \mathcal{N}_n$, direct calculation yields*

$$B_\varphi(P_2\|P_1) = D_{KL}(P_1\|P_2).$$

2.3. Mean of Parameter Point Clouds

The main idea of the traditional K-means algorithm is that for a given data cloud with the scale m,

$$C_m = \{p_i \in \mathbb{R}^n \mid i = 1, \cdots, m\},$$

which is abbreviated as C, by using the clustering algorithm, we divide the point cloud into K classes. The effect of the traditional K-means algorithm is mainly affected by the selection of initial cluster centers, the expression of data and the difference function.

In order to avoid the shortage of the traditional K-means algorithm, we will consider the clustering algorithm on the Riemannian space instead of the Euclidean space so that we can use the geodesic distance and KL divergence but the Euclidean distance and obtain better clustering results.

Now, we give the definition of the geometric mean of point cloud C in $\mathcal{N}_n$ under different difference functions D.

Definition 5. *The geometric mean $c(C)$ of point cloud $C = \{(\mu_1, \Sigma_1), \cdots, (\mu_m, \Sigma_m)\}$ in $\mathcal{N}_n$ is*

$$c(C) := \operatorname*{argmin}_{(\mu, \Sigma) \in \mathcal{N}_n} \frac{1}{m}\sum_{i=1}^{m} D((\mu_i, \Sigma_i), (\mu, \Sigma)).$$

In practical problems, the calculation of the geometric mean of some difference functions may be very complicated; thus, we will use the arithmetic mean instead of the geometric mean.

Definition 6. *The parameter space $\mathbb{R}^n \times \text{SPD}(n)$ of $\mathcal{N}_n$ is a convex set. Hence, the arithmetic mean $\bar{c}(C)$ of the parameter point cloud $C = \{(\mu_1, \Sigma_1), \cdots, (\mu_m, \Sigma_m)\}$ in $\mathcal{N}_n$ can be defined as*

$$\bar{c}(\tilde{C}) = \frac{1}{m} \sum_{i=1}^{m} (\mu_i, \Sigma_i).$$

Now, we introduce the geometric mean of the point cloud C with respect to the KL divergence.

From (5), we can obtain the following proposition [16].

Proposition 2. *The geometric mean of the point cloud C with respect to the KL divergence exists and is unique, and is equal to the arithmetic mean in the above natural coordinates.*

Furthermore, we can see that the geometric mean of the point cloud C with respect to the Bregman divergence B_φ exists and is unique, and it is equal to the arithmetic mean in natural coordinates, hence the geometric mean of point cloud C about KL divergence exists and is unique, and it is equal to the arithmetic mean in natural coordinates, that is,

$$c(C) = \underset{P \in \mathcal{N}_n}{\operatorname{argmin}} \frac{1}{m} \sum_{i=1}^{m} D_{KL}(P \| P_i) = P\left(x_1, x_2; \frac{1}{m} \sum_{i=1}^{m} \theta_i \right). \quad (6)$$

In the following K-means algorithm with KL divergence as the difference function, the Proposition 2 ensures that the geometric mean of the parameter point cloud can be explicitly given by the arithmetic mean after parameter transformation.

2.4. Gaussian Mixture Models

The mixture model is a probability model that can be used to represent an overall distribution with K sub-distributions. In other words, the mixture model represents the probability distribution of observational data overall, which is a mixture of K sub-distributions. The mixture model does not require the observational data to provide information about the sub-distributions to calculate the probability that the observational data are in the overall distribution.

In general, a mixture model can use any probability distribution, but due to the good mathematical properties and good computational performance of the Gaussian distribution, the Gaussian mixture model is the most widely used model in practice [17].

Definition 7. *The probability distribution of Gaussian mixture models is*

$$P(x \mid \Theta) = \sum_{i=1}^{K} \alpha_i p_i(x \mid \theta_i), \quad (7)$$

where $\Theta = (\alpha_1, \ldots, \alpha_K, \theta_1, \ldots, \theta_K)$ such that $\alpha_i \geq 0$, $\sum_{i=1}^{K} \alpha_i = 1$, α_i is the probability that the observational data belong to the i-th submodel and p_i is the Gaussian distribution density function of the i-th submodel, whose parameter is θ_i.

3. Statistical K-Means Algorithm

The K-means algorithm on statistical manifolds, which we refer to as the SKM algorithm, consists of three parts: local statistical method, K-means algorithm, and selection of difference function. This section first introduces the K-nearest neighbor local statistical method and then introduces the details of the SKM algorithm.

3.1. Local Statistical Method

The point cloud is a sampling of some specified features in the objective world, each of which we consider to have the same properties within a small neighborhood. Mathematically, we obtain neighborhood properties through local statistics. Specifically, we use local statistics as parameters to describe a parameter distribution. Two sets of different local statistics can determine two different distributions on the same parameter distribution family. This idea is equivalent to finding a distribution for any point in the point cloud and its neighbors in the point cloud (subclouds of the point cloud) such that the subcloud is a sample of that distribution.

For the initial point cloud without any annotation, we have no reason to think that its local statistics conform to some special distribution. We believe that the factors affecting the local distribution of point clouds in their natural background are complex enough; consequently, the local statistics can be generated from a multivariate normal distribution according to the Central Limit Theorem. Therefore, we only need to calculate the mean and covariance matrix of each point of the point cloud in its local area to determine a normal distribution. By doing this, the entire point cloud will be projected as a parameter point cloud on the family of multivariate normal distribution, and then, the K-means algorithm is used on the parameter point cloud to cluster the original data. The data are then classified using their differences in neighborhood densities [18–21].

For the selection of the neighborhood in the point cloud, we use the *k*-nearest neighbor method: that is, for any positive integer *k*, find a *k* Euclidean nearest neighbor of some point in the point cloud. This method can reflect the number density of local point clouds. Next, we introduce the selection method of k-nearest neighbors.

Definition 8. *Let $C_m = \{p_i \in \mathbb{R}^n \mid i = 1, 2, \cdots, m\}$ be a point cloud of scale m, abbreviated C. For any $p \in C_m$,*

$$k\text{-}N(p,k) = \{p_j \in C_m, j \in [i_1, \cdots, i_k] \mid \|p_l - p\| \geq \|p_j - p\|, \forall l \notin [i_1, \cdots, i_k]\}$$

is called the k-nearest neighbor of p in C_m, abbreviated as k-N, and $p \in k\text{-}N \subseteq C$.

Denote $\mu(k\text{-}N) = E[k\text{-}N(p,k)] - p$ and $\Sigma(k\text{-}N) = \text{Cov}[k\text{-}N(p,k)]$ as the mean and covariance matrices of the distances between data points in p and $N(p, k)$, respectively, thus defining the local statistical map

$$\Psi_k : C \to \mathcal{N}_n, \tag{8}$$

where $\Psi_k(p) := f(\mu(k\text{-}N), \Sigma(k\text{-}N)) = \frac{1}{\sqrt{(2\pi)^n \det(\Sigma)}} \exp\left\{-\frac{(x-\mu)^T \Sigma^{-1}(x-\mu)}{2}\right\}$. It is worth noting that we refer to the image of point cloud C under the local statistical map Ψ_k

$$\widetilde{kC} := \Psi_k[C], \widetilde{kC} \subseteq \mathcal{N}_n$$

as the parameter point cloud under the k-nearest neighbor method in this paper.

3.2. Details of the SKM Algorithm

Giving the image of point cloud C under the k-nearest neighbor and local statistical mapping $\widetilde{kC} = \Psi_k[C]$, which is the parameter point cloud in $\mathcal{N}_n$, it is reasonable that we cluster the parameter points to gain the potential classifications among the original data, and the core idea of the SKM algorithm is the application of the K-means algorithm together with non-Euclidean difference functions. The SKM algorithm's performance depends on the choice of difference functions, which makes the SKM algorithm flexible for various tasks.

The specific steps of the SKM algorithm are as Algorithm 1:

Algorithm 1 Statistical K-Means Cluster Algorithm

Input: point cloud C, k-nearest neighbor indicator k, initial cluster center $c_1^0, \cdots, c_k^0$, threshold ε

Output: a K division of point cloud C

1: By local statistics methods, the point cloud C is represented as a point cloud in the manifold of n-dimensional normal distribution family $\widetilde{kC}$
2: Input the initial cluster centers $c_1^0, \cdots, c_k^0$ and, based on the selected difference function, apply the K-means algorithm to $\widetilde{kC}$, where the distances between parameter points are given by the difference function, and the centroid c_j^i is updated to the current geometric mean of each division
3: According to the indicator division of $\widetilde{kC}$ clustering $l_1, \cdots, l_k$, the output $C[l_1], \cdots, C[l_k]$ is a division of the origin cloud C

4. Data Pre-Processing and Preparations

After the introduction of the SKM algorithm, we can prepare the data for our method to simulate on. This section mainly explains the work of data pre-processing and the criteria to assess the cluster results.

4.1. Data Pre-Processing

Here, the original data of the experiment are selected among the top 20 universities in mainland China in terms of scientific research funding in 2021. A total of 32 types of indicators from 2010 to 2019 are taken into account. Data sources are the WOS and CSSCI databases alongside the analysis platform of CNKI [22–24]. The names of universities and statistical indicators are as Tables 1 and 2.

Table 1. The names of the twenty universities and their abbreviations.

University Name	Abbreviation
Tsinghua University	THU
Zhejiang University	ZJU
Peking University	PKU
Sun Yat-sen University	SYSU
Shanghai Jiao Tong University	SJU
Fudan University	FDU
Shandong University	SDU
Huazhong University of Science and Technology	HUST
Xi'an Jiaotong University	XJU
Southeast University	SEU
Beihang University	BUAA
Harbin Institute of Technology	HIT
Tongji University	TJU
Wuhan University	WHU
Northwestern Polytechnical University	NPU
Jilin University	JLU
Beijing Normal University	BNU
Central South University	CSU
Beijing Institute of Technology	BIT

Table 2. Selection of thirty-two statistical indicators.

Category	Indicator
SCI	Total Posts
	Total Cited
SSCI	Total Posts
	Total Cited
CSCD	Total Posts
	Total Cited
CSSCI	Total Posts
Patent	Number of Patent Applications
	Number of Invention Patent Applications
	Number of Utility Model Patent Applications
	Number of Industrial Design Patent Applications
	Number of Patent Authorizations
	Number of Invention Patent Authorizations
	Number of Utility Model Patent Authorizations
	Number of Industrial Design Patent Authorizations
Funding	Amount of State-Level Funding
	Amount of Ministrial Funding
	Amount of Provincial Funding
	Number of National Natural Science Funds
	Amount of National Natural Science Funding
	Number of National Social Science Funds
Newspaper	Number of Posts
	Number of Citations
	Average Cited
	Number of Downloads
	Average Downloads
	Posts on Local Newspaper
	Posts on Central Newspaper
Rewards	The State Science and Technology Awards
	State-Level Teaching Award
	Honors from Ministry and Province
	Academic Association Awards

Assuming that x_i as the i-th indicator, the numerical expression of academic performance of a university s in the year y is denoted by

$$X_{s,y} = (x_1, x_2, \cdots, x_k)^T.$$

It is natural that we make up a matrix $X(s,y)$ whose element is the academic performance vector $X_{s,y}$. Hence, the row represents different universities, and the column represents the different years. Since our indicators are in different dimensions, we apply the z-score normalization on the indicators of every column: namely, normalize the same indicator of different universities in the year.

$$x_{nor} = \frac{x - mean(X)}{std(X)}, \ x \in X.$$

The normalization makes indicators among different years comparable, which forms the basis of clustering.

4.2. Clustering Assessment Criteria

The commonly used clustering assessment criteria can be generally devided into two classes, external assessment and internal assessment. The external assessment needs a reference model as the benchmark, while the internal assessment simply measures the clustering results from the perspective of compactness, connectivity and so on. Since there is no state-of-the-art reference model or ranking in this field, it is convincing to choose proper internal assessment criteria. In this paper, we use the Davies–Bouldin Index (DBI), Dunn Index (DI) and Silhouette Score (SC) as the clustering assessment criteria, which have been proved to be effective in such problems [25,26].

Assume that $C = \{C_1, C_2, \cdots, C_k\}$ as the cluster result, where $|C|$ represents the number of samples in C, $dist(x_i, x_j)$ represents the distance metric of sample x_i and x_j, μ_i represents the center of cluster C_i. Giving definitions as follows

$$avg(C) = \frac{2}{|C|(|C|-1)} \sum_{1 \leq i \leq j \leq |C|} dist(x_i, x_j),$$

$$diam(C) = \max_{1 \leq i \leq j \leq |C|} \{dist(x_i, x_j)\},$$

$$d_{min}(C_i, C_j) = \min_{x_i \in C_i, x_j \in C_j} \{dist(x_i, x_j)\},$$

$$d_{cen}(C_i, C_j) = dist(\mu_i, \mu_j).$$

Then, we can define DBI, DI and SC as

$$DBI = \frac{1}{k} \sum_{i=1}^{k} \max_{i \neq j} \left(\frac{avg(C_i) + avg(C_j)}{d_{cen}(\mu_i, \mu_j)} \right),$$

$$DI = \frac{\min_{1 \leq i \leq j \leq m} \{d_{min}(C_i, C_j)\}}{\max_{1 \leq l \leq m} \{diam(C_l)\}},$$

$$s(x_i) = \frac{b-a}{max(a,b)}, \ a = \frac{1}{|C_q|-1} \sum_{x_i, x_j \in C_q} dist(x_i, x_j),$$

$$b = \frac{1}{\sum |C| - |C_q|} \sum_{x_i \in C_q, x_j \notin C_q} dist(x_i, x_j), \ SC = \frac{\sum s(x_i)}{\sum |C|}.$$

The three indicators evaluate the clustering results from different perspectives. DBI measures the maximum similarity between clusters; hence, the smaller DBI is, the better the clustering result is; DI calculates the ratio of the minimum cluster distance and the largest intra-class discrete distance, and a good clustering result should make the value as big as possible; the SC value of each sample represents the degree of matching relationship between the sample and its cluster; therefore, the higher the SC value in general, the better the clustering result.

5. Data Cloud Simulation

In this section, we will respectively apply the traditional K-means, GMM and the SKM algorithm on the processed data. By analyzing the cluster results and calculating the assessment criteria scores, we can compare the performance of different algorithms as well as give the academic levels of the 20 universities. The estimation of university academic level is given by the most reasonable cluster result, as all these cluster algorithms evolve random processes.

5.1. The K-Means Algorithm Clustering

To avoid the influence of sparse data and speed up the process of convergence, PCA is used at first to reduce the data dimension [27]. The PCA scree plot is displayed as Figure 1.

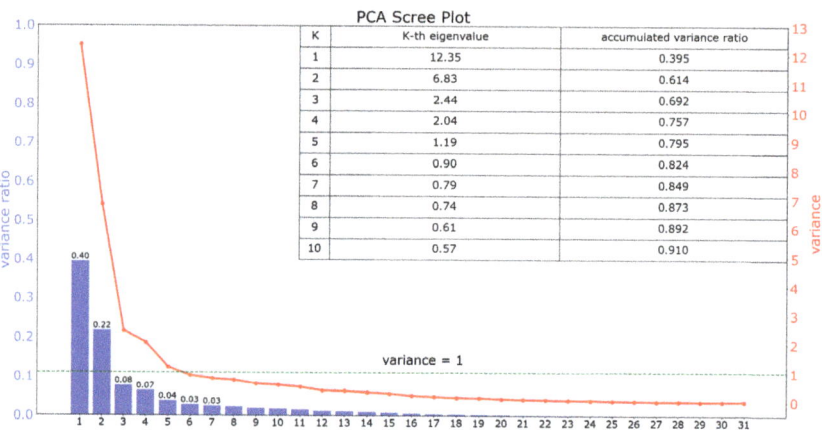

Figure 1. PCA Scree Plot. The red line is the variance plot and explains the proportion of variation by each component from PCA; the green dotted line is the split line to better present components that have variance bigger than 1.

Often, there are two ways to obtain the number of principal components, that is, to retain a certain percentage of the variance of the original data or to retain only the principal components with eigenvalues greater than 1 according to Kraiser's rule [28,29]. It can be seen in the shown PCA results that there are five principal components with eigenvalues greater than 1, and when the number of principal components is 6, the cumulative variance contribution rate reaches more than 0.8. We finally choose to keep six principal components, that is, compress the 32-dimension original data to six dimensions. It is worth mentioning that several indicators ignored in previous research prove to contribute signficantly according to the PCA results, which are shown above. This is a strong testament to the effectiveness of big data.

There are many methods for deciding the number of clusters K. One simple way is to observe the sum of the squarred errors (SSE) with the change of K and select the point where SSE changes from steep to gentle. However, the Figure 2 shows that there is no very clear elbow point. As a consequence, we choose to use the Gap Statistic method [30]. Every K corresponds to a Gap_k and s_k, and K is selected as the minimal K that makes $Gap_k - Gap_{k+1} + s_{k+1} \geq 0$. We conduct simulations 50 times, as random sampling is also used in the Gap Statistic. The results are shown in Figure 3, and Figure 4 shows the most common case. It can be seen that when $K = 4, 6$, the GapDiffs are most likely to be greater than 0. Although inferior to $K = 4, 6$, $K = 5$ also shows a considerable frequency. Considering that academic performance evaluation needs an adequate K to produce reasonable results, we finally chose K as 4, 5 and 6.

In order to obtain credible results, we limit the iteration times of each simulation to 20, so as to avoid bad cases caused by random initialization. In addition, we merge those simulations that have very similar initialization and cluster results. We select the most representative case by comparing their clustering evaluation criteria [31,32]. This strategy makes it easier for us to analyze the performance of different algorithms. For eack K, we conduct 30 independent simulations and give the cluster details. To better visualize the clusters, we map the original data points to a plane using PCA. The results are shown in the table and graph below.

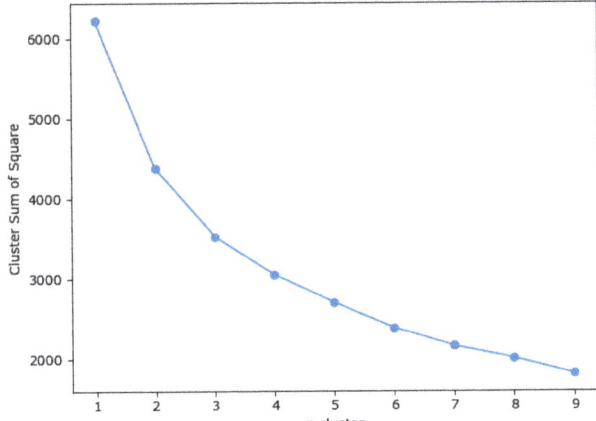

Figure 2. Sum of the Squared Errors Plot.

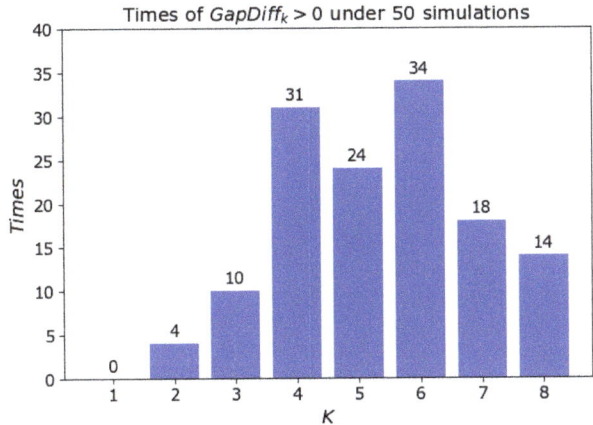

Figure 3. Results of Gap Statistic Simulations.

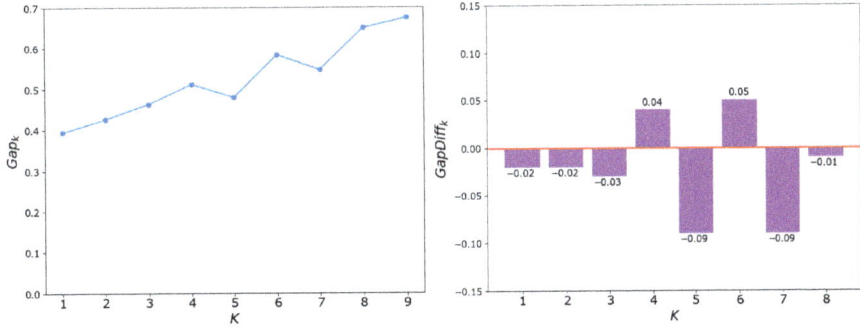

Figure 4. Gap Statistic Typical Result.

When $K = 4$, we can see from Figure 5 that the cluster completeness is well preserved. Only Xi'an Jiaotong University and Tongji University have small parts divided into different clusters, and the rest of the data points of the same university are all in the same cluster.

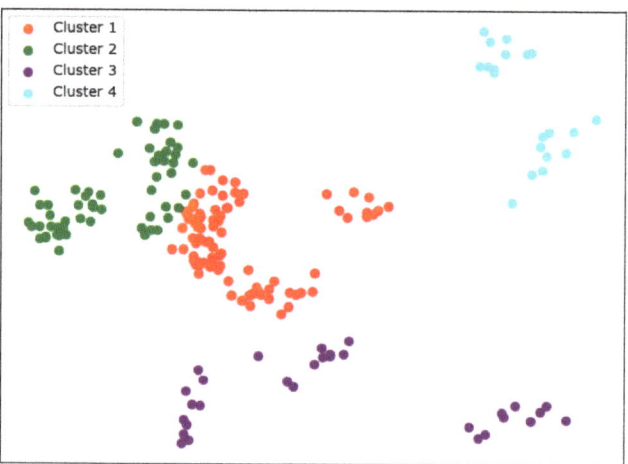

Figure 5. Clustering results of K-means when $K = 4$.

When $K = 5$, the cluster result Figure 6 still shows very good completeness. However, some universities have changed from one cluster to another. Peking University itself becomes one new cluster, and Wuhan University becomes clustered with Beijing Normal University and Fudan University.

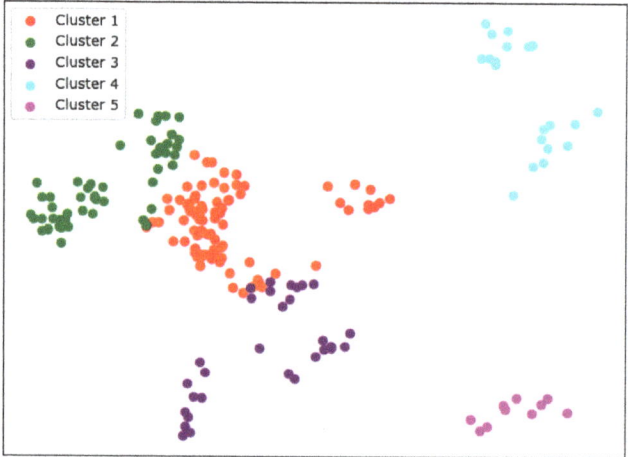

Figure 6. Clustering results of K-means when $K = 5$.

When $K = 6$, things begin to change. We can see from Figure 7 that so-called rag bags, which mean small parts of data points that cannot be well clustered, begin to increase. This actually has a bad effect on the cluster homogenity. Shanghai Jiao Tong University and Sun Yat-sen University now also change the cluster and join with Fudan University, while Wuhan University and Beijing Normal University remain together.

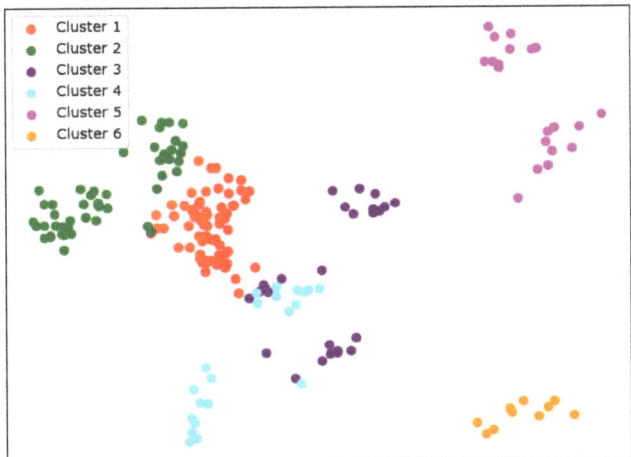

Figure 7. Clustering results of K-means when $K = 6$.

It can be seen from Table 3 that the clustering indicators of the K-means algorithm are relatively stable. DBI is basically maintained between 1.3 and 1.6, DI is basically maintained between 0.05 and 0.08, and SC is mostly distributed above 0.3. It is in line with the previous SSE result and proves the cluster result to be reasonable. For results, with the change of K, the data points of Tsinghua University and Zhejiang University in all years are always the only two in the same cluster, which indicates that the academic level of these two universities is very close and there is a large gap between the two and the remaining universities. In addition, in all years data points of Central South University, Jilin University, Sichuan University, Huazhong University of Science and Technology, Shandong University, Tongji University, etc. always appear in the same cluster, indicating their academic level is close; Northwestern Polytechnical University, Beihang University, Beijing Institute of Technology, Harbin Institute of Technology and Southeast University are in the same situation, and the difference between these two clusters may be that the universities in the latter cluster have a strong color of science and engineering along with a national defense background. Considering that Xi'an Jiaotong University has a relatively uniform distribution in the two clusters with the change of K, it is likely that the academic level is close. We also notice that the clustering results of Wuhan University, Sun Yat-sen University, Fudan University, Shanghai Jiao Tong University, Beijing Normal University, Peking University and other universites changed greatly with the change of K. When $K = 4$, Beijing Normal University and Peking University are in the same cluster, but it is then divided as K increases. One explanation is that when K is small, Beijing Normal University and Peking University are clustered together because they have similar backgrounds in humanities and social sciences. However, because of the huge difference of academic level, the two are then divided. This also explains the cluster variance for Fudan University, Sun Yat-sen University, Wuhan University, and Shanghai Jiao Tong University. These are all comprehensive universities, and characteristics of both (1) humanities and social science and (2) science and engineering are relatively distinct. Therefore, for different K, they can be in the same cluster with Beijing Normal University or in the cluster of science and engineering backgrounds.

Table 3. K-means clustering results.

K	Number of Cases	Samples in Different Clusters	DBI	DI	SC
4	27	90 60 30 20	1.56	0.06	0.30
4	3	84 65 31 20	1.68	0.06	0.29
5	14	91 50 29 20 10	1.45	0.07	0.33
5	7	86 55 29 20 10	1.47	0.08	0.33
5	4	84 56 30 20 10	1.49	0.07	0.32
5	4	75 67 28 20 10	1.50	0.06	0.32
5	1	82 57 30 20 11	1.40	0.06	0.32
6	10	71 51 27 21 20 10	1.41	0.07	0.34
6	7	74 51 30 20 15 10	1.40	0.07	0.34
6	5	78 51 28 22 11 10	1.39	0.07	0.34
6	4	81 58 20 20 11 10	1.30	0.07	0.35
6	4	78 51 30 20 11 10	1.35	0.07	0.35

5.2. The GMM Clustering

Different from the K-means algorithm, the Gaussian mixture model uses Gaussian distributions as feature descriptors, and it is able to softly assign weights for each component thanks to the Expectation Maximization (EM) algorithm. Consequently, the GMM can form clusters of more complicated shapes, which makes it suitable for the university academic data. Under the consideration of consistence with K-means and from the experience of previous work [33], we take the same simulation conditions as the K-means. The Gap Statistic method can also be applied to the GMM, so it is reasonable to choose the same K values. The results are shown in the table and graph below.

We can see from Table 4 that the overall performance of the GMM is better than the K-means in terms of clustering criteria. During the change of N-class, we can see that there are actually two patterns. The results of Figures 8 and 9 are actually very similar to that of the K-means. However, Figures 10 and 11 present a very unbalanced result. In thier case, almost all the universities of science and technology are clustered together, and the rest of the universites are actually always the same ones. Although good cluster criteria scores are obtained, the results of the GMM actually cannot be used for university academic evaluation, as they make no effective divisions. This indicates that a different feature extraction method is needed, and we use the SKM algorithm.

Table 4. GMM clustering results.

N Class	Number of Cases	Samples in Different Clusters	DBI	DI	SC
4	14	102 48 30 20	1.52	0.08	0.31
4	8	95 75 20 10	1.61	0.08	0.29
4	5	140 20 20 20	1.35	0.18	0.34
4	3	102 48 30 20	1.52	0.08	0.31
5	11	102 48 20 20 10	1.31	0.10	0.33
5	7	91 49 30 20 10	1.46	0.15	0.32
5	6	89 47 30 20 11	1.40	0.06	0.33
5	4	55 53 52 20 20	1.68	0.03	0.27
5	2	120 20 20 20 20	1.34	0.16	0.36

Table 4. *Cont.*

N Class	Number of Cases	Samples in Different Clusters	DBI	DI	SC
6	11	91 49 20 20 10 10	1.34	0.17	0.33
6	5	83 47 30 20 10 10	1.32	0.07	0.36
6	4	70 51 49 10 10 10	1.50	0.15	0.30
6	4	70 49 40 20 11 10	1.40	0.15	0.33
6	3	118 41 11 10 10 10	1.19	0.14	0.38
6	2	120 20 20 20 10 10	1.19	0.16	0.38
6	1	120 20 20 20 20	1.18	0.21	0.38

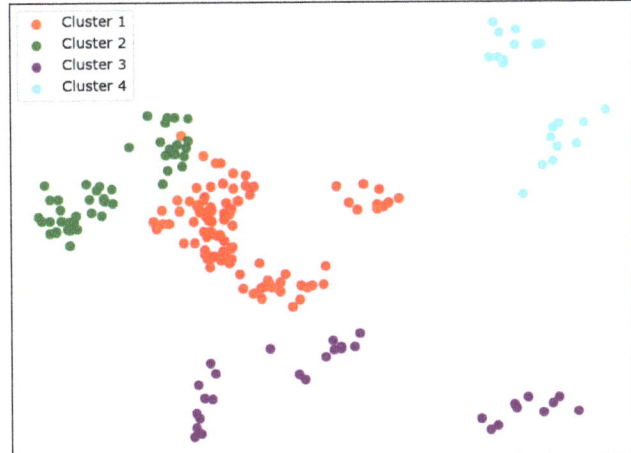

Figure 8. One case of the GMM when N = 4.

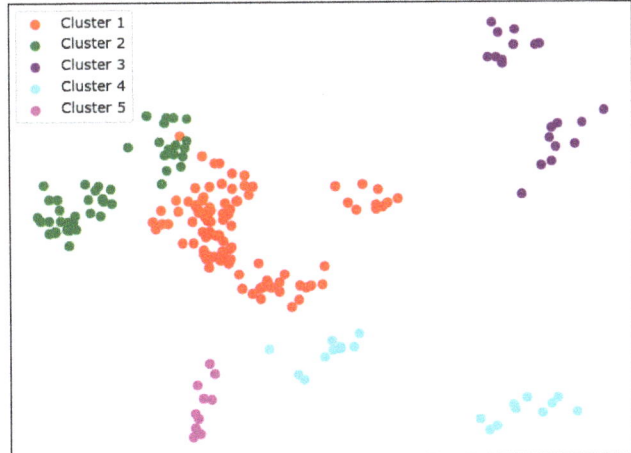

Figure 9. One case of the GMM when N = 5.

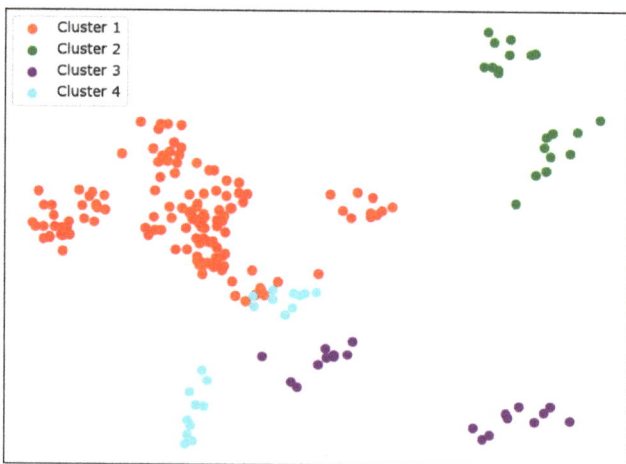

Figure 10. The other case of the GMM when N = 4.

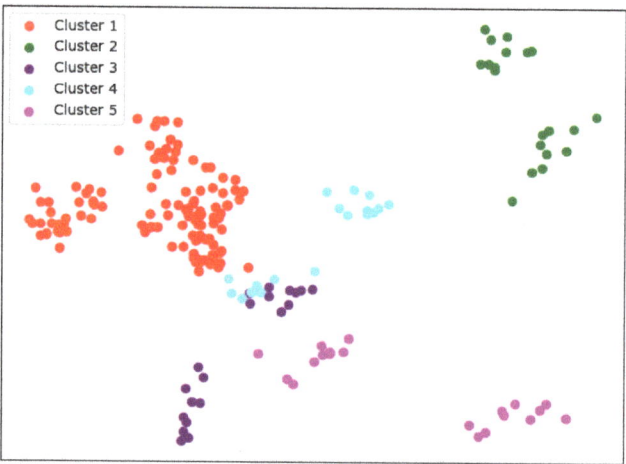

Figure 11. The other case of the GMM when N = 5.

5.3. The SKM Algorithm Clustering

The idea of the SKM algorithm is based on the assumption that in the original data point cloud, the neighborhood of each point should have a convergent property with this point. The point cloud is the sampling and discretization of real physical quantities, so the rationality of this assumption is quite natural. In our simulation, we firstly use the k-nearest neighbor method to select points near each data point and map this subcloud to an N-dimensional normal distribution family manifold. Then, we apply the SKM algorithm with non-Euclidean difference functions and analyze their clustering results. For the selection of k, we simply choose $k = 10$, which is the number of the points in the origin point cloud for every university. The choice not only enables the points from the same university to be mapped to one distribution on statistical manifolds in theory: it also has been proven in our simulation that when $k = 10$, the SKM algorithm could achieve convergence faster compared to other k-values.

In this simulation, we use the KL divergence and the Wasserstein difference functions. Due to the use of the local statistical method, there is no need for dimension reduction;

in other words, the application of PCA is skipped. Especially, as there is a one-to-one correspondence between the point clouds on Euclidean space and on manifolds, and in the Euclidean space we have obtained K values, we just keep it unchanged as our simulation parameters[34]. The other simulation strategies are the same as those in Section 4.1. The results are shown in the table and graph below.

The first is the result of using KL divergence.

When $K = 4$, we can see similar results with K-means from Figure 12; the cluster completeness is also well preserved. However, this time, Peking University is divided into a separate cluster, and Beijing Normal University is divided into a large cluster.

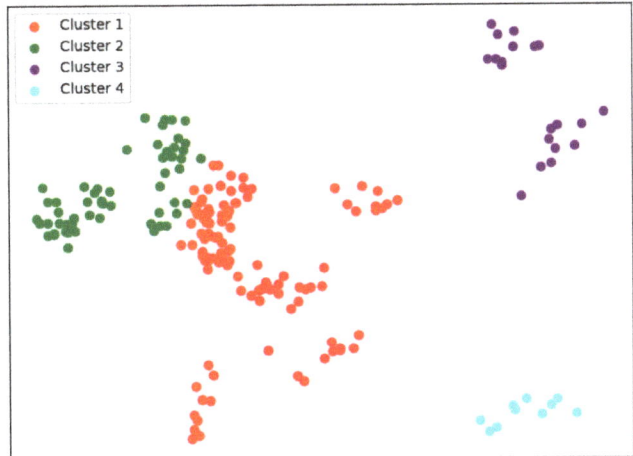

Figure 12. Clustering results of SKM about KL divergence when $K = 4$.

Compared with K-means, we can see from Figure 13 that the biggest difference when $K = 5$ is that this time, Sun Yat-sen University, Fudan University, and Shanghai Jiao Tong University are in the same cluster. Except for Peking University, Zhejiang University, and Tsinghua University, the rest are divided into two main clusters.

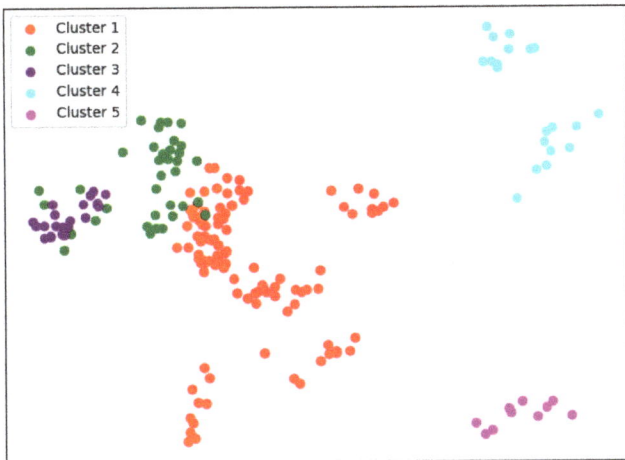

Figure 13. Clustering results of SKM about KL divergence when $K = 5$.

When $K = 6$, it also fails to cluster a small number of data points well. In Figure 14, Peking University, Tsinghua University, and Zhejiang University were each divided into a cluster.

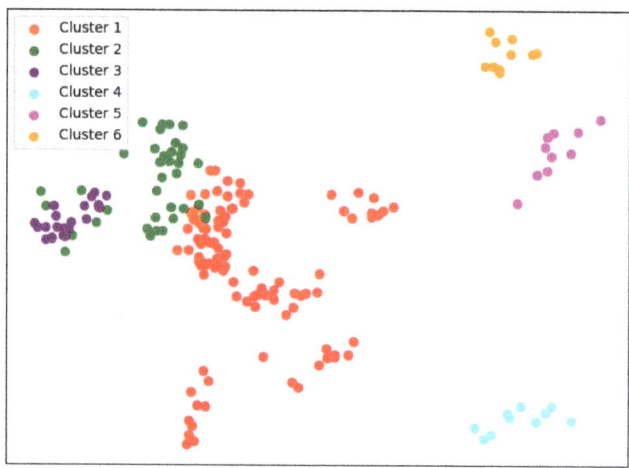

Figure 14. Clustering results of SKM about KL divergence when $K = 6$.

The result for the Wasserstein distance is below.

When $K = 4$, we can see from Figure 15 that the difference between using Wasserstein distance and KL divergence is that when using Wasserstein distance, Fudan University is divided into the same cluster as Peking University. The rest of the results are basically the same.

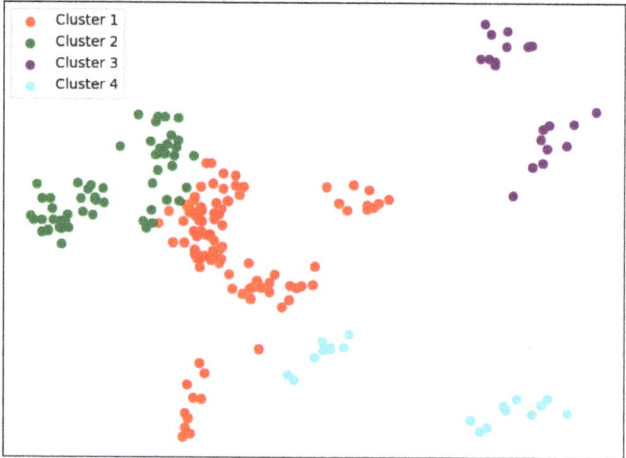

Figure 15. Clustering results of SKM about Wasserstein distance when $K = 4$.

When $K = 5$, the SKM results in Figure 16 are basically the same with using Wasserstein distance and KL divergence, but with using KL divergence, it is more likely that small parts of data points cannot be well clustered.

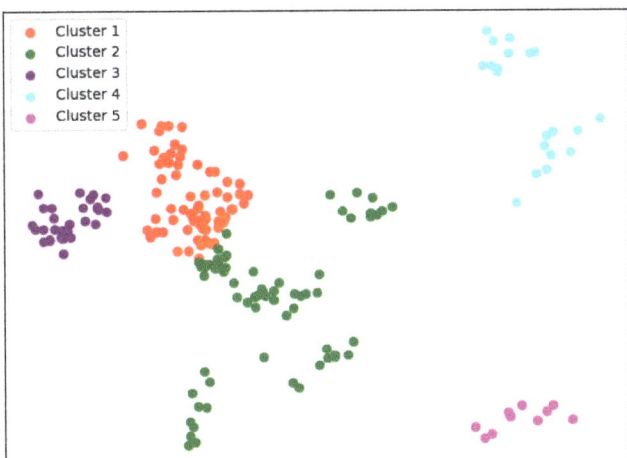

Figure 16. Clustering results of SKM about Wasserstein distance when K = 5.

When $K = 6$, the clustering results with using Wasserstein distance in Figure 17 are less stable relative to KL divergence. In addition, the Wasserstein distance produce clusters with a very small number of samples, which indicates that it cannot distinguish the mainfolds on this problem very well.

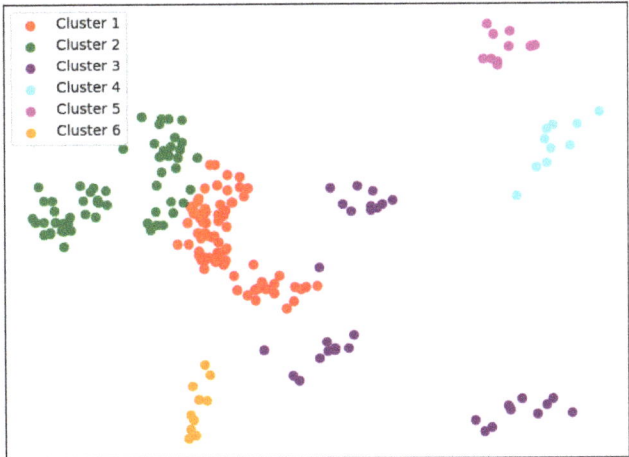

Figure 17. Clustering results of SKM about Wasserstein distance when K = 6.

We can see from Tables 5 and 6 that the SKM algorithm is inferior to the K-means and GMM method on the two indicators of DBI and DI. From the definitions of DBI and DI, we speculate that this can be caused by the local statistical methods. During the process of selecting a local point cloud, we use the K-nearest neighbor strategy. It can better reflect the statistical density characteristics of a local point cloud, but on the other hand, it may also cause the selected area to be non-convex, resulting in a diffrent distribution in parameter space from the original space. However, the SC indicator of both metrics for the SKM algorithm performs better than that in K-means and GMM. We attribute this to the introduction of non-Euclidean metrics, which achieve a more granular comparison. It can also be seen from the degree of dispersion of the statistical indicators that the two indicators in this section fluctuate considerably, as the selection of the initial cluster center will greatly affect the final clustering, which is a manifestation of the high sensitivity of the SKM algorithm. Between the two metric functions of the SKM algorithm, the KL divergence performs better, as it gives more stable results and better interpretability, while the Wasserstein distance has greatly varied indicators and gives clusters of high similarities.

Table 5. SKM clustering results with KL divergence.

K	Number of Cases	Samples in Different Clusters	DBI	DI	SC
4	17	110 60 20 10	2.51	0.04	0.65
4	8	103 67 20 10	2.77	0.04	0.63
4	5	100 60 20 20	3.23	0.03	0.64
5	12	104 46 20 20 10	2.87	0.04	0.66
5	11	109 38 23 20 10	3.40	0.03	0.65
5	4	58 57 55 20 10	3.10	0.04	0.67
5	3	87 52 31 20 10	3.08	0.05	0.66
6	13	109 39 22 10 10 10	3.12	0.04	0.66
6	10	84 43 25 20 18 10	4.55	0.02	0.64
6	7	68 41 39 22 20 10	3.54	0.03	0.69

Table 6. SKM clustering results with Wasserstein distance.

K	Number of Cases	Samples in Different Clusters	DBI	DI	SC
4	21	119 61 10 10	2.03	0.07	0.54
4	5	140 40 10 10	1.78	0.11	0.58
4	4	101 60 20 19	2.66	0.02	0.54
5	15	101 54 20 19 6	2.34	0.02	0.56
5	8	84 59 37 10 10	2.68	0.04	0.54
5	7	73 67 30 20 10	3.11	0.03	0.55
6	17	101 54 19 10 10 6	2.17	0.04	0.58
6	7	84 59 37 10 9 1	2.37	0.02	0.56
6	6	92 63 19 10 10 6	2.66	0.05	0.56

In terms of clustering results, the clusters given by the SKM algorithm are generally similar to the results of K-means and general cases of GMM, and they actually have better discrimination on the universities of science and technology than the other case of GMM, but there are still some interesting phenomena. After verification and comparison, it can be seen that using several Riemann metrics defined on symmetric positive definite manifolds, the obtained clustering effect is not as good as KL divergence. Hence, we choose KL divergence as the distance function for clustering. In the results of KL divergence, the clustering results are relatively more stable and have no university spans from one cluster to another. The biggest difference is that the KL divergence does not give a division among comprehensive universities; instead, it further divides universities of science and engineering, resulting in the cluster of Peking University, Beihang University and Northwestern Polytechnical University as well as Harbin Institute of Technology, Southeast University, Xi'an Jiaotong University. As for Wasserstein distance, it has unsatifactory indicators and results. Especially when $K = 6$, the Wasserstein metric produce clusters with a very small number of samples, which indicates that it cannot distinguish the mainfolds on this problem very well. It is worth noting that the dimension of the data on which the SKM algorithm is applied is 32 compared to six for the traditional K-means and GMM algorithms. In this case, the SKM algorithm still obtains remarkable clustering results, which proves the potential of the SKM algorithm in terms of processing large amounts of high-dimensional data.

To further assess the three algorithms quantitatively, we apply them on a UCI ML dataset [35] and compare the accuracies. We choose to use the 'Steel Plates Faults Data Set' provided by Semeion from the Research Center of Sciences of Communication, Via Sersale 117, 00128, Rome, Italy. Every sample in the dataset consists of 27 features, and the task is to classify whether a sample has any of the seven faults. We choose this dataset because it has similar feature dimensions with our origin problem and it provides various indicators to classify, which can better assess the different clustering algorithms. The results are produced under the same condition as the simulation set above, including data pre-processing methods and cluster parameters. The classification accuracies of different algorithms on the seven faults are shown in Table 7.

Table 7. Classification Accuracies on the Fault Dataset.

Fault Type	K-Means	GMM	SKM (KL Div.)	SKM (Wass)
Pastry	0.7208	0.7398	0.7450	0.9181
Z-Scratch	0.7084	0.7244	0.7400	0.9016
K-Scatch	0.9366	0.9521	0.9547	0.7991
Stains	0.7609	0.7810	0.7979	0.9624
Dirtiness	0.7697	0.7897	0.7970	0.9711
Bumps	0.5971	0.6131	0.6318	0.7924
Other Faults	0.6033	0.6121	0.6479	0.6528
Ave. Accu.	0.7281	0.7433	0.7592	0.8568

We can see that the SKM algorithm is greatly advantageous over the K-means and the GMM algorithm on accuracy scores. In comparison, the dataset provider's model has an average accuracy of 0.77 on this dataset [36]. In addition, in terms of cluster indicators, we can see from Table 8 that the SKM algorithm has better performance on the SC score, but it does not perform well on the DBI score, which is basically consistent with the results on the Chinese University dataset. The result exactly reveals the great potential of the SKM algorithm on the application of many other fields. It could be a great replacement of traditional Euclidean-based cluster methods in a certain problem.

Table 8. DBI, DI and SC Indicators on the Fault Dataset.

Indicator	K-Means	GMM	SKM (KL Div.)	SKM (Wass)
DBI	1.53	1.43	2.99	2.67
DI	0.01	0.02	0.01	0.02
SC	0.36	0.37	0.54	0.49

6. Conclusions and Future Work

In this paper, we propose a university academic evaluation method based on statistical manifold combined with the K-means algorithm, which quantifies the academic achievement indicators of universities into point clouds and performs clustering on Euclidean space and the family of multivariate normal distributions manifolds, respectively. The simulation results show that in terms of DBI and DI, the SKM algorithm is inferior to the method of direct PCA weight reduction and K-means clustering in Euclidean space. On the SC indicator, the SKM algorithm is significantly better than the traditional K-means method in both difference functions. The GMM has a slightly better performance than the K-means, but it still lacks necessary discrimination to tell apart the universites of similar backgrounds. This shows that the SKM algorithm can extract features that are hard to capture in Euclidean space, thus achieving more fine-grained feature recognition and clustering. The great ability is attributed to the process of mapping original data to the local statistics, which forms the parameter distribution on statistical manifold.

By analyzing the cluster results, we can also demonstrate that most of the universities evaluated have very similar academic levels, and their main differences come from their developing backgrounds. This conclusion explains the reason why university ratings could vary greatly in different leaderboards, and it indicates that different evaluation perspectives may be taken for different universites. Clustering would be useful when seperating different types of universities, and this paper provides a promising way.

In the future, we need to strictly construct the theoretical model of the point cloud and explain the principle of local statistics according to the theory of probability theory. On this basis, we try to propose other local statistical methods and analyze their effectiveness. Furthermore, this paper discusses the case where KL divergence and Wasserstein distance are used as difference functions, and other distance functions can be discussed as difference functions later, which may lead to better clustering algorithms. Finally, the explicit expression of the geometric mean of the Wasserstein distance adopted in this paper is still an unsolved problem, and we replace its geometric mean with the arithmetic mean. If this problem is solved, it is possible that the simulation results of the algorithm will be more accurate.

Author Contributions: Conceptualization, D.Y. and H.S.; Data curation, Y.P. and Z.N.; Formal analysis, D.Y., X.Z. and Z.N.; Investigation, H.S.; Methodology, D.Y.; Project administration, H.S.; Software, X.Z. and Y.P.; Supervision, Z.N.; Visualization, X.Z. and Y.P.; Writing—original draft, D.Y. and Y.P.; Writing—review & editing, H.S. All authors have read and agreed to the published version of the manuscript.

Funding: This research was funded by National Key Research and Development Plan of China, grant number 2019YFB1406303; National Natural Science Fundation of China, grant number 61370137.

Institutional Review Board Statement: Not applicable.

Informed Consent Statement: Not applicable.

Data Availability Statement: Restrictions apply to the availability of these data. Data was obtained from CNKI and are available at https://usad.cnki.net/, accessed on 12 June 2022 with the permission of CNKI.

Conflicts of Interest: The authors declare no conflict of interest.

References

1. Mingers, J.; Leydesdorff, L. A Review of Theory and Practice in Scientometrics. *Eur. J. Oper. Res.* **2015**, *246*, 1–19. [CrossRef]
2. Xia, M.; Wang, Q. Research on the Evaluating Index System of University Knowledge Creation Capability. *Sci. Sci. Technol. Manag.* **2010**, *31*, 156–161.
3. Zhang, Y. Empirical Study on the Network Indexes of Topping University in China. *Inf. Sci.* **2008**, *26*, 604–611.
4. Liu, J.; Liu, Y.; Zeng, C. Research on University Innovation Indicators with the Factor Analysis. *Sci. Sci. Technol. Manag.* **2007**, *28*, 111–114.
5. Chen, H.; Lin, C.; Xia, C. Construction of Performance Evaluation System for Sci-Tech Achievements Transformation in High-level Engineering Colleges Based on PCA and Comprehensive Index Method. *Sci. Technol. Manag. Res.* **2019**, *39*, 48–54.
6. Zhang, J.; Wang, G.; Wu, J. Research on Evaluation of Scientific and Technological Innovation Ability of Universities Based on Entropy Weight-DEMATEL in Jiangsu. *Sci. Technol. Manag. Res.* **2018**, *38*, 47–54.
7. Li, H.; Liu, A. Study on Evaluation Index System of Transformation of Scientific and Technological Achievements in CAS. *Sci. Technol. Dev.* **2017**, *13*, 773–778.
8. Faraki, M.; Harandi, M.T.; Porikli, F. More about VLAD: A leap from Euclidean to Riemannian manifolds. In Proceedings of the IEEE Conference on Computer Vision and Pattern Recognition, Boston, MA, USA, 7–12 June 2015.
9. Kastaniotis, D.; Theodorakopoulos, I.; Economou, G.; Fotopoulos, S. Gait based recognition via fusing information from Euclidean and Riemannian manifolds. *Pattern Recognit. Lett.* **2016**, *84*, 245–251. [CrossRef]
10. Loohach, R.; Garg, K. Effect of Distance Functions on Simple K-means Clustering Algorithm. *Int. J. Comput. Appl.* **2012**, *49*, 7–9. [CrossRef]

11. Li, Y.; Wong, K. Riemannian Distances for Signal Classification by Power Spectral Density. *IEEE J. Sel. Top. Signal Process.* **2013**, *7*, 655–669. [CrossRef]
12. Zhang, S.; Cao, Y.; Li, W.; Yan, F.; Luo, Y.; Sun, H. A New Riemannian Structure in SPD(n). In Proceedings of the 2019 IEEE International Conference on Signal, Information and Data Processing (ICSIDP), Chongqing, China, 11–13 December 2019.
13. Malag, L.; Montrucchio, L.; Pistone, G. Wasserstein Riemannian Geometry of Gaussian densities. *Inf. Geom.* **2018**, *1*, 137–179. [CrossRef]
14. Do Carmo, M.P. *Riemannian Geometry*; Springer: Boston, MA, USA, 1992.
15. Amari, S.I. *Information Geometry and Its Applications*; Springer: Tokyo, Japan, 2016.
16. Sun, H.; Song, Y. A Clustering Algorithm Based on Statistical Manifold. *Trans. Beijing Inst. Technol.* **2021**, *41*, 226–230.
17. He, X.; Cai, D.; Shao, Y.; Bao, H.; Han, J. Laplacian Regularized Gaussian Mixture Model for Data Clustering. *IEEE Trans. Knowl. Data Eng.* **2011**, *23*, 1406–1418. [CrossRef]
18. Zhu, Y.; Ting, K.M.; Carman, M.J. Density-Ratio Based Clustering for Discovering Clusters with Varying Densities. *Pattern Recognit.* **2016**, *60*, 983–997. [CrossRef]
19. Rodriguez, A.; Laio, A. Clustering by Fast Search and Find of Density Peaks. *Science* **2014**, *344*, 1492–1496. [CrossRef] [PubMed]
20. Aryal, A.M.; Wang, S. Discovery of Patterns in Spatio-Temporal Data Using Clustering Techniques. In Proceedings of the 2017 2nd International Conference on Image, Vision and Computing (ICIVC), Chengdu, China, 2–4 June 2017; pp. 990–995.
21. Aggarwal, C.C.; Reddy, C.K. *Data Clustering: Algorithms and Applications*; Chapman & Hall/CRC Data Mining and Knowledge Discovery Series; Chapman & Hall/CRC: London, UK, 2014.
22. Clarivate Analytics. Web of Science. 1997. Available online: http://www.webofscience.com/ (accessed on 1 November 2021).
23. Nanjing University. Chinese Social Sciences Citation Index. 2000. Available online: http://cssci.nju.edu.cn/ (accessed on 5 November 2021).
24. Tongfang Co., Ltd. China National Knowledge Infrastructure. 1999. Available online: https://www.cnki.net/ (accessed on 3 November 2021).
25. Singh, A.K.; Mittal, S.; Malhotra, P.; Srivastava, Y.V. Clustering Evaluation by Davies-Bouldin Index(DBI) in Cereal data using K-Means. In Proceedings of the 2020 Fourth International Conference on Computing Methodologies and Communication (ICCMC), Erode, India, 11–13 March 2020; pp. 306–310.
26. Gupta, T.; Panda, S.P. Clustering Validation of CLARA and K-Means Using Silhouette & DUNN Measures on Iris Dataset. In Proceedings of the 2019 International Conference on Machine Learning, Big Data, Cloud and Parallel Computing (COMITCon), Faridabad, India, 14–16 February 2019; pp. 10–13.
27. Jain, A.K. Data clustering: 50 years beyond K-means. *Pattern Recognit. Lett.* **2010**, *31*, 651–666. [CrossRef]
28. Khan, S.S.; Ahmad, A. Cluster center initialization algorithm for K-means clustering. *Pattern Recognit. Lett.* **2004**, *25*, 1293–1302. [CrossRef]
29. Ye, Y.; Huang, J.Z.; Chen, X.; Zhou, S.; Williams, G.; Xu, X. Neighborhood Density Method for Selecting Initial Cluster Centers in K-Means Clustering. In *Advances in Knowledge Discovery and Data Mining*; Springer: Berlin/Heidelberg, Germany, 2006.
30. Tibshirani, R.; Walther, G.; Hastie, T. Estimating the Number of Clusters in a Data Set via the Gap Statistic. *J. R. Stat. Soc. Ser. B (Stat. Methodol.)* **2001**, *63*, 411–423. [CrossRef]
31. Tzortzis, G.; Likas, A. The global kernel k-means clustering algorithm. In Proceedings of the 2008 IEEE International Joint Conference on Neural Networks, Hong Kong, China, 1–8 June 2008.
32. Zhang, R.; Rudnicky, A.I. A large scale clustering scheme for kernel K-Means. In Proceedings of the 2002 International Conference on Pattern Recognition, Quebec City, QC, Canada, 11–15 August 2002.
33. Khan, M.H.; Farid, M.S.; Grzegorzek, M. A generic codebook based approach for gait recognition. *Multimed. Tools Appl.* **2019**, *78*, 35689–35712. [CrossRef]
34. Rao, C.R. Information and the Accuracy Attainable in the Estimation of Statistical Parameters. *Reson. J. Sci. Educ.* **1945**, *20*, 78–90.
35. Dua, D.; Graff, C. *UCI Machine Learning Repository*; University of California, School of Information and Computer Science: Irvine, CA, USA, 2019. Available online: http://archive.ics.uci.edu/ml (accessed on 1 July 2022).
36. Buscema, M.; Terzi, S.; Tastle, W. A new meta-classifier. In Proceedings of the Annual Meeting of the North American Fuzzy Information Processing Society, Toronto, ON, Canada, 12–14 July 2010; pp. 1–7.

Article

Some Information Measures Properties of the GOS-Concomitants from the FGM Family

Florentina Suter [1,2,*], Ioana Cernat [1] and Mihai Drăgan [1]

[1] Faculty of Mathematics and Computer Science, University of Bucharest, Academiei 14, 010014 Bucharest, Romania
[2] "Gheorghe Mihoc-Caius Iacob" Institute of Mathematical Statistics and Applied Mathematics of Romanian Academy, Calea 13 Septembrie, 13, 050711 Bucharest, Romania
* Correspondence: florentina.suter@g.unibuc.ro

Abstract: In this paper we recall, extend and compute some information measures for the concomitants of the generalized order statistics (GOS) from the Farlie–Gumbel–Morgenstern (FGM) family. We focus on two types of information measures: some related to Shannon entropy, and some related to Tsallis entropy. Among the information measures considered are residual and past entropies which are important in a reliability context.

Keywords: concomitants; GOS; FGM family; Shannon entropy; Tsallis entropy; Awad entropy; residual entropy; past entropy; Fisher–Tsallis information number; Tsallis divergence

Citation: Suter, F.; Cernat, I.; Drăgan, M. Some Information Measures Properties of the GOS-Concomitants from the FGM Family. *Entropy* **2022**, *24*, 1361. https://doi.org/10.3390/e24101361

Academic Editors: Karagrigoriou Alexandros, Makrides Andreas, Yong Deng and Takuya Yamano

Received: 19 July 2022
Accepted: 21 September 2022
Published: 26 September 2022

Publisher's Note: MDPI stays neutral with regard to jurisdictional claims in published maps and institutional affiliations.

Copyright: © 2022 by the authors. Licensee MDPI, Basel, Switzerland. This article is an open access article distributed under the terms and conditions of the Creative Commons Attribution (CC BY) license (https://creativecommons.org/licenses/by/4.0/).

1. Introduction

The notion of concomitants or induced order statistics arose in the early 1970s in the works of David [1] and Bhattacharya [2]. Briefly, when there is a sample from a bivariate distribution ordered by the first variate, the second variate paired with the r-th first variate is called the concomitant of the r-th-order statistic. Concomitants are important in situations in which are implied two characteristics and measuring one of them can influence the other. Therefore, they have applications in many fields such as selection procedures, inference problems, double sampling plans and systems reliability. For example, in [3,4] are studied from a reliability point of view complex systems with components which have two sub-components that performs different tasks, and in [5], the distribution theory of lifetimes of two component systems is discussed. In studies regarding the concomitants there are two elements that have to be mentioned: the kind of dependence between first and second variate, and the kind of order for the first variate. The majority of studies are based on the hypothesis of simple order statistics, but there are also studies that assume different kinds of orders such as as record values order or generalized order statistics.

Generalized order statistics (GOS) was introduced by Kamps [6] and it is a unifying concept for various types of order statistics such as simple order statistics, record values, sequential order statistics.

In this paper, we focus on the concomitants of GOS and with the dependence structure between the first variate and the second variate given by the Fairlie–Gumbel–Morgenstern (FGM) family. This family is a flexible family of bivariate distributions used as a modeling tool for bivariate data in many fields [7], one such field being Reliability, see [3–5]. The FGM family has a simple analytical form, but it can describe only relatively weak dependence because the correlation coefficient between the two components cannot exceed 1/3. To prevent this limitation, extensions of FGM family have been proposed, for example, iterative FGM distributions or Huang–Kotz FGM distributions [8–12]. The results obtained in our paper will be generalized for these extensions of FGM family in a future work.

For the concomitants mentioned above, we recall and determine properties that some information measures have. The information measures that we deal with are in two categories, information measures related to Shannon entropy and information measures related to Tsallis entropy.

Since it was introduced in physics and adapted to information theory by Shannon in 1948, the concept of entropy has become more and more important in fields such as information theory, code theory, probability and statistics, reliability.

In probability and statistics, entropy measures the uncertainty associated to a random variable. Taking as a starting point Shannon entropy, a series of entropies have been defined as a generalization of it. For the concomitants of GOS from the FGM family, we will look at Shannon-derived and Tsallis-derived entropies, and our main aim is to determine Awad-type extensions for all the considered entropies, because Awad entropies do not have several drawbacks that Shannon entropy, for example, has: different systems with the same entropy, possible negative values for continuous distributions, different results in discrete and continuous case of linear random variable transformation, etc.

Furthermore, for the concomitants of GOS from FGM, we will determine not only entropies, but also other information measures such as Tsallis divergence and shift-invariant Fisher–Tsallis information number.

In the following sections, we recall some definitions and properties of GOS and their concomitants, in particular, when the bivariate distribution is in the FGM family. Then, we will discuss Shannon-type entropies, Tsallis-type entropies, Fisher information and divergences for concomitants of GOS from the FGM family. For these concomitants, in the last section, we will introduce new extensions and results on information measures.

2. Generalized Order Statistics and Their Concomitants for the FGM Family

2.1. Generalized Order Statistics

The concept of GOS was introduced by Kamps [6], in 1995, who proposed an unifying pattern of various order statistics:

Definition 1. *The random variables $X(1, n, \tilde{m}, k), \ldots, X(n, n, \tilde{m}, k)$ are called GOS based on distribution function F with density function f, if their joint density function is given by:*

$$f(x_1, \ldots, x_n) = k \left(\prod_{j=1}^{n-1} \gamma_j \right) \left(\prod_{i=1}^{n-1} (1 - F(x_i))^{m_i} f(x_i) \right) (1 - F(x_n))^{k-1} f(x_n) \quad (1)$$

on the cone $F^{-1}(0) < x_1 \leq x_2 \cdots \leq x_n < F^{-1}(1)$ of $\mathbb{R}^n$ with parameters $n \in \mathbb{N}, n \geq 2, k > 0$, $\tilde{m} = (m_1, \ldots, m_{n-1}), \gamma_r = k + n - r + \sum_{j=r}^{n-1} m_j > 0$, for all $r \in \{1, 2, \ldots, n-1\}$.

Some particular cases of GOS are:
- Simple order statistics with $m_1 = m_2 = \cdots = m_{n-1} = 0$ and $k = 1$;
- Common record values with $m_1 = m_2 = \cdots = m_{n-1} = -1$ and $k = 1$;
- Sequential order statistics with $\gamma_i = (n - i + 1)\alpha_i, \alpha_1, \alpha_2, \ldots, \alpha_n > 0$;
- Progressive type II censored order statistics based on censoring scheme $(R_1, R_2, \ldots, R_n)$ with $\gamma_n = k = R_n + 1, \gamma_r = n - r + 1 - \sum_{i=r}^{n} R_i, 1 \leq r \leq n$ and $m_r = R_r, 1 \leq r \leq n$, [13,14].

As a result of the complex formula of the joint density, finding the marginal distributions of (1) is a difficult task, but in some particular cases, marginal densities can be found. In [6], the marginal densities are determined for $m_1 = m_2 = \ldots m_{n-1} = m$, and in [15] for $\gamma_i \neq \gamma_j, 1 \leq i \neq j \leq n$. In the following, we will suppose that $m_1 = m_2 = \ldots m_{n-1} = m$, i.e., we are in the m-GOS case where simple order statistics, record values and progressive type II censored order statistics with equi-balanced censoring scheme are included. Now, the density (1) becomes:

$$f(x_1, \ldots, x_n) = k \left(\prod_{j=1}^{n-1} \gamma_j \right) \left(\prod_{i=1}^{n-1} (1 - F(x_i))^m f(x_i) \right) (1 - F(x_n))^{k-1} f(x_n) \quad (2)$$

on the cone $F^{-1}(0) < x_1 \leq x_2 \cdots \leq x_n < F^{-1}(1)$ of $\mathbb{R}^n$ with parameters $n \in \mathbb{N}, n \geq 2$, $k > 0, m, \gamma_r = k + (n-r)(m+1) > 0$, for all $r \in \{1, 2, \ldots, n-1\}$.

The marginal density function of the r-th GOS, $r = 1, 2, \ldots, n$, in this case, is given by [6]:
$$f_r(x) = \frac{c_{r-1}}{(r-1)!}(1-F(x))^{\gamma_r - 1} f(x) g_m^{r-1}(F(x)) \qquad (3)$$
where $c_{r-1} = \prod_{j=1}^{r} \gamma_j$ and for $x \in [0, 1)$:
$$g_m(x) = \begin{cases} \frac{1}{m+1}(1 - (1-x)^{m+1}), & m \neq -1 \\ \log\left(\frac{1}{1-x}\right) & m = -1. \end{cases}$$

Remark 1. *For $m = 0$ and $k = 1$, i.e., the case of simple order statistics, we have $\gamma_r = n - r + 1$, $c_{r-1} = \gamma_1 \gamma_2 \ldots \gamma_r = n(n-1)\ldots(n-r+1)$, $g_0(F(x)) = F(x)$, and (3) becomes the well-known marginal density of the r-th-order statistic.*

For $m = -1$ and $k = 1$, i.e., the case of record values, (3) becomes
$$f_r(x) = \frac{1}{(r-1)!} f(x)[-\ln(1-F(x))]^{n-1}, \qquad (4)$$

the marginal density of the r-th record value.

For progressive type II censored order statistics with equi-balanced censoring scheme, the form of the marginal density is the same as the form of (3), with $m = R$, R being the removal number.

2.2. Concomitants

The term concomitant was introduced by David (1973) [1] and has the following definition:

Definition 2. *Let $(X_1, Y_1), (X_2, Y_2), \ldots, (X_n, Y_n)$ be iid bivariate random variables with cumulative distribution function $F(x, y)$. Then, the Y variate associated to the r-th-order statistic of X-s, $X_{(r:n)}$, denoted by $Y_{[r:n]}$, is the concomitant of $X_{(r:n)}$.*

A natural use of concomitants is in selection procedures when k individuals are chosen on the basis of their X-values. Then, the corresponding Y-values represent performance on an associated characteristics. In Reliability Theory, the role of the concomitants is emphasized in [3–5].

2.3. Concomitants of FGM Family

The FGM bivariate distribution family has a flexible form and it was studied by Farlie [16], Gumbel [17], Morgenstern [18], and Johnson and Kotz [19].

Definition 3. *Let X and Y be two random variables with distribution functions F_X and F_Y, respectively. Additionally, let α be a real number. Then, the FGM family has the distribution function:*
$$F_{X,Y}(x,y) = F_X(x)F_Y(y)[1 + \alpha(1 - F_X(x))(1 - F_Y(y))]. \qquad (5)$$

The corresponding probability density function (pdf) of (5) is:
$$f_{X,Y}(x,y) = f_X(x)f_Y(y)[1 + \alpha(1 - F_X(x))(1 - F_Y(y))], \qquad (6)$$
where $f_X(x) f_Y(y)$ are the marginals of $f_{X,Y}(x,y)$.

The parameter $\alpha \in [-1, 1]$ is known as the association parameter and the two random variables X and Y are independent when $\alpha = 0$. For $\alpha \neq 0$, there is a dependence between the two variables, characterized by the FGM-copula whose properties were studied in [20].

Concomitants of FGM family, related to GOS, started to come into notice with the work of Beg and Ahsanullah in 2008 [21] where the density $g_{[r,n,m,k]}$ of the concomitant of the r-th GOS is derived:

$$g_{[r,n,m,k]}(y) = f_Y(y) + \alpha(2F_Y(y) - 1)f_Y(y)C^*(r,n,m,k), \qquad (7)$$

where

$$C^*(r,n,m,k) = 1 - 2\frac{c_{r-1}}{(\gamma_1 + 1)(\gamma_2 + 1)\ldots(\gamma_r + 1)}$$

is a constant.

Remark 2. If $m = 0, k = 1$, then $C^*(r,n,0,1) = -(n - 2r + 1)/(n + 1)$ and

$$g_{[r,n,0,1]}(y) = f_Y(y) - \alpha\frac{n - 2r + 1}{n + 1}(2F_Y(y) - 1)f_Y(y) \qquad (8)$$

is the density of the concomitant of r-th-order statistic from the FGM family.
If $m = -1, k = 1$, then $C^*(r,n,-1,1) = 1 - 2^{1-r}$ and

$$g_{[r,n,-1,1]}(y) = f_Y(y) - \alpha(2^{1-r} - 1)(2F_Y(y) - 1)f_Y(y). \qquad (9)$$

If we are in the case of progressive type II censoring order statistics with equi-balanced censoring scheme, the density of the concomitant of r-th-order statistic from the FGM family is (7) with $m = R$, the removal number.

The cumulative distribution function and the survival function of the concomitant of r-th-order statistic can also be computed:

$$G_{[r,n,m,k]}(y) = f_Y(y) + \alpha(1 - F_Y(y))f_Y(y)C^*(r,n,m,k), \qquad (10)$$

$$\overline{G}_{[r,n,m,k]}(y) = 1 - f_Y(y) - \alpha(1 - F_Y(y))f_Y(y)C^*(r,n,m,k). \qquad (11)$$

In the following, in order to make it easier to read computations, we make the notations: $Y^*_{[r]} = Y_{[r,n,m,k]}, g_{[r]} = g_{[r,n,m,k]}, G_{[r]} = G_{[r,n,m,k]}, \bar{G}_{[r]} = \bar{G}_{[r,n,m,k]}, C^*_r = C^*(r,n,m,k)$.

3. Information Measures for the Concomitants from the FGM Family, Existing Results

In this section, we will recall some definitions and results for the information measures of the concomitants of GOS from the FGM family.

3.1. Shannon and Shannon-Related Entropies

Shannon entropy was introduced by Shannon in 1948 [22], it has multiple applications and it can be defined as:

$$H^S(X) = -E[\log f(X)] \qquad (12)$$

Information measures for concomitants derived from the FGM family have been studied by Tahmasebi and Behboodian: in [23] for concomitants of order statistics, and in [24] for concomitants of GOS. Using (7), they proved that for the Shannon entropy of $Y_{[r]}$, the concomitant of the r-th generalized order statistics is:

$$H^S(Y^*_{[r]}) = W(r,\alpha,n,m,k) + H^S(Y)(1 - \alpha C^*_r) - 2\alpha C^*_r \phi_f(u), \qquad (13)$$

where

$$W(r,\alpha,n,m,k) = \frac{1}{4\alpha C^*_r}\{(1 - C^*_r\alpha)^2 \log(1 - C^*_r\alpha) - (1 + C^*_r\alpha)^2 \log(1 + C^*_r\alpha)\} + \frac{1}{2}, \qquad (14)$$

and

$$\phi_f(u) = \int_0^1 \log f_Y(F_Y^{-1}(u))du. \qquad (15)$$

Remark 3. In [23] are analyzed the properties of (13) in the particular case when $m = 0$ and $k = 1$, i.e., when the GOS reduces to the simple order statistics, and therefore, the entropy from (13) in this case is the Shannon entropy of the concomitant of r-th-order statistic:

$$H^S(Y_{[r]}) = W(r, \alpha, n, 0, 1) + H^S(Y)\left(1 + \alpha \frac{n - 2r + 1}{n + 1}\right) + 2\alpha \frac{n - 2r + 1}{n + 1} \phi_f(u) \quad (16)$$

In [24], Shannon entropy for record values is also mentioned:

$$H^S(R_{[r]}) = W(r, \alpha, n, -1, 1) + H^S(Y)(1 + \alpha(2^{1-r} - 1)) + 2\alpha(2^{1-r} - 1)\phi_f(u). \quad (17)$$

If we are in the case of progressive type II censoring order statistics with an equi-balanced censoring scheme, the Shannon entropy of the concomitant of r-th-order statistic from the FGM family is (13) with $m = R$, the removal number.

Awad, in 1987, ref. [25] noticed that Shannon entropy, in the continuous case, does not fulfill the condition that the entropy is preserved under the linear transformation and proposed the following entropy known also in the literature as Sup-entropy:

$$H^{SA}(X) = -E\left[\log \frac{f(X)}{\delta}\right] \quad (18)$$

where $\delta = \sup\{f(x) | x \in \mathbb{R}\}$. We will call this entropy **Shannon–Awad entropy**.

Residual and past Shannon entropies were defined in the context of reliability, being important in measuring the amount of information that a residual life or a past life of a unit has. In the following, the random variable X with pdf f, cdf F, and survival function $\bar{F}$, is considered positive and it has the meaning of a lifetime of a unit.

Residual entropy is introduced and its properties are analyzed in the works of Ebrahimi [26] and Ebrahimi and Pellerey [27]. Residual entropy is based on the idea of measuring the expected uncertainty contained in the conditional density of $X - t$ given $X > t$ [27]:

$$H^S(X; t) = -E\left[\log \frac{f(X)}{\bar{F}(t)} \middle| X > t\right]. \quad (19)$$

In terms of failure rate, the residual entropy can be written as:

$$H^S(X; t) = 1 - E[\log \lambda_F(X) | X > t],$$

where $\lambda_F(\cdot) = f(\cdot)/\bar{F}(\cdot)$ is the failure rate function.

Similar to the definition of the residual entropy, DiCrescenzo and Longobardi [28] introduced past entropy as a dual to the residual entropy. Past entropy measures the uncertainty about past life of a failed unit:

$$\bar{H}^S(X; t) = -E\left[\log \frac{f(X)}{F(t)} \middle| X < t\right]. \quad (20)$$

In terms of reversed failure rate, past entropy can be written as:

$$\bar{H}^S(X; t) = 1 - E[\log \tau_F(X) | X < t],$$

where $\tau_F(\cdot) = f(\cdot)/F(\cdot)$ is the reversed failure rate function.

Residual and past entropies for concomitants of GOS from the FGM family were determined by Mohie EL-Din et al. in [29]. They considered also concomitants of other types of GOS, but the form of the entropies is similar. The residual entropy of the r-th concomitant of GOS from the FGM family is [29]:

$$H^S(Y^*_{[r]};t) = \log \overline{G}_{[r]}(t) - \frac{1}{\overline{G}_{[r]}(t)} \{(1 - \alpha C^*_r)[\overline{F}_Y(t)(\log \overline{F}_Y(t) - H^S(Y;t))] + \quad (21)$$
$$+ 2\alpha C^*_r \phi_f(t) + K_1(r,t,\alpha,n,m,k)\},$$

where

$$K_1(r,t,\alpha,n,m,k) = \frac{1}{2\alpha C^*_r} \left\{ \frac{-1}{4}[(1+\alpha C^*_r)^2 - (1+\alpha C^*_r(2F_Y(t)-1))^2] + \quad (22) \right.$$
$$\left. + \frac{1}{2}[(1+\alpha C^*_r)^2 \log(1+\alpha C^*_r) - (1+\alpha C^*_r(2F_Y(t)-1))^2 \log(1+\alpha C^*_r(2F_Y(t)-1))]\right\},$$

and

$$\phi_f(t) = \int_t^\infty F_Y(y) f_Y(y) \log f_Y(y) dy. \quad (23)$$

We notice that for $t = 0$, the residual entropy (21) becomes the entropy (13).

Remark 4. For $m = 0$ and $k = 1$, we obtain residual Shannon entropy for the concomitant of r-th-order statistic:

$$H^S(Y_{[r]};t) = \log \overline{G}_{[r]}(t) - \frac{1}{\overline{G}_{[r]}(t)} \left\{ \left(1 - \alpha \frac{n-2r+1}{n+1}\right)[\overline{F}_Y(t)(\log \overline{F}_Y(t) - H^S(Y;t))] - \quad (24) \right.$$
$$\left. - 2\alpha \frac{n-2r+1}{n+1} \phi_f(t) + K_1(r,t,\alpha,n,0,1)\right\}.$$

For $m = -1$ and $k = 1$, we obtain residual Shannon entropy for the concomitant of r-th record value:

$$H^S(R_{[r]};t) = \log \overline{G}_{[r]}(t) - \frac{1}{\overline{G}_{[r]}(t)} \{(1 - \alpha(2^{1-r}-1))[\overline{F}_Y(t)(\log \overline{F}_Y(t) - H^S(Y;t))] - \quad (25)$$
$$- 2\alpha(2^{1-r}-1)\phi_f(t) + K_1(r,t,\alpha,n,-1,1)\}.$$

In the case of progressive type II censoring order statistics with equi-balanced censoring scheme, the residual Shannon entropy of the concomitant of r-th-order statistic from the FGM family is (21) with $m = R$, the removal number.

In a similar way, the past entropy for the concomitant of the r-th GOS from the FGM family is defined as [29]:

$$\overline{H}^S(Y^*_{[r]};t) = \log G_{[r]}(t) - \frac{1}{G_{[r]}(t)} \{(1 - \alpha C^*_r)[F_Y(t)(\log F_Y(t) - \overline{H}^S(Y;t))] + \quad (26)$$
$$+ 2\alpha C^*_r \overline{\phi}_f(t) + K_2(r,t,\alpha,n,m,k)\},$$

where

$$K_2(r,t,\alpha,n,m,k) = \frac{1}{2\alpha C^*_r} \left\{ \frac{-1}{4}[(1+\alpha C^*_r(2F_Y(t)-1))^2 - (1-\alpha C^*_r)^2] + \quad (27) \right.$$
$$\left. + \frac{1}{2}[(1+\alpha C^*_r(2F_Y(t)-1))^2 \log(1+\alpha C^*_r(2F_Y(t)-1)) - (1-\alpha C^*_r)^2 \log(1-\alpha C^*_r)]\right\},$$

and

$$\overline{\phi}_f(t) = \int_0^t F_Y(y) f_Y(y) \log f_Y(y) dy. \quad (28)$$

We notice that for $t \to \infty$, the past entropy (26) becomes the entropy (13).

3.2. Tsallis and Tsallis-Related Entropies

For the first time, Tsallis entropy was introduced and used in the context of Cybernetics Theory by Harvda and Charvat [30], but it has become well known since its definition as a generalization of Boltzmann–Gibbs statistics, in the context of thermodynamics, by Tsallis in 1988 [31]. Being the starting point of the field of non-extensive statistics, Tsallis entropy is a non-additive generalization of the Shannon entropy and for a continuous random variable X with density function f, it can be defined as:

$$H^T(X) = \frac{1}{q-1}\left\{1 - \int_{-\infty}^{+\infty} [f(x)]^q dx\right\} \quad q > 0, \; q \neq 1. \tag{29}$$

When $q \to 1$, Tsallis entropy approaches to Shannon entropy. Tsallis entropy has, in turn, various generalizations, see, for example, [32].

Another important element in non-extensive statistics is $\log_q$ function:

$$\log_q x = \frac{x^{1-q} - 1}{1-q}, \quad x > 0, \; q \neq 1, \tag{30}$$

and Tsallis entropy can be obtained using this function in two ways:

$$H^T(X) = E\left[\log_q \frac{1}{f(X)}\right] = \frac{1}{q-1} E\left[1 - [f(X)]^{q-1}\right].$$

Tsallis entropy has applications in many fields, from statistical mechanics and thermodynamics, to image processing and reliability, sometimes being more suited to measuring uncertainty than classical Shannon entropy [33,34].

In [35], Tsallis entropy was computed and its properties obtained for record values and their concomitants when the bivariate distribution is in the FGM family.

Similar to the Shannon case, we can think about residual and past variants of the Tsallis entropy in the context of reliability. In [36], Nanda and Paul introduced **residual Tsallis entropy** as the 'first kind residual entropy of order β''. In our notation, β is q:

$$H^T(X;t) = \frac{1}{q-1}\left\{1 - \int_t^\infty \left[\frac{f(x)}{\overline{F}(t)}\right]^q dx\right\} = \frac{1}{q-1}\left\{1 - \frac{1}{[\overline{F}(t)]^q}\int_t^\infty [f(x)]^q dx\right\}. \tag{31}$$

In addition to entropy type information measures, there are another two types information measures that can be associated to probability distributions—Fisher measures and divergence measures [37].

3.3. Fisher Information Number

Fisher information measures the amount of information that we can obtain from a sample about an unknown parameter and therefore, it measures the uncertainty included in a unknown characteristic of a population. If the parameter is a location one, then Fisher information is shift-invariant and has the form:

$$I_f = \int_{-\infty}^{+\infty} \left(\frac{\partial}{\partial x}\log f(x)\right)^2 f(x) dx = E\left[\left(\frac{\partial}{\partial x}\log f(x)\right)^2\right]. \tag{32}$$

Shift-invariant Fisher information, also called Fisher Information Number (FIN), was studied in [38]. It has applications in statistical physics where it is also known by the name extreme physical information [39], and it is used in analyzing the evolution of dynamical systems.

For the concomitants of GOS from the FGM family, the Fisher information number was determined in [40].

3.4. Divergence Measures

Divergences are useful tools when a measure of the difference between two probability distributions is needed and therefore, they have applications in various fields, from inference for Markov chains, [41–43] to machine learning [44,45]. One of the best-known divergence is Kullback–Leibler divergence [46,47], which for two continuous random variables Z_1, with probability density f_1, and Z_2 with probability density f_2 is :

$$KLD(Z_1, Z_2) = \int_{-\infty}^{+\infty} f_1(z) \log\left(\frac{f_1(z)}{f_2(z)}\right) dz. \tag{33}$$

Kullback–Leibler divergence for the concomitants of GOS from the FGM family was computed in [24] and the result is distribution-free.

One of the generalizations of Kullback–Leibler divergence measure is Tsallis divergence, which expands Kullback–Leibler divergence in a similar way to that in which Tsallis entropy extends Shannon entropy. There is a very rich literature on Tsallis divergence or Tsallis relative entropy in the case of the discrete distributions, see, for example, [48–50]. Tsallis divergence for continuous distributions does not appear so frequently in the literature, being studied mainly in Machine Learning context, [44,45]. Tsallis divergence for the concomitants will be determined in this paper in the next section.

4. Information Measures for the Concomitants from FGM Family, New Results

In this section, we will provide some generalizations of the existing results on the information measures for the concomitants of GOS from the FGM family, results that are mentioned in previous section. We are interested in Awad-type extensions of the entropies, in residual and past Tsallis entropies, in Tsallis type extension of the FIN, and in Tsallis divergence.

4.1. Shannon and Shannon-Related Entropies

One can easily notice that the relationship between Shannon–Awad entropy (18) and Shannon entropy (12) is:

$$H^{SA}(X) = H^S(X) + \log \delta. \tag{34}$$

In the following, we provide natural extensions of the results obtained in [24], considering Shannon–Awad entropy instead of Shannon entropy. Thus, **Shannon–Awad entropy** of the concomitant of the r-th GOS from the FGM family is:

$$H^{SA}(Y^*_{[r]}) = W(r, \alpha, n, m, k) + (H^{SA}(Y) - \log \delta)(1 - \alpha C^*_r) - 2\alpha C^*_r \phi_f(u) + \log \delta^{[r]}, \tag{35}$$

where $W(r, \alpha, n, m, k)$ and ϕ_f are given by (14) and (15) and

$$\delta = \sup\{f_Y(x) | x > 0\}, \quad \delta^{[r]} = \sup\{g_{[r]}(x) | x > 0\}.$$

Remark 5. *For the simple OS, the r-th OS concomitant from the FGM family, Shannon–Awad entropy is:*

$$H^{SA}(Y_{[r]}) = W(r, \alpha, n, 0, 1) + (H^{SA}(Y) - \log \delta)\left(1 + \alpha \frac{n - 2r + 1}{n + 1}\right) + \tag{36}$$
$$+ 2\alpha \frac{n - 2r + 1}{n + 1} \phi_f(u) + \log \delta_{[r]},$$

with $\delta_{[r]} = \sup\{g_{[r]}(x) | x > 0\}$ and $g_{[r]}$ being here the pdf of the concomitant r-th-order statistics.

For the record values, the r-th record value concomitant from the FGM family, Shannon–Awad entropy is:

$$H^{SA}(R_{[r]}) = W(r,\alpha,n,-1,1) + (H^{SA}(Y) - \log \delta)\left[1 + \alpha(2^{1-r} - 1)\right] + \qquad (37)$$
$$+ 2\alpha(2^{1-r} - 1)\phi_f(u) + \log \delta_{[r]}$$

with $\delta_{[r]} = \sup\{g_{[r]}(x)|x > 0\}$ and $g_{[r]}$ being here the pdf of the concomitant r-th record value.

In the case of progressive type II censoring order statistics with equi-balanced censoring scheme, the Shannon–Awad entropy of the concomitant of r-th-order statistic from the FGM family is (35) with $m = R$, the removal number.

An extension of the above entropies are **residual and past Shannon–Awad entropies**. We define residual Shannon–Awad entropy as:

$$H^{SA}(X;t) = -E\left[\log \frac{f(X)}{\overline{F}(t)\delta^F_{(t,\infty)}} \Big| X > t\right], \qquad (38)$$

where

$$\delta^F_{(t,\infty)} = \frac{1}{\overline{F}(t)} \sup\{f(x)|x \in (t,\infty)\}. \qquad (39)$$

In terms of failure rate, residual Shannon–Awad entropy can be obtained:

$$H^{SA}(X;t) = 1 - E[\log \lambda(X)|X > t] + \log \delta^F_{(t,\infty)}. \qquad (40)$$

We notice that the relationship between residual Shannon entropy and residual Shannon–Awad entropy is similar to (34) and it is:

$$H^{SA}(X;t) = H^S(X;t) + \log \delta^F_{(t,\infty)}. \qquad (41)$$

In a similar way, we can extend past Shannon entropy to past Shannon–Awad entropy:

$$\overline{H}^{SA}(X;t) = -E\left[\log \frac{f(X)}{F(t)\delta^F_{(0,t)}} \Big| X < t\right], \qquad (42)$$

where

$$\delta^F_{(0,t)} = \frac{1}{F(t)} \sup\{f(x)|x \in (0,t)\}. \qquad (43)$$

As a function of reversed failure rate, past Shannon–Awad entropy can be written:

$$\overline{H}^{SA}(X;t) = 1 - E[\log \tau(X)|X < t] + \log \delta^F_{(0,t)}. \qquad (44)$$

We can write also the relationship between past Shannon–Awad entropy and past Shannon entropy:

$$\overline{H}^{SA}(X;t) = \overline{H}^S(X;t) + \log \delta^F_{(0,t)}. \qquad (45)$$

Taking into account the above relationships, (21), and (26), we can obtain the Awad-type extension of the Shannon entropy for the concomitant of r-th GOS from the FGM family, when the concomitant represents the residual life or the past life of a unit.

Theorem 1. *Residual Shannon–Awad entropy for the concomitant of r-th GOS from the FGM family is:*

$$H^{SA}(Y^*_{[r]};t) = \log \overline{G}_{[r]}(t) - \frac{1}{\overline{G}_{[r]}(t)} \{(1 - \alpha C^*_r)[\overline{F}_Y(t)(\log \overline{F}_Y(t) - H^{SA}(Y;t) + \delta^{F_Y}_{t,\infty})] + \qquad (46)$$

$$+ 2\alpha C^*_r \phi_f(t) + K_1(r,t,\alpha,n,m,k)\} + \log \delta^{\overline{G}_{[r]}}_{(t,\infty)}$$

where $K_1(r,t,\alpha,n,m,k)$ and $\phi_f(t)$ are given by (22), (23) respectively, and

$$\delta^{F_Y}_{(t,\infty)} = \frac{1}{\overline{F}_Y(t)} \sup\{f_Y(x)|x \in (t,\infty)\}, \quad \delta^{G_{[r]}}_{(t,\infty)} = \frac{1}{\overline{G}_{[r]}(t)} \sup\{g_{[r]}(x)|x \in (t,\infty)\}.$$

Past Shannon–Awad entropy for the concomitant of r-th GOS from the FGM family is:

$$\overline{H}^{SA}(Y^*_{[r]};t) = \log G_{[r]}(t) - \frac{1}{G_{[r]}(t)} \{(1 - \alpha C^*_r)[F_Y(t)(\log F_Y(t) - \overline{H}^{SA}(Y;t) + \delta^{F_Y}_{(0,t)})] + \qquad (47)$$

$$+ 2\alpha C^*_r \overline{\phi}_f(t) + K_2(r,t,\alpha,n,m,k)\} + \log \delta^{G_{[r]}}_{(0,t)}$$

where $K_2(r,t,\alpha,n,m,k)$ and $\overline{\phi}_f(y)$, and $\delta_{(0,t)}$ are given by (22) and (23) respectively, and

$$\delta^{F_Y}_{(0,t)} = \frac{1}{F_Y(t)} \sup\{f_Y(x)|x \in (0,t)\}, \quad \delta^{G_{[r]}}_{(0,t)} = \frac{1}{G_{[r]}(t)} \sup\{g_{[r]}(x)|x \in (0,t)\}.$$

Corollary 1. *The residual Shannon–Awad entropy for the concomitant of r-th-order statistic is:*

$$H^{SA}(Y_{[r]};t) = \log \overline{G}_{[r]}(t) - \frac{1}{\overline{G}_{[r]}(t)} \left\{ \left(1 + \alpha \frac{n-2r+1}{n+1}\right)[\overline{F}_Y(t)(\log \overline{F}_Y(t) - H^{SA}(Y;t) + \delta^{F_Y}_{t,\infty})] + \qquad (48) \right.$$

$$\left. - 2\alpha \frac{n-2r+1}{n+1} \phi_f(t) + K_1(r,t,\alpha,n,0,1) \right\} + \log \delta^{\tilde{G}_{[r]}}_{(t,\infty)}.$$

The residual Shannon–Awad entropy for the concomitant of r-th record value is:

$$H^{SA}(R_{[r]};t) = \log \overline{G}_{[r]}(t) - \frac{1}{\overline{G}_{[r]}(t)} \{(1 + \alpha(2^{1-r} - 1))[\overline{F}_Y(t)(\log \overline{F}_Y(t) - H^{SA}(Y;t) + \delta^{F_Y}_{t,\infty})] + \qquad (49)$$

$$- 2\alpha(2^{1-r} - 1)\phi_f(t) + K_1(r,t,\alpha,n,-1,1)\} + \log \delta^{\tilde{G}_{[r]}}_{(t,\infty)}.$$

In the case of progressive type II censoring order statistics with equi-balanced censoring scheme, the residual Shannon–Awad entropy of the concomitant of r-th-order statistic from the FGM family is (46) with $m = R$, the removal number.

Similar results can be obtained also for past Shannon–Awad entropy.

4.2. Tsallis and Tsallis-Related Entropies

Information measures related to Tsallis entropy for the concomitants are very few in the literature. In [35], Tsallis entropy and residual Tsallis entropy for the concomitants of the record values from the FGM family are obtained. In this subsection, we will obtain more general results, computing Tsallis entropies for the concomitants of generalized order statistics and, furthermore, considering Awad-type extensions of the Tsallis entropies.

Theorem 2. *Tsallis entropy for the concomitant of the r-th GOS from the FGM family is:*

$$H^T(Y^*_{[r]}) = \frac{1}{q-1} \left\{ 1 - \sum_{k=0}^{q} \sum_{s=0}^{k} (-1)^s \binom{q}{k} \binom{k}{s} 2^{k-s} \alpha^k C^{*k}_r E_U \left[f_Y(F_Y^{-1}(U))^{q-1} U^{k-s} \right] \right\}, \quad (50)$$

where U is an $U(0,1)$ random variable and E_U is the expectation of $f_Y(F_Y^{-1}(U))^{q-1}U^{k-s}$.

Proof. Taking into account the definitions of Tsallis entropy (29) and the density of the concomitants (6), we obtain:

$$H^T(Y_{[r]}^*) = \frac{1}{q-1}\left\{1 - \int_0^\infty [g_{[r]}(y)]^q dy\right\} =$$
$$= \frac{1}{q-1}\left(1 - \int_0^\infty [f_Y(y)]^q (1 + \alpha C_r^*(2F_Y(y) - 1))^q dy\right).$$

We have that:

$$(1 + \alpha C_r^*(2F_Y(y) - 1))^q = \sum_{k=0}^q \sum_{s=0}^k (-1)^s \binom{q}{k}\binom{k}{s} 2^{k-s} \alpha^k C_r^{*k} [F_Y(y)]^{k-s}.$$

Additionally, if we consider the transformation

$$F_Y(y) = u;\ y = F_Y^{-1}(u),\ f_Y(y)dy = du,$$

the result (50) follows. □

Corollary 2. *The Tsallis entropy for the concomitant of r-th-order statistic is:*

$$H^T(Y_{[r]}) = \frac{1}{q-1}\left\{1 - \sum_{k=0}^q \sum_{s=0}^k (-1)^s \binom{q}{k}\binom{k}{s} 2^{k-s} \alpha^k (-1)^k \left(\frac{n - 2r + 1}{n+1}\right)^k \times \right. \quad (51)$$
$$\left. \times E_U\left[f_Y(F_Y^{-1}(U))^{q-1} U^{k-s}\right]\right\}.$$

The Tsallis entropy for the concomitant of r-th record value is:

$$H^T(R_{[r]}) = \frac{1}{q-1}\left\{1 - \sum_{k=0}^q \sum_{s=0}^k (-1)^s \binom{q}{k}\binom{k}{s} 2^{k-s} \alpha^k (-1)^k (2^{1-r} - 1)^k \times \right. \quad (52)$$
$$\left. \times E_U\left[f_Y(F_Y^{-1}(U))^{q-1} U^{k-s}\right]\right\}.$$

In the case of progressive type II censoring order statistics with equi-balanced censoring scheme, the Tsallis entropy of the concomitant of r-th-order statistic from the FGM family is (50) with $m = R$, the removal number.

We now discuss some Tsallis-related entropies. First, we give an Awad-type extension of Tsallis entropy and then we focus on Residual Tsallis, Past Tsallis entropies and their Awad-type extensions.

Several Awad-type extensions have been proposed in the literature ([51,52]). Now, we introduce this type of extension for Tsallis entropy and we define **Tsallis–Awad entropy** for a continuous random variable X which take values in $\mathbb{R}$:

$$H^{TA}(X) = \frac{1}{q-1}\left\{1 - \int_{-\infty}^{+\infty}\left[\frac{f(x)}{\delta}\right]^{q-1} f(x)dx\right\} = \frac{1}{q-1}\left\{1 - \frac{1}{\delta^{q-1}}\int_{-\infty}^{+\infty}[f(x)]^q dx\right\}, \quad (53)$$

where $\delta = \sup\{f(x)|x \in \mathbb{R}\}$.

We notice that the relationship between Tsallis–Awad entropy and Tsallis entropy is:

$$H^{TA}(X) = \delta^{1-q} H^T(X) + \log_q \delta. \quad (54)$$

Using (50) and (54), we can obtain the expression of Tsallis–Awad entropy for the concomitant of the r-th GOS from the FGM family:

Theorem 3. *Tsallis–Awad entropy for the concomitant of the r-th GOS from the FGM family is:*

$$H^{TA}(Y^*_{[r]}) = \frac{\delta^{1-q}}{q-1}\left\{1 - \sum_{k=0}^{q}\sum_{s=0}^{k}(-1)^s\binom{q}{k}\binom{k}{s}2^{k-s}\alpha^k C^{*k}_r E_U\left[f_Y(F_Y^{-1}(U))^{q-1}U^{k-s}\right]\right\} + \log_q \delta, \quad (55)$$

where U is an U(0,1) random variable, and, in this case, $\delta = \sup\{g_{[r]}(x)|x > 0\}$.

Corollary 3. *The Tsallis–Awad entropy for the concomitant of r-th-order statistic is:*

$$H^T(Y_{[r]}) = \frac{\delta^{1-q}}{q-1}\left\{1 - \sum_{k=0}^{q}\sum_{s=0}^{k}(-1)^s\binom{q}{k}\binom{k}{s}2^{k-s}\alpha^k(-1)^k\left(\frac{n-2r+1}{n+1}\right)^k \times \right. \quad (56)$$

$$\left. \times E_U\left[f_Y(F_Y^{-1}(U))^{q-1}U^{k-s}\right]\right\} + \log_q \delta.$$

The Tsallis–Awad entropy for the concomitant of r-th record value is:

$$H^T(R_{[r]}) = \frac{\delta^{1-q}}{q-1}\left\{1 - \sum_{k=0}^{q}\sum_{s=0}^{k}(-1)^s\binom{q}{k}\binom{k}{s}2^{k-s}\alpha^k(-1)^k(2^{1-r}-1)^k \times \right. \quad (57)$$

$$\left. \times E_U\left[f_Y(F_Y^{-1}(U))^{q-1}U^{k-s}\right]\right\} + \log_q \delta.$$

In the case of progressve type II censoring order statistics with equi-balanced censoring scheme, the Tsallis–Awad entropy of the concomitant of r-th-order statistic from the FGM family is (55) with $m = R$, the removal number.

In a similar way to the definition of **residual Tsallis** (31), we can consider the **past Tsallis entropy**:

$$\overline{H}^T(X;t) = \frac{1}{q-1}\left\{1 - \int_0^t\left[\frac{f(x)}{F(t)}\right]^q dx\right\} = \frac{1}{q-1}\left\{1 - \frac{1}{F(t)^q}\int_0^t [f(x)]^q dx\right\}. \quad (58)$$

Taking into account Theorem 2, the following theorem is naturally deduced:

Theorem 4. *Residual Tsallis entropy for the concomitant of the r-th GOS from the FGM family is:*

$$H^T(Y^*_{[r]};t) = \frac{1}{q-1}\left\{1 - \frac{1}{(\bar{G}_{[r]}(t))^q}\sum_{k=0}^{q}\sum_{s=0}^{k}(-1)^s\binom{q}{k}\binom{k}{s}2^{k-s}\alpha^k C^{*k}_r \times \right. \quad (59)$$

$$\left. \times E_U\left[f_Y(F^{-1}(U))^{q-1}U^{k-s}|U > F_Y(t)\right]\right\},$$

where U is an U(0,1) random variable and E_U is the conditional expectation of $f_Y(F^{-1}(U))^{q-1}U^{k-s}$, given $U > F_Y(t)$.

Past Tsallis entropy for the concomitant of the r-th GOS from the FGM family is:

$$\overline{H}^T(Y^*_{[r]};t) = \frac{1}{q-1}\left\{1 - \frac{1}{(G_{[r]}(t))^q}\sum_{k=0}^{q}\sum_{s=0}^{k}(-1)^s\binom{q}{k}\binom{k}{s}2^{k-s}\alpha^k C^{*k}_r \times \right. \quad (60)$$

$$\left. \times E_U\left[f_Y(F_Y^{-1}(U))^{q-1}U^{k-s}|U < F_Y(t)\right]\right\},$$

where U is a U(0,1) random variable and E_U is the conditional expectation of $f_Y(F^{-1}(U))^{q-1}U^{k-s}$, given $U < F_Y(t)$.

Corollary 4. The residual Tsallis entropy for the concomitant of r-th-order statistic is:

$$H^T(Y_{[r]};t) = \frac{1}{q-1}\left\{1 - \frac{1}{\left(\bar{G}_{[r]}(t)\right)^q}\sum_{k=0}^{q}\sum_{s=0}^{k}(-1)^s\binom{q}{k}\binom{k}{s}2^{k-s}\alpha^k(-1)^k\left(\frac{n-2r+1}{n+1}\right)^k \times \right. \quad (61)$$
$$\left. \times E_U\left[f_Y(F^{-1}(U))^{q-1}U^{k-s}|U > F_Y(t)\right]\right\},$$

The residual Tsallis entropy for the concomitant of r-th record value is:

$$H^T(R_{[r]};t) = \frac{1}{q-1}\left\{1 - \frac{1}{\left(\bar{G}_{[r]}(t)\right)^q}\sum_{k=0}^{q}\sum_{s=0}^{k}(-1)^s\binom{q}{k}\binom{k}{s}2^{k-s}\alpha^k(-1)^k(2^{1-r}-1)^k \times \right. \quad (62)$$
$$\left. \times E_U\left[f_Y(F^{-1}(U))^{q-1}U^{k-s}|U > F_Y(t)\right]\right\}.$$

In the case of progressive type II censoring order statistics with equi-balanced censoring scheme, the residual Tsallis entropy of the concomitant of r-th-order statistic from the FGM family is (59) with $m = R$, the removal number.

Similar results can be obtained for past Tsallis entropy.

We now introduce **Residual Tsallis–Awad entropy**:

$$H^{TA}(X;t) = \frac{1}{q-1}\left\{1 - \frac{1}{\left(\delta^{\bar{F}}_{(t,+\infty)}\right)^{q-1}}\int_t^{+\infty}\left[\frac{f(x)}{\bar{F}(t)}\right]^q dx\right\} \quad (63)$$

$$= \frac{1}{q-1}\left\{1 - \frac{1}{\bar{F}(t)}E\left[\left[\frac{f(X)}{\bar{F}(t)\delta^{\bar{F}}_{(t,\infty)}}\right]^{q-1}\bigg|X > t\right]\right\}, \quad (64)$$

where $\delta^{\bar{F}}_{(t,\infty)} = \frac{1}{\bar{F}(t)}\sup\{f(x)|x \in (t,+\infty)\}$.

Past Tsallis–Awad entropy can also be defined:

$$\bar{H}^{TA}(X;t) = \frac{1}{q-1}\left[1 - \frac{1}{\left(\delta^{F}_{(0,t)}\right)^{q-1}}\int_0^t\left[\frac{f(x)}{F(t)}\right]^q dx\right] \quad (65)$$

$$= \frac{1}{q-1}\left\{1 - \frac{1}{F(t)}E\left[\left[\frac{f(X)}{F(t)\delta^{F}_{(0,t)}}\right]^{q-1}\bigg|0 < X < t\right]\right\}. \quad (66)$$

where $\delta^F_{(0,t)} = \frac{1}{F(t)}\sup\{f(x)|x \in (0,t)\}$.

We notice that a similar relationship to (54) can be written for residual Tsallis entropies and for past Tsallis entropies:

$$H^{TA}(X;t) = \left(\delta^{\bar{F}}_{(t,\infty)}\right)^{1-q}H^T(X;t) + \log_q \delta^{\bar{F}}_{(t,\infty)}, \quad (67)$$

$$\bar{H}^{TA}(X;t) = \left(\delta^{F}_{(0,t)}\right)^{1-q}\bar{H}^T(X;t) + \log_q \delta^{F}_{(0,t)}, \quad (68)$$

and the following theorem can be proven:

Theorem 5. *Residual Tsallis–Awad entropy for the concomitant of the r-th GOS from the FGM family is:*

$$H^{TA}(Y^*_{[r]};t) = \frac{(\delta^{\overline{G}_{[r]}}_{(t,\infty)})^{1-q}}{q-1}\left\{1 - \frac{1}{(\overline{G}_{[r]}(t))^q}\sum_{k=0}^{q}\sum_{s=0}^{k}(-1)^s\binom{q}{k}\binom{k}{s}2^{k-s}\alpha^k C^{*k}_r \times \right. \tag{69}$$

$$\left. \times E_U\left[f_Y(F_Y^{-1}(U))^{q-1}U^{k-s}|U > F_Y(t)\right]\right\} + \log_q \delta^{\overline{G}_{[r]}}_{(t,\infty)},$$

where U is an U(0,1) random variable, and $\delta^{\overline{G}_{[r]}}_{(t,\infty)} = \frac{1}{\overline{G}_{[r]}(t)}\sup\{g_{[r]}(x)|x \in (t,+\infty)\}$.

Past Tsallis–Awad entropy for the concomitant of the r-th GOS from the FGM family is:

$$\overline{H}^{TA}(Y^*_{[r]};t) = \frac{(\delta^{G_{[r]}(t)}_{(0,t)})^{1-q}}{q-1}\left\{1 - \frac{1}{(G_{[r]}(t))^q}\sum_{k=0}^{q}\sum_{s=0}^{k}(-1)^s\binom{q}{k}\binom{k}{s}2^{k-s}\alpha^k C^{*k}_r \times \right. \tag{70}$$

$$\left. \times E_U\left[f_Y(F_Y^{-1}(U))^{q-1}U^{k-s}|U < F_Y(t)\right]\right\} + \log_q \delta^{G_{[r]}}_{(0,t)},$$

where U is an U(0,1) random variable, and $\delta^{G_{[r]}}_{(0,t)} = \frac{1}{G_{[r]}}\sup\{g_{[r]}(x)|x \in (0,t)\}$.

Corollary 5. *The residual Tsallis–Awad entropy for the concomitant of r-th-order statistic is:*

$$H^{TA}(Y_{[r]};t) = \frac{(\delta^{\overline{G}_{[r]}}_{(t,\infty)})^{1-q}}{q-1}\left\{1 - \frac{1}{(\overline{G}_{[r]}(t))^q}\sum_{k=0}^{q}\sum_{s=0}^{k}(-1)^s\binom{q}{k}\binom{k}{s}2^{k-s}\alpha^k(-1)^k\left(\frac{n-2r+1}{n+1}\right)^k \times \right. \tag{71}$$

$$\left. \times E_U\left[f_Y(F_Y^{-1}(U))^{q-1}U^{k-s}|U > F_Y(t)\right]\right\} + \log_q \delta^{\overline{G}_{[r]}}_{(t,\infty)}.$$

The residual Tsallis–Awad entropy for the concomitant of r-th record value is:

$$H^{TA}(Y_{[r]};t) = \frac{(\delta^{\overline{G}_{[r]}}_{(t,\infty)})^{1-q}}{q-1}\left\{1 - \frac{1}{(\overline{G}_{[r]}(t))^q}\sum_{k=0}^{q}\sum_{s=0}^{k}(-1)^s\binom{q}{k}\binom{k}{s}2^{k-s}\alpha^k(-1)^k(2^{1-r}-1)^k \times \right. \tag{72}$$

$$\left. \times E_U\left[f_Y(F_Y^{-1}(U))^{q-1}U^{k-s}|U > F_Y(t)\right]\right\} + \log_q \delta^{\overline{G}_{[r]}}_{(t,\infty)}.$$

In the case of progressive type II censoring order statistics with equi-balanced censoring scheme, the residual Tsallis entropy of the concomitant of r-th-order statistic from the FGM family is (59) with $m = R$, the removal number.

Similar results can be obtained for past Tsallis entropy.

4.3. Fisher–Tsallis Information Number

Various generalizations of FIN have been proposed, see, for example, [53–55]. In [53], the FIN is generalized, replacing the expectation and the logarithm functions with their q variants, and in [54], a (β,q)-Fisher information is defined. We here consider the following extension FIN, which we call **Fisher–Tsallis information number**:

$$I_f = E_f\left[\left(\frac{\partial}{\partial x}\log_q f(x)\right)^2\right], \tag{73}$$

where $\log_q$ is given by (30). This extension is a type of extension from [54], with $\beta = 2$ and $q = 1$.

For the concomitants of the GOS from FGM family, we have the following theorem which can be seen as an extension of the results obtained in [40]:

Theorem 6. *For the r-th concomitant $Y^*_{[r]}$ of GOS from a FGM family, the Tsallis–Fisher information number for a location parameter is:*

$$I_{g_{[r]}} = I_1 + I_2 + I_3, \qquad (74)$$

where

$$I_1 = E_U\left[(f_Y(F^{-1}(U)))^{-2q}(f'_Y(F_Y^{-1}(U)))^2(1+C^*_r\alpha(1-2U))^{2-2q}\right],$$

$$I_2 = 4C^{*2}_r\alpha^2 \cdot E_U\left[(f_Y(F^{-1}(U)))^{4-2q}(1+C^*_r\alpha(1-2U))^{-2q}\right],$$

$$I_3 = -4C^{*2}_r\alpha \cdot E_U\left[f_Y(F^{-1}(U)))^{2-2q}f'_Y(F_Y^{-1}(U))(1+C^*_r\alpha(1-2U))^{1-2q}\right].$$

Proof. From (73), we have

$$I_{g_{[r]}} = E_{g_{[r]}}\left[(g_{[r]}(Y))^{-2q}(g'_{[r]}(Y))^2\right].$$

Using the expression (7) for the density $g_{[r]}$, it results in

$$I_{g_{[r]}} = E_{g_{[r]}}\left[f_Y(Y)^{-2q}\left[1+C^*_r\alpha(1-2F_Y(Y))\right]^{-2q}\left[f'_Y(Y)(1+C^*_r\alpha(1-2F_Y(Y)))-2(f_Y(Y))^2 C^*_r\alpha\right]^2\right].$$

Thus,

$$I_{g_{[r]}} = E_{g_{[r]}}\Big[(f_Y(Y))^{-2q}\left[1+C^*_r\alpha(1-2F_Y(Y))\right]^{-2q}$$
$$\cdot \left[(f'_Y(Y))^2(1+C^*_r\alpha(1-2F_Y(Y)))^2+4(f_Y(Y))^4 C^{*2}_r\alpha^2-\right.$$
$$\left.-4f'_Y(Y)(f_Y(Y))^2 C^*_r\alpha(1+C^*_r\alpha(1-2F_Y(Y)))\right]\Big].$$

After some computations,

$$I_{g_{[r]}} = E_{g_{[r]}}\left[(f_Y(Y))^{-2q}(f'_Y(Y))^2(1+C^*_r\alpha(1-2F_Y(Y)))^{2-2q}\right] +$$
$$+ 4C^{*2}_r\alpha^2 E_{g_{[r]}}\left[f_Y(Y)^{4-2q}(1+C^*_r\alpha(1-2F_Y(Y)))^{-2q}\right] -$$
$$- 4C^*_r\alpha E_{g_{[r]}}\left[(f_Y(Y))^{2-2q}f'_Y(Y)(1+C^*_r\alpha(1-2F_Y(Y)))^{1-2q}\right].$$

After the transformation $U = F_Y(Y)$, with $U \sim U(0,1)$ we obtain (74). □

4.4. Tsallis Divergence

We consider **Tsallis divergence** for two densities, f_1 and f_2, as it is defined in [44]:

$$TD(Z_1, Z_2) = \int_{-\infty}^{+\infty} f_1(z)\log_q\left(\frac{f_2(z)}{f_1(z)}\right)dz \qquad (75)$$

that can also be expressed as:

$$TD(Z_1, Z_2) = \frac{1}{1-q}E_{f_1}\left[\left(\frac{f_1(z)}{f_2(z)}\right)^{q-1}-1\right]. \qquad (76)$$

We notice that this divergence is the divergence considered in [36], with $\phi(x) = \log_q(1/x)$, it is the divergence analyzed in [56], with $k = 1 - q$, and it is Tsallis Relative Entropy from [57].

When $q \to 1$, Tsallis entropy becomes Shannon entropy and also Tsallis divergence becomes Kullback–Leibler divergence (33). The next theorem generalizes the results from [23], computing Tsallis divergence for two concomitants of GOS from the FGM family.

Theorem 7. *Let $Y_{[r]}$ and $Y_{[s]}$ the r-th and the s-th concomitants of the GOS from the FGM family with the densities $g_{[r]}$ and $g_{[s]}$. Then, the Tsallis divergence of $g_{[s]}$ from $g_{[r]}$ has the following form:*

$$TD(Y_{[r]}, Y_{[s]}) = \frac{1}{1-q}[D_1 - D_2 - 1], \quad (77)$$

where

$$D_1 = \frac{1}{q(q+1)}\left(\frac{C_r^*}{C_r^* - C_s^*}\right)^{q-1}(1 + C_r^*\alpha)^{q+1}F_1\left(q+1, q-1, q+1, -\frac{C_s^*(1 + C_r^*\alpha)}{C_r^* - C_s^*}\right),$$

$$D_2 = \frac{1}{q(q+1)}\left(\frac{C_r^*}{C_r^* - C_s^*}\right)^{q-1}(1 - C_r^*\alpha)^{q+1}F_1\left(q+1, q-1, q+1, -\frac{C_s^*(1 - C_r^*\alpha)}{C_r^* - C_s^*}\right),$$

with F_1 being the hypergeometric function.

Proof. In (76), we replace f_1 and f_2 with the concomitants densities:

$$g_{[r]}(y) = f_Y(y)[1 + C_r^*\alpha(2F_y(y) - 1)],$$

$$g_{[s]}(y) = f_Y(y)[1 + C_s^*\alpha(2F_y(y) - 1)],$$

and we compute the expectation:

$$E_{g_{[r]}}\left[\left(\frac{g_{[r]}(Y)}{g_{[s]}(Y)}\right)^{q-1}\right] = \int_0^\infty g_{[r]}(y)\left(\frac{g_{[r]}(Y)}{g_{[s]}(Y)}\right)^{q-1} dy \quad (78)$$

$$= \int_0^\infty f_Y(y)[1 + C_r^*\alpha(2F_Y(y) - 1)]\left(\frac{f_Y(y)[1 + C_r^*\alpha(2F_Y(y) - 1)]}{f_Y(y)[1 + C_s^*\alpha(2F_Y(y) - 1)]}\right)^{q-1} dy.$$

First, we make the transformation:

$$F_Y(y) = u, \quad y = F_Y^{-1}(u), \quad f_Y(y)dy = du,$$

and we obtain

$$E_{g_{[r]}}\left[\left(\frac{g_{[r]}(Y)}{g_{[s]}(Y)}\right)^{q-1}\right] = \int_0^1 \frac{[1 + C_r^*\alpha(2u - 1)]^q}{[1 + C_s^*\alpha(2u - 1)]^{q-1}}du. \quad (79)$$

Then, we make the transformation:

$$2u - 1 = v, \quad u = (v+1)/2, \quad 2du = dv,$$

and we obtain:

$$E_{g_{[r]}}\left[\left(\frac{g_{[r]}(Y)}{g_{[s]}(Y)}\right)^{q-1}\right] = \frac{1}{2}\int_{-1}^1 \frac{[1 + C_r^*\alpha v]^q}{[1 + C_s^*\alpha v]^{q-1}}dv. \quad (80)$$

We use the general formula:

$$\frac{1}{2}\int_{-1}^{1}\frac{(1+ax)^A}{(1+bx)^B}dx = \qquad(81)$$

$$= \frac{1}{A(A+1)}\left\{(1+a)^{A+1}(1+b)^{-B}\left[\frac{a(1+b)}{a-b}\right]^{B} F_1\left(A+1,B,A+1,-\frac{b(1+a)}{a-b}\right) - \right.$$
$$\left. -(1-a)^{A+1}(1-b)^{-B}\left[\frac{a(1-b)}{a-b}\right]^{B} F_1\left(A+1,B,A+1,-\frac{b(1-a)}{a-b}\right)\right\},$$

where F_1 is the hypergeometric function. It results in:

$$E_{g_{[r]}}\left[\left(\frac{g_{[r]}(Y)}{g_{[s]}(Y)}\right)^{q-1}\right] = D_1 - D_2.$$

□

5. Conclusions

This paper is focused on information measures related to Shannon entropy, Tsallis entropy, Fisher information, and divergences for the concomitants of GOS from the FGM family. We review the literature on the mentioned information measures and we generalize existing results. The study of the concomitants, pairs of the order statistics in a sample from a bivariate distribution, ordered by one variate, could have applications in reliability, for example, in the analysis of the lifetime uncertainty of complex systems. For this reason, we also discuss residual and past versions of the entropies. Considering generalized order statistics (GOS) results in an increasing complexity of computations, but it gives a general form of the computed measures that can be applied for the concomitants of various order statistics.

Author Contributions: All authors contributed equally to the paper. All authors have read and agreed to the published version of the manuscript.

Funding: This research received no external funding.

Institutional Review Board Statement: Not applicable.

Data Availability Statement: Not applicable.

Acknowledgments: The authors are grateful to the referees for their comments and suggestions which improved the presentation of this paper.

Conflicts of Interest: The authors declare no conflict of interest.

References

1. David, H.A. Concomitants of order statistics. *Bull. Inst. Int. Statist.* **1973**, *45*, 295–300.
2. Bhattacharya, P. Convergence of sample paths of normalized sums of induced order statistics. *Ann. Stat.* **1974**, *2*, 1034–1039. [CrossRef]
3. Bayramoglu, I. Reliability and mean residual life of complex systems with two dependent components per element. *IEEE Trans. Reliab.* **2013**, *62*, 276–285. [CrossRef]
4. Ozkut, M. The (n- k+ 1)-out-of-n concomitant system having m subcomponents and its reliability. *J. Comput. Appl. Math.* **2021**, *386*, 113251. [CrossRef]
5. Scaria, J.; Mohan, S. Dependence concepts and Reliability application of concomitants of order statistics from the Morgenstern family. *J. Stat. Theory Appl.* **2021**, *20*, 193–203. [CrossRef]
6. Kamps, U. A concept of generalized order statistics. *J. Stat. Plan. Inference* **1995**, *48*, 1–23. [CrossRef]
7. Balakrishnan, N.; Lai, C.D. *Continuous Bivariate Distributions*; Springer Science & Business Media: Berlin, Germany, 2009.
8. Kotz, S.; Johnson, N.L. Propriétés de dépendance des distributions itérées généralisées à deux variables Farlie-Gumbel-Morgenstern. *C. R. Acad. Sci. Paris A* **1977**, *285*, 277–280.
9. Huang, J.; Kotz, S. Correlation structure in iterated Farlie-Gumbel-Morgenstern distributions. *Biometrika* **1984**, *71*, 633–636.
10. Huang, J.S.; Kotz, S. Modifications of the Farlie-Gumbel-Morgenstern distributions. A tough hill to climb. *Metrika* **1999**, *49*, 135–145. [CrossRef]

11. Bairamov, I.; Kotz, S.; Bekci, M. New generalized Farlie-Gumbel-Morgenstern distributions and concomitants of order statistics. *J. Appl. Stat.* **2001**, *28*, 521–536. [CrossRef]
12. Bairamov, I.; Kotz, S. Dependence structure and symmetry of Huang-Kotz FGM distributions and their extensions. *Metrika* **2002**, *56*, 55–72. [CrossRef]
13. Aggarwala, R.; Balakrishnan, N. Recurrence relations for single and product moments of progressive Type-II right censored order statistics from exponential and truncated exponential distributions. *Ann. Inst. Stat. Math.* **1996**, *48*, 757–771. [CrossRef]
14. Balakrishnan, N.; Cramer, E. *The Art of Progressive Censoring*; Statistics for Industry and Technology; Birkhäuser: Basel, Switzerland; Springer Science + Business Media: New York, NY, USA, 2014.
15. Cramer, E.; Kamps, U. Marginal distributions of sequential and generalized order statistics. *Metrika* **2003**, *58*, 293–310. [CrossRef]
16. Farlie, D.J.G. The performance of some correlation coefficients for a general bivariate distribution. *Biometrika* **1960**, *47*, 307–323. [CrossRef]
17. Gumbel, E. Bivariate exponential distributions. *J. Am. Statist. Assoc.* **1960**, *55*, 698–707. [CrossRef]
18. Morgenstern, D. Einfache Beispiele Zweidimensionaler Verteilungen. *Mitt. Fur Math. Stat.* **1956**, *8*, 234–235.
19. Johnson, N.L.; Kotz, S. On some generalized Farlie-Gumbel-Morgenstern distributions-II regression, correlation and further generalizations. *Commun. Stat.-Theory Methods* **1977**, *6*, 485–496. [CrossRef]
20. Nelsen, R.B. *An Introduction to Copulas*; Springer Science + Business Media: New York, NY, USA, 2007.
21. Beg, M.; Ahsanullah, M. Concomitants of generalized order statistics from Farlie–Gumbel–Morgenstern distributions. *Stat. Methodol.* **2008**, *5*, 1–20. [CrossRef]
22. Shannon, C.E. A mathematical theory of communication. *Bell Syst. Tech. J.* **1948**, *27*, 379–423. [CrossRef]
23. Tahmasebi, S.; Behboodian, J. Information properties for concomitants of order statistics in Farlie–Gumbel–Morgenstern (FGM) family. *Commun. Stat.-Theory Methods* **2012**, *41*, 1954–1968. [CrossRef]
24. Tahmasebi, S.; Behboodian, J. Shannon information for concomitants of generalized order statistics in Farlie–Gumbel–Morgenstern (FGM) family. *Bull. Malays. Math. Sci. Soc.* **2012**, *35*, 975–981.
25. Awad, A. A statistical information measure. *Dirasat (Sci.)* **1987**, *14*, 7–20.
26. Ebrahimi, N.; Pellerey, F. New partial ordering of survival functions based on the notion of uncertainty. *J. Appl. Probab.* **1995**, *32*, 202–211. [CrossRef]
27. Ebrahimi, N. How to measure uncertainty in the residual life time distribution. *Sankhyā Indian J. Stat. Ser. A* **1996**, *58*, 48–56.
28. Di Crescenzo, A.; Longobardi, M. Entropy-based measure of uncertainty in past lifetime distributions. *J. Appl. Probab.* **2002**, *39*, 434–440. [CrossRef]
29. Mohie EL-Din, M.M.; Amein, M.M.; Ali, N.S.A.; Mohamed, M.S. Residual and past entropy for concomitants of ordered random variables of Morgenstern family. *J. Probab. Stat.* **2015**, *2015*, 1–6. [CrossRef]
30. Havrda, J.; Charvát, F. Quantification method of classification processes. Concept of structural a-entropy. *Kybernetika* **1967**, *3*, 30–35.
31. Tsallis, C. Possible generalization of Boltzmann-Gibbs statistics. *J. Stat. Phys.* **1988**, *52*, 479–487. [CrossRef]
32. Hirica, I.E.; Pripoae, C.L.; Pripoae, G.T.; Preda, V. Weighted Relative Group Entropies and Associated Fisher Metrics. *Entropy* **2022**, *24*, 120. [CrossRef]
33. Wilk, G.; Włodarczyk, Z. Example of a possible interpretation of Tsallis entropy. *Phys. A Stat. Mech. Its Appl.* **2008**, *387*, 4809–4813. [CrossRef]
34. Calì, C.; Longobardi, M.; Ahmadi, J. Some properties of cumulative Tsallis entropy. *Phys. A Stat. Mech. Its Appl.* **2017**, *486*, 1012–1021. [CrossRef]
35. Paul, J.; Thomas, P.Y. Tsallis entropy properties of record values. *Calcutta Stat. Assoc. Bull.* **2015**, *67*, 47–60. [CrossRef]
36. Nanda, A.K.; Paul, P. Some results on generalized residual entropy. *Inf. Sci.* **2006**, *176*, 27–47. [CrossRef]
37. Zografos, K. On reconsidering entropies and divergences and their cumulative counterparts: Csiszár's, DPD's and Fisher's type cumulative and survival measures. *Probab. Eng. Infor. Sci.* **2022**, 1–28. [CrossRef]
38. Papaioannou, T.; Ferentinos, K. On two forms of Fisher's measure of information. *Commun. Stat.-Theory Methods* **2005**, *34*, 1461–1470. [CrossRef]
39. Frieden, B.R. *Physics from Fisher information: A Unification*; Cambridge University Press: New York, NY, USA, 1998.
40. Tahmasebi, S.; Jafari, A.A. Fisher information number for concomitants of generalized order statistics in Morgenstern family. *J. Inform. Math. Sci.* **2013**, *5*, 15–20.
41. Barbu, V.S.; Karagrigoriou, A.; Preda, V. Entropy and divergence rates for Markov chains: I. The Alpha-Gamma and Beta-Gamma case. *Proc. Rom. Acad.-Ser. A* **2017**, *4*, 293–301.
42. Barbu, V.S.; Karagrigoriou, A.; Preda, V. Entropy and divergence rates for Markov chains: II. The weighted case. *Proc. Rom. Acad.-Ser. A* **2018**, *19*, 3–10.
43. Barbu, V.S.; Karagrigoriou, A.; Preda, V. Entropy and divergence rates for Markov chains: III. The Cressie and Read case and applications. *Proc. Rom. Acad.-Ser. A* **2018**, *2*, 413–421.
44. Villmann, T.; Haase, S. Mathematical Aspects of Divergence Based Vector Quantization Using Fréchet-Derivatives. Master's Thesis, University of Applied Sciences Mittweida, Mittweida, Germany, 2010.
45. Póczos, B.; Schneider, J. On the estimation of alpha-divergences. In Proceedings of the Fourteenth International Conference on Artificial Intelligence and Statistics, Fort Lauderdale, FL, USA, 11–13 April 2011; pp. 609–617.

46. Kullback, S.; Leibler, R.A. On information and sufficiency. *Ann. Math. Stat.* **1951**, *22*, 79–86. [CrossRef]
47. Kullback, S. *Information Theory and Statistics*; Dover Publications, Inc.: Mineola, NY, USA, 1959.
48. Furuichi, S.; Yanagi, K.; Kuriyama, K. Fundamental properties of Tsallis relative entropy. *J. Math. Phys.* **2004**, *45*, 4868–4877. [CrossRef]
49. Furuichi, S.; Mitroi, F.C. Mathematical inequalities for some divergences. *Phys. A Stat. Mech. Its Appl.* **2012**, *391*, 388–400. [CrossRef]
50. Vigelis, R.F.; De Andrade, L.H.; Cavalcante, C.C. Properties of a generalized divergence related to Tsallis generalized divergence. *IEEE Trans. Inf. Theory* **2019**, *66*, 2891–2897. [CrossRef]
51. Awad, A.; Alawneh, A. Application of entropy to a life-time model. *IMA J. Math. Control Inf.* **1987**, *4*, 143–148. [CrossRef]
52. Sfetcu, R.C.; Sfetcu, S.C.; Preda, V. Ordering Awad–Varma Entropy and Applications to Some Stochastic Models. *Mathematics* **2021**, *9*, 280. [CrossRef]
53. Furuichi, S. On the maximum entropy principle and the minimization of the Fisher information in Tsallis statistics. *J. Math. Phys.* **2009**, *50*, 013303. [CrossRef]
54. Bercher, J.F. Some properties of generalized Fisher information in the context of nonextensive thermostatistics. *Phys. A Stat. Mech. Its Appl.* **2013**, *392*, 3140–3154. [CrossRef]
55. Kharazmi, O.; Balakrishnan, N.; Jamali, H. Cumulative Residual q-Fisher Information and Jensen-Cumulative Residual χ^2 Divergence Measures. *Entropy* **2022**, *24*, 341. [CrossRef]
56. Sfetcu, R.C.; Sfetcu, S.C.; Preda, V. On Tsallis and Kaniadakis Divergences. *Math. Phys. Anal. Geom.* **2022**, *25*, 1–23. [CrossRef]
57. Koukoumis, C.; Karagrigoriou, A. On entropy-type measures and divergences with applications in engineering, management and applied sciences. *Int. J. Math. Eng. Manag. Sci.* **2021**, *6*, 688. [CrossRef]

Article

Probabilistic Pairwise Model Comparisons Based on Bootstrap Estimators of the Kullback–Leibler Discrepancy

Andres Dajles *,†, Joseph Cavanaugh †

Department of Biostatistics, University of Iowa, 145 N. Riverside Drive, Iowa City, IA 52242, USA
* Correspondence: andres-dajles@uiowa.edu
† These authors contributed equally to this work.

Abstract: When choosing between two candidate models, classical hypothesis testing presents two main limitations: first, the models being tested have to be nested, and second, one of the candidate models must subsume the structure of the true data-generating model. Discrepancy measures have been used as an alternative method to select models without the need to rely upon the aforementioned assumptions. In this paper, we utilize a bootstrap approximation of the Kullback–Leibler discrepancy (BD) to estimate the probability that the fitted null model is closer to the underlying generating model than the fitted alternative model. We propose correcting for the bias of the BD estimator either by adding a bootstrap-based correction or by adding the number of parameters in the candidate model. We exemplify the effect of these corrections on the estimator of the discrepancy probability and explore their behavior in different model comparison settings.

Keywords: bootstrap discrepancy comparison probability (BDCP); discrepancy comparison probability (DCP); likelihood ratio test (LRT); model selection; *p*-value

1. Introduction

Hypothesis testing and *p*-values are routinely used in applied, empirically oriented research. However, practitioners of statistics often misinterpret *p*-values, particularly in settings where hypothesis tests are used for model comparisons. Riedle, Neath and Cavanaugh [1] attempt to address this issue by providing an alternate conceptualization of the *p*-value. The authors introduce and investigate the concept of the discrepancy comparison probability (DCP) and its bootstrapped estimator, called the bootstrap discrepancy comparison probability (BDCP). The authors establish a clear connection between the BDCP based on the Kullback–Leibler discrepancy (KLD) and the *p*-values derived from likelihood ratio tests. However, this connection only exists when using the bootstrap discrepancy (BD) that arises from the "plug-in" principle, which yields a biased approximation to the KLD. Similarly to complexity penalization of the Akaike Information Criterion (AIC), we establish that an intuitive bias correction to the BD is the addition of k, the number of functionally independent parameters in the candidate model. We also propose utilizing a bootstrap-based correction, which can be justified under less stringent assumptions. We analyze how well the bootstrap approach corrects the bias of the BDCP and the BD, and we show that, in most settings, its performance is comparable to simply adding k.

2. Methodological Development

2.1. Background

When faced with the task of choosing amongst competing models, statisticians often use discrepancy or divergence functions. One of the most flexible and ubiquitous divergence measures is the Kullback–Leibler information. To introduce this measure in the present context, consider a vector of independent observations $y = (y_1, y_2, \ldots, y_n)^T$ such that y is generated from an unknown distribution $g(y)$. Suppose that a candidate

model $f(y|\theta)$ is proposed as an approximation for $g(y)$, and that this model belongs to the parametric class of densities

$$F = [f(y|\theta) : \theta \in \Theta],$$

where Θ is the parameter space for θ. The Kullback–Leibler information, given by

$$I_{KL}(g,\theta) = E_g\left[\log \frac{g(y)}{f(y|\theta)}\right],$$

captures the separation between the proposed model $f(y|\theta)$ and the true data-generating model $g(y)$.

Although not a formal metric, $I_{KL}(g,\theta)$ is characterized by two desirable properties. First, by Jensen's inequality, $I_{KL}(g,\theta) \geq 0$ with equality if and only if $g(y) = f(y|\theta)$. Second, as the dissimilarity between $g(y)$ and $f(y|\theta)$ increases, $I_{KL}(g,\theta)$ increases accordingly.

Note that we can write

$$2I_{KL}(g,\theta) = E_g[-2\log(f(y|\theta))] - E_g[-2\log(g(y))]$$
$$= E_g[-2\ell(\theta|y)] - E_g[-2\log(g(y))],$$

where $\log(f(y|\theta)) = \ell(\theta|y)$. In the preceding relation, for any proposed candidate model, the quantity $E_g[-2\log(g(y))]$ is constant. Only the quantity $E_g[-2\ell(\theta|y)]$ changes across different models, which means it is the only quantity needed to distinguish among various models. The expression

$$d(g,\theta) = E_g[-2\ell(\theta|y)]$$

is known as the Kullback–Leibler discrepancy (KLD) and is often used as a substitute for $I_{KL}(g,\theta)$.

In practice, the goal is to determine the propriety of fitted models of the form $f(y|\hat{\theta})$, where $\hat{\theta} = \text{argmax}_{\theta \in \Theta}\, \ell(\theta|y)$. The KL discrepancy for the fitted model is given by

$$d(g,\hat{\theta}) = E_g[-2\ell(\theta|y)]|_{\theta=\hat{\theta}}.$$

2.2. The Discrepancy Comparison Probability and Bootstrap Discrepancy Comparison Probability

Suppose that we have two nested models that are formulated to characterize the sample y, and we designate one of the models the null, represented by θ_1, and the other model the alternative, represented by θ_2. The discrepancies under the fitted null and alternative models are given by $d(g,\hat{\theta}_1)$ and $d(g,\hat{\theta}_2)$, respectively. We can use these discrepancies to define the Kullback–Leibler discrepancy comparison probability (KLDCP), which is given by

$$P = \Pr[d(g,\hat{\theta}_1) < d(g,\hat{\theta}_2)].$$

The KLDCP evaluates the probability that the fitted null model is closer to the true data-generating model than the fitted alternative. The values of $d(g,\hat{\theta}_1)$ and $d(g,\hat{\theta}_2)$ are calculated from the same sample. For example, a KLDCP of 0.8 means that the fitted null has a smaller discrepancy than the fitted alternative in 80% of the samples drawn from the same distribution and of the same size. The development and interpretation of the KLDCP is presented in depth by Riedle, Neath and Cavanaugh [1].

We can estimate the KLDCP using the bootstrap approximation of the joint distribution of $d(g,\hat{\theta}_1)$ and $d(g,\hat{\theta}_2)$. The bootstrap joint distribution is based on the discrepancy estimators that arise from the "plug-in" principle, as described by Efron and Tibshirani [2], which replaces all the elements of the KLD by their bootstrap analogues. Specifically, we replace g by the empirical distribution $\hat{g}$; y by the bootstrap sample from $\hat{g}$, which we call y^*; and finally, $\hat{\theta}$ by the maximum likelihood estimate (MLE) derived under the bootstrap sample y^*, which we call $\hat{\theta}^*$. With these replacements, the bootstrap version of the KLD is given by

$$d(\hat{g}, \hat{\theta}^*) = E_{\hat{g}}[-2\ell(\theta|y)]|_{\theta=\hat{\theta}^*}$$
$$= \sum_{i=1}^{n} -2\ell_i(\hat{\theta}^*|y_i) \text{ (because each } y_i \text{ is independent.)}$$
$$= -2\ell(\hat{\theta}^*|y),$$

where ℓ_i represents the contribution to the likelihood based on the ith response y_i.

Now, in order to build a bootstrap distribution, we must draw various bootstrap samples from y. Suppose that we draw $j = 1, 2, \ldots, J$ bootstrap samples, and for each of these samples, we calculate the MLE of θ, which we denote as $\hat{\theta}^*(j)$. This allows us to obtain a set of J different bootstrap discrepancies; this set is defined as

$$\{d(\hat{g}, \hat{\theta}^*(j)) : j = 1, \ldots, J\},$$

and these variates can be used to construct the bootstrap analogue of the discrepancy distribution.

Finally, we can extend this procedure to the setting of the null and alternative models. For each bootstrap sample, we calculate $\hat{\theta}_2^*(j)$ and $\hat{\theta}_1^*(j)$, which are the bootstrap sample MLEs of θ_2 and θ_1, respectively. We then compute the discrepancies $d(\hat{g}, \hat{\theta}_2^*(j))$ and $d(\hat{g}, \hat{\theta}_1^*(j))$ for the null and alternative models, respectively. This collection of J pairs of null and alternative bootstrap discrepancies defines the set

$$\{(d(\hat{g}, \hat{\theta}_1^*(j)), d(\hat{g}, \hat{\theta}_2^*(j))) : j = 1, \ldots, J\},$$

which characterizes the bootstrap analogue of the joint distribution of $d(\hat{g}, \hat{\theta}_1)$ and $d(\hat{g}, \hat{\theta}_2)$. The bootstrap distribution can be utilized to estimate the bootstrap analogue of the DCP, given by

$$P^* = \text{Pr}^*[d(\hat{g}, \hat{\theta}_1^*) < d(\hat{g}, \hat{\theta}_2^*)].$$

By the law of large numbers, we can approximate P^* by calculating the proportion of times when $d(\hat{g}, \hat{\theta}_1^*(j)) < d(\hat{g}, \hat{\theta}_2^*(j))$ in the J bootstrap samples that were drawn. Thus, if I is an indicator function, we can define an estimator of the DCP, which we call the bootstrap discrepancy comparison probability (BDCP), as follows:

$$\text{BDCP} = \frac{1}{J} \sum_{j=1}^{J} I[d(\hat{g}, \hat{\theta}_1^*(j)) < d(\hat{g}, \hat{\theta}_2^*(j))]. \tag{1}$$

3. Bias Corrections for the BDCP

An important issue that arises in the bootstrap estimation of the KLD is the negative bias of the discrepancy estimators that materializes from the "plug-in" principle. The following lemma establishes and quantifies this bias for large-sample settings under an appropriately specified candidate model.

Lemma 1. *For a large sample size, assuming that the candidate model subsumes the true model, we have*

$$E_g\{E_*[-2\ell(\hat{\theta}^*|y)]\} \approx E_g[d(g, \hat{\theta})] - k,$$

where E_* is the expectation with respect to the bootstrap distribution, and k is the dimension of the model.

Proof. For a maximum likelihood estimator $\hat{\theta}$, it is well known that for a large sample size and under certain regularity conditions, we have

$$(\hat{\theta} - \theta)^T I(\theta|y)(\hat{\theta} - \theta) \sim \chi_k^2, \tag{2}$$

provided that the model is adequately specified. In the preceding, χ_k^2 denotes a centrally distributed chi-square random variable with k degrees-of-freedom.

Now, consider the second-order Taylor series expansion of $-2\ell(\hat{\theta}^*|y)$ about $\hat{\theta}$, which results in

$$-2\ell(\hat{\theta}^*|y) \approx -2\ell(\hat{\theta}|y) + (\hat{\theta}^* - \hat{\theta})^T I(\hat{\theta}|y)(\hat{\theta}^* - \hat{\theta}). \qquad (3)$$

By taking the expected value of both sides of (3) with respect to the bootstrap distribution of $\hat{\theta}^*$, we obtain

$$E_*\left(-2\ell(\hat{\theta}^*|y)\right) \approx -E_*\left(2\ell(\hat{\theta}|y)\right) + E_*\left((\hat{\theta}^* - \hat{\theta})^T I(\hat{\theta}|y)(\hat{\theta}^* - \hat{\theta})\right)$$
$$\approx -2\ell(\hat{\theta}|y) + k \quad \text{(by the approximation in (2))},$$
$$= \text{AIC} - k,$$

where AIC denotes the Akaike information criterion.

Finally, it has been established that if the true model is contained in the candidate class at hand, and if the large sample properties of MLEs hold, then AIC serves as an asymptotically unbiased estimator of the KLD. Thus,

$$E_g\left(E_*\left(-2\ell(\hat{\theta}^*|y)\right)\right) \approx E_g(\text{AIC}) - k$$
$$\approx E_g(d(g, \hat{\theta})) - k.$$

□

The preceding expression can be re-written as

$$E_g(d(g, \hat{\theta})) \approx E_g\left(E_*\left(-2\ell(\hat{\theta}^*|y)\right)\right) + k,$$

which implies that the bias correction k must be added to the bootstrap discrepancy in the estimation of the KLD. The BD estimator corrected by the addition of k will be called BDk.

Now, focus again on Equation (3). By subtracting $(-2\ell(\hat{\theta}|y))$ from both sides of the equation, we obtain

$$-2\ell(\hat{\theta}^*|y) - (-2\ell(\hat{\theta}|y)) \approx (\hat{\theta}^* - \hat{\theta})^T I(\hat{\theta}|y)(\hat{\theta}^* - \hat{\theta}). \qquad (4)$$

As mentioned previously, if the candidate model is adequately specified, then the distributional approximation in (2) holds true. However, if this model specification assumption is not met, then we can utilize the approximation in (4) to find a suitable bias correction via the bootstrap. The bootstrap has been used for bias corrections in similar problem contexts [3,4].

By applying the expected value with respect to the bootstrap distribution of $\hat{\theta}^*$ to both sides of (4), we obtain

$$E_*\left(-2\ell(\hat{\theta}^*|y)\right) - (-2\ell(\hat{\theta}|y)) \approx E_*\left((\hat{\theta}^* - \hat{\theta})^T I(\hat{\theta}|y)(\hat{\theta}^* - \hat{\theta})\right). \qquad (5)$$

The goal is then to find an approximation of $E_*\left(-2\ell(\hat{\theta}^*|y)\right) - (-2\ell(\hat{\theta}|y))$. Note that by the law of large numbers, we have that when $J \to \infty$,

$$\frac{1}{J} \sum_{j=1}^{J} -2\ell(\hat{\theta}^*(j)|y) \to E_*(-2\ell(\hat{\theta}^*|y)).$$

Thus, for $J \to \infty$, we can assert

$$\frac{1}{J} \sum_{j=1}^{J} -2\ell(\hat{\theta}^*(j)|y) - (-2\ell(\hat{\theta}|y)) \to E_*(-2\ell(\hat{\theta}^*|y)) - (-2\ell(\hat{\theta}|y)).$$

The preceding result shows that $\frac{1}{J}\sum_{j=1}^{J} -2\ell(\hat{\theta}^*(j)|y) - (-2\ell(\hat{\theta}|y))$ serves as an asymptotically unbiased estimator of $E_*(-2\ell(\hat{\theta}^*|y)) - (-2\ell(\hat{\theta}|y))$. We therefore propose using

$$k_b = \frac{1}{J}\sum_{j=1}^{J} -2\ell(\hat{\theta}^*(j)|y) - (-2\ell(\hat{\theta}|y))$$

as a bootstrap-based correction of the BD. A more in-depth derivation and exploration of the k_b correction can be found in Cavanaugh and Shumway [5].

Subsequently, the bootstrap approximation of the KLD with a bootstrap-based bias correction is expressed by $E_*(-2\ell(\hat{\theta}^*|y)) + k_b$, and is estimated by

$$\text{BDb} = \frac{1}{J}\sum_{j=1}^{J} -2\ell(\hat{\theta}^*(j)|y) + k_b.$$

It follows that the bootstrap bias-corrected BDCP would be defined as

$$\text{BDCPb} = \frac{1}{J}\sum_{j=1}^{J} I\left[d(\hat{g},\hat{\theta}_1^*(j)) + k_{1b} < d(\hat{g},\hat{\theta}_2^*(j)) + k_{2b}\right], \quad (6)$$

where k_{1b} and k_{2b} correspond to the bootstrap-based corrections for the null and alternative models, respectively.

Similarly, the k bias-corrected BD is expressed as

$$\text{BDk} = \frac{1}{J}\sum_{j=1}^{J} -2\ell(\hat{\theta}^*(j)|y) + k,$$

and the k bias-corrected BDCP is given by

$$\text{BDCPk} = \frac{1}{J}\sum_{j=1}^{J} I\left[d(\hat{g},\hat{\theta}_1^*(j)) + k_1 < d(\hat{g},\hat{\theta}_2^*(j)) + k_2\right], \quad (7)$$

where k_1 and k_2 are the number of functionally independent parameters that define the null and alternative models, respectively.

4. Simulation Studies

The following simulation sets are designed to explore the bias when estimating both the DCP based on the Kullback–Leibler discrepancy (KLDCP) and the expected value of the KLD. We present different hypothesis testing scenarios, not all of which are conventional, under a linear data-generating model and for varying sample sizes. Each setting exhibits three different approaches to formulating the BD: adding the bootstrap-based correction (BDb), adding k (BDk), and leaving the estimator uncorrected.

4.1. Settings for Simulation Sets

For Sets 1 to 5, the true data-generating model is of the form

$$y_i = x_i^T \beta_0 + \epsilon_i,$$

with $\beta_0^T = \begin{bmatrix} \beta_{0,1} & \beta_{0,2} & \cdots & \beta_{0,p} \end{bmatrix}$, $x_i^T = \begin{bmatrix} 1 & x_{i2} & \cdots & x_{ip} \end{bmatrix}$, and

$$\begin{bmatrix} x_{i2} & \cdots & x_{ip} \end{bmatrix}^T \sim N_{p-1}(\mu, \Sigma), \quad (8)$$

where the entries of μ are chosen from $\{-1,1\}$ with equal probability, and $\Sigma = \text{diag}_{p-1}(100)$. For Sets 1 to 4, we have $\epsilon_i \sim N(0, \sigma_0^2)$; for Set 5, we have that $\epsilon_i \sim t_{df=5}$, where t_{df} denotes the Student's t distribution based on df degrees of freedom; and for Set 6, we have that $\epsilon_i \sim Z \cdot N(0,1) + (1-Z) \cdot N(0,50)$, where $Z \sim \text{Bernoulli}(\pi)$ with $\pi = 0.85$.

In the setting at hand, the true data-generating model g has parameters $\theta = (\beta_0^T, \sigma_0^2)^T$. Hurvich and Tsai [6] showed that for the family of approximating models $y = X\beta + \epsilon$, where X is the design matrix and $\epsilon \sim N(0, \sigma^2 I_n)$, with maximum likelihood estimators given by

$$\hat{\beta} = (X^T X)^{-1} X^T y$$

and

$$\hat{\sigma}^2 = \frac{(y - X\hat{\beta})^T (y - X\hat{\beta})}{n},$$

the KLD measure $d(g, \hat{\theta})$ is given by

$$d(g, \hat{\theta}) = n \log(2\pi\hat{\sigma}^2) + \frac{n\sigma_0^2}{\hat{\sigma}^2} + \frac{(X\beta_0 - X\hat{\beta})^T (X\beta_0 - X\hat{\beta})}{\hat{\sigma}^2}. \quad (9)$$

The expected value of the KLD for the null and the alternative models was approximated by averaging the KLD over 5000 samples generated from g. These 5000 KLD values, computed using (9), approximate the joint distribution of $d(g, \hat{\theta}_1)$ and $d(g, \hat{\theta}_2)$; hence, the simulation-based estimator of the KLDCP is given by

$$\hat{P} = \frac{1}{5000} \sum_{i=1}^{5000} I[d(g, \hat{\theta}_1(i)) < d(g, \hat{\theta}_2(i))]. \quad (10)$$

This KLDCP estimate is calculated 100 times in order to estimate the KLDCP distribution and its expected value.

Finally, for each of the 5000 samples, we calculate the BD and the BDb using 200 bootstrap samples. However, to attenuate the simulation variability incurred by the mixture distribution, the number of bootstrap samples in Set 6 was increased to 500. The results displayed in the tables are based on averages over the 5000 samples.

Set 1: *Null hypothesis is correctly specified, and alternative hypothesis is overspecified.*

Consider the true data-generating model given by

$$y_i = \beta_{0,1} + \beta_{0,2} x_{i2} + \beta_{0,3} x_{i3} + \epsilon_i,$$

where $\epsilon_i \sim N(0, 50)$, $\beta_{0,1} = 1$, $\beta_{0,2} = \beta_{0,3} = 0.5$ and $\begin{bmatrix} x_{i2} & x_{i3} \end{bmatrix}^T$ is sampled as indicated in (8).

For the hypothesis testing setting in Set 1, the null and alternative models are defined as

$$H_1 : y_i = \beta_1 + \beta_2 x_{2i} + \beta_3 x_{i3},$$
$$H_2 : y_i = \beta_1 + \beta_2 x_{i2} + \beta_3 x_{i3} + \beta_4 x_{i4} + \beta_5 x_{i5} + \beta_6 x_{i6} + \beta_7 x_{i7}.$$

Note that the null model is adequately specified, while the alternative model contains the true model plus four additional explanatory variables. These extra explanatory variables are generated from the distribution indicated in (8).

Set 2: *Null hypothesis is underspecified, and alternative hypothesis is correctly specified.*

Consider the true data-generating model given by

$$y_i = \beta_{0,1} + \beta_{0,2} x_{i2} + \beta_{0,3} x_{i3} + \beta_{0,4} x_{i4} + \beta_{0,5} x_{i5} + \epsilon_i,$$

where $\epsilon_i \sim N(0, 45)$, $\beta_{0,1} = 1, \beta_{0,2} = 0.11, \beta_{0,3} = 0.13, \beta_{0,4} = 0.12, \beta_{0,5} = -0.11$, and $\begin{bmatrix} x_{i2} & x_{i3} & \cdots & x_{i5} \end{bmatrix}^T$ is sampled as indicated in (8).

For the hypothesis testing setting in Set 2, the null and alternative models are

$$H_1 : y_i = \beta_1 + \beta_2 x_{2i} + \beta_3 x_{i3} + \beta_4 x_{i4},$$
$$H_2 : y_i = \beta_1 + \beta_2 x_{i2} + \beta_3 x_{i3} + \beta_4 x_{i4} + \beta_5 x_{i5}.$$

Here, the alternative model has the same structure as the data-generating model, but the null model is missing one of the explanatory variables in the true model, namely x_5.

Set 3: *Both null and alternative models are underspecified, but the null is closer to the data-generating model.*

Consider the true data-generating model given by

$$y_i = \beta_{0,1} + \beta_{0,2} x_{i2} + \beta_{0,3} x_{i3} + \beta_{0,4} x_{i4} + \beta_{0,5} x_{i5} + \beta_{0,6} x_{i6} + \epsilon_i,$$

where $\epsilon_i \sim N(0, 50)$, $\beta_{0,1} = 1, \beta_{0,2} = \beta_{0,3} = 0.5, \beta_{0,4} = \beta_{0,5} = -0.5, \beta_{0,6} = 0.1$, and $\begin{bmatrix} x_{i2} & x_{i3} & \cdots & x_{i6} \end{bmatrix}^T$ is sampled as indicated in (8).

For the hypothesis testing setting in Set 3, the null and alternative models are

$$H_1 : y_i = \beta_1 + \beta_2 x_{2i} + \beta_3 x_{i3},$$
$$H_2 : y_i = \beta_1 + \beta_4 x_{i4} + \beta_6 x_{i6}.$$

In this setting, both the null and alternative candidate models have the same number of explanatory variables, and they are both missing variable x_4. However, there is a slight difference in the effect sizes of the variables for these models. For the alternative, the effect sizes are -0.5 and 0.1 for x_4 and x_6, respectively. On the other hand, the effect size for the null model is 0.5 for both x_2 and x_3. When comparing the null and alternative models, the smaller effect size on x_6 sets the alternative further away from the true model.

Set 4: *Both null and alternative models are equally underspecified.*

Consider the true data-generating model given by

$$y_i = \beta_{0,1} + \beta_{0,2} x_{i2} + \beta_{0,3} x_{i3} + \beta_{0,4} x_{i4} + \beta_{0,5} x_{i5} + \beta_{0,6} x_{i6} + \beta_{0,7} x_{i7} + \epsilon_i,$$

with $\epsilon_i \sim N(0, 50)$, $\beta_{0,1} = 1, \beta_{0,2} = \beta_{0,3} = \beta_{0,6} = \beta_{0,7} = 0.5, \beta_{0,4} = \beta_{0,5} = -0.5$, and $\begin{bmatrix} x_{i1} & x_{i2} & \cdots & x_{i7} \end{bmatrix}^T$ is sampled as indicated in (8).

For the hypothesis testing setting in Set 4, the null and alternative models are

$$H_1 : y_i = \beta_1 + \beta_2 x_{2i} + \beta_3 x_{i3},$$
$$H_2 : y_i = \beta_1 + \beta_4 x_{i4} + \beta_5 x_{i5}.$$

Here, the null and alternative candidate models are equally underspecified because they have the same number of explanatory variables with the same effect sizes, and neither model captures the true data-generating model.

Set 5: *Null model has correct mean specification and alternative model is overspecified, but both are misspecified with respect to the error distribution, which is a Student's t distribution.*

Consider the true data generating model given by

$$y_i = \beta_{0,1} + \epsilon_i,$$

with $\epsilon_i \sim t_{df=5}$ and $\beta_{0,1} = 1$. Therefore, $\sigma_0^2 = \frac{5}{3}$.

For the hypothesis testing setting in Set 5, the null and alternative models are

$$H_1 : y_i = \beta_1,$$
$$H_2 : y_i = \beta_1 + \beta_2 x_{i2},$$

where $x_{i2} \sim N(1, 100)$. This setting is similar to the one displayed in Set 1, where the null is properly specified while the alternative is overspecified. However, the models in the setting at hand inadequately specify the distribution of the errors.

Set 6: *Null model has correct mean specification, and the alternative model is overspecified, but both are misspecified with respect to the error distribution, which is a mixture of normals.*

Consider the true data-generating model given by

$$y_i = \beta_{0,1} + \epsilon_i,$$

with $\epsilon_i \sim Z \cdot N(0, 1) + (1 - Z) \cdot N(0, 50)$, where $Z \sim Bernoulli(\pi)$ with $\pi = 0.85$. Therefore,

$$\sigma_0^2 = 0.85(1) + 0.15(50)$$
$$= 8.35.$$

For the hypothesis testing setting in Set 6, the null and alternative models are

$$H_1 : y_i = \beta_1,$$
$$H_2 : y_i = \beta_1 + \beta_2 x_{i2},$$

where $x_{i2} \sim N(1, 100)$. This setting is similar to the one featured in Set 5. However, the errors in the setting at hand are generated from a mixture of normal distributions.

4.2. KLDCP Estimates From Simulations

For the tables showing the KLDCP simulation results, the columns are labeled as follows.

(1) **KLDCP** corresponds to results based on the distribution of 100 replicates of KLDCP, where each KLDCP is calculated using (10). Note that the null and alternative KLD joint distribution is characterized based on discrepancy replicates obtained through (9).
(2) **BDCPb** corresponds to results based on the distribution of 5000 replicates of BDCPb. Each BDCPb is computed using (6) with 200 bootstrap samples for Sets 1–5 and 500 bootstrap samples for Set 6.
(3) **BDCPk** corresponds to results based on the distribution of 5000 replicates of BDCPk. Each BDCPk is computed using (7) with 200 bootstrap samples for Sets 1–5 and 500 bootstrap samples for Set 6.
(4) **BDCP** corresponds to results based on the distribution of 5000 replicates of the uncorrected BDCP. Each BDCP is computed using (1) with 200 bootstrap samples for Sets 1–5 and 500 bootstrap samples for Set 6.

4.3. Estimates of the Expected KLD From Simulations

For the tables showing the KLD results, the columns are labeled as follows.

(1) **E(KLD)** corresponds to the average of 5000 discrepancies calculated using (9).
(2) **E(BD)** corresponds to the average of 5000 replicates of BD, where each BD is calculated by

$$\frac{1}{M} \sum_{m=1}^{M} -2\ell(\hat{\theta}^*(m)|y).$$

We have that $M = 200$ for Sets 1–5 and $M = 500$ for Set 6.

(3) **ΔBDb** corresponds to the difference between the estimate of $E(BD)$, with each BD corrected by k_b and the estimate of $E(KLD)$ described in (1). In other words, if we let $j \in \{1, 2 \ldots, 5000\}$ be the number of simulated data sets, $\widetilde{BD}_j$ be the BD estimate for each data set j, and k_{jb} be the k_b correction for data set j, then

$$\Delta \text{BDb} = \frac{1}{5000} \sum_{j=1}^{5000} \left[\widetilde{BD}_j + k_{jb} \right] - E(KLD).$$

(4) **ΔBDk** shows the same difference described in (3), but using k instead of k_b, which results in

$$\Delta \text{BDk} = \frac{1}{5000} \sum_{j=1}^{5000} \left[\widetilde{BD}_j + k \right] - E(KLD).$$

4.4. Discussion of Simulation Results

As mentioned previously, in the conventional hypothesis testing scenario for comparing nested models, Riedle, Neath and Cavanaugh [1] established that the uncorrected BDCP approximates the p-value derived from the likelihood ratio test. Therefore, in the case where the null candidate model is correctly specified, both the uncorrected BDCP and the p-value have a $Uniform(0, 1)$ distribution. This behavior is displayed in Table 1, where for large sample sizes, the mean and median of the BDCP distribution are around 0.5. This is a problematic feature of the uncorrected BDCP and p-values because the measure does not reliably favor the null model in those settings where the null is true. However, we see that for large sample sizes, both the BDCPk and the BDCPb values are close to 1, which clearly favors the null model.

Table 2 shows the results from the setting where the alternative hypothesis is correctly specified, while the null is underspecified. Here, we would expect all the discrepancy probabilities to be close to 0, as seen in the case where the sample size is $N = 500$. However, for smaller sample sizes, i.e., $N = 25$ and $N = 50$, we observe larger values for the discrepancy probabilities. In fact, for $N = 25$, the BDCPb is 0.89 and, with a mean and median close to 0.5, the uncorrected BDCP exhibits similar behavior to the case where the null is true. This phenomenon is expected within the framework of model selection, where additional explanatory variables are favorable if there is a sufficient sample size to adequately estimate their effects. If the sample size is too small to construct reliable estimates, then it is best to choose smaller models, even at the expense of model misspecification.

The results from Tables 1, 3–6 show that when estimating the KLDCP with a small sample size ($N = 25$ to $N = 100$), the BDb performs either better than or as well as the BDk. For large sample sizes, all simulation sets exhibit a similar performance for both corrections.

For discrepancy estimation, Tables 7–10 show that across all sample sizes, k_b overcorrects for the bias of the discrepancy approximation, and the over correction is more prominent for small sample sizes. It is worth noting that this evident over-estimation from the BDb is accompanied by a superior bias reduction of the corresponding KLDCP estimator. For instance, Table 7 shows a significant over-estimation by BDb compared to BDk, especially in the small sample settings. However, the corresponding estimator of the KLDCP, displayed in Table 1, exhibits less bias for BDCPb than for BDCPk.

Finally, Tables 11 and 12 show that, across all sample sizes, the correction by k_b markedly reduces the bias compared to the correction by k. This means that in the setting where the mean structure is correctly specified for the null and overspecified for the alternative, but both models are incorrectly specified with respect to the error distribution, the bootstrap-based correction evidently outperforms the simple correction of k.

In most cases, however, the bias reductions resulting from the k_b and the k corrections are comparable. Therefore, our simulation studies suggest that if the null and/or the alternative models are misspecified, then correcting by either k_b or k will generally yield comparable estimators of the expected KLDCP.

Table 1. Distribution approximations for Set 1, where the null model is correctly specified, while the alternative model is overspecified.

Statistic	KLDCP	BDCPb	BDCPk	BDCP
N = 500				
Mean	1.000	0.878	0.868	0.515
Median	1.000	1.000	1.000	0.515
SD	0.000	0.233	0.241	0.282
N = 100				
Mean	1.000	0.918	0.864	0.564
Median	1.000	1.000	0.995	0.580
SD	0.000	0.186	0.225	0.256
N = 50				
Mean	1.000	0.966	0.875	0.631
Median	1.000	1.000	0.980	0.650
SD	0.000	0.111	0.193	0.220
N = 25				
Mean	1.000	0.999	0.886	0.739
Median	1.000	1.000	0.955	0.755
SD	0.000	0.012	0.144	0.156

Table 2. Distribution approximations for Set 2, where the null model is underspecified, while the alternative model is correctly specified.

Statistic	KLDCP	BDCPb	BDCPk	BDCP
N = 500				
Mean	0.001	0.022	0.021	0.011
Median	0.001	0.000	0.000	0.000
SD	0.000	0.088	0.085	0.043
N = 100				
Mean	0.156	0.470	0.428	0.264
Median	0.156	0.340	0.280	0.170
SD	0.005	0.390	0.378	0.257
N = 50				
Mean	0.372	0.691	0.597	0.409
Median	0.372	0.905	0.630	0.360
SD	0.007	0.350	0.354	0.266
N = 25				
Mean	0.617	0.890	0.698	0.536
Median	0.617	0.990	0.785	0.535
SD	0.006	0.213	0.280	0.222

Table 3. Distribution approximations for Set 3, where the null and alternative models are underspecified, but the null model is closer to the true data-generating model.

Statistic	KLDCP	BDCPb	BDCPk	BDCP
N = 500				
Mean	1.000	1.000	1.000	1.000
Median	1.000	1.000	1.000	1.000
SD	0.000	0.013	0.013	0.013
N = 100				
Mean	0.979	0.910	0.910	0.910
Median	0.979	1.000	1.000	1.000
SD	0.002	0.244	0.244	0.244
N = 50				
Mean	0.916	0.807	0.808	0.808
Median	0.916	0.970	0.970	0.970
SD	0.004	0.311	0.309	0.309
N = 25				
Mean	0.804	0.692	0.699	0.699
Median	0.805	0.845	0.840	0.840
SD	0.005	0.314	0.303	0.303

Table 4. Distribution approximations for Set 4, where the null and alternative models are equally underspecified.

Statistic	KLDCP	BDCPb	BDCPk	BDCP
N = 500				
Mean	0.498	0.507	0.507	0.507
Median	0.498	0.570	0.580	0.580
SD	0.007	0.478	0.478	0.478
N = 100				
Mean	0.500	0.510	0.509	0.509
Median	0.500	0.562	0.567	0.567
SD	0.007	0.442	0.442	0.442
N = 50				
Mean	0.500	0.502	0.502	0.502
Median	0.500	0.505	0.515	0.515
SD	0.007	0.407	0.406	0.406
N = 25				
Mean	0.501	0.501	0.501	0.501
Median	0.501	0.490	0.495	0.495
SD	0.007	0.353	0.345	0.345

Table 5. Distribution approximations for Set 5, where the null and alternative models are misspecified with respect to the error distribution. Here, the errors are generated from a Student's t distribution.

Statistic	KLDCP	BDCPb	BDCPk	BDCP
N = 500				
Mean	1.000	0.794	0.794	0.499
Median	1.000	1.000	1.000	0.500
SD	0.000	0.329	0.328	0.289
N = 100				
Mean	1.000	0.807	0.794	0.507
Median	1.000	1.000	1.000	0.515
SD	0.000	0.318	0.323	0.284
N = 50				
Mean	1.000	0.825	0.790	0.508
Median	1.000	1.000	0.995	0.505
SD	0.000	0.301	0.315	0.273
N = 25				
Mean	1.000	0.862	0.790	0.525
Median	1.000	1.000	0.985	0.530
SD	0.000	0.270	0.306	0.261

Table 6. Distribution approximations for Set 6, where the null and alternative models are misspecified with respect to the error distribution. Here, the errors are generated from a mixture of normal distributions.

Statistic	KLDCP	BDCPb	BDCPk	BDCP
N = 500				
Mean	1.000	0.783	0.786	0.487
Median	1.000	1.000	1.000	0.484
SD	0.000	0.338	0.335	0.289
N = 100				
Mean	1.000	0.808	0.793	0.495
Median	1.000	1.000	0.998	0.496
SD	0.000	0.322	0.325	0.283
N = 50				
Mean	1.000	0.851	0.793	0.502
Median	1.000	1.000	0.994	0.494
SD	0.000	0.286	0.311	0.269
N = 25				
Mean	1.000	0.906	0.787	0.509
Median	1.000	1.000	0.986	0.490
SD	0.000	0.229	0.300	0.246

Table 7. Expected value of the KLD, its bootstrap estimate, and the bias of the corrected bootstrap estimates for the null and alternative models in Set 1. Here, the null model is correctly specified, while the alternative model is overspecified.

Hypothesis	E(KLD)	E(BD)	ΔBDb	ΔBDk
N = 500				
Null	3378.949	3375.407	0.488	0.411
Alternative	3383.138	3375.578	0.686	0.362
N = 100				
Null	679.282	675.291	0.385	−0.030
Alternative	684.115	676.667	2.518	0.521
N = 50				
Null	342.167	338.498	1.267	0.268
Alternative	348.245	342.348	7.476	2.065
N = 25				
Null	174.334	171.169	3.657	0.910
Alternative	183.828	193.249	43.328	17.290

Table 8. Expected value of the KLD, its bootstrap estimate, and the bias of the corrected bootstrap estimates for the null and alternative models in Set 2. Here, the null model is underspecified, while the alternative model is correctly specified.

Hypothesis	E(KLD)	E(BD)	ΔBDb	ΔBDk
N = 500				
Null	3340.491	3335.733	0.410	0.290
Alternative	3328.467	3322.581	0.319	0.143
N = 100				
Null	672.373	667.928	1.210	0.520
Alternative	671.137	665.628	1.493	0.454
N = 50				
Null	339.515	334.726	1.891	0.226
Alternative	339.923	334.181	2.888	0.305
N = 25				
Null	174.136	171.376	7.446	2.223
Alternative	176.073	174.320	13.270	4.106

Table 9. Expected value of the KLD, its bootstrap estimate, and the bias of the corrected bootstrap estimates for the null and alternative models in Set 3. Here, the null and alternative models are underspecified, but the null model is closer to the true data-generating model.

Hypothesis	E(KLD)	E(BD)	ΔBDb	ΔBDk
N = 500				
Null	3726.902	3726.159	3.401	3.332
Alternative	3832.770	3832.395	3.704	3.626

Table 9. Cont.

Hypothesis	E(KLD)	E(BD)	ΔBDb	ΔBDk
N = 100				
Null	745.967	745.809	4.358	3.943
Alternative	766.212	766.813	4.947	4.528
N = 50				
Null	373.419	373.704	5.309	4.325
Alternative	383.156	384.020	5.843	4.858
N = 25				
Null	187.563	188.745	8.082	5.245
Alternative	191.924	194.082	8.878	6.088

Table 10. Expected value of the KLD, its bootstrap estimate, and the bias of the corrected bootstrap estimates for the null and alternative models in Set 4. Here, the null and alternative models are equally underspecified.

Hypothesis	E(KLD)	E(BD)	ΔBDb	ΔBDk
N = 500				
Null	3923.423	3923.908	5.022	4.948
Alternative	3923.580	3924.705	5.475	5.399
N = 100				
Null	784.021	784.917	5.080	4.670
Alternative	784.042	785.026	5.241	4.823
N = 50				
Null	391.751	393.155	6.335	5.343
Alternative	391.753	393.131	6.222	5.239
N = 25				
Null	195.732	198.616	9.602	6.821
Alternative	195.862	198.690	9.598	6.804

Table 11. Expected value of the KLD, its bootstrap estimate, and the bias of the corrected bootstrap estimates for the null and alternative models in Set 5. Here, the null and alternative models are misspecified with respect to the error distribution, and the errors are generated from a Student's t distribution.

Hypothesis	E(KLD)	E(BD)	ΔBDb	ΔBDk
N = 500				
Null	1678.652	1672.369	−2.224	−4.178
Alternative	1679.695	1672.387	−2.248	−4.231
N = 100				
Null	338.728	334.154	−0.920	−2.471
Alternative	339.866	334.300	−0.728	−2.438

Table 11. *Cont.*

Hypothesis	E(KLD)	E(BD)	ΔBDb	ΔBDk
N = 50				
Null	171.377	167.500	−0.231	−1.839
Alternative	172.640	167.847	0.283	−1.714
N = 25				
Null	87.689	83.577	−0.434	−2.077
Alternative	89.311	84.495	0.869	−1.785

Table 12. Expected value of the KLD, its bootstrap estimate, and the bias of the corrected bootstrap estimates for the null and alternative models in Set 6. Here, the null and alternative models are misspecified with respect to the error distribution, and the errors are generated from a mixture of normal distributions.

Hypothesis	E(KLD)	E(BD)	ΔBDb	ΔBDk
N = 500				
Null	2488.932	2480.154	−0.389	6.554
Alternative	2490.012	2480.141	−0.310	6.659
N = 100				
Null	508.122	497.000	−0.383	8.404
Alternative	509.426	497.237	−0.597	8.459
N = 50				
Null	263.382	252.424	−2.852	8.590
Alternative	264.974	253.245	−3.930	8.361
N = 25				
Null	144.895	131.870	−4.361	10.842
Alternative	147.551	134.298	−7.782	9.956

5. Application: Creatine Kinase Levels during Football Preseason

In this section, we apply the BDCP to a data set from a biomedical setting. The goal of this application is to understand the changes in creatine kinase (CK) levels observed on the blood samples of college football players during preseason training. In order to properly explain the variation of CK, we must select between competing models that use different demographic and clinical variables. We will analyze the models selected by the k_b corrected, the k corrected and the uncorrected BDCP, and we will compare the results to the selection of models via the more conventional p-value approach.

5.1. Overview of Application

During strenuous exercise, skeletal muscle cells break down and release a variety of intracellular contents. When in excess, a condition known as exertional rhabdomyolysis (ER) can occur, which may result in life-threatening complications such as renal failure, cardiac arrhythmia and compartment syndrome. Creatine kinase (CK) is one of the proteins released during muscle breakdown, and measuring its levels is the most sensitive test for assessing muscular damage that could lead to ER [7].

During the off-season workouts in January 2011, a group of 13 University of Iowa football players developed ER. This event led to a prospective study where 30 University of Iowa football athletes were followed during a 34-day preseason workout camp. Variables such as body mass index (BMI) and CK levels were obtained from blood samples that were drawn at the first, third, and seventh day of the camp. Other demographic and clinical variables such as age, number of semesters in the program and history of rhabdomyolysis were also collected.

The initial results of the study, published by Smoot et al. [8], show that the CK levels at later time points were significantly different than the levels at earlier times. However, most of the clinical and demographic variables were not significant in explaining the levels of CK. One of the underlying issues with this type of modeling analysis is that the significance of each variable can only be assessed by hypothesis tests with nested models. For example, suppose that we wish to determine the significance of BMI in the presence of semesters in the program. To obtain a p-value for BMI, we need to formulate a hypothesis test where the null model only contains semesters in the program, while the alternative model contains both BMI and semesters in the program.

Although this setting may be useful in some scenarios, it is too limiting. For instance, suppose that we wish to choose between two non-nested models where one contains BMI and the other contains semesters in the program. Although a conventional test based on linear regression models would not be able to answer this question, the BDCP approach could indeed determine the propriety of either model in this type of non-nested setting.

In the analysis of this data set, we let $CK3$ be the log of CK levels measured at the seventh day of the camp, $CK1$ be the log of CK levels measured at the first day of the camp, and *Semesters* be the number of semesters at the program. Of note, the log transformation is routinely applied in studies involving CK levels in order to justify approximate normality, as the raw levels tend to have heavily right-skewed distributions.

Now, consider the following hypothesis testing settings.

Setting 1: *Testing the propriety of the model containing $CK1$.*

$$H_1 : CK3 = \beta_1,$$
$$H_2 : CK3 = \beta_1 + \beta_2 \, CK1.$$

Setting 2: *Testing the propriety of the model containing $CK1$ and Semesters over the model containing only $CK1$.*

$$H_1 : CK3 = \beta_1 + \beta_2 \, CK1,$$
$$H_2 : CK3 = \beta_1 + \beta_2 \, CK1 + \beta_3 \, Semesters.$$

Setting 3: *Head-to-head comparison of non-nested models.*

$$H_1 : CK3 = \beta_1 + \beta_2 \, CK1 + \beta_3 \, BMI,$$
$$H_2 : CK3 = \beta_1 + \beta_2 \, CK1 + \beta_3 \, Semesters.$$

5.2. Results of Application

The results for the application are summarized in Table 13. Settings 1 and 2 illustrate the congruence between BDCP and p-values in the case of hypothesis testing based on nested models. Setting 1 assesses the propriety of a model that includes only the intercept against a model that includes both the intercept and the levels of $CK1$. The p-value for $CK1$ in this setting is 0.001, which means that, using a level α of 0.05, $CK1$ is significant in explaining the variation in $CK3$ levels. Both the BDCPk and BDCPb are 0.075, which means that there is a 7.5% chance that the null model is preferred over multiple bootstrap samples, indicating that the model containing $CK1$ is superior.

Once we establish that $CK1$ is an important variable to include in our model, the next step is to determine if additional variables can improve our model fit. Setting 2 displays a hypothesis test where the null model only contains $CK1$, while the alternative contains both $CK1$ and *Semesters*. The p-value for *Semesters* is 0.734, which means that *Semesters* is not statistically significant, and a reasonable investigator would choose to exclude *Semesters* from the final model. The corrected BDCP values arrive at the same conclusion. For instance, the BDCPb is 0.995, which indicates that the across multiple bootstrap samples, the null model is chosen 99.5% of the time; therefore, the BDCP encourages us to choose the model that excludes *Semesters*.

Table 13. From left to right: results for Setting 1, Setting 2, and Setting 3. BDCPk is the BDCP corrected by k, BDCPb is the BDCP corrected by k_b, and BDCP is the uncorrected BDCP. Results are based on 200 bootstraps samples.

			BDCP		
BDCPk	0.075	BDCPk	0.990	BDCPk	0.815
BDCPb	0.075	BDCPb	0.995	BDCPb	0.780
BDCP	0.055	BDCP	0.495	BDCP	0.815
			p-Value		
CK1	0.001	CK1	0.001	CK1	0.001
		Semesters	0.734	BMI	0.176
				Semesters	0.936

The rationale for testing *Semesters* is based on the idea that more senior athletes tend to rigorously maintain their workout habits during the off season, mostly because of experience and maturity. Therefore, *Semesters* is a variable that may confound the effects of *CK*1 on the variation of *CK*3. Additionally, medical literature has shown that BMI highly correlates with CK levels and the development of ER [9], which means that one should also test for the propriety of models that include *BMI*. Thus, one could ask if a model featuring *BMI* would be better than a model featuring *Semesters*. This results in a hypothesis testing scenario where the null and alternative models are non-nested, as exhibited in Setting 3.

First, note that the *p*-values displayed in the table for Setting 3 do not answer the question at hand. These *p*-values are obtained from partial tests applied to the full model containing both variables. On the other hand, the BDCP gives us meaningful information about the performance of adding *BMI* versus adding *Semesters*. The BDCPb tells us that there is a 78% probability that the model containing *BMI* is a better fit than the model containing *Semesters*. If we use the BDCPk instead, the probability increases to 81.5%. In both cases, if we are debating weather to include *BMI* or *Semesters* as an adjusting variable, the BDCP clearly favors the inclusion of *BMI*.

6. Conclusions

When deciding between two competing models, practitioners of statistics normally utilize traditional hypothesis testing methods that rely on the assumption that one of the candidate models is properly specified. This approach is problematic because it is unreasonable to assume that one of the proposed models is precisely true. In addition, these methods are only applicable for nested models. To avoid any underlying assumptions and model structure limitations, Riedle, Neath and Cavanaugh [1] propose the use of the bootstrap discrepancy probability (BDCP) to assess the propriety of the fit of two candidate models. However, the bootstrap discrepancy (BD) utilized in this work provides a biased estimator of the Kullback–Leibler discrepancy (KLD).

When hypothesis testing assumptions are met, the BDCP asymptotically approximates the likelihood ratio test *p*-value. Therefore, similarly to *p*-values, the distribution of the BDCP is uniform if the null hypothesis is true. Hence, in settings when the null is true, the BDCP would be of limited value in choosing the appropriate model.

In this paper, we proposed utilizing the k_b or the k corrected BDCP, namely BDCPb and BDCPk, respectively. The BDCPb employs the BDb, a bootstrap corrected estimator of the

KLD, while the BDCPk uses the BDk, a BD corrected by adding the number of functionally independent parameters in the candidate model. We showed that for most settings, the BDb serves as an over-corrected estimator of the KLD, but the corresponding BDCPb is less biased than the BDCPk for the estimation of the KLDCP. However, in the case when there is distributional misspecification, we showed that the BDb has negligible bias for the estimation of expected value of the KLD.

Moreover, the estimation of the bootstrap correction k_b utilizes the same bootstrap samples that were used to calculate the BD; therefore, we argue that the computational requirements of estimating k_b are not too burdensome. However, if the sample size is moderately large compared to the number of parameters in the model, then we showed that using k to correct the bias generally results in comparable values of the KLDCP estimates.

Author Contributions: Conceptualization, A.D. and J.C.; Formal analysis, A.D. and J.C.; Methodology, A.D. and J.C.; Supervision, J.C.; Writing—original draft, A.D. and J.C.; Writing—review and editing, A.D. and J.C. All authors have read and agreed to the published version of the manuscript.

Funding: This research received no external funding.

Institutional Review Board Statement: Not applicable.

Data Availability Statement: The R code used in generating the data for the simulation study is available on request from the corresponding author. The data for the application are not publicly available since the dataset is confidential.

Conflicts of Interest: The authors declare no conflict of interest.

References

1. Riedle, B.; Neath, A.; Cavanaugh, J.E. Reconceptualizing the *p*-Value From a Likelihood Ratio Test: A Probabilistic Pairwise Comparison of Models Based on Kullback-Leibler Discrepancy Measures. *J. Appl. Stat.* **2020**, *47*, 13–15. [CrossRef] [PubMed]
2. Efron, B.; Tibshirani, R. *An Introduction to the Bootstrap*, 2nd ed.; Chapman Hall: New York, NY, USA, 1993; pp. 31–37.
3. Efron, B. Estimating the Error Rate of a Prediction Rule: Improvement on Cross-Validation. *J. Am. Stat. Assoc.* **1983**, *78*, 316–331. [CrossRef]
4. Efron, B. How Biased is the Apparent Error Rate of a Prediction Rule? *J. Am. Stat. Assoc.* **1986**, *81*, 461–470. [CrossRef]
5. Cavanaugh, J.E.; Shumway, R.H. A Bootstrap Variant of AIC for State-Space Model Selection. *Stat. Sin.* **1997**, *7*, 473–496.
6. Hurvich, C.M.; Tsai, C. Regression and Time Series Model Selection in Small Samples. *Biometrika* **1989**, *76*, 297–307. [CrossRef]
7. Torres, P; Helmstetter, J; Kaye, A; Kaye A. Rhabdomyolysis: Pathogenesis, Diagnosis, and Treatment. *Ochsner J. Spring* **2015**, *15*, 58–69.
8. Smoot M.K.; Cavanaugh J.E.; Amendola A.; West D.R.; Herwaldt L.A. Creatine Kinase Levels During Preseason Camp in National Collegiate Athletic Association Division I Football Athletes. *Clin. J. Sport Med.* **2014**, *5*, 438–440. [CrossRef] [PubMed]
9. Vasquez C.R.; DiSanto T.; Reilly J.P.; Forker C.M.; Holena D.N.; Wu Q.; Lanken P.N.; Christie J.D.; Shashaty M.G.S. Relationship of Body Mass Index, Serum Creatine Kinase, and Acute Kidney Injury After Severe Trauma. *J. Trauma Acute Care Surg.* **2020**, *89*, 179–185. [CrossRef] [PubMed]

Communication

Spatial Information-Theoretic Optimal LPI Radar Waveform Design

Jun Chen [1,*], Jie Wang [1,*], Yidong Zhang [1], Fei Wang [2] and Jianjiang Zhou [2]

1 School of Electronic and Information Engineering, Nanjing University of Information Science and Technology, Nanjing 210044, China
2 Key Laboratory of Radar Imaging and Microwave Photonics, Ministry of Education, Nanjing University of Aeronautics and Astronautics, Nanjing 210016, China
* Correspondence: junchen@nuist.edu.cn (J.C.); 002915@nuist.edu.cn (J.W.)

Abstract: In this paper, the design of low probability of intercept (LPI) radar waveforms considers not only the performance of passive interception systems (PISs), but also radar detection and resolution performance. Waveform design is an important considerations for the LPI ability of radar. Since information theory has a powerful performance-bound description ability from the perspective of information flow, LPI waveforms are designed in this paper within the constraints of the detection performance metrics of radar and PISs, both of which are measured by the Kullback–Leibler divergence, and the resolution performance metric, which is measured by joint entropy. The designed optimization model of LPI waveforms can be solved using the sequential quadratic programming (SQP) method. Simulation results verify that the designed LPI waveforms not only have satisfactory target-detecting and resolution performance, but also have a superior low interception performance against PISs.

Keywords: LPI; radar waveform; passive interception systems; Kullback–Leibler divergence; joint entropy

1. Introduction

Low probability of intercept (LPI) radar waveforms have been developed to combat passive interception systems (PISs) for several decades [1–3]. Common LPI waveforms include FM/PM signals, FSK/PSK signals, etc. [2,4–7], which utilize wideband modulations to spread the energy in a frequency. LPI radar waveform design is a primary means of affecting the interception performance of PISs, which is actually a compromise between radar performance (which contains detection and resolution performance) and the interception performance of the PIS. In this paper, the dispersion of waveform energy in a frequency can be implemented through the compromise between the optimal detection performance, resolution performance, and LPI performance of radar by adjusting their frequency amplitudes.

In frequency amplitude adjustment modeling, it is crucial to establish the performance metrics of both the radar and the PIS. For radar detection performance, besides metrics such as output signal-to-noise ratio (SNR), relative entropy, and mean square error, the method of maximizing mutual information has been widely used in optimal radar waveform design (see [8–11] and references therein). Zhu et al. [12] presented the Kullback–Leibler divergence (KLD) as more appropriate than mutual information to describe optimal radar detection performance. The KLD is defined as

$$D(\mathbf{x};\mathbf{n}_1) = E_{\mathbf{y}}[D(\mathbf{x};\mathbf{n}_1|\mathbf{y})] - I(\mathbf{x};\mathbf{y}), \qquad (1)$$

where $\mathbf{x} = \mathbf{y} + \mathbf{n}_1$ is the received radar signal, $\mathbf{y}$ is the target response, $\mathbf{n}_1$ is the background radar noise, $E(\cdot)$ denotes capture expectation, $I(\cdot)$ denotes mutual information, and $D(\cdot)$ denotes the KLD. For radar resolution performance, the most classic and common metric is the ambiguity function [13]. In this paper, we will design a simpler resolution metric for radar by using joint entropy. For PISs, the common interception performance metric includes the peak-to-average power ratio, time–bandwidth product, and so on (see [2,7,14] and references therein). Here, we regard the KLD, denoted by $D(\mathbf{z}; \mathbf{n}_2)$, between the intercept signal $\mathbf{z}$ and background noise $\mathbf{n}_2$ of a PIS as the effective interception performance metric of a PIS for LPI radar waveform design. Thus, by maximizing the detection and resolution performance of radar and minimizing the interception performance of the PIS, an optimization problem of frequency amplitudes can be established and solved with the constraint of a fixed transmission power.

2. LPI Radar Waveform Design Method

We presume the real radar signal $s(t)$ is emitted by the transmitting antenna with gain G_t in the target direction. It can be scattered and intercepted by the target, which is equipped with a PIS. We denote $x(t) = y(t) + n_1(t)$ as the signal received by the receiving antenna of the radar with gain G_r, where $y(t) = \alpha s(t) * h(t)$ is the target response, $h(t)$ is the target impulse response, $\alpha = \sqrt{\frac{G_t G_r \lambda^2 L_1}{(4\pi)^3 R^4}}$ is the energy attenuation coefficient, λ is the wavelength, R is the distance to the target, L_1 is the total radar path loss, and the symbol "$*$" denotes convolution. Meanwhile, the signal intercepted by the receiving antenna of the PIS with gain G_i can be denoted as $z(t) = \beta s(t) + n_2(t)$, where $\beta = \sqrt{\frac{G_t G_i \lambda^2 L_2}{(4\pi)^2 R^2}}$, L_2 is the path loss between radar and target. We also assume that $h(t)$, $n_1(t)$, and $n_2(t)$ are zero-mean Gaussian random processes.

For the convenience of analysis, we split the frequency interval $\mathcal{W}$ of the radar waveform into a large number of sufficiently small and disjoint frequency intervals $\mathcal{F}_k = [f_k, f_k + \delta f]$, so that for all $f \in \mathcal{F}_k$, we have $S(f) \approx S(f_k)$, where $S(f)$ is the frequency domain waveform of $s(t)$. We denote $\mathbf{z}_k$ and $\mathbf{n}_{2,k}$ as components of $\mathbf{z}$ and $\mathbf{n}_2$, with frequencies in $\mathcal{F}_k$, where $\mathbf{z}$ is the received signal vector of the PIS whose elements are the samplings of $z(t)$, and $\mathbf{n}_2$ is the corresponding background noise vector of the PIS. Based on sampling theory, we suppose the sampling frequency is $2\delta f$, and therefore the sample size is $2\delta fT$, where T denotes the duration of signals.

According to the expressions of the KLD between two Gaussian probability density functions (PDFs) and the entropy of a Gaussian random variable, the terms in Equation (1) can be calculated as

$$E_\mathbf{y}[D(\mathbf{x}; \mathbf{n}_1 | \mathbf{y})] = T \int_\mathcal{W} \frac{2\alpha^2 |S(f)|^2 \sigma_H^2(f)}{T P_{N_1}(f)} df, \quad (2)$$

$$I(\mathbf{x}; \mathbf{y}) = T \int_\mathcal{W} \ln\left[1 + \frac{2\alpha^2 |S(f)|^2 \sigma_H^2(f)}{T P_{N_1}(f)}\right] df, \quad (3)$$

where $\sigma_H^2(f)$ is the variance of $H(f)$, which is the Fourier transform of $h(t)$, and $P_{N_1}(f)$ is the one-sided power spectral density (PSD) of $n_1(t)$.

Thus, the KLD between $\mathbf{x}$ and $\mathbf{n}_1$ can be written as

$$D(\mathbf{x}; \mathbf{n}_1) = T \int_\mathcal{W} \left\{ \frac{2\alpha^2 |S(f)|^2 \sigma_H^2(f)}{T P_{N_1}(f)} - \ln\left[1 + \frac{2\alpha^2 |S(f)|^2 \sigma_H^2(f)}{T P_{N_1}(f)}\right] \right\} df. \quad (4)$$

In the design of LPI radar waveforms, the resolution performance should also be considered, which is another quite important performance measure for radar. In this paper, we use autocorrelation to describe radar resolution performance, which is a more concise way of representing the ambiguity function. For time, the worse the autocorrelation is, the better the range resolution is. Correspondingly, for frequency, the worse the autocorrelation is, the better the velocity resolution is. Next, we will utilize joint entropy to describe the autocorrelation.

Suppose the samplings of the transmitted waveform $\mathbf{s} = [s(1), s(2), \cdots, s(L)]^T$ come from the normal distribution with mean 0 and variance σ_l^2. Then, the entropy of sample $s(l)$ can be computed as

$$\text{Entropy}[s(l)] = \frac{1}{2}[\log 2\pi + 1] + \frac{1}{2}\log \sigma_l^2. \tag{5}$$

Since the joint probability density function of these samples is $p(\mathbf{s}) = (2\pi)^L |\mathbf{R}|_{-\frac{1}{2}} \exp\left(-\frac{1}{2}\mathbf{s}^T |\mathbf{R}|^{-1}\mathbf{s}\right)$, the joint entropy of these samples can be calculated as

$$\text{Entropy}[\mathbf{s}] = \frac{L}{2}[\log 2\pi + 1] + \frac{1}{2}\log |\mathbf{R}|, \tag{6}$$

where $\mathbf{R}$ is the sample covariance matrix of transmitted waveform $\mathbf{s}$, which can be estimated as $\hat{\mathbf{R}} = (r_{i,j})_{i=1,j=1}^{L,L}$, $r_{i,j} = \frac{1}{L}\sum_{l=1}^{L-|i-j|} s(l)s(l+|i-j|)$, and $\mathbf{R}$ is a Toeplitz and symmetric matrix.

If the designed waveform has a perfect resolution performance, then the samples are independent. It means that the joint entropy is equal to the sum of the entropy of each sample, that is: $\text{Entropy}[\mathbf{s}] = \sum_{l=1}^{L} \text{Entropy}[s(l)]$. In fact, the designed waveform cannot have a perfect resolution performance. The joint entropy and the sum of the entropy of each sample have a relationship as follows: $\text{Entropy}[\mathbf{s}] \leq \sum_{l=1}^{L} \text{Entropy}[s(l)]$. Therefore, we use the difference between the joint entropy and the sum of the entropy of each sample as the metric of resolution performance, which can be expressed as

$$\Delta E_s = \sum_{l=1}^{L} \text{Entropy}[s(l)] - \text{Entropy}[\mathbf{s}] = \frac{1}{2}\sum_{l=1}^{L}\log \sigma_l^2 - \frac{1}{2}\log |\mathbf{R}|, \tag{7}$$

where $\Delta E_s \geq 0$.

From Equation (7), we find that the smaller the value of the metric, the better the resolution performance of the transmitted waveform, and when the transmitted waveform is white Gaussian noise, the value of the metric ΔE_s is equal to zero, which means the white Gaussian noise has a perfect resolution performance. In the design of LPI waveforms, we need to minimize ΔE_s. For solving it conveniently, since $\mathbf{R}$ is a Toeplitz and symmetric matrix, we can simplify the metric ΔE_s to a convex function, which can be expressed as

$$\widehat{\Delta E_s} = \frac{\sum_{j=2}^{c} r_{1,j}}{(c-1)P_S} = \frac{\sum_{j=2}^{c}\sum_{l=1}^{L-|1-j|} s(l)s(l+|1-j|)}{(c-1)LP_S}, \tag{8}$$

where c is the constraint number of the time delay or Doppler shift, which can be set according to the practical application, since we do not need to constrain the autocorrelation for each time delay and Doppler shift, and P_S is the average power spectral density of the transmitted waveform, which is used for the purpose of normalization, that is, the upper bound of $\widehat{\Delta E_s}$ is equal to one.

For frequency, resolution performance has the same computational procedure. We only need to substitute $s(l)$ with $S(f_l)$, and we denote the metric of resolution performance for frequency as ΔE_s.

It is a common view that white noise is the best LPI waveform. The closer the distance between intercept signal $\mathbf{z}$ and background noise $\mathbf{n}_2$, the more difficult it is to detect and recognize the intercept signal. The KLD has been confirmed to be a powerful and accurate tool to measure the information of multivariate data, with lesser complexity and superior performance among the existing distance measures, such as $\mathcal{L}^1$, Bhattacharyya distance, Hellinger distance, $f-$ divergence, etc. [15–17]. Therefore, here we use KLD as the PDF distance measure, which is denoted as $D(\mathbf{z}; \mathbf{n}_2)$.

The KLD between $\mathbf{z}_k^m$ and $\mathbf{n}_{2,k}^m$, which are samples of $\mathbf{z}_k$ and $\mathbf{n}_{2,k}$ in each frequency $f_m \in \mathcal{F}_k$ can be written as $D\left(\mathbf{z}_k^m; \mathbf{n}_{2,k}^m\right) = \frac{\beta^2 |S(f_k)|^2}{P_{N_2}(f_k)}$, where $P_{N_2}(f)$ is the one-sided power spectral density (PSD) of $n_2(t)$, that is a function of SNR. The lower SNR a waveform possesses in each frequency, the harder it is for a PIS to intercept it. This agrees with our common knowledge and experience. In order to solve the following optimization problem smoothly, we take the natural exponential function of $D\left(\mathbf{z}_k^m; \mathbf{n}_{2,k}^m\right)$, which can maintain the monotonicity near $|S(f_k)|^2$. It can be denoted as $\widetilde{D}\left(\mathbf{z}_k^m; \mathbf{n}_{2,k}^m\right) = \exp\left\{\frac{\beta^2 |S(f_k)|^2}{P_{N_2}(f_k)}\right\}$. Thus, the modified KLD between component $\mathbf{z}_k$ and $\mathbf{n}_{2,k}$ is

$$D(\mathbf{z}_k; \mathbf{n}_{2,k}) = 2\delta f\, T \widetilde{D}\left(\mathbf{z}_k^m; \mathbf{n}_{2,k}^m\right) = 2\delta f T \exp\left\{\frac{\beta^2 |S(f_k)|^2}{P_{N_2}(f_k)}\right\}. \tag{9}$$

When $\delta f \to 0$, the modified KLD between $\mathbf{z}$ and $\mathbf{n}_2$ can be obtained as

$$D(\mathbf{z}; \mathbf{n}_2) = 2T \int_{\mathcal{W}} \exp\left\{\frac{\beta^2 |S(f)|^2}{P_{N_2}(f)}\right\} df. \tag{10}$$

Since the KLDs $D(\mathbf{x}; \mathbf{n}_1)$ and $D(\mathbf{z}; \mathbf{n}_2)$ can be used to measure the detection performance of radar and a PIS respectively, and $\widehat{\Delta E_s}$ and $\widetilde{\Delta E_s}$ can be used to measure the resolution performance of radar, we can design an LPI radar waveform which not only has superior target detecting and resolution performance, but also has superior LPI performance against PIS interception based on these four metrics. The optimization problem of LPI radar waveform design can be straightforwardly described as $\mathbf{s}^\star = arg\{\max_\mathbf{s} D(\mathbf{x}; \mathbf{n}_1), \min_\mathbf{s} \widehat{\Delta E_s}, \min_\mathbf{s} \widetilde{\Delta E_s}, \min_\mathbf{s} D(\mathbf{z}; \mathbf{n}_2)\}$, under the constraint that the average transmitted power is fixed, denoted by $\int_{\mathcal{W}} |S(f)|_2 df = \mathbf{P}_s$.

LPI radar waveform design is a trade-off between the performance of radar and of PISs, which is to maximize the detection and resolution performance of radar and minimize the interception performance of PISs. In fact, the primary task of the emitted waveform is to accomplish target detection and resolution. The designed radar waveform should be considered for its LPI capability under the condition of meeting radar performance. Therefore, we minimize the KLD $D(\mathbf{z}; \mathbf{n}_2)$ of the PIS in the situation that the KLD $D(\mathbf{x}; \mathbf{n}_1)$, $\widehat{\Delta E_s}$, and $\widetilde{\Delta E_s}$ of radar make some concessions, which can be expressed as

$$\mathbf{s}^\star = arg\left\{\min_{\mathbf{s}} D(\mathbf{z}; \mathbf{n}_2)\right\}$$
$$\text{s.t. } D(\mathbf{x}; \mathbf{n}_1) \geq \gamma, \quad \widehat{\Delta E_s} \leq \nu_1, \quad \widetilde{\Delta E_s} \leq \nu_2, \quad \int_{\mathcal{W}} |S(f)|_2 df = \mathbf{P}_s, \tag{11}$$

where γ is the value of $D(\mathbf{x}; \mathbf{n}_1)$ required to meet radar detection performance, and ν_1 and ν_2 are the values of $\widehat{\Delta E_s}$ and $\widetilde{\Delta E_s}$ needed to meet the radar resolution performance for range and velocity, respectively. All of them can be set to various values in different competing scenarios.

In order to achieve the optimal solution of Equation (11), the discrete form of the optimization problem first needs to be obtained, which can be written as

$$\mathbf{s}^{\star} = arg\left\{\min_{\mathbf{s}} 2Tb \sum_{l=1}^{L} e^{\frac{\beta^2 |S(f_l)|^2}{P_{N_2}(f_l)}}\right\},$$

$$s.t. \begin{cases} Tb \sum_{l=1}^{L} \left\{ \frac{2\alpha^2 |S(f_l)|^2 \sigma_H^2(f_l)}{TP_{N_1}(f_l)} - \ln\left[1 + \frac{2\alpha^2 |S(f_l)|^2 \sigma_H^2(f_l)}{TP_{N_1}(f_l)}\right]\right\} \geq \gamma \\ \frac{\sum_{j=2}^{c} \sum_{l=1}^{L-|1-j|} s(l)s(l+|1-j|)}{(c-1)LP_S} \leq \nu_1, \quad \frac{\sum_{j=2}^{c} \sum_{l=1}^{L-|1-j|} S(f_l)S(f_{l+|1-j|})}{(c-1)LP_S} \leq \nu_2, \\ b \sum_{l=1}^{L} |S(f_l)|^2 = \mathbf{P_s} \\ 0 \leq |S(f_l)|_2 \leq \frac{\mathbf{P_s}}{b}, l = 1, \cdots, L \end{cases} \quad (12)$$

where $f_l, l = 1, \cdots, L$ are the uniform partition points in the frequency interval $\mathcal{W}$ and $b = f_{l+1} - f_l$.

When $\gamma = 0, \nu_1 = 1$, and $\nu_2 = 1$, that is, the LPI waveform is optimized without regard to radar detection and resolution performance, the optimized waveform—considering only the interception performance of the PIS—is $|S^\star(f)|_2 = \mathbf{P_s}/\mathcal{W}$, under the assumption that the background noise $\mathbf{n}_2$ is a white Gaussian noise, whose PSD $P_{N_2}(f)$ is a constant. Thus, in this case we can draw a conclusion that for PISs, it is most difficult to intercept a radar waveform whose power is distributed equally within the whole bandwidth $\mathcal{W}$. When the radar resolution and interception performance of the PIS are not considered, and only the radar detection performance is considered, the radar detection performance metric $D(\mathbf{x}; \mathbf{n}_1)$ is maximized, and the optimized waveform concentrates all waveform energies at the frequency where $\sigma_H^2(f_l)/P_{N_1}(f_l)$ achieves the maximum value. The optimized LPI waveform in Equation (12) should be a compromise between one optimized solution, i.e., energy is distributed equally in all frequencies, considering only the interception performance of the PIS, and another optimized solution, i.e., energy is concentrated at a certain frequency, considering only radar detection performance.

An efficient method for solving nonlinear constrained optimization problems is the combination of the interior point and sequential quadratic programming (SQP) methods. Here, we use the algorithm proposed by Byrd [18] to solve the optimization problem in Equation (12), which jointly utilizes trust regions to ensure the robustness of iterations.

3. Simulation Results

In this section, several simulation experiments are provided. The simulation parameters are: $G_t = G_r = 30$ dB, $G_i = 0$ dB, $\lambda = 0.03$ m, $\mathcal{W} = 512$ MHz, $T = 25$ ns, $L_1 = -20$ dB, $L_2 = -10$ dB, and $R = 100$ km. We suppose the target heading for the radar is an F-16 aircraft, whose variance $\sigma_H^2(f), f \in [9.744, 10.252]$ GHz with azimuth $0.05°$ and elevation $5°$ between the radar and the target has been calculated by electromagnetic software, which is shown as the grey dotted line in Figure 1.

In order to verify the superiority of our proposed LPI radar waveform design method, SNR loss is treated as a performance degradation metric for radar and the PIS, which can be defined as $\delta_{snr} = snr_{opt} - snr_{pro}$, where snr_{opt} is the output SNR for the optimized waveforms proposed by Zhu et al. [12], which just considers the maximization of radar detection performance, and snr_{pro} is the output SNR for the proposed optimized LPI radar waveforms, which not only consider optimal radar detection performance, but also consider the resolution performance of the radar and interception performance of the PIS. The output SNRs are obtained by matched filtering of the radar and time–frequency analysis of the PIS.

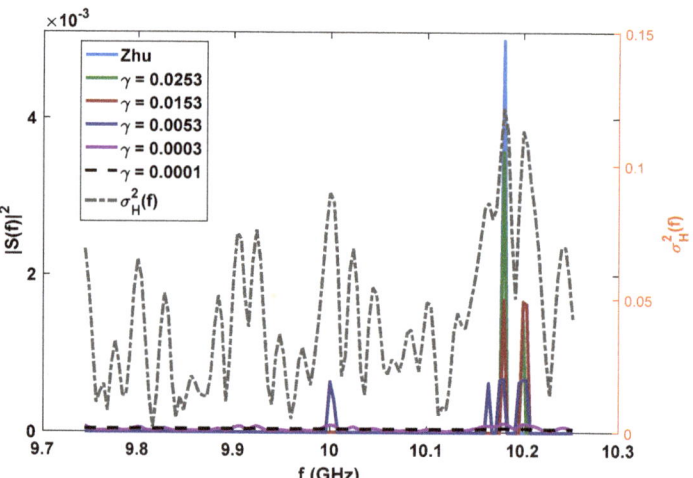

Figure 1. Optimized LPI radar waveforms under the constraint of radar detection performance (white Gaussian noise, $P_{N1} = P_{N2} = 1.9531 \times 10^{-18}$, $\mathbf{P_s} = 20$ kw), the variance of target impulse response $\sigma_H^2(f)$.

3.1. LPI Waveform Design Considering Radar Detection Performance and the PIS

The baby-blue dotted lines (only one-sided PSDs are shown) in Figure 1 (experiment 1: white Gaussian noise) and Figure 2 (experiment 2: colored Gaussian noise) are the optimal radar waveforms for target detection proposed by Zhu et al. [12], which place all their power at the frequency where $\sigma_H^2(f)/P_{N1}(f)$ (denoted by $C(f)$) is maximum. The aim of the proposed LPI waveform design method is to reduce the peak power under a certain loss of radar detection and resolution performance and a fixed transmission power, in order to decrease the interception performance of the PIS. That is, some power will be placed at other frequencies. In this subsection, we first consider radar detection performance, and the combination of radar detection and resolution performance is considered in the next subsection.

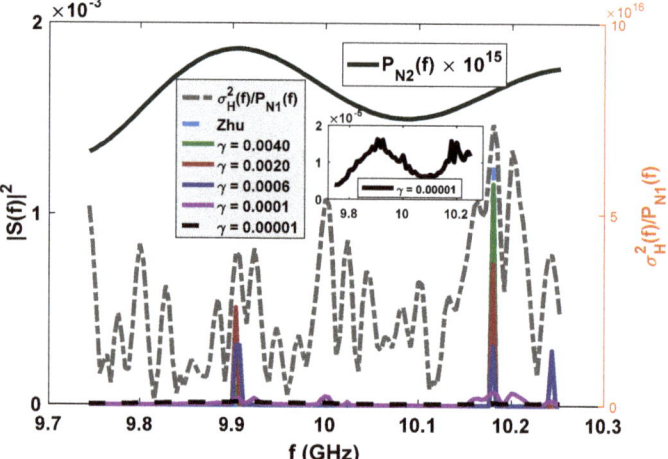

Figure 2. Optimized LPI radar waveforms under the constraint of the radar detection performance (colored Gaussian noise, $P_{N1} = P_{N2}$, $\mathbf{P_s} = 5$ kw), target-to-noise ratio $\sigma_H^2(f)/P_{N1}(f)$ of radar, PSD of colored Gaussian noise $P_{N2}(f)$.

For experiment 1, since $P_{N2}(f)$ is a constant, only by putting some power at the frequency where $C(f)$ is the secondary maximum can we furthest reduce the peak power to minimize $D(\mathbf{z}; \mathbf{n}_2)$ under a given radar detection performance constraint γ, as the green and red lines show in Figure 1. With the relaxing of constraint γ, the power of the optimized LPI waveform will be put at the corresponding frequencies in a descending order of $C(f)$ (as the deep blue and purple lines show in Figure 1) until the energy is distributed equally within the whole bandwidth (as the black dotted line shows in Figure 1). *For experiment 2*, since $P_{N2}(f)$ is not a constant anymore, the frequencies at which the power reduced from the baby-blue dotted line can be placed are related to both $C(f)$ and $P_{N2}(f)$. As the light green and red lines show in Figure 2, the reduced power is first placed at the frequency where $P_{N2}(f)$ is maximum, which can minimize the $D(\mathbf{z}; \mathbf{n}_2)$ in Equation (10). With the decrease in the value of the radar detection performance constraint γ, the optimized LPI waveforms are the result of the combined effects of $P_{N2}(f)$ and $C(f)$ (as the deep blue and purple lines show in Figure 2). When γ tends to zero, the optimized waveform is almost completely influenced by $P_{N2}(f)$, and they have the same shape, as the black dotted line shows in Figure 2.

Since the PIS has no prior information about the transmitted waveform, a reduction in peak power may have a serious effect on its output SNR. In contrast, radar can reduce the effect significantly using the matched filtering technique. As shown in Figure 3, with the decrease in radar detection performance constraint γ, the performance degradation δ_{snr} gradually increases and remains unchanged in the end. The degradation of radar performance for experiment 1 and 2 stays within 5 dB, while that of the PIS can finally reach 20 dB. As there is such a large performance degradation gap between the radar and the PIS, the optimized radar waveform can achieve a superior LPI performance.

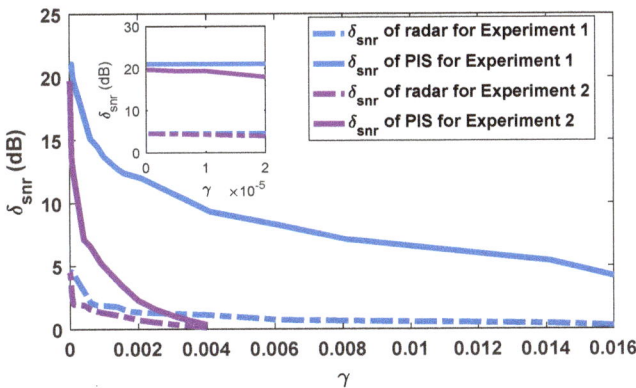

Figure 3. Performance degradation versus radar detection performance constraint.

3.2. LPI Waveform Design Considering Radar Detection and Resolution Performance and PIS Interception Performance

Since the LPI waveforms (which are designed to minimize the interception performance of a PIS with a certain loss of radar detection performance) do not have good range and velocity resolution, we also need to further design LPI radar waveforms to satisfy a given requirement of radar resolution performance. In this subsection, we further optimize the LPI radar waveforms, which are designed in *experiment 2* of Section 3.1, to meet the requirements of radar detection and resolution performance simultaneously. Under the background of colored Gaussian noise, whose PSD is displayed in Figure 2, the designed LPI waveforms are shown in Figure 4 with different values of resolution constraints ν_1 and ν_2, and a given radar detection performance constraint $\gamma = 0.0001$. In these designs, the constrained normalized Doppler shifts are in the interval $[-2, 2]$, and the constrained normalized time delays are in the interval $[-0.1575, 0.1575]$, the length of which can be set according to the actual demands, which is the reflection of parameter c in Equation (8).

As shown in Figure 4, the power of these optimized LPI waveforms has been put at the frequencies where $C(f)$ has a local extremum to implement the maximization of the radar detection performance. In Figure 4, we can also find that the smaller the value of the resolution performance constraints ν_1 and ν_2, that is, the higher the requirement level of radar resolution performance, the more the power is put at the frequencies where $C(f)$ has a local extremum. This is because it is meant to satisfy the higher requirement of resolution performance by sacrificing more LPI performance, that is to put more power at the frequencies where $C(f)$ has a local extremum, under a certain requirement $\gamma = 0.0001$ of radar detection performance. There are the same conclusions when the constrained normalized Doppler shifts and normalized time delays are extended to the intervals $[-3, 3]$ and $[-0.2362, 0.2362]$, respectively, as Figure 5 shows.

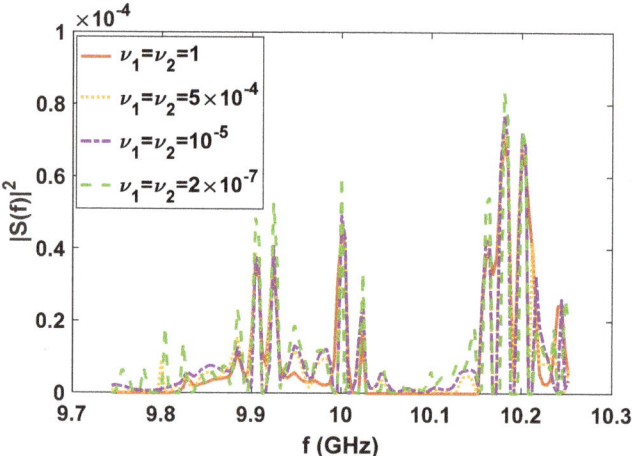

Figure 4. Optimized LPI radar waveforms under the constraint of radar detection and resolution performance (colored Gaussian noise, $P_{N1} = P_{N2}$, $\mathbf{P_s} = 5$ kw, $\gamma = 0.0001$; constrained normalized Doppler shifts are in $[-2, 2]$; constrained normalized time delays are in $[-0.1575, 0.1575]$).

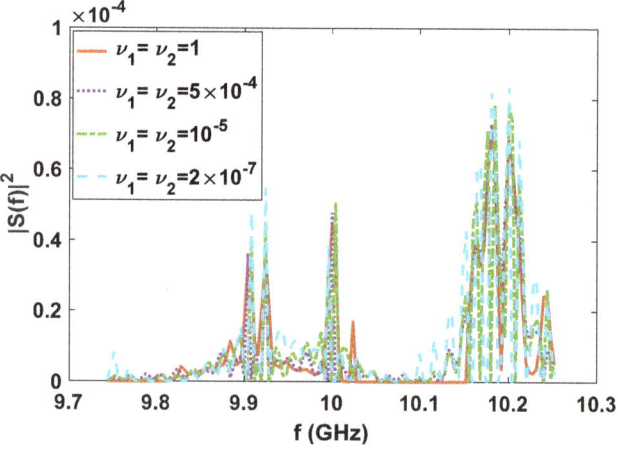

Figure 5. Optimized LPI radar waveforms under the constraint of radar detection and resolution performance (colored Gaussian noise, $P_{N1} = P_{N2}$, $\mathbf{P_s} = 5$ kw, $\gamma = 0.0001$; constrained normalized Doppler shifts are in $[-3, 3]$; constrained normalized time delays are in $[-0.2362, 0.2362]$).

The one-dimensional zero-delay and zero-Doppler cuts of the ambiguity function of these optimized LPI radar waveforms are shown in Figures 6 and 7 for different intervals of constrained normalized Doppler shifts and normalized time delays. Figure 6a displays the one-dimensional zero-delay cuts of the ambiguity function of those optimized LPI radar waveforms, whose constrained normalized Doppler shifts are in the interval $[-2, 2]$. From Figure 6a, we find that the peak values of each sidelobe become smaller and smaller with the fall in the value of resolution performance metrics v_1 and v_2 in the constrained interval $[-2, 2]$, which means velocity resolution can be improved effectively under the constraint of resolution performance. From Figure 6a, we can find that the first sidelobe can be suppressed to -20 dB below the maximum of the mainlobe with the resolution performance constraint $v_1 = v_2 = 2 \times 10^{-7}$, while the first sidelobe is -4.2 dB without a resolution performance constraint. Figure 7a shows the one-dimensional zero-delay cuts of the ambiguity function, whose constrained normalized Doppler shifts are in the interval $[-3, 3]$. In the same way, we can find the sidelobes have better suppression, with reduction of the values of resolution performance metrics v_1, and v_2, in a wider range $[-3, 3]$ of normalized Doppler shift. From Figure 7a, we can see that the first sidelobe can be suppressed to -22 dB below the maximum of the mainlobe with the resolution performance constraint $v_1 = v_2 = 2 \times 10^{-7}$, while the first sidelobe is -4.3 dB without resolution performance constraint. Figures 6b and 7b give the one-dimensional zero-Doppler cuts of the ambiguity function of those optimized LPI radar waveforms with the constrained intervals $[-0.1575, 0.1575]$ and $[-0.2362, 0.2362]$ of normalized time delay, respectively. In Figure 6b, we see that the sidelobes can acquire better suppression with reduction of the values of the resolution performance metrics v_1 and v_2 in the constrained normalized time delay interval $[-0.1575, 0.1575]$, which means the range resolution of radar can be effectively improved under the constraint of resolution performance. From Figure 6b, we see that the first sidelobe can be suppressed from -51 dB to -62 dB below the maximum of the mainlobe with the resolution performance constraint $v_1 = v_2 = 2 \times 10^{-7}$. In Figure 7b, we have the same result in a wider constrained normalized time delay interval $[-0.2362, 0.2362]$. Thus, we can draw the conclusion that the LPI radar waveforms can be designed to effectively satisfy the given requirements of radar detection and resolution performance, which can also be verified in Figures 8–10. These three figures furnish the ambiguity functions with different radar detection performance constraints $\gamma = 0.0001$ (Figures 8 and 9) and $\gamma = 0.0005$ (Figure 10), and different constrained intervals for radar resolution performance (Figures 8 and 10: normalized Doppler shifts $[-2, 2]$, normalized time delays $[-0.1575, 0.1575]$; Figure 9: normalized Doppler shifts $[-3, 3]$, normalized time delays $[-0.2362, 0.2362]$). In each figure, different constraint levels of resolution performance have been simulated, and we can see that the sidelobe in the constraint interval has been effectively suppressed with $v_1 = v_2 = 2 \times 10^{-7}$ compared to other subfigures, which can be suppressed in more Doppler shifts and time delays by increasing the value of parameter c in Equation (8).

In order to verify the superiority of LPI performance of the designed radar waveforms, we calculate the performance degradations δ_{snr} for radar and PIS in different constraint parameters and compare the optimized waveforms with a common LPI radar waveform (Frank, P1–P4). In Table 1, we find that there is a huge gap in performance degradation between the radar and the PIS for the optimized waveforms (radar detection constraint $\gamma = 0.0001$; resolution performance constraint $v_1 = v_2 = 2 \times 10^{-7}$; optimized waveform 1: constrained normalized Doppler shifts are in $[-2, 2]$, constrained normalized time delays are in $[-0.1575, 0.1575]$; optimized waveform 2: constrained normalized Doppler shifts are in $[-3, 3]$, constrained normalized time delays are in $[-0.2362, 0.2362]$). The performance degradation of radar is 2.6 dB, while the performance degradation of the PIS is 11.2 dB. As there are such huge gaps, the optimized waveforms can achieve a superior LPI performance. Compared with the common LPI radar waveforms, our designed waveforms still have a significant LPI superiority, as shown in Table 1. For each compared LPI radar waveform (Frank, P1–P4), we can find the SNR loss of radar for optimized waveforms is approximately equal to that of the compared waveform, as the second row shows. However, the SNR losses of the PIS are different between compared waveforms and the optimized waveforms.

As the third row shows, the SNR loss of the PIS of each compared waveform is nearly 3 dB less than that of the optimized waveforms. Therefore, we can conclude that our designed waveforms can maximize the performance degradations of PISs when they meet the requirements of radar detection and resolution performance.

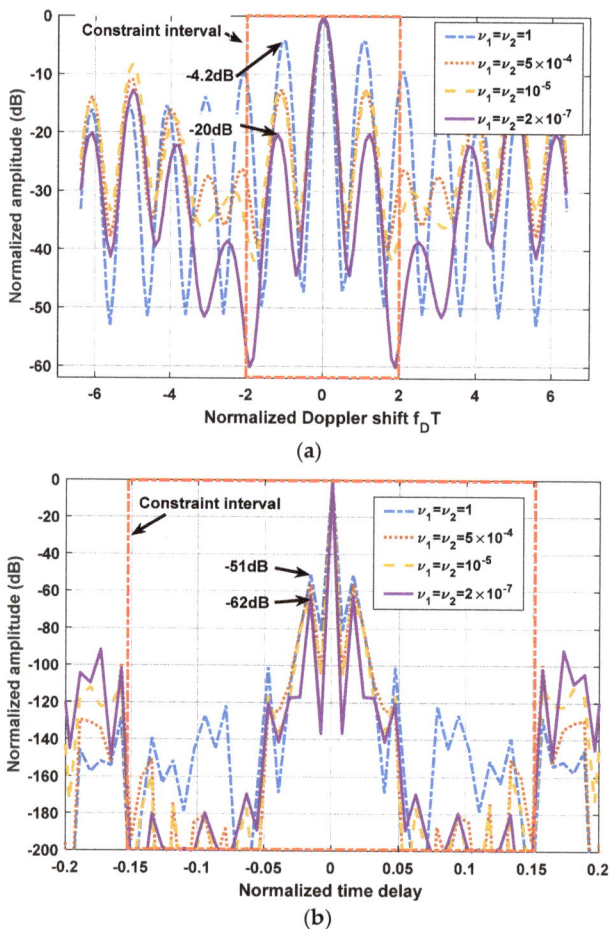

Figure 6. (**a**) One-dimensional zero-delay cuts of the ambiguity function of optimized LPI radar waveforms; (**b**) One-dimensional zero-Doppler cuts of the ambiguity function of optimized LPI radar waveforms; (colored Gaussian noise, $P_{N1} = P_{N2}$, $\mathbf{P_s} = 5$ kw, $\gamma = 0.0001$; constrained normalized Doppler shifts are in $[-2, 2]$; constrained normalized time delays are in $[-0.1575, 0.1575]$).

Table 1. SNR losses for the common low probability of intercept (LPI) radar waveforms and optimized waveforms (radar detection constraint $\gamma = 0.0001$; resolution performance constraint $\nu_1 = \nu_2 = 2 \times 10^{-7}$; optimized waveform 1: constrained normalized Doppler shifts are in $[-2, 2]$, constrained normalized time delays are in $[-0.1575, 0.1575]$; optimized waveform 2: constrained normalized Doppler shifts are in $[-3, 3]$, constrained normalized time delays are in $[-0.2362, 0.2362]$).

	Optimized Waveform 1	Optimized Waveform 2	Frank	P1	P2	P3	P4
δ_{snr} of radar (dB)	2.63	2.64	2.63	2.63	2.61	2.63	2.63
δ_{snr} of PIS (dB)	11.22	11.25	8.15	8.12	7.96	8.12	8.12

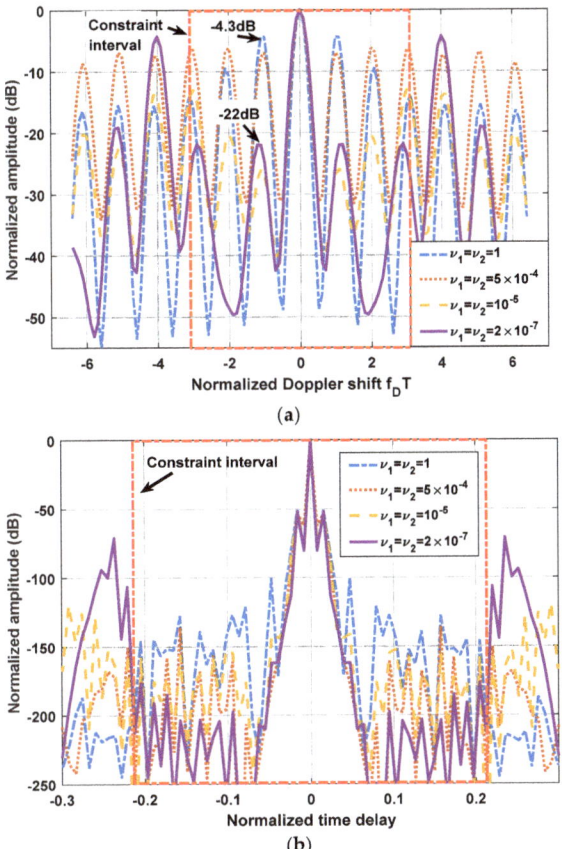

Figure 7. (a) One-dimensional zero-delay cuts of the ambiguity function of optimized LPI radar waveforms; (b) One-dimensional zero-Doppler cuts of the ambiguity function of optimized LPI radar waveforms; (colored Gaussian noise, $P_{N1} = P_{N2}$, $\mathbf{P_s} = 5$ kw, $\gamma = 0.0001$; constrained normalized Doppler shifts are in $[-3, 3]$; constrained normalized time delays are in $[-0.2362, 0.2362]$).

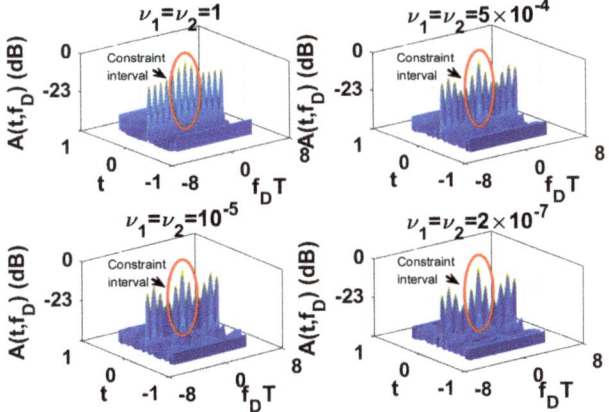

Figure 8. Ambiguity function of optimized LPI radar waveforms for different resolution performance constraints ν_1 and ν_2 (colored Gaussian noise, $P_{N1} = P_{N2}$, $\mathbf{P_s} = 5$ kw, $\gamma = 0.0001$; constrained normalized Doppler shifts are in $[-2, 2]$; constrained normalized time delays are in $[-0.1575, 0.1575]$).

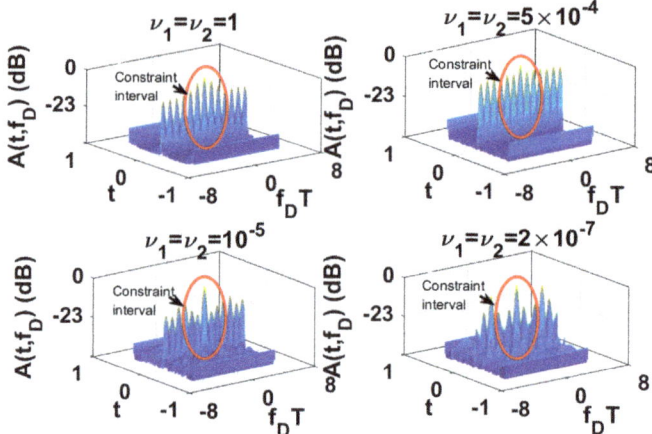

Figure 9. Ambiguity function of optimized LPI radar waveforms for different resolution performance constraints v_1 and v_2 (colored Gaussian noise, $P_{N1} = P_{N2}$, $\mathbf{P_s} = 5$ kw, $\gamma = 0.0001$; constrained normalized Doppler shifts are in $[-3, 3]$; constrained normalized time delays are in $[-0.2362, 0.2362]$).

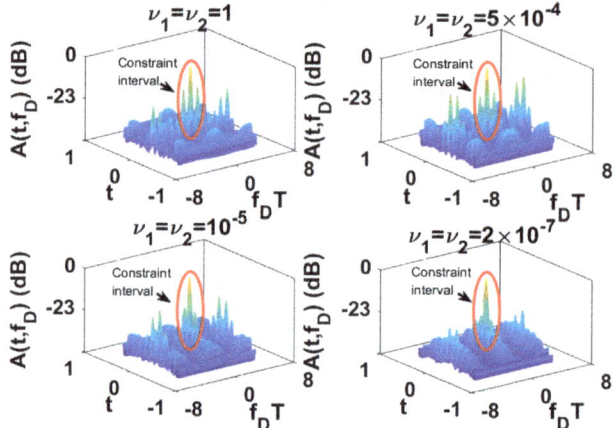

Figure 10. Ambiguity function of optimized LPI radar waveforms for different resolution performance constraints v_1 and v_2 (colored Gaussian noise, $P_{N1} = P_{N2}$, $\mathbf{P_s} = 5$ kw, $\gamma = 0.0005$; constrained normalized Doppler shifts are in $[-2, 2]$; constrained normalized time delays are in $[-0.1575, 0.1575]$).

4. Conclusions

In response to the LPI requirements of modern military radar, waveforms with a fixed average power constraint have been designed from the perspective of information flow to minimize the interception performance of a PIS (which is measured by the KLD in this paper) under the condition that both the detection performance and resolution performance of the radar make some concessions. In this paper, we presented a simple information theoretic metric to measure the resolution performance of radar by utilizing the joint entropy theory. Simulations verify the superiority of the designed radar waveforms in radar detection, resolution performance, and the LPI performance.

Author Contributions: Conceptualization, J.C. and F.W.; methodology, J.C.; software, J.C., Y.Z. and J.W.; validation, J.C., F.W. and J.Z.; formal analysis, Y.Z. and J.C.; investigation, Y.Z.; resources, J.Z.; data curation, J.Z.; writing—original draft preparation, J.C.; writing—review and editing, J.W. and F.W.; visualization, Y.Z.; supervision, J.Z.; funding acquisition, J.C., J.W. and F.W. All authors have read and agreed to the published version of the manuscript.

Funding: This work was supported in part by the National Natural Science Foundation of China under grant 62171229, in part by the Natural Science Foundation of Jiangsu Province under grant BK20190772, and in part by the National Aerospace Science Foundation of China under grant 20200020052005.

Institutional Review Board Statement: Not applicable.

Data Availability Statement: Not applicable.

Conflicts of Interest: The authors declare no conflict of interest.

References

1. Schrick, G.; Wiley, R.G. Interception of LPI radar signals. In Proceedings of the IEEE International Conference on Radar, Arlington, VA, USA, 7–10 May 1990; pp. 108–111.
2. David, L., Jr. *An Introduction to RF Stealth*, 2nd ed.; SciTech: Raleigh, NC, USA, 2021; pp. 5–10.
3. Lou, M.; Zhong, T.; Li, M.; Li, X.; Li, Z.; Wu, J.; Yang, J. Low Probability of Intercept Waveform Optimization Method for Sar Imaging. In Proceedings of the 2021 IEEE International Geoscience and Remote Sensing Symposium IGARSS, Brussels, Belgium, 11–16 July 2021; pp. 3963–3966.
4. LeMieux, J.A.; Ingels, F.M. Analysis of FSK/PSK modulated radar signals using Costas arrays and complementary Welti codes. In Proceedings of the IEEE International Conference on Radar, Arlington, VA, USA, 7–10 May 1990; pp. 589–594.
5. Kim, I.; Park, K.; Song, M.K.; Song, H.; Lee, J.Y. Design of LPI signals using optimal families of perfect polyphase sequences. In Proceedings of the 2016 International Symposium on Information Theory and Its Applications (ISITA), Monterey, CA, USA, 30 October 2016–2 November 2016; pp. 261–264.
6. Warnke, L.; Correll, B., Jr.; Swanson, C.N. The density of Costas arrays decays exponentially. *IEEE Trans. Inf. Theory* **2022**, 1–7. [CrossRef]
7. Chen, J.; Wang, F.; Zhou, J. The metrication of LPI radar waveforms based on the asymptotic spectral distribution of Wigner matrices. In Proceedings of the 2015 IEEE International Symposium on Information Theory (ISIT), Hong Kong, China, 14–19 June 2015; pp. 331–335.
8. Bell, M.R. Information theory and radar waveform design. *IEEE Trans. Inf. Theory* **1993**, *39*, 1578–1597. [CrossRef]
9. Xiao, Y.; Deng, Z.; Wu, T. Information–theoretic radar waveform design under the SINR constraint. *Entropy* **2020**, *22*, 1182. [CrossRef] [PubMed]
10. Qian, J.; Zhao, L.; Shi, X.; Fu, N.; Wang, S. Cooperative design for MIMO radar-communication spectral sharing system based on mutual information optimization. *IEEE Sens. J.* **2022**, *22*, 17184–17193. [CrossRef]
11. Tang, B.; Zhang, Y.; Tang, J. An efficient minorization maximization approach for MIMO radar waveform optimization via relative entropy. *IEEE Trans. Signal Process.* **2018**, *66*, 400–411. [CrossRef]
12. Zhu, Z.; Kay, S.; Raghavan, R.S. Information-theoretic optimal radar waveform design. *IEEE Signal Process. Lett.* **2017**, *24*, 274–278. [CrossRef]
13. Chen, Z.; Liang, J.; Wang, T.; Tang, B.; So, H.C. Generalized MBI algorithm for designing sequence set and mismatched filter bank with ambiguity function constraints. *IEEE Trans. Signal Process.* **2022**, *70*, 2918–2933. [CrossRef]
14. Shu, Y.; Chen, Z. Evaluation and simulation of LPI radar signals' low probability of exploitation. In Proceedings of the 2nd International Conference on Image, Vision and Computing (ICIVC), Chengdu, China, 2–4 June 2017; pp. 842–846.
15. Tang, J.; Cheng, J.; Xiang, D.; Hu, C. Large-difference-scale target detection using a revised Bhattacharyya distance in SAR images. *IEEE Geosci. Remote Sens. Lett.* **2022**, *19*, 1–5. [CrossRef]
16. Hilali, A.E.; Chergui, M.; Wahbi, B.E.; Ayoub, F. A study of the relative operator entropy via some matrix versions of the Hellinger distance. In Proceedings of the 4th International Conference on Advanced Communication Technologies and Networking (CommNet), Rabat, Morocco, 3–5 December 2021; pp. 1–6.
17. Nomura, R.; Yagi, H. Optimum intrinsic randomness rate with respect to f-divergences using the smooth min entropy. In Proceedings of the IEEE International Symposium on Information Theory (ISIT), Melbourne, Australia, 12–20 July 2021; pp. 1784–1789.
18. Byrd, R.H.; Gilbert, J.C.; Nocedal, J. A trust region method based on interior point techniques for nonlinear programming. *Math. Program.* **2000**, *89*, 149–185. [CrossRef]

Article

Some Properties of Weighted Tsallis and Kaniadakis Divergences

Răzvan-Cornel Sfetcu [1,*], Sorina-Cezarina Sfetcu [1] and Vasile Preda [1,2,3]

[1] Faculty of Mathematics and Computer Science, University of Bucharest, Str. Academiei 14, 010014 Bucharest, Romania
[2] "Gheorghe Mihoc-Caius Iacob" Institute of Mathematical Statistics and Applied Mathematics, Calea 13 Septembrie 13, 050711 Bucharest, Romania
[3] "Costin C. Kirițescu" National Institute of Economic Research, Calea 13 Septembrie 13, 050711 Bucharest, Romania
* Correspondence: razvan.sfetcu@fmi.unibuc.ro

Abstract: We are concerned with the weighted Tsallis and Kaniadakis divergences between two measures. More precisely, we find inequalities between these divergences and Tsallis and Kaniadakis logarithms, prove that they are limited by similar bounds with those that limit Kullback–Leibler divergence and show that are pseudo-additive.

Keywords: Tsallis logarithm; Kaniadakis logarithm; weighted Tsallis divergence; weighted Kaniadakis divergence

1. Introduction

Shannon entropy, in the form we know it, was introduced by Boltzmann and used by Shannon in the context of Information Theory. This entropy has applications in Statistical Thermodynamics, Combinatorics and Machine Learning. In Machine Learning, Shannon entropy represents the basis for building decision trees and fitting classification models.

In the last couple of years, many generalizations of Shannon entropy appeared: Tsallis entropy, Kaniadakis entropy, Rényi entropy, Varma entropy, weighted entropy, relative entropy, cumulative entropy, etc. These entropies have applications in areas such as Physics, Information Theory, Probabilities, Communication Theory, and Statistics.

Tsallis entropy was introduced by C. Tsallis in [1] and is applied to: Income distribution (see [2,3]), Internet (see [4]), Non-coding human DNA (see [5]), Plasma (see [6]), and Stock exchanges (see [7,8]).

Kaniadakis entropy was introduced by G. Kaniadakis in [9] and is useful in many areas like: Finance (see [10–12]), Astrophysics (see [13,14]), Networks (see [15,16]), Economics (see [17,18]), and Statistical Mechanics (see [19–21]).

S. Kullback and R.A. Leibler were concerned "to measure" "the distance" or "the divergence" between statistical populations and they generalized Shannon entropy by defining, in [22], a nonsymmetric measure, called Kullback–Leibler divergence. This divergence between two probability measures μ_1 and μ_2 on a measurable non-negligible set A is additive, non-negative and greater than $\log\left(\frac{\mu_1(A)}{\mu_2(A)}\right)$, where log is the classical logarithm function. Divergences are a key tool in Information Geometry (see [23]).

The goodness of fit test is based on the Corrected Weighted Kullback–Leibler divergence (see [24]) and, as a consequence, it inherits all special characteristics of this divergence measure. Narowcki and Harding proposed the use of weighted entropy as a measure of investment risk (see [25]). Afterwards, Guiașu used the weighted entropy to group data with respect to the importance of specific regions of the domain (see [26]), Di Crescenzo and Longobardi propose the weighted residual and past entropies (see [27]) and Suhov and

Zohren proposed the quantum version of weighted entropy and its properties in Quantum Statistical Mechanics (see [28]).

Working with the Kullback–Leibler divergence formula and using the same technique like in the cases of Tsallis and Kaniadakis entropies (i.e., classical logarithm is replaced by Tsallis logarithm, respectively, by Kaniadakis logarithm), Tsallis and Kaniadakis divergences were introduced in some papers (see [29–32]).

Motivated by the aforementioned facts and by the papers [33–35], we deal with the weighted Tsallis and Kaniadakis divergences in this article.

In the following, we briefly describe the structure of the paper. Section 2 is dedicated to preliminaries. In Section 3, using some inequalities concerning the Tsallis logarithm, we obtain inequalities between the weighted Tsallis and Kaniadakis divergences on a non-negligible measurable arbitrary set and Tsallis logarithm, respectively, Kaniadakis logarithm (see Theorem 1). Finally, we prove that the weighted Tsallis and Kaniadakis divergences are limited by bounds that are similar to those that limit Kullback–Leibler divergence (see Theorem 2). In Section 4, we define the weighted Tsallis and Kaniadakis divergences for product measure spaces and prove some pseudo-additivity properties for them (see Theorem 3).

Other interesting results related to the present topics can be found in: [36–40].

2. Preliminary Facts

Definition 1. *Let $k \in \mathbb{R}^*$. We consider the Tsallis logarithm given by*

$$\log^T x = \begin{cases} \dfrac{x^k - 1}{k} & \text{if } x > 0 \\ 0 & \text{if } x = 0 \end{cases}$$

and the Kaniadakis logarithm given via

$$\log^K x = \begin{cases} \dfrac{x^k - x^{-k}}{2k} & \text{if } x > 0 \\ 0 & \text{if } x = 0. \end{cases}$$

Remark 1. *It is easy to see that $\log_k^K x = \dfrac{1}{2}\left(\log_k^T x + \log_{-k}^T x\right)$ for any $x \geq 0$.*

We have $\lim_{k \to 0} \log_k^T x = \lim_{k \to 0} \log_k^K x = \log x$ for any $x > 0$ ("log" is the classical logarithm function).

Definition 2. *Let $(\Omega, \mathcal{T})$ be a measurable space and $\mu, \nu : \mathcal{T} \to \overline{\mathbb{R}}_+ = [0, \infty) \cup \{\infty\}$ two measures. We say that μ is absolutely continuous with respect to ν if, for any $A \in \mathcal{T}$ such that $\nu(A) = 0$, one has $\mu(A) = 0$.*

Notation 1. *If μ and ν are absolutely continuous with respect to each other, we denote this fact by $\mu \sim \nu$.*

In the absence of other mentions, we work in the following scenario: Let $(\Omega, \mathcal{T}, \mu_i)$, $i = 1, 2$ be two measure spaces and λ a measure on $(\Omega, \mathcal{T})$ such that $\mu_i \sim \lambda$ for any $i = 1, 2$. With the help of Radon–Nikodým Theorem we find two non-negative measurable functions f_1 and f_2 defined on Ω such that $\mu_i(A) = \int_A f_i d\lambda$ for any $A \in \mathcal{T}$ and any $i = 1, 2$. Consider $w : \Omega \to (0, \infty)$ a weight function (i.e., w is a non-negative measurable function).

Definition 3. Let $A \in \mathcal{T}$. The weighted Tsallis divergence on A between μ_1 and μ_2 is defined via

$$D_k^{w,T}(\mu_1|\mu_2, A) = \begin{cases} \dfrac{1}{\int_A w d\mu_1} \int_A w \log_k^T\left(\dfrac{f_1}{f_2}\right) d\mu_1 & \text{if } \mu_1(A) \neq 0 \\ 0 & \text{if } \mu_1(A) = 0 \end{cases}$$

and the weighted Kaniadakis divergence on A between μ_1 and μ_2 is given by

$$D_k^{w,K}(\mu_1|\mu_2, A) = \begin{cases} \dfrac{1}{\int_A w d\mu_1} \int_A w \log_k^K\left(\dfrac{f_1}{f_2}\right) d\mu_1 & \text{if } \mu_1(A) \neq 0 \\ 0 & \text{if } \mu_1(A) = 0. \end{cases}$$

Remark 2. We assume that all divergences and integrals which appear in this paper are finite.

Remark 3. We can see that the values of $D_k^{w,T}(\mu_1|\mu_2, A)$ and $D_k^{w,K}(\mu_1|\mu_2, A)$ do not depend on the choice of reference measure λ (because $\dfrac{f_1}{f_2} = \dfrac{d\mu_1/d\lambda}{d\mu_2/d\lambda} = \dfrac{d\mu_1}{d\mu_2}$).

3. Bounds of the Weighted Tsallis and Kaniadakis Divergences

The proof of the following lemma is elementary and is omitted.

Lemma 1. For any $x \in (0, \infty) \setminus \{1\}$, let $\varphi_x : \mathbb{R} \setminus \{0\} \to \mathbb{R}$,

$$\varphi_x(t) = \frac{x^t - 1}{t}.$$

The function φ_x is strictly increasing.

The next two corollaries are very useful in this article.

Corollary 1. Let $x > 0$ and $k \in (-1, \infty) \setminus \{0\}$. Then,

$$x \log_k^T x \geq x - 1$$

and the equality is valid if and only if $x = 1$.

Corollary 2. Let $x > 0$ and $k \in \left(-\dfrac{1}{2}, 1\right) \setminus \{0\}$. Then,

$$\frac{2(\sqrt{x} - 1)}{\sqrt{x}} \leq \log_k^T x \leq x - 1.$$

We have equality in these inequalities if and only if $x = 1$.

Theorem 1. Let $A \in \mathcal{T}$ such that $\mu_i(A) \neq 0$ for any $i = 1, 2$.
(a) Assume that $k \in (-1, \infty) \setminus \{0\}$. Then,

$$D_k^{w,T}(\mu_1|\mu_2, A) \geq \log_k^T\left(\frac{\int_A w d\mu_1}{\int_A w d\mu_2}\right).$$

(b) Assume that $k \in (-1, 1) \setminus \{0\}$. Then,

$$D_k^{w,K}(\mu_1|\mu_2, A) \geq \log_k^K\left(\frac{\int_A w d\mu_1}{\int_A w d\mu_2}\right).$$

In both cases, the equality holds if and only if $\dfrac{f_1(\omega)}{f_2(\omega)} = \dfrac{\int_A w d\mu_1}{\int_A w d\mu_2}$ λ − a.e. for $\omega \in A$.

Proof. (a) We will make the proof in two steps.

Step 1. Assume that $\int_A w d\mu_1 = \int_A w d\mu_2$. Because $\log_k^T\left(\dfrac{\int_A w d\mu_1}{\int_A w d\mu_2}\right) = 0$, we have to show that $D_k^{w,T}(\mu_1|\mu_2, A) \geq 0$.

According to Corollary 1, we have

$$D_k^{w,T}(\mu_1|\mu_2, A) = \dfrac{1}{\int_A w d\mu_1} \int_A w \log_k^T\left(\dfrac{f_1}{f_2}\right) d\mu_1 = \dfrac{1}{\int_A w d\mu_1} \int_A w \cdot \dfrac{f_2}{f_1} \cdot \dfrac{f_1}{f_2} \log_k^T\left(\dfrac{f_1}{f_2}\right) d\mu_1 \geq$$

$$\dfrac{1}{\int_A w d\mu_1} \int_A w \cdot \dfrac{f_2}{f_1}\left(\dfrac{f_1}{f_2} - 1\right) d\mu_1 = \dfrac{1}{\int_A w d\mu_1} \int_A w \left(1 - \dfrac{f_2}{f_1}\right) d\mu_1 =$$

$$1 - \dfrac{1}{\int_A w d\mu_1} \int_A w \cdot \dfrac{f_2}{f_1} d\mu_1 = 1 - \dfrac{\int_A w d\mu_2}{\int_A w d\mu_1} = 0.$$

The equality holds if and only if $\dfrac{f_1(\omega)}{f_2(\omega)} = 1$ μ_1 − a.e, i.e., if and only if $\dfrac{f_1(\omega)}{f_2(\omega)} = 1$ λ − a.e.

Step 2. Let $A \in \mathcal{T}$ with $\mu_i(A) \neq 0$ for any $i = 1, 2$. We define the measures $\widetilde{\mu}_1$ and $\widetilde{\mu}_2$ via

$$\widetilde{\mu}_i(B) = \dfrac{\mu_i(B)}{\int_A w d\mu_i} \text{ for any } B \in \mathcal{T} \text{ and any } i = 1, 2.$$

We remark that $\int_A w d\widetilde{\mu}_1 = \int_A w d\widetilde{\mu}_2 = 1$.

Hence the weighted Tsallis divergence between $\widetilde{\mu}_1$ and $\widetilde{\mu}_2$ on A is

$$D_k^T(\widetilde{\mu}_1|\widetilde{\mu}_2, A) = \int_A w \cdot \dfrac{f_1}{\int_A w d\mu_1} \cdot \log_k^T\left(\dfrac{\dfrac{f_1}{\int_A w d\mu_1}}{\dfrac{f_2}{\int_A w d\mu_2}}\right) d\lambda =$$

$$\int_A w \cdot \dfrac{f_1}{\int_A w d\mu_1} \cdot \log_k^T\left(\dfrac{f_1 \int_A w d\mu_2}{f_2 \int_A w d\mu_1}\right) d\lambda.$$

We deduce from Step 1 that $D_k^T(\widetilde{\mu}_1|\widetilde{\mu}_2, A) \geq 0$.

So,

$$0 \leq \int_A w \cdot \frac{f_1}{\int_A w d\mu_1} \cdot \log_k^T \left(\frac{f_1 \int_A w d\mu_2}{f_2 \int_A w d\mu_1} \right) d\lambda = \int_A w \cdot \frac{f_1}{\int_A w d\mu_1} \cdot \frac{\left(\frac{f_1 \int_A w d\mu_2}{f_2 \int_A w d\mu_1} \right)^k - 1}{k} d\lambda =$$

$$\int_A w \cdot \frac{f_1}{\int_A w d\mu_1} \cdot \frac{\left(\frac{\int_A w d\mu_2}{\int_A w d\mu_1} \right)^k \cdot \left(\frac{f_1}{f_2} \right)^k - 1}{k} d\lambda =$$

$$\int_A w \cdot \frac{f_1}{\int_A w d\mu_1} \cdot \frac{\left(\frac{\int_A w d\mu_2}{\int_A w d\mu_1} \right)^k \cdot \left[\left(\frac{f_1}{f_2} \right)^k - 1 + 1 \right] - 1}{k} d\lambda =$$

$$\int_A w \cdot \frac{f_1}{\int_A w d\mu_1} \cdot \left[\left(\frac{\int_A w d\mu_2}{\int_A w d\mu_1} \right)^k \cdot \frac{\left(\frac{f_1}{f_2} \right)^k - 1}{k} + \frac{\left(\frac{\int_A w d\mu_2}{\int_A w d\mu_1} \right)^k - 1}{k} \right] d\lambda =$$

$$\left(\frac{\int_A w d\mu_2}{\int_A w d\mu_1} \right)^k D_k^{w,T}(\mu_1|\mu_2, A) + \frac{\left(\frac{\int_A w d\mu_2}{\int_A w d\mu_1} \right)^k - 1}{k}.$$

Hence, $D_k^{w,T}(\mu_1|\mu_2, A) \geq \left(\frac{\int_A w d\mu_1}{\int_A w d\mu_2} \right)^k \cdot \frac{1 - \left(\frac{\int_A w d\mu_2}{\int_A w d\mu_1} \right)^k}{k} = \log_k^T \left(\frac{\int_A w d\mu_1}{\int_A w d\mu_2} \right).$

The equality holds if and only if $\frac{f_1(\omega)}{\int_A w d\mu_1} = \frac{f_2(\omega)}{\int_A w d\mu_2}$ $\lambda - a.e.$ for $\omega \in A$, i.e., if and only if $\frac{f_1(\omega)}{f_2(\omega)} = \frac{\int_A w d\mu_1}{\int_A w d\mu_2}$ $\lambda - a.e.$ for $\omega \in A$.

(b) Because $\log_k^K x = \frac{1}{2} \left(\log_k^T x + \log_{-k}^T x \right)$, we obtain

$$D_k^{w,K}(\mu_1|\mu_2) = \frac{1}{2} \left(D_k^{w,T}(\mu_1|\mu_2) + D_{-k}^{w,T}(\mu_1|\mu_2) \right) \geq$$
$$\frac{1}{2} \left(\log_k^T \left(\frac{\int_A w d\mu_1}{\int_A w d\mu_2} \right) + \log_{-k}^T \left(\frac{\int_A w d\mu_1}{\int_A w d\mu_2} \right) \right) = \log_k^K \left(\frac{\int_A w d\mu_1}{\int_A w d\mu_2} \right) \text{ (see } (a) \text{)}.$$

We have equality in the preceding inequality if and only if

$$\frac{1}{2}\left(D_k^{w,T}(\mu_1|\mu_2, A) + D_{-k}^{w,T}(\mu_1|\mu_2, A)\right) = \frac{1}{2}\left(\log_k^T\left(\frac{\int_A w d\mu_1}{\int_A w d\mu_2}\right) + \log_{-k}^T\left(\frac{\int_A w d\mu_1}{\int_A w d\mu_2}\right)\right),$$

which is equivalent to $D_k^{w,T}(\mu_1|\mu_2, A) = \log_k^T\left(\frac{\int_A w d\mu_1}{\int_A w d\mu_2}\right)$ and $D_{-k}^{w,T}(\mu_1|\mu_2, A) = \log_{-k}^T\left(\frac{\int_A w d\mu_1}{\int_A w d\mu_2}\right)$ and these are equivalent to $\frac{f_1(\omega)}{f_2(\omega)} = \frac{\int_A w d\mu_1}{\int_A w d\mu_2}$ λ − a.e. for $\omega \in A$. □

Theorem 2. Let $A \in \mathcal{T}$ such that $\mu_i(A) \neq 0$ for any $i = 1, 2$ and $\int_A w d\mu_1 = \int_A w d\mu_2$.

(a) Assume that $k \in \left(-\frac{1}{2}, 1\right) \setminus \{0\}$. Then,

$$\frac{1}{\int_A w d\mu_1} \int_A w \left(\sqrt{\frac{d\mu_1}{d\mu_2}} - 1\right)^2 d\mu_2 \leq D_k^{w,T}(\mu_1|\mu_2) \leq \frac{1}{\int_A w d\mu_1} \int_A w \left(\frac{d\mu_1}{d\mu_2} - 1\right)^2 d\mu_2.$$

(b) Assume that $k \in \left(-\frac{1}{2}, \frac{1}{2}\right) \setminus \{0\}$. Then,

$$\frac{1}{\int_A w d\mu_1} \int_A w \left(\sqrt{\frac{d\mu_1}{d\mu_2}} - 1\right)^2 d\mu_2 \leq D_k^{w,K}(\mu_1|\mu_2) \leq \frac{1}{\int_A w d\mu_1} \int_A w \left(\frac{d\mu_1}{d\mu_2} - 1\right)^2 d\mu_2.$$

Proof. (a) We have (see Corollary 2)

$$D_k^{w,T}(\mu_1|\mu_2) = \frac{1}{\int_A w d\mu_1} \int_A w \cdot \frac{f_1}{f_2} \cdot \log_k^T\left(\frac{f_1}{f_2}\right) d\mu_2 \geq$$

$$\frac{1}{\int_A w d\mu_1} \int_A w \cdot \frac{f_1}{f_2} \cdot \frac{2\left(\sqrt{\frac{f_1}{f_2}} - 1\right)}{\sqrt{\frac{f_1}{f_2}}} d\mu_2 = \frac{1}{\int_A w d\mu_1} \int_A 2w \cdot \sqrt{\frac{f_1}{f_2}} \cdot \left(\sqrt{\frac{f_1}{f_2}} - 1\right) d\mu_2 =$$

$$\frac{1}{\int_A w d\mu_1} \int_A 2w \cdot \sqrt{\frac{d\mu_1}{d\mu_2}} \cdot \left(\sqrt{\frac{d\mu_1}{d\mu_2}} - 1\right) d\mu_2 = \frac{1}{\int_A w d\mu_1} \int_A w \cdot \left(2 \cdot \frac{d\mu_1}{d\mu_2} - 2\sqrt{\frac{d\mu_1}{d\mu_2}}\right) d\mu_2 =$$

$$\frac{1}{\int_A w d\mu_1} \int_A w \cdot \frac{d\mu_1}{d\mu_2} d\mu_2 - 2 \cdot \frac{1}{\int_A w d\mu_1} \int_A w \cdot \sqrt{\frac{d\mu_1}{d\mu_2}} d\mu_2 + \frac{1}{\int_A w d\mu_1} \int_A w d\mu_2 =$$

$$\frac{1}{\int_A w d\mu_1} \int_A w \cdot \left(\sqrt{\frac{d\mu_1}{d\mu_2}} - 1\right)^2 d\mu_2.$$

On the other hand (see again Corollary 2),

$$D_k^{w,T}(\mu_1|\mu_2) = \frac{1}{\int_A w d\mu_1} \int_A w \cdot \frac{f_1}{f_2} \cdot \log_k^T\left(\frac{f_1}{f_2}\right) d\mu_2 \leq \frac{1}{\int_A w d\mu_1} \int_A w \cdot \frac{f_1}{f_2} \cdot \left(\frac{f_1}{f_2} - 1\right) d\mu_2 =$$

$$\frac{1}{\int_A w d\mu_1} \int_A w \cdot \frac{d\mu_1}{d\mu_2} \cdot \left(\frac{d\mu_1}{d\mu_2} - 1\right) d\mu_2 = \frac{1}{\int_A w d\mu_1} \int_A w \cdot \left(\left(\frac{d\mu_1}{d\mu_2}\right)^2 - \frac{d\mu_1}{d\mu_2}\right) d\mu_2 =$$

$$\frac{1}{\int_A w d\mu_1} \int_A w \cdot \left(\frac{d\mu_1}{d\mu_2}\right)^2 d\mu_2 - 2 \cdot \frac{1}{\int_A w d\mu_1} \int_A w \cdot \frac{d\mu_1}{d\mu_2} d\mu_2 + \frac{1}{\int_A w d\mu_1} \int_A w d\mu_2 =$$

$$\frac{1}{\int_A w d\mu_1} \int_A w \left(\frac{d\mu_1}{d\mu_2} - 1\right)^2 d\mu_2.$$

(b) Using (a) we obtain

$$\frac{1}{2} \cdot \frac{1}{\int_A w d\mu_1} \int_A w \left(\sqrt{\frac{d\mu_1}{d\mu_2}} - 1\right)^2 d\mu_2 + \frac{1}{2} \cdot \frac{1}{\int_A w d\mu_1} \int_A w \left(\sqrt{\frac{d\mu_1}{d\mu_2}} - 1\right)^2 d\mu_2 \leq$$

$$\frac{1}{2} D_k^{w,T}(\mu_1|\mu_2) + \frac{1}{2} D_{-k}^{w,T}(\mu_1|\mu_2) \leq$$

$$\frac{1}{2} \cdot \frac{1}{\int_A w d\mu_1} \int_A w \left(\frac{d\mu_1}{d\mu_2} - 1\right)^2 d\mu_2 + \frac{1}{2} \cdot \frac{1}{\int_A w d\mu_1} \int_A w \left(\frac{d\mu_1}{d\mu_2} - 1\right)^2 d\mu_2.$$

Hence,

$$\frac{1}{\int_A w d\mu_1} \int_A w \left(\sqrt{\frac{d\mu_1}{d\mu_2}} - 1\right)^2 d\mu_2 \leq D_k^{w,K}(\mu_1|\mu_2) \leq \frac{1}{\int_A w d\mu_1} \int_A w \left(\frac{d\mu_1}{d\mu_2} - 1\right)^2 d\mu_2.$$

□

4. Pseudo-Additivity of the Weighted Tsallis and Kaniadakis Divergences

Let $(\Omega, \mathcal{T}, \mu_i)$, $i = 1, 2$ be two measure spaces and λ_1 a measure on $(\Omega, \mathcal{T})$ such that $\mu_i \sim \lambda_1$ for any $i = 1, 2$. We consider Radon–Nikodým derivatives $f_1^{(1)}$ and $f_2^{(1)}$ on Ω, i.e., $f_i^{(1)} = \frac{d\mu_i}{d\lambda_1}$ for any $i = 1, 2$. Let also $(S, \mathcal{S}, \nu_j)$, $j = 1, 2$ be two measure spaces and λ_2 a measure on $(S, \mathcal{S})$ such that $\nu_j \sim \lambda_2$ for any $j = 1, 2$. We apply Radon–Nikodým Theorem and find the non-negative measurable functions $f_1^{(2)}$ and $f_2^{(2)}$ defined on S such that $f_j^{(2)} = \frac{d\nu_j}{d\lambda_2}$ for any $j = 1, 2$. We take $w_1 : \Omega \to (0, \infty)$ and $w_2 : S \to (0, \infty)$ two weight functions.

We consider the measure λ on $(\Omega \times S, \mathcal{T} \times \mathcal{S})$ induced by λ_1 and λ_2. Because $\mu_i \times \nu_i$ is absolutely continuous with respect to λ, we apply Radon–Nikodým Theorem and find two non-negative measurable functions f_1 and f_2 on $\Omega \times S$ such that $f_i = \frac{d(\mu_i \times \nu_i)}{d\lambda}$ for any $i = 1, 2$.

The uniqueness from Radon–Nikodým Theorem assures us that $f_i(\omega, s) = f_i^{(1)}(\omega) f_i^{(2)}(s)$ for any $\omega \in \Omega$, $s \in S$ and any $i = 1, 2$.

Let $A \in \mathcal{T}$ and $B \in \mathcal{S}$.

We define the weighted Tsallis divergence for product measures via

$$D_k^{w_1 w_2, T}(\mu_1 \times \nu_1 | \mu_2 \times \nu_2, A \times B) =$$

$$\frac{1}{\iint_{A \times B} w_1 w_2 d(\mu_1 \times \nu_1)} \iint_{A \times B} w_1(\omega) w_2(s) \log_k^T \left(\frac{f_1(\omega, s)}{f_2(\omega, s)}\right) d(\mu_1 \times \nu_1)(\omega, s) =$$

$$\frac{1}{\int_A w_1 d\mu_1 \int_B w_2 d\nu_1} \iint_{A \times B} w_1(\omega) w_2(s) f_1(\omega, s) \log_k^T \left(\frac{f_1(\omega, s)}{f_2(\omega, s)}\right) d\lambda(\omega, s) \text{ if}$$

$$(\mu_1 \times \nu_1)(A \times B) \neq 0$$

and

$$D_k^{w_1 w_2, T}(\mu_1 \times \nu_1 | \mu_2 \times \nu_2, A \times B) = 0 \text{ if } (\mu_1 \times \nu_1)(A \times B) = 0.$$

The weighted Kaniadakis divergence for product measures is given by

$$D_k^{w_1 w_2, K}(\mu_1 \times \nu_1 | \mu_2 \times \nu_2, A \times B) =$$
$$\frac{1}{\iint_{A \times B} w_1 w_2 d(\mu_1 \times \nu_1)} \iint_{A \times B} w_1(\omega) w_2(s) \log_k^K \left(\frac{f_1(\omega, s)}{f_2(\omega, s)} \right) d(\mu_1 \times \nu_1)(\omega, s) =$$
$$\frac{1}{\int_A w_1 d\mu_1 \int_B w_2 d\nu_1} \iint_{A \times B} w_1(\omega) w_2(s) f_1(\omega, s) \log_k^K \left(\frac{f_1(\omega, s)}{f_2(\omega, s)} \right) d\lambda(\omega, s) \text{ if}$$
$$(\mu_1 \times \nu_1)(A \times B) \neq 0$$

and

$$D_k^{w_1 w_2, K}(\mu_1 \times \nu_1 | \mu_2 \times \nu_2, A \times B) = 0 \text{ if } (\mu_1 \times \nu_1)(A \times B) = 0.$$

Lemma 2 (see [41]). *We have the following pseudo-additivity property for Tsallis logarithm (valid for any $x, y > 0$):*

$$\log_k^T(xy) = \log_k^T x + \log_k^T y + k(\log_k^T x)(\log_k^T y).$$

Theorem 3. *Let $A \in \mathcal{T}$ and $B \in \mathcal{S}$ such that $(\mu_1 \times \nu_1)(A \times B) \neq 0$. The weighted Tsallis and Kaniadakis divergences for product measures satisfy the following pseudo-additivity properties:*

(a) $D_k^{w_1 w_2, T}(\mu_1 \times \nu_1 | \mu_2 \times \nu_2, A \times B) = D_k^{w_1, T}(\mu_1 | \mu_2, A) + D_k^{w_2, T}(\nu_1 | \nu_2, B) + k D_k^{w_1, T}(\mu_1 | \mu_2, A) D_k^{w_2, T}(\nu_1 | \nu_2, B).$

(b) $D_k^{w_1 w_2, K}(\mu_1 \times \nu_1 | \mu_2 \times \nu_2, A \times B) = D_k^{w_1, K}(\mu_1 | \mu_2, A) + D_k^{w_2, K}(\nu_1 | \nu_2, B) + \frac{k}{2} \left(D_k^{w_1, T}(\mu_1 | \mu_2, A) D_k^{w_2, T}(\nu_1 | \nu_2, B) - D_{-k}^{w_1, T}(\mu_1 | \mu_2, A) D_{-k}^{w_2, T}(\nu_1 | \nu_2, B) \right).$

(c) $D_k^{w_1 w_2, K}(\mu_1 \times \nu_1 | \mu_2 \times \nu_2, A \times B) = \frac{1}{\int_B w_2 d\nu_1} \left(\int_B w_2(s) f_1^{(2)}(s) \left(\frac{f_1^{(2)}(s)}{f_2^{(2)}(s)} \right)^k d\lambda_2(s) \right) \cdot$
$D_k^{w_1, K}(\mu_1 | \mu_2, A) + \frac{1}{\int_A w_1 d\mu_1} \left(\int_A w_1(\omega) f_1^{(1)}(\omega) \left(\frac{f_1^{(1)}(\omega)}{f_2^{(1)}(\omega)} \right)^{-k} d\lambda_1(\omega) \right) D_k^{w_2, K}(\nu_1 | \nu_2, B).$

Proof. (a) According to Lemma 2, we have

$$D_k^{w_1 w_2, T}(\mu_1 \times \nu_1 | \mu_2 \times \nu_2, A \times B) =$$
$$\frac{1}{\int_A w_1 d\mu_1 \int_B w_2 d\nu_1} \iint_{A \times B} w_1(\omega) w_2(s) f_1(\omega, s) \log_k^T \left(\frac{f_1(\omega, s)}{f_2(\omega, s)} \right) d\lambda(\omega, s) =$$
$$\frac{1}{\int_A w_1 d\mu_1} \cdot \frac{1}{\int_B w_2 d\nu_1} \iint_{A \times B} w_1(\omega) w_2(s) f_1^{(1)}(\omega) f_1^{(2)}(s) \log_k^T \left(\frac{f_1^{(1)}(\omega)}{f_2^{(1)}(\omega)} \right) d\lambda_1(\omega) d\lambda_2(s) +$$
$$\frac{1}{\int_A w_1 d\mu_1} \cdot \frac{1}{\int_B w_2 d\nu_1} \iint_{A \times B} w_1(\omega) w_2(s) f_1^{(1)}(\omega) f_1^{(2)}(s) \log_k^T \left(\frac{f_1^{(2)}(s)}{f_2^{(2)}(s)} \right) d\lambda_1(\omega) d\lambda_2(s) + k \cdot$$
$$\frac{1}{\int_A w_1 d\mu_1} \cdot \frac{1}{\int_B w_2 d\nu_1} \cdot$$
$$\iint_{A \times B} w_1(\omega) w_2(s) f_1^{(1)}(\omega) f_1^{(2)}(s) \left(\log_k^T \left(\frac{f_1^{(1)}(\omega)}{f_2^{(1)}(\omega)} \right) \right) \left(\log_k^T \left(\frac{f_1^{(2)}(s)}{f_2^{(2)}(s)} \right) \right) d\lambda_1(\omega) d\lambda_2(s) =$$
$$\frac{1}{\int_A w_1 d\mu_1} \left(\int_A w_1(\omega) f_1^{(1)}(\omega) \log_k^T \left(\frac{f_1^{(1)}(\omega)}{f_2^{(1)}(\omega)} \right) d\lambda_1(\omega) \right) \cdot \frac{1}{\int_B w_2 d\nu_1} \cdot$$
$$\left(\int_B w_2(s) f_1^{(2)}(s) d\lambda_2(s) \right) +$$

$$\frac{1}{\int_A w_1 d\mu_1}\left(\int_A w_1(\omega)f_1^{(1)}(\omega)d\lambda_1(\omega)\right)\frac{1}{\int_B w_2 dv_1}\left(\int_B w_2(s)f_1^{(2)}(s)\log_k^T\left(\frac{f_1^{(2)}(s)}{f_2^{(2)}(s)}\right)d\lambda_2(s)\right)+$$

$$k\cdot\frac{1}{\int_A w_1 d\mu_1}\left(\int_A w_1(\omega)f_1^{(1)}(\omega)\log_k^T\left(\frac{f_1^{(1)}(\omega)}{f_2^{(1)}(\omega)}\right)d\lambda_1(\omega)\right)\frac{1}{\int_B w_2 dv_1}\cdot$$

$$\left(\int_B w_2(s)f_1^{(2)}(s)\log_k^T\left(\frac{f_1^{(2)}(s)}{f_2^{(2)}(s)}\right)d\lambda_2(s)\right)=$$

$$D_k^{w_1,T}(\mu_1|\mu_2,A)+D_k^{w_2,T}(\nu_1|\nu_2,B)+kD_k^{w_1,T}(\mu_1|\mu_2,A)D_k^{w_2,T}(\nu_1|\nu_2,B).$$

(b) Because $\log_k^K x = \frac{1}{2}\left(\log_k^T x + \log_{-k}^T x\right)$, we have

$$D_k^{w_1 w_2,K}(\mu_1\times\nu_1|\mu_2\times\nu_2,A\times B)=$$

$$\frac{1}{\int_A w_1 d\mu_1 \int_B w_2 dv_1}\iint_{A\times B} w_1(\omega)w_2(s)f_1(\omega,s)\log_k^K\left(\frac{f_1(\omega,s)}{f_2(\omega,s)}\right)d\lambda(\omega,s)=$$

$$\frac{1}{\int_A w_1 d\mu_1}\cdot\frac{1}{\int_B w_2 dv_1}\cdot\iint_{A\times B} w_1(\omega)w_2(s)f_1^{(1)}(\omega)f_1^{(2)}(s)\cdot$$

$$\frac{1}{2}\left(\log_k^T\left(\frac{f_1^{(1)}(\omega)f_1^{(2)}(s)}{f_2^{(1)}(\omega)f_2^{(2)}(s)}\right)+\log_{-k}^T\left(\frac{f_1^{(1)}(\omega)f_1^{(2)}(s)}{f_2^{(1)}(\omega)f_2^{(2)}(s)}\right)\right)d\lambda_1(\omega)d\lambda_2(s)=$$

$$\frac{1}{2}\left(D_k^{w_1 w_2,T}(\mu_1\times\nu_1|\mu_2\times\nu_2,A\times B)+D_{-k}^{w_1 w_2,T}(\mu_1\times\nu_1|\mu_2\times\nu_2,A\times B)\right).$$

Using (a), we get

$$D_k^{w_1 w_2,K}(\mu_1\times\nu_1|\mu_2\times\nu_2,A\times B)=$$

$$\frac{1}{2}\left(D_k^{w_1,T}(\mu_1|\mu_2,A)+D_k^{w_2,T}(\nu_1|\nu_2,B)+kD_k^{w_1,T}(\mu_1|\mu_2,A)D_k^{w_2,T}(\nu_1|\nu_2,B)\right)+$$

$$\frac{1}{2}\left(D_{-k}^{w_1,T}(\mu_1|\mu_2,A)+D_{-k}^{w_2,T}(\nu_1|\nu_2,B)-kD_{-k}^{w_1,T}(\mu_1|\mu_2,A)D_{-k}^{w_2,T}(\nu_1|\nu_2,B)\right)=$$

$$D_k^{w_1,K}(\mu_1|\mu_2,A)+D_k^{w_2,K}(\nu_1|\nu_2,B)+$$

$$\frac{k}{2}\left(D_k^{w_1,T}(\mu_1|\mu_2,A)D_k^{w_2,T}(\nu_1|\nu_2,B)-D_{-k}^{w_1,T}(\mu_1|\mu_2,A)D_{-k}^{w_2,T}(\nu_1|\nu_2,B)\right).$$

(c) It is easy to prove that

$$\log_k^K(xy)=y^k\cdot\frac{x^k-x^{-k}}{2k}+x^{-k}\cdot\frac{y^k-y^{-k}}{2k}=y^k\log_k^K x+x^{-k}\log_k^K y \text{ for any } x,y\in(0,\infty).$$

Hence,

$$D_k^{w_1 w_2,K}(\mu_1\times\nu_1|\mu_2\times\nu_2,A\times B)=$$

$$\frac{1}{\int_A w_1 d\mu_1 \int_B w_2 dv_1}\iint_{A\times B} w_1(\omega)w_2(s)f_1(\omega,s)\log_k^K\left(\frac{f_1(\omega,s)}{f_2(\omega,s)}\right)d\lambda(\omega,s)=$$

$$\frac{1}{\int_A w_1 d\mu_1}\cdot\frac{1}{\int_B w_2 dv_1}\iint_{A\times B} w_1(\omega)w_2(s)f_1^{(1)}(\omega)f_1^{(2)}(s)\left[\left(\frac{f_1^{(2)}(s)}{f_2^{(2)}(s)}\right)^k\log_k^K\left(\frac{f_1^{(1)}(\omega)}{f_2^{(1)}(\omega)}\right)+\right.$$

$$\left.\left(\frac{f_1^{(1)}(\omega)}{f_2^{(1)}(\omega)}\right)^{-k}\log_k^K\left(\frac{f_1^{(2)}(s)}{f_2^{(2)}(s)}\right)\right]d\lambda_1(\omega)d\lambda_2(s)=$$

$$\frac{1}{\int_A w_1 d\mu_1}\left(\int_A w_1(\omega)f_1^{(1)}(\omega)\log_k^K\left(\frac{f_1^{(1)}(\omega)}{f_2^{(1)}(\omega)}\right)d\lambda_1(\omega)\right)\cdot$$

$$\frac{1}{\int_B w_2 d\nu_1}\left(\int_B w_2(s)f_1^{(2)}(s)\left(\frac{f_1^{(2)}(s)}{f_2^{(2)}(s)}\right)^k d\lambda_2(s)\right)+$$

$$\frac{1}{\int_A w_1 d\mu_1}\left(\int_A w_1(\omega)f_1^{(1)}(\omega)\left(\frac{f_1^{(1)}(\omega)}{f_2^{(1)}(\omega)}\right)^{-k} d\lambda_1(\omega)\right)\cdot$$

$$\frac{1}{\int_B w_2 d\nu_1}\left(\int_B w_2(s)f_1^{(2)}(s)\log_k^K\left(\frac{f_1^{(2)}(s)}{f_2^{(2)}(s)}\right)d\lambda_2(s)\right)=$$

$$\frac{1}{\int_B w_2 d\nu_1}\left(\int_B w_2(s)f_1^{(2)}(s)\left(\frac{f_1^{(2)}(s)}{f_2^{(2)}(s)}\right)^k d\lambda_2(s)\right)D_k^{w_1,K}(\mu_1|\mu_2,A)+$$

$$\frac{1}{\int_A w_1 d\mu_1}\left(\int_A w_1(\omega)f_1^{(1)}(\omega)\left(\frac{f_1^{(1)}(\omega)}{f_2^{(1)}(\omega)}\right)^{-k} d\lambda_1(\omega)\right)D_k^{w_2,K}(\nu_1|\nu_2,B).$$

□

5. Conclusions

With the help of some inequalities concerning Tsallis logarithm, we obtained inequalities between the weighted Tsallis and Kaniadakis divergences on an arbitrary measurable non-negligible set and Tsallis logarithm, respectively, Kaniadakis logarithm (Theorem 1). We showed that the aforementioned divergences are limited by similar bounds with those that limit Kullback–Leibler divergence (Theorem 2) and proved that are pseudo-additive (Theorem 3).

Author Contributions: Conceptualization, R.-C.S., S.-C.S. and V.P.; Formal analysis, V.P.; Investigation, R.-C.S., S.-C.S. and V.P.; Methodology, R.-C.S.; Validation, S.-C.S.; Writing—original draft, R.-C.S.; Writing—review and editing, S.-C.S. and V.P. All authors contributed equally to the paper. All authors have read and agreed to the published version of the manuscript.

Funding: This research received no external funding.

Institutional Review Board Statement: Not applicable.

Informed Consent Statement: Not applicable.

Data Availability Statement: Not applicable.

Acknowledgments: The authors are very much indebted to the anonymous referees and to the editors for their most valuable comments and suggestions which improved the quality of the paper.

Conflicts of Interest: The authors declare no conflict of interest.

References

1. Tsallis, C. Possible generalization of Boltzmann-Gibbs statistics. *J. Stat. Phys.* **1988**, *52*, 479–487. [CrossRef]
2. Preda, V.; Dedu, S.; Gheorghe, C. New classes of Lorenz curves by maximizing Tsallis entropy under mean and Gini equality and inequality constraints. *Physics A* **2015**, *436*, 925–932. [CrossRef]
3. Soares, A.D.; Moura, N.J., Jr.; Ribeiro, M.B. Tsallis statistics in the income distribution of Brazil. *Chaos Solitons Fractals* **2016**, *88*, 158–171. [CrossRef]
4. Abe, S.; Suzuki, N. Itineration of the Internet over nonequilibrium stationary states in Tsallis statistics. *Phys. Rev. E* **2003**, *67*, 016106. [CrossRef] [PubMed]
5. Oikonomou, N.; Provata, A.; Tirnakli, U. Nonextensive statistical approach to non-coding human DNA. *Physics A* **2008**, *387*, 2653–2659. [CrossRef]
6. Lima, J.; Silva, R., Jr.; Santos, J. Plasma oscillations and nonextensive statistics. *Phys. Rev. E* **2000**, *61*, 3260. [CrossRef]
7. Jiang, Z.Q.; Chen, W.; Zhou, W.X. Scaling in the distribution of intertrade durations of Chinese stocks. *Physics A* **2008**, *387*, 5818–5825. [CrossRef]
8. Kaizoji, T. An interacting-agent model of financial markets from the viewpoint of nonextensive statistical mechanics. *Physics A* **2006**, *370*, 109–113. [CrossRef]

9. Kaniadakis, G. Non-linear kinetics underlying generalized statistics. *Physics A* **2001**, *296*, 405–425. [CrossRef]
10. Preda, V.; Dedu, S.; Sheraz, M. New measure selection for Hunt-Devolder semi-Markov regime switching interest rate models. *Physics A* **2014**, *407*, 350–359. [CrossRef]
11. Trivellato, B. The minimal k-entropy martingale measure. *Int. J. Theor. Appl. Financ.* **2012**, *15*, 1250038. [CrossRef]
12. Trivellato, B. Deformed exponentials and applications to finance. *Entropy* **2013**, *15*, 3471–3489. [CrossRef]
13. Abreul, E.M.C.; Neto, J.A.; Barboza, E.M., Jr.; Nunes, R.C. Jeans instability criterion from the viewpoint of Kaniadakis' statistics. *EPL* **2016**, *114*, 55001. [CrossRef]
14. Cure M.; Rial, D.F.; Christen, A.; Cassetti, J. A method to deconvolve stellar rotational velocities. *Astron. Astrophys.* **2014**, *564*, A85.
15. Macedo-Filho, A.; Moreira, D.A.; Silva, R.; da Silva, L.R. Maximum entropy principle for Kaniadakis statistics and networks. *Phys. Lett. A* **2013**, *377*, 842–846. [CrossRef]
16. Stella, M.; Brede, M. A kappa-deformed model of growing complex networks with fitness. *Physics A* **2014**, *407*, 360–368. [CrossRef]
17. Clementi, F.; Gallegati, M.; Kaniadakis, G. A k-generalized statistical mechanics approach to income analysis. *J. Stat. Mech.* **2009**, *2009*, P02037. [CrossRef]
18. Modanese, G. Common origin of power-law tails in income distributions and relativistic gases. *Phys. Lett. A* **2016**, *380*, 29–32. [CrossRef]
19. Kaniadakis, G. Statistical mechanics in the context of special relativity. *Phys. Rev. E* **2002**, *66*, 056125. [CrossRef]
20. Kaniadakis, G. Statistical mechanics in the context of special relativity. II. *Phys. Rev. E* **2005**, *72*, 036108. [CrossRef]
21. Kaniadakis, G.; Scarfone, A.M.; Sparavigna, A.; Wada, T. Composition law of k-entropy for statistically independent systems. *Phys. Rev. E* **2017**, *95*, 052112. [CrossRef]
22. Kullback, S.; Leibler, R.A. On information and sufficiency. *Ann. Math. Stat.* **1951**, *22*, 79–86. [CrossRef]
23. Amari, S.; Nagaoka, H. *Methods of Information Geometry (Translated from the Japanese by Daishi Harada)*; American Mathematical Society: Providence, RI, USA, 2000. [CrossRef]
24. Gkelsinis, T.; Karagrigoriou, A.; Barbu, V.S. Statistical inference based on weighted divergence measures with simulations and applications. *Stat. Pap.* **2022**, *63*, 1511–1536. [CrossRef]
25. Nawrocki, D.N.; Harding, W.H. State-value weighted entropy as a measure of investment risk. *Appl. Econ.* **1986**, *18*, 411–419. [CrossRef]
26. Guiaşu, S. Grouping data by using the weighted entropy. *J. Stat. Plan. Inference* **1990**, *15*, 63–69. [CrossRef]
27. Di Crescenzo, A.; Longobardi, M. On weighted residual and past entropies. *arXiv* **2007**, arXiv:math/0703489. [CrossRef]
28. Suhov, Y.; Zohren, S. Quantum weighted entropy and its properties. *arXiv* **2014**, arXiv:11411.0892. [CrossRef]
29. Furuichi, S.; Yanagi, K.; Kuriyama, K. Fundamental properties of Tsallis relative entropy. *J. Math. Phys.* **2004**, *45*, 4868–4877. [CrossRef] [PubMed]
30. Huang, J.; Yong, W.-A.; Hong, L. Generalization of the Kullback-Leibler divergence in the Tsallis statistics. *J. Math. Anal. Appl.* **2016**, *436*, 501–512. [CrossRef]
31. Sfetcu, R.-C. Tsallis and Rényi divergences of generalized Jacobi polynomials. *Physics A* **2016**, *460*, 131–138.
32. Sfetcu, R.-C.; Sfetcu, S.-C.; Preda, V. On Tsallis and Kaniadakis divergences. *Math. Phys. Anal. Geom.* **2022**, *25*, 23. [CrossRef]
33. Barbu, V.S.; Karagrigoriou, A.; Preda, V. Entropy and divergence rates for Markov chains. II: The weighted case. *Proc. Rom. Acad. Ser. A Math. Phys. Tech. Sci. Inf. Sci.* **2018**, *19*, 3–10. [CrossRef]
34. Beliş M.; Guiaşu S. A quantitative-qualitative measure of information in cybernetic systems. *IEEE Trans. Inf. Theory* **1968**, *14*, 593–594. [CrossRef]
35. Guiaşu, S. Weighted entropy. *Rep. Math. Phys.* **1971**, *2*, 165–179.
36. Barbu, V.S.; Karagrigoriou, A.; Makrides, A. Semi-Markov modelling for multi-state systems. *Methodol. Comput. Appl. Probab.* **2017**, *19*, 1011–1028.
37. Bulinski, A.; Dimitrov, D. Statistical estimation of the Kullback-Leibler divergence. *Mathematics* **2021**, *9*, 544. [CrossRef]
38. Gkelsinis, T.; Karagrigoriou, A. Theoretical aspects on measures of directed information with simulations. *Mathematics* **2020**, *8*, 587. [CrossRef]
39. Toma, A. Optimal robust M-estimators using divergences. *Stat. Probab. Lett.* **2009**, *79*, 1–5. [CrossRef]
40. Toma, A. Model selection criteria using divergences. *Entropy* **2014**, *16*, 2686–2698. [CrossRef]
41. Tsallis, C. *Introduction to Nonextensive Statistical Mechanics*; Springer Science Business Media LLC: Berlin/Heidelberg, Germany, 2009.

Article

Transversality Conditions for Geodesics on the Statistical Manifold of Multivariate Gaussian Distributions

Trevor Herntier * and Adrian M. Peter

Department of Computer Engineering and Sciences, Florida Institute of Technology, 150 W. University Blvd., Melbourne, FL 32940, USA
* Correspondence: therntier2007@my.fit.edu; Tel.: +1-321-536-0317

Abstract: We consider the problem of finding the closest multivariate Gaussian distribution on a constraint surface of all Gaussian distributions to a given distribution. Previous research regarding geodesics on the multivariate Gaussian manifold has focused on finding closed-form, shortest-path distances between two fixed distributions on the manifold, often restricting the parameters to obtain the desired solution. We demonstrate how to employ the techniques of the calculus of variations with a variable endpoint to search for the closest distribution from a family of distributions generated via a constraint set on the parameter manifold. Furthermore, we examine the intermediate distributions along the learned geodesics which provide insight into uncertainty evolution along the paths. Empirical results elucidate our formulations, with visual illustrations concretely exhibiting dynamics of 1D and 2D Gaussian distributions.

Keywords: geodesic; Fisher information; differential geometry; transversality; multivariate Gaussian

Citation: Herntier, T.; Peter, A.M. Transversality Conditions for Geodesics on the Statistical Manifold of Multivariate Gaussian Distributions. *Entropy* **2022**, *24*, 1698. https://doi.org/10.3390/e24111698

Academic Editors: Karagrigoriou Alexandros and Makrides Andreas

Received: 30 September 2022
Accepted: 18 November 2022
Published: 21 November 2022

Publisher's Note: MDPI stays neutral with regard to jurisdictional claims in published maps and institutional affiliations.

Copyright: © 2022 by the authors. Licensee MDPI, Basel, Switzerland. This article is an open access article distributed under the terms and conditions of the Creative Commons Attribution (CC BY) license (https://creativecommons.org/licenses/by/4.0/).

1. Introduction

The importance of a metric to measure the similarity between two distributions has weaved itself into a plethora of applications. Fields concerning statistical inference [1–3], model selection [4–6] and machine learning have found it necessary to quantify the likeness of two distributions. A common approach to measure this similarity is to define a distance or divergence between distributions using the tenets of information geometry, e.g., the Fisher–Rao distance or the f-divergence [7], respectively. To the best of our knowledge, research and results in information geometry have predominantly focused on establishing similarities between two given distributions. Here, we consider an important class of problems where one or both endpoint distributions are not fixed, but instead, constrained to live on subset of the parameter manifold.

When one relaxes the fixed endpoint requirements, the development of finding the shortest path between a given distribution and constraint surface (not single distribution) must be reconsidered using transversality conditions [8,9] for the standard length-minimizing functional. This is precisely the focus of the present work, where we derive the transversality conditions for working in the Riemannian space of multivariate Gaussian distributions. This approach opens new avenues for research and application areas where one no longer needs to provide the ending distribution but rather a description of the constraint set where the most similar model must be discovered. For example, applications such as domain adaptation [10–12] can be reformulated such that the optimal target domain distribution is discovered among a constraint family starting from a known source distribution estimated from training data, or even model selection [4–6,13,14], where a search in a constrained family of distributions may be better aligned with the desired objective versus evaluating the MLE fit penalized by parameter cardinality.

In this work, we have purposefully chosen to work in the natural parameter space of multivariate Gaussians (mean vector, μ, and covariance matrix, Σ) and address the problem formulation in a completely Riemannian context. We are aware of the usual dually flat constructions [2,15,16] afforded by information geometry using divergence measures and the Legendre transformation. Though elegant in their algebraic constructions, these alternate parameterizations have yet to be employed in most statistical and machine-learning applications. Hence, we develop all geometric motivations and consequential mathematical derivations using Riemannian geometry and the natural parameter space, i.e., we employ the Fisher information matrix metric tensor and find the length-minimizing curve to the constraint set.

The remainder of this paper is organized as follows. In Section 2, we give a summary of important results concerning geodesics on manifolds. In Section 3, we provide a brief introduction to the techniques of calculus of variations with the goal of developing the Euler-Lagrange equations necessary to find the shortest path between two multivariate Gaussian distributions. In this section, we restrict ourselves to problems in which both the initial and final distributions are known exactly. Following this, in Section 3.3, we develop the conditions required to satisfy transversality constraints, or constraints where either the initial and/or final distribution are determined from those residing on a defined subsurface of the manifold rather than being exactly known. The results from these sections are employed in Section 4, where we explore various constraint surfaces and numerical experiments to demonstrate the utility of our variable-endpoint framework. Finally, some closing perspectives and remarks are given in Section 5.

2. Related Works

Most efforts towards measuring distances on statistical manifolds build on the foundation started by Fisher in [17], in which he introduces the idea of the information matrix. In [18] Kullback and Leibler published a pioneering effort to describe this distance. Works such as [19,20], endowed statistical distributions with geometrical properties. However, it was Rao [21] that expanded on the ideas of Fisher that defined a metric for statistical models based on the information matrix. The information matrix satisfies the conditions of a metric on a Riemannian statistical manifold, and is widely used because of its invariance [22]. This connection between distance and distributions encouraged others to explore the distance between specific families of distributions [23]. Among these families include special cases of the multivariate normal model [24], the negative binomial distribution [25], the gamma distribution [26,27], Poisson distribution [28], among others.

In [29], the authors offer a detailed exploration of geodesics on a multivariate Gaussian manifold. They show that there exists a geodesic connecting any two distributions on a Gaussian manifold. However, a closed-form solution for the most general case remains an open problem.

In [30] and expanded on in [31], the authors offer a very detailed discussion, focusing primarily on the univariate normal distribution for which a closed-form solution for the Fisher–Rao distance is known. Here, the authors focus on a geometrical approach, abandoning the "proposition-proof" format offered in previous research. With this geometric approach, closed-form solutions to various special cases are derived: univariate Gaussian distributions, isotropic Gaussian distributions, and Gaussian distributions with diagonal covariance matrix.

Another novel application of geodesics on a Gaussian statistical manifold is explored in [32], where the authors use information geometry for shape analysis. Shapes were represented using a *K*-component Gaussian Mixture Model, with the number of components being the same for each shape. With this, each shape occupied a unique point on a common statistical manifold. Upon mapping two shapes to their points on this manifold, the authors use an iterative approach to calculate the geodesic between these two points, with the length of the geodesic offering a measure of similarity of the shapes. Furthermore, because of the iterative approach to solving for the geodesic, all intermediate points along path are revealed. These points can be mapped to their own unique shapes, essentially showing the evolution from one shape to another. This shape deformation exhibits the benefit of analyzing more than just the distance between points on a manifold and that "walk" along the path has real substance.

In [33], the authors explore the complexity of Gaussian geodesic paths, with the ultimate goal of relating the complexity of a geodesic path on a manifold to the correlation of the variables labeling its macroscopic state. Specifically, the authors show that, if there is a dependence between the variables, the complexity of the geodesic path decreases. Complexity, for these purposes is defined as the volume of the manifold traversed by the geodesic connecting a known initial state to a future state, which is well defined. It is shown that this volume decays by a power law at a rate that is determined by the correlation between the variables on the Gaussian manifold.

In [34], the authors use the geometry of statistical manifolds to study how the quantum characteristics of a system are affected by its statistical properties. Similar to our work, the authors prescribe an initial distribution on the manifold of Gaussians and examine the geodesics emanating from it, without dictating a specific terminating distribution. The authors show that these paths tend to terminate at distributions that minimize Shannon entropy. However, unlike our work, these paths are free to roam on the manifold and are not required to terminate on a specific surface on the manifold. Furthermore, the most relevant part of the author's work considers only univariate Gaussians with a two-dimensional parameter manifold, without ever considering higher dimensions.

Though we have chosen to work with Riemannian geometry, it is worth mentioning that information geometry often employs dualistic geometries that can be established using divergence measures. In [35], the authors detail the use of divergence measures to obtain the dual coordinates for space of multivariate Gaussians. However, they point out that the choice of divergence measure is not unique and resulting geometries lack the same interpretative power of the natural parameterization.

Though these previous works operate in the space of multivariate Gaussians and deriving geodesics therein, they all require defining the initial and terminal distributions on the manifold. In this work, we address a novel problem of finding the geodesics when the terminal conditions are hypersurface constraints rather than a single point. Technically, these transversality conditions are variable boundary conditions placed on the initial and final distributions requiring them to reside on a parametric surface typically defined by constraining the coordinates. The usefulness of these variable boundary conditions has emerged in many areas including physics [36] in which the author studied wetting phenomenon on rough surfaces and in [37], where the authors studied the elasticity of materials. Additionally, in [8,38,39], transversality conditions were employed in economic optimal control problems with a free-time terminal condition. However, as practical as transversality conditions have been in the above fields, their application in information geometry literature is deficient.

3. Geodesics for Fixed-Endpoint Problems

We begin by briefly developing standard calculus of variation results for discovering the shortest path between fixed points on a differentiable manifold. Then, the result is applied to the space of multivariate Gaussians, with detailed derivations for the case of bivariate Gaussians. We finally extend the formulation to show how to incorporate variable-endpoint boundary conditions.

3.1. General Euler-Lagrange Equations

Among differential calculus' many applications are problems regarding finding the maxima and minima of functions. Analogously, techniques of calculus of variation operates on *functionals*, which are mappings from a space of functions to its underlying field of scalars. considering the functional $L[y]$, the typical formulation of a calculation of variations problem is

$$\min \quad L[y] = \int_{x_0}^{x_1} F(x, y, \dot{y}) dx \tag{1}$$
$$y(x_0) = y_0 \qquad y(x_1) = y_1$$

where initial and terminal values are defined as (x_0, y_0) and (x_1, y_1), respectively and $\dot{y}$ is notation for the derivative. In general, y can be a vector of functions dependent on x, a vector of independent variables. The theory behind finding the extremum to problems such as these are analogous to single variable calculus, in which we a vanishing first derivative to locate critical points. Here, we locate the extremal functions using functional derivatives, leading to solving the Euler-Lagrange equations outlined in Section 3.2.

Though the formulation of finding the shortest path as a calculus of variations problem is rather elementary, its solution is involved. Obviously, in Euclidean geometry, this path is a straight line, and this distance is easily found. However, moving these ideas onto statistical manifolds complicates both the geometry and the calculus of this seemingly elementary problem. Analogous to the Euclidean setting, in a Riemannian manifold such as our space of Gaussians, solving for the shortest path L, involves the summation of many infinitely small arc lengths, ds

$$ds^2 = \dot{\theta}^T g(\theta) \dot{\theta}, \tag{2}$$

where θ is a parameter vector, $g(\theta)$ is a metric tensor dependent on the parameter vector and $(\cdot)^T$ represents the transpose of a vector. The metric tensor for Euclidean space is the identity matrix but on the multivariate Gaussian manifold, this metric tensor is the Fisher information matrix, discussed later in Section 3.2.

This makes the functional we wish to minimize

$$P = \int_{x_0}^{x_1} \sqrt{\dot{\theta}^T g(\theta) \dot{\theta}} dx \tag{3}$$

or, because the square root is a monotonically increasing function, we can conveniently use

$$\mathcal{F} = \int_{x_0}^{x_1} \dot{\theta}^T g(\theta) \dot{\theta} dx. \tag{4}$$

With this, the calculus of variation problem that solves for the minimum distance on a manifold is

$$\min \quad \mathcal{F}[\theta] = \int_{x_0}^{x_1} \dot{\theta}^T g(\theta) \dot{\theta} dx \tag{5}$$
$$\theta(x_0) = [\theta_{01}, \theta_{02}, \ldots, \theta_{0n}] \qquad \theta(x_1) = [\theta_{11}, \theta_{12}, \ldots, \theta_{1n}]$$

In the present context, the Fisher information metric tensor $g(\theta) = g(\mu, \Sigma)$, the natural parameterization for multivariate Gaussians. Moreover, θ_0 and θ_1 are the parameters of the initial and final distributions.

The minimizer to Equation (5) is the well-known Euler-Lagrange equation, a system of second-order differential equations. These equations operate on the function in Equation (4). Accordingly, we define

$$K = \dot{\theta}^T g(\theta) \dot{\theta} \tag{6}$$

With this, the Euler-Lagrange equations are

$$K_\theta - \frac{d}{dx} K_{\dot{\theta}} = 0. \tag{7}$$

where K_θ and $K_{\dot{\theta}}$ are the functional derivatives with respect the curve $\theta(x)$.

3.2. Euler-Lagrange Equation for Gaussian Distributions

The Fisher information matrix is a measure of how much information about the parameter of interest from a multivariate distribution is revealed from random data space. Intuitively, it can be considered an indication of how "peaked" a distribution is around a parameter. If the distribution is sharply peaked, very few data points are required to locate it. As such, each data point carries a lot of information.

For a multivariate probability distribution, the Fisher information matrix is given by

$$g_{i,j}(\theta) = \int f(x;\theta) \frac{\partial}{\partial \theta_i} \log f(x;\theta) \frac{\partial}{\partial \theta_j} \log f(x;\theta) dx, \tag{8}$$

where the index (i, j) represents the appropriate parameter pair of the multivariate parameter vector θ.

Alternatively, there are additional useful forms of the Fisher information, provided that certain regularity conditions are satisfied. First, the Fisher information matrix is the expectation of the Hessian of the log likelihood of the density function. Specifically,

$$g_{i,j}(\theta) = -\mathcal{E}\left[\frac{\partial^2}{\partial \theta_i \partial \theta_j} \log f(x;\theta)\right] = -\mathcal{E}[H], \tag{9}$$

where H is the Hessian matrix of the log-likelihood.

Second, the Fisher information can be calculated from the variance of the score function

$$g(\theta) = \text{Var}(S_f(x;\theta)), \tag{10}$$

where

$$S_f(x;\theta) = \nabla \log f(x;\theta). \tag{11}$$

Most importantly and for our purposes, the Fisher information matrix is the metric tensor that will define distances on Riemannian Gaussian manifold. Given a distribution on a manifold, by use of this metric tensor, we can minimize an appropriate functional to find a closest second distribution residing on a constrained subset the manifold. A class of problems covered by variable-endpoint conditions in the calculus of variations.

Consider the n-dimensional multivariate Gaussian with density given by

$$f(x_n : \mu_n, \Sigma) = 2\pi^{-\frac{n}{2}} \det(\Sigma)^{-\frac{1}{2}} \exp -\frac{(X-\mu)^T \Sigma^{-1}(X-\mu)}{2} \tag{12}$$

where X is the random variable vector, $\mu = \mu_1, \mu_2, ..., \mu_n$ is the n-dimensional mean vector of the distribution and Σ is the $n \times n$ covariance matrix.

Since the covariance matrix is symmetric, it contains $\frac{(n+1)(n)}{2}$ number of unique parameters, i.e., the number of diagonal and the upper (or lower) triangular elements. With the n-dimensional mean vector, the total number of scalar parameters in an n-dimensional multivariate Gaussian is $\frac{(n+3)n}{2}$, which will be the size of the Fisher information matrix. For all further developments in the parameter space, these parameters are collected in a single vector, θ such that

$$\theta = \{\underbrace{\mu_1, \mu_2, ... \mu_n}_{\theta_1, \theta_2, ..., \theta_n}, \underbrace{\sigma_{1,1}^2, \sigma_{1,2}^2, ..., \sigma_{n,n}^2}_{\theta_{n+1}, ..., \theta_{\frac{(n+3)n}{2}}}\} \tag{13}$$

To clarify, this new parameter θ has the mean vector μ as its first n components and the resulting components are made up of the unique elements of the covariance matrix, starting with the first row, followed, by the second row but without the first entry, since $\Sigma_{1,2} = \Sigma_{2,1}$ and $\Sigma_{1,2}$ is already included in θ. We capture all the parameters of the multivariate Gaussian distribution in this non-traditional vector form because it is more conceptually in line with the calculation of the Fisher information matrix defined in Equation (8).

Therefore, using Equations (8) and (12), the Fisher information for the general multivariate Gaussian distribution is

$$g_{ij}(\mu, \Sigma) = \frac{1}{2} tr\left[\left(\Sigma^{-1} \frac{\partial \Sigma}{\partial \theta_i} \right) \left(\Sigma^{-1} \frac{\partial \Sigma}{\partial \theta_j} \right) \right] + \frac{\partial \mu}{\partial \theta_i}^T \Sigma^{-1} \frac{\partial \mu}{\partial \theta_j} \qquad (14)$$

for which a very detailed proof can be found in the Appendix A of this paper. In the case of the bivariate Gaussian distribution, this 5×5 matrix has only 15 unique elements, because of its symmetry. Once again, the detailed derivation of each of the elements is provided in the Appendix A. The resulting metric tensor elements are

$$\begin{aligned}
g_{11} &= \frac{\sigma_2^2}{\sigma_1^2 \sigma_2^2 - \sigma_{12}^2} \\
g_{22} &= \frac{\sigma_1^2}{\sigma_1^2 \sigma_2^2 - \sigma_{12}^2} \\
g_{33} &= \frac{1}{2} \left(\frac{\sigma_2^2}{\sigma_1^2 \sigma_2^2 - \sigma_{12}^2} \right)^2 \\
g_{44} &= \frac{1}{2} \left(\frac{\sigma_1^2}{\sigma_1^2 \sigma_2^2 - \sigma_{12}^2} \right)^2 \\
g_{55} &= \frac{\sigma_1^2 \sigma_2^2 + \sigma_{12}^2}{(\sigma_1^2 \sigma_2^2 - \sigma_{12}^2)^2} \\
g_{12} &= -\frac{\sigma_{12}}{\sigma_1^2 \sigma_2^2 - \sigma_{12}^2} = g_{21} \\
g_{34} &= \frac{1}{2} \left(\frac{\sigma_{12}}{\sigma_1^2 \sigma_2^2 - \sigma_{12}^2} \right)^2 = g_{43} \\
g_{35} &= -\frac{\sigma_{12} \sigma_2^2}{(\sigma_1^2 \sigma_2^2 - \sigma_{12}^2)^2} = g_{53} \\
g_{45} &= -\frac{\sigma_{12} \sigma_1^2}{(\sigma_1^2 \sigma_2^2 - \sigma_{12}^2)^2} = g_{54}
\end{aligned} \qquad (15)$$

All elements dealing with the information between a component of μ and an element of Σ vanish, which is a property extended to every multivariate Gaussian distribution of higher dimensions as well.

3.3. Variable-Endpoint Formulation: Transversality Boundary Conditions

Our development so far has focused on summarizing the usual situation of finding the length-minimizing path between two fixed points on a Riemannian manifold. We now shift to the situation of allowing one or both of the initial or final endpoints (distributions in this context) to be variable. This changes both the scope and the mathematics of the problem and requires the use of transversality boundary conditions.

Transversality conditions have been useful in other applications. In economics, the conditions are needed to solve the infinite horizon [40,41] problems. Other applications are found in biology [42] and physics [43]. However, to the best of our knowledge, there is little to no prior work investigating variable-endpoint formulations in the domain of information geometry. As we will demonstrate, the crux of employing these methods revolves around appropriately defining the parameter constraint surface. Though our results here provide concrete examples of interesting constraint surfaces, guidance on prescribing these subsets or developing techniques for automatically learning them will be important areas for future research.

The transversality conditions take into account the constrained hypersurface, $\phi(\theta)$, from the coordinates parameterizing the distributions of the statistical manifold. If, for example, we are given an initial distribution and are asked to find which distribution on $\phi(\theta)$ is closest, the usual geodesic problem formulated in Equation (5) now becomes

$$\min \quad \mathcal{F}[\theta] = \frac{1}{2}\int_{x_0}^{x_1} \dot{\theta}^T g(\theta) \dot{\theta} dx \tag{16}$$

$$\theta(x_0) = [\theta_{01}, \theta_{02}, \ldots, \theta_{0n}] \qquad \theta(x_1) = \phi(\theta)$$

Therefore, in addition to satisfying the Euler-Lagrange equation, now with transversality conditions, the optimal solution must also satisfy

$$\begin{bmatrix} K_{\dot{\theta}_1} \\ K_{\dot{\theta}_2} \\ \vdots \\ K_{\dot{\theta}_n} \end{bmatrix} = \alpha \begin{bmatrix} \phi_{\theta_1} \\ \phi_{\theta_2} \\ \vdots \\ \phi_{\theta_n} \end{bmatrix} \tag{17}$$

In Equation (17), the left-hand side is a vector tangent to the optimal path and the vector on the right right-hand side is the gradient of the terminal surface, which is orthogonal to the surface. Considering that the optimal path and the constraint surface intersect at the terminal distribution, this view of the transversality requirement implies that the tangent vector to the optimal path and the gradient of the constraint surface be collinear at the intersecting distribution. The scalar multiple α affects that magnitude of the vector and, from a geometric perspective, there is no loss of generality by setting $\alpha = 1$.

4. Results: Transversal Euler-Lagrange Equations for Bivariate Gaussian Distributions

We now turn our attention to various use cases of the transversal boundary conditions on the Gaussian manifold. We limit our derivations to bivariate Gaussians to make the calculations tractable and for visualization purposes. However, the same development is applicable to higher-dimensional Gaussians. It is worth mentioning that even in the fixed-endpoint scenario, there are no closed-form solutions for the geodesic when manifold coordinates include μ and Σ, with analytical solutions existing only for special cases such zero-mean distributions.

Using the Fisher information matrix defined in Equation (14), more specifically for the bivariate Gaussian distribution discussed in the Appendix, and employing the general form of the geodesic functional in Equation (4), we can define the integrand of the arc-length-minimizing function on the space of bivariate Gaussian distribution as

$$K(\theta) = \frac{\sigma_2^2 \dot{\mu}_1^2}{k} + \frac{\sigma_1^2 \dot{\mu}_2^2}{k} + \frac{(\sigma_2^2)^2(\dot{\sigma}_1^2)^2}{2k^2} + \frac{(\sigma_1^2)^2(\dot{\sigma}_2^2)^2}{2k^2} + \frac{\sigma_1^2 \sigma_2^2 \dot{\sigma}_{12}^2}{k^2} + \frac{\sigma_{12}^2 \dot{\sigma}_{12}^2}{k^2} \\ - \frac{2\sigma_{12}\dot{\mu}_1\dot{\mu}_2}{k} + \frac{\sigma_{12}^2 \dot{\sigma}_1^2 \dot{\sigma}_2^2}{k^2} - \frac{2\sigma_{12}\sigma_2^2 \dot{\sigma}_1^2 \dot{\sigma}_{12}}{k^2} - \frac{2\sigma_{12}\sigma_1^2 \dot{\sigma}_2^2 \dot{\sigma}_{12}}{k^2} \tag{18}$$

where $k = \sigma_1^2 \sigma_2^2 - \sigma_{12}^2$.

We can use Equation (18) to derive the system of second-order differential equations, solutions to which yield the shortest path between two distributions.

$$\ddot{\mu}_1 = \frac{\dot{\mu}_1 \dot{\sigma}_1^2 \sigma_2^2 + \dot{\mu}_2 \sigma_1^2 \dot{\sigma}_{12} - \dot{\mu}_2 \dot{\sigma}_1^2 \sigma_{12} - \dot{\mu}_1 \sigma_{12} \dot{\sigma}_{12}}{\sigma_1^2 \sigma_2^2 - \sigma_{12}^2} \tag{19}$$

$$\ddot{\mu}_2 = \frac{\dot{\mu}_2 \sigma_1^2 \dot{\sigma}_2^2 + \dot{\mu}_1 \sigma_2^2 \dot{\sigma}_{12} - \dot{\mu}_1 \dot{\sigma}_2^2 \sigma_{12} - \dot{\mu}_2 \sigma_{12} \dot{\sigma}_{12}}{\sigma_1^2 \sigma_2^2 - \sigma_{12}^2} \tag{20}$$

$$\ddot{\sigma}_1^2 = \frac{\dot{\mu}_1^2 \sigma_{12}^2 + \dot{\sigma}_1^2 \sigma_2^2 + \sigma_1^2 \dot{\sigma}_{12}^2 - \dot{\mu}_1^2 \sigma_1^2 \sigma_2^2 - 2\dot{\sigma}_1^2 \sigma_{12} \dot{\sigma}_{12}}{\sigma_1^2 \sigma_2^2 - \sigma_{12}^2} \tag{21}$$

$$\ddot{\sigma}_2^2 = \frac{\mu_2^2 \sigma_{12}^2 + \dot{\sigma}_2^2 \dot{\sigma}_1^2 + \sigma_2^2 \dot{\sigma}_{12}^2 - \dot{\mu}_2^2 \sigma_1^2 \sigma_2^2 - 2\dot{\sigma}_2^2 \sigma_{12} \dot{\sigma}_{12}}{\sigma_1^2 \sigma_2^2 - \sigma_{12}^2} \tag{22}$$

$$\ddot{\sigma}_{12} = -\frac{\sigma_{12} \dot{\sigma}_{12}^2 - \dot{\mu}_2 \mu_2 \sigma_{12}^2 - \sigma_1^2 \dot{\sigma}_2^2 \dot{\sigma}_{12} - \dot{\sigma}_1^2 \sigma_2^2 \dot{\sigma}_{12} + \dot{\sigma}_1^2 \dot{\sigma}_2^2 \sigma_{12} + \dot{\mu}_2 \mu_2 \sigma_1^2 \sigma_2^2}{\sigma_1^2 \sigma_2^2 - \sigma_{12}^2} \tag{23}$$

Along with satisfying this system of equations, the solutions presented here must satisfy transversality conditions at one or both the terminal and initial boundaries. In what follows, those conditions will be prescribed accordingly, considering various applications of interest.

4.1. Isotropic Terminal Distribution

Working with the full parameterization of a multivariate Gaussian distribution can be computationally expensive, especially when calculating their Fisher information matrix. For example, the number of parameters grows quadratically with dimension. However, isotropic Gaussian distributions, defined below in Equation (24) grow only linearly with the mean vector's size, orders of magnitude more favorable. In addition to being computationally efficient, isotropic Gaussian distributions provide a submanifold prescribable by a tractable transversality condition. Accordingly, we formulate the following variable-endpoint problem: Given a general multivariate Gaussian distribution, what is the closest (in a geodesic sense) isotropic distribution?

Let Σ_i be the covariance matrix of a multivariate Gaussian distribution with n mean components. This distribution is *isotropic* if

$$\Sigma_i = \sigma^2 I_n \tag{24}$$

where I_n is the n-dimensional identity matrix.

Formally, let θ capture all the parameters of a multivariate Gaussian distribution according to Equation (13). The functional to minimize is given be

$$\min \quad \mathcal{F}[\theta] = \frac{1}{2} \int_{x_0}^{x_1} \dot{\theta}^T g(\theta) \dot{\theta} \, dx$$
$$\theta_0 = [\mu_0, \Sigma_0] \qquad \theta_1 = \phi(\mu_1, \Sigma_1) \tag{25}$$

where μ_0 and Σ_0 are the known parameters of the starting distribution, but μ_1 and Σ_1 are identified by solving the Euler-Lagrange equations while satisfying the transversal condition in Equation (24).

For the bivariate Gaussian distribution, the terminal surface described in Equation (24) can be defined by

$$\Phi(\sigma_1^2, \sigma_2^2) = \sigma_1^2 - \sigma_2^2 = 0, \tag{26}$$

with μ_1 free and $\sigma_{12} = 0$. Appling Equation (17) to this surface, we obtain the condition

$$(\sigma_2^2)^2 \dot{\sigma}_1^2 + (\sigma_1^2)^2 \dot{\sigma}_2^2 + \sigma_{12}^2 \dot{\sigma}_2^2 + \sigma_{12}^2 \dot{\sigma}_1^2 - 2\sigma_{12} \sigma_1^2 \dot{\sigma}_{12} - 2\sigma_{12} \sigma_2^2 \dot{\sigma}_{12} = 0. \tag{27}$$

Therefore, in addition to the Euler-Lagrange equations in Equation (19) through Equation (23), requiring the final distribution to be isotropic implies the geodesic must also satisfy Equation (27). Additionally, the terminal distribution must satisfy the conditions of constraint surface in Equation (26).

4.1.1. Constant Mean Vector with Initial Isotropic Covariance

In this use case, we introduce a slight modification of the previous scenario, where now we set the mean vector of the initial and final distributions to be $\mu_0 = \mu_1 = [0,0]$. We are still interested in finding the closed isotropic Gaussian, but now not allowing the curve evolution to move the distribution's mode.

For example, let us assume an initial distribution with

$$\mu_0 = [0,0], \quad \Sigma_0 = \begin{bmatrix} 7 & 0 \\ 0 & 2 \end{bmatrix} \tag{28}$$

and the final distribution lie on the surface defined in Equation (26).

Applying the Euler-Lagrange equation with the transversality conditions to the problem above results in a final isotropic distribution with $\sigma^2 = 3.74$. Figure 1a shows the information path (dashed and curved) from the initial distribution to the chosen distribution on the isotropic constraint. A Euclidean path would end with a distribution with an isotropic variance equivalent to the average of the original variances. The geodesic path calculated under the Fisher information matrix is an indication of the curvature of the manifold in this region of the parameter space. It is possible in this special zero-mean case to analytically calculate the ending variance on the isotropic constraint surface. Given initial variances of σ_1^2, σ_2^2, it can be shown that the final variance, σ_f^2 is given by

$$\sigma_f^2 = \sqrt{\sigma_1^2 \sigma_2^2}. \tag{29}$$

In Figure 1b, we can see the evolution of all the parameters, starting from the initial distribution to end. Noteworthy is that, even though σ_{12} is not required to stay at 0, there is no benefit for it deviating from 0, as seen in Figure 1b. The Fisher information matrix is independent of the mean vector and, since the values of the mean vector are also not part of our isotropic constraint on the final distribution, the mean vector is not compelled to change from the original distribution, justifying the exclusion of the mean vector's path in Figure 1.

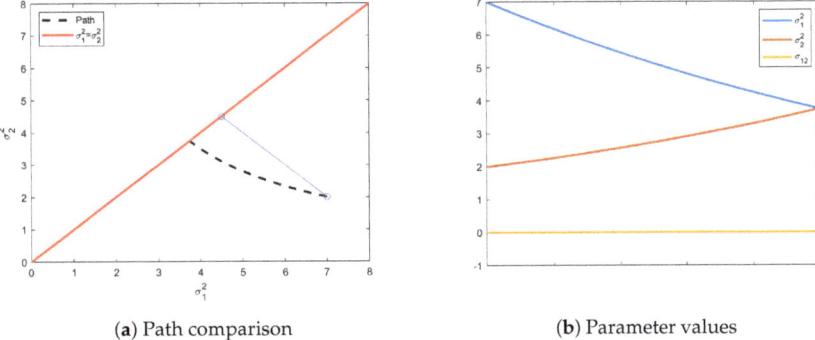

(a) Path comparison   (b) Parameter values

Figure 1. Shown above in (**a**) is the shortest path (dashed line) from a prescribed initial distribution with diagonal covariance matrix, $\sigma_1^2 = 7$, $\sigma_2^2 = 2$, to the closest isotropic distribution. The final distribution has $\sigma_1^2 = \sigma_2^2 = 3.74$. The red solid line above is the transversality constraint $\sigma_1^2 = \sigma_2^2$, represents the isotropic submanifold. Additionally illustrated, in blue, is the Euclidean path, which is clearly the straight-line path resulting from an identity metric tensor. In (**b**) are the paths showing the value of each element of Σ as the distributions move towards the transversality constraint.

4.1.2. Constant Mean Vector with Initial Full Covariance

In the example above, the distributions move along a 2-dimensional manifold parameterized just by the individual variances of the variables. Neither the mean vector, nor the off-diagonal values of the covariance matrices are considered by the Euler-Lagrange equation and therefore remain static. However, starting with a full covariance matrix changes the problem appreciably. For comparison, we will start with same diagonal elements of the covariance matrix but now incorporate the off-diagonal element.

The problem formulation is analogous to Equation (25) subject to the isotropic constraint in Equation (26). Furthermore, we define the initial distribution as

$$\mu_0 = [0,0], \quad \Sigma_0 = \begin{bmatrix} 7 & -3 \\ -3 & 2 \end{bmatrix} \qquad (30)$$

As seen in Figure 2, including $\sigma_{12} = -3$ alters where the geodesic terminates on the transversality constraint, with the final covariance matrix having diagonal elements of $\sigma_1^2 = \sigma_2^2 = 2.24$. In Figure 2a, the effects of including the off-diagonal value σ_{12} are clearly visible on the path of the geodesic causing it to deviate significantly. Figure 2b shows all values of the parameters along the geodesic. As mentioned before, the mean vector remains constant at all intermediate values of the distribution. Unlike before, the value for σ_{12} must evolve to satisfy the terminal constraint surface, illustrated in Figure 2b and emphasized in Figure 2c.

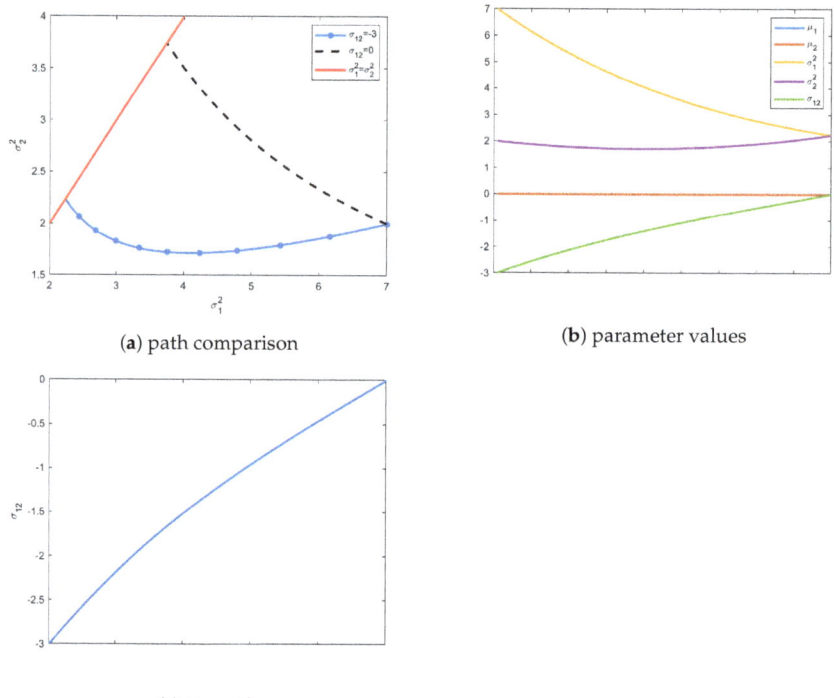

(a) path comparison

(b) parameter values

(c) σ_{12} path

Figure 2. In (**a**) is the shortest path (blue line) from a prescribed initial distribution with an off-diagonal covariance element of $\sigma_{12} = -3$. Additionally, the path from (**a**) (dashed black) is shown to illustrate differences in the variances of the terminal distribution. The final distribution, when starting with a full covariance, has $\sigma_1^2 = \sigma_2^2 = 2.24$. The red line above is the transversality constraint $\sigma_1^2 = \sigma_2^2$, and represents the isotropic submanifold. Figure (**b**) captures the path of all parameters from the initial to the final distribution. Figure (**c**) highlights the values of σ_{12} for each distribution in the geodesic on the manifold.

4.1.3. Starting on the Constraint Surface

When searching for the isotropic boundary condition, interesting paths occur if we start with an initial isotropic distribution, but require the mean vector to change. That is, if the initial distribution already resides on the terminal constraint surface, it would seem counter-intuitive if the geodesic is compelled to leave this constraint. However, as seen in Figure 3, this is exactly what happens.

Employing the same modeling equations as the previous example, we define the initial distribution as

$$\mu_0 = [-3, 3], \quad \Sigma_0 = \begin{bmatrix} 1 & 0 \\ 0 & 1 \end{bmatrix} \tag{31}$$

which is already isotropic. We search for the closest final distribution that is isotropic but with a mean vector $\mu_1 = [3, -4]$. If we track evolution of just the mean vector, it starts in Quadrant II and moves to a distribution in Quadrant IV. Qualitatively, the initial and final distributions are geometrically symmetric. However, the isotropic uncertainty is considerably different.

The insights gleaned from this example shed new light into information evolution. Naively, one would think the shortest path would be one that maintains its current shape and just moves along the constraint surface to reach the desired μ. However, as shown in Figure 3, this is not the case. In fact, intermediate distributions obtain covariance matrices with $\sigma_{12} < 0$, as demonstrated in Figure 3c. Instead of just staying on the constraint surface, the distributions stretch in the direction of the desired mean, which explains negative values of the covariance between the variables. This elongation of the covariance in the direction of final mean vector suggests that the information metric prefers uncertainty reduction in regions with few plausible solutions. Instead, the distributions along the geodesic "reach" for their destination, i.e., the initial mean vector in Quadrant II and final in Quadrant IV. This behavior is illustrated by the intermediate (red) ellipse in Figure 4.

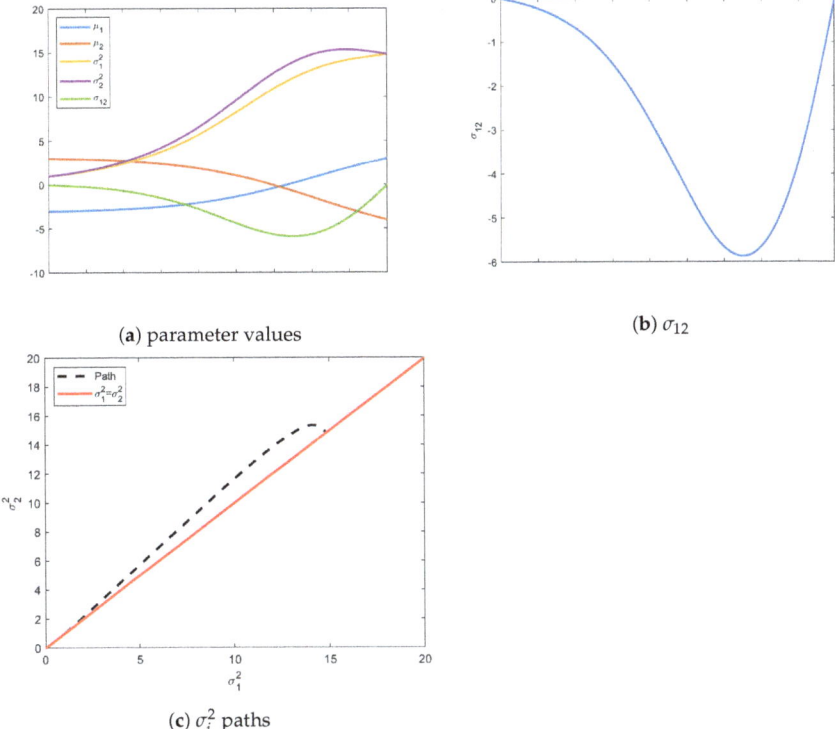

(a) parameter values

(b) σ_{12}

(c) σ_i^2 paths

Figure 3. Above are evolutions of the geodesic from an initial isotropic distribution to a final isotropic distribution with a different mean vector. In (**a**), the values of all five parameters are shown at each iteration. Figure (**b**) highlights the values of σ_{12} showing that it leaves the constraint surface and acquires negative values. The individual variances of the variables also temporarily abandon their required isotropicity as seen in (**c**). In (**c**), the dotted line shows the path of the σ_1^2 and σ_2^2 and the solid line shows the isotropic constraint surface.

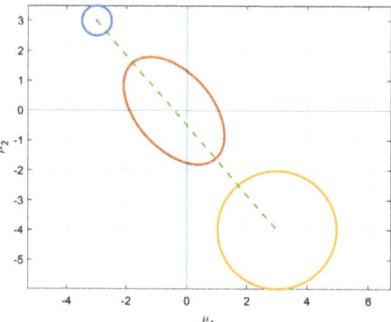

Figure 4. The ellipses above illustrate uncertainty contour for three different density functions along the geodesic. The initial distribution shown in the top left and final distribution in the bottom right are isotropic. The uncertainty evolution is clearly visible in the intermediate distribution which acquires negative covariance values as it "reaches" towards the final distribution.

To reiterate this insightful behavior of information flow, a second example was conducted with a mean vector that starts in Quadrant III, $\mu_0 = [-3, -3]$, and seeks out a final mean vector in Quadrant I, $\mu_1 = [3, 4]$, as shown in Figure 5. The initial distribution is still isotropic and the requirement to end isotropic remains. However, as seen in Figure 6, the values of σ_{12} acquire positive values along the geodesic. The path of the main diagonal variances remains unchanged.

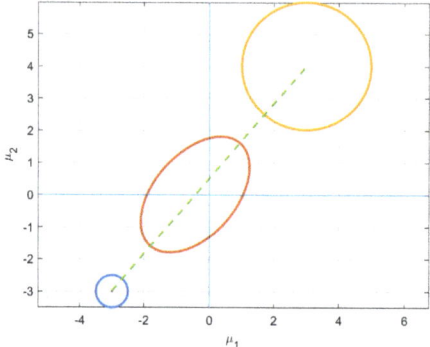

Figure 5. Similar to Figure 4, uncertainty level curves of three densities along the geodesic are shown. This time, the intermediate distribution acquires $\sigma_{12} > 0$ along the geodesic as the distributions move from Quadrant III to Quadrant I along the dotted path.

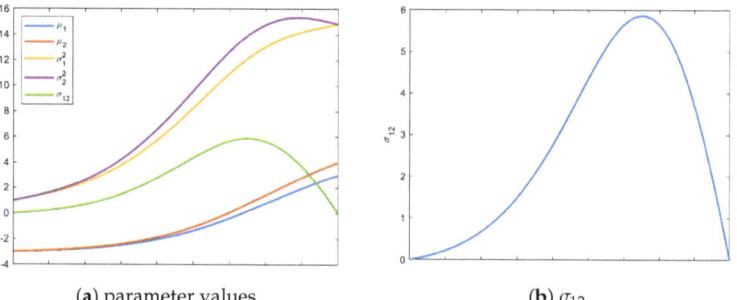

(**a**) parameter values

(**b**) σ_{12}

Figure 6. *Cont.*

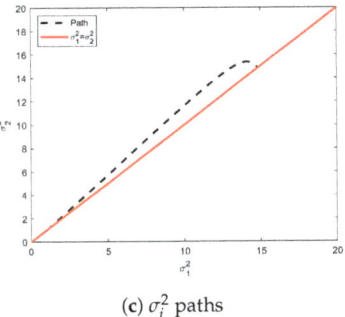

(c) σ_i^2 paths

Figure 6. Illustration of geodesic paths from an initial isotropic distribution with a mean vector in Quadrant III and a final isotropic distribution with a mean vector Quadrant I. In (**a**), the evolutions of all five parameters are shown. Figure (**b**) highlights the values of σ_{12} showing that it leaves the constraint surface and acquires positive values in contrast to the previous example. The individual variances of the variables also temporarily abandon their required isotropicity as seen in Figure 3c. In (**c**), the dotted line shows the path of the σ_1^2 and σ_2^2, with the solid red line representing the isotropic constraint surface.

4.2. Initial and Terminal Variable-Endpoint Conditions

It is possible to place transversality conditions on both the initial and final boundaries, with each being entirely independent of the other. Essentially, we are searching for a geodesic between two almost unknown distributions, with only minimal knowledge about the constraint set characterizing the initial and final hypersurfaces.

We consider the example where the final distribution is prescribed to be isotropic as before, but now the initial distribution must have a mean vector with equal components. This enforcement has the practical benefit of reducing the parameter dimensionality of allowable distributions. The problem is formulated as

$$\min \quad \mathcal{F}[\theta] = \frac{1}{2}\int_{x_0}^{x_1} \dot\theta^T g(\theta)\dot\theta \, dx \qquad (32)$$
$$\theta_0 = \phi_0(\mu_0, \Sigma_0), \qquad \theta_1 = \phi_1(\mu_1, \Sigma_1)$$

where ϕ_0 and ϕ_1 represent the initial and final transversality constraint surfaces, such that

$$\phi_0(\mu_{01}, \mu_{02}) = \mu_{01} - \mu_{02} = 0 \quad \text{and} \quad \phi_1(\sigma_1^2, \sigma_2^2) = \sigma_1^2 - \sigma_2^2 = 0. \qquad (33)$$

To demonstrate this concretely, the initial distribution with unknown mean vector is prescribed with the following covariance matrix

$$\Sigma_0 = \begin{bmatrix} 10 & 0 \\ 0 & 2 \end{bmatrix}. \qquad (34)$$

Similarly, the unknown isotropic terminal distribution is given the mean vector $\mu_1 = [-3, 13]$.

Using Equation (17), the constraint requiring the initial distribution to reside on ϕ_0 imposes that the geodesic satisfy

$$(\sigma_2^2 - \sigma_{12})\dot\mu_1 + (\sigma_1^2 - \sigma_{12})\dot\mu_2 = 0. \qquad (35)$$

As shown in Figure 7, the unknown initial mean vector satisfying the ϕ_1 is $\mu_0 = [7.4, 7.4]$ and the final isotropic distribution has $\sigma_1^2 = \sigma_2^2 = 26.4$. The behavior of the geodesic under these variable-endpoint conditions is shown in Figure 8.

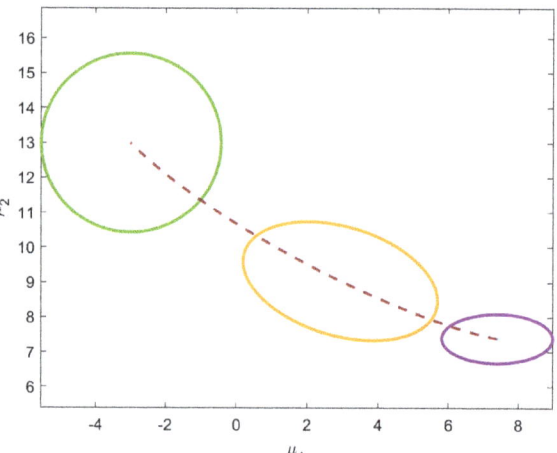

Figure 7. Alternate visualization of the resulting geodesic when both endpoints are allowed to vary. The uncertainty contour ellipses of the initial, intermediate and final distribution are also shown. The initial distribution represented by the bottom right ellipse, has components of the mean vector that are equal. The final distribution, at the top left of the path, isotropic.

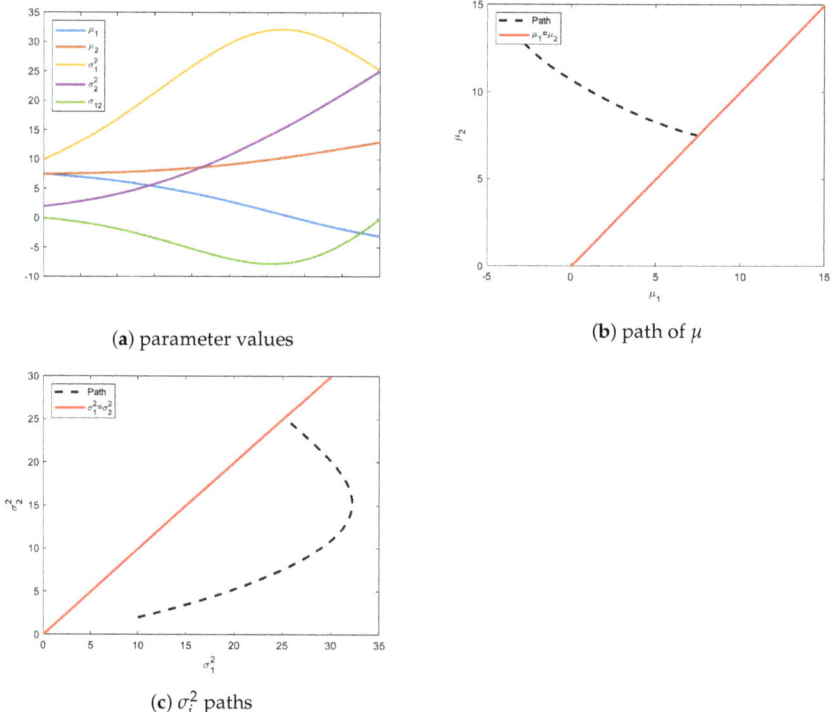

Figure 8. Illustration of geodesics resulting from initial and terminal variable-endpoint boundary conditions. Figure (**a**) shows the behavior of all parameters along the geodesic. Figure (**b**) shows how the geodesic (dashed) evolves the *initial* distribution to reach the constraint (solid) surface defined by the means. Similarly, Figure (**c**) shows the evolution of *final* distribution to the isotropic covariance constraint.

5. Conclusions

In this work, we have explored new formulations for working on information geometric manifolds. Previous and contemporary work using the Riemannian geometry of statistical manifolds has focused on establishing geodesics between two fixed-endpoint distributions. Here, by employing techniques from the calculus of variations, we have developed constructions that allow variable endpoints that are prescribed by a constraint set rather than fixed points.

These transversality conditions on initial and final distributions, enable new insights into how information evolves under different constraint use cases. Though this present effort focused on just a small variety of constraints on Gaussian manifolds, this approach can be readily extended to other statistical families. This novel approach of relaxing fixed endpoints and moving constraint sets has the potential to impact several application domains that employ information geometric models. In future research, we plan to recast the problem of optimal distribution discovery, in areas such as model selection and domain adaptation, using the presented framework, which allows for greater expressive power. We also plan to investigate observational data scenarios where parameters must be estimated and impacts uncertainty modeling of the manifold parameters.

Author Contributions: Conceptualization: T.H. and A.M.P.; Investigation: T.H. and A.M.P.; Formal Analysis: T.H. and A.M.P.; Methodology: T.H. and A.M.P.; Validation and Software: T.H. and A.M.P.; Original Draft Preparation: T.H.; Writing (Review and Editing): T.H. and A.M.P. All authors have read and agreed to the published version of the manuscript.

Funding: This research received no external funding.

Institutional Review Board Statement: Not applicable.

Informed Consent Statement: Not applicable.

Data Availability Statement: Not applicable.

Conflicts of Interest: The authors declare no conflict of interest.

Appendix A. Fisher Information for Multivariate Gaussian

Here, we consider the structure of the Fisher information matrix for n-dimensional multivariate Gaussian with density given by

$$f(x_n : \mu_n, \Sigma) = 2\pi^{-\frac{n}{2}} \det(\Sigma)^{-\frac{1}{2}} \exp -\frac{(X-\mu)^T \Sigma^{-1}(X-\mu)}{2} \tag{A1}$$

where X is a data vector, $\mu = [\mu_1, \mu_2, ..., \mu_n]$ is the n-dimensional mean vector of the distribution and Σ is the $n \times n$ covariance matrix.

These define an n-dimensional multivariate Gaussian. This distribution has $\frac{(n+3)n}{2}$ unique parameters, which we will capture as a single vector θ such that

$$\theta = \{\underbrace{\mu_1, \mu_2, ... \mu_n}_{\theta_1, \theta_2, ..., \theta_n}, \underbrace{\sigma^2_{1,1}, \sigma^2_{1,2}, ..., \sigma^2_{n,n}}_{\theta_{n+1}, ... \theta_{\frac{(n+3)n}{2}}}\}. \tag{A2}$$

The log-likelihood associated with Equation (A1) is

$$\log f = L(\theta) = \frac{n}{2} \ln 2\pi - \frac{1}{2} \ln \det \Sigma - \frac{1}{2}(x-\mu)^T \Sigma^{-1}(x-\mu). \tag{A3}$$

As stated, we will find an equation that will yield each element of the Fisher information matrix using the following definition

$$g_{ij}(\theta) = E\left[\frac{\partial}{\partial \theta_i} \log f(x;\theta) \frac{\partial}{\partial \theta_j} \log f(x;\theta)\right]. \tag{A4}$$

Equation (A4) requires the partial derivative of each parameter in the log-likelihood defined in Equation (A3).

$$\frac{\partial L}{\partial \theta_i} = \underbrace{-\frac{1}{2} tr\left[\Sigma^{-1}\frac{\partial \Sigma}{\partial \theta_i}\right]}_{A} + \underbrace{\frac{1}{2}(x-\mu)^T \Sigma^{-1}\frac{\partial \Sigma}{\partial \theta_i}\Sigma^{-1}(x-\mu)}_{B}$$
$$+ \underbrace{\frac{\partial \mu}{\partial \theta_i}^T \Sigma^{-1}(x-\mu)}_{C} \quad (A5)$$

Similarly, we can take the partial derivative with respect to a different parameter, θ_j and obtain the same result, indexed with j instead of i. The below equation labels A, B, C will provide clarity in the proof.

To find each g_{ij} in the Fisher information matrix, we need to find the expectation of the product of every combination two partial derivatives which will result in nine terms. However, upon taking the expectation, some of these terms will vanish to 0, because the expectation of data vector x approaches the mean vector μ. Specifically, let us denote A_i, B_i, C_i to be the terms of $\frac{\partial L}{\partial \theta_i}$ and A_j, B_j, C_j to be the terms of $\frac{\partial L}{\partial \theta_j}$. Upon taking the expectation of the product, $A_i C_j = C_i A_j = B_i C_j = B_j C_i = 0$. Ignoring these, we will look individually at each of the remaining terms. Starting with $A_i A_j$

$$A_i A_j = \left(-\frac{1}{2} tr\left[\Sigma^{-1}\frac{\partial \Sigma}{\partial \theta_i}\right]\right)\left(-\frac{1}{2} tr\left[\Sigma^{-1}\frac{\partial \Sigma}{\partial \theta_j}\right]\right)$$
$$= \frac{1}{4} tr\left[\Sigma^{-1}\frac{\partial \Sigma}{\partial \theta_i}\right] tr\left[\Sigma^{-1}\frac{\partial \Sigma}{\partial \theta_j}\right] \quad (A6)$$

Next, calculating $B_i B_j$,

$$B_i B_j = \left[\frac{1}{2}(x-\mu)^T \Sigma^{-1}\frac{\partial \Sigma}{\partial \theta_i}\Sigma^{-1}(x-\mu)\right]\left[\frac{1}{2}(x-\mu)^T \Sigma^{-1}\frac{\partial \Sigma}{\partial \theta_j}\Sigma^{-1}(x-\mu)\right]$$
$$= \frac{1}{4}\left[(x-\mu)^T \Sigma^{-1}\frac{\partial \Sigma}{\partial \theta_i}\Sigma^{-1}(x-\mu)(x-\mu)^T \Sigma^{-1}\frac{\partial \Sigma}{\partial \theta_j}\Sigma^{-1}(x-\mu)\right] \quad (A7)$$

We are required to take the expectation of this, which is a fourth moment of the multivariable normal distribution. The result of this is

$$B_i B_j = \frac{1}{4}\left[tr\left(\Sigma^{-1}\frac{\partial \Sigma}{\partial \theta_i}\right) tr\left(\Sigma^{-1}\frac{\partial \Sigma}{\partial \theta_j}\right) + 2tr\left[\left(\Sigma^{-1}\frac{\partial \Sigma}{\partial \theta_i}\right)\left(\Sigma^{-1}\frac{\partial \Sigma}{\partial \theta_j}\right)\right]\right]. \quad (A8)$$

Turning attention to $C_i C_j$,

$$C_i C_j = \frac{\partial \mu}{\partial \theta_i}^T \Sigma^{-1}(x-\mu)(x-\mu)^T \Sigma^{-1}\frac{\partial \mu}{\partial \theta_j}$$
$$= \frac{\partial \mu}{\partial \theta_i}^T \Sigma^{-1} \Sigma \Sigma^{-1}\frac{\partial \mu}{\partial \theta_j} \quad (A9)$$
$$= \frac{\partial \mu}{\partial \theta_i}^T \Sigma^{-1}\frac{\partial \mu}{\partial \theta_j}.$$

The final set of non-vanishing terms, $A_i B_j + B_i A_j$ are considered simultaneously.

$$A_iB_j + B_iA_j = \left(-\frac{1}{2}tr\left[\Sigma^{-1}\frac{\partial\Sigma}{\partial\theta_i}\right]\right)\left(\frac{1}{2}(x-\mu)^T\Sigma^{-1}\frac{\partial\Sigma}{\partial\theta_j}\Sigma^{-1}(x-\mu)\right)$$
$$+ \left(\frac{1}{2}(x-\mu)^T\Sigma^{-1}\frac{\partial\Sigma}{\partial\theta_i}\Sigma^{-1}(x-\mu)\right)\left(-\frac{1}{2}tr\left[\Sigma^{-1}\frac{\partial\Sigma}{\partial\theta_j}\right]\right)$$
$$= -\frac{1}{4}\left\{\left(tr\left[\Sigma^{-1}\frac{\partial\Sigma}{\partial\theta_i}\right]\right)\left((x-\mu)^T\Sigma^{-1}\frac{\partial\Sigma}{\partial\theta_j}\Sigma^{-1}(x-\mu)\right)\right.$$
$$\left. + \left((x-\mu)^T\Sigma^{-1}\frac{\partial\Sigma}{\partial\theta_i}\Sigma^{-1}(x-\mu)\right)\left(tr\left[\Sigma^{-1}\frac{\partial\Sigma}{\partial\theta_j}\right]\right)\right\} \quad (A10)$$

Now, we use the identity
$$b^T A b = tr(bb^T A) \quad (A11)$$
on all terms of Equation (A10) that do not yet involve the trace of a matrix. Doing so, Equation (A10) becomes

$$A_iB_j + B_iA_j = -\frac{1}{4}\left\{\left(tr\left[\Sigma^{-1}\frac{\partial\Sigma}{\partial\theta_i}\right]\right)\left(tr\left[(x-\mu)(x-\mu)^T\Sigma^{-1}\frac{\partial\Sigma}{\partial\theta_j}\Sigma^{-1}\right]\right)\right.$$
$$\left. + \left(tr\left[(x-\mu)(x-\mu)^T\Sigma^{-1}\frac{\partial\Sigma}{\partial\theta_i}\Sigma^{-1}\right]\right)\left(tr\left[\Sigma^{-1}\frac{\partial\Sigma}{\partial\theta_j}\right]\right)\right\}$$
$$= -\frac{1}{4}\left\{\left(tr\left[\Sigma^{-1}\frac{\partial\Sigma}{\partial\theta_i}\right]\right)\left(tr\left[\Sigma\Sigma^{-1}\frac{\partial\Sigma}{\partial\theta_j}\Sigma^{-1}\right]\right)\right.$$
$$\left. + \left(tr\left[\Sigma\Sigma^{-1}\frac{\partial\Sigma}{\partial\theta_i}\Sigma^{-1}\right]\right)\left(tr\left[\Sigma^{-1}\frac{\partial\Sigma}{\partial\theta_j}\right]\right)\right\} \quad (A12)$$
$$= -\frac{1}{4}\left\{\left(tr\left[\Sigma^{-1}\frac{\partial\Sigma}{\partial\theta_i}\right]\right)\left(tr\left[\frac{\partial\Sigma}{\partial\theta_j}\Sigma^{-1}\right]\right)\right.$$
$$\left. + \left(tr\left[\frac{\partial\Sigma}{\partial\theta_i}\Sigma^{-1}\right]\right)\left(tr\left[\Sigma^{-1}\frac{\partial\Sigma}{\partial\theta_j}\right]\right)\right\}.$$

Once again, we took the expectation as required to find the Fisher information. Finally, we use the commutative property of trace to clean up the expression in Equation (A12)

$$A_iB_j + B_iA_j = -\frac{1}{4}\left\{\left(tr\left[\Sigma^{-1}\frac{\partial\Sigma}{\partial\theta_i}\right]\right)\left(tr\left[\Sigma^{-1}\frac{\partial\Sigma}{\partial\theta_j}\right]\right) + \left(tr\left[\Sigma^{-1}\frac{\partial\Sigma}{\partial\theta_i}\right]\right)\left(tr\left[\Sigma^{-1}\frac{\partial\Sigma}{\partial\theta_j}\right]\right)\right\}$$
$$= -\frac{1}{2}\left(tr\left[\Sigma^{-1}\frac{\partial\Sigma}{\partial\theta_i}\right]\right)\left(tr\left[\Sigma^{-1}\frac{\partial\Sigma}{\partial\theta_j}\right]\right). \quad (A13)$$

Combining Equations (A6), (A7, (A9 and (A13) into Equation (A5), we obtain

$$\begin{aligned}
g_{i,j}(\theta) =& \frac{1}{4} tr\left[\Sigma^{-1}\frac{\partial \Sigma}{\partial \theta_i}\right] tr\left[\Sigma^{-1}\frac{\partial \Sigma}{\partial \theta_j}\right] \\
&+ \frac{1}{4}\left[tr\left(\Sigma^{-1}\frac{\partial \Sigma}{\partial \theta_i}\right) tr\left(\Sigma^{-1}\frac{\partial \Sigma}{\partial \theta_j}\right)\right] + 2tr\left[\left(\Sigma^{-1}\frac{\partial \Sigma}{\partial \theta_i}\right)\left(\Sigma^{-1}\frac{\partial \Sigma}{\partial \theta_j}\right)\right] \\
&+ \frac{\partial \mu}{\partial \theta_i}^T \Sigma^{-1} \frac{\partial \mu}{\partial \theta_j} \\
&+ -\frac{1}{2}\left(tr\left[\Sigma^{-1}\frac{\partial \Sigma}{\partial \theta_i}\right]\right)\left(tr\left[\Sigma^{-1}\frac{\partial \Sigma}{\partial \theta_j}\right]\right) \\
=& \frac{1}{2} tr\left[\left(\Sigma^{-1}\frac{\partial \Sigma}{\partial \theta_i}\right)\left(\Sigma^{-1}\frac{\partial \Sigma}{\partial \theta_j}\right)\right] + \frac{\partial \mu}{\partial \theta_i}^T \Sigma^{-1} \frac{\partial \mu}{\partial \theta_j}.
\end{aligned} \quad (A14)$$

Appendix B. Fisher Information of a 2-Dimensional Gaussian

The usefulness of Equation (A14) lies in the ability of calculating the individual terms in the equation. Here, the inverse of a covariance matrix is extremely illusive for a high-dimensional Gaussian distribution, even after leveraging its symmetric properties.

Considering just a 2 × 2 covariance matrix, Equation (A14) is tractable, since its inverse is known exactly and is reasonably manageable. Furthermore, we will collect all the parameters of a general bivariate Gaussian into a single vector, to facilitate the calculation of each element of the Fisher information matrix.

$$\begin{aligned}
\theta &= [\theta_1, \theta_1, \theta_1, \theta_1, \theta_1] \\
&= [\mu_1, \mu_2, \sigma_1^2, \sigma_2^2, \sigma_{12}]
\end{aligned} \quad (A15)$$

Starting with the diagonal elements, g_{11} and g_{22} share similar structures. Focusing just on g_{11}, and consider a 2-dimensional Gaussian with mean vector $\mu^T = [\mu_1, \mu_2]$ and covariance matrix

$$\Sigma = \begin{pmatrix} \sigma_1^2 & \sigma_{12} \\ \sigma_{12} & \sigma_2^2 \end{pmatrix}$$

which will be indexed according to Equation (A15). We now have, using the standard definition of the inverse

$$\Sigma^{-1} = \frac{1}{\sigma_1^2 \sigma_2^2 - \sigma_{12}^2} \begin{pmatrix} \sigma_2^2 & -\sigma_{12} \\ -\sigma_{12} & \sigma_1^2 \end{pmatrix}.$$

For succinctness, we will let $k = \frac{1}{\sigma_1^2 \sigma_2^2 - \sigma_{12}^2}$.

Conveniently, the means are not involved in the covariance matrix, so the first term of Equation (A14) vanishes. To find g_{11} we need

$$\begin{aligned}
g_{11} &= \frac{1}{k}\left[\frac{\partial \mu}{\partial \mu_1}^T \begin{pmatrix} \sigma_2^2 & -\sigma_{12} \\ -\sigma_{12} & \sigma_1^2 \end{pmatrix} \frac{\partial \mu}{\partial \mu_1}\right] \\
&= \frac{1}{k}\left[(1 \; 0)\begin{pmatrix} \sigma_2^2 & -\sigma_{12} \\ -\sigma_{12} & \sigma_1^2 \end{pmatrix}\begin{pmatrix} 1 \\ 0 \end{pmatrix}\right] \\
&= \frac{\sigma_2^2}{k} \\
&= \frac{\sigma_2^2}{\sigma_1^2 \sigma_2^2 - \sigma_{12}^2}.
\end{aligned} \quad (A16)$$

Finding g_{22} easily follows the above, resulting in

$$g_{22} = \frac{\sigma_1^2}{\sigma_1^2 \sigma_2^2 - \sigma_{12}^2}. \tag{A17}$$

Finding the remaining diagonal elements involve the just the first term of Equation (A14). For the variance of the first variable, we will need to find

$$\begin{aligned}
g_{33} &= \frac{1}{2} \left(tr \left[\Sigma^{-1} \frac{\partial \Sigma}{\partial \sigma_1^2} \right]^2 \right) \\
&= \frac{1}{2} \left(tr \left[\frac{1}{k} \begin{pmatrix} \sigma_2^2 & -\sigma_{12} \\ -\sigma_{12} & \sigma_1^2 \end{pmatrix} \begin{pmatrix} 1 & 0 \\ 0 & 0 \end{pmatrix} \right]^2 \right) \\
&= \frac{1}{2k^2} \left(tr \left[\begin{pmatrix} \sigma_2^2 & 0 \\ -\sigma_{12} & 0 \end{pmatrix} \right]^2 \right) \\
&= \frac{1}{2k^2} \left(tr \left[\begin{pmatrix} (\sigma_2^2)^2 & 0 \\ (\sigma_{12}\sigma_2^2)^2 & 0 \end{pmatrix} \right] \right) \\
&= \frac{1}{2k^2} (\sigma_2^2)^2 \\
&= \frac{1}{2} \left(\frac{\sigma_2^2}{\sigma_1^2 \sigma_2^2 - \sigma_{12}^2} \right)^2.
\end{aligned} \tag{A18}$$

Once again, the element of the Fisher information matrix for the variance of the second variable mirrors the above exactly.

$$g_{44} = \frac{1}{2} \left(\frac{\sigma_1^2}{\sigma_1^2 \sigma_2^2 - \sigma_{12}^2} \right)^2. \tag{A19}$$

The covariance component will complete the diagonal elements of the Fisher information matrix.

$$\begin{aligned}
g_{55} &= \frac{1}{2} \left(tr \left[\Sigma^{-1} \frac{\partial \Sigma}{\partial \sigma_{12}} \right]^2 \right) \\
&= \frac{1}{2} \left(tr \left[\frac{1}{k} \begin{pmatrix} \sigma_2^2 & -\sigma_{12} \\ -\sigma_{12} & \sigma_1^2 \end{pmatrix} \begin{pmatrix} 0 & 1 \\ 1 & 0 \end{pmatrix} \right]^2 \right) \\
&= \frac{1}{2k^2} \left(tr \left[\begin{pmatrix} -\sigma_{12} & \sigma_2^2 \\ \sigma_1^2 & -\sigma_{12} \end{pmatrix} \right]^2 \right) \\
&= \frac{1}{2k^2} \left(tr \left[\begin{pmatrix} \sigma_1^2 \sigma_2^2 + \sigma_{12}^2 & 2\sigma_2^2 \sigma_{12} \\ 2\sigma_1^2 \sigma_{12} & \sigma_1^2 \sigma_2^2 + \sigma_{12}^2 \end{pmatrix} \right] \right) \\
&= \frac{1}{2k^2} 2(\sigma_1^2 \sigma_2^2 + \sigma_{12}^2) \\
&= \frac{\sigma_1^2 \sigma_2^2 + \sigma_{12}^2}{(\sigma_1^2 \sigma_2^2 - \sigma_{12}^2)^2}.
\end{aligned} \tag{A20}$$

The off-diagonal elements are only slightly more involved. However, because the terms in Equation (A14) involve the partial derivatives, and because the mean vector and the covariance matrix have no overlapping terms, many of the off-diagonal elements vanish, specifically the ones that involve both a mean component and a variance component, i.e., $g_{ij} = 0$ for $i \in (1, 2)$ and $j \in (3, 4, 5)$. For the other off-diagonal components, we will employ all the conveniences of symmetry to complete the Fisher information matrix.

Turning our attention to the g_{12}, the element concerning the two means:

$$\begin{aligned} g_{12} &= \frac{\partial \mu}{\partial \theta_1}^T \Sigma^{-1} \frac{\partial \mu}{\partial \theta_2} \\ &= \frac{1}{k}(1\ 0)\begin{pmatrix} \sigma_2^2 & -\sigma_{12} \\ -\sigma_{12} & \sigma_1^2 \end{pmatrix}\begin{pmatrix} 0 \\ 1 \end{pmatrix} \\ &= -\frac{1}{k}\sigma_{12} \\ &= -\frac{\sigma_{12}}{\sigma_1^2 \sigma_2^2 - \sigma_{12}^2} = g_{21}. \end{aligned} \qquad (A21)$$

Next, we consider the elements of the Fisher information matrix involving both variances, g_{34}

$$\begin{aligned} g_{34} &= \frac{1}{2}\left(tr\left[\Sigma^{-1}\frac{\partial \Sigma}{\partial \sigma_1^2}\Sigma^{-1}\frac{\partial \Sigma}{\partial \sigma_2^2}\right]\right) \\ &= \frac{1}{2k^2}\left(tr\left[\begin{pmatrix} \sigma_2^2 & -\sigma_{12} \\ -\sigma_{12} & \sigma_1^2 \end{pmatrix}\begin{pmatrix} 1 & 0 \\ 0 & 0 \end{pmatrix}\begin{pmatrix} \sigma_2^2 & -\sigma_{12} \\ -\sigma_{12} & \sigma_1^2 \end{pmatrix}\begin{pmatrix} 0 & 0 \\ 0 & 1 \end{pmatrix}\right]\right) \\ &= \frac{1}{2k^2}\left(tr\left[\begin{pmatrix} \sigma_2^2 & 0 \\ -\sigma_{12} & 0 \end{pmatrix}\begin{pmatrix} 0 & -\sigma_{12} \\ 0 & \sigma_1^2 \end{pmatrix}\right]\right) \\ &= \frac{1}{2k^2}\left(tr\left[\begin{pmatrix} 0 & -\sigma_2^2\sigma_{12} \\ 0 & \sigma_{12}^2 \end{pmatrix}\right]\right) \\ &= \frac{1}{2}\left(\frac{\sigma_{12}}{\sigma_1^2\sigma_2^2 - \sigma_{12}^2}\right)^2 = g_{43}. \end{aligned} \qquad (A22)$$

The variance/covariance elements of the Fisher information matrix will all have similar structures. We calculate one of them below

$$\begin{aligned} g_{35} &= \frac{1}{2}\left(tr\left[\Sigma^{-1}\frac{\partial \Sigma}{\partial \sigma_1^2}\Sigma^{-1}\frac{\partial \Sigma}{\partial \sigma_{12}}\right]\right) \\ &= \frac{1}{2k^2}\left(tr\left[\begin{pmatrix} \sigma_2^2 & -\sigma_{12} \\ -\sigma_{12} & \sigma_1^2 \end{pmatrix}\begin{pmatrix} 1 & 0 \\ 0 & 0 \end{pmatrix}\begin{pmatrix} \sigma_2^2 & -\sigma_{12} \\ -\sigma_{12} & \sigma_1^2 \end{pmatrix}\begin{pmatrix} 0 & 1 \\ 1 & 0 \end{pmatrix}\right]\right) \\ &= \frac{1}{2k^2}\left(tr\left[\begin{pmatrix} \sigma_2^2 & 0 \\ -\sigma_{12} & 0 \end{pmatrix}\begin{pmatrix} -\sigma_{12} & \sigma_2^2 \\ \sigma_1^2 & -\sigma_{12} \end{pmatrix}\right]\right) \\ &= \frac{1}{2k^2}\left(tr\left[\begin{pmatrix} -\sigma_{12}\sigma_2^2 & \sigma_{12}^2 \\ \sigma_{12}^2 & -\sigma_{12}\sigma_2^2 \end{pmatrix}\right]\right) \\ &= -\frac{\sigma_{12}\sigma_2^2}{(\sigma_1^2\sigma_2^2 - \sigma_{12}^2)^2} = g_{53}. \end{aligned} \qquad (A23)$$

Similarly, the element involving the second variance with the covariance is

$$g_{45} = g_{54} = -\frac{\sigma_{12}\sigma_1^2}{(\sigma_1^2\sigma_2^2 - \sigma_{12}^2)^2}. \qquad (A24)$$

References

1. Kass, R.E. The geometry of asymptotic inference. *Stat. Sci.* **1989**, *4*, 188–234. [CrossRef]
2. Amari, S.I. *Differential Geometric Methods in Statistics*; Springer: Berlin/Heidelberg, Germany, 1995.
3. Critchley, F.; Marriott, P. Information Geometry and Its Applications: An Overview. In *Computational Information Geometry: For Image and Signal Processing*; Nielsen, F., Critchley, F., Dodson, C.T.J., Eds.; Springer International Publishing: Cham, Switzerland, 2017; pp. 1–31.
4. Akaike, H. A new look at the statistical model identification. *IEEE Trans. Autom. Control.* **1974**, *19*, 716–723. [CrossRef]
5. Rissanen, J. Modeling by shortest data description. *Automatica* **1978**, *14*, 465–471. [CrossRef]

6. Herntier, T.; Ihou, K.E.; Smith, A.; Rangarajan, A.; Peter, A.M. Spherical minimum description length. *Entropy* **2018**, *20*, 575. [CrossRef] [PubMed]
7. Rényi, A. On measures of entropy and information. In Proceedings of the Fourth Berkeley Symposium on Mathematical Statistics and Probability, Berkeley, CA, USA, 1961 June 20; Volume 1.
8. Miller, R.E. *Dynamic Optimization and Economic Applications*; McGraw-Hill Inc.: New York, NY, USA, 1979.
9. Gel'fand, I.; Fomin, S. *Calculus of Variations by I.M. Gelfand and S.V. Fomin*; Selected Russian Publications in the Mathematical Sciences; Prentice-Hall: Upper Saddle River, NJ, USA, 1964.
10. Ben-David, S.; Blitzer, J.; Crammer, K.; Kulesza, A.; Pereira, F.; Vaughan, J. A theory of learning from different domains. *Mach. Learn.* **2010**, *79*, 151–175. [CrossRef]
11. Ganin, Y.; Ustinova, E.; Ajakan, H.; Germain, P.; Larochelle, H.; Laviolette, F.; Marchand, M.; Lempitsky, V. Domain-adversarial training of neural networks. *J. Mach. Learn. Res.* **2016**, *17*, 2096–2130.
12. Sun, B.; Feng, J.; Saenko, K. Return of frustratingly easy domain adaptation. In Proceedings of the AAAI Conference on Artificial Intelligence, Phoenix, AZ, USA, 12–17 February 2016; Volume 30.
13. Rissanen, J. Stochastic complexity. *J. R. Stat. Soc.* **1987**, *49*, 223–239. [CrossRef]
14. Schwarz, G. Estimating the dimension of a model. *Ann. Stat.* **1978**, *6*, 461–464. [CrossRef]
15. Efron, B. Defining the curvature of a statistical problem (with applications to second order efficiency). *Ann. Stat.* **1975**, *3*, 1189–1242. [CrossRef]
16. Felice, D.; Ay, N. Towards a canonical divergence within information geometry. *Inf. Geom.* **2021**, *4*, 65–130. [CrossRef]
17. Fisher, R.A. On the mathematical foundations of theoretical statistics. *Philos. Trans. R. Soc. Lond. A* **1922**, *222*, 309–368.
18. Kullback, S.; Leibler, R.A. On information and sufficiency. *Ann. Math. Stat.* **1951**, *22*, 79–86. [CrossRef]
19. Bhattacharyya, A. On a measure of divergence between two multinomial populations. *Sankhyā: Indian J. Stat. (1933–1960)* **1946**, *7*, 401–406.
20. Hotelling, H. Spaces of statistical parameters. *Bull. Am. Math. Soc.* **1930**, *36*, 191.
21. Rao, C.R. Information and accuracy attainable in estimation of statistical parameters. *Bull. Calcutta Math. Soc.* **1945**, *37*, 81–91.
22. Čencov, N. Algebraic foundation of mathematical statistics. *Ser. Stat.* **1978**, *9*, 267–276. [CrossRef]
23. Isham, V.; Murray, M. *Differential Geometry and Statistics*; Routledge: London, UK, 2017.
24. Skovgaard, L.T. A Riemannian geometry of the multivariate normal model. *Scand. J. Stat.* **1984**, *11*, 211–223.
25. Manté, C. The Rao's distance between negative binomial distributions for exploratory analyses and Goodness-of-Fit testing. In Proceedings of the 61st World Statistics Congress—ISI2017, Marrakech, Maroc, 16–21 July 2017.
26. Reverter, F.; Oller, J. Computing the Rao distance for Gamma distributions. *J. Comput. Appl. Math.* **2003**, *157*, 155–167. [CrossRef]
27. Arwini, K.A.; Dodson, C.T. *Information Geometry*; Springer: Berlin/Heidelberg, Germany, 2008.
28. Nielsen, F. The many faces of information geometry. *Not. Am. Math. Soc.* **2022**, *69*, 36–45. [CrossRef]
29. Calvo, M.; Oller, J.M. An explicit solution of information geodesic equation for the multivatriate normal model. *Stat. Risk Model.* **1991**, *9*, 119–138.
30. Burbea, J. Informative geometry of probability spaces. *Expo. Math.* **1986**, *4*, 347–378.
31. Costa, S.I.R.; Santos, S.A.; Strapasson, J.E. Fisher information distance: A geometrical reading. *Discret. Appl. Math.* **2015**, *197*, 59–69. [CrossRef]
32. Peter, A.M.; Rangarajan, A. Information geometry for landmark shape analysis: Unifying shape representation and deformation. *IEEE Trans. PAMI* **2009**, *31*, 337–350. [CrossRef]
33. Cafaro, C.; Mancini, S. Quantifying the complexity of geodesic paths on curved statistical manifolds through information geometric entropies and Jacobi fields. *Phys. Nonlinear Phenom.* **2011**, *240*, 607–618. [CrossRef]
34. Ciaglia, F.M.; Cosmo, F.D.; Felice, D.; Mancini, S.; Marmo, G.; Pérez-Pardo, J.M. Aspects of geodesical motion with Fisher-Rao metric: Classical and quantum. *Open Syst. Inf. Dyn.* **2018**, *25*, 1850005. [CrossRef]
35. Yoshizawa, S.; Tanabe, K. Dual differential geometry associated with the Kullback-Leibler information on the Gaussian distributions and its 2-parameter deformations. *SUT J. Math.* **1999**, *35*, 113–137. [CrossRef]
36. Bormashenko, E. Contact angles of sessile droplets deposited on rough and flat surfaces in the presence of external fields. *Math. Model. Nat. Phenom.* **2012**, *7*, 1–5. [CrossRef]
37. Gladkov, S.O. A contribution to the computation of the Young Modulus. *J. Eng. Phys. Thermophys.* **2003**, *76*, 1126–1130. [CrossRef]
38. Halkin, H. Necessary conditions for optimal control problems with infinite horizons. *Econometrica* **1974**, *42*, 267–272. [CrossRef]
39. Kamihigashi, T. Transversality Conditions and Dynamic Economic Behaviour. In *The New Palgrave Dictionary of Economics*; Palgrave Macmillan: London, UK, 2018; pp. 13858–13862.
40. Michel, P. On the transversality condition in infinite horizon optimal problems. *Econometrica* **1982**, *50*, 975–985. [CrossRef]
41. Leung, S.F. Transversality condition and optimality in a class of infinite horizon continuous time economic models. *J. Econ. Theory* **1991**, *54*, 224–233. [CrossRef]
42. Moroz, A. 2-Some general optimal control problems useful for biokinetics. In *The Common Extremalities in Biology and Physics*, 2nd ed.; Moroz, A., Ed.; Elsevier: London, UK, 2012; pp. 43–110.
43. Li, C.F. A key role of transversality condition in quantization of photon orbital angular momentum. *arXiv* **2016**, arXiv:1609.07717.

Article

Robust Z-Estimators for Semiparametric Moment Condition Models

Aida Toma [1,2]

[1] Department of Applied Mathematics, Bucharest University of Economic Studies, 010374 Bucharest, Romania; aida.toma@csie.ase.ro

[2] "Gheorghe Mihoc-Caius Iacob" Institute of Mathematical Statistics and Applied Mathematics of the Romanian Academy, 050711 Bucharest, Romania

Abstract: In the present paper, we introduce a class of robust Z-estimators for moment condition models. These new estimators can be seen as robust alternatives for the minimum empirical divergence estimators. By using the multidimensional Huber function, we first define robust estimators of the element that realizes the supremum in the dual form of the divergence. A linear relationship between the influence function of a minimum empirical divergence estimator and the influence function of the estimator of the element that realizes the supremum in the dual form of the divergence led to the idea of defining new Z-estimators for the parameter of the model, by using robust estimators in the dual form of the divergence. The asymptotic properties of the proposed estimators were proven, including here the consistency and their asymptotic normality. Then, the influence functions of the estimators were derived, and their robustness is demonstrated.

Keywords: moment condition models; divergences; robustness

1. Introduction

A moment condition model is a family $\mathcal{M}^1$ of probability measures, all defined on the same measurable space $(\mathbb{R}^m, \mathcal{B}(\mathbb{R}^m))$, such that

$$\int g(x,\theta)dQ(x) = 0, \quad \text{for all} \quad Q \in \mathcal{M}^1. \tag{1}$$

The parameter θ belongs to $\Theta \subset \mathbb{R}^d$; the function $g := (g_1, \ldots, g_l)^\top$ is defined on $\mathbb{R}^m \times \Theta$, each of the g_i's being real-valued, $l \geq d$, and the functions $g_1, \ldots, g_l$ and $\mathbf{1}_\mathcal{X}$ are supposed to be linearly independent. Denote by M^1 the set of all probability measures on $(\mathbb{R}^m, \mathcal{B}(\mathbb{R}^m))$ and

$$\mathcal{M}^1_\theta := \{Q \in M^1 : \int g(x,\theta)dQ(x) = 0\}, \tag{2}$$

such that

$$\mathcal{M}^1 = \bigcup_{\theta \in \Theta} \mathcal{M}^1_\theta. \tag{3}$$

Let $X_1, \ldots, X_n$ be an i.i.d. sample on the random vector X with unknown probability distribution P_0. We considered the problem of the estimation of the parameter θ_0 for which the constraints of the model are satisfied:

$$\int g(x,\theta_0)dP_0(x) = 0. \tag{4}$$

We supposed that θ_0 is the unique solution of Equation (4). Thus, we assumed that information about θ_0 and P_0 is available in the form of $l \geq d$ functionally independent unbiased estimating functions, and we used this information to estimate θ_0.

Among the best-known estimation methods for moment condition models, we mention the generalized method of moments (GMM) [1], the continuous updating (CU) estimator [2], the empirical likelihood (EL) estimator [3,4], the exponential tilting (ET) estimator [5], and the generalized empirical likelihood (GEL) estimators [6]. Although the EL estimator is superior to other estimators in terms of higher-order asymptotic properties, these properties hold only under the correct specification of the moment conditions. In [7] was proposed the exponentially tilted empirical likelihood (ETEL) estimator, which has the same higher-order property as the EL estimator under the correct specification, while maintaining the usual asymptotic properties such as the consistency and asymptotic normality under misspecification. The so-called information and entropy econometric techniques have been proposed to improve the finite sample performance of the GMM-estimators and tests (see, e.g., [4,5]).

Some recent methods for the estimation and testing of moment condition models are based on using divergences. Divergences between probability measures are widely used in statistics and data science in order to perform inference in models of various kinds, parametric or semiparametric. Statistical methods based on divergence minimization extend the likelihood paradigm and often have the advantage of providing a trade-off between efficiency and robustness [8–11]. A general methodology for the estimation and testing of moment condition models was developed in [12]. This approach is based on minimizing divergences in their dual form and allows the asymptotic study of the estimators, called minimum empirical divergence estimators, and of the associated test statistics, both under the model and under misspecification of the model. The approach based on minimizing dual forms of divergences was initially used in the case of parametric models, the results being published in a series of articles [13–16]. The broad class of minimum empirical divergence estimators contains in particular the EL estimator, the CU estimator, as well as the ET estimator mentioned above. Using the influence function as the robustness measure, it has been shown that the minimum empirical divergence estimators are not robust, because the corresponding influence functions are generally not bounded [17]. On the other hand, the minimum empirical divergence estimators have the same efficiency of first order, and moreover, the EL estimator, which belong to this class, is superior in higher-order efficiency. Therefore, proposing robust versions of the minimum empirical divergence estimators would bring a trade-off between robustness and efficiency. These aspects motivated our studies in the present paper.

Some robust estimation methods for moment condition models have been proposed in the literature, for example in [18–22]. In the present paper, we introduce a class of robust Z-estimators for moment condition models. These new estimators can be seen as robust alternatives for the minimum empirical divergence estimators. By using the multidimensional Huber function, we first define robust estimators of the element that realizes the supremum in the dual form of the divergence. A linear relationship between the influence function of a minimum empirical divergence estimator and the influence function of the estimator of the element that realizes the supremum in the dual form of the divergence led to the idea of defining new Z-estimators for the parameter of the model, by using robust estimators in the dual form of the divergence. The asymptotic properties of the proposed estimators were proven, including here the consistency and their asymptotic normality. Then, the influence functions of the estimators were derived, and their robustness is demonstrated.

The paper is organized as follows. In Section 2, we briefly recall the context and the definitions of the minimum empirical divergence estimators, these being necessary for defining the new estimators. In Section 3, the new Z-estimators for moment condition models are defined. The asymptotic properties of these estimators were proven, including here the consistency and their asymptotic normality. Then, the influence functions of the estimators were derived, and their robustness is demonstrated. The proofs of the theoretical results are deferred in Appendix A.

2. Minimum Empirical Divergence Estimators
2.1. Statistical Divergences

Let φ be a convex function defined on $\mathbb{R}$ and $[0, \infty]$-valued, such that $\varphi(1) = 0$, and let $P \in M^1$ be some probability measure. For any signed finite measure Q defined on the same measurable space $(\mathbb{R}^m, \mathcal{B}(\mathbb{R}^m))$, absolutely continuous (a.c.) with respect to P, the φ divergence between Q and P is defined by

$$D_\varphi(Q, P) := \int \varphi\left(\frac{dQ}{dP}(x)\right) dP(x). \tag{5}$$

When Q is not a.c. with respect to P, we set $D_\varphi(Q, P) = \infty$. This extension, for the case when Q is not absolutely continuous with respect to P, was considered in order to have a unique definition of divergences, appropriate for both cases—that of continuous probability laws and that of discrete probability laws.

This definition extends the one of divergences between probability measures [23], and the necessity of working with signed finite measures will be explained in Section 2.2.

Largely used in information theory, the Kullback–Leibler divergence is associated with the real convex function $\varphi(x) := x \log x - x + 1$ and is defined by

$$KL(Q, P) := \int \log\left(\frac{dQ}{dP}\right) dQ.$$

The modified Kullback–Leibler divergence is associated with the convex function $\varphi(x) := -\log x + x - 1$ and is defined through

$$KL_m(Q, P) := \int -\log\left(\frac{dQ}{dP}\right) dP.$$

Other divergences, largely used in inferential statistics, are the χ^2 and the modified χ^2 divergences, namely

$$\chi^2(Q, P) := \frac{1}{2} \int \left(\frac{dQ}{dP} - 1\right)^2 dP,$$

$$\chi^2_m(Q, P) := \frac{1}{2} \int \frac{\left(\frac{dQ}{dP} - 1\right)^2}{\frac{dQ}{dP}} dP,$$

these being associated with the convex functions $\varphi(x) := \frac{1}{2}(x-1)^2$ and $\varphi(x) := \frac{1}{2}(x-1)^2/x$, respectively. The Hellinger distance and the L_1 distance are also φ divergences. They are associated with the convex functions $\varphi(x) := 2(\sqrt{x} - 1)^2$ and $\varphi(x) := |x - 1|$, respectively.

All the preceding examples, except the L_1 distance, belong to the class of power divergences introduced by Cressie and Read [24] and defined by the convex functions:

$$x \in \mathbb{R}^*_+ \mapsto \varphi_\gamma(x) := \frac{x^\gamma - \gamma x + \gamma - 1}{\gamma(\gamma - 1)}, \tag{6}$$

for $\gamma \in \mathbb{R} \setminus \{0, 1\}$ and $\varphi_0(x) := -\log x + x - 1$, $\varphi_1(x) := x \log x - x + 1$. The Kullback–Leibler divergence is associated with φ_1, the modified Kullback–Leibler with φ_0, the χ^2 divergence with φ_2, the modified χ^2 divergence with φ_{-1}, and the Hellinger distance with $\varphi_{1/2}$. When φ_γ is not defined on $(-\infty, 0)$ or when φ_γ is not convex, the definition of the corresponding power divergence function $Q \in M^1 \mapsto D_{\varphi_\gamma}(Q, P)$ can be extended to the whole set of signed finite measures by taking the following extension of φ_γ:

$$\varphi_\gamma : x \in \mathbb{R} \mapsto \varphi_\gamma(x) \mathbf{1}_{[0, \infty)}(x) + (+\infty) \mathbf{1}_{(-\infty, 0)}(x).$$

The φ divergence between some set Ω of signed finite measures and a probability measure P is defined by
$$D_\varphi(\Omega, P) = \inf_{Q \in \Omega} D_\varphi(Q, P). \tag{7}$$
Assuming that $D_\varphi(\Omega, P)$ is finite, a measure $Q^* \in \Omega$ is called a φ-projection of P on Ω if
$$D_\varphi(Q^*, P) \leq D_\varphi(Q, P), \text{ for all } Q \in \Omega.$$

2.2. Minimum Empirical Divergence Estimators

Let $X_1, \ldots, X_n$ be an i.i.d. sample on the random vector X with the probability distribution P_0. The "plug-in" estimator of the φ divergence $D_\varphi(\mathcal{M}_\theta^1, P_0)$ between the set $\mathcal{M}_\theta^1$ and the probability measure P_0 is defined by replacing P_0 with the empirical measure associated with the sample. More precisely,
$$\widehat{D}_\varphi(\mathcal{M}_\theta^1, P_0) = \inf_{Q \in \mathcal{M}_\theta^1} D_\varphi(Q, P_n) = \inf_{Q \in \mathcal{M}_\theta^1} \int \varphi\left(\frac{dQ}{dP_n}(x)\right) dP_n(x), \tag{8}$$

where $P_n := \frac{1}{n} \sum_{i=1}^n \delta_{X_i}$ is the empirical measure associated with the sample, δ_x being the Dirac measure putting all mass at x. If the projection of the measure P_n on $\mathcal{M}_\theta^1$ exists, it is a law a.c. with respect to P_n. Then, it is natural to consider
$$\mathcal{M}_\theta^{(n)} = \{Q \in M^1 : Q \text{ a.c. with respect to } P_n \text{ and } \sum_{i=1}^n g(X_i, \theta) Q(X_i) = 0\}, \tag{9}$$
and then, the plug-in estimator (8) can be written as
$$\widehat{D}_\varphi(\mathcal{M}_\theta^1, P_0) = \inf_{Q \in \mathcal{M}_\theta^{(n)}} \frac{1}{n} \sum_{i=1}^n \varphi(nQ(X_i)). \tag{10}$$

The infimum in the above expression (10) may be achieved at a point situated on the frontier of the set $\mathcal{M}_\theta^{(n)}$, a case in which the Lagrange method for characterizing the infimum and computing $\widehat{D}_\varphi(\mathcal{M}_\theta^1, P_0)$ cannot be applied. In order to avoid this difficulty, Broniatowski and Keziou [12,25] proposed to work on sets of signed finite measures and defined
$$\mathcal{M}_\theta := \{Q \in M : \int dQ = 1 \text{ and } \int g(x, \theta) dQ(x) = 0\}, \tag{11}$$
where M denotes the set of all signed finite measures on the measurable space $(\mathbb{R}^m, \mathcal{B}(\mathbb{R}^m))$, and
$$\mathcal{M} := \bigcup_{\theta \in \Theta} \mathcal{M}_\theta. \tag{12}$$

They showed that, if Q_1^* the projection of P_n on $\mathcal{M}_\theta^1$ is an interior point of $\mathcal{M}_\theta^1$ and Q^* the projection of P_n on $\mathcal{M}_\theta$ is an interior point of $\mathcal{M}_\theta$, then both approaches based on signed finite measures, respectively on probability measures, for defining minimum divergence estimators coincide. On the other hand, in the case when Q_1^* is a frontier point of $\mathcal{M}_\theta^1$, the estimator of the parameter θ_0 defined using the context of signed finite measures converges to θ_0. These aspects justify the substitution of $\mathcal{M}_\theta^1$ by $\mathcal{M}_\theta$.

In the following, we briefly recall the definitions of the estimators for the moment condition proposed in [12] in the context of signed finite measure sets.

Denote by $\overline{g}$ the function defined on $\mathbb{R}^m \times \Theta$ and $\mathbb{R}^{l+1}$-valued:
$$\overline{g}(x, \theta) := (\mathbf{1}_\mathcal{X}(x), g_1(x, \theta), \ldots, g_l(x, \theta))^\top. \tag{13}$$

Given a φ divergence, when the function φ is strictly convex on its domain, denote

$$\varphi^*(u) := u\varphi'^{-1}(u) - \varphi(\varphi'^{-1}(u)),$$

the convex conjugate of the function φ. For a given probability measure $P \in \mathcal{M}^1$ and a fixed $\theta \in \Theta$, define

$$\Lambda_\theta(P) := \{t \in \mathbb{R}^{l+1} : \int |\varphi^*(t_0 + \sum_{j=1}^l t_j g_j(x,\theta))| dP(x) < \infty\}. \tag{14}$$

We also use the notations Λ_θ for $\Lambda_\theta(P_0)$ and $\Lambda_\theta^{(n)}$ for $\Lambda_\theta(P_n)$.

Supposing that P_0 admits a projection Q_θ^* on $\mathcal{M}_\theta$ with the same support as P_0 and that the function φ is strictly convex on its domain, then the φ divergence $D_\varphi(\mathcal{M}_\theta, P_0)$ admits the dual representation:

$$D_\varphi(\mathcal{M}_\theta, P_0) = \sup_{t \in \Lambda_\theta} \int m(x, \theta, t) dP_0(x), \tag{15}$$

where $m(x, \theta, t) := t_0 - \varphi^*(t^\top \overline{g}(x, \theta))$.

The supremum in (15) is unique and is reached at a point that we denote as $t_\theta = t_\theta(P_0)$:

$$t_\theta := \arg\sup_{t \in \Lambda_\theta} \int m(x, \theta, t) dP_0(x). \tag{16}$$

Then, $D_\varphi(\mathcal{M}_\theta, P_0)$, t_θ, $D_\varphi(\mathcal{M}, P_0)$ and θ_0 can be estimated respectively by

$$\widehat{D}_\varphi(\mathcal{M}_\theta, P_0) := \sup_{t \in \Lambda_\theta^{(n)}} \int m(x, \theta, t) dP_n(x), \tag{17}$$

$$\widehat{t}_\theta := \arg\sup_{t \in \Lambda_\theta^{(n)}} \int m(x, \theta, t) dP_n(x), \tag{18}$$

$$\widehat{D}_\varphi(\mathcal{M}, P_0) := \inf_{\theta \in \Theta} \sup_{t \in \Lambda_\theta^{(n)}} \int m(x, \theta, t) dP_n(x), \tag{19}$$

$$\widehat{\theta}_\varphi := \arg\inf_{\theta \in \Theta} \sup_{t \in \Lambda_\theta^{(n)}} \int m(x, \theta, t) dP_n(x). \tag{20}$$

The estimators defined in (20) are called minimum empirical divergence estimators. We refer to [12] for the complete study of the existence and of the asymptotic properties of the above estimators.

The influence functions of these estimators and corresponding robustness properties were studied in [17]. According to those results, for $\theta \in \Theta$ fixed, the influence function of the estimator $\widehat{t}_\theta$ is given by

$$\text{IF}(x; t_\theta, P_0) = -\left[\int \frac{\partial^2}{\partial^2 t} m(y, \theta, t_\theta(P_0)) dP_0(y)\right]^{-1} \frac{\partial}{\partial t} m(x, \theta, t_\theta(P_0)), \tag{21}$$

where

$$\frac{\partial}{\partial t} m(x, \theta, t) = (1, 0_l)^\top - \varphi'^{-1}(t^\top \overline{g}(x, \theta)) \overline{g}(x, \theta), \tag{22}$$

$$\frac{\partial^2}{\partial^2 t} m(x, \theta, t) = -\frac{1}{\varphi''(\varphi'^{-1}(t^\top \overline{g}(x, \theta)))} \overline{g}(x, \theta) \overline{g}(x, \theta)^\top, \tag{23}$$

with the particular case $\theta = \theta_0$:

$$\text{IF}(x; t_{\theta_0}, P_0) = -\varphi''(1) \left[\int \overline{g}(y, \theta_0) \overline{g}(y, \theta_0)^\top dP_0(y) \right]^{-1} (0, g(x, \theta_0)^\top)^\top. \tag{24}$$

On the other hand, the influence function of the estimator $\widehat{\theta}_\varphi$ is given by

$$\text{IF}(x; T_\varphi, P_0) = -\left\{ \left[\int \tfrac{\partial}{\partial \theta} g(y, \theta_0) dP_0(y) \right]^\top \left[\int g(y, \theta_0) g(y, \theta_0)^\top dP_0(y) \right]^{-1} \int \tfrac{\partial}{\partial \theta} g(y, \theta_0) dP_0(y) \right\}^{-1} \\ \cdot \left[\int \tfrac{\partial}{\partial \theta} g(y, \theta_0) dP_0(y) \right]^\top \left[\int g(y, \theta_0) g(y, \theta_0)^\top dP_0(y) \right]^{-1} g(x, \theta_0). \tag{25}$$

Since the function $x \mapsto g(x, \theta)$ is usually not bounded, for example, when we have linear constraints, the influence function $\text{IF}(x; T_\varphi, P_0)$ is not bounded; therefore, the minimum empirical divergence estimators $\widehat{\theta}_\varphi$ defined in (20) are generally not robust.

Through the calculations, it can be seen that there is a connection between the influence functions $\text{IF}(x; t_{\theta_0}, P_0)$ and $\text{IF}(x; T_\varphi, P_0)$, namely the relation

$$\left[\int \tfrac{\partial}{\partial \theta} \overline{g}(y, \theta_0) dP_0(y) \right]^\top \cdot \left\{ \tfrac{\partial}{\partial \theta} t(\theta_0, P_0) \text{IF}(x; T_\varphi, P_0) + \text{IF}(x; t_{\theta_0}, P_0) \right\} = 0.$$

Since $\text{IF}(x; T_\varphi, P_0)$ is linearly related to $\text{IF}(x; t_{\theta_0}, P_0)$, using a robust estimator of $t_\theta = t_\theta(P_0)$ in the original duality Formula (15) would lead to a new robust estimator of θ_0. This is the idea at the basis of our proposal in this paper, for constructing new robust estimators for moment condition models.

3. Robust Estimators for Moment Condition Models

3.1. Definitions of New Estimators

In this section, we define robust versions of the estimators $\widehat{t}_\theta$ from (18) and robust versions of minimum empirical divergence estimators $\widehat{\theta}_\varphi$ from (20). First, we define robust estimators of t_θ, by using a truncated version of the function $x \mapsto \tfrac{\partial}{\partial t} m(x, \theta, t)$, and then, we insert such a robust estimator in the estimating equation corresponding to the minimum empirical divergence estimator. The truncated function is based on the multidimensional Huber function and contains a shift vector τ_θ and a scale matrix A_θ to calibrate t_θ and, thus, t_θ, which realizes the supremum in the duality formula, will also be the solution of a new equation based on the new truncated function.

For simplicity, for fixed $\theta \in \Theta$, we also use the notation $m_\theta(x, t) := m(x, \theta, t)$. With this notation, $t_\theta = t_\theta(P_0)$ defined in (16) is the unique solution of the equation:

$$\int \tfrac{\partial}{\partial t} m_\theta(x, t_\theta(P_0)) dP_0(x) = 0. \tag{26}$$

Consider the system

$$\int \tfrac{\partial}{\partial t} m_\theta(y, t) dP_0(y) = 0 \tag{27}$$

$$\int H_c(A[\tfrac{\partial}{\partial t} m_\theta(y, t) - \tau]) dP_0(y) = 0 \tag{28}$$

$$\int H_c(A[\tfrac{\partial}{\partial t} m_\theta(y, t) - \tau]) H_c(A[\tfrac{\partial}{\partial t} m_\theta(y, t) - \tau])^\top dP_0(y) = I_{\ell+1} \tag{29}$$

where

$$H_c(y) := \begin{cases} y \cdot \min\left(1, \tfrac{c}{\|y\|}\right) & \text{if } y \neq 0 \\ 0 & \text{if } y = 0 \end{cases} \tag{30}$$

is the multidimensional Huber function, with $c > 0$, $I_{\ell+1}$ the identity matrix, A is a $(l+1) \times (l+1)$ matrix, and $\tau \in \mathbb{R}^{l+1}$. For fixed θ, this system admits a unique solution $(t, A, \tau) = (t_\theta(P_0), A_\theta(P_0), \tau_\theta(P_0))$ (according to [18], p. 17).

The multidimensional Huber function is useful to define robust estimators; it transforms each point outside a hypersphere of c radius to the nearest point of it and leaves those inside unchanged (see [26], p. 239, [27]). By applying the multidimensional Huber function to the function $y \mapsto \frac{\partial}{\partial t} m_\theta(y, t)$, together with considering the scale matrix A_θ and the shift vector τ_θ, a modification is produced there, where the norm exceeds the bound c, and in the meantime, the original t_θ remains the solution of the equation based on the new truncated function. For parametric models, the multidimensional Huber function was also used in other contexts, for example to define optimal B_s-robust estimators or optimal B_i-robust estimators (see [26], p. 244).

The above arguments can be used for each probability measure P from the moment condition model $\mathcal{M}^1$. This context allows defining the truncated version of the function $y \mapsto \frac{\partial}{\partial t} m_\theta(y, t)$, which we denote by $\psi_\theta(y, t)$, such that the original $t_\theta(P_0)$, the solution of Equation (26), is also the solution of the equation $\int \psi_\theta(y, t_\theta(P_0)) dP_0(y) = 0$.

For θ fixed and P a probability measure, the equation $\int \frac{\partial}{\partial t} m_\theta(y, t) dP(y) = 0$ has a unique solution $t = t_\theta(P) \in \Lambda_\theta(P)$ assuring the supremum in the dual form of the divergence $D_\varphi(\mathcal{M}_\theta, P)$ (see [12]). For each t, we define the $A_\theta(t)$ and $\tau_\theta(t)$ solutions of the system:

$$\int H_c(A_\theta(t)[\frac{\partial}{\partial t} m_\theta(y, t) - \tau_\theta(t)]) dP(y) = 0 \quad (31)$$

$$\int H_c(A_\theta(t)[\frac{\partial}{\partial t} m_\theta(y, t) - \tau_\theta(t)]) H_c(A_\theta(t)[\frac{\partial}{\partial t} m_\theta(y, t) - \tau_\theta(t)])^\top dP(y) = I_{\ell+1}. \quad (32)$$

We define a new estimator $\widehat{t}_\theta^c$ of $t_\theta = t_\theta(P_0)$, as a Z-estimator corresponding to the ψ-function:

$$\psi_\theta(x, t) := H_c(A_\theta(t)[\frac{\partial}{\partial t} m_\theta(x, t) - \tau_\theta(t)]); \quad (33)$$

more precisely, $\widehat{t}_\theta^c$ is defined by

$$\int \psi_\theta(y, \widehat{t}_\theta^c) dP_n(y) = 0 \text{ or } \sum_{i=1}^n H_c(A_\theta(\widehat{t}_\theta^c)[\frac{\partial}{\partial t} m_\theta(X_i, \widehat{t}_\theta^c) - \tau_\theta(\widehat{t}_\theta^c)]) = 0, \quad (34)$$

the theoretical counterpart of this estimating equation being

$$\int \psi_\theta(y, t_\theta(P_0)) dP_0(y) = 0. \quad (35)$$

For a given probability measure P, the statistical functional $t_\theta^c(P)$ associated with the estimator $\widehat{t}_\theta^c$, whenever it exists, is defined by

$$\int \psi_\theta(y, t_\theta^c(P)) dP(y) = \int H_c(A_\theta(t_\theta^c(P))[\frac{\partial}{\partial t} m_\theta(y, t_\theta^c(P)) - \tau_\theta(t_\theta^c(P))]) dP(y) = 0. \quad (36)$$

Note that

$$t_\theta^c(P_0) = t_\theta(P_0), \quad (37)$$

by construction.

Remark 1. *We notice a similarity between the Z-estimator defined in (34) and the classical optimal Bs-robust estimator for parametric models from [26]. In the case of the parametric models, the M-estimator corresponding to the ψ-function (33), but defined for the classical score function $\frac{\partial}{\partial t}(\ln f_t(x)) = \frac{\frac{\partial}{\partial t} f_t(x)}{f_t(x)}$ instead of the function $\frac{\partial}{\partial t} m_\theta(x, t)$ (inclusively in the system (31) and (32) defining $A_\theta(t)$ and $\tau_\theta(t)$), is the classical optimal Bs-robust estimator ($f_t(x)$ denotes the density* corresponding to a parametric model indexed by the parameter t). The classical optimal Bs-robust estimator for parametric models has the optimal property that minimizes a measure of the asymptotic mean-squared error, among all the Fisher-consistent estimators with a self-standardized sensitivity smaller than the positive constant c.

In the following, for a given divergence, using the estimators $\widehat{t}_\theta^c$ for $t_\theta(P_0)$, we constructed new estimators of the parameter θ_0 of the model. In Section 3.3, we prove that all the estimators $\widehat{t}_\theta^c$ are robust, and this property will be transferred to the new estimators that we define for the parameter θ_0.

To define new estimators for θ_0, we used the dual representation (15) of the divergence $D_\varphi(\mathcal{M}_\theta, P_0)$. Since

$$\theta_0 = \arg\inf_{\theta\in\Theta} D_\varphi(\mathcal{M}_\theta, P_0) = \arg\inf_{\theta\in\Theta}\sup_{t\in\Lambda_\theta}\int m_\theta(y,t)dP_0(y) \tag{38}$$

$$= \arg\inf_{\theta\in\Theta}\int m_\theta(y,t_\theta(P_0))dP_0(y), \tag{39}$$

$\theta = \theta_0$ is the solution of the equation:

$$\int \frac{\partial}{\partial \theta}[m(y,\theta,t(\theta,P_0))]dP_0(y) = 0, \tag{40}$$

where we used the notation $t(\theta,P) := t_\theta(P)$. Equation (40) may be written as

$$\int \frac{\partial}{\partial\theta}m(y,\theta_0,t(\theta_0,P_0))dP_0(y) + \frac{\partial}{\partial\theta}t(\theta_0,P_0)^\top\int \frac{\partial}{\partial t}m(y,\theta_0,t(\theta_0,P_0))dP_0(y) = 0. \tag{41}$$

On the basis of the definition of $t_\theta(P_0) = t(\theta,P_0)$, for $\theta = \theta_0$, we have

$$\int \frac{\partial}{\partial t}m(y,\theta_0,t(\theta_0,P_0))dP_0(y) = 0; \tag{42}$$

therefore, we deduce that $\theta = \theta_0$ is the solution of equation:

$$\int \frac{\partial}{\partial\theta}m(y,\theta,t(\theta,P_0))dP_0(y) = 0. \tag{43}$$

Using (37), namely $t^c(\theta,P_0) = t(\theta,P_0)$, we obtain that $\theta = \theta_0$ is in fact the solution of equation:

$$\int \frac{\partial}{\partial\theta}m(y,\theta,t^c(\theta,P_0))dP_0(y) = 0. \tag{44}$$

Then, we define a new estimator $\widehat{\theta}_\varphi^c$ of θ_0, as a plug-in estimator solution of the equation:

$$\int \frac{\partial}{\partial\theta}m(y,\widehat{\theta}_\varphi^c, t^c(\widehat{\theta}_\varphi^c, P_n))dP_n(y) = 0. \tag{45}$$

For a probability measure P, the statistical functional T^c corresponding to the estimator $\widehat{\theta}_\varphi^c$, whenever it exists, is defined by

$$\int \frac{\partial}{\partial\theta}m(y,T^c(P),t^c(T^c(P),P))dP(y) = 0. \tag{46}$$

The functional T^c is Fisher-consistent, because

$$T^c(P_0) = \theta_0. \tag{47}$$

This equality is obtained by using (46) for $P = P_0$, the fact that $t^c(T^c(P_0),P_0) = t(T^c(P_0),P_0)$, and the definition of $t_\theta(P_0) = t(\theta,P_0)$ for $\theta = T^c(P_0)$, all these leading to

$$\int \frac{\partial}{\partial \theta} m(y, T^c(P_0), t(T^c(P_0), P_0)) dP_0(y) + \frac{\partial}{\partial \theta} t(T^c(P_0), P_0)^\top \int \frac{\partial}{\partial t} m(y, T^c(P_0), t(T^c(P_0), P_0)) dP_0(y) = 0. \quad (48)$$

Since θ_0 is the unique solution of Equation (41) and, according to (48), $T^c(P_0)$ would be another solution to the same equation, we deduce (47).

From (34) and (45), we have

$$\int \psi_{\widehat{\theta}^c_\varphi}(y, t^c(\widehat{\theta}^c_\varphi, P_n)) dP_n(y) = 0,$$
$$\int \frac{\partial}{\partial \theta} m(y, \widehat{\theta}^c_\varphi, t^c(\widehat{\theta}^c_\varphi, P_n)) dP_n(y) = 0,$$

and then,

$$\int \psi(y, \widehat{\theta}^c_\varphi, \widehat{t}^c_{\widehat{\theta}^c_\varphi}) dP_n(y) = 0,$$
$$\int \frac{\partial}{\partial \theta} m(y, \widehat{\theta}^c_\varphi, \widehat{t}^c_{\widehat{\theta}^c_\varphi}) dP_n(y) = 0,$$

with $\psi(y, \theta, t) := \psi_\theta(y, t)$. The couple of estimators $\widehat{\theta}^c_\varphi, \widehat{t}^c_{\widehat{\theta}^c_\varphi}$ can be viewed as a Z-estimator solution of the above system. Denoting

$$\Psi(y, \theta, t) := (\psi(y, \theta, t)^\top, (\frac{\partial}{\partial \theta} m(y, \theta, t))^\top)^\top, \quad (49)$$

the Z-estimators $\widehat{\theta}^c_\varphi, \widehat{t}^c_{\widehat{\theta}^c_\varphi}$ are the solutions of the system:

$$\int \Psi(y, \widehat{\theta}^c_\varphi, \widehat{t}^c_{\widehat{\theta}^c_\varphi}) dP_n(y) = 0, \quad (50)$$

and the theoretical counterpart is given by

$$\int \Psi(y, \theta_0, t_{\theta_0}) dP_0(y) = 0. \quad (51)$$

3.2. Asymptotic Properties

In this section, we establish the consistency and the asymptotic distributions for the estimators $\widehat{\theta}^c_\varphi$ and $\widehat{t}^c_{\widehat{\theta}^c_\varphi}$. In order to prove the consistency of the estimators, we adopted the results from the general theory of Z-estimators as presented for example in [28]. Then, using the consistency of the estimators, as well as supplementary conditions, we proved that the asymptotic distributions of the estimators are multivariate normal:

Assumption 1.

(a) There exist compact neighbourhoods V_{θ_0} of θ_0 and $V_{t_{\theta_0}}$ of t_{θ_0} such that

$$\int \sup_{\theta \in V_{\theta_0}, t \in V_{t_{\theta_0}}} \|\Psi(y, \theta, t)\| dP_0(y) < \infty.$$

(b) For any positive ε, the following condition holds

$$\inf_{(\theta, t) \in M} \|\int \Psi(y, \theta, t) dP_0(y)\| > 0 = \|\int \Psi(y, \theta_0, t_{\theta_0}) dP_0(y)\|,$$

where $M := \{(\theta, t) \text{ s.t. } \|(\theta, t) - (\theta_0, t_{\theta_0})\| > \varepsilon\}$.

Proposition 1. *Under Assumption 1, $\widehat{\theta}^c_\varphi$ converges in probability to θ_0 and $\widehat{t}^c_{\widehat{\theta}^c_\varphi}$ converges in probability to t_{θ_0}.*

Assumption 2.

(a) Both estimators $\widehat{\theta}^c_\varphi$ and $\widehat{t}^c_{\widehat{\theta}^c_\varphi}$ converge in probability to θ_0 and t_{θ_0}, respectively.

(b) The function $(\theta, t) \mapsto \psi(x, \theta, t)$ is C^2 on some neighbourhood $V(\theta_0, t_{\theta_0})$ for all x (P_0 a.s.), and the partial derivatives of order two of the functions $\{(\theta, t) \mapsto \psi(x, \theta, t); (\theta, t) \in V(\theta_0, t_{\theta_0})\}$ are dominated by some P_0-integrable function $H_1(x)$.

(c) The function $(\theta, t) \mapsto m(x, \theta, t)$ is C^3 on some neighbourhood $U(\theta_0, t_{\theta_0})$ for all x (P_0 a.s.), and the partial derivatives of order three of the functions $\{(\theta, t) \mapsto m(x, \theta, t); (\theta, t) \in U(\theta_0, t_{\theta_0})\}$ are dominated by some P_0-integrable function $H_2(x)$.

(d) $\int \|\frac{\partial}{\partial \theta} m(y, \theta_0, t_{\theta_0})\|^2 dP_0(y)$ is finite, and the matrix:

$$S := \begin{pmatrix} S_{11} & S_{12} \\ S_{21} & S_{22} \end{pmatrix}, \qquad (52)$$

with $S_{11} := (\int \frac{\partial}{\partial t} \psi(y, \theta_0, t_{\theta_0}) dP_0(y))^\top$, $S_{12} := (\int \frac{\partial}{\partial \theta} \psi(y, \theta_0, t_{\theta_0}) dP_0(y))^\top$, $S_{21} := (\int \frac{\partial^2}{\partial \theta \partial t} m(y, \theta_0, t_{\theta_0}) dP_0(y))^\top$ and $S_{22} := \int \frac{\partial^2}{\partial^2 \theta} m(y, \theta_0, t_{\theta_0}) dP_0(y)$, exists and is invertible.

Proposition 2. *Let P_0 belong to the model $\mathcal{M}^1$, and suppose that Assumption 2 holds. Then, both $\sqrt{n}(\widehat{\theta}^c_\varphi - \theta_0)$ and $\sqrt{n}(\widehat{t}^c_{\widehat{\theta}^c_\varphi} - t_{\theta_0})$ converge in distribution to a centred multivariate normal variable with covariance matrices given by*

$$[[S_{21} S_{11}^{-1} S_{12}]^{-1} S_{21} S_{11}^{-1}] \times [[S_{21} S_{11}^{-1} S_{12}]^{-1} S_{21} S_{11}^{-1}]^\top, \qquad (53)$$

and

$$[S_{11}^{-1} - S_{11}^{-1} S_{12} [S_{21} S_{11}^{-1} S_{12}]^{-1} S_{21} S_{11}^{-1}] \times [S_{11}^{-1} - S_{11}^{-1} S_{12} [S_{21} S_{11}^{-1} S_{12}]^{-1} S_{21} S_{11}^{-1}]^\top. \qquad (54)$$

The condition of Type (a) from Assumption 1 is usually considered to apply the uniform law of large numbers. For many choices of divergence (for example, those from the Cressie–Read family), the function Ψ is continuous in (θ, t), and consequently, this condition is verified. The second condition from Assumption 1 is imposed for the uniqueness of (θ_0, t_{θ_0}) as a solution of the equation and is verified, for example, whenever Ψ is continuous and the parameter space is compact ([28], p. 46). Furthermore, the conditions of Type (b)–(d), included in Assumption 2, are often imposed in order to apply the law of large numbers or the central limit theorem and can be verified for the functions appearing in the definitions of estimators proposed in the present paper.

3.3. Influence Functions and Robustness

In this section, we derive the influence functions of the estimators $\widehat{t}^c_{\widehat{\theta}}$ and $\widehat{\theta}^c_\varphi$ and prove their B-robustness. The corresponding statistical functionals are defined by (36) and (46), respectively.

Recall that, a map T, defined on a set of probability measures and parameter-space-valued, is a statistical functional corresponding to an estimator $\widehat{\theta}$ of the parameter θ_0 from the model P_0, if $\widehat{\theta} = T(P_n)$, P_n being the empirical measure corresponding to the sample. The influence function of T at P_0 is defined by

$$\text{IF}(x; T, P_0) := \left. \frac{\partial T(\widetilde{P}_{\varepsilon x})}{\partial \varepsilon} \right|_{\varepsilon = 0},$$

where $\widetilde{P}_{\varepsilon x} := (1 - \varepsilon) P_0 + \varepsilon \delta_x$, δ_x being the Dirac measure. An unbounded influence function implies an unbounded asymptotic bias of a statistic under single-point contamination of the model. Therefore, a natural robustness requirement on a statistical functional is the boundedness of its influence function. Whenever the influence function is bounded with respect to x, the corresponding estimator is called B-robust [26].

Proposition 3. *For fixed θ, the influence function of the functional t_θ^c is given by*

$$\text{IF}(x; t_\theta^c, P_0) = -\left\{ \int \frac{\partial}{\partial t} \psi_\theta(y, t_\theta(P_0)) dP_0(y) \right\}^{-1} \cdot \psi_\theta(x, t_\theta(P_0)). \tag{55}$$

Proposition 4. *The influence function of the functional T^c is given by*

$$\text{IF}(x; T^c, P_0) = \left\{ \left[\int \frac{\partial}{\partial \theta} \overline{g}(y, \theta_0) dP_0(y) \right]^\top \left[\int \overline{g}(y, \theta_0) \overline{g}(y, \theta_0)^\top dP_0(y) \right]^{-1} \left[\int \frac{\partial}{\partial \theta} \overline{g}(y, \theta_0) dP_0(y) \right] \right\}^{-1}$$
$$\cdot \left[\int \frac{\partial}{\partial \theta} \overline{g}(y, \theta_0) dP_0(y) \right]^\top \frac{1}{\varphi''(1)} \text{IF}(x; t_{\theta_0}^c, P_0). \tag{56}$$

On the basis of Propositions 3 and 4, since $x \mapsto \psi_\theta(x, t_\theta(P_0))$ is bounded, all the estimators $\widehat{\theta}_\varphi^c$ are B-robust.

4. Conclusions

We introduced a class of robust Z-estimators for moment condition models. These new estimators can be seen as robust alternatives for the minimum empirical divergence estimators. By using truncated functions based on the multidimensional Huber function, we defined robust estimators of the element that realizes the supremum in the dual form of the divergence, as well as new robust estimators for the parameter of the model. The asymptotic properties were proven, including the consistency and the limit laws. The influence functions for all the proposed estimators are bounded; therefore, these estimators are B-robust. The truncated function that we used to define the new robust Z-estimators contains functions implicitly defined, for which analytic forms are not available. The implementation of the estimation method will be addressed in a future research study. The idea of using the multidimensional Huber function, together with a scale matrix and a shift vector, to create a bounded version of the function corresponding to the estimating equation for the parameter of interest, could be considered in other contexts as well and would lead to new robust Z-estimators. As one of the Referees suggested, some other bounded functions could be used to define new robust Z-estimators for moment condition models. For example, the Tukey biweight function used together with a norm inside, in order to be appropriate to be applied to functions with vector values, could also be considered. Again, the original parameter of interest should remain the solution of the estimating equation based on the new bounded function. Such an idea is interesting to be analysed in future studies, in order to provide new robust versions of minimum empirical divergence estimators or robust Z-estimators in other contexts.

Funding: This work was supported by a grant of the Ministry of Research, Innovation and Digitization, CNCS CCCDI — UEFISCDI, Project Number PN-III-P4-ID-PCE-2020-1112, within PNCDI III.

Data Availability Statement: Not applicable.

Acknowledgments: We are very grateful to the Referees for their helpful comments and suggestions.

Conflicts of Interest: The author declares no conflict of interest.

Abbreviations

The following abbreviations are used in this manuscript:

i.i.d. independent and identically distributed
a.c.   absolutely continuous
GMM   generalized method of moments
CU   continuous updating
EL   empirical likelihood
ET   exponential tilting
GEL   generalized empirical likelihood
ETEL exponentially tilted empirical likelihood

Appendix A

Proof of Proposition 1. Since $(\theta, t) \mapsto \Psi(y, \theta, t)$ is continuous, by the uniform law of large numbers, Assumption 1 (a) implies

$$\sup_{\theta \in V_{\theta_0}, t \in V_{t_{\theta_0}}} \left\| \int \Psi(y, \theta, t) dP_n(y) - \int \Psi(y, \theta, t) dP_0(y) \right\| \to 0, \quad (A1)$$

in probability. This result together with Assumption 1 (b) ensures the convergence in probability of the estimators $\hat{\theta}^c_\varphi$ and $\hat{t}^c_{\hat{\theta}^c_\varphi}$ toward θ_0 and t_{θ_0}, respectively. The proof is the same as the one for Theorem 5.9 from [28], p. 46. □

Proof of Proposition 2. By the definitions of $\hat{\theta}^c_\varphi$ and $\hat{t}^c_{\hat{\theta}^c_\varphi}$, they both satisfy

$$\int \psi(y, \hat{\theta}^c_\varphi, \hat{t}^c_{\hat{\theta}^c_\varphi}) dP_n(y) = 0 \quad (E1)$$

$$\int \frac{\partial}{\partial \theta} m(y, \hat{\theta}^c_\varphi, \hat{t}^c_{\hat{\theta}^c_\varphi}) dP_n(y) = 0 \quad (E2)$$

Using a Taylor expansion in (E1), there exists $(\tilde{\theta}^c_\varphi, \tilde{t}^c_\varphi)$ inside the segment that links $(\hat{\theta}^c_\varphi, \hat{t}^c_{\hat{\theta}^c_\varphi})$ and (θ_0, t_{θ_0}) such that

$$0 = \int \psi(y, \theta_0, t_{\theta_0}) dP_n(y) + \left[\left(\int \frac{\partial}{\partial t} \psi(y, \theta_0, t_{\theta_0}) dP_n(y) \right)^\top, \left(\int \frac{\partial}{\partial \theta} \psi(y, \theta_0, t_{\theta_0}) dP_n(y) \right)^\top \right] \cdot a_n + \frac{1}{2} a_n^\top A_n a_n, \quad (A2)$$

where

$$a_n := \left((\hat{t}^c_{\hat{\theta}^c_\varphi} - t_{\theta_0})^\top, (\hat{\theta}^c_\varphi - \theta_0)^\top \right)^\top, \quad (A3)$$

and

$$A_n := \begin{pmatrix} \int \frac{\partial^2}{\partial^2 t} \psi(y, \tilde{\theta}^c_\varphi, \tilde{t}^c_\varphi) dP_n(y) & \int \frac{\partial^2}{\partial \theta \partial t} \psi(y, \tilde{\theta}^c_\varphi, \tilde{t}^c_\varphi) dP_n(y) \\ \int \frac{\partial^2}{\partial t \partial \theta} \psi(y, \tilde{\theta}^c_\varphi, \tilde{t}^c_\varphi) dP_n(y) & \int \frac{\partial^2}{\partial^2 \theta} \psi(y, \tilde{\theta}^c_\varphi, \tilde{t}^c_\varphi) dP_n(y) \end{pmatrix}. \quad (A4)$$

By Assumption 2 (b), the law of large numbers implies that $A_n = O_P(1)$. Then, using Assumption 2 (a), the last term in (A2) can be written $o_P(1) a_n$. On the other hand, by Assumption 2 (d), using the law of large numbers, we can write

$$\left[\left(\int \frac{\partial}{\partial t} \psi(y, \theta_0, t_{\theta_0}) dP_n(y) \right)^\top, \left(\int \frac{\partial}{\partial \theta} \psi(y, \theta_0, t_{\theta_0}) dP_n(y) \right)^\top \right]$$
$$= \left[\left(\int \frac{\partial}{\partial t} \psi(y, \theta_0, t_{\theta_0}) dP_0(y) \right)^\top, \left(\int \frac{\partial}{\partial \theta} \psi(y, \theta_0, t_{\theta_0}) dP_0(y) \right)^\top \right] + o_P(1).$$

Consequently, (A2) becomes

$$-\int \psi(y, \theta_0, t_{\theta_0}) dP_n(y)$$
$$= \left[\left(\int \frac{\partial}{\partial t} \psi(y, \theta_0, t_{\theta_0}) dP_0(y) \right)^\top + o_P(1), \left(\int \frac{\partial}{\partial \theta} \psi(y, \theta_0, t_{\theta_0}) dP_0(y) \right)^\top + o_P(1) \right] \cdot a_n. \quad (A5)$$

In the same way, using a Taylor expansion in (E2), there exists $(\overline{\theta}_\varphi^c, \overline{t}_\varphi^c)$ inside the segment that links $(\widehat{\theta}_{\widehat{\theta}_\varphi^c}^c, \widehat{t}_{\widehat{\theta}_\varphi^c}^c)$ and (θ_0, t_{θ_0}) such that

$$0 = \int \frac{\partial}{\partial \theta} m(y, \theta_0, t_{\theta_0}) dP_n(y) + \left[\left(\int \frac{\partial^2}{\partial \theta \partial t} m(y, \theta_0, t_{\theta_0}) dP_n(y) \right)^\top, \right. \\ \left. \left(\int \frac{\partial^2}{\partial^2 \theta} m(y, \theta_0, t_{\theta_0}) dP_n(y) \right)^\top \right] \cdot a_n + \tfrac{1}{2} a_n^\top B_n a_n, \quad (A6)$$

where

$$B_n := \begin{pmatrix} \int \frac{\partial^3}{\partial \theta \partial^2 t} m(y, \overline{\theta}_\varphi^c, \overline{t}_\varphi^c) dP_n(y) & \int \frac{\partial^3}{\partial^2 \theta \partial t} m(y, \overline{\theta}_\varphi^c, \overline{t}_\varphi^c) dP_n(y) \\ \int \frac{\partial^3}{\partial \theta \partial t \partial \theta} m(y, \overline{\theta}_\varphi^c, \overline{t}_\varphi^c) dP_n(y) & \int \frac{\partial^3}{\partial^3 \theta} m(y, \overline{\theta}_\varphi^c, \overline{t}_\varphi^c) dP_n(y) \end{pmatrix}. \quad (A7)$$

Similarly, as in (A5), we obtain

$$-\int \frac{\partial}{\partial \theta} m(y, \theta_0, t_{\theta_0}) dP_n(y) \\ = \left[\left(\int \frac{\partial^2}{\partial \theta \partial t} m(y, \theta_0, t_{\theta_0}) dP_0(y) \right)^\top + o_P(1), \int \frac{\partial^2}{\partial^2 \theta} m(y, \theta_0, t_{\theta_0}) dP_0(y) + o_P(1) \right] \cdot a_n. \quad (A8)$$

Using (A5) and (A8), we obtain

$$\sqrt{n} a_n = \sqrt{n} \begin{pmatrix} \left(\int \frac{\partial}{\partial t} \psi(y, \theta_0, t_{\theta_0}) dP_0(y) \right)^\top & \left(\int \frac{\partial}{\partial \theta} \psi(y, \theta_0, t_{\theta_0}) dP_0(y) \right)^\top \\ \left(\int \frac{\partial^2}{\partial \theta \partial t} m(y, \theta_0, t_{\theta_0}) dP_n(y) \right)^\top & \int \frac{\partial^2}{\partial^2 \theta} m(y, \theta_0, t_{\theta_0}) dP_n(y) \end{pmatrix}^{-1} \\ \times \begin{pmatrix} -\int \psi(y, \theta_0, t_{\theta_0}) dP_n(y) \\ -\int \frac{\partial}{\partial \theta} m(y, \theta_0, t_{\theta_0}) dP_n(y) \end{pmatrix} + o_P(1). \quad (A9)$$

Consider S the $(l + 1 + d) \times (l + 1 + d)$ matrix:

$$S := \begin{pmatrix} S_{11} & S_{12} \\ S_{21} & S_{22} \end{pmatrix}, \quad (A10)$$

with $S_{11} := \left(\int \frac{\partial}{\partial t} \psi(y, \theta_0, t_{\theta_0}) dP_0(y) \right)^\top$, $S_{12} := \left(\int \frac{\partial}{\partial \theta} \psi(y, \theta_0, t_{\theta_0}) dP_0(y) \right)^\top$, $S_{21} := \left(\int \frac{\partial^2}{\partial \theta \partial t} m(y, \theta_0, t_{\theta_0}) dP_0(y) \right)^\top$, and $S_{22} := \int \frac{\partial^2}{\partial^2 \theta} m(y, \theta_0, t_{\theta_0}) dP_0(y)$. Through calculations, we have

$$S_{21} = -[0_d, \int \frac{\partial}{\partial \theta} g(y, \theta_0) dP_0(y)], \quad (A11)$$

$$S_{22} = [0_d, \ldots, 0_d]. \quad (A12)$$

From (A9), we deduce that

$$\sqrt{n} \begin{pmatrix} \widehat{t}_{\widehat{\theta}_\varphi^c}^c - t_{\theta_0} \\ \widehat{\theta}_\varphi^c - \theta_0 \end{pmatrix} = S^{-1} \sqrt{n} \begin{pmatrix} -\int \psi(y, \theta_0, t_{\theta_0}) dP_n(y) \\ 0_d \end{pmatrix} + o_P(1). \quad (A13)$$

On the other hand, under assumption Assumption 2 (d), using the central limit theorem,

$$\sqrt{n} \begin{pmatrix} -\int \psi(y, \theta_0, t_{\theta_0}) dP_n(y) \\ 0_d \end{pmatrix} \quad (A14)$$

converges in distribution to a centred multivariate normal variable with covariance matrix:

$$M := \begin{pmatrix} M_{11} & M_{12} \\ M_{21} & M_{22} \end{pmatrix}, \quad (A15)$$

with

$$M_{11} := \mathrm{cov}[\psi(X,\theta_0,t_{\theta_0})], \quad M_{12} := \begin{pmatrix} 0_d^\top \\ \vdots \\ 0_d^\top \end{pmatrix}, \quad M_{21} := \begin{pmatrix} 0 & 0_l^\top \\ \vdots & \vdots \\ 0 & 0_l^\top \end{pmatrix}, \quad M_{22} := \begin{pmatrix} 0_d^\top \\ \vdots \\ 0_d^\top \end{pmatrix}.$$

Since $E[\psi(X,\theta_0,t_{\theta_0})] = 0$ by the construction of ψ, we obtain

$$M_{11} = \mathrm{cov}[\psi(X,\theta_0,t_{\theta_0})] = \int \psi(y,\theta_0,t_{\theta_0})\psi(y,\theta_0,t_{\theta_0})^\top dP_0(y) = I_{l+1}, \quad (A16)$$

on the basis of (29) for $\theta = \theta_0$.

Using then (A13) and the Slutsky theorem, we obtain that

$$\sqrt{n}\begin{pmatrix} \widehat{t}^c_{\widehat{\theta}_\varphi} - t_{\theta_0} \\ \widehat{\theta}^c_\varphi - \theta_0 \end{pmatrix} \quad (A17)$$

converges in distribution to a centred multivariate normal variable with the covariance matrix given by

$$C = S^{-1}M[S^{-1}]^\top. \quad (A18)$$

If we denote

$$C := \begin{pmatrix} C_{11} & C_{12} \\ C_{21} & C_{22} \end{pmatrix}, \quad (A19)$$

through calculation, we obtain

$$C_{11} = [S_{11}^{-1} - S_{11}^{-1}S_{12}[S_{21}S_{11}^{-1}S_{12}]^{-1}S_{21}S_{11}^{-1}] \times [S_{11}^{-1} - S_{11}^{-1}S_{12}[S_{21}S_{11}^{-1}S_{12}]^{-1}S_{21}S_{11}^{-1}]^\top, \quad (A20)$$
$$C_{12} = [S_{11}^{-1} - S_{11}^{-1}S_{12}[S_{21}S_{11}^{-1}S_{12}]^{-1}S_{21}S_{11}^{-1}] \times [[S_{21}S_{11}^{-1}S_{12}]^{-1}S_{21}S_{11}^{-1}]^\top, \quad (A21)$$
$$C_{21} = [[S_{21}S_{11}^{-1}S_{12}]^{-1}S_{21}S_{11}^{-1}] \times [S_{11}^{-1} - S_{11}^{-1}S_{12}[S_{21}S_{11}^{-1}S_{12}]^{-1}S_{21}S_{11}^{-1}]^\top, \quad (A22)$$
$$C_{22} = [[S_{21}S_{11}^{-1}S_{12}]^{-1}S_{21}S_{11}^{-1}] \times [[S_{21}S_{11}^{-1}S_{12}]^{-1}S_{21}S_{11}^{-1}]^\top. \quad (A23)$$

□

Proof of Proposition 3. For the contaminated model $\widetilde{P}_{\varepsilon x} = (1-\varepsilon)P_0 + \varepsilon \delta_x$, whenever it exists, $t_\theta^c(\widetilde{P}_{\varepsilon x})$ is defined as the solution of equation:

$$\int H_c(A_\theta(t_\theta^c(\widetilde{P}_{\varepsilon x})))[\frac{\partial}{\partial t}m_\theta(y,t_\theta^c(\widetilde{P}_{\varepsilon x})) - \tau_\theta(t_\theta^c(\widetilde{P}_{\varepsilon x}))]d\widetilde{P}_{\varepsilon x}(y) = 0. \quad (A24)$$

It follows that

$$\begin{aligned}&(1-\varepsilon)\int H_c(A_\theta(t_\theta^c(\widetilde{P}_{\varepsilon x})))[\tfrac{\partial}{\partial t}m_\theta(y,t_\theta^c(\widetilde{P}_{\varepsilon x})) - \tau_\theta(t_\theta^c(\widetilde{P}_{\varepsilon x}))]dP_0(y)\\ &+\varepsilon H_c(A_\theta(t_\theta^c(\widetilde{P}_{\varepsilon x})))[\tfrac{\partial}{\partial t}m_\theta(x,t_\theta^c(\widetilde{P}_{\varepsilon x})) - \tau_\theta(t_\theta^c(\widetilde{P}_{\varepsilon x}))]) = 0.\end{aligned} \quad (A25)$$

Derivation with respect to ε in (A25) yields

$$\begin{aligned}&-\int H_c(A_\theta(t_\theta(P_0)))[\tfrac{\partial}{\partial t}m_\theta(y,t_\theta(P_0)) - \tau_\theta(t_\theta(P_0))]dP_0(y)\\ &+\int \tfrac{\partial}{\partial t}[H_c(A_\theta(t))[\tfrac{\partial}{\partial t}m_\theta(y,t) - \tau_\theta(t)]]|_{t=t_\theta(P_0)}dP_0(y)\mathrm{IF}(x;t_\theta^c,P_0)\\ &+H_c(A_\theta(t_\theta(P_0)))[\tfrac{\partial}{\partial t}m_\theta(x,t_\theta(P_0)) - \tau_\theta(t_\theta(P_0))]).\end{aligned} \quad (A26)$$

Since the first integral in (A26) equals zero, we obtain

$$\begin{aligned}\mathrm{IF}(x;t_\theta^c,P_0) &= -\left\{\int \tfrac{\partial}{\partial t}[H_c(A_\theta(t))[\tfrac{\partial}{\partial t}m_\theta(y,t) - \tau_\theta(t)]]|_{t=t_\theta(P_0)}dP_0(y)\right\}^{-1}\\ &\quad \cdot H_c(A_\theta(t_\theta(P_0)))[\tfrac{\partial}{\partial t}m_\theta(x,t_\theta(P_0)) - \tau_\theta(t_\theta(P_0))])\\ &= -\left\{\int \tfrac{\partial}{\partial t}\psi_\theta(y,t_\theta(P_0))dP_0(y)\right\}^{-1} \cdot \psi_\theta(x,t_\theta(P_0)).\end{aligned} \quad (A27)$$

For each θ, the influence function (55) is bounded with respect to x; therefore, the estimators $\widehat{t}_\theta^c$ are B-robust.
□

Proof of Proposition 4. For the contaminated model $\widetilde{P}_{\varepsilon x} = (1-\varepsilon)P_0 + \varepsilon\delta_x$, $T^c(\widetilde{P}_{\varepsilon x})$ is defined as the solution of equation:

$$\int \frac{\partial}{\partial \theta} m(y, T^c(\widetilde{P}_{\varepsilon x}), t^c(T^c(\widetilde{P}_{\varepsilon x}), \widetilde{P}_{\varepsilon x})) d\widetilde{P}_{\varepsilon x}(y) = 0, \tag{A28}$$

whenever this solution exists. Then,

$$(1-\varepsilon)\int \frac{\partial}{\partial \theta} m(y, T^c(\widetilde{P}_{\varepsilon x}), t^c(T^c(\widetilde{P}_{\varepsilon x}), \widetilde{P}_{\varepsilon x})) dP_0(y) + \varepsilon \frac{\partial}{\partial \theta} m(x, T^c(\widetilde{P}_{\varepsilon x}), t^c(T^c(\widetilde{P}_{\varepsilon x}), \widetilde{P}_{\varepsilon x})) = 0. \tag{A29}$$

Derivation with respect to ε in (A29) yields

$$\begin{aligned}&-\int \tfrac{\partial}{\partial \theta} m(y,\theta_0,t^c(\theta_0,P_0)) dP_0(y) + \int \tfrac{\partial^2}{\partial^2\theta} m[y,\theta,t]_{\theta=\theta_0,t=t_{\theta_0}(P_0)} dP_0(y)\mathrm{IF}(x;T^c,P_0)+\\ &+\int \tfrac{\partial^2}{\partial\theta\partial t} m[y,\theta,t]_{\theta=\theta_0,t=t_{\theta_0}(P_0)} dP_0(y)\cdot\left\{\tfrac{\partial}{\partial \theta} t^c(\theta_0,P_0)\mathrm{IF}(x;T^c,P_0)+\right.\\ &\left.+\mathrm{IF}(x;t^c_{\theta_0},P_0)\right\} + \tfrac{\partial}{\partial \theta}[m(x,\theta,t)]_{\theta=\theta_0,t=t_{\theta_0}(P_0)} = 0.\end{aligned} \tag{A30}$$

Some calculations show that

$$\frac{\partial}{\partial \theta}[m(x,\theta,t)]_{\theta=\theta_0,t=t_{\theta_0}(P_0)} = 0 \text{ and } \frac{\partial^2}{\partial^2\theta}[m(x,\theta,t)]_{\theta=\theta_0,t=t_{\theta_0}(P_0)} = 0, \tag{A31}$$

for any x; therefore, (A30) reduces to

$$\int \frac{\partial^2}{\partial\theta\partial t} m[y,\theta,t]_{\theta=\theta_0,t=t_{\theta_0}(P_0)} dP_0(y) \cdot \left\{\frac{\partial}{\partial \theta} t^c(\theta_0,P_0)\mathrm{IF}(x;T^c,P_0) + \mathrm{IF}(x;t^c_{\theta_0},P_0)\right\} = 0. \tag{A32}$$

On the other hand,

$$\begin{aligned}\int \tfrac{\partial^2}{\partial\theta\partial t} m[y,\theta,t]_{\theta=\theta_0,t=t_{\theta_0}(P_0)} dP_0(y) &= -\psi'(\varphi'(1))\int \tfrac{\partial}{\partial \theta}\overline{g}(y,\theta_0) dP_0(y)\\ &= -\int \tfrac{\partial}{\partial \theta}\overline{g}(y,\theta_0) dP_0(y),\end{aligned}$$

since $\psi'(u) = \varphi'^{-1}(u)$.

Taking into account that $t^c(\theta, P_0) = t(\theta, P_0)$ and $t(\theta, P_0)$ verifies

$$\int \frac{\partial}{\partial t} m(y,\theta,t(\theta,P_0)) dP_0(y) = 0, \tag{A33}$$

and the derivation with respect to θ yields

$$\int \frac{\partial^2}{\partial t\partial\theta} m(y,\theta,t(\theta,P_0)) dP_0(y) + \int \frac{\partial^2}{\partial^2 t} m(y,\theta,t(\theta,P_0)) dP_0(y) \cdot \frac{\partial}{\partial \theta} t(\theta,P_0) = 0, \tag{A34}$$

which implies

$$\begin{aligned}\tfrac{\partial}{\partial \theta} t^c(\theta_0, P_0) = \tfrac{\partial}{\partial \theta} t(\theta_0, P_0) &= -\left\{\int \tfrac{\partial^2}{\partial^2 t} m(y,\theta_0,t(\theta_0,P_0)) dP_0(y)\right\}^{-1}\int \tfrac{\partial^2}{\partial t\partial\theta} m(y,\theta_0,t(\theta_0,P_0)) dP_0(y)\\ &= -\varphi''(1)\left\{\int \overline{g}(y,\theta_0)\overline{g}(y,\theta_0)^\top dP_0(y)\right\}^{-1}\int \tfrac{\partial}{\partial \theta}\overline{g}(y,\theta_0) dP_0(y),\end{aligned}$$

because

$$\int \frac{\partial^2}{\partial^2 t} m(y,\theta_0,t(\theta_0,P_0)) dP_0(y) = -\frac{1}{\varphi''(1)}\int \overline{g}(y,\theta_0)\overline{g}(y,\theta_0)^\top dP_0(y). \tag{A35}$$

Then, (A32) becomes

$$\left[\int \tfrac{\partial}{\partial\theta}\overline{g}(y,\theta_0)dP_0(y)\right]^\top\left[-\varphi''(1)\{\int \overline{g}(y,\theta_0)\overline{g}(y,\theta_0)^\top dP_0(y)\}\right]^{-1}\int \tfrac{\partial}{\partial\theta}\overline{g}(y,\theta_0)dP_0(y)\mathrm{IF}(x;T^c,P_0)$$
$$+\mathrm{IF}(x;t^c_{\theta_0},P_0)\Big]=0,$$

and consequently,

$$\mathrm{IF}(x;T^c,P_0)=\left\{\left[\tfrac{\partial}{\partial\theta}\overline{g}(y,\theta_0)dP_0(y)\right]^\top\left[\int \overline{g}(y,\theta_0)\overline{g}(y,\theta_0)^\top dP_0(y)\right]^{-1}\left[\tfrac{\partial}{\partial\theta}\overline{g}(y,\theta_0)dP_0(y)\right]\right\}^{-1}$$
$$\cdot\left[\tfrac{\partial}{\partial\theta}\overline{g}(y,\theta_0)dP_0(y)\right]^\top \tfrac{1}{\varphi''(1)}\mathrm{IF}(x;t^c_{\theta_0},P_0).$$
(A36)

References

1. Hansen, L.P. Large sample properties of generalized method of moments estimators. *Econometrica* **1982**, *50*, 1029–1054. [CrossRef]
2. Hansen, L.; Heaton, J.; Yaron, A. Finite-sample properties of some alternative gmm estimators. *J. Bus. Econ. Stat.* **1996**, *14*, 262–280.
3. Qin, J.; Lawless, J. Empirical likelihood and general estimating equations. *Ann. Stat.* **1994**, *22*, 300–325. [CrossRef]
4. Imbens, G.W. One-step estimators for over-identified generalized method of moments models. *Rev. Econ. Stud.* **1997**, *64*, 359–383. [CrossRef]
5. Kitamura, Y.; Stutzer, M. An information-theoretic alternative to generalized method of moments estimation. *Econometrica* **1997**, *65*, 861–874. [CrossRef]
6. Newey, W.K.; Smith, R.J. Higher order properties of GMM and generalized empirical likelihood estimators. *Econometrica* **2004**, *72*, 219–255. [CrossRef]
7. Schennach, S.M. Point estimation with exponentially tilted empirical likelihood. *Ann. Stat.* **2007**, *35*, 634–672. [CrossRef]
8. Pardo, L. *Statistical Inference Based on Divergence Measures*; Chapman & Hall: London, UK, 2006.
9. Basu, A.; Shioya, H.; Park, C. *Statistical Inference: The Minimum Distance Approach*; Chapman & Hall: London, UK, 2011.
10. Pardo, L.; Martín, N. Robust procedures for estimating and testing in the framework of divergence measures. *Entropy* **2021**, *23*, 430. [CrossRef]
11. Riani, M.; Atkinson, A.C.; Corbellini, A.; Perrotta, D. Robust regression with density power divergence: Theory, comparisons, and data analysis. *Entropy* **2020**, *22*, 399. [CrossRef]
12. Broniatowski, M.; Keziou, A. Divergences and duality for estimation and test under moment condition models. *J. Stat. Plan. Inference* **2012**, *142*, 2554–2573. [CrossRef]
13. Broniatowski, M.; Keziou, A. Parametric estimation and tests through divergences and the duality technique. *J. Multivar. Anal.* **2009**, *100*, 16–36. [CrossRef]
14. Toma, A.; Broniatowski, M. Dual divergence estimators and tests: Robustness results. *J. Multivar. Anal.* **2011**, *102*, 20–36. [CrossRef]
15. Toma, A.; Leoni-Aubin, S. Robust tests based on dual divergence estimators and saddlepoint approximations. *J. Multivar. Anal.* **2010**, *101*, 1143–1155. [CrossRef]
16. Toma, A. Model selection criteria using divergences. *Entropy* **2014**, *16*, 2686–2698. [CrossRef]
17. Toma, A. Robustness of dual divergence estimators for models satisfying linear constraints. *C. R. Math. Acad. Sci. Paris* **2013**, *351*, 311–316. [CrossRef]
18. Ronchetti, E.; Trojani, F. Robust inference with GMM estimators. *J. Econom.* **2001**, *101*, 37–69. [CrossRef]
19. Lô, S.N.; Ronchetti, E. Robust small sample accurate inference in moment condition models. *Comput. Stat. Data Anal.* **2012**, *56*, 3182–3197. [CrossRef]
20. Felipe, A.; Martín, N.; Miranda, P.; Pardo, L. Testing with exponentially tilted empirical likelihood. *Methodol. Comput. Appl. Probab.* **2018**, *20*, 1319–1358. [CrossRef]
21. Keziou, A.; Toma, A. A robust version of the empirical likelihood estimator. *Mathematics* **2021**, *9*, 829. [CrossRef]
22. Keziou, A.; Toma, A. Robust Empirical Likelihood. In *Geometric Science of Information, Proceedings of the 5th International Conference, GSI 2021, Paris, France, 21–23 July 2021*; Springer International Publishing: Cham, Switzerland, 2021.
23. Rüschendorf, L. On the minimum discrimination information theorem. *Stat. Decis.* **1984**, 263–283.
24. Cressie, N.; Read, T.R.C. Multinomial goodness-of-fit tests. *J. R. Stat. Soc. Ser. B* **1984**, *46*, 440–464. [CrossRef]
25. Broniatowski, M.; Keziou, A. Minimization of ϕ divergences on sets of signed measures. *Stud. Sci. Math. Hung.* **2006**, *43*, 403–442.
26. Hampel, F.R.; Ronchetti, E.; Rousseeuw, P.J.; Stahel, W. *Robust Statistics: The Approach Based on Influence Functions*; Wiley: New York, NY, USA, 1986.
27. Ronchetti, E. M.; Huber, P.J. *Robust Statistics*; John Wiley & Sons: Hoboken, NJ, USA, 2009.
28. van der Vaart, A. W. *Asymptotic Statistics*; Cambridge Series in Statistical and Probabilistic Mathematics; Cambridge University Press: Cambridge, UK, 1998.

Disclaimer/Publisher's Note: The statements, opinions and data contained in all publications are solely those of the individual author(s) and contributor(s) and not of MDPI and/or the editor(s). MDPI and/or the editor(s) disclaim responsibility for any injury to people or property resulting from any ideas, methods, instructions or products referred to in the content.

MDPI
St. Alban-Anlage 66
4052 Basel
Switzerland
Tel. +41 61 683 77 34
Fax +41 61 302 89 18
www.mdpi.com

Entropy Editorial Office
E-mail: entropy@mdpi.com
www.mdpi.com/journal/entropy

www.ingramcontent.com/pod-product-compliance
Lightning Source LLC
LaVergne TN
LVHW070140100526
838202LV00015B/1857